S0-BPF-628

COLLECTED WORKS OF JOHN STUART MILL

VOLUME XXVIII

The Collected Edition of the Works of John Stuart Mill has been planned and is being directed by an editorial committee appointed from the Faculty of Arts and Science of the University of Toronto, and from the University of Toronto Press. The primary aim of the edition is to present fully collated texts of those works which exist in a number of versions, both printed and manuscript, and to provide accurate texts of works previously unpublished or which have become relatively inaccessible.

Public and Parliamentary Speeches

by JOHN STUART MILL

November 1850 – November 1868

Edited by

JOHN M. ROBSON

University Professor and Professor of English,
Victoria College, University of Toronto

and

BRUCE L. KINZER

Associate Professor of History
University of North Carolina at Wilmington

Introduction by

BRUCE L. KINZER

Textual Introduction by

JOHN M. ROBSON

UNIVERSITY OF TORONTO PRESS

ROUTLEDGE

Toronto and Buffalo
Printed in Canada

ISBN 0-8020-2693-1

London: Routledge
ISBN 0-415-03791-3
ISBN 0-415-03793-X (set)

Printed on acid-free paper

Canadian Cataloguing in Publication data
Mill, John Stuart, 1806–1873.
[Works]
Collected works of John Stuart Mill
Includes bibliographies and indexes.
PARTIAL CONTENTS: v. 28–29.
Public & parliamentary speeches /
edited by John M. Robson and Bruce L. Kinzer.
ISBN 0-8020-2693-1 (v. 28–29).
1. – Collected works. 2. – Collected works.
I. Robson, John M., 1927–
II. Title.
B1602.A2 1963 192 C65-188-2 rev.

This volume has been published
with the assistance of a grant
from the Social Sciences
and Humanities Research Council
of Canada

Contents

*

* *

July 1869 to March 1873

APPENDICES

FACSIMILES

"Westminster Election: The Nomination in Covent-Garden"
Illustrated London News, 22 July, 1865, p. 56
Metropolitan Toronto Library

Introduction

BRUCE L. KINZER

WERE IT NOT for his Westminster years (1865-68), there would be very little to do in the way of editing or introducing John Stuart Mill's post-London Debating Society speeches. Mill had an impressive facility for putting thoughts into words, written or spoken, but he recognized that he could usually accomplish much more with his pen than with his tongue. He also understood that formal prose was the only medium capable of doing complete justice to the ideas and arguments he wished to convey to his audience. It can be assumed that Mill felt more comfortable at his desk than on the platform or in the House of Commons. The psychological security offered by his study, however, is not responsible for the marked preference he showed for the written word. Mill's sense of public duty was such that there would have been a great deal more labour for the editors of these volumes had he been persuaded that his goals could be better advanced through speeches than through essays.

Mill delivered very few public speeches before 1865. Those that he did give were of modest length and ambition; they did not attract much notice at the time and they do not call for special analysis now. From his defeat at the 1868 general election until his death in 1873, Mill was certainly a much more active and prominent speech-maker than he had been prior to the 1865 Westminster campaign. The content and context of that activity constitute a distinctive phase in his life-long experience of political engagement. Even so, the intervening parliamentary career, which established Mill as a highly visible figure in the political world of mid-Victorian England, goes far towards explaining the disparity in quantity and dimensions between the pre-1865 and post-1868 public speeches. Of paramount concern are the origin, character, and significance of that career.

THE *AUTOBIOGRAPHY* AND THE WESTMINSTER YEARS

THE TEMPTATION EXISTS to dismiss J.S. Mill's three years in the House of Commons as a relatively insignificant episode in a life distinguished by extraordinarily influential writings on virtually every subject central to the intellectual discourse of his age. Whereas the *Autobiography* has induced a literature of impressive proportions on Mill's education, his mental crisis, and his association with Harriet Taylor, nothing like commensurate attention has been paid to the section of this peculiar work that discusses his years in the House of Commons. Such neglect is not the result of the brevity of the treatment he provides. The account of the 1865 to 1868 period of his life, an account that concentrates heavily on his experiences as a candidate and Member of Parliament, constitutes over a tenth of the entire *Autobiography* (eighteen printed pages are given to these four years–approximately two-thirds of the space allocated to the preceding quarter-century).[1] It is not how much Mill says but what he says and how he says it that has made scholars generally indifferent to Mill's portrayal of his parliamentary career. Although a conception of purpose with regard to his political objectives imparts a focus and a measure of unity to the parliamentary paragraphs, their content lacks the personal dimension so singularly displayed in the early chapters. The cumulative effect of the self-satisfied detachment with which Mill describes his support of parliamentary reform and purity of election, women's suffrage and personal representation, justice for Ireland and no less for Jamaica, can produce mild irritation, unrelieved by anything twentieth-century readers are disposed to find absorbing or provocative.

The formality and flatness of tone characteristic of Mill's consideration of these years cannot be attributed to temporal distance. Written less than two years after his defeat at the November 1868 general election, the exposition of the Westminster period drew upon eminently fresh recollections. The distance is rather psychological and rhetorical, serving an argumentative function that is not without paradox. The final portion of the *Autobiography* embraces an explanation and justification of his political conduct between 1865 and 1868. If the need to explain and justify is responsible for the disproportionate length of the account, that need itself is a consequence of his failure to secure re-election in 1868. Mill patiently builds up his case, making it abundantly clear, if only by implication, that while he lost nothing of substance at the 1868 general election, the electors of Westminster denied themselves the opportunity of being represented by one whose integrity, intellectual weight, and moral authority did honour to his constituents and his country.

An intellectual and moralist in politics? So much can be taken for granted. But the real interest of his parliamentary career lies in its illumination of Mill as politician. The ultimate objectives invariably involved a commitment to the "improvement" or "regeneration" of mankind. His head might be in the air, but Mill always saw himself as a man whose feet were firmly planted on the ground. The successful moralist had to be an able tactician. Mill's labours, whether in or

[1]*Autobiography* [*A*], in *Autobiography and Literary Essays*, ed. John M. Robson and Jack Stillinger, *Collected Works of John Stuart Mill* [*CW*], I (Toronto: University of Toronto Press, 1981), 229-90.

out of the House of Commons, always assumed a form consistent with his understanding of the obligation to marry theory and practice. His grasp of political realities may have sometimes been deficient; his sense of politics as "the art of the possible" remained a constant.

Whatever doubts Mill had respecting the advisability of his entering the House of Commons, they did not spring from an apprehension of personal unfitness. A passage in the *Autobiography* remote from the parliamentary section makes explicit Mill's supreme confidence in his capacities as a practical man of business. Evaluating the benefits he gained from his long service in the East India Company, Mill observes:

> as a Secretary conducting political correspondence, I could not issue an order or express an opinion, without satisfying various persons very unlike myself, that the thing was fit to be done. I was thus in a good position for finding out by practice the mode of putting a thought which gives it easiest admittance into minds not prepared for it by habit; while I became practically conversant with the difficulties of moving bodies of men, the necessities of compromise, the art of sacrificing the non-essential to preserve the essential. I learnt how to obtain the best I could, when I could not obtain everything; instead of being indignant or dispirited because I could not have entirely my own way, to be pleased and encouraged when I could have the smallest part of it; and when even that could not be, to bear with complete equanimity the being overruled altogether. I have found, through life, these acquisitions to be of the greatest possible importance for personal happiness, and they are also a very necessary condition for enabling any one, either as theorist or as practical man, to effect the greatest amount of good compatible with his opportunities.[2]

A disadvantage of his position at India House, however, was that it excluded him "from Parliament, and public life," an exclusion to which he "was not indifferent."[3]

Mill never questioned his ability to function effectively in the House of Commons. Although there are very good reasons for viewing the nineteenth-century House as a unique institution with distinctive traditions, conventions, and assumptions that had to be learned and understood before a member could feel at home there, Mill in 1865 never considered the possibility that his full acceptance and recognition would require a period of apprenticeship. He not only entered the House as an established public figure; he also, as his remarks indicate, had a

[2]*Ibid.*, 87.

[3]*Ibid.*, 85. In 1842 Mill had written to Comte: "la question de participation au moins directe, au mouvement politique, se trouve pour moi à peu près décidée par ma position individuelle. Je remettrai à un autre temps l'exposition de mes vues sur les circonstances politiques de mon pays, qui malgré la force incontestable de vos objections, font encore à mes yeux de la tribune parlementaire la meilleure chaire d'enseignement public pour un philosophe sociologiste convenablement placé, et qui chercherait peut être à faire des ministères ou à les diriger dans sons sens, mais en s'abstenant d'en faire partie, sinon probablement dans des moments critiques que je ne crois pas, chez nous, très éloignés." (*Earlier Letters of John Stuart Mill* [*EL*], ed. Francis E. Mineka, *CW*, XII-XIII [Toronto: University of Toronto Press, 1963], XIII, 503.) In 1851 Mill declined an offer, made by Charles Gavan Duffy and Frederick Lucas, to stand for an Irish county constituency. Mill writes in the *Autobiography* that "the incompatibility of a seat in Parliament with the office I then held in the India House precluded even consideration of the proposal" (*A*, 272).

consciousness of himself as a mature and experienced politician. Servant of the East India Company from 1823 until its demise as an agency of government in 1858; erstwhile active member of the London Debating Society; political journalist and editor of the *Westminster Review* in the 1830s; political theorist habitually aware of the need to comprehend contemporary developments and relate them to his analytical objectives—the Mill of the mid-1860s thought he possessed the credentials and qualities necessary to demonstrate what a member of Parliament should be (as opposed to what most members generally were).

MILL'S 1865 CANDIDACY

IN MARCH of 1865 Mill received a request from James Beal, representing a Committee organized to serve the Radical interest in Westminster, to allow his name to be put forward as a possible candidate for the general election expected to occur before the year was out.[4] Beal's association with Mill was not personal. He believed Mill's name could carry Westminster and sought to use Mill's presence in the House to advertise the programme of the Metropolitan Municipal Reform Association, founded by Beal in this same year.[5] In *Representative Government* Mill had criticized both the Corporation of the City of London ("that union of modern jobbery and antiquated foppery") and the Metropolitan Board of Works,[6] the primary targets of Beal's reform campaign. Assuming he could be elected, Mill's sponsorship of the Association's proposals in the House would boost the visibility of the issue and the organization that worked to publicize it.[7]

In response to Beal's approach, Mill indicated that he would be willing to stand should a majority of Liberal electors so wish. But he told Beal in no uncertain terms that his would be no ordinary candidacy. Having implied that they were not doing him a favour in offering him the prospect of a seat in Parliament—"All

[4]Beal led a group of "New Reformers" in Westminster that wished to challenge the dominance of the "Old Reformers" who had virtually dictated the representation of the constituency since 1837. Captain Grosvenor was the candidate of the "Old Reformers." See Marc Bradley Baer, "The Politics of London, 1852-1868: Parties, Voters and Representation," Ph.D. diss., 2 vols., University of Iowa, 1976, I, 156-62.

[5]See David Owen, *The Government of Victorian London, 1855-1889: The Metropolitan Board of Works, the Vestries and the City Corporation* (Cambridge, Mass.: Harvard University Press, 1982), 196.

[6]*Essays on Politics and Society*, *CW*, XVIII-XIX (Toronto: University of Toronto Press, 1977), XIX, 538-9.

[7]While in the House of Commons Mill actively promoted Beal's municipal reform programme. He did so as a member of the Select Committee on Metropolitan Local Government (see App. B), and as a metropolitan member of the House. For his initiatives on the question see Nos. 56, 82, 93, and 105. In the *Autobiography* Mill refers to his attempt to obtain a Municipal Government for the Metropolis: "on that subject the indifference of the House of Commons was such that I found hardly any help or support within its walls. On this subject, however, I was the organ of an active and intelligent body of persons outside, with whom and not with me the scheme originated, who carried on all the agitation on the subject and drew up the Bills." (*A*, 276.)

private considerations are against my accepting it"—Mill said that, if elected, he would not undertake to look after the constituency's "local business" in the House of Commons. He went on to observe that a seat in the House interested him only as a vehicle for the promotion of his opinions. The electors were entitled to know the nature of those opinions but they should have no expectation that he would modify them to conform with their own. At this time, however, Mill probably thought more about the contribution he could make as a candidate than as an M.P. If he did not win the opportunity to exemplify the correct *modus operandi* of a parliamentarian, he might at least draw attention not only to his substantive views on major questions but also to his prescriptive conception of the electoral process. Mill intimated that because it was not quite right for an individual to "want" to be in Parliament, he would do nothing to assist any committee formed to secure his return.

It is the interest of the constituencies to be served by men who are not aiming at personal objects, either pecuniary, official, or social, but consenting to undertake gratuitously an onerous duty to the public. That such persons should be made to pay for permission to do hard & difficult work for the general advantage, is neither worthy of a free people, nor is it the way to induce the best men to come forward. In my own case, I must even decline to offer myself to the electors in any manner; because, proud as I should be of their suffrages, & though I would endeavour to fulfil to the best of my ability the duty to which they might think fit to elect me, yet I have no wish to quit my present occupations for the H. of C. unless called upon to do so by my fellow-citizens.[8]

Elections should involve the qualifications of the candidates—their principles, opinions, and capabilities. They should not be decided by the longest purse.

Mill was deeply disturbed by what he perceived as the growing influence of money at elections. He informed Beal of his conviction "that there can be no Parliamentary Reform worthy of the name, so long as a seat in Parliament is only attainable by rich men, or by those who have rich men at their back."[9] A man whose Liberal credentials Mill held suspect,[10] and whose financial resources were considerable, had already entered the field in Westminster. Captain Robert Wellesley Grosvenor, a nephew of the Marquess of Westminster, had declared his intention of seeking to represent the constituency.[11] An inexperienced Liberal barely more than thirty years of age, Grosvenor had little to recommend him but his name and flush connections (usually sufficient recommendations at mid-

[8]Letter to James Beal, *Later Letters of John Stuart Mill* [*LL*], ed. Francis E. Mineka and Dwight N. Lindley, *CW*, XIV-XVII (Toronto: University of Toronto Press, 1972), XVI, 1005-6 (7 Mar., 1865).

[9]*Ibid.*

[10]In February of 1865 Kate Amberley recorded in her journal: "Mill said they could not have one [a candidate] worse than Mr. Grosvenor, for at a meeting he had been at he had been as illiberal as possible for a liberal to be" (*The Amberley Papers*, ed. Bertrand and Patricia Russell, 2 vols. [London: Woolf, 1937], I, 369).

[11]One of the sitting Liberal members for Westminster, Sir George De Lacy Evans, had previously announced his retirement. The other sitting Liberal, Sir John Shelley, would subsequently withdraw from the field.

Victorian elections). That Mill felt a special affinity for the Radical tradition of Westminster[12] can be accepted as a given; that Grosvenor would do less than justice to that tradition few of advanced persuasion could doubt. If Westminster wished to reclaim its status as the fulcrum of English Radicalism, Mill was inclined to assist if asked.

By mid-April the decision had been made—Beal's electoral Committee wanted Mill to be their candidate.[13] Even before the invitation was issued, Mill had sensed the momentum building in his favour. On 6 April he sanguinely reported to J.E. Cairnes on recent developments:

> there is something very encouraging in the enthusiasm which has been excited, both in Westminster and elsewhere, not simply for me, but for the opinion respecting the proper position of a candidate, which I expressed in my letter [to Beal]. . . . The greatest pleasure which public life could give me would be if it enabled me to shew that more can be accomplished by supposing that there is reason and good feeling in the mass of mankind than by proceeding on the ordinary assumption that they are fools and rogues.[14]

Mill could scarcely have been in a more satisfactory position. He had no intention of allowing the campaign to interfere with his Avignon spring. Beal's Committee had promoted his candidacy and they could now get on with the task of helping Westminster electors prove themselves something other than "fools and rogues." As a matter of principle Mill would do nothing to help himself. He could best instruct the voters of England in the value of purity of election by refusing to allow the Westminster contest to distract him from his work in Avignon.[15] He planned to return to London in early July[16] to await the judgment of the electorate—a judgment less on his qualifications as a candidate than on the wisdom of the Committee that nominated him and the virtue of the electors to whom that Committee made their appeal.[17]

By the end of April there were three candidates in the field—Grosvenor, Mill, and W.H. Smith. Smith, the son of Victorian England's most innovative bookseller and now the effective head of the firm, offered himself to the electors as a "Liberal-Conservative." Tories did not win seats in Westminster, and Smith, while he hoped to win Tory votes, did not come forward as a follower of Lord Derby. He claimed to be "unconnected with either of the great political parties"; he

[12]William Thomas, *The Philosophic Radicals: Nine Studies in Theory and Practice, 1817-1841* (Oxford: Clarendon Press, 1979), 46-94; and E.P. Thompson, *The Making of the English Working Class* (London: Gollancz, 1963), 451-71.

[13]For Mill's response, see letter to James Beal, *LL*, *CW*, XVI, 1031-5 (17 Apr., 1865).

[14]*Ibid.*, 1026-7.

[15]John M. Robson has noted that "more editions of Mill's works appeared in 1865 than in any other year" (Textual Introduction, *Essays on Politics and Society*, *CW*, XVIII, lxxxix).

[16]Letter to William Hickson, *LL*, *CW*, XVI, 1044-5 (3 May, 1865).

[17]In an 1868 article Edward Dicey observed that over £2000 was spent on behalf of Mill's candidacy in 1865. Mill might have considered that too much, but as Dicey points out, it was Mill's name that made it possible to win on such a small investment ("The Candidates for Next Parliament," *Macmillan's Magazine*, XVIII [Sept. 1868], 445).

desired to act "as an independent member at liberty to vote for measures rather than for men"; he declared that he would "not be a party to any factious attempt to drive Lord Palmerston from power."[18] Smith's aim was to combine the votes of the Conservative minority in Westminster with those of Palmerstonian moderates in sufficient number to outdistance Mill. If the Tories had a candidate in this contest, Smith was it.

What did Mill think of his chances as he passed the month of May in Avignon? He does not seem to have taken Smith very seriously. On 11 May he wrote Edwin Chadwick: "I do not think the Tories expect their man to come in, otherwise some more considerable person would have started in that interest."[19] Yet at the end of the month he informed Max Kyllman that he thought "it hardly possible" his own candidacy "should succeed,"[20] a view echoed by Helen Taylor two days later in a letter to Kate Amberley.[21] With two seats open and only three candidates, one of whom Mill two weeks earlier had lightly dismissed, it is not easy to see how such pessimism could be justified.

A letter from Chadwick in late May could account for it. Chadwick reported that Mill's Committee wanted him to return to London to meet with them and the electors. Inasmuch as Mill had given clear indication of his unwillingness to play the part of candidate, the approach through Chadwick did not augur well. Mill, nonetheless, held his ground.

> If I were now to attend meetings and make speeches to the electors in the usual . . . manner, it would seem as if there had been no truth in my declaration that I did not personally seek to be in Parliament; as if I had merely been finessing to get myself elected without trouble and expense, and having found more difficulty than I expected, had at last shewn myself in my true colours.[22]

Shortly thereafter Mill's Committee became increasingly uneasy about the charges of atheism being levelled against Mill by elements of the metropolitan press. The controversy stemmed from a passage in the recently published *Examination of Sir William Hamilton's Philosophy*. Attacking H.L. Mansel's theology, Mill had stated that he could not worship a God whose goodness could not be comprehended in relation to human morality: "I will call no being good, who is not what I mean when I apply that epithet to my fellow-creatures; and if such a being can sentence me to hell for not so calling him, to hell I will go."[23] In

[18]Quoted in Viscount Chilston, *W.H. Smith* (London: Routledge & Kegan Paul, 1965), 50. H.J. Hanham notes that Smith "was in some demand as a Liberal candidate" in the early sixties (*Elections and Party Management: Politics in the Time of Disraeli and Gladstone* [London: Longmans, 1959], 226).

[19]*LL*, *CW*, XVI, 1050.

[20]*Ibid.*, 1063 (30 May, 1865).

[21]*Amberley Papers*, I, 434.

[22]Letter to Chadwick, *LL*, *CW*, XVI, 1059 (28 May, 1865).

[23]*An Examination of Sir William Hamilton's Philosophy*, *CW*, IX (Toronto: University of Toronto Press, 1979), 103.

the late spring and early summer of 1865 perhaps no passage in print received more attention.[24] Charles Westerton, a prominent member of Mill's Committee, suggested that he return to England to answer the allegations of irreligion being hurled at him. On 21 June Mill told Westerton that a candidate's private religious opinions were no business of the electors. As for his published work, he would not disavow anything he had written, but added that the refusal to worship any God "but a good God" did not make him an atheist. He indignantly declined to dignify the charges brought against him by the likes of the *Record* and *Morning Advertiser* by issuing a response.[25]

Less than a week later, however, Mill agreed to return early to meet with his Committee and to address the electors of Westminster.[26] He explained to Chadwick that an urgent letter had arrived from Westerton that left him little choice: "it is due to those who have taken so much trouble about me that I should not give them the impression that for my own convenience I expose them to the probable frustration of all their endeavours."[27] Mill's Committee had evidently persuaded him that he could win, but not without helping himself. Smith's candidacy jeopardized Mill's election because of the strained relations prevailing between the Committees of Grosvenor and Mill.[28] Few doubted that Grosvenor would top the poll when the day was done, and Mill's Committee feared that in the absence of cooperation between the two Liberal candidates many Whiggish Westminster electors would split their two votes between Grosvenor and Smith, leaving Mill odd man out. The Committee therefore wanted Mill to take up the fight against Smith, and to sanction negotiations with Grosvenor's Committee.

On 30 June Mill, now back at Blackheath Park, told Westerton that he would not meet with either Grosvenor or Grosvenor's Committee. But if he would not support cooperation between the two Committees, neither would he forbid it. He insisted that the campaign was theirs, not his, and it was for them to decide how to conduct it.[29] Before the first week of July was out, an arrangement with

[24]For the press controversy on this passage, see the *Spectator*, 27 May, 585, and 10 June, 1865, 631-2; the *Record*, 2 June, 3; 14 June, 2; and 19 June, 1865, 2; *Morning Advertiser*, 3 June, 5; and 28 June, 1865, 2.

[25]*LL*, *CW*, XVI, 1069-70.

[26]See letter to Westerton, *ibid.*, 1073 (26 June, 1865).

[27]*Ibid.*, 1072 (26 June, 1865).

[28]In May Mill had said of Lord Amberley: "It is really a fine thing in him to have withdrawn from Grosvenor's Committee and come over to me" (letter to Chadwick, *ibid.*, 1050 [15 May, 1865]).

[29]*Ibid.*, 1073-4. Helen Taylor wrote to Kate Amberley on 2 July, "Mr. Mill has undergone a sort of persecution from his Committee to show himself and speak at meetings, which, in moderation, however, he is willing to do; but others want him to combine with Captain Grosvenor which he thinks quite out of the question. He has no objection to the Committee co-operating with Captain Grosvenor's committee if they themselves think fit, since he leaves the conduct of the election in their hands, but any personal combination between himself and a man who (as well as the Tory candidate) is employing all the old corrupt practices would be an utter dereliction of the principle on which he declared himself willing to stand." (*Amberley Papers*, I, 437.)

Grosvenor's Committee had been concluded. Mill tersely disclosed to Chadwick: "there was nothing for me to do but acquiesce in it."[30]

Mill's "acquiescence" in the deal that was cut by the Committees was the product of the same forces that had moved him to become an "active" candidate. His Committee believed that such a course of action was indispensable to the success of their cause. And now that he was in the thick of it, Mill realized that he too wanted that cause to succeed. He felt most comfortable on the high ground, surveying the battle from an elevated vantage point. But a detachment born of disinterest could not be effectively maintained once the struggle had reached a decisive stage. The role of observer had to be abandoned for that of participant, and Mill descended warily into the contested zone. Having done so, he would not veto the negotiations considered necessary to ensure his return to the House of Commons.

THE ELECTION SPEECHES OF 1865

THERE ARE several noteworthy features about Mill's election speeches in July 1865. Not at all surprising is the element of defensiveness in his explanation to his audience of why he had come among them after declaring emphatically that he would not be a candidate in the usual sense. "I was told by those who had good means of judging that many of you desired to know more of me than you have been able to collect from what I have written. Such a statement as that left me no option, for you have a right to know my opinions and to have an opportunity of judging for yourself what man you are to select." (21.) Mill would not admit to his listeners or to himself that he harboured any ambition to sit in the House of Commons. There is more self-deception than fine calculation or hypocrisy in the way he makes bedfellows of disinterestedness and self-advertisement.

> When I stated in my letter [to Beal] that for my own sake I should not desire to sit in Parliament, I meant what I said. I have no personal objects to be promoted by it. It is a great sacrifice of my personal tastes and pursuits, and of that liberty which I value the more because I have only recently acquired it after a life spent in the restraints and confinements of a public office; for, as you may not perhaps know it, and as many people think that a writer of books, like myself, cannot possibly have any practical knowledge of business, it is a fact that I have passed many hours of every day for thirty-five years in the actual business of government. (19-20.)

Characteristically, the interpretation Mill offers of the contest at hand focuses on issues of principle and morality, not personality. If Grosvenor figures in this interpretation at all, it is only by implication. The arrangement made by their respective Committees notwithstanding, Mill could not at this stage recommend

[30] *LL*, *CW*, XVI, 1075 (6 July, 1865).

Grosvenor to the electors of Westminster. After what had transpired, however, neither could he condemn him. The best Mill could do was ignore Grosvenor and behave as though the choice before the voters was between Smith and himself, each representing diametrically opposed versions of what the electoral process was about. If Westminster's virtue was for sale, Mill suggested, Smith could meet the price. Emphasizing the symbolic importance of the decision Westminster had to make, Mill urged her electors in flattering terms to demonstrate that they could not be bought, by supporting the candidate who preferred the public to the private interest.

It is no exaggeration to say that all eyes are upon you. Every friend of freedom and purity of election in the country is looking to you with anxious feelings. . . . If you elect me and I should turn out a failure . . . you would have nothing to be ashamed of. You would have acted an honest part and done that which at the time seemed to be best for the public good. Can the same thing be said if you return the candidate of a party against which for a century past Westminster has in the most emphatic manner protested, for his money? If this great constituency should so degrade itself it will not only be the deepest mortification to all who put faith in popular institutions, but Westminster will have fallen from her glory, and she can never hold her head as high as she has done, because the progress of popular institutions, which cannot possibly be stopped, will have to go on in future without her. (25-6.)

Mill repeatedly hammered away in his election speeches at the unwholesome influence of money in the British political system. His rhetoric was often quite unlike that he adopted later in the House of Commons. Although he certainly did not hesitate to express his views frankly and forcefully in parliamentary debates, he for the most part phrased his thoughts with a judiciousness frequently absent from his extra-parliamentary speeches. He may have sometimes misjudged his audiences but he invariably sought to manifest a sensitivity to their character and expectations. On 8 July Mill asked his hearers whether they thought it a good thing that the House of Commons should be the preserve of the rich or (an oblique reference to Grosvenor?) "men with rich connections?" Admitting that the rich showed a paternalistic concern for the poor, Mill nonetheless insisted that their fundamental sympathies lay with their own kind. In language that some would probably have considered inflammatory, inciting bad feeling between the poor and their betters, Mill revealed his capacity for platform oratory. The rich

had almost universally a kind of patronising and protective sympathy for the poor, such as shepherds had for their flocks—only that was conditional upon the flock always behaving like sheep. But if the sheep tried to have a voice in their own affairs, he was afraid that a good many shepherds would be willing to call in the wolves. (32.)

That Mill had a certain relish for polemical combat had been evident long before his candidature; but he had no time for polemic for the sake of polemic. Moral purpose always informed his engagement in controversy. He might have welcomed the opportunity to pitch his message at a level somewhat beneath that he thought suitable for the printed page or the House of Commons, but for all that, the moral intent of the message was not blunted. Mill felt very strongly that purity of election was essential to a healthy political order. Something nobler than money should determine the outcome of elections. As he saw it, his candidacy was undertaken to promote the integrity of the electoral process, and he would have been derelict had he not drawn attention to this aspect of his campaign.

Mill did not eschew the philosophical in these election speeches, setting forth with clarity and directness the method of his politics and offering his prospective constituents a line of vision that looked beyond the pressures, constraints, and opportunities of the moment. He would readily confess that good will and altruistic motives in themselves did not make the ideal politician—a realistic grasp of immediate difficulties, limitations, and contingencies was essential to working a representative political system to progressive advantage. In effect Mill argued that the best politician was one who used the possibilities inherent in a particular political context to further ultimate objectives favourable to the public interest.

In the nature of things, however, many could not see what the future required of the present. Even well-intentioned and liberal-minded politicians could all too easily succumb to the demands, details, and routines of day-to-day political life, and conclude that acting upon principle was a luxury they could ill afford. Progress could not result from subordinating principle to practice, but from seeking the maximum good in each specific set of circumstances. Mill laid out the essence of his political method to the electors of Westminster on 5 July in St. James's Hall.

> Believing as I do that society and political institutions are, or ought to be, in a state of progressive advance; that it is the very nature of progress to lead us to recognise as truths what we do not as yet see to be truths; believing also that . . . it is possible to see a certain distance before us, and to be able to distinguish beforehand some of these truths of the future, and to assist others to see them—I certainly think there are truths which the time has now arrived for proclaiming, although the time may not yet have arrived for carrying them into effect. That is what I mean by advanced Liberalism. But does it follow that, because a man sees something of the future, he is incapable of judging of the past? . . . I venture to reverse the proposition. The only persons who can judge for the present . . . are those who include to-morrow in their deliberations. We can see the direction in which things are tending, and which of those tendencies we are to encourage and which to resist. . . . But while I would refuse to suppress one iota of the opinions I consider best, I confess I would not object to accept any reasonable compromise which would give me even a little of that of which I hope in time to obtain the whole. (23.)

One could compromise one's principles or one could compromise in the interest of one's principles. While in the House of Commons Mill would strive to avoid the former and pursue willingly the latter, which he deemed both honourable and wise.

Of course the impact of Mill's appearances on the results of the Westminster contest cannot be known. It is safe to say they did him no harm. On polling day, 12 July, only nine votes separated Mill and Grosvenor (the latter headed the poll with

4,534 votes), while Smith trailed by seven hundred. In his speech following the declaration of the poll, Mill retroactively gave his imprimatur to the compact that encouraged Liberal electors to support both Mill and Grosvenor rather than plump for either or split their votes between Grosvenor and Smith.[31] Mill approvingly observed that the electors of Westminster had "shown that whatever differences of opinion may exist amongst the several shades of Liberals, whatever severe criticisms they may occasionally make on each other, they are ready to help and co-operate with one another when the time of need arrives" (45). Part of the politician's art is to make a virtue of necessity.

Yet it may be that cooperation with Grosvenor was not vital to Mill's victory. It had been some time since Westminster had had an opportunity to put its mark on a general election. It did so in 1865 by electing Mill; it did so in 1868 by defeating him. A month before polling day in the first election Lord Russell had written to Amberley: "I expect Mill to come in for Westminster, & tho' I am far from agreeing with him, I think he is too distinguished a man to be rejected."[32] Mill's triumph did not reflect any deep personal commitment to him among the mass of Westminster electors. Bagehot remarked on Mill's success in *The English Constitution*: "what did the electors of Westminster know of Mr. Mill? What fraction of his mind could be imagined by any percentage of their minds? They meant to do homage to mental ability, but it was the worship of an unknown god—if ever there was such a thing in the world."[33]

MILL AND PARTY

THE MILL ELECTED by Westminster in 1865 represented no identifiable group, interest, or party in England. He could fairly be described as a Radical or advanced Liberal, but he occupied an unequivocally independent and highly personal position within the spectrum of left-wing liberalism. The weight of his established

[31]Grosvenor's Committee offered more than advice to Liberal electors. Cabs, paid for by Grosvenor, transported supporters of the Liberal candidates to the polls. See Leslie Stephen, "On the Choice of Representatives by Popular Constituencies," in *Essays on Reform*, ed. Leslie Stephen (London: Macmillan, 1867), 111-12.

[32]*Amberley Papers*, I, 394.

[33]*The English Constitution*, in *Political Essays*, ed. Norman St. John Stevas, *Collected Works of Walter Bagehot*, V-VIII (London: The Economist, 1974), V, 302. In 1867 Leslie Stephen asserted that "the efficient cause of Mr. Mill's election was the enthusiasm which his name excited in a large number of thinking and educated men; that the zeal with which they supported him induced the electors to accept him upon their recommendation; and that, in short, whatever were the intermediate steps by which Mr. Mill's reputation was brought to bear upon the electors' votes, that reputation really caused his election" ("On the Choice of Representatives," 112). In a similar vein, Henry Taylor wrote that Mill "furnished the first example of a man sought out by a large constituency to represent them in the House of Commons, without any proposal or desire of his own to do so, partly on account of his political opinions no doubt, but chiefly on the ground of his eminence as a political philosopher" (*Autobiography*, 2 vols. [London: Longmans, Green, 1885], I, 80).

intellectual and moral authority had been employed to promote certain principles and propositions, not to further the political interests or ambitions of a particular set of men who defined their aims in relation to institutional party objectives. Mill did not lack the rudimentary elements of a theory of party,[34] nor was he opposed to organized cooperation among men pursuing common goals (his chairmanship of the Jamaica Committee and, later, of the Land Tenure Reform Association come immediately to mind). Although he generally preferred Liberals to Tories, Mill did not find much to choose between Palmerston and Derby,[35] and the divisions within Radical ranks were such as to render impossible an affiliation with any specific segment of advanced opinion.

The peculiar character of Mill's radicalism was highlighted by Bagehot in the latter's *Economist* article of 29 April, 1865. Mill's letter of 17 April to Beal, outlining his position on some of the major issues of the day, was intended for publication (it appeared in the *Daily News*, *Morning Advertiser*, and *The Times* on 21 April). This letter served as Mill's election address, which Bagehot considered "one of the most remarkable . . . ever delivered by any candidate to any constituency,—especially in respect to the qualities of honesty, simplicity, and courage." According to Bagehot, Mill's radicalism, grounded in "a thorough logical capacity, unflinching integrity of purpose, and a profound knowledge of the facts and principles involved," amounted to a shattering indictment of the creed of the advanced wing of the Liberal party. Bagehot proceeded to cite the opinions expressed by Mill in his letter to Beal and to contrast them with the views of the "Radicals" on the subjects concerned. He observed that the Radicals want the ballot whereas Mill does not; the Radicals want government revenues to be drawn exclusively from direct taxation whereas Mill prefers a mixture of direct and indirect taxes; the Radicals stand for a foreign policy based on the principle of non-intervention whereas Mill asserts that there are circumstances in which English intervention on behalf of freedom abroad may be justified; the Radicals recommend drastic reductions in military expenditure whereas Mill favours only

[34]See Bruce L. Kinzer, "J.S. Mill and the Problem of Party," *Journal of British Studies*, XXI (1981), 106-22.

[35]Mill's hostility to the party environment of the Palmerstonian ascendancy was profound. On the change at the top from Derby to Palmerston in June of 1859 Mill wrote: "I see no prospect of anything but mischief from the change of ministry. . . . The new cabinet will never be able to agree on anything but the well worn useless shibboleths of Whig mitigated democracy. . . . The Liberals, by refusing to take the [Reform] bill of the late government as the foundation for theirs, have given redoubled force to the mischievous custom almost universal in Parliament, that whatever one party brings forward, the other is sure to oppose. . . . All parties seem to have joined in working the vices and weak points of popular representation for their miserably low selfish ends, instead of uniting to free representative institutions from the mischief and discredit of them." (Letter to Thomas Hare, *LL*, *CW*, XV, 626-7 [17 June, 1859].) Of the parliamentary politics of the late 1850s Norman Gash has said: "Majorities in divisions were composed to a large extent of men to whom the matter in dispute was less important than the result. Factious votes were justified by disingenuous arguments in support of dishonest resolutions." (*Aristocracy and People: Britain, 1815-1865* [Cambridge, Mass.: Harvard University Press, 1979], 266.)

those economies that will in no respect weaken England's capacity to defend her national interests in the face of aggressive and potentially hostile European despotisms; the Radicals urge abolition of purchase in the army whereas Mill cautions that thought must be given to ensure that the cure for the disease not be more damaging than the disease itself; the Radicals call for the complete abolition of flogging whereas Mill thinks it an appropriate punishment for certain crimes; the Radicals strongly oppose whereas Mill ardently supports the representation of minorities.[36]

Bagehot is using Mill to slam the radicalism of Bright and the Manchester School. In doing so he occasionally distorts the content of Mill's letter. Mill's preference for a combination of direct and indirect taxation is qualified by his assertion that taxes should not be placed on "the necessaries of life."[37] From Bagehot's discussion of Mill's views on purchase in the army one would not infer Mill's confidence that a satisfactory means could be devised for terminating "the monopoly by certain classes of the posts of emolument." To flogging Mill is "entirely opposed . . . except for crimes of brutality."[38] Yet Mill would have no wish to deny Bagehot's basic contention: his radicalism was not Bright's. Apart from their differences on specific issues, there is evidence to show that Mill regarded Bright as a demagogue[39] who represented an inferior brand of radicalism from which Mill desired to distance himself.

How can this depiction of Mill as an independent agent in 1865, a depiction that in the *Autobiography* he by implication extends to his entire parliamentary career,[40] be squared with John Vincent's treatment of Mill as "a good party man in Parliament"?[41] By "a good party man" Vincent means an admirer and supporter of Gladstone. When Mill took his seat in February of 1866 the House of Commons was led not by Palmerston, who had died the previous autumn, but by Gladstone, who together with Russell headed a Liberal government pledged to introduce a reform bill. In Palmerston's hand had lain the key to both the stability and sterility of the politics of the early 1860s, and he held it firmly in his grasp to the very end, knowing there was no one to whom he could safely pass it on.[42] Gladstone and Palmerston had been at odds before and after the former accepted the Chancellor-

[36]"Mr. Mill's Address to the Electors of Westminster," in *Historical Essays*, ed. Norman St. John Stevas, *Collected Works of Walter Bagehot*, III-IV (London: The Economist, 1968), III, 541-6.

[37]Letter to Beal, *LL*, *CW*, XVI, 1032 (17 Apr., 1865).

[38]*Ibid.*, 1034.

[39]Letter to Chadwick, *ibid.*, XV, 654-5 (20 Dec., 1859).

[40]*A*, 275-6.

[41]John Vincent, *The Formation of the Liberal Party, 1857-1868* (London: Constable, 1966), 158-61.

[42]In June of 1865 *Blackwood's Magazine* observed that Palmerston "has long arrived at the conviction that after him will come chaos; and as far as his own party is concerned, we believe him to be right. . . . [I]t is certain that to the future he looks forward with an alarm which he scarcely takes the trouble to disguise, and that his great bugbear of all is the almost certain advance of democracy." (G.R. Gleig, "The Government and the Budget," *Blackwood's Magazine*, CXVII [June 1865], 754.)

ship of the Exchequer in the Liberal administration formed in 1859.[43] By comparison with Palmerston, Gladstone, notwithstanding his Tory antecedents and instincts, represented the politics of movement. Palmerston's departure dramatically transformed the political context within which Mill found himself. Many whose liberalism was so moderate as to verge on the nominal had comfortably followed Palmerston. These could not help but be uneasy at the prospect of a government subject to the pre-eminent influence of a man thought by more than a few to be constitutionally (in both senses of the word) unsound.[44] The Conservatives, relegated to minority status since the split over the Corn Laws, would now prepare to exploit the fissures opening in Liberal ranks. Their animus against Gladstone was vehement. That Mill should be drawn to a politician of Gladstone's intellectual stature and great abilities with enemies such as these is no great mystery. The vulnerability of the Russell-Gladstone government led Mill to limit his independence. For much of the eighteen months following the resignation of Russell and Gladstone in June 1866, the latter's leadership of the party was not secure. On those issues Gladstone chose to stake his authority on, Mill circumspectly avoided action that might weaken Gladstone's position.

Vincent therefore is not wrong to see Mill as "a good party man," but he may be misleading. Mill could back Gladstone and yet retain a good deal of independence. On a whole range of subjects upon which Mill felt strongly—Jamaica, women's suffrage, proportional representation, metropolitan government—he could not look to Gladstone to take the lead. But because these were not "party" questions, in striking an independent line on them Mill in no way jeopardized Gladstone's leadership. The character of the House of Commons and the party system of the 1860s gave Mill scope to exercise a marked degree of autonomy. The initiatives he took, many of which had no chance of attracting Gladstone's endorsement, were often on subjects that fell outside the sphere of party questions as defined by the political world Mill had entered in February of 1866.

Mill has various things to say about his mission in the House of Commons. In the *Autobiography* he emphasizes an independent strategy based on the premise that he should concentrate on doing what others would not or could not do so well. He was less interested in parliamentary influence for himself than in gaining exposure for views that would remain unexpressed were it not for his presence. An element of isolation was inherent in his approach. He often found himself taking up subjects "on which the bulk of the Liberal party, even the advanced portion of it, either were of a different opinion from mine, or were comparatively indifferent."[45] Mill suggests that he chose a role that required more courage than

[43]See Richard Shannon, *Gladstone, I, 1809-1865* (London: Hamish Hamilton, 1982), 336-7, 358, 359, and Chaps. vii and viii, *passim*.

[44]To make matters worse, Gladstone had recently descended from the rarefied atmosphere of Oxford University, where he had been defeated in 1865, into South Lancashire, a pit of popular politics.

[45]*A*, 275.

most of his Radical colleagues could muster. His duty was "to come to the front in defence of advanced Liberalism on occasions when the obloquy to be encountered was such as most of the advanced Liberals in the House, preferred not to incur."[46]

Associated with this role was a larger ambition: the construction of an advanced Liberal party, which, he told Theodor Gomperz, could not be done "except in the House of Commons."[47] Mill had to use his opportunity to show Liberals in the House and in the country that his brand of liberalism could practically contribute to the formation of a Gladstone-led party built on a foundation of sound Radical doctrine. In essence, Mill saw himself as a shaper of future public and party opinion. He explained to a correspondent, in language rather more grandiose than he employed in the *Autobiography*: "I look upon the House of Commons not as a place where important practical improvements can be effected by anything I can do there, but as an elevated Tribune or Chair from which to preach larger ideas than can at present be realised."[48] Hence Mill's objectives in the House were much like those in his political writings. They were educative in nature. He had moved into a new forum in the hope that he could reach more people more effectively than he had hitherto.

There is no reason to question the sincerity of Mill's statements about purpose. Yet they convey a conception of his part in the parliamentary history of these years that is altogether too static and abstract. No politician in this Parliament functioned within a fixed political context. The major players—Russell, Gladstone, Derby, Disraeli, Bright—had a good deal to do with what Parliament would or would not do, but even they could not control the ebb and flow of political currents that swept through the House of Commons in 1866-67. On many important questions Mill became enmeshed in a web not of his own making. He might be able to affect the web's configuration but he could not alter its constitution in any fundamental way. He could exercise no influence whatsoever if he pretended that the web had nothing to do with him. His handling of the overwhelmingly dominant issue of parliamentary reform reveals him working those strands that seemed to him most promising.

PARLIAMENTARY REFORM

MILL HAD AN AGENDA of reform but it was not his agenda that counted. He might want adult suffrage limited only by a literacy qualification, and a redistribution modelled at least in part on Thomas Hare's scheme of personal representation.[49]

[46]*Ibid.*, 276.

[47]*LL*, *CW*, XVI, 1197 (22 Aug., 1866). Mill admitted to Gomperz doubts concerning the value "of chipping off little bits of one's thought, of a size to be swallowed by a set of diminutive practical politicians incapable of digesting them" (*ibid.*, 1196).

[48]Letter to Arnold Ruge, *ibid.*, 1234 (7 Feb., 1867).

[49]Letter to Kyllman, *ibid.*, 998 (15 Feb., 1865).

But only a government bill could pass through Parliament and Mill would not be one of its draughtsmen.

The 1866 Bill of record would be the work of Russell and Gladstone. Mill cared much about the content of a reform measure but in 1866 he cared more about supporting Gladstone. In February of 1865, five months before his triumph at Westminster and eight months before Palmerston's death, Mill told Max Kyllman, "no Reform Bill which we are likely to see for some time to come, will be worth moving hand or foot for."[50] By the end of the year he had come to view the matter rather differently, admitting to Chadwick,

> The whole of our laws of election from top to bottom require to be reconstructed on new principles: but to get those principles into people's heads is work for many years, and they will not wait that time for the next step in reform. . . . And perhaps some measure of reform is as likely to promote as to delay other improvements in the representative system.[51]

Mill had not changed his ideas concerning what should go into a reform bill. Nor did he expect that any bill emerging from the deliberations of the Liberal government would remotely resemble what he wanted. But Mill was now member for Westminster; Palmerston was dead; Russell and Gladstone had left no doubt that parliamentary reform would be the centrepiece of their 1866 legislative programme. Where Gladstone led on this critical party question, Mill would follow.

A comparison of a letter Mill wrote to Hare in January of 1866 with his response to Gladstone's Reform Bill shows the extent to which he had chained himself to Gladstone's slow-moving chariot. To Hare Mill expatiated on the dangers a bill confined to franchise extension presented to their position. The proposal and passage of such a bill, Mill argued, would exclude the subject of personal representation from the sphere of parliamentary discussion. Once a reform bill had been enacted "the whole subject of changes in the representation will be tabooed for years to come."[52] (Chadwick, after receiving Mill's letter of December 1865, would presumably not have attributed such an opinion to his friend.) Mill did not expect the Liberal government to offer a measure that incorporated the views he and Hare held, but he did hope the bill would be sufficiently broad in scope to justify raising the issues that he wanted to air in the House of Commons.

The Bill Gladstone introduced on 12 March provided for a reduction in the borough household qualification from £10 to £7 and for a county occupation franchise of £14. It was a franchise bill and nothing more.[53] Had it passed,

[50]*Ibid.*, 997 (15 Feb., 1865).

[51]*Ibid.*, 1129 (29 Dec., 1865).

[52]*Ibid.*, 1138-9 (11 Jan., 1866).

[53]For the cabinet's decision not to take up redistribution, see Maurice Cowling, *1867: Disraeli, Gladstone and Revolution: The Passing of the Second Reform Bill* (Cambridge: Cambridge University Press, 1967), 99-100. After indicating in March that it would offer a Seats Bill only after the second reading of the Franchise Bill, the government introduced the measure on 7 May. On 31 May Mill spoke on this Bill and briefly argued the case for personal representation. He did not oppose Gladstone's redistribution scheme.

working-class voters would have constituted approximately a quarter of the total electorate of England and Wales (a doubling of working-class electoral weight). The Tories were not inclined to mount a frontal assault on the measure. They were more than happy to let Robert Lowe and the band of Liberal renegades hostile to parliamentary reform, whom Bright referred to as the "Adullamites," make the running. Although the bulk of Mill's fine 13 April speech (No. 16) focused on the need for working-class enfranchisement, the occasion for it was a motion tabled by Lord Grosvenor (an Adullamite) and seconded by Lord Stanley (a Conservative for whom Mill had considerable regard) that called for postponement of the Bill's second reading until a redistribution package had been presented. Mill, knowing that the Adullamites and their Tory sympathizers wanted to wreck the Bill, apprehended that from such a wreckage Gladstone would not emerge without serious injury. That Mill must have agreed with the substance of Grosvenor's motion did not move him to support it. The preface to his elegant argument on behalf of parliamentary reform was devoted to a defence of the ministry's exclusive concentration on the franchise. Mill insisted that the Bill, though "far more moderate than is desired by the majority of reformers," significantly enlarged working-class electoral power and was therefore "not only a valuable part of a scheme of Parliamentary Reform, but highly valuable even if nothing else were to follow" (60-1).[54]

The government and its Bill survived for another two months. On 18 June Lord Dunkellin's amendment to substitute a rating for a rental franchise in the boroughs was carried against the ministry by a vote of 315 to 304.[55] A week later the Russell-Gladstone government resigned. Throughout their difficulties over the reform question, Mill had steadfastly adhered to the Gladstonian line.[56]

Mill's behaviour should not be attributed to servility. He knew what he was doing and why he was doing it. He admired Gladstone and cast him as the future leader of a radicalized Liberal party. That radicalization could occur only in conjunction with a marked increase of working-class political power. Mill had grave misgivings about class power of any sort and did not advocate working-class political ascendancy.[57] The enormous appeal Hare's scheme had for Mill lay

[54]Gladstone's diary entry for 13 April includes: "Reform Debate. Mill admirable." (*Gladstone Diaries*, ed. H.C.G. Matthew, Vol. VI: *1861-1868* [Oxford: Clarendon Press, 1978], 430.)

[55]A rating value of seven pounds was approximately equivalent to an eight-pound rental value. The intent of the amendment was to restrict the extent of working-class enfranchisement. Mill's prediction that the Bill would be "carried by increasing instead of diminishing majorities" proved mistaken (57).

[56]Kate Amberley recorded in her journal on 23 June a conversation with Gladstone. "I told him that Mill was so grieved at the Govt. going out, and said that . . . he had never hoped to be under a leader with whom he could feel so much sympathy and respect as he did for Gladstone, and Gladstone answered 'Poor fellow, he has all through been most kind and indulgent to me'" (*Amberley Papers*, I, 516).

[57]To David Urquhart Mill wrote: "I doubt not that they would be corrupted like other classes by becoming the predominant power in the country, though probably in a less degree because in a multitude the general feelings of human nature are usually more powerful & class feeling less so than in a small body. But I do not want to make them predominant." (*LL, CW*, XVI, 1209 [26 Oct., 1866].)

partly in its capacity to promote both democratic political participation and meritocratic government.[58] Aristocratic and middle-class prejudices retarded social and political improvement. A sizeable injection of working-class influence was required to achieve the accelerated rate of progress Mill wished to foster. He sensed the growth of working-class activism, as manifested in the Reform League, and put this together with Gladstonian leadership and franchise extension to come up with a new and better political order. In January of 1866 he told H.S. Chapman,

> English statesmanship will have to assume a new character, and to look in a more direct way than before to the interests of posterity. We are now . . . standing on the very boundary line between this new statesmanship and the old; and the next generation will be accustomed to a very different set of political arguments and topics from those of the present and past.[59]

In 1866 and 1867 Mill was prepared to serve as a bridge between Gladstonian parliamentary Liberalism and working-class political agitation. There were other bridges (Bright was unquestionably the most important). But Mill's conduct inside and outside the House of Commons in relation to both Gladstone's position and the aspirations of the politically conscious members of the working classes resonates with an acute sensitivity to new forces at work and their potential for constructive political engagement.

The resignation of Russell and Gladstone was followed by the formation of a minority Conservative government under Derby and Disraeli. The public agitation for parliamentary reform, led by the Manchester based middle-class dominated Reform Union and the metropolitan based artisan dominated Reform League, heated up in response.[60] The Reform League, eager to impress upon the new government the earnestness of the working classes on the question of the franchise, announced their sponsorship of a mass public demonstration to be held in Hyde Park on 23 July. The right to hold public meetings had been one of the issues galvanizing those reponsible for organizing the Reform League. The view of the Derby ministry, one supported by Sir George Grey, Home Secretary in previous Liberal administrations, was that Royal Parks were not appropriate locations for public meetings, and that such gatherings were prohibited by law.[61] The Tory Home Secretary, Spencer Walpole, authorized Sir Richard Mayne, Metropolitan Police Commissioner, to issue an order forbidding the meeting.[62] At about 6 p.m. on 23 July the Leaguers, led by their President, Edmond Beales, arrived at the

[58]For a discussion of Hare's scheme in relation to Mill's preoccupations with participation and competence, see Dennis F. Thompson, *John Stuart Mill and Representative Government* (Princeton: Princeton University Press, 1976), 102-12.

[59]*LL*, *CW*, XVI, 1137 (6 Jan., 1866).

[60]For the public agitation, see Cowling, *1867*, 242-86; Frances Elma Gillespie, *Labor and Politics in England, 1850-1867* (Durham, N.C.: Duke University Press, 1927), 235-88; and Royden Harrison, *Before the Socialists: Studies in Labour and Politics, 1861-1881* (London: Routledge & Kegan Paul, 1965), 78-136. Both the Union and the League had endorsed Gladstone's Reform Bill.

[61]See Grey's speech of 19 July, 1866: *Parliamentary Debates* [*PD*], 3rd ser., Vol. 184, cols. 1074-5.

[62]*Ibid.*, 1073-4.

locked gates of Hyde Park and were confronted by a police barricade. Beales did not mind the government's thinking he carried the match that could ignite an agitation of truly dangerous proportions, but he had no intention of striking that match. On being informed that the demonstrators would not be admitted to the Park, Beales led his forces off to Trafalgar Square. The confusion arising from the shift, aggravated by the turbulence of a crowd that apparently included more than a few ruffians out for a bit of fun, resulted in the felling of the Park railings. Three days of commotion in Hyde Park ensued. Damage to the grounds was fairly extensive and some two hundred people were injured.[63]

In his speech of 24 July, given while the tumult was still in progress, Mill laid responsibility at the government's door. In attempting to enforce an exclusion for which there could be no justification, the ministry had precipitated the disturbance and heightened bad feeling between the governing classes and the masses. "Noble Lords and right honourable Gentlemen opposite may be congratulated on having done a job of work last night which will require wiser men than they are, many years to efface the consequences of" (100).

Under the circumstances, Mill's speech, delivered in a House many of whose members felt they had good cause to be alarmed at the recent turn of events, was remarkably bold.[64] Disraeli, cognizant that Mill's opinions on this matter were shared by few M.P.s on either side of the House, rose when Mill resumed his seat, and opened with an observation designed to accentuate Mill's isolation: "I take it for granted . . . that the speech we have just heard is one of those intended to be delivered in Hyde Park, and if I may judge from it as a sample, we can gather a very good idea of the rhetoric which will prevail at those periodical meetings we are promised." In a masterful brief speech calculated to highlight the contrast between the responsible conduct of ministers of the crown and the irresponsible language of the member for Westminster, Disraeli rejected Mill's imputations. He denied that the government was opposed to working-class political meetings, but declared that these should be held "at the proper time and place." The 23rd of July at Hyde Park, Disraeli implied, was neither, as the "riot, tumult, and disturbance" unleashed by the League's initiative unhappily demonstrated.[65]

Mill devotes more than a page of the *Autobiography* to the curious and rather enigmatic aftermath of the Hyde Park riots. A trace of bitterness enters into his account of the part he played in dissuading the League from endeavouring to hold a meeting in Hyde Park on 31 July in defiance of the government. Mill thought it

[63]Henry Broadhurst, who was present, gives a useful account of the riots in his autobiography, *The Story of His Life from a Stonesmason's Bench to the Treasury Bench* (London: Hutchinson, 1901), 33-40; see also the full report in the *Daily News*, 24 July, 1866, 5.

[64]Matthew Arnold's linking of Mill and Jacobinism in *Culture and Anarchy* derived at least in part from Arnold's hostile response to the Hyde Park riots and Mill's defence of the Reform League. See *Culture and Anarchy with Friendship's Garland and Some Literary Essays*, ed. R.H. Super, *Complete Prose Works of Matthew Arnold*, V (Ann Arbor: University of Michigan Press, 1965), 111, 132-3.

[65]*PD*, 3rd ser., Vol. 184, cols. 1412-14.

highly probable that serious violence would erupt from such a confrontation and that nothing good could come of it. Having successfully made his case, he agreed to address a League meeting at the Agricultural Hall on the 30th (No. 32). He believed that he had been "the means of preventing much mischief." His bitterness was directed not against the League but against certain elements of the metropolitan press that had accused him of being "intemperate and passionate." "I do not know," he said, "what they expected from me; but they had reason to be thankful to me if they knew from what I had in all probability preserved them. And I do not believe it could have been done, at that particular juncture, by any one else."[66]

The object of reviewing this well-known episode is not to assess the accuracy of Mill's claims. Evelyn L. Pugh, after a searching and sympathetic enquiry into Mill's connection with the Hyde Park affair, concedes that there is no evidence to corroborate Mill's assessment of his effectiveness. What Mill reported no doubt did occur, but his interpretation perhaps assigns too much weight to his intervention.[67] Whatever the practical import of Mill's involvement with the League in late July of 1866, the whole business usefully illuminates the purposeful intent that fashioned his response to the reform crisis of 1866-67.

The political coin minted by Mill in answer to the franchise question had Gladstone on one side and the working classes on the other. Through Gladstone the working classes could be integrated into the political process. The mode of achieving this objective could also contribute to a transformation of the Liberal party into an effective instrument of social and political reform.[68] But for Gladstone to keep in the air a sufficient number of balls to secure his ascendancy over other ambitious jugglers, he had to put a respectable distance between himself and the radicalism of the Reform League. To some degree both Bright and Mill consciously acted as Gladstone's surrogates.[69]

Not too much should be made of Mill's refusal to join the Reform League. Considering the strong exception he took to its programme of manhood (rather than adult) suffrage and the ballot, his identification with its struggle is impressive. In declining the invitation to join the League, Mill observed that "the general promotion of the Reform cause is the main point at present, and . . . advanced reformers, without suppressing their opinions on the points on which

[66]*A*, 278-9.

[67]Evelyn L. Pugh, "J.S. Mill's *Autobiography* and the Hyde Park Riots," *Research Studies*, L (Mar. 1982), 1-20. Pugh rightly emphasizes the central role Mill played in killing the 1867 government bill to prohibit public meetings in Royal Parks.

[68]Mill wrote to Fawcett: "One of the most important consequences of giving a share in the government to the working classes, is that there will then be some members of the House with whom it will no longer be an axiom that human society exists for the sake of property in land—a grovelling superstition which is still in full force among the higher classes" (*LL*, *CW*, XVI, 1130 [1 Jan., 1866]).

[69]For a stimulating discussion of Bright, Mill, and the emergence of the Gladstonian Liberal party, see Vincent, *Formation of the Liberal Party*, 149-211.

they may still differ, should act together as one man in the common cause."[70] Not only did Mill defend the League in the Commons on the Hyde Park question, but he sent a £5 donation to assist those arrested by the police on 23 July.[71] In February of 1867 he participated in a deputation whose purpose was to persuade Walpole to appoint a working man to the Royal Commission on Trades Unions.[72] In the summer of 1867 Mill subscribed to a Reform League fund established to organize the newly enfranchised electors on behalf of advanced Liberalism.[73] The League also had cause to appreciate Mill's role in the successful fight to stop the 1867 Parks Bill from getting through the House of Commons.

In late July of 1866, in urging caution on the League, Mill had drawn on some of the moral and political capital he had invested in the working-class movement. He had done what he could to prevent violence and to ease the war of nerves between the authorities and the agitators. Mill asserted himself not merely for the sake of peace. Indeed, he had no desire to moderate the conflict between the government and the League; rather, he sought to enclose the League's expression of that conflict within bounds prescribed by the need to build and sustain an unofficial and necessarily unacknowledged alliance between Gladstone and the working-class reform movement.

The same concern prompted Mill to call upon the League to exercise self-restraint in early 1867. At a League-organized conference of late February, delegates representing the League and the trades unions passed a resolution threatening that, in the event of governmental resistance to working-class enfranchisement, it would "be necessary to consider the propriety of those classes adopting a universal cessation from labour until their political rights are conceded."[74] The *Morning Star* reported that the speeches given at the meeting were demagogic.[75] On reading this report Mill wrote to William Randal Cremer, a leading figure in trades union and radical political circles, protesting against the extreme rhetoric employed on the occasion. Mill argued that any reform bill acceptable to Parliament would in the nature of things have to be a compromise. Violent language hinting at "revolutionary expedients" should not be indulged in by those leading the agitation. The conditions that might justify revolution, Mill unequivocally stated, did not exist in England.[76] He did not deny that League

[70]Letter to [George Howell?], *LL*, *CW*, XVII, 2010-11 (22 July, 1865).

[71]Letter to Edmond Beales, *ibid.*, XVI, 1186 (26 July, 1866).

[72]See 133-4, and letter to George Jacob Holyoake, *LL*, *CW*, XVI, 1242-3 (16 Feb., 1867).

[73]Letter to Beales, *ibid.*, 1291-2 (22 July, 1867).

[74]Quoted in Gillespie, *Labor and Politics*, 284.

[75]*Morning Star*, 28 Feb., 1867, 2.

[76]What conditions could justify revolution? "One is personal oppression & tyranny & consequent personal suffering of such intensity that to put an immediate stop to them is worth almost any amount of present evil & future danger. The other is when either the system of government does not permit the redress of grievances to be sought by peaceable & legal means, or when those means have been perseveringly exerted to the utmost for a long series of years, & their inefficacy has been demonstrated by experiment." (Letter to W.R. Cremer, *LL*, *CW*, XVI, 1248 [1 Mar., 1867].)

members had been given "ample provocation and abundant excuse" for their "feelings of irritation." To allow such irritation to rob them of their sense of proportion, however, was likely to harm the cause of reform. Especially arousing Mill's displeasure was the message carried in the speeches of "a determined rejection beforehand of all compromise on the Reform question, even if proposed by the public men in whose sincerity & zeal as reformers you have repeatedly expressed the fullest confidence."[77] Mill feared that the rather tenuous line joining Gladstone to the working-class reform movement was beginning to fragment. The course pursued by Derby and Disraeli in 1867 further jeopardized the enterprise to which Mill had committed himself.

The parliamentary struggle over the details of the Conservative Reform Bill centred on the borough householders and their payment of rates. Derby and Disraeli offered borough household suffrage, subject to the stipulation that only householders who paid their rates directly should be eligible for the franchise. In 171 boroughs the composition of rates, whereby the local authorities compounded with the landlords for the payment of the occupier's rates, had proved a highly convenient mechanism.[78] These compound householders, whose names did not appear on the rating book, would be excluded from the vote under clause 3 of the Tory Bill. Disraeli would show himself to be infinitely flexible in committee but he rigidly maintained that on the principle of ratepaying the Bill would stand or fall.[79]

Gladstone was appalled by what he took to be the dishonest and fraudulent character of the Bill. Early in the debate on clause 3 he moved to eliminate for electoral purposes the distinction between direct ratepayers and compounders. Gladstone held no brief for household suffrage "pure and simple." His humiliating setback of the previous session doubtless very much with him, Gladstone was now ready to put his strength to the test in opposition to the aspect of the Tory Bill that he thought most unacceptable. The outcome he looked for was a defeat of the government and settlement of the question on terms that satisfied his own preferences. But his reach exceeded his grasp. In the division of 12 April forty-seven Liberals, a number of Radicals among them, rejected Gladstone's

[77]*Ibid.*, 1247-8.

[78]There were approximately 486,000 compound householders in parliamentary boroughs. The system spared the occupier the bother of putting aside money to meet his quarterly rating obligations. What was in it for the landlord and local authority? "A deduction of twenty or twenty-five per cent was allowed when the rate was compounded, so that the owner of fifty or a hundred small houses derived no small profit by calling on his tenants to pay the full rate in their rent, while he had a discount in paying it over to the parish. Naturally it was convenient for the parish to be saved the trouble of collecting from the small occupiers." (Charles Seymour, *Electoral Reform in England and Wales: The Development and Operation of the Parliamentary Franchise, 1832-1885* [New Haven: Yale University Press, 1915], 149.)

[79]"The bill as it went into committee included no lodger franchise. . . . The Act enfranchised all £10 lodgers in parliamentary boroughs. The county occupation franchise in the bill began at £15 p.a. In the Act it was lowered to £12 and supplemented by a £5 franchise for copyholders. The period of qualifying residence was two years in the bill, one in the Act. The provision to allow voters to vote by voting papers, which was included in the bill, was removed by the time it was passed." (Cowling, *1867*, 223.)

leadership and the amendment went down by a vote of 310 to 289. Suspecting that, although he would do no business with Gladstone, Disraeli would find it necessary to do business with them, these Radicals put the survival of the Bill before a parliamentary victory for Gladstone. In his diary Gladstone recorded: "A smash perhaps without example."[80] Mill voted with the minority.[81]

Mill's sole major speech on the ratepaying issue was delivered in the debate that saw Gladstone empty his barrels in a final attempt to wound the measure fatally. On 6 May Disraeli informed the House that the government could not accept the amendment of J.T. Hibbert, Radical M.P. for Oldham, that would allow compounders who wished to opt out of composition to pay a reduced rate. Instead, he indicated, the government would offer an amendment providing that the full rate would have to be paid by those opting out of composition, but that amount could be deducted from the rent received by their landlords. If defeated on the amendment, Disraeli announced, the government would dissolve. Gladstone took up the challenge and advised the House to reject Disraeli's amendment. That advice was not heeded by fifty-eight Liberals who voted with the government, which sailed through the division with a majority of sixty-six.[82]

A correct deciphering of Mill's speech of 9 May hinges on an understanding of what was at stake in this debate. The Tory Bill had sent tremors through Liberal ranks, as Derby and Disraeli had intended that it should. Mill vehemently criticized Disraeli for politicizing the ratepaying issue and sponsoring an amendment calculated to increase electoral corruption. But Mill's words were directed less at the government than at the Radicals. "I hope that honourable Gentlemen on this side of the House, who, loving household suffrage not wisely but too well, have brought matters to this state, intend to come down handsomely to the registration societies in their own neighbourhoods; for the registration societies are destined henceforth to be one of the great institutions of the country" (147). Shortly thereafter Mill warned those Radicals who had shown a tendency to act on the supposition that more of what they wanted could be had from Disraeli than from Gladstone that they would pay a heavy price at the polls (monetarily and politically) for their determination "to outwit the Chancellor of the Exchequer, and make his Bill bring forth pure and simple household suffrage, contrary to the intentions of everybody except themselves who will vote for it" (147).

These sentiments did not originate in a conviction that household suffrage was a bad idea. Mill wanted his free-wheeling Radical colleagues to realize they were gambling on getting a form of household suffrage they could live with. More importantly, he wanted them to understand that purchasing any bill of goods from Disraeli at Gladstone's political expense could severely damage the prospects for the formation of an effective advanced Liberal party.

[80]*Gladstone Diaries*, VI, 513.
[81]For the division, see *PD*, 3rd ser., Vol. 186, col. 1700 (12 Apr., 1867).
[82]Cowling, *1867*, 269-71.

Disraeli had managed to put Gladstone on the defensive. The stepped-up pace of the agitation out of doors may for a time have had a similar effect. In 1866 the leaders of the League might have thought a £7 franchise bill from Gladstone preferable to anything the Tories were likely to offer. By April of 1867 they could not be so sure. Frances Gillespie notes that in this month the League "utterly denounced" Gladstone's proposal of a £5 rating franchise.[83] On 6 May the League defied the government and held a demonstration in Hyde Park. Feelings were running high inside and outside the House. Gladstone could make no overt move towards the League. Mill had to take up ground distinct from that occupied by the League while doing everything possible to convince its supporters that Gladstone was the man to whom they must turn for leadership.

Gladstone made that task somewhat easier after the defeat of 9 May. His "reaction to this second defeat," Cowling observes, "was to abandon the £5 rating line altogether . . . and to deliver a sarcastic address to the Reform Union on 11 May in which he attacked the Adullamite Whigs for the first time in public . . . and went as near as a responsible politician could to committing himself as soon as he returned to office to reject the personal payment principle."[84]

On 17 May Disraeli made his stunning announcement to the House that the government intended to accept the principle of Grosvenor Hodgkinson's amendment for the abolition of compounding. The amendment was not incompatible with Disraeli's insistence on retaining the ratepaying principle, but its acceptance swept away the restrictive effects of the Bill's distinction between direct ratepayers and compounders. The fuss that ensued, in which Mill took part (see Nos. 54, 58, 59), focused on the procedure by which the abolition of compounding was to be implemented.[85]

Disraeli's bravura performance on 17 May obviated Radical obstruction and ensured the passage of the Bill. Once again he had caught Gladstone off guard and made it appear that the House could carry on very well without Gladstone's assistance. In his speech to a London meeting of the Reform Union on 25 May, Mill tried to counteract this impression by emphasizing who had done what for whom in 1866 and 1867. He complained of the government's unfair treatment of the compounder and suggested that Disraeli had been consistent only in his unwillingness to play straight.

> This is very like all that has been going on ever since the beginning of these reform discussions. It has been a succession—I will not say of tricks, because I do not like to use hard words, especially when I cannot prove them, but of what is called in the vernacular, trying it on. The object is just to see what you will bear, and anything that you will bear you

[83]*Labor and Politics*, 278n.

[84]*1867*, 272.

[85]In the end the 1867 Act abolished composition in parliamentary boroughs. The confusion and inconvenience caused by the change, however, led to the passage in 1869 of a measure (32 & 33 Victoria, c. 41) that reinstated composition and also provided that compound occupiers have their names recorded in the rate-book.

shall have to bear, but if you show that you will not bear it, then perhaps it may not be required of you. (169.)

No better could perhaps be expected of Disraeli; but Mill thought it vital that he not be rewarded for a technique designed to conceal the identity of the real author of reform. Reformers should have no patience for the leader of the House of Commons

when he gibes at those to whom we really owe all this, when he . . . talks of their "blundering hands," and gives it to be understood that they have not been able to carry reform and he can, and that it is not their measure. He is quite satisfied if he can say to Mr. Gladstone, "You did not do it." But Mr. Gladstone did do it. He could not carry his measure last year because Mr. Disraeli and his friends opposed it; Mr. Disraeli can carry his Reform Bill because Mr. Gladstone will not oppose anything but that which is not real reform, and will support to the utmost that which is. I have no objection to thank everybody for their part in it when once we have got it, but I will always thank most those to whom we really owe it. The people of England know that but for the late government this government would have gone one hundred miles out of their way before they would have brought in any Reform Bill at all. And every good thing we have got in this bill, even that which seems to be more than Mr. Gladstone was prepared to give, has only been given for the purpose of outbidding Mr. Gladstone. (170-1.)

Ideas and ideals were central to Mill's liberalism, but politics was an indispensable medium for their having practical effect. The Liberal party was important to Mill for what it could become. Its development in a direction consonant with his objectives required, he believed, both a leadership dominated by Gladstone and an active influential rank and file with a strong working-class contingent. His response to the reform crisis of 1866-67 followed from this conviction.

Mill, disappointed by the fortunes of radicalism at the 1868 general election, gave scant indication in the *Autobiography* of the motives that governed his general political disposition in 1867. There he writes not of party political purposes but of independent advocacy of fundamental principles concerning women's suffrage and the representation of minorities. "In the general debates on Mr. Disraeli's Reform Bill, my participation was limited to the one speech [on 9 May] already mentioned; but I made the Bill an occasion for bringing the two greatest improvements which remain to be made in representative government formally before the House and the nation."[86] Mill invariably stressed the non-party character of these initiatives, but the "occasion" for bringing them forward was coloured by party considerations. On 7 June 1866, he presented to the House a women's suffrage petition signed by 1521 women. He also gave notice of a motion for a return of the number of women who met the existing property qualifications but were barred from the vote by reason of their sex.[87] Mill had no

[86]*A*, 284.
[87]Mill put this motion on 17 July; see No. 25.

intention of pressing the issue beyond this point in the 1866 session, explaining to a fellow M.P. (C.D. Griffith) that "there is no chance that we can succeed in getting a clause for admitting women to the suffrage introduced with the present Reform Bill." The object was "merely to open the subject this year, without taking up the time of the House and increasing the accusation of obstructiveness by forcing on a discussion which cannot lead to a practical result."[88] Had the Reform Bill of 1866 carried it is possible that Mill would never have proposed the enfranchisement of women in the House of Commons ("perhaps the only really important public service I performed in the capacity of a Member of Parliament").[89] Much the same can be said of the personal representation amendment. In November of 1866 Mill wrote to Hare:

> There will, in all probability, be a Tory Reform Bill, and whatever may be its quality, no moving of amendments or raising of new points will in the case of a Tory bill be regarded by Liberals as obstructiveness, or as damaging to the cause. Then will be the very time to bring forward and get discussed, everything which we think ought to be put into a good Reform Bill.[90]

JAMAICA AND IRELAND

NO ONE was obliged to treat seriously Mill's views on women's suffrage and personal representation. Those who disliked such opinions could regard their propagation as foolish but not as dangerous. For the trouble he took on these matters he may have attracted the admiration of some, the derision of others. Few politicians would care to have the measure of their power taken by reference to either the esteem they inspire or the ridicule they provoke. Whatever political power Mill commanded was inseparable from the intellectual and moral authority he could bring to bear on issues that the governing classes could not easily shrug off. Jamaica and Ireland were such issues, and the high moral line Mill adopted on both is well known.[91] But his course of action on these questions too was not unaffected by his sensitivity to party and personal struggles, and to their possible implications for the future of Gladstone and the Liberal party.

On no subject that he addressed during his Westminster years did Mill feel more strongly than that of the conduct of Governor Eyre and the Jamaican authorities in October of 1865, following the uprising at Morant Bay.[92] The intensity of Mill's

[88] *LL*, *CW*, XVI, 1175 (9 June, 1866).

[89] *A*, 285.

[90] *LL*, *CW*, XVI, 1215 (18 Nov., 1866).

[91] See *A*, 280-2; Bernard Semmel, *The Governor Eyre Controversy* (London: Macgibbon and Lee, 1962), esp. Chap. iii; Lynn Zastoupil, "Moral Government: J.S. Mill on Ireland," *Historical Journal*, XXVI (1983), 707-17.

[92] For a good general treatment of the Jamaican background, see W.P. Morrell, *British Colonial Policy in the Mid-Victorian Age: South Africa, New Zealand, and the West Indies* (Oxford: Clarendon Press, 1969), 399-432.

reaction to the reports from Jamaica and his assumption that consideration of Eyre's behaviour did not lie beyond the parliamentary pale were evident as early as December, when he wrote to a correspondent: "There seems likely to be enough doing in Parliament, this session, to occupy all one's thoughts. There is no part of it all, not even the Reform Bill, more important than the duty of dealing justly with the abominations committed in Jamaica."[93]

When Mill took his seat in February the Royal Commission appointed to investigate the Jamaica troubles had not completed its work. The ministry, preoccupied with the Reform Bill, hoped that all parties, including the anti-Eyre Jamaica Committee, of which Mill was a prominent member, would hold their fire until the Commission had reported.[94] It is perhaps not surprising that Mill kept himself in check while the Commission took evidence and deliberated, even though he seems to have already made up his mind that Eyre was responsible for the terrible things that had been done and that the rule of law demanded he be punished accordingly. When the Report reached London on 30 April, its content did nothing to soften Mill's view of Eyre.[95] His self-imposed silence on the subject for nearly three months after the Report became public was probably dictated by his resolution that Gladstone's friends should refrain from aggravating in any way their leader's formidable difficulties in the House of Commons.[96]

With the defeat of the Reform Bill and the fall of Russell and Gladstone, Mill's role in the anti-Eyre movement was transformed. At the end of June Charles Buxton resigned as Chairman of the Jamaica Committee, having vainly argued that the Committee should not attempt to prosecute Eyre for murder. The burden of Buxton's case was that conviction was highly improbable and, if obtained, would be followed by a royal pardon. While prosecution could produce but meagre results, it would alienate public opinion, which would come to see Eyre as a dutiful servant of the crown, hounded by a vindictive group who failed to appreciate the heavy responsibility borne by the governor of an island whose predominantly black population could present a grave threat to the life and property of the white minority. The Jamaica Committee, Buxton urged, would best serve the interests of the victims and the cause of justice by working to secure an official condemnation

[93]To William Fraser Rae, *LL*, *CW*, XVI, 1126 (14 Dec., 1865). Two weeks later he observed to Henry Fawcett: "The two great topics of the year will be Jamaica and Reform, and there will be an immensity to be said and done on both subjects" (*ibid.*, 1131 [1 Jan., 1866]).

[94]For a valuable discussion of the governmental response to the Eyre difficulties, see B.A. Knox, "The British Government and the Governor Eyre Controversy, 1865-1875," *Historical Journal*, XIX (1976), 877-900.

[95]Among its other findings the Commission concluded that "the punishment of death was unnecessarily frequent"; "the floggings were reckless, and at Bath positively barbarous"; "the burning of 1,000 houses was wanton and cruel." For these findings, see "Report of the Jamaica Royal Commission," *PP*, 1866, XXX, 489-531.

[96]If Mill assumed that Gladstone was deeply disturbed by what had occurred in Jamaica he was right. Knox has noted that "Gladstone leaned towards a sterner view of Eyre's conduct than did his colleagues" ("The British Government and the Governor Eyre Controversy," 880).

of Eyre and those who had used the declaration and continuance of martial law to inflict unwarrantable and cruel suffering on thousands of British subjects. That condemnation could form the basis of a campaign to win financial compensation for the victims and their families.[97]

Mill and Bright (also a member of the executive committee) held that the course Buxton saw as impolitic offered the only means by which the principles of law, morality, and justice could be vindicated. Eyre's removal from the governorship (he had been temporarily superseded in January of 1866 and his successor would be commissioned in July) fell far short of what was required. Compensation for victims should be sought, but such compensation could not restore the moral authority of British imperial government. If the government refused to prosecute, then the Committee must, as was explained to the public in a document issued by the Committee not long after Buxton's resignation as Chairman.

In undertaking to discharge this duty, so far as circumstances and the means at their disposal may permit, the Committee are not . . . activated by vindictive feelings towards those whom they believe to have violated the law. Their aim, besides upholding the obligation of justice and humanity towards all races beneath the Queen's sway, is to vindicate, by an appeal to judicial authority, the great legal and constitutional principles which have been violated in the late proceedings, and deserted by the Government.[98]

Mill and Bright carried the executive with them on 26 June. On 9 July Mill was elected to replace Buxton.[99] Ten days later Mill put his Jamaica questions to the government in the House of Commons.[100] On 31 July he delivered his single major speech (No. 33) on the subject in the debate occasioned by the introduction of four resolutions by Buxton.[101]

Mill could hardly have acted as he did on the Jamaica question in July had the fragile Russell-Gladstone government still been in office. Certainly the object in pressing the issue was to rescue England's moral reputation, not to irritate the Conservative ministry. The fact remains that however strongly Mill felt about the matter, he abstained during the first half of the year from venting his feelings in the

[97]See Semmel, *Governor Eyre Controversy*, 68-9.

[98]"Jamaica Documents," in *Essays on Equality, Law, and Education*, *CW*, XXI (Toronto: University of Toronto Press, 1984), 423.

[99]For a report of the meeting at which he was elected, see *The Times*, 10 July, 1866, 5.

[100]Disraeli insisted that Mill state in full each of the questions, into which were built allegations the justification of which Mill seemed to take for granted. Disraeli's masterful response charged Mill with having assumed guilt where none had yet been legally established. He also made it clear that the government had no intention of taking any further action against Eyre. For Disraeli's speech of 19 July, 1866, see *PD*, 3rd ser., Vol. 184, cols. 1064-9.

[101]The first of Buxton's resolutions, which the government agreed to accept on the understanding that he would withdraw the other three, deplored the excessive punishments inflicted in Jamaica. The second asked that the conduct of military, naval, and colonial officers responsible for such excesses "be inquired into with a view to their punishment." The third concerned compensation for victims or their families, and the last the treatment of Jamaicans held in connection with the disturbances. For the motion and the debate, see *ibid.*, cols. 1763-1840. In the *Autobiography* Mill says that his Jamaica speech "is that which I should probably select as the best of my speeches in Parliament" (*A*, 281).

House of Commons. Had a perfectly secure Liberal government been in office he surely would not have held back. The spectacle of a vulnerable Gladstone harassed by anti-reform forces persuaded Mill that the assertion of principles dear to him had to be subordinated, at least momentarily, to political exigencies.

The Eyre question never acquired a significant parliamentary status.[102] Irish subjects, especially the land question, had such a status and Mill came to think that he had an important role to play in making England aware of the remedies appropriate to Irish problems.

Very soon after first taking his seat in the House of Commons Mill spoke on the suspension of habeas corpus in Ireland (February 1866). He did not offer remedies on this occasion; instead he made very plain his belief that England had abysmally failed to reconcile Ireland to British rule. Mill's words did not sit well with the House.[103] His general condemnation of English government in Ireland, however,

[102]No government, Liberal or Tory, would have been prepared to act upon the recommendations of the Jamaica Committee. No criminal convictions followed from the prosecutions launched by the Committee. As Buxton had feared, the policy pushed by Mill aroused sympathy for Eyre, led to the formation of the Eyre Defence Committee, and engendered a good deal of hostility towards members of the Jamaica Committee, Mill included. He had no regrets, observing in the *Autobiography*, "we had given an emphatic warning to those who might be tempted to similar guilt hereafter, that though they might escape the actual sentence of a criminal tribunal, they were not safe against being put to some trouble and expense in order to avoid it. Colonial Governors and other persons in authority will have a considerable motive to stop short of such extremities in future." (*Ibid.*, 282.)

[103]Particular exception, it seems, was taken to the following: "Every foreigner, every continental writer, would believe for many years to come that Ireland was a country constantly on the brink of revolution, held down by an alien nationality, and kept in subjection by brute force" (53). Mill alludes to the occasion in the *Autobiography*. "I did no more than the general opinion of England now admits to have been just; but the anger against Fenianism was then in all its freshness; any attack on what Fenians attacked was looked upon as an apology for them; and I was so unfavourably received by the House, that more than one of my friends advised me (and my own judgment agreed with the advice) to wait, before speaking again, for the favourable opportunity that would be given by the first great debate on the Reform Bill" (*A*, 277). The third reading of the Habeas Corpus Suspension Bill passed the House of Commons by a vote of 354 to 6. Mill abstained.

Among those urging Mill, after the habeas corpus debate, to hold his tongue until the second reading of the Reform Bill was J.A. Roebuck. No longer the friend he had once been, Roebuck "did not presume to address him directly," but instead went through Chadwick. Roebuck, always ready to speak his mind, plainly stated that the debate on the Reform Bill should have been the occasion for Mill's "debut." Whatever mistakes Mill might have made in February, the opportunity to establish himself as a force in the House had not been conclusively lost. All would depend on his Reform Bill speech. "Having determined what to say, he ought to plant himself steadily on his feet, give the right pitch & tone of voice, then earnestly and with perfect simplicity, make his opening statement. The House will be anxious to hear him—Let him shew, that he is no mere puppet, that he is no man's follower—but one possessed of strong opinions—well thought opinions—and really anxious to have those opinions fairly & honestly laid before his country. . . . Let him give all the body he can to his voice. He should above all things be manly, quiet [?], self-possessed & earnest. . . . I know that he is able to teach the House, but he must not appear to be a teacher. He ought to seem merely desirous of laying his whole heart before the House, honestly, fearlessly & in all sincerity. If he follows these badly expressed counsels, he will succeed." (9 Mar., 1866, Mill Collection, Yale University Library.)

That Roebuck felt such advice was called for suggests that Mill had gotten off to a shaky start. The word going around in late February of 1866, according to William White, Door-Keeper of the House of Commons, was "failure." From this judgment White dissented. "To ascertain whether a man is a

did not translate into a criticism of the particular Liberal ministry then in office. That suspension of habeas corpus should be necessary pointed up the inadequacy of what had hitherto been done for Ireland, but Mill did not question the necessity. A notable feature of the speech is his separation of Russell and Gladstone from the causes that had brought Ireland to the edge of rebellion.

> He was not prepared to vote against granting to Her Majesty's Government the powers which, in the state to which Ireland had been brought, they declared to be absolutely necessary. . . . They did not bring Ireland into its present state—they found it so, through the misgovernment of centuries and the neglect of half a century. [Such words gave Gladstone more cover than they did Russell.] He did not agree with his honourable Friend the Member for Birmingham [Bright] in thinking that Her Majesty's Ministers, if they could not devise some remedy for the evils of Ireland, were bound to leave their seats on the Treasury Bench and devote themselves to learning statesmanship. From whom were they to learn it? From the Gentlemen opposite, who would be their successors, and who, if they were to propose anything which his honourable Friend or himself would consider as remedies for Irish evils, would not allow them to pass it? (53.)

If Mill's tolerance stretched so far as to accommodate Jamaica during the first half of 1866, it would not snap over Ireland.

Mill's solicitude for the beleaguered Russell-Gladstone ministry is evident in his speech on the government's 1866 Irish Land Bill. Introduced on 30 April by Chichester Fortescue,[104] Irish Chief Secretary, this "extremely mild measure"[105] proposed to invest Irish tenants with a legal claim to compensation for

---

failure we must ascertain what he aims at. Mr. Mill never thought to startle and dazzle the House by his oratory, as Disraeli did when he first rose to speak. Mr. Mill has no oratorical gifts, and he knows it. Nor can he be called a rhetorician. He is a close reasoner, and addresses himself directly to our reasoning powers; and though he has great command of language, as all his hearers know, he never condescends to deck out his arguments in rhetorical finery to catch applause. His object is to convey his thoughts directly to the hearer's mind, and to do this he uses the clearest medium—not coloured glass, but the best polished plate, because through that objects may be best seen. . . . What Mr. Mill intended to do was to reason calmly with his opponents, and this he succeeded in doing. . . . He has not a powerful voice, but then it is highly pitched and very clear; and this class of voice goes much further than one of lower tone—as the ear-piercing fife is heard at a greater distance than the blatant trombone. The giant, then, is not a failure; no, except in the eyes of the pigmies." (William White, ***The Inner Life of the House of Commons***, 2 vols. [1897] [Freeport, N.Y.: Books for Libraries Press, 1970], II, 31-3.)

White and Roebuck agreed on the quality and impact of Mill's Reform Bill speech on 13 April. The former confessed that it was not in his power to give "an adequate description of Mr. Mill's great reform speech." He considered it "something entirely new in the debates of the House. Search Hansard from the time that record first began, and you will find nothing like it for purity of style and closeness of reasoning; and, secondly, as we venture to think, nothing like it for the effect it produced upon the House. . . . When Mr. Mill sat down the House cleared. As the Liberal members passed the gangway, not a few stepped out of their way to thank Mr. Mill." (*Ibid.*, 42-3.) Roebuck was no less impressed. Writing to Chadwick on the day after Mill's speech, he described it as "the outpouring of a great, honest, yet modest mind; the vigorous expression of well-considered & accurate thought." The speech, "an epoch in parliamentary oratory," had "settled for sure the position Mill is to hold in the House & I believe lays open to him the highest offices in the administration of the country" (14 Apr., 1866, Mill Collection, Yale University Library).

[104]See *PD*, 3rd ser., Vol. 183, cols. 214-22.

[105]*A*, 279.

improvements in those cases where there existed no written contract between landlord and tenant denying the latter's right to such compensation.[106] On the second reading of the Bill Mill "delivered one of [his] most careful speeches . . . in a manner calculated less to stimulate friends, than to conciliate and convince opponents."[107]

Mill's opponents could be forgiven for wondering what it was he was trying to convince them of in this speech of 17 May. He began with an assertion that may have inadvertently done Gladstone and Fortescue more harm than good. "I venture to express the opinion that nothing which any Government has yet done, or which any Government has yet attempted to do, for Ireland . . . has shown so true a comprehension of Ireland's real needs, or has aimed so straight at the very heart of Ireland's discontent and of Ireland's misery" (75). Such an endorsement from Mill of an Irish land scheme in a House of Commons that had its full complement of landlords was something the Liberal government might have preferred to manage without. Nonetheless, Mill meant to do well by the government and that intention gave rise to a very curious speech on a Bill whose place in the history of the Irish land question is deservedly obscure.

Two themes uneasily cohabit in Mill's speech. The first concerns the need for English legislators to think seriously about whether Ireland could be best governed according to English principles. Mill argued that Irish conditions resembled those on the Continent and that English assumptions concerning the ordering of agricultural society were unorthodox. "Irish circumstances and Irish ideas as to social and agricultural economy are the general ideas and circumstances of the human race; it is English circumstances and English ideas that are peculiar" (76). Continental experience had shown that where the tenant was also the cultivator of the soil his welfare depended on his having "the protection of some sort of fixed usage. The custom of the country has determined more or less precisely the rent which he should pay, and guaranteed the permanence of his tenure as long as he paid it." (77.) But if Mill seemed to be saying that Irish tenants should be given fixity of tenure, that is not what he proceeded to advocate. Instead, and here emerges the second theme, Mill defended the ministerial measure on the premise that it would contribute to achieving the aim supported by the English governing class: the promotion of the English system of agriculture in Ireland. Such a goal, whose wisdom Mill openly questioned, entailed making prosperous farmers of the most capable of the Irish tenantry. Indispensable to this process was the provision

[106]The government hoped the Bill would encourage improvements and discourage evictions.

[107]*A*, 279. For the background to Mill's involvement with the Irish land question, see T.A. Boylan and T.P. Foley, "John Elliot Cairnes, John Stuart Mill and Ireland: Some Problems for Political Economy," *Hermathena*, CXXXV (1983), 96-119; Bruce L. Kinzer, "J.S. Mill and Irish Land: A Reassessment," *Historical Journal*, XXVII (1984), 111-27; E.D. Steele, "J.S. Mill and the Irish Question: The Principles of Political Economy, 1848-1865," *ibid.*, XIII (1970), 216-36; and Zastoupil, "Moral Government."

of compensation for improvements, without which tenants would lack the incentive to act the part of Anglicized tenant farmers.

Mill knew the House of Commons would not sanction fixity of tenure and he had to admit that he knew it. He could not remain silent when the opportunity arose to tell the House that Ireland needed fixity of tenure. He would not, however, use the occasion to criticize the government's feeble proposal. On the contrary he would bestow extravagant praise upon its authors. His admission that fixity of tenure would not fly in the House served to justify a course of action consistent with an allegiance to political ends that could not be dissociated from the fate of Gladstone.[108]

Towards the end of 1867 Mill concluded that the time for pulling his punches had passed. The Fenian outbursts in Ireland and England in 1867 convinced him that England could not and should not keep Ireland unless she could furnish a satisfactory settlement of the land question. In his pamphlet *England and Ireland*, published in early 1868, Mill eloquently and trenchantly pleaded the case for fixity of tenure.[109] Dr. Steele has documented the hostile reception given this pamphlet and has argued that Mill, realizing that he had gone too far, retreated from his exposed position on 12 March in his speech on the state of Ireland.[110]

Mill's speech reads differently from his pamphlet but the difference does not come from his having had second thoughts about fixity of tenure for Irish tenants. Rather it arises from the distinct roles Mill assigned the pamphlet and the speech in his campaign. The scheme he proposed in *England and Ireland* was deliberately presented simply, boldly, directly. Mill wanted to get people's attention—the

[108]The constraints affecting Mill at this time were evident in connection with another dimension of the Irish question that deeply concerned him: Irish universities. Mill was anxious to see preserved the non-denominational integrity of the Queen's Colleges in Ireland that together made up the Queen's University. Every encouragement should be given to bringing "youths of different religions to live together in colleges" (letter to Cairnes, *LL*, *CW*, XVI, 1134 [6 Jan., 1866]). Just before leaving office Russell's government issued a supplemental charter to the Queen's University, which was empowered to set matriculation examinations independent of those held at the Queen's Colleges and to award degrees to suitably qualified candidates who had not studied in any of those Colleges. Mill's unhappiness at this development was pronounced. Writing to Cairnes on 3 July he declared: "We, who were holding back on account of the Reform Bill, certainly were led to expect a further notice [before the issuing of the supplemental charter]: otherwise we should have brought the matter before the House at once, which would have been very disagreeable to the Govt." (*ibid.*, 1178). Sir Robert Peel, a member of the Queen's University Senate and son of the Prime Minister who had established the Queen's Colleges, was determined to fight the implementation of the supplemental charter. Mill was ready to do what he could to support Peel's effort but he did not want to be "*the* prominent person in a move which is very likely to break up the alliance between the Irish Catholics and the English Liberals, and perhaps keep the Tories in office for years" (*ibid.*, 1184 [15 July, 1866]). See Bruce L. Kinzer, "John Stuart Mill and the Irish University Question," *Victorian Studies*, XXXI (1987), 59-77.

[109]*England and Ireland*, in *Essays on England, Ireland, and the Empire*, *CW*, VI (Toronto: University of Toronto Press, 1982), 505-32. For differing perspectives on the significance of *England and Ireland*, see E.D. Steele, "J.S. Mill and the Irish Question: Reform and the Integrity of the Empire, 1865-1870," *Historical Journal*, XIII (1970), 419-50; and Kinzer, "J.S. Mill and Irish Land," 121-7.

[110]Steele, "Reform and the Integrity of the Empire," 437-48.

fleshing out of details belonged to a later stage. The primary function of the speech was to answer the criticisms and misapprehensions the pamphlet had incited, and to emphasize the flexible application to which its principle was subject. The relation of the pamphlet to the speech was plainly laid out by Mill in a letter to Cairnes, written only hours before the opening of the debate on Ireland. "The object [of *England and Ireland*] was to strike hard, and compel people to listen to the largest possible proposal. This has been accomplished, and now the time is come for discussing in detail the manner in which the plan, if adopted, would work."[111] The generally conciliatory tone of the speech does not represent any backtracking on Mill's part. He did not hesitate to announce to the House that "Great and obstinate evils require great remedies" (249), nor did he decline the opportunity to reiterate his defence of peasant proprietorship (259-61).

Before March of 1868 Gladstone's political star, apparently on the descent during the Reform Bill struggle, had begun to regain altitude in a climb that by December would carry him to the premiership with a large majority at his back. At Christmas 1867 Lord Russell resigned the leadership of the party, and Gladstone succeeded to a position that conferred on him an authority he had hitherto been denied. The dissension caused by the controversy over reform had largely dissipated and the prospect of a general election provided ample incentive for the party to put its house in order and unite behind a strong leader. Gladstone was ready to provide that leadership. In February of 1868 he introduced his Bill for the abolition of compulsory church rates, which would not long thereafter become law. Four days after Mill spoke on Irish land, Gladstone committed himself in the House to Irish Church disestablishment, which he made the subject of the resolutions he proposed on 23 March. His grip on the party, so unsure in 1866 and 1867, had tightened noticeably. Mill no longer had to tread softly for Gladstone's sake. Indeed, Mill's shift into high gear on the Irish land question reflected his understanding that Gladstone's growing strength had opened up a fast lane to the leader's left.

In the drive towards a Liberalism more programmatic than anything yet seen, Mill attempted to set a pace that he hoped would keep him within Gladstone's sight while helping the latter gain acceptance for measures that would have horrified Palmerston. Mill's lunge on Irish land did something to make the question ripe for serious legislation and also enlarged the framework of debate. That Gladstone got as much as he did on Irish land in 1870 (he did not get all that he wanted)[112] owed a little (maybe more) to *England and Ireland*. Mill may have had less reason than Gladstone to applaud the legislation of 1870, but he had known better than to entertain expectations incapable of immediate fulfilment. As he told Cairnes in March of 1868: "I do not share your hopes that anything much short of what I have

[111] *LL*, *CW*, XVI, 1373 (10 Mar., 1868).

[112] For the making of the 1870 Irish Land Act, see E.D. Steele's excellent study, *Irish Land and British Politics: Tenant-Right and Nationality, 1865-70* (Cambridge: Cambridge University Press, 1974).

proposed, would give peace or prosperity to Ireland in union with England: but if there is any intermediate course which would do so, its adoption is likely to be very much promoted by frightening the Government and the landlords with something more revolutionary."[113]

CORRUPT PRACTICES

THE IRISH LAND QUESTION, however important to Mill in 1868, was overshadowed by his immersion in the issue of corrupt electoral practices. Disraeli had promised a bill on the subject for 1868.[114] The depth of Mill's detailed involvement with this measure exceeded that of any other he encountered during his years in Parliament. Believing that a number of advanced Liberals shared his interest, he was disposed to assume responsibility for directing and coordinating their strategy and tactics. In November of 1867 he wrote to Chadwick:

> The great question of next session will be the promised bill against electoral corruption. The advanced Liberals must have *their* rival bill, and I am anxious that all who have thought on the subject . . . should put down, as heads of a bill, all that has occurred to them as desirable on this subject. When all suggestions have been got together, the most feasible may be selected, and the best radicals in and out of the House may be urged to combine in forcing them on the government.[115]

Later that month Mill was in touch with W.D. Christie, whom he considered the leading authority on the subject.[116] He asked Christie to draw up a measure that could serve as an instrument of discussion for advanced Liberals, who might meet on the reassembling of Parliament "and produce an outline of a Bill which might be circulated among the Liberal party. It might be possible to prevail on Mr. Gladstone to introduce it: but . . . the bill will only be a rallying point: the fight will . . . be . . . on the attempt to engraft its provisions on the bill of the Tory Government."[117]

In late December Mill, having heard from Christie, clearly felt the time had come to talk about details. The major points Christie wished to press concerned the inclusion of municipal elections within the bill's purview and the desirability of conducting a post-election enquiry into all contests regardless of whether or not a

[113] *LL*, *CW*, XVI, 1373 (10 Mar., 1868).

[114] The Conservative government had actually introduced a bill on the subject in 1867, which had been referred to a select committee of the House. It was, however, withdrawn on 29 July, and on 16 August Disraeli informed the House of the government's intention to deal with the matter early in the following session. See *PD*, 3rd ser., Vol. 189, col. 1606.

[115] *LL*, *CW*, XVI, 1325 (4 Nov., 1867).

[116] In February of 1864 Christie had read a paper, "Suggestions for an Organization for the Restraint of Corruption at Elections" before the Jurisprudence Department of the National Association for the Promotion of Social Science. Less than two months later Mill attended a meeting of the Law Amendment Society, at which Christie's paper "Corruption at Elections" was discussed. For Mill's brief remarks on this occasion, see No. 3.

[117] Letter to William Dougal Christie, *LL*, *CW*, XVI, 1331 (20 Nov., 1867).

complaint had been lodged. Mill agreed that corruption at parliamentary elections often fed off the unsavoury techniques used at the municipal level and that any bill that did not apply to both would be highly unsatisfactory. As for a uniform and comprehensive enquiry process, Mill admitted the idea was new to him. "One can at once see many reasons in its favour, but it will be a difficult thing to get carried, owing to the habitual objection to 'fishing' enquiries, and to enquiries when there is no complaint. It is, however, evident that the absence of complaint is, in such a case, no evidence of the absence of mischief." Mill also raised other questions with Christie at this time: what punishment should be imposed on the convicted briber? should all money spent by candidates and their agents at elections "pass through a public officer, so that the mere fact of incurring expenditure in which he is passed over should be legal proof of an unlawful purpose?"[118]

At the beginning of the new year Mill received and read Christie's pamphlet *Election Corruption and Its Remedies* (1867), whose recommendations he considered "excellent." Of these Mill deemed Christie's proposal for the appointment of an official in each constituency to supervise all aspects of the local electoral process to be of central importance.[119] On 17 January Christie learned of Mill's preference for his plan "of an investigation after every election, parliamentary or municipal, by a special officer, with the addition of an appeal from that officer to one of the Judges."[120]

Disraeli, unlike Mill, did not look to Christie for instruction on this matter. The key question addressed by the government's Election Petitions and Corrupt Practices at Elections Bill concerned jurisdiction over controverted elections.[121] The measure proposed to transfer jurisdiction from Election Committees of the House of Commons to a judicial tribunal.[122] What little opposition there was to the principle of the Bill was not party motivated. Gladstone accepted the need for such a change and did not take a leading part in the debates. Mill himself endorsed the measure, declaring that "though it does in reality only one thing, that thing is a vigorous one, and shows an adequate sense of the emergency" (262). Mill had no wish to see the Bill defeated; rather, he sought to expand its scope so that it could be made into a powerful weapon in the fight against the corrupt influence of money at elections.

The campaign organized by Mill secured none of its objectives.[123] Nothing could be done to establish the enquiry mechanism urged by Christie. The Act of

[118]*Ibid.*, 1337 (28 Dec., 1867).

[119]*Ibid.*, 1348 (8 Jan., 1868).

[120]*Ibid.*, 1353.

[121]Cornelius O'Leary provides a good account of the Bill and its passage in *The Elimination of Corrupt Practices in British Elections, 1868-1911* (Oxford: Clarendon Press, 1962), 27-43.

[122]The Act provided that the judges of each of the three superior courts at Westminster annually select one of their members to try election petitions.

[123]Mill's correspondence during the first half of 1868 testifies to his vigilance on behalf of the cause. See his letters to Christie: *LL*, *CW*, XVI, 1381-2 (31 Mar.), 1383-4 (3 Apr.), 1397 (8 May), 1398 (11 May), 1399-1400 (20 May), 1403 (25 May), 1409 (6 June), and 1425 (27 July).

1868 did not prohibit paid canvassers or limit each candidate to one paid agent; it did not apply to municipal elections; it did not transfer official election expenses from the candidates to the rates, an alteration advocated by Mill in *Thoughts on Parliamentary Reform* and in *Representative Government*.[124]

The account of this episode in the *Autobiography*, no doubt coloured by Mill's experience of the general election of 1868, carries the full weight of his disappointment. Referring to the "fight kept up by a body of advanced Liberals," he blames the Liberal party for the futility to which that fight was condemned.

> The Liberal party in the House was greatly dishonoured by the conduct of many of its members in giving no help whatever to this attempt to secure the necessary conditions of an honest representation of the people. With their large majority in the House they could have carried all the amendments, or better ones if they had better to propose. But it was late in the Session; members were eager to set about their preparations for the impending General Election: and while some . . . honourably remained at their post . . . a much greater number placed their electioneering interests before their public duty. . . . From these causes our fight . . . was wholly unsuccessful, and the practices which we sought to render more difficult, prevailed more widely than ever in the first General Election held under the new electoral law.[125]

Implicit in the passage is a criticism of Gladstone's leadership, the quality of which Mill would do nothing to impugn during 1868.

That Mill should seek to strike a blow for purity of election can surprise no one; that he should identify the cause so exclusively with a group of advanced Liberals reveals something of his underlying hopes for political realignment. A less narrow identification could have been made. Radicals may have been the most aggressive advocates of a systematic attack on corrupt practices but such advocacy was not confined to them. Beresford-Hope, a Tory, proposed an amendment to forbid the use of public houses as committee rooms. The *Saturday Review*, not known to sympathize with advanced Liberalism, expressed regret that the Bill did not go further. "The truth is that the Government Bill is only a half-measure. The whole of our election system requires overhauling. It is better to do what is proposed than to do nothing, but far more will yet have to be done before we have exhausted all reasonable legal efforts to put down or to detect bribery."[126] *The Times*, not one of Mill's favourite newspapers, could write that "the great increase in the number of the moneyed class is as threatening a spring of danger as the adoption of Household Suffrage."[127] There could be an aristocratic as well as a democratic bias against money at elections.

Mill's was emphatically of the latter sort. In *Considerations on Representative Government* he had written:

[124]*CW*, XIX, 320, 496. Henry Fawcett's amendment for placing official election expenses on the rates was actually carried in a small House by a vote of 84 to 76. On the third reading, however, the government managed to reverse that decision, defeating Fawcett's amendment 102 to 91.

[125]*A*, 283-4.

[126]Quoted in O'Leary, *Elimination of Corrupt Practices*, 39n-40n.

[127]Quoted *ibid.*, 38.

There has never yet been, among political men, any real and serious attempt to prevent bribery, because there has been no real desire that elections should not be costly. Their costliness is an advantage to those who can afford the expense, by excluding a multitude of competitors; and anything, however noxious, is cherished as having a conservative tendency, if it limits the access to Parliament to rich men. . . . They care comparatively little who votes, as long as they feel assured that none but persons of their own class can be voted for.[128]

Mill's objection to the Palmerstonian ascendancy was that it seemed impervious to politics as he understood the term. Palmerston's House of Commons was a club of complacent comfortable gentlemen who felt strongly only about preserving an order of things that they found highly congenial. The broad appeal of the Palmerstonian Liberal party emanated from its standing for an ill-defined "progress" in general and nothing very much in particular. Politics without principles might serve nicely the interests of the rich but could not foster the social and moral improvement that Mill prized.

The transformation of the Liberal party into a vehicle of radical reform was vital to the creation of a politics of principle. The entry into the political arena of men of intelligence wedded to ideas and ideals had to be encouraged. Working-class participation in an advanced Liberal party purged of Palmerstonians was also requisite. If these objectives could be secured, the Liberal party would become something different from and far better than the loose combination of individuals who had followed Palmerston. Indispensable to this achievement, however, was a dramatic reduction in the cost of contesting elections, the end to which each of the amendments put forward by Mill and his associates was directed. The substitution of plutocracy for aristocracy could not make English government or English society what it should be; indeed, Mill was inclined to think that plutocracy aggravated the worst tendencies of aristocracy while introducing new ones to which aristocracy was not normally prone. "They desired to diminish the number of men in this House, who came in, not for the purpose of maintaining any political opinions whatever, but solely for the purpose, by a lavish expenditure, of acquiring the social position which attended a seat in this House, and which, perhaps, was not otherwise to be attained by them" (280).

THE 1868 WESTMINSTER ELECTION

THE IMPACT (if not the existence) of corrupt practices in the Westminster election of 1868 remains open to doubt. W.H. Smith's great wealth contributed to his success in 1868, but its failure to obtain the desired result in 1865 suggests that other factors were at work in Mill's second Westminster contest.

Parliament was prorogued on 31 July and formally dissolved on 11 November. The prorogation accelerated an election campaign that had indeed already begun,

[128] *CW*, XIX, 497-8.

and lasted over three months. Mill left London for Avignon at the beginning of August and did not return to England until early November, two and a half weeks before polling day. His absence handicapped his Committee, which had just cause for irritation at Mill's posture. His removal from the scene of action suggested an aloofness from the proceedings that probably did his cause no good. It did not, however, prevent him from making seemingly desultory thrusts into the electoral terrain—without consulting those who were working to secure his re-election—that his Committee understandably considered ill-advised.

In late August Mill sent a ten-pound contribution to Charles Bradlaugh's Northampton election fund.[129] Not only was Bradlaugh a notorious atheist, Malthusian, and Radical, but his candidacy in a constituency already represented by two well-established Liberals (Charles Gilpin and Lord Henley) would inevitably provoke discord in local Liberal ranks. Prudence dictated that a candidate standing in the Gladstonian interest should refrain from promoting challenges to Liberal incumbents, especially when the challenger was Charles Bradlaugh. Mill either failed to see the potentially destructive ramifications of his identification with Bradlaugh or he was indifferent to the consequences. A Bradlaugh victory could only be had at the expense of one of the sitting Liberals, and Gilpin (a member of the Jamaica Committee executive), an advanced Liberal himself though certainly not in Bradlaugh's league, respectfully expressed his unease to Mill in a letter of 7 September. In response, Mill assured Gilpin that Bradlaugh wanted Henley's seat and assumed, along with Mill, that Gilpin's position at Northampton was unassailable. He went on to say that Bradlaugh was a man of ability with distinctive opinions that should be heard in the House of Commons, adding that though "it is most important to uphold honest & honourable men, faithful supporters of our own party, like Lord Henley against Tories & lukewarm Liberals, [he did] not think that their claims ought to be allowed to prevail against the claims of exceptional men."[130]

By late September Mill had learned from his Committee that the subscription for Bradlaugh had provoked considerable fuss in Westminster and created difficulties for his supporters. Mill, "exceedingly sorry" that there should have been "trouble or annoyance," was not penitent. Had he not been a candidate he would have assisted Bradlaugh and he could not allow his own candidacy at Westminster to interfere with a course of action he thought right. It would be wrong for people to infer, Mill maintained, that his sympathy for Bradlaugh had any connection with the latter's religious opinions. What Mill admired in Bradlaugh was his thoughtfulness, his "ardour," his independence of mind. He was a "strenuous supporter of representation of minorities" and an "earnest" Malthusian. "If the capability of taking & the courage of maintaining such views as these is not a

[129]Letter to Austin Holyoake, *LL*, *CW*, XVI, 1433 (28 Aug., 1868).
[130]*Ibid.*, 1434-5 (12 Sept., 1868).

recommendation, to impartial persons, of an extreme radical politician, what is?" Admitting that the first priority should be the return of supporters of Gladstone, Mill observed that opponents of Gladstone were not contesting Northampton and that it was necessary to look beyond "the immediate struggle." He expressed the hope that the House of Commons elected in 1868 would embark on "a general revision of our institutions" and begin to act "against the many remediable evils which infest the existing state of society."

Already the too exclusive attention to one great question [the Irish Church] has caused it to be generally remarked, by friends & enemies, that there will be very little new blood in the future Parlt, that the new H. of C. will be entirely composed of the same men, or the same kind of men, as the old one. Now I do not hesitate to say that this is not what ought to happen. We want, in the first place, representatives of the classes, now first admitted to the representation. And in the next place we want men of understanding whose minds can admit ideas not included in the conventional creed of Liberals or of Radicals, & men also of ardent zeal.[131]

In a letter of 1 October Mill again turned to the need for a real representation of working-class "opinions and feelings," which he was not at all sure the result of the 1868 general election would secure. It would be the responsibility of the new House to pass legislation that would improve the quality of life for the masses. "This cannot be expected unless the suffering as well as the prosperous classes are represented."[132]

That Bradlaugh, if elected, would do useful work in the House of Commons, Mill did not doubt; Edwin Chadwick's services there, Mill believed, would be invaluable. Their longstanding friendship made him keenly conscious both of Chadwick's ambition to sit in the House and of England's shabby treatment of a man who had done much for the betterment of his society. Mill encouraged Chadwick to stand for Kilmarnock against E.P. Bouverie, an Adullamite, and Mill's intervention in this contest would give rise to nearly as much unfavourable comment as did his support of Bradlaugh.[133]

Chadwick took with him to Kilmarnock a glowing letter of recommendation from Mill. On 16 and 22 October *The Times* published the exchange of correspondence that ensued between Bouverie and Mill. In his letter of 25 September the former conveyed his surprise and chagrin that Mill should instigate a division among the Liberals at Kilmarnock, who had supported Bouverie as their member for more than two decades. Acknowledging that he and Mill had their political differences, he observed that these had not prevented him, as an elector in Westminster, from endorsing Mill's candidacy. "Toleration for minor differ-

[131]Letter to Thomas Beggs, *ibid.*, 1449-50 (27 Sept., 1868).

[132]Letter to Samuel Warren Burton, *ibid.*, 1452.

[133]See *The Times*, 21 Oct., 1868, 9. On 29 October Mill would admit to Cairnes that he was "more attacked for helping Chadwick against Bouverie . . . than even for subscribing to Bradlaugh; though the latter proceeding is the more likely of the two to alienate voters in Westminster" (*LL*, *CW*, XVI, 1465).

ences, union for common public objects, such, at least, is the doctrine I entertain with regard to party action, and without a practical adhesion to it, I believe the Liberals will be powerless for good."[134]

In his response of 4 October Mill did not say what he thought of Bouverie's notion of party. Instead, he concentrated on Chadwick's special claims as an "exceptional man," asserting that "I would very gladly put him in my place if I saw a probability of success." Chadwick's qualities were such that considerations of party were, in his case, of secondary importance. Mill implied, however, that he could, if pressed, defend his intervention on party grounds.[135]

Bouverie did press him. On 13 October he accused Mill of setting himself up as an authority competent to determine the best interests of the electors of Kilmarnock. "If I were to act on your advice [by withdrawing], the result would be a substitution of your individual opinion for the free choice of the constituency." As the electors of Westminster, presumably, did not want Chadwick as their representative, there might be good reason to suppose that he would be no more acceptable to Kilmarnock. In effect, Bouverie charged Mill with an arrogant presumption that threatened to harm the Liberal interest, affirming that "the best hope of our common political adversaries lies in the Liberal constituencies being exposed to a contest among Liberals."[136]

Mill issued a very lengthy rejoinder on 19 October, in which he projected a conception of the Liberal party from which he knew Bouverie must dissent. He laid bare the significance he attached to the general election, placing personal considerations well into the background, and announcing that "we are not now in ordinary times." There were new electors and "new questions to be decided." Parliament required men who understood "the wants of the country" and the remedies for "the most pressing existing evils." The challenge to the Palmerstonians was unmistakable. If the "recognised candidates of the party" did not include "a reasonable number of men of advanced opinions, or possessing the confidence of the working classes," then they should not be surprised to face competition from unrecognized candidates. The Adullamites had wounded the Liberal party in the preceding Parliament and "if a similar result should befall it in the next there will be cause for bitter regret that the liberal party did not fight out its battles at the polling booths rather than in the lobby of the H. of C." Mill's strident conclusion stated as bluntly as could be stated under the circumstances his view that the Liberal party could well afford to do without Bouverie and those who sympathized with his politics.

> We do not want men who cast reluctant looks back to the old order of things, nor men whose liberalism consists chiefly in a warm adherence to all the liberal measures already passed, but men whose heart & soul are in the cause of progress, & who are animated by that ardour

[134]*The Times*, 16 Oct., 1868, 10.
[135]*LL*, *CW*, XVI, 1453-4; *The Times*, 16 Oct., 1868, 10.
[136]*The Times*, 16 Oct., 1868, 10.

which in politics as in war kindles the commander to his highest achievements & makes the army at his command worth twice its numbers; men whose zeal will encourage their leader to attempt what their fidelity will give him strength to do. It would be poor statesmanship to gain a seeming victory at the poll by returning a majority numerically large but composed of the same incompatible elements as the last.[137]

Mill hoped that the general election would initiate a Radical take-over of the Liberal party.

He may have felt fairly confident of his own success during the months in Avignon. By late October, however, the concern of Liberal organizers over the effort being mounted by W.H. Smith led to Mill's being summoned to London for the final fortnight of the campaign.[138] Only upon his return did he comprehend the seriousness of his predicament. The tone and content of his election speeches suggest that leading figures on the Liberal Committee, believing that Mill had put himself in a dangerously exposed position and desiring to undo some of the damage that had been done, counselled moderation, restraint, and discretion. That such advice should be proffered is entirely understandable; that Mill should have taken it to heart is perhaps a little baffling.

The most striking characteristic of Mill's November election speeches is that they are indistinguishable in message from what orthodox Liberal candidates were saying up and down the country. They are highly conventional partisan speeches. Praise for Gladstone, cuts for the Tories, the obligatory reference to the Irish Church, vague allusions to Irish land and social reform—these are the staple of Mill's election addresses.[139] He had little to say about Jamaica, women's suffrage, personal representation, or the radicalization of the Liberal party. Something approaching defensiveness crept into both the speeches and the letters he wrote for publication at this time. In reiterating his hostility to the ballot, Mill expressed regret that he should find himself "conscientiously opposed to many of the Liberal party, though not in principle, upon the ballot question." (Mill stood on principle in rejecting the ballot; where this left the multitude of Liberals who favoured secret voting—from whom he pointedly declined to separate himself "in principle"—it is not easy to know.) His audience, in any case, need not worry about his position on the issue: "If he was wrong, he would be beaten in the end; so they could afford to let him have his way" (344). More revealing yet is Mill's letter of 9 November on the Bradlaugh connection that appeared two days later in *The Times*, *Daily News*, and *Morning Star*. Written in response to the fuss over the matter being

[137] *LL*, *CW*, XVI, 1460-4; *The Times*, 22 Oct., 1868, 3.

[138] See his letter to Cairnes, *LL*, *CW*, XVI, 1465 (29 Oct., 1868).

[139] Laudatory remarks on Gladstone were a commonplace in the election speeches of Liberal candidates, and Mill certainly was not remiss in this respect. Bagehot observes: "Mr. Gladstone's personal popularity was such as has not been seen since the time of Mr. Pitt, and such as may never be seen again. . . . A bad speaker is said to have been asked how he got on as a candidate. 'Oh,' he answered, 'when I do not know what to say, I say "Gladstone," and then they are sure to cheer, and I have time to think'" (Introduction to 2nd ed. of *The English Constitution*, *Works*, V, 171).

kicked up by the Tories, it says much for his state of mind a week before polling day.

I suppose the persons who call me an Atheist are the same who are impudently asserting that Mr. Gladstone is a Roman Catholic. . . . An attempt was made to raise the same cry against me at my first election, & the defence which I did not choose to make for myself was made for me by several eminent dignitaries of the C[hurch] of England. . . . If any one again tells you that I am an atheist, I would advise you to ask him, how he knows and in what page of my numerous writings he finds anything to bear out the assertion.[140]

Helen Taylor, on discovering that Mill had penned such a letter for publication, was not a little indignant. "I cannot tell you how ashamed I feel. . . . Do not disgrace yourself as an open and truthful man; do not shut the door to all future power of usefulness on religious liberty by such mean & wretched subterfuges as this letter."[141]

Helen Taylor did not walk in Mill's shoes (though she may have tied them for him). In early November Mill had become acutely aware of the difficulties that in the preceding months had not penetrated his Avignon refuge. He held his cards close to his chest in the fortnight before the election because he lacked faith in the hand he had dealt himself. It was by no means a hand to be ashamed of—the pursuit of Eyre, fixity of tenure for Irish tenants, the contribution to Bradlaugh's campaign, and the endorsement of Chadwick—and Mill was not ashamed of it. He feared, however, that it might be a losing hand. Mill wanted to win in 1868 in order to be part of a new Liberal dispensation to which he felt he had much to offer.

Neither Mill nor perhaps anyone else could have known in early November that W.H. Smith was not beatable. In the interval between the 1865 and 1868 elections Smith and his people had been assiduously nursing Westminster. His commitment and money, the latter drawn from a purse so deep as to approximate bottomlessness, generated the foundation of the London and Westminster Constitutional Association and fuelled the high level of activity it sustained in the lead-up to and during the 1868 election.[142] Excluding the money spent on this effort prior to the summer of 1868 and the money spent by the London and Westminster Constitutional Association on behalf of Smith's candidacy while the election was in progress, expenditure directly attributable to Smith at the contest came to £9000, more than four times what the Liberal Committee spent for Grosvenor and Mill.[143]

[140]Letter to Frederick Bates, *LL, CW,* XVI, 1483.

[141]Helen Taylor to Mill, Mill-Taylor Collection, British Library of Political and Economic Science, Vol. LIII (12 Nov., 1868).

[142]See Hanham, *Elections and Party Management*, 107-8. The Hambleden Papers (W.H. Smith and Son, London) for these years supply abundant evidence of the buildup of a formidable Tory machine in Westminster under Smith's leadership.

[143]Mill's supporters filed a petition against Smith's return, claiming that the Smith campaign had bought votes. The petition was heard by Baron Martin, who ruled that although the bribing of voters seemed to figure among the practices of the London and Westminster Constitutional Association,

The Liberals got many more votes for their money than did Smith, but they were not enough to carry Mill: Smith, 7648; Grosvenor, 6584; Mill, 6284. Smith's victory marked the beginning of a trend that would establish Westminster as a virtually invincible Tory stronghold in the late nineteenth century. Two Tories would be returned at the 1874 election, Smith on this occasion polling 9371 votes, nearly 5000 more than the stronger of the two Liberal candidates.[144] When viewed from this perspective, a perspective unavailable in 1868 to Westminster Liberals disappointed with their showing, it can be seen that Mill did not do at all badly. Might he have won had he known that Grosvenor and not Smith was the man to beat and acted accordingly?

Mill did not run against Grosvenor in 1868 nor could he have done so. In 1865 animosity between their respective Committees had been overcome shortly before polling day in the interest of mutual assistance, from which Mill stood to benefit more than Grosvenor. In 1868 there was a single Liberal Committee sponsoring both candidates. It could not be said that Grosvenor had distinguished himself in the House of Commons, but then no one had expected him to. Unlike his kinsman, the future Duke of Westminster,[145] Captain Grosvenor had kept his distance from the Adullamite camp and done nothing to give offence to either Gladstone or advanced Liberals. In July of 1868 the leader of the Liberal party, aware that Grosvenor intended to stand again, sent a letter to the Chairman of the Westminster Liberal Committee recommending Grosvenor to the electors of the constituency.[146] A unilateral decision by Mill to take on Grosvenor would have created havoc in Liberal ranks and probably harmed Mill more than Grosvenor, who might have attracted more Tory votes than he did if Mill had gone after him. Most Conservatives clearly plumped for Smith, but those who did not would be far more likely to split their votes between Smith and Grosvenor than between Smith and Mill. If Liberals of whatever stripe could find little to complain of in Grosvenor's conduct, he was inconsequential enough to generate much less hostility among Tories than did his Liberal associate. Mill, in short, had almost no room for manoeuvre in November of 1868; that he finished only three hundred votes behind Grosvenor was in itself a triumph of sorts.

Although Mill was the most eminent of the Radicals denied admission to the Gladstonian host elected in 1868, he had plenty of worthy company. Bradlaugh and Chadwick were defeated. George Odger, in whose candidacy Mill had taken a

---

Smith could not be held responsible for the conduct of this "independent agency." Smith's election stood. See O'Leary, *Elimination of Corrupt Practices*, 50-1.

[144]See John Biddulph Martin, "The Elections of 1868 and 1874," *Royal Statistical Society Journal*, XXXVII (1874), 197. The combined total of votes for the two Liberal candidates at Westminster in 1874 was only 8184; the two Tories polled 18,052 between them.

[145]Hugh Lupus Grosvenor; see xxx above.

[146]"Captain Grosvenor . . . has shewn himself to be an able and faithful representative, whom his constituents might well have chosen from his personal merits and ability alone" (Hanham, *Elections and Party Management*, 80).

special interest,[147] retired from the field in Chelsea to prevent a Conservative victory there. Edmond Beales, George Howell, and W.R. Cremer—leading figures (as was Odger) in the political world of working-class activists—failed to win their contests. The university Liberals—G.C. Brodrick, E.A. Freeman, Auberon Herbert, George Young, Godfrey Lushington, Charles Roundell—were also unsuccessful.[148] None of this was lost on Mill, who found little to celebrate in the results. In a letter to Charles Eliot Norton, Mill remarked on "the defeat of the radical party throughout the country."[149]

A Liberal party, even one led by Gladstone, that did not include a substantial battalion of Radicals in the House of Commons (working-class representatives among them) was of limited use to Mill. The experience of 1868 compelled him to recognize that Liberal constituency organizations, largely dominated by men of means, would resist the changes in personnel and policy that he wished to promote.[150] He also believed that such short-sightedness would ultimately alienate the working-class electorate and enfeeble the Liberal party. In early November he asserted to John Plummer that the "Liberal party will have cause to repent of not having adopted the best leaders of the working men and helped them to seats."[151] Mill urged working-class political organizations to use their influence to insist on representation equal to that of the higher classes within the party. "Where a place returns two members, one of these should be a candidate specially acceptable to the working classes: where there is but one, he shd be selected in concert by both sections of Liberals."[152] Mill's loyalty to a Gladstonian Liberal party that refused to give the working classes their due did not extend very far. By February of 1870 he was ready to sanction tactics that emphasized his complete detachment from the Liberal establishment. Writing to George Odger, Mill declared: "It is plain that the Whigs intend to monopolise political power as long as they can without coalescing in any degree with the Radicals. The working men are quite right in allowing Tories to get into the House to defeat this exclusive feeling of the Whigs, and may do it without sacrificing any principle."[153]

When Mill came to write the concluding section of the *Autobiography* he had been disabused of the notion that the 1867 Reform Act and a Gladstonian ascendancy would usher in a new political era responsive to his sense of priorities. He conceived of the years immediately following his defeat as the beginning of a

[147]See letter to W.R. Cremer, *LL*, *CW*, XVI, 1485 (10 Nov., 1868).

[148]For a valuable study of the university liberals, see Christopher Harvie, *The Lights of Liberalism: University Liberals and the Challenge of Democracy* (London: Penguin, 1976).

[149]*LL*, *CW*, XVI, 1493 (28 Nov., 1868).

[150]The leading item on Mill's list of policy changes would probably have been the land question, Irish and English. For Mill's relation to this subject, see David Martin, *John Stuart Mill and the Land Question* (Hull: University of Hull Publications, 1981).

[151]*LL*, *CW*, XVI, 1479 (5 Nov., 1868).

[152]Letter to R.C. Madge (Secretary of the Chelsea Working Men's Parliamentary Electoral Association), *ibid.*, 1514 (7 Dec., 1868).

[153]*Ibid.*, XVII, 1697 (19 Feb., 1870).

transitional period, the outcome of which could not be confidently predicted.[154] Mill's post-election uncertainty manifestly distorted the account he gave of his parliamentary career by refracting it through a lens that elevated the independent aspects of his conduct at the expense of the pattern of action moulded from his interpretation of the ongoing party struggle and its possible implications. Such a pattern did exist, and its source resided in Mill's view of himself as a progressive politician functioning within a system that seemed to offer unprecedented opportunities for a fundamental reshaping of the Liberal party.

In retrospect it may appear that Mill should have known better than to think that things could have turned out other than they did in 1868. His hopes and illusions, it might be supposed, were those of an amateur lacking a sound grasp of the English political world and the social forces that shaped it. Such condescension would be misplaced. The mid-Victorian equilibrium and the reassurance it gave the governing classes concerning the stability of English society made the granting of borough household suffrage a conceivable option in 1867. But those who conceded so much were by no means sure that nothing untoward would flow from it. Mill's perhaps unreasonable hopes were matched by equally unreasonable fears on the part of some whose miscalculations could not be ascribed to political naïveté. Lord Derby meant what he said when he spoke of "a leap in the dark." Mill was looking for a leap into the light, and from 1866 through 1868 he had done what he thought best to help prepare the way for it.

THE LATE PUBLIC SPEECHES

RELEASED from parliamentary constraints and responsibilities, Mill redirected his political activism in the last five years of his life to focus on several abiding passions: women's suffrage, education, and land reform.[155] As assessment of

[154]In January of 1869 Mill wrote that he had "never felt more uncertainty about the immediate future of politics" (part of a passage deleted from a letter to W.T. Thornton, *ibid.*, 1548 [16 Jan., 1869]). Two months later he admitted to Fawcett that he had "considerable difficulty in judging . . . of any question of political tactics, during the present transitional state of politics" (*ibid.*, 1579 [22 Mar., 1869]).

[155]Whereas Mill was central in initiating the organized movements for women's suffrage and land reform, his taking up of the education question was prompted by the government's 1870 Education Bill. Although he spoke on education, he did not publish material on the subject during these years, as he did on the other two. *The Subjection of Women* appeared in print in 1869. Relevant to his association with the land question in this period are two essays written for the *Fortnightly Review*, "Professor Leslie on the Land Question," n.s., VII (1870), 641-54 (in *Essays on Economics and Society*, *CW*, IV-V [Toronto: University of Toronto Press, 1967], V, 669-85); "Mr. Maine on Village Communities," n.s., IX (1871), 543-56; the 1871 *Programme of the Land Tenure Reform Association, with an Explanatory Statement by John Stuart Mill* (in *CW*, V, 687-95); and three contributions to the *Examiner* in 1873: "Advice to Land Reformers," 4 Jan., 1-2; "Should Public Bodies Be Required to Sell Their Lands?" 11 Jan., 29-30; "The Right of Property in Land," 19 July, 725-8 (in *Newspaper Writings*, ed. Ann P. and John M. Robson, *CW*, XXII-XXV [Toronto: University of Toronto Press, 1986], XXV, 1227-43).

Mill's parliamentary career shows in its abundant variety those elements that defined its essential unity, so analysis of the late public speeches reveals features common to the core of Mill's radicalism. Hitherto, the fundamental question has been: What do the Westminster years demonstrate about the character of Mill's political objectives in the second half of the 1860s and the means by which he sought to give them effect? Emphasis has been placed on Mill's conception of the party struggle and its relation to his ultimate purposes. The claim is not that the meaning of each and every speech he gave in the House of Commons can be uncovered only through a penetration of the political layers within which the words were often embedded, but that on those critical issues determining the rise and fall of party fortunes Mill acted as a politician in pursuit of fairly precise political aims. Even though the parliamentary context is not especially germane to most of the late public speeches, when viewed as a group they can be seen to encapsulate themes basic to what Mill had been doing from 1865 through 1868.

The speeches on women's suffrage, education, and land reform manifest Mill's commitment to a politics of inclusion. The exclusion of women from the franchise "is a last remnant of the old bad state of society—the regimen of privileges and disabilities" (407). Mill wants a sound elementary education made available to all children. He stoutly rejects the claims of religious sectarianism to rate-money designated for educational ends. The exclusionist tendencies of sectarianism were anathema to Mill. The existing distribution of landed property in England, buttressed by such artificial contrivances as primogeniture, entail, and strict settlement, unjustly excluded the vast majority of people from what should be accessible to all. Mill, speaking on behalf of the Land Tenure Reform Association, denounced such contrivances. The Association's programme, in the drawing up of which Mill had been instrumental, also called for preservation of the commons, government supervision of the waste lands in the interest of the public and the agricultural labourers (to whom allotments on favourable terms should be offered), and—most radical of all—a tax on the unearned increment of rent.[156] Landed property must no longer be treated "as if it existed for the power and dignity of the proprietary class and not for the general good" (417).

Unquestionably, a strain of old anti-establishment radicalism lingered in Mill. Privileges, monopolies, exclusiveness—in his mind, these were linked inextricably to the pernicious consequences of aristocratic government. Mill, however, was more interested in elucidating the advantages of progressive change than he was in savaging what remained (quite a lot) of the establishment.

Mill's politics of inclusion sprang from a profoundly democratic civic

[156]For a stimulating assessment of the general controversy over land reform and its political significance, see Harold Perkin, "Land Reform and Class Conflict in Victorian Britain," in his *The Structured Crowd: Essays in English Social History* (Brighton: Harvester Press, 1981), 100-35. For Mill in particular, see Martin, *John Stuart Mill and the Land Question*, and Samuel Hollander, *The Economics of John Stuart Mill*, 2 vols. (Toronto: University of Toronto Press, 1985), II, 833-55.

consciousness. Participation was integral to political education. An educated citizenry was vital to the creation and perpetuation of a healthy body politic. The expansive ideal of citizenship inculcated by Mill put a premium on a widely diffused energy, virtue, and intelligence. The achievement of a higher politics required, among other things, opportunities for personal growth, which entailed bringing more and better schooling, more civic participation, more material benefits, and more beauty within the reach of more and more people. Thus Mill ardently supported working-class enfranchisement and women's suffrage; universal elementary education, which should be in no way inferior to the best primary education bought by the rich; the election of women and working men to school boards; generous allotments for agricultural labourers; public access to parks and commons; and, indeed, a citizen army ("Henceforth our army should be our whole people trained and disciplined") (413). Political development, personal growth, and an increase in the total sum of human happiness were to advance together.

Mill appreciated that very practical considerations respecting political power had to be attacked by a reformer with an agenda such as this. Abraham Hayward, in his obituary on Mill for *The Times*, observed that "of late years Mill has not come before the world with advantage. When he appeared in public it was to advocate the fanciful rights of women, or to propound some impracticable reform or revolutionary change in the laws relating to land."[157] It should be borne in mind that Hayward and *The Times* would have cheered the resurrection of Palmerston. The picture of the later Mill as a crotchety philosopher promoting hare-brained schemes comforted those who wanted no part of his radicalism. That radicalism deliberately cultivated a hard-headedness that Hayward's shallow dismissal cannot obscure. Mill persistently grappled with issues of power: political, intellectual, and economic. A state that withheld the franchise from women, quality elementary education from the masses, and land reform from the agricultural labourers of England and the tenant farmers of Ireland illegitimately denied to these groups the power needed for self-protection. The liberal state advocated by Mill would confer that power upon the disadvantaged and dispossessed. Mill's political speeches, no less than his political writings, evince a readiness to tackle the problem of power. "Safety does not lie in excluding some, but in admitting all, that contrary errors and excesses may neutralise one another" (390-1). With the suffrage, women "cannot long be denied any just right, or excluded from any fair advantage: without it, their interests and feelings will always be a secondary consideration, and it will be thought of little consequence how much their sphere is circumscribed, or how many modes of using their faculties are denied to them" (380). Mill is encouraged by signs of an awakening agricultural labouring class, the "most neglected, and, as it has hitherto seemed, most helpless portion of the labouring population." They had at last "found a

[157]*The Times*, 10 May, 1873, 5.

voice, which can, and which will, make itself heard by the makers of our laws" (430). There is plenty of room for disagreement among commentators concerning how successfully Mill assayed the problem of power; it cannot be persuasively argued that he overlooked or evaded it.

The theoretical and practical tenability of a politics of inclusion partly hinged upon its enlistment of a valid principle *and* process of authority.[158] The final authority for public policy must reside in the will of the democracy. The exercise of that will in the public interest, however, necessitated the acceptance by the demos of a conspicuous role for individuals with superior abilities, knowledge, and experience.

> Different people had very different ideas of popular government; they thought that it meant that public men should fling down all the great subjects among the people, let every one who liked have his word about them, and trust that out of the chaos there would form itself something called public opinion, which they would have nothing to do but to carry into effect. That was not his idea of popular government, and he did not believe that popular government thus understood and carried on would come to good. His idea of popular government was, a government in which statesmen, and thinking and instructed people generally pressed forward with their best thoughts and plans, and strove with all their might to impress them on the public mind. What constituted the government a free and popular one was, not that the initiative was left to the general mass, but that statesmen and thinkers were obliged to carry the mind and will of the mass along with them; they could not impose these ideas by compulsion as despots could. (395.)

In Parliament and out, Mill strove with all his might.

[158]Although a theory of authority is implicit in much that Mill wrote, he never furnished an extensive or systematic treatment of the issue. For a valuable exploration of the problem, see Richard B. Friedman, "An Introduction to Mill's Theory of Authority," in *Mill: A Collection of Critical Essays*, ed. J.B. Schneewind (Notre Dame: University of Notre Dame Press, 1969), 379-425.

Textual Introduction

JOHN M. ROBSON

MOST OF MILL'S LATER SPEECHES have never been republished.[1] Those here collected[2] are mainly from *Parliamentary Debates* and newspapers; one uniquely exists in manuscript and one in typescript, and four others are also extant in manuscript as well as in print; a handful appeared in pamphlets, and one was reprinted in *Dissertations and Discussions*.

Our goal, to include all Mill's speeches in the House of Commons and in public,[3] remains ideal, for several reasons. First, Mill kept no record of his speeches, and we have had to follow many trails, some clear, others overgrown. Locating the public, non-parliamentary speeches gave most difficulty. The existence of a few is signalled in correspondence and other documents, some are found in manuscript or in newspaper clippings in the Mill-Taylor Collection, and others have been located through that indispensable but tormenting aid, *Palmer's Index to The Times*. *The Times*, however, did not report all Mill's speeches, and we have had to search through files of other London (and occasionally provincial) papers. Under current and abiding conditions, such a search can never be final, and we have asked for and received help from scholars and institutions. Our success will be tested by time and the industry of others; our certain claim is only that we have found many more than were previously known. Locating Mill's speeches in the House of Commons presents no comparable difficulty, the basic guide being the index in *Parliamentary Debates*. Even here, however, a couple of minor items appeared only after a search through *St. Stephen's Chronicle*, a short-lived journal of parliamentary affairs.

A second problem lies in definition. What is "a speech"? Surely some interjections cannot qualify, and what of questions and replies, or series of short comments? No logical fineness seems here necessary, and our short answer is that

[1]Headnotes to the individual items give details of publication and republication during Mill's lifetime. In his unpublished Ph.D. dissertation, "The Collected Speeches of John Stuart Mill with Introduction and Notes" (Wisconsin, 1955), John Ellery included a substantial but incomplete collection of the speeches in raw form.

[2]His other extant speeches, all from the 1820s, are in *Journals and Debating Speeches*, Vols. XXVI-XXVII of the *Collected Works*.

[3]The only exception is the *Inaugural Address at St. Andrews*, which is included with Mill's other educational writings in *Essays on Equality, Law, and Education*, *CW*, Vol. XXI, on the grounds that it was prepared for publication.

all Mill's remarks are of value in a complete record of his parliamentary career. For convenience we have ruled that all Mill's recorded words on a specific subject of debate on one day constitute a speech. This policy would prove annoying if he had often made an isolated comment on an issue, which we would by this rule dignify as a speech; fortunately, almost all his interventions can be merged with others as part of a continuing discussion in Committee of the Whole. In fact, we have preserved only a few potentially irritating instances, of which Nos. 30, 35, and 78 are most likely to peeve; if there were more, another practice would be justifiable. The impatient will be grateful that Mill's one recorded silent intervention is mentioned only in a footnote (No. 22, n1). And one intended speech is recorded only here: on 12 March, 1868, the Speaker was faced with several Members, including Mill, Agon-Ellis, and Pim, who wished to offer remarks on the Irish Church. Bernal Osborne moved that the Honourable Member for Westminster be next heard, thus occasioning "some laughter, mingled with cries of 'Order'"; however, the Speaker ceded the floor to Agon-Ellis.[4]

Though a secondary goal is to give, through our text and editorial apparatus, a skeletal guide to Mill's activities in the House of Commons, we have not elevated to textual status his seconding of an unsuccessful motion for a return of the number of times since the Act of Union the Habeas Corpus Act had been suspended in Ireland or the number of acts of repression there since then, and of the number of Irish people sentenced for political offences, indicating which acts had been applied in each case (19 Mar., 1868; *PD*, 3rd ser., Vol. 190, col. 1939). We also have not given as textual items his notices of motion.[5] All of these except two are mentioned in notes to speeches when the motions were made; in two cases, however, no speech was reported. On 5 March, 1867, on Mill's motion, a return was ordered of the number of robberies of pillar letter-boxes in the metropolis and city of London, giving the number for each year separately from the period of the establishment of the system.[6] And on 16 May, 1867, he gave notice of motion that certain petitions against the National Gallery Enlargement Bill be referred to a Select Committee on the Bill.[7]

THE TYPESCRIPT AND MANUSCRIPTS

THE TYPESCRIPT is that of "Secular Education," the first item. It transcribes a manuscript, not now located, formerly in the possession of Harold J. Laski, who

[4]*The Times*, 13 Mar., 7.

[5]It should be recorded, however, that when he gave notice of motion on 8 June, 1866, for a return of the numbers of those, otherwise qualified, who were denied the franchise because of their sex, the House responded with "Laughter" (*The Times*, 9 June, 6), and that when he gave notice of his motion to replace "man" with "person" in the Reform Bill of 1867, the response was mixed "Laughter and cheers" (*The Times*, 20 Mar., 6).

[6]Reported in *The Times*, 6 Mar., 6.

[7]*Ibid.*, 17 May, 8.

published it in an appendix to his edition of Mill's *Autobiography*.[8] He had bought it as part of Lot 719 in Sotheby's sale on 29 March, 1922, of the effects of Mary Taylor, Mill's step-granddaughter.[9] The extant manuscripts are printed here in Appendix D; a fragment is given as a variant note to No. 26; and a speech of Helen Taylor's appears as Appendix F. The manuscript of No. 6, "The Westminster Election of 1865 [2]," was part of Lot 669 in the second Sotheby's sale of Mary Taylor's effects, on 27 July, 1927. Described as "SPEECH to the Electors of Westminster, Auto. Notes, 4 pp. 8vo," it was bought in 1956 for the Mill-Taylor Collection from Myers for £46. The Houghton Library, Harvard, obtained the manuscript of No. 16, "Representation of the People [2]," as a gift from George Herbert Palmer, who bought it (as a sticker indicates) at the sale of Mill's books and papers by the Avignon bookseller, Roumanille, on 21-28 May, 1905, after Helen Taylor had moved back to England. The fragment of No. 26, "The Disturbances in Jamaica [1]," in the Yale University Library, was presumably part of Lot 730 in the Sotheby's sale of 29 March, 1922, which included "various unfinished MSS. in the hand of J.S. Mill, and various essays on the Education of Women, etc., by Helen Taylor *a large parcel*." The provenance of the manuscript of No. 144, "Women's Suffrage [1]," in the Mill-Taylor Collection, is not known. The Houghton Library, Harvard, also has the manuscript of No. 145, "The Education Bill," which was donated by Mrs. Norman Himes; it was, like that of No. 6, part of Lot 669 in the Sotheby's sale of 27 July, 1927, "AUTO. NOTES for a Speech of [*sic*] the Education League, 9 pp. 4to." The fragment of Helen Taylor's speech, "War and Peace," our Appendix F, also part of the Himes donation to Harvard, is not identifiable as an item from these sales.

THE TEXTS

EACH ITEM consists of a headnote, the text, and notes. The headnote gives the provenance of the copy-text, lists other versions, and provides the immediate context, with other closely relevant information. The notes, at the foot of the page, are substantive and textual. The substantive notes include Mill's own (in the sequence *, †, etc.) and the editors' (in numerical sequence, beginning anew in each item or section of an item). The textual notes normally record variant readings, with alphabetic markers in the text signalling the word or words for which the variant reading is a substitute; these too begin anew in each item or section of an item.

The texts themselves have been determined in ways appropriate to their kind and provenance. No overall principle presents itself, although in places our methods

[8]Oxford University Press, 1924, 326-30.

[9]For a full account of this collection, see the Textual Introduction to *Journals and Debating Speeches*, *CW*, Vols. XXVI-XXVII.

parallel those based on established principles; for reasons that will become obvious, new rules (with their exceptions) have had to be devised.

The problems originate in the recording and transmission of texts.[10] Leaving aside for the moment the few instances where there is a holograph manuscript, we are faced in the non-parliamentary speeches with one or more reports taken in shorthand by recorders for the press or, in rare instances, for special interest groups, including the organizers of the meetings at which Mill spoke. If there is but one report, there are no decisions to make other than those resulting from a study of possible errors. But usually there is more than one report, and when there is, there are large as well as small differences. Most significantly, the reports differ in the length of the main text, in the reporting of answers to questions, and in incidental details. Also, there are differences in the emphasis given to particular parts of speeches, and in summary as against what purports to be (and undoubtedly sometimes is) a verbatim account. Furthermore, some reports are in direct speech, that is, the first person, present tense, but most are in indirect speech, that is, the third person, which by convention carries the past tense.[11]

Attempts to establish one text consequently must involve an initial choice of copy-text, and then a collation of goats and cabbages, as the French seem to say. If Mill indicates elsewhere, as he occasionally does, which text is to be preferred, we have followed his choice. The same decision might seem to be entailed when there is a pamphlet or other reprint; however, such a document may represent in places what he wished he had said rather than what he actually said. The latter elusive goal being ours, careful consideration must be given to internal criteria. The two most significant of these are comparative length and voice.

As to length, it may with reasonable certainty be assumed that reporters did not normally add (except perhaps transitional words); indeed the established rule was "When in doubt leave out."[12] So we have tended to accept the fullest account as copy-text. It is equally probable, however, that first-person are closer than third-person accounts to verbatim reporting, and are to be preferred for those portions of a speech that they cover. Fortunately, these two criteria seldom conflict, because first-person accounts are generally longer as well. Still, collation is necessary, for often reports that are inferior on these two grounds include matter not found in the copy-text. Consequently, it is necessary to compare what purport to be direct quotations with summaries, because the latter sometimes contain not merely ideas but words that seem *prima facie* and even after examination to represent something that was said. This comparison leaves one with a decision as

[10]For a fuller discussion of these matters, with special reference to *Parliamentary Debates*, see John M. Robson, *What Did He Say? Editing Nineteenth-Century Speeches from Hansard and the Newspapers* (Lethbridge: University of Lethbridge Press, 1988).

[11]More precisely, not the past tense, but one tense further back than would be used in reporting direct speech.

[12]Michael MacDonagh, *The Reporters' Gallery* (London: Hodder and Stoughton, n.d. [1928?]), 73.

to which substantives should be included in the final text; that is, which words or passages should be added from versions other than the copy-text, and which substituted for what are judged to be inferior wordings. In accidentals the copy-text is followed except in demonstrable deficiencies (which are less frequent than the major provenance, newspapers, would suggest). The result is inescapably eclectic, but, given the facts, all the better for its mixed parentage.

It is physically impossible to record all the variant readings without printing parallel texts of each version, a solution both economically impossible and morally inutile.[13] Our decision has therefore been to give in variant notes (a) all the readings from the copy-text for which alternate versions have been preferred, (b) alternate readings that, while they have not seemed sufficiently grounded to justify elevation to the text, are possibly what Mill said, or may have influenced judgments of what he said, and (c) manuscript versions that, though probably not uttered, might have been (the recorded version being a mishearing or reporter's "improvement"), or that have interest as suggesting an *ad hoc* change of mind.

The question will have arisen in editors' minds as to why the extant manuscripts are not chosen as copy-text. The reason is simply stated, although its simplicity will not convince traditionalists. As indicated above, what we aim at, looking up to admit and so ensure that we cannot hit the target, is a record of what Mill actually said. A manuscript, even if he read from it (and that option was usually not open and seldom followed), gives only what he apparently intended to say—"apparently" because most speakers consciously leave open the possibility of departing from a text when, as is normally the case, the occasion calls for an alteration. Further, the intention, no matter how fixed, is often frustrated by circumstances, such as lack of time, and faltering memory or tongue.[14] It would be foolish to assert that what Mill actually uttered always better fulfilled the intentions he had when he planned a speech, but certainly most of the modifications found in our collations suggest a later intention consciously if rapidly cancelling or modifying the earlier one. To enable others to test our judgments, however, we give the full manuscript texts in Appendix D.

Given our view that the best version of a speech reflects its circumstances, we have also recorded, in italic type, the audiences' responses.[15] Here again we have followed the copy-text, except in adding responses not there contained and in substituting wordings that are fuller or more precise. In choosing the wording of responses from among differing accounts, we have taken that which is most expressive and full, and not given the others in variant notes, except in the rare

[13]One example, No. 4, of a comparatively short text in three versions, is given as an Appendix in Robson, *What Did He Say?*

[14]This frequent malaise was identified by a friend as being "tongue-struck."

[15]In the parliamentary speeches, the names of Members, when added in parentheses after their constituencies, are also given in italics, as additions to the spoken word, as are the insertions of "(Mr. Mill)" following "he" in third-person reports.

cases when there is some difference of tone or even full contradiction,[16] or when the response can be seen as tied to a particular textual variant.[17] The specific sources of the responses are given only when they form part of larger variants. The actual form of course reflects the different reporters' (and perhaps editors') views of how to indicate what happened;[18] in surprisingly few cases do different versions suggest a bias towards or against Mill and his positions, but almost always they add not just colour but understanding to one's reading. I hope, for instance, that the frequency with which audiences are reported to have responded with "(*Laughter*)" will modify at least interstitially the uninformed judgment that Mill was without humour.

A summary of the events leading up to Mill's remarks is given in the headnotes. Except for the copy-texts, the dates of texts from daily newspapers are given only when they differ from that of the copy-text. Within the text itself the concluding events and remarks by others, and when appropriate intervening events and remarks, are supplied in italic type and, when summarized rather than quoted directly from the copy-text, also in square brackets. (This practice is quite straightforward except in the uncommon cases when a report moves from an apparent attempt to convey the main ideas, if not the words, into an obvious attempt to summarize the flow of the speech.) We have included in these summaries all references to Mill, sometimes embedded in long quotations.

In turning to Mill's parliamentary speeches, it may be thought that one is leaving behind the excitement and weariness of textual problems. There is, after all, *Hansard's Parliamentary Debates* on which to rely. What is not generally known is that T.C. Hansard Jr., who was responsible for the series from the 1830s through the period when Mill was in the Commons, had no official mandate and, apart from rare occasions, no reporters of his own.[19] In fact, Hansard proceeded in just the way we have, collating newspaper accounts and giving an eclectic text; he, however, indicates the sources of his texts only in the rare instances when an asterisk signals that a speech was sent to him by the Member; almost always one is left with the choice of taking his text as gospel or trying to unravel what he has

[16]See No. 58^{i-i} and $^{x-x}$, the latter odd, as both contradictory responses may be read as the same answer to a rhetorical question.

[17]See No. 11^{d-d} and $^{e-e}$.

[18]That national habits and predilections are not irrelevant will occur to those with experience of the debates in the French Chambers, which are more Gallically dramatic. One must envy French editors who can choose, for example: "Voix des extrémités: Ce n'est pas la question!"; "De toutes parts: Aux voix l'amendement!"; "Bruits divers"; "Vif mouvement d'adhésion"; "Sensation prolongée"; "Rires aux extrémités"; "Hilarité générale et prolongée"; "Violente interruption"; "Profond silence" (less commonly found); "Vives réclamations à gauche"—and so on. The English satirical paper *Judy* commented: "the French press always keeps in type the following phrases during the sittings of the *Corps Législatif*:—'Uproar,' 'Continued uproar,' 'Fresh uproar,' 'Signs of Denial,' 'Emotion,' 'Violence from the Opposition,' 'Offensive expressions from the left,' in order that they may be 'distributed' among the speeches" (4 Mar., 1868, 240).

[19]The history of his operations and of the confusions resulting is given in Robson, *What Did He Say?*, with examples of abiding conundrums.

given and then knitting all together again in a new—or perhaps the same?—pattern. Neither of these choices is attractive, and we have fallen somewhere between. His resources, being immediate and concerted, were better than ours can be, and he and his collators were extraordinarily practised in their craft; therefore we have taken his versions as copy-text, looking for confirmation in the few extant manuscript and pamphlet versions. As a check, however, we have compared the versions in *The Times*, which is thought to have been Hansard's main source, because generally it provided the fullest record. To our surprise, it appears that almost never does Hansard's text agree with that of *The Times*; indeed, in Mill's case, we have found only a handful of speeches, all very short, where there is coincidence.[20] As a further check, we have made a comparison with the versions in *St. Stephen's Chronicle*, which reported parliamentary matters in 1867; here again there is but rare agreement with *Parliamentary Debates*, although there is not infrequent agreement with *The Times*.[21] This search produced, as mentioned above, two minor speeches by Mill (on 8 March and 4 July), neither of which is in *Parliamentary Debates* or in *Palmer's Index to The Times*, though both are summarized in *The Times*.

The results of all these comparisons are not trivial, but are also not sufficiently significant for us to adopt anything other than *Parliamentary Debates* as copy-text. It must not be thought that this decision removes all problems, for even the difficulty over person and tense arises: in No. 120, for instance, which combines several of Mill's interventions, the first passage in *Parliamentary Debates* is in the first person, present tense, while the next two are in the third person, past tense; consequently, in adding a fourth from *The Times* that is not in *Parliamentary Debates*, we decided to leave it in the third person, past tense, to match what immediately preceded it.

As in the public speeches, we have accepted some variants to complement or replace parts of the copy-text, and have used the alternate texts for the responses in the House. The newspapers' record of responses is, indeed, much fuller than *Parliamentary Debates* provides, and gives more to think about.[22]

Mill, as a prominent Member, was solicited for texts, and at least some of the reports in the *Morning Star*, the *Daily News*, and the *Daily Telegraph* may have had the benefit of his manuscript notes. Writing in June 1866 to Charles Ross, the chief parliamentary reporter for *The Times*, who had evidently asked him to supply such manuscript, Mill said that, so far as he had examined *The Times*'s report, it

[20]Instances are No. 110, which has only two sentences of Mill's, and No. 127, where there are five sentences, with one accidental difference. No. 57 exemplifies cases where the report in *The Times* differs markedly in arrangement as well as wording from that in *Parliamentary Debates*.

[21]In one case, No. 56, *St. Stephen's Chronicle* is much closer to *Parliamentary Debates* than is *The Times*.

[22]See, for instance, No. 72, where we have added from *The Times* in one place, "(*Loud cries of Oh!*)", and in several others, "(*Oh, oh.*)", and cf. No. 88[t–t]. No. 62 illustrates cases where there are more responses in *The Times*, which here adds three to the one in *Parliamentary Debates*.

seemed so good that it had not suffered by the lack of his script. He continued:

If I understand your note correctly it would not be open to you, if you took a speech from myself, to give slips to the other papers. I am afraid, if this is so, that it will generally prevent me from availing myself of your obliging offer to receive such communications from me. It is of much more importance to be well reported in the Times than anywhere else, but one is so much more certain of being so, that if one has to choose between sending one's notes to the Times or to the other papers one would rather do it to the others.[23]

He explained his practice to W.F. Rae on 2 June:

The reason I do not give my speeches to the Times, is that the Times would keep them to itself, while the other papers give slips to one another. It would be a great piece of servility to give anything that depends on me to the Times alone; denying it to the papers with whose politics I agree, and which have acted in the most friendly manner to me throughout.[24]

As mentioned above, occasionally Mill gave the nod to one or another account, crediting with the best report the *Morning Star* (Nos. 47 and 124) or the *Daily Telegraph* (No. 133), and it may be assumed that they were, as most sympathetic to his views, generally fuller in their accounts. But the presumption is not strong enough to override, in the case of the public speeches, the evidence from collation, or, in the case of the parliamentary speeches, the superior resources of Hansard.

In brief summary, we conclude that the text of public and parliamentary speeches, when there are competing authorities, must be eclectic, in the interest of providing the reader with the fullest account possible in one place. The assumptions behind particular choices of text are that (a) Mill did not normally give reporters a text (exceptions, as indicated above, are given special authority), and even when he did, his final intentions, which we respect, are better indicated in the reports of what he said than in what he planned to say; (b) normally reporters made no attempt at verbatim reporting (their highest goal being that of T.C. Hansard, a "full and accurate" account),[25] but summarized and revised, taking little time over decisions, aiming to fill the available space with what in their view their editors and readers would find most important; (c) reporters and editors for various newspapers differed in their views of what was most important; (d) reporters and editors did not normally add passages, though they added transitional words or phrases to make their summaries coherent; and (e) as a result, the fullest text from any source probably contains more of what Mill actually said, and so should be used as copy-text, though any variant found in another version may accurately represent what Mill said in that particular passage.

[23]*LL*, *CW*, XVI, 1173. The reference is presumably to No. 52, given in the House of Commons on 31 May, in which case the letter should be dated 1 or 2 June (see the next letter quoted). The only known speech by Mill in June was No. 53, delivered on the 23rd.

[24]*Ibid.*, 1174.

[25]"Report from the Select Committee on Parliamentary Reporting," *Parliamentary Papers*, 1878-79, XII, 30.

EMENDATIONS TO THE TEXTS

IN GENERAL, contractions and abbreviations are expanded to conform to what would be spoken. Other changes are listed in Appendix G, with explanations except when the change has been made for obvious reasons of sense (including easily identified typographical errors).

In conformity with modern practice, italic type is used for the titles of works published separately, while quotation marks are placed around titles of parts of separate publications. Foreign words and phrases are normalized to italic, as are the abbreviations for currency.

In the appendices giving questions and petitions, the dates that begin entries are styled uniformly. When a speech is reported in the first person, the introductory "Mr. J.S. Mill:" is not recorded.

VARIANT NOTES

THE SYSTEM of recording variant readings used throughout this edition is based on superscript letters in the text; these appear in pairs around words or phrases, or singly centred between words or between a word and punctuation. As explained above, in the few cases where there are manuscripts, these are printed in Appendix D, but some passages, interesting for various reasons, are also given as variants. The practice for the public speeches is illustrated in No. 4, where the *Morning Star* provides the copy-text, but alternate readings are adopted from the *Daily News* and *The Times*. For instance, on 12 a superscript italic letter [a] appears in the text at the beginning and end of a two-sentence passage; the variant note, beginning "[a–a]DN" gives the alternative reading from the *Daily News* (three sentences) and then, following a closing square bracket and "TT", the alternative reading from *The Times* (two sentences). At 12[d–d] a sentence from the *Daily News*, not paralleled in the other version, is given in the text; the variant note reads "[d–d]+DN". At 12[e–e] another passage from the *Daily News* is given in the text; the note indicates again the source and that it is an addition by "[e–e]+DN", and then continues after a closing square bracket to give the alternative reading from *The Times*, beginning "TT". When an alternative reading is not given in the text (as is the case with manuscript versions), a single centred superscript appears in the text at the place where the reading occurs. For example, at 20, [b] is centred between "debauching" and "the constituents"; the variant note reads "[b]Manuscript (by strictly legal means of course)". The interpretation is that the manuscript reads "debauching (by strictly legal means of course) the constituents", and that, as reported in the copy-text, Mill omitted the parenthesis. The parliamentary speeches, again for reasons explained above, take *Parliamentary Debates* for copy-text, with a few variants noted from *The Times* and (for 1867) *St. Stephen's Chronicle*; these are based on the same principles as those in the public speeches.

APPENDICES

APPENDIX A gives the physical details about the manuscripts. Appendices B and C fill in the detail of Mill's parliamentary career by giving his questions as a member of Select Committees, and the origins, subjects, and dates of the petitions he presented. Appendix D contains the full manuscript texts of speeches that are represented in the text proper by printed sources. Appendix E calls attention to occasions when it is known that Mill spoke, but no record is extant of his remarks. Appendix F supplies the text of a manuscript speech that is in Mill's hand, but undoubtedly was prepared by his step-daughter, Helen Taylor, for her use. Appendix G lists and explains the textual emendations, while Appendix H is an index of persons and works cited in the text and Appendices B-D and F. Finally, there is an analytic Index, prepared by Dr. Jean O'Grady with her customary categorical and alphabetic skill.

ABBREVIATIONS

THE FOLLOWING short forms are used, mainly in the variant notes, the headnotes, and in Appendix H. To avoid confusion with "MS" signalling the *Morning Star*, "Manuscript" is spelled out in full.

35="Rationale of Representation" (1835)
B=*The Beehive*
CW=*Collected Works of J.S. Mill*
CS=*Chapters and Speeches on the Irish Land Question*
D&D=*Dissertations and Discussions*
DN=*Daily News*
DT=*Daily Telegraph*
JP=*Jamaica Papers*
JSM=John Stuart Mill
MET=*Manchester Examiner and Times*
MP=*Morning Post*
MS=*Morning Star*
P=a pamphlet
P^1=the 1st ed. of a pamphlet
P^2=the 2nd ed. of a pamphlet
PD=*Parliamentary Debates* (Hansard)

PMG=*Pall Mall Gazette*
PP=*Parliamentary Papers*
R=*Reasoner*
S=*Standard*
SC=Mill's library in Somerville College, Oxford
Scot=*Scotsman*
SSC=*St. Stephen's Chronicle*
TT=*The Times*
W=*Women's Suffrage: Great Meeting in Edinburgh in the Music Hall, on 12th January 1871, under the Auspices of the Edinburgh Branch of the National Society for Women's Suffrage* (Edinburgh: printed Greig, 1871).

ACKNOWLEDGMENTS

FOR PERMISSION to publish manuscript materials, we are indebted to the National Provincial Bank, residual legatees of Mary Taylor, Mill's step-granddaughter, and (for specific manuscripts) the British Library of Political and Economic Science, the Harvard University Library, and the Yale University Library. In addition to these, we are indebted to the librarians and staff of the British Library, the Institute of Historical Research (University of London), the Newspaper Library and the India Office Library and Records of the British Library, Somerville College Oxford, the University of London Library, the University of Toronto Library, and the Victoria University Library.

As ever our work has been gladdened and lessened by the warming and unstinted aid of individuals, among the host, Robin Alston, Sue Grace, J.R. de J. Jackson, Trevor Lloyd, Ray Maycock, Mary S. Miller, the late Francis E. Mineka, Pamela G. Nunn, Walter O'Grady, Helene E. Roberts, and Ann Christine Robson. Among the always helpful members of the Editorial Committee we are especially indebted to J.B. Conacher and Ann P. Robson, the former a mentor and guide to both, the latter a source of wise advice appreciated by one and almost always heeded by the other. The generous financial support of the Social Sciences and Humanities Research Council of Canada was essential to the preparation and production of these volumes. The staff of the Mill Project are part of the efficient and indeed material causes, especially the Senior Research Assistant, Marion Filipiuk, and the Post-doctoral Fellow, Jean O'Grady, with the Editorial Assistant Rea Wilmshurst, each of whom showed in her individual way the constant and dedicated watchfulness, the inventive intelligence, and not least the interest that make our work a pleasure. The part-time junior members, Jonathan Cutmore, Michele Green, Margaret Paternek, Jannifer Smith-Rubenzahl, Elizabeth King, Marion Halmos, John Huxley, and John Sipos, all contributed to our pleasure and the edition's profit.

PUBLIC AND PARLIAMENTARY SPEECHES

1850–1873

· · · November 1850 to July 1865 · · ·

1. Secular Education

AFTER 4 NOVEMBER, 1850?

Fabian Society typescript, headed in ink, "Secular Education." The occasion is not known. Printed by Laski in his edition of Mill's *Autobiography*, pp. 326–30, with the comment, "Not delivered," and dated 1849 (no evidence given). Laski's dating is clearly wrong, as Mill refers to events later than 1849. There are no substantive differences between the two versions; the typescript is followed in accidentals.

SIR, the commencement at Manchester of a movement for a national education not under the control or management of either established or non-established clergy has already, it would seem, made no inconsiderable impression on the public, or else *The Times* has made a false move and miscalculated the signs of the coming public opinion; for already at the very beginning of the agitation that journal has discovered, what it did not find out in the case of the Corn Law League until the fourth or fifth year of its existence, that the thing is not merely a good thing, but what is so much better in the estimation of *The Times*, a thing destined to succeed.[1] The promoters doubtless thought no less, but they probably did not expect so early a recognition of their prospects. How much then it is to be lamented that an enterprise of so much promise should have been inaugurated by an act of truckling and compromise; that for the sake of conciliating people who are not to be conciliated and whom it ought not to have been an object to conciliate, the Association should have let itself be persuaded by Mr. Cobden, aided by some dissenting ministers, to sacrifice its distinctive flag, and instead of calling itself an Association for secular education should have sheltered its timidity under the ambiguous designation of *unsectarian*.[2]

[1]For its prediction of success for the movement for non-sectarian national education, see its leading article on the question, *The Times*, 4 Nov., 1850, p. 4. Its belated prediction of success for the Anti-Corn Law League (which was founded in 1839) is in a leader of 19 Dec., 1845, p. 4.

[2]On 30 October, 1850, during a conference of the Lancaster Public School Association at which its name was changed to the National Public School Association, Richard Cobden (1804–65), the well-known free-trader, a founder of the anti-corn law campaign, successfully objected to the use of the word "secular" because it suggested "not religious" rather than "non-sectarian." See "Conference at the Mechanics Institution on Secular Education," *The Times*, 31 Oct., 1850, p. 5.

If this is only a change in words and means nothing it deserves no better name than that of deception; if it does mean anything, if by *unsectarian* is to be understood something different from secular education, the broad principle of religious freedom which was to be the foundation of this great educational movement is abandoned.

In the debates of the Conference there was a good deal of misunderstanding, some of it I fear rather wilful on the part of Mr. Cobden and his supporters respecting the import of the word *secular*. There is no uncertainty about it. There is not a better defined word in the English language. *Secular* is whatever has reference to this life. Secular instruction is instruction respecting the concerns of this life. Secular subjects therefore are all subjects except religion. All the arts and sciences are secular knowledge. To say that *secular* means irreligious implies that all the arts and sciences are irreligious, and is very like saying that all professions except that of the law are illegal. There is a difference between irreligious and not religious, however it may suit the purposes of many persons to confound it. Now on the principles of religious freedom which we were led to believe that it was the purpose of this Association to accept, instruction on subjects not religious is as much the right of those who will not accept religious instruction as of those who will. To know the laws of the physical world, the properties of their own bodies and minds, the past history of their species, is as much a benefit to the Jew, the Mussulman, the Deist, the Atheist, as to the orthodox churchman; and it is as iniquitous to withhold it from them. Education provided by the public must be education for all, and to be education for all it must be purely secular education.

When, then, the Association refuses to say that their education is secular but are willing to say that it shall be unsectarian, what do they mean? Doubtless that it is still to be exclusive, though in a minor degree. That religion is to be taught, but not sectarian religion. That they are not to have Church of England teaching, or Catholic teaching, or Baptist, or Methodist, or Unitarian teaching, but I suppose Christian teaching; that is, whatever common elements of Christianity are supposed to be found in all these sects alike. How far this is likely to conciliate the various classes of sectarians the Association will probably hear loudly enough from the sectarians themselves. I am much mistaken if they will be at all thankful for any religious teaching which expresses no opinion on a subject on which Christians differ in opinion, or if the substratum of universal Christianity which it is proposed to teach will appear to them at all different from Deism. But this is their concern. I take higher ground. I maintain that if you could carry all the sects with you by your compromise you would have effected nothing but a compact among the more powerful bodies to cease fighting among themselves and join in trampling on the weaker. You would have contrived a national education not for all, but for believers in the New Testament. The Jew and the unbeliever would be excluded from it though they would not the less be required to pay for it. I do not hear that their money is to be refused, that they are to be exempted from the school rate. Religious exclusion and inequality are as odious when practised towards minorities as majorities. I thought the principle of the Association had been that of justice, but I find it is that of being unjust to those alone who are not numerous enough to resist.

I cannot help remarking how much less confidence professed Christians appear to have in the truth and power of their principles than infidels generally have in theirs. Disbelievers in Christianity almost always hail the advance of public intelligence as favourable to them; the more informed and exercised a mind is, the more likely they account it to adopt their opinions: but I cannot find a trace of similar confidence in most of the professedly religious. If they hold their belief with the same full assurance as the others their disbelief, surely infidels and the children of infidels are those to whom, even more than to any others, they would be eager to give all instruction which could render their minds more capable of pursuing and recognising truth. A person is without religious belief, or in other words is in their estimation in a state of the most pitiable, the most calamitous ignorance by which anyone can possibly be afflicted, and for this reason they refuse him instruction, they refuse him knowledge and the cultivation and discipline of the intellect, as if they thought that mental cultivation could not possibly be favourable to Christianity, unless the mind is first strongly pre-possessed on its behalf. Such sentiments as these are not complimentary to Christianity nor to the sincerity of their belief in it. Its greatest enemy could say nothing worse of it than that either ignorance or early prejudice is the soil it must have to flourish in, and that to instruct unbelievers, to make them rational and thinking beings, is but to confirm them in unbelief. I hoped that the founders of the Lancaster Association[3] had been persons who thought that mental cultivation opens the mind to all truth, whether expressly taught or not. Let us hope that this conviction is still theirs and will guide and animate their labours; but they have missed through pusillanimity a splendid opportunity for inscribing it on their banner and proclaiming it in the face of the world.

2. Cooperation

28 MARCH, 1864

The Reasoner (then subtitled *The Secular World and Social Economist*), XXVIII (1 May, 1864), 116–17. Dated in text "Easter Monday." Headed: "Great Co-operative Soiree in London. / Speech of Mr. J.S. Mill." Also in *The Co-operator*, No. 52 (June 1864), pp.

[3]Two of the main founders of the Association were active at the meeting of 30 October: Samuel Lucas (1811–65), author of works on education, and William McKerrow (1803–78), a liberal Presbyterian minister.

4–6. Both journals were the property of George Jacob Holyoake, who says, in his *J.S. Mill as Some of the Working Classes Knew Him* (London: Trübner, 1873), p. 5: "The first time [Mill] appeared at a public meeting and made a speech was at the Whittington Club, before a large tea gathering of co-operators with their wives and families. I was asked to urge him to speak. . . . [H]ad it not been for the evidence of so many women taking part in co-operative economy, . . . he, I suspect had not spoken then." The organizing group was the London Society for Promoting Co-operation. The Chair was taken by Edward Vansittart Neale. His speech was followed by those of Lloyd Jones, Dr. Bowker, and Henry Pitman (editor of *The Reasoner*). Then Mill spoke.

I HAVE VERY LITTLE TO SAY, but that little will be to express my sense of the great value of such societies as this is, as a central organ in London, and possibly for much more than London. It appears to me that the value of such a society consists not solely or principally in the great advantage it affords, to bring into a single focus the interests and efforts of its members, so as to carry on, as this purposes to do, that joint operation for their common benefit; it is not this merely which seems to me to constitute the principal value of a central organ like this—but it is also to be a moral organ, to keep before the eyes of co-operators true principles. What does this mean? Does it mean merely a contrivance by which a small number of persons, or a small number of societies can eat or drink that which is wholesome, and eat and drink it at the lowest price? This is certainly not an unimportant thing; but this is a small thing, and co-operation is a great thing. No doubt it is very desirable, and, indeed, important, that some hundreds of persons or societies should improve their condition—if they should do so, I would be very glad, and should greatly rejoice at it,—and that they should purchase what they want more cheaply and of better quality than they have been accustomed to do. But this is not co-operation. It is not co-operation between a few persons to join for the purpose of making a profit from cheap purchases, by which one, two, or more might benefit. Co-operation is where the whole of the produce is divided. [a]We want, not to benefit a few, but to elevate the whole working class.[a] This principle has been so well stated before, that I should not venture to insist upon it after the admirable manner in which it has been put by previous speakers; but it is absolutely necessary to insist upon it, and it is impossible to insist upon it too strongly. It is not [b]genuine[b] co-operation, where any of the [c]co-operators are excluded from the division of the whole produce[c]. Anything else than such participation in the produce, is nothing more than raising working people into the position of employers. Now, what is wanted is, that the whole of the working classes should partake of the profits of labour. (*Cheers.*) We want that the whole produce of labour shall, as far as the nature of things will permit, be divided among the

[a–a]+C
[b–b]+C
[c–c]C producers are excluded from the profits

workers. The nature, however, of things [d]fixes certain limitations. But the whole of the produce of labour can be divided amongst the workers only to the extent that it is obtained from[d] their own industry. So long as profits are thus obtained, and the workers are in possession of capital, they will naturally receive,—as they are entitled to receive,—the whole of the produce; but as long as they are not in possession of means sufficient, or cannot employ their labour, they will need to be aided by greater means—by the capital of those [e]who, or[e] whose progenitors have accumulated it by their labour [f]or acquired it by their intelligence. Those[f] who furnish a portion of the capital, will, no doubt, be entitled to a portion of the profit. The earnings of capital are not large—its remuneration is not great. Three per cent. is but little for its use; that is the rate with the Government, where the security is the best given. Capitalists are satisfied with four per cent. from some of the railway companies, where the security is not so good. This is all that can be obtained for the risk implied in its investment. Now, we are not to suppose that co-operation may not be made as safe as railway companies. Indeed, you may ultimately hope that the workers will be able to divide among themselves the whole produce, with the exception of the small amount I have mentioned. Three, or four, or five per cent., five pounds out of £100, is but a small deduction. Who can say that this is too much, or that it is unreasonable for the use of capital to be applied to the purposes of labour? Few societies would think of offering a less consideration [g]than that to their own members to induce them to save, and put their savings into the joint concern[g]. Many people think, although the co-operatives have very judiciously and very rightly shown no hostility to any other class—no desire on their own account to bring any other class down, yet that their aims are unattainable. A difficulty is felt; and it is said, what is to become of capital, if you succeed to the extent you hope for? In the first place, it is necessary to state that this is a gradual process; for as long as there are [h]any working people who are dishonest—as long as there are any who are idle, who are intemperate, who are spendthrifts—so long there will be working people who are only fit to be[h] receivers of wages. We are enabled to judge of those who are honest and trustworthy in the same way as we are to judge who is untrustworthy, so that, while we ought not to give our confidence rashly, there is also a danger in withdrawing it rashly when it has been once reasonably, and after due consideration, given. Here are two dangers; and it follows, that, so long as there are persons unworthy to take a part in great

[d-d]C which is too strong for all of us, will not allow that the labourers should have the whole produce of labour, unless they own the capital; and they can only do this when they have acquired it by

[e-e]+C

[f-f]C and intelligence, and accumulated it by their own frugality; and those

[g-g]C] R for it than that

[h-h]C] R working people, there will also be the idle, the imprudent, and the spendthrift, who will remain the

operations, there must be persons receivers of wages. [i]It is only when the entire working class shall be as much improved as the best portion of them now are that our hopes will be realised, and the whole mass of the people will practically adopt co-operation.[i] There is no fear that there will be any disturbance of existing interests, that there will be any disposition to avoid taking part in the working out the problem. Nothing will last any longer than the circumstances which necessitate it. There is no fear that co-operation will spread faster than the co-operators [j]improve[j]. It is not an easy thing. It is certain there will be, for many generations a great scope for labour in common way of wages. It is only in proportion as the lower grades rise to the level of the higher classes—it is only in proportion as that great change takes place, that the advantages of co-operation will be individually felt; and persons will become ashamed of not taking their due share in the work; and no difficulty whatever will be felt of obtaining capital to co-operate with labour. This will be a new millennium, which it requires but little knowledge to comprehend as entirely practical. We want, then, the co-operation of all workers—such ought to be our object. We ought to proceed towards this cautiously and tentatively, and never attempt to do an act which we feel will not be recommended by right principle. We ought to be content with steady persevering co-operation. I do not mean that the industrial or commercial operations of co-operatives can or ought to be carried on on some gigantic scale; for all such operations as you contemplate are in their essence limited. That which can be carried on from your side, must be necessarily small. The duty of all such co-operative societies is first, that they should help one another, that they should encourage those who have gone first, and shown the others the way to go,—how to succeed, and the sort of success worth having. (*Cheers.*) How to succeed will be learned by degrees. Co-operators will learn by practice. It is not an easy thing: if it had been, people would not have waited until this period for it. It cannot advance further than the minds and morals of the people engaged in it [k]nor faster than honest and competent men and women can find how[k] to manage its concerns. It cannot progress faster than the [l]ability to distinguish those who are trustworthy, and the willingness to trust them when found[l]. These are the points on which co-operators are most in danger of failing—in the first place in not having competent and trustworthy managers; and, in the next place, to have them and not to know them. (*Hear.*) Then, what is the success to be kept in view! [m]But when this great improvement in the mind of the people has taken place,—when all have become capable of co-operation, and most have adopted it,—I believe that the

[i-i]C] R We are looking forward to the time when the whole mass of the people shall adopt the true principles of co-operation.
[j-j]C] R desire
[k-k]C , than honest men and women can be found
[l-l]C] R power to trust a person when you find him trustworthy
[m-m]+C

owners of property will be ashamed to be the only persons who do not take their share in the useful work of the world, and will be willing to invest their capital in co-operative societies, receiving a fair interest for its use. This is the millennium towards which we should strive. I do not mean that the industrial or commercial operations of particular co-operative societies can or ought to be carried out upon some gigantic scale. All that such societies as this can do, is in its nature limited. But this co-operative societies *can* do—they can help one another. Those who have succeeded can encourage and show the way to others; and they can keep constantly in view both the way to succeed, and the sort of success worth having. How to succeed will be learned by degrees—co-operators will learn by practice. [m] I confess, if there were no other object in view than that persons who are original members should make themselves a little better off, I should not be addressing you to-night. I should be glad of it. I should be rejoiced at any person being improved in his position. This, however, is a small thing compared with co-operation. What we ought to aim at is, not to enable a small number of persons to rise, but all workers to share in the profits of labour. It all depends upon keeping right principles in view. All depends upon the disposition to put into practice the excellent principles that Mr. Lloyd Jones has expounded.[1] I believe there are many co-operators who are fully imbued with these principles, and I believe that the number is increasing. It is because I believe this [n]—and therefore feel assured that[n] co-operation will ultimately regenerate the masses of the country, and through them society itself, that I have ventured to address you this evening. (*Loud cheering.*)

[*Following Mill, the Rev. Henry Solly (a long-time friend of Mill's family) and George Jacob Holyoake spoke.*]

3. Corruption at Elections

4 APRIL, 1864

In Frederick D. Maurice, *Corruption at Elections* (London: Faithful, 1864), pp. 14–16. Briefly noted in the *Daily Telegraph*, 5 April, 1864 (copied in the *Beehive*, 9 April, p. 2), and the *Law Times*, 16 April, p. 277. The Department of Jurisprudence and Amendment of the Law, a section of the National Association for the Promotion of Social Science, met at its offices, 3 Waterloo Place, Edwin Chadwick (1800–91) in the Chair, to consider the standing committee's report on the paper by William Dougal Christie (1816–74), which is included, with Chadwick's speech, in the pamphlet and was issued as *Suggestions for an Organization for the Restraint of Corruption at Elections* (London: N.A.P.S.S., 1864).

[1]The speech by Lloyd Jones (1811–86), socialist activist and author, which preceded Mill's, is given in *The Reasoner*, XXVIII, 116.

[n-n]C] R , that I believe

After mention by G.W. Hastings of registration in Ireland, letters were read in support of the report, and then Mill spoke.

IT IS UNNECESSARY HERE, though it might be necessary in some other places, to insist upon the magnitude of the evil to which this report relates. What is at stake is nothing less than the vitality of representative government. If the majority or a preponderant portion of the House of Commons represented only their own pockets, we should, indeed, have what Mr. Disraeli called a Venetian Constitution,[1] and that in a very bad form. It would be a great mistake to suppose that we have seen the worst of this evil. I am persuaded that we are only in the beginning of it. When we consider the rapid growth of manufacture and commerce, and the number of persons that are constantly becoming wealthy, whose sole ambition is to obtain what wealth alone has not yet given them, namely, position, we see what a rapidly increasing number of persons there is to whom it is worth any money to acquire the only thing purchaseable by money, which will give them the grand object of their desire. I have been told by one who has filled a distinguished position in Australia[2] that there were within his knowledge five or six persons, Australians, who were only waiting for a general election to offer themselves to English constituencies, with the object I have mentioned. I mean nothing uncomplimentary to Australians. I believe them to be a very intelligent community. But the instance suggests the class of persons who make this evil an increasing one—the vulgar rich, to whom it is worth while to spend any amount of money for the sake of station in society. Persons of established position are often wishing to spend money corruptly, but there is a limit to the amount they will spend. They can gain comparatively little in importance by lavish expenditure. Their position is made, and they may even impair instead of advancing it if they spend too lavishly. But to a person of the other kind a seat in Parliament may be worth half his fortune. Now I think the Society must feel that, saving exceptions (admirable exceptions there are sure to be,) this class of persons, whether they act the part of flunkies, crouching at the feet of the aristocracy, or of envious demagogues anxious to bring them down, or, as will often be the case, are ready to turn from either of these parts to the other, according to convenience, are about the most undesirable and the most dangerous class of persons who can obtain admission to Parliament. It may be thought that the only evils to be apprehended from them are those of what may be called plutocracy; but, in reality, we should

[1]See *Vindication of the English Constitution, in a Letter to a Noble and Learned Lord* (London: Saunders and Otley, 1835), pp. 139, 168, 173, and 176, and *Coningsby; or, The New Generation*, 3 vols. (London: Colburn, 1844), Vol. II, pp. 229–31, and Vol. III, pp. 128–30, by Benjamin Disraeli (1804–81), Conservative statesman and author.

[2]Possibly Charles Gavan Duffy (1816–1903), Irish nationalist, a correspondent of Mill's, who emigrated to Australia in 1855, and had served in the Victoria government as Minister of Land and Works; or perhaps Henry Samuel Chapman (1803–81), another correspondent, who had been a politician and lawyer in Australia since 1851.

have those of democracy too, for if the costliness of elections limited the choice to such men, the electors, finding no one to vote for whom they could trust to act according to his own judgment and conscience, if they themselves have any regard to their own particular opinions, will bind them strictly by pledges to abide by subjects which the electors care about. The House of Commons would be an assembly of delegates, while on other subjects the member would vote according to his own interests or caprice, or according to the questions in which he desired to curry favour. Now as to the remedying of this, I am not one of those who think that legal means would necessarily be insufficient. I think there are legal measures which could be made effectual, but only if backed by a moral demonstration of a sufficient number of honest men, who would league themselves together against the political crime, expressly or virtually pledging themselves both to abstain from it personally, and to use all their influence to prevent it. They would probably be able to obtain from the Legislature any such enactments as may be desirable, while they would supply the only powers which could enable those enactments to be enforced. Great credit is due to Mr. Christie for having, as it seems to me, "hit the right nail on the head." As to the persons who should take this in hand, I think there is none so fit as this Society. [a]No individual, and no self-elected committee could address themselves to the leaders of parties, and to influential politicians throughout the country, nor would they be listened to if they did. But this Association, not to mention the larger society of which it now forms a part, could address itself to anyone.[a]

[*Mill concluded by moving the reception and adoption of the report; the motion was seconded by Frederick Hill, and adopted after discussion. A report on Walter Crofton's paper on the convict question was read, received, and adopted, and the meeting adjourned.*]

4. Hare's Plan for the Metropolis

10 APRIL, 1865

Morning Star, 11 April, 1865, p. 3. Headed: "Corrupt and Pernicious Influences at Elections." Also reported in summary form on 11 April in the *Daily News*, and *The Times*, and (apparently copied from the *Morning Star*) in *The National Reformer*, 16 April, pp. 250–1. The well-attended evening meeting, with many women members present, of the National Association for the Promotion of Social Science and the Society for Promoting the Amendment of the Law was held in the Rooms, Adam Street, Adelphi, with Lord Stanley in the Chair. The principal speaker was Thomas Hare (1806–91), author of *A Treatise on the Election of Representatives, Parliamentary and Municipal* (London: Longman, *et al.*,

[a-a]DT,B The Law Amendment Society had the power of aiding this, not being a self-elected body, but deriving authority from the eminence of its members.

1859), which had a profound effect on Mill (see *Autobiography*, *CW*, I, 262–3). Hare read his paper, "On such an organisation of the metropolitan elections as would call into exercise the knowledge and judgment of the constituencies, and as far as possible discourage all corrupt and pernicious influences" (*The Times*, 11 Apr., p. 10). In the ensuing discussion seven members spoke before Mill.

MR. J. STUART MILL dilated at much length on the details of the plan submitted by Mr. Hare, and pointed out that the objections raised to it were caused by a misapprehension on the part of those who, either through a want of interest in the matter or a determination to adhere to the present state of things, neglected to pay sufficient attention, so as to properly understand it. [a]It seemed to him that the plan proposed was as simple as possible, easy to be understood, and if given a trial would be found to be effectual and salutary in its results. Mr. Mill then referred in caustic terms to the manner in which contending parties under the present system get themselves represented, dwelling particularly on the part the great clubs play during election times.[a] [b]For instance, he remarked that no sooner a vacancy for a Liberal or Conservative candidate occurred than some one went down from a club with 3,000*l*. or 4,000*l*. at his back, saying, "I am a Liberal," "I am a Conservative," as the case might be.[b] But by the plan proposed by Mr. Hare this system would be checked. [c]Boobies would no longer be able to go down to constituencies with any chance of success; and besides, public interest would be elicited to a far greater extent than at present.[c] [d]He referred to the injustice of the existing system, in leaving the minority, say 19,000 out of 40,000—the election being carried by 21,000—practically unrepresented.[d] He considered the proposition of Mr. Hare both feasible and just, and he trusted the discussion that evening, and a little better understanding of the plan submitted, would have the effect of gaining for it that public support it so well deserved, and that the result would be that it would at all events get a fair trial. [e]This evil would be remedied by the

[a-a]DN It was the great merit of the plan that it did not contemplate the elected representing only the opinions and interests of those who voted for them. It would not leave the House of Commons the representatives of only three shades of opinion—whig, tory, and radical—but the opinions of the whole country would be represented, and property as well as numbers. The voter would no longer be compelled to vote for any booby sent down by the dominant party.] TT The great beauty and merit of Mr. Hare's system was that it would not leave the election to mere political opinion—to the three shades of opinion, Whig, Tory, and Radical. The voters would have the choice of the whole country—of all the eminent men in the country.

[b-b]TT The clubs would no longer be able to send a mere booby with 3,000*l*. or 4,000*l*. in his pocket.

[c-c]DN Boobies would no longer be sent down as candidates—men of merit would be sent down, or if they were not, the constituencies would find men of merit for themselves.] TT If they did not send down a man of merit, the electors would choose a man of merit for themselves. At present the Liberals must vote for the Liberal candidate, and the Tories for the Tory candidate, though each of the two candidates might be nothing more than a booby.

[d-d]+DN

[e-e]+DN] TT It was enough to put one out of temper to hear intelligent gentlemen say they could not understand Mr. Hare's plan. It was not anything like so difficult as the multiplication table.

proposed plan, which, in answer to the objection that it was complex and impracticable, he said was much more simple than the multiplication table, and might be easily understood by anyone who took the trouble to examine it fairly. Mr. Hare's plan, he knew, was anxiously thought of by some of the leaders of the working classes, and he should not be surprised if, before long, it became part of their political programme. He claimed for it the merit of giving ascendancy to none and justice to all.[e] He considered that the metropolitan constituencies offered a good field for the purpose of trying the experiment, and he urged the desirability of doing so.

[*After discussion, Hare replied. A motion of thanks to Hare, calling for his paper to be printed and circulated to members, was passed, and the meeting concluded with a vote of thanks to the Chair.*]

5. The Westminster Election of 1865 [1]

3 JULY, 1865

Daily Telegraph, 4 July, 1865, p. 3. Headed: "Election Intelligence. / Westminster." The evening meeting was called by Mill's general committee in one of the large rooms of St. James's Hall. This was Mill's first speech on his return to England to stand for election, and, as he indicates, it was impromptu; he had prepared for a speech on the 5th (see No. 6). This occasion clearly involved a surprise: "although it was only what was termed a meeting of the general committee, it was to all intents and purposes an open meeting, between 300 and 400 gentlemen being present" (*Daily News*). There "were present on the platform most of the leading Reformers not only of the city of Westminster but of the metropolis at large." Though many were present "who formed no part of the body invited to meet Mr. Mill, . . . the proceedings throughout were undisturbed" (*The Times*). "The chair was taken at eight o'clock by Dr. Brewer [William Brewer (d. 1881), a prominent physician and medical writer, a consistent supporter of Mill], who introduced Mr. Mill in a highly eulogistic speech." Then Mill, who "was received with great cheering," spoke.

GENTLEMEN, I can most sincerely say that our excellent chairman has not in the slightest degree exaggerated anything in what he has said respecting my want of preparation for a speech to-night. I did not at all expect that I should be called upon to make an address. I understood there was a day appointed when I should make a speech and express my sentiments as far as you desire to hear them. I thought that I should only be expected to meet you to-night as friends, and for the purpose of joining in friendly conversation—(*hear, hear*)—and thus have the opportunity of giving any explanation that you might wish respecting my political views—upon points which I have not sufficiently made known, or may not have sufficiently explained. For this, I was ready, but I was not in the least aware of the public character of this meeting (*referring to the reporters*). Therefore, I hope you will, in consideration of my want of experience in such cases, excuse the imperfections which must necessarily arise from my want of preparation. (*Applause.*) Let me begin by saying, that if our chairman has not made any exaggeration in that respect, I am afraid that he has in many others, for I do not know how it will be possible that I should fulfil all that he has said respecting me, in case I have the honour of being elected your representative. I say it will be difficult for me to fulfil the high expectations which must have been raised—(*no*)—by the friendly and favourable opinions which have been uttered respecting me throughout the whole of this election—friendly and favourable opinions, too, from quarters whence I could little expect them. The mere fact of the number of distinguished persons who have consented to have their names placed on my committee is a matter for which personally I cannot possibly be too thankful. It is a most distinguished honour itself, besides the fact of having been selected by such a body, as a candidate for the important post of representing Westminster, perhaps the most important seat in the whole House of Commons. (*Hear, hear.*) A higher honour than this can scarcely be conceived. But, though one of the highest, it ought not to be considered as a favour. (*Applause.*) If it be considered as a favour I have no right to ask it [a], and the electors would have no right to confer it[a]. It is not a favour; it is an onerous duty which you are anxious to impose upon me, and which I cannot but feel flattered to the highest degree at being thought worthy and capable of properly holding. (*Cheers.*) If I should receive your support and be elected to the House of Commons, I feel that I must fall below your expectations. (*Loud cries of No, no.*) Notwithstanding the utmost exertions which I could make, I feel that I must necessarily remain behind. (*Renewed cries of No, no.*) One thing I will say, no one can feel stronger than I do the importance of that part in the contest which has nothing to do with me individually—and that is purity of election. (*Cheers.*) I am obliged to say that you give me too much honour when you bestow on me the glory of that. If you are victorious, the praise will not be mine, the praise will be wholly yours. (*No.*) It is all very well for me to say how desirable are these things, but you have to accomplish them, therefore to you will be the credit. You have to maintain the fight to elect me on what you suppose are my qualifications, and which are my only recommendation. I am a person almost entirely unknown to you except through my writings. You have not only undertaken to elect a person on these grounds, but you have also undertaken to do it and bear all those expenses—ordinary expenses—which ought never to be borne by the candidate. (*Great applause.*) For those charges which are legitimate ought to be borne by the public or the municipal body—(*hear, hear*)—and those which are illegitimate ought never to be incurred at all. (*Cheers.*) You have undertaken to abstain from the illegitimate expenses, and to bear the burden of the legitimate. (*Yes, and cheerfully.*) This you have performed, and not only so, but you have done it

[a-a]+DN

having to bear up against a candidature which is conducted on opposite principles[1]—a candidature conducted on principles of the most lavish expenditure. (*Hear, hear, and cheers.*) And neither is this all, for you have not only to contend against this, but you have to evoke a spirit in the constituency which shall rise superior to those opposite principles, and to a level with those which you have adopted. (*Hear, hear.*) Therefore the praise will be yours. It is easy for me to say that I will use no illegitimate or even [b]what were usually considered[b] legitimate means. Yours will be the deserved credit. I do not think that it is right a candidate should make any other pledge than a complete sincerity [c]and that he ought not to canvass the electors[c]. (*Hear, hear.*) It costs me nothing to say this, but it costs you much, for it is you who have to bear the burden. (*Cheers.*) Whatever honour I may receive, it will be you who have gained it for me. I cannot help thanking the worthy chairman for having paid the tribute he has done to one to whom in my early life I owe everything—to my father (*applause*)—a man who has done more, infinitely more, for the public cause than I can ever do; because he lived in times when there were few to do it—when the fact of being Liberal—Liberalism which was worth anything—stood most seriously in the way of a man's advancement in life, and especially of men who had their bread to gain.[2] He had to win his bread by his pen, and had to do this at a time when his opinions were such as necessarily to produce not only the ill-favour of the chiefs and recognised leaders of political parties, but to compromise him with all the powerful classes of this country. I say he did this at a time when there were very few to favour or praise him. Nothing that I can do will compare with this—it will not have a tenth, a hundredth, a thousandth part of the merit which belongs to those who went before me. To him I am indebted for everything which has made me at all capable of following in his footsteps. As it is, I may say, if there is a time when a person may be allowed to speak of himself, it is on such an occasion as this. I may perhaps say something which may make you better satisfied with me, when I affirm that I have sat by the cradle of all the great political reforms of this and the last generation; and I have not only sat by the cradle of these reforms, but before I was out of my teens I was up and stirring, and writing about them. (*Hear.*) I have stood by these reforms, which now count followers by millions when their followers did not count tens of thousands, nay, not thousands, nor hundreds. (*Cheers.*) When they only counted tens I was

[1]I.e., that of William Henry Smith (1825–91), proprietor and son of the founder of W.H. Smith and Son, who was running as a Liberal Conservative, or Conservative Liberal (both labels were used).

[2]James Mill (1772–1836), an active propagandist for radical Benthamite and Ricardian views through articles, pamphlets, books, and personal influence, had lived by his pen until he joined the East India Company in 1819, rising to the head of the Examiner's Office, a position J.S. Mill also attained.

[b-b]+DN
[c-c]+DN

amongst them. Nay, I may say, when their followers only counted units—when that which is now the universally received principle respecting the government of our colonies was not always so. I can recollect the time when there were two men amongst the active political writers of this country who recognised it—two men, Mr. Roebuck and myself.[3] (*Great cheering.*) I can remember another thing which many of you may—which, indeed, you must have heard—the Wakefield doctrine for finding funds for supplying the population of the colonies.[4] The Wakefield principle is to put a price on uncultivated land, and employ the proceeds in paying the expenses of immigration [d], which would prevent them from settling down as Irish cottiers[d]; the price, at the same time, being an obstacle to the too great dispersion of the inhabitants. That was in 1831, when there were three persons who held that—Mr. Wakefield, the inventor or discoverer, myself, and one other.[5] And we so worked the principle that in four years a new colony, South Australia, was founded on the principle. (*Cheers.*) [e]In a few years afterwards it was a principle which was very greatly extended over all our Australian Colonies. From that date, long before the discovery of the gold mines, these colonies entered upon a career of prosperity which has continued, and those colonies now constitute one of the most splendid offshoots of the English people.[e] (*Cheers.*) I have said this for the purpose of showing I have never been one of those who have left difficult things for others. (*Cheers.*) I have never been one of those who have left things alone when they have been an uphill fight, but I have left them when the fight was no longer difficult. When the thing was prosperous I have left it for a time, and have said, "This matter no longer requires me," and I have therefore transferred my services to those who did. (*Loud cheers.*) I have left that prosperous thing, and have turned to something else—to something that was still a crotchet, still an abstraction, still something that no practical person would battle with. (*Hear, hear.*) For I have been accustomed even in my life—and all history confirms the same thing—I have been accustomed to see that the crotchet of

[3]John Arthur Roebuck (1801–79) had been a close associate—initially a disciple—of Mill's in the late 1820s; he was a leading Radical in the House of Commons after the Reform Act of 1832. Though personally estranged from Mill during most of their adult lives, he remained an admirer, joined in the movement for Mill's election, and offered him advice on effective performance in the Commons.

[4]See, e.g., Edward Gibbon Wakefield, *Plan of a Company to Be Established for the Purpose of Founding a Colony in Southern Australia* (London: Ridgway, 1831).

[5]Robert Gouger (1802–66), early and ardent advocate of Wakefield's scheme; for evidence that he is the one intended, see Wakefield, *A Letter from Sydney* (London: Cross, *et al.*, 1829), pp. 169–80, and Appendix, pp. iii-xxiv.

[d-d]+DN] TT , and the application of this prevented the people from settling on the land like Irish cottiers

[e-e]DN After that, but not to a very great extent, it was applied to all our Australian colonies, and some of the colonies which had languished revived. Western Australia, which had been a failure, had entered upon a career of prosperity.

to-day, the crotchet of one generation, becomes the truth of the next and the truism of the one after. (*Cheers.*) I have lived long enough to see the three steps of this process taking place with a number of my opinions. I have told you a number of my crotchets now, and perhaps they will be truisms by-and-by. (*Hear, hear.*) I think, gentlemen, as all of you have consented to be members of my committee, I may take it for granted that you have a sufficient general idea of my political opinions for you to be aware what course I should take if you do me the honour of electing me. (*We will.*) But if there is anything respecting which you wish to know more, or anything upon which you would wish further explanation, and to ask my sentiments, here I am to answer. (*Hear, hear.*) Coming, as I said, unprepared, I have stated that which came uppermost in my mind. It rests with you upon what other topic I shall speak. If any of you will do me the honour of putting any question, I will endeavour to answer it. (*Cheers.*)

Mr. Probyn said that a rumour had been circulated by the Conservatives that Mr. Mill did not intend to go to the poll. [f]*This was utterly false; for not only did they intend to go to the poll, but they believed by next Tuesday night that Mr. Mill would be one of the members for Westminster. (Cheers.)*[f] *He would simply venture to mention the American question as one upon which he would wish to ask Mr. Mill to give them some little explanation*—viz., *with respect to the doctrine of non-intervention. He read a paper of Mr. Mill's, which in 1857 was published in* Fraser's Magazine, *and which well pleased him.*[6] *Its doctrine was that we as a country ought not to intervene in the domestic, in the purely internal events which occurred in any particular country, whatever our sympathies might be; but this did not preclude our interfering in the affairs of the continent when any one power or any two by their attitude or acts jeopardised a third power, and which might be a free power. In that case we ought to interfere for the sake of freedom, and in so doing we did not contravene the real doctrine of non-intervention.*

Mr. Mill said that this was a correct quotation from his writings. [g]He did not think it was possible for a nation more than an individual to say that if it should cost anything, it would not help people who were struggling in a good cause. He thought intervention was generally wrong, not on account of the nation interfering, but of the nation with which it interfered. He thought every nation was the best judge of its own affairs.[g] (*Cheers.*)

Professor Masson strongly advocated the claims of Mr. Mill.

[6]"A Few Words on Non-Intervention," *Fraser's Magazine*, LX (Dec. 1859), 766–76 (*CW*, Vol. XXI, pp. 109–24).

[f-f]DN *He assured the electors that he would poll to the last hour, and that he would then be found at its head. (Loud cheers.)*

[g-g]DN] DT He thought a people were much the best judges of their own internal affairs but this spirit of non-intervention did not apply in the case which had been put forward.] TT [He] considered no nation should interfere in the internal affairs of another nation; but that when a despotic government interfered with a nation which desired to be free, then a free country would be in duty bound to interfere on the side of right.

A gentleman in the body of the room asked the honourable candidate's views respecting Church and State and the Maynooth grant.[7]

Mr. Mill said that as he had said before he would not give a pledge; but this would not prevent him from stating what was his sincere opinion. His sincere opinion was that it was best that Church and State should be perfectly distinct. He was against all connection between Church and State. As things stood, he did not think this was a practicable object. [h]He thought their object should be to exercise all the influence the State had over the Church, to improve its spirit.[h] He thought most present would agree with him that the State was considerably more Liberal than the Church. (*Cheers.*) [i]There had been occasions on which the State had tended to corrupt the Church, but at present matters stood the other way.[i] He had a great opinion that at present those who held the most liberal sentiments—and by liberal he did not mean lax, but who took the most Christian view of religion—had a much greater chance of being in the highest places of the Church than if the Church were separated from the State. Respecting the Maynooth grant, he should be quite ready to discontinue it as soon as no State endowment was granted to any other religion. (*Hear, hear.*) As long as there was, and especially that [j]utterly condemnable[j] body, the Irish Church Establishment—(*hear, hear*)—he should think it a very great shame to take away from the religion of the body of the people the small pittance which they were allowed. (*Applause.*)

[k]*No resolutions were moved, and the proceedings concluded by the announcement of a series of meetings which Mr. Mill would attend.*[k][8]

6. The Westminster Election of 1865 [2]

5 JULY, 1865

Morning Star, 6 July, 1865, p. 2. Headed: "Election Intelligence. / Meeting of Mr. J.S. Mill with the Electors of Westminster." The speech exists in a shorter version in manuscript (Mill-Taylor Collection, printed in Appendix D), and was reported fully on 6 July also in the *Daily Telegraph*, the *Daily News*, and *The Times* (the last in the third person). The meeting was held in St. James's Hall in the evening. "A considerable time before the hour for the commencement of the meeting the hall was crowded to excess by an audience, a large portion of whom seemed to be electors. The meeting displayed a feature not common

[7]8 & 9 Victoria, c. 25 (1845) provided Maynooth College, a Roman Catholic seminary in Ireland, with a special building grant of £30,000, and increased its annual subsidy from £9,000 to £26,000.

[8]See Nos. 6, 7, 8, and 10.

[h-h]+DN

[i-i]+DN

[j-j]DN anomalous and contemptible

[k-k]DN] DT *The Committee then proceeded with private business.*

at election assemblies. Both side galleries were occupied by ladies, who appeared to take a warm interest in the proceedings." (*Morning Star.*) Edwin Lankester (1814–74), surgeon, coroner for central Middlesex, and professor of natural history, long known to Mill, was in the Chair. He said "it gave him great pleasure in introducing Mr. John Stuart Mill as a candidate for the suffrages of the electors of the ancient city of Westminster. (*Cheers.*) Mr. Mill was not unknown to them by name; he was not unknown to the people of England by reputation. (*Hear.*) He was known wherever the interests of humanity lay deep in the hearts of men, wherever progress and civilisation formed an element in the thoughts of men. (*Hear, hear.*)" (*Morning Star.*) "They saw before them the great philosopher of the day, and he should have been still better pleased if they could have elected him without seeing him" (*Daily News*). "They would find that Mr. Mill was not an advocate of chimerical theories as had been represented, but a man of large and practical views. He was a great politician and a great practical philosopher, ["and though some of his ideas were termed crotchets, they would turn out to be the seed from which they would hereafter have abundant results" (*Daily News*)]; and he trusted they would not from any imaginary difference of religious views push him from the pedestal on which he now stood. (*Cheers.*) The opposition to Mr. Mill on account of his religious opinions was disgraceful to Westminster. (*Loud and prolonged cheers.*)" He mentioned the "great religious teachers of the day": Charles Kingsley (1819–75), Anglican priest and author; Frederick Denison Maurice (1805–72), also priest and author, an acquaintance of Mill's since the 1820s; Connop Thirlwall (1797–1875), historian and Bishop of St. David's since 1840, also known to Mill since the 1820s; and Arthur Penrhyn Stanley (1815–81), author and professor of ecclesiastical history at Oxford, Dean of Westminster since 1864: all had publicly expressed support for Mill's candidature, in the face of his anti-Church attitudes. Those men, Lankester said, "had perfect confidence in his opinions; and he hoped therefore that they would away with the wickedness and uncharitableness which sought to reject Mr. Mill on account of his religious views. (*Loud cheers.*)" (*Morning Star.*) "Mr. Mill, on rising to address the meeting, was received with the utmost enthusiasm. The people rose en masse, and waved their hats and cheered, and again and again renewed the cheers. When silence was restored" (*The Times*), Mill spoke.

LADIES AND GENTLEMEN, it is probable that many persons present desire that I should explain why I have hitherto abstained from all the ordinary practices of candidates, and from appearing at public meetings of the electors. My reasons for doing so have been stated in the letter in which I consented to be made a candidate;[1] but that is no reason why I should not repeat them here. When I stated in my letter that for my own sake I should not desire to sit in Parliament, I meant what I said. I have no personal objects to be promoted by it. It is a great sacrifice of my personal tastes and pursuits, and of that liberty which I value the more because I have only recently acquired it after a life spent in the restraints and confinements of a public office; for, as you may not perhaps know it, and as many people think that a writer of books, like myself, cannot possibly have any practical knowledge of business, it is a fact that I have passed [a]many hours of every day for[a] thirty-five years in the

[1]To James Beal (7 Mar., 1865), published *inter alia* in the *Daily News*, 23 Mar., p. 1 (*CW*, Vol. XVI, pp. 1005–7).

[a-a]DN] MS my days for the last [*reporter's error*]

actual business of government.[2] These personal considerations I have cast aside—(*cheers*)—but there is one thing which it is not so easy to cast aside—a rooted dislike to the mode in which the suffrages of electors are ordinarily sought. To be selected by a great community as the representative of what is highest in their minds, their consciences, and their understanding—of their sincere convictions and their patriotic sentiments—is one of the highest honours which it is possible for the citizen of a free country to receive. (*Hear, hear.*) But to be sent into Parliament as representative of that part of the electors whose minds are to be got at by money—who are to be reached by trickery—by saying one thing and meaning another—by making professions which are not intended to be acted upon, and which being contrary to one's own convictions it would be a greater breach of morality to keep than to violate—that I regard not as an honour but as a disgrace. (*Cheers.*) Therefore, when a body of this great constituency did me the honour to make the most unexpected and flattering proposal of presenting me as a candidate for your suffrages, I answered that I should not be willing to spend £10,000 in corrupting and debauching [b] the constituents who are debauchable and corruptible; that neither would I give any pledge except the single pledge to be always open and above board (*loud cheers*); and that neither would I solicit your votes. I hold the whole system of personal solicitation to be a mistake. Not that I would condemn those who merely have conformed to a bad custom, and have done nothing to make that custom worse than they found it. A seat in Parliament ought not to be a matter of solicitation, because it cannot be a matter of favour. I have no right to ask it as a favour; you have no right to grant it [c]. You have no right but to select the man who appears to you to be fittest. That was my answer, and to the honour of Westminster—I may say that much, though I am a party concerned—a body of men were found who were sufficiently alive to what is due to public principle, who were sufficiently solicitous for their own honour, and for the honour of this constituency, to say [d]that not the man who did those things, but the man who would not do them, was the man of their choice. (*Cheers.*) It remained to be seen if the electors of Westminster thought so too. (*Cheers.*)[d] That, gentlemen, is the way in which I became a candidate, and it would have been quite inconsistent with a candidature grounded on these considerations to have gone about amongst you and asked for your votes [e]. (*Hear, hear.*) My principle is that you are bound to elect the fittest man. Would it have been decent in me to have gone among you and said, "I am the fittest man"? (*Hear, hear.*) What would have been thought of the candidate who said, "It is your duty to elect a man of merit; here am I, elect

[2]I.e., from 1823 to 1858 in the Examiner's Office of the East India Company.

[b]Manuscript (by strictly legal means of course)

[c]Manuscript : you are conferring a solemn trust

[d-d]TT] MS that no man who would do these things ought to represent Westminster. (*Cheers.*) We will see if the electors don't think so too.

[e]Manuscript directly and personally

me." (*A laugh and cheers.*) Gentlemen, I am not here because I proposed myself; I am here because I am proposed by others. I hope you don't suppose that I think all the fine things true about me which have been said and written with so much exaggeration, but with a depth and strength of kind feeling towards myself, for which I never can be sufficiently grateful, by numbers of persons almost all personally unknown to me. I know that you will excuse [f]these strong encomiums[f], knowing how much a man is liable to be overpraised, as well as unjustly attacked, at a contested election. (*Hear, hear.*)

Perhaps you may ask, since for those reasons I have during all these weeks not come among you, why I come now. I come for two reasons. I was told by those who had good means of judging that many of you desired to know more of me than you have been able to collect from what I have written. Such a statement as that left me no option, for you have a right to know my opinions and to have an opportunity of judging for yourself what man you are to select. Whatever you think right to ask concerning my political opinions it is my duty to tell you, I stand pledged to answer you—and it is the only pledge I will give—not only truly, but with perfect openness. (*Cheers.*) It would have been as easy for me, as it is for many others, to have put forth a plausible profession of political faith. It need not have been one of those wishy-washy, meaningless, and colourless addresses—(*cheers*)—of which the papers are now so full, and which a Tory, Whig and Radical might equally have signed—which bind them to nothing, and which are consistent with almost any vote that they can give. (*Cheers.*) I need not have been reduced to such an extremity. (*Hear, hear.*) I might have made out a long [g]*bona fide*[g] list of political questions on which I have the high satisfaction of believing that I entirely agree with you. I might have passed gently over all subjects of possible difference and observed a discreet silence about any opinion that might possibly have startled anybody. (*Laughter and cheers.*) [h] I did the very reverse. I put forth no address, but instead I undertook that whatever questions you put to me concerning my political opinions I would answer fully. (*Hear, hear.*) The questions that you did put to me I answered with a degree of unreserve which has been a sort of scandal in the electioneering world. (*A laugh and cheers.*) What compelled me to say anything about women's votes or the representation of minorities? Is it likely that any one would have questioned me upon those points? Not one of you probably would, but you asked what my opinions on Reform were, and being asked, I did not think it consistent with plain dealing to keep back any of them. (*Cheers.*) I dare say I lowered myself prodigiously in the eyes of those persons who think that the cleverest thing in a candidate is to dissemble, to finesse, and to commit himself to nothing if he can possibly help it. "How injudicious!" said one; "How impractical!" said another; "How can he possibly expect to be elected on such a

[f-f]Manuscript what is excessive in these eulogiums
[g-g]+DN,Manuscript
[h]Manuscript Did I do this?

programme?" thought even sincere friends. In answer to all that I beg them to consider—1st, that perhaps if I had the choice I would rather be honest than be elected—(*loud cheers, which continued for several minutes*); and 2nd, that perhaps the electors of Westminster have a taste for honesty and may think that man who deals honestly with them before he is elected is the more likely person to deal honestly with them after he is elected. (*Renewed cheers.*) Of one thing I am sure—that [i], even though a man should lose his election by it,[i] the most practical thing in the world is honesty [j], and perhaps they would live to learn this lesson[j]. (*Hear, hear.*)

I suppose you would hardly expect me to travel over a whole catalogue of political questions, and tell you things which you know quite as well as I do. [k]It would be better that I should answer questions afterwards, and give you any explanations that you may desire on particular points. What I will do now is to attempt to give you an idea of the general tendency of my opinions.[k] I am here as the candidate of advanced Liberalism—(*cheers*)—and I should like to tell you what in my estimation these words mean. Mr. Gladstone (*cheers*) in one of those memorable speeches which have made every sincere reformer look to him as our future Parliamentary leader—(*cheers*)—has given us a definition of the difference between Tory and Liberal. He has said that Liberalism is trust in the people, limited only by prudence; that Toryism is distrust of the people, limited only by fear. (*Cheers.*)[3] That is a distinction which in one of its aspects is a most important one; but there is a still larger view that may be taken of the difference. A Liberal is he who looks forward for his principles of government; a Tory looks backward. (*Cheers.*) A Tory is of opinion that the real model of government lies somewhere behind us in the region of the past, from which we are departing further and further. Toryism means the subjection and dependence of the great mass of the community in temporal matters upon the hereditary possessors of wealth, and in spiritual matters to the Church, and therefore it is opposed [l]to the last moment,[l] to everything which could lead us further away from this model. When beaten the Tory may accept defeat by a necessity of the age, but he still hankers after the past, and still thinks that good government means the restoration in some shape [m]or other[m] of the feudal principle—(*hear, hear*)—and continues to oppose all further

[3]William Ewart Gladstone (1809–98), who was, following the death of Lord Palmerston, to become the leading Liberal in the Commons in the next session, Speech at Chester, 1 June, 1865 (*The Times*, 2 June, p. 5).

[i-i]+DN] DT , even if a man loses by it,] Manuscript *as* DN . . . man may now and then lose his election by it, in the long run]

[j-j]+TT] Manuscript and this is a lesson politicians will have to learn

[k-k]DN] MS What I will do now is to give you an idea of the general tendency of my political opinions.] DT It is better that I should confine myself to questions you ask me; but I will attempt to show you the general tendency of my opinions.] Manuscript It is better that I should confine myself to giving explanations on any points on which you think they are needed.

[l-l]+DT,DN,TT] Manuscript , up to the last moment

[m-m]Manuscript , perhaps a shape better adapted to the time

progress in a new direction. The Liberal is something very different from this. [n]The probability is,[n] that we have not yet arrived at the perfect model of government—that it lies before us and not behind us—that we are too far from it to be able to see it distinctly except in outline, but that we can see very clearly in what direction it lies—not in the direction of some new form of dependence, but in the emancipation of the dependent classes—more freedom, more equality, and more responsibility of each person for himself. (*Loud cheers.*) That, gentlemen, is the first article of my political creed. Now for the second. Believing as I do that [o]society and[o] political institutions are, or ought to be, in a state of progressive advance; that it is the very nature of progress to lead us to recognise as truths what we do not as yet see to be truths; believing also that [p]by diligent study, by attention to the past, by constant application,[p] it is possible to see a certain distance before us, and to be able to distinguish beforehand some of these truths of the future, and to assist others to see them—I certainly think there are truths which [q]the time has now arrived for[q] proclaiming, although the time may not yet have arrived for carrying them into effect. (*Cheers.*) That is what I mean by [r]advanced[r] Liberalism. [s]But does it follow that, because a man sees something of the future, he is incapable of judging of the past? Does it follow that, because a man thinks of to-morrow, he knows nothing of to-day?[s] That is what the dunces will tell you. (*Cheers and laughter.*) I venture to reverse the proposition. The only persons who can judge for the present—who can judge for the day truly and safely—are those who include to-morrow in their deliberations. [t]We can see the direction in which things are tending, and which of those tendencies we are to encourage and which to resist. That is a policy to which we look for all the greater good of the future.[t] But while I would refuse to suppress one iota of the opinions I consider best, I confess I would not object to accept any reasonable compromise which would give me even a little of that of which I hope in time to obtain the whole. (*Cheers.*)

[n-n]DT] MS,DN He probably thinks] TT He was of opinion] Manuscript He thinks

[o-o]+DT,DN,Manuscript

[p-p]+DT] DN by patient study of the past and a sufficient application of our thoughts to a great subject,] Manuscript by a diligent study of the past, and application of thought to great questions

[q-q]DN which a few are now holding and

[r-r]+DT,DN,Manuscript

[s-s]DT] MS Does it follow that because a man sees something of to-morrow he can do nothing about to-day?] DN But does it follow that because a man can see something of the future he is not capable of judging of to-day?] Manuscript But does it follow, because a person has something to say about the future, that he must be incapable of judging of the present? That if he thinks for tomorrow, he can know nothing about today?

[t-t]DT I can see much tendency now which we ought to encourage, much to resist; but we ought to take care that the policy of the moment will be such as to fit us, and not unfit us, for the policy of the future. (*Hear, hear.*)] DN If we see towards what things are tending, what the tendencies are which we ought to encourage and what to resist, we shall take care that the policy of the moment shall be such as to fit us, and not unfit us, for the future. (*Cheers.*)] Manuscript : who can see what things we are tending to; which of the tendencies we should favour and which resist; and who will take care that his policy of the moment shall fit us instead of unfitting us for the greater good of the future. [*The clause previous to this passage is in the singular.*]

There is one more topic upon which I have something to say. I have told you one reason why I have now come amongst you. There is another. The contest has changed its character. It [u]no longer relates to me personally[u]. What you are called upon to decide is not whether you prefer me to somebody else: it is whether the representation of Westminster, up to this time the most honourable seat in the House of Commons, is to continue hereafter, as it has been heretofore, to be obtained by the honest choice of the constituents, or is to be had for money? (*Cheers.*) The very fact that such a question can be put—much more that there should be a doubt as to the result—is enough to fill with shame any inhabitant of Westminster who knows the ancient reputation of his city. (*Cheers.*) [v]We[v] Reformers have been accustomed to demand that the great landed nobility and gentry should no longer have it in their power to hoist their sons and *protégés* into Parliament over the heads of the constituents, passing over their minds, and addressing themselves either to their personal interests or to their hereditary subserviency. [w]We object to this, and with reason[w]; but what shall we gain, what will it profit us, to weaken aristocratic ascendancy if seats in Parliament are to be put up to auction? (*Hear, hear.*) What is it but putting them up to auction if they are to be knocked down to the man [x]with the longest purse, and who is willing to spend his money[x]? (*Cheers.*) Of all the political nuisances of the day this is one which it most behoves everyone to make a stand against, because it is the only one which is increasing while almost all the others are rapidly diminishing. The great facilities for money-getting which arise from the unexampled prosperity of the country are raising up a crowd of persons who have made large fortunes or whose fathers have made large fortunes for them—(*laughter*)—and whose main object in life is by means of these fortunes to purchase position—that is to say, admission into the society of persons of higher rank than themselves. In this country there is only one way in which that can be done by money, and that is by getting a seat in Parliament: Was it for this purpose that the House of Commons was instituted? (*Cheers.*) I am the very last person to say anything disparaging of the class of persons I am speaking of and to assert that they have no business in Parliament. Many of them have strong claims [y], by their knowledge and abilities,[y] to a seat in the House of Commons, and are an element which it could ill spare. (*Hear, hear.*) But the mischief is that it is precisely those who have the least chance of getting elected on their own merits [z]who have no chance of getting into good society by

[u-u]DT is no longer a mere personal matter] DN now no longer regards me] Manuscript is no longer foremost to myself

[v-v]+DN,Manuscript] DT What

[w-w]+DT] Manuscript This we object to, and with reason

[x-x]+DN] Manuscript who has the longest purse, and is willing to open it widest

[y-y]+DN, Manuscript

[z-z]DT , and who have no chance of getting into society by their talents or their education,] DN , who have no chance whatever of getting into society by their own talents, or education, or influence,] Manuscript —who have no chance of making their way into what is called good society by . . . *as* MS . . . breeding—it is exactly those

their talents, their education, and their breeding. It is exactly those persons[z] who are under the strongest temptation to employ the only other means open to them—*viz.*, a lavish expenditure of money, in corrupting the electors—I say corrupting, not meaning necessarily a violation of the law. There is a great deal of corruption which is not technically bribery. (*Hear, hear.*) [a]It makes no difference if a working man is paid for his vote or paid for putting a placard in his window.[a] Everyone who gets into Parliament by such means as these—by opening the public-houses—goes there to represent the vices of the constituency. (*Cheers.*) It is vain to hope that men will be shamed out of these things as long as they are not cut in society [b]. But if you cannot prevent them from doing these things you can prevent them from succeeding. (*Cheers.*) The experiment is being tried upon you. A strong effort is being made to bring in a Tory candidate by an expenditure of money more profuse than a Tory ever attempted in this city. (*Cheers.*) It is tolerably well known that the majority of the electors of Westminster are not Tories—(*a laugh*)—and it is not uncharitable to suppose that the supporters of the Tory candidate rested their hopes upon money. If they thought that you had turned Conservative, that you had had enough of Reform, that constitutional improvements had gone far enough, and that it was now time to stop—(*a laugh*)—they would have selected for the distinction of representing this city one of their eminent men—one of the men who are an honour to their party—such a man as Lord Stanley.[4] (*Cheers.*) When, instead of the man of the greatest merit they offer you a man who is willing to spend most profusely, they show plainly in what it is that they put their trust. (*Cheers.*)

Will you let them succeed? (*Cries of No, no.*) It is no exaggeration to say that all eyes are upon you. Every friend of freedom and purity of election in the country is looking to you with anxious feelings. There is another class of persons who are also looking at you, and they are those [c]—and there are many of them—[c] who cultivate contempt of the people. All these are watching you, and hoping to find you worthy of their contempt. They are chuckling in the hope of succeeding in the attempt to debauch you. They say [d]that it is not in you to elect any man except he is willing to spend his money, that[d] you have no public virtue, and that public

[4]Edward Henry Stanley (1826–93), the son and heir of the 14th Earl of Derby, at this time M.P. for King's Lynn, known for his abilities and his political moderation.

[a-a]DT It makes no difference to a working man whether he be paid for working or be paid for putting a placard in his window.] DN It is not more corruption to give money to get into parliament than it is to pay a man for exhibiting a placard in his window for the purpose of inducing him to vote for the man who pays him.] Manuscript To gain a seat by giving money to the electors is not less corruption because the elector does not receive the money for his vote, but for ostensible services; it makes no moral difference whether a working man is paid for voting, or for putting, for instance, a placard in his window.

[b]MS for doing them

[c-c]+DT] Manuscript (they are very numerous)

[d-d]+DN] Manuscript that you have it not in you to elect any person but the man who will spend most money among you—that

virtue is not to be expected from such people as you are. They are waiting eagerly and anxiously for you to justify their opinion. I hope you will disappoint them. (*Cheers.*) If you elect me and I should turn out a total failure—if I disappointed every expectation—you would have nothing to be ashamed of. You would have acted an honest part and done that which at the time seemed to be best for the public good. Can the same thing be said if you return the candidate of a party against which for a century past Westminster has in the most emphatic manner protested, for his money? If this great constituency should so degrade itself it will not only be the deepest mortification to all who put faith in popular institutions, but Westminster will have fallen from her glory, and she can never hold her head as high as she has done, because the progress of popular institutions, which cannot possibly be stopped, will have to go on [e]in future[e] without her. (*Mr. Mill resumed his seat amid loud and prolonged cheers.*)

[f]*Mr. Harrow (a non-elector) asked what were Mr. Mill's views with respect to marriage with a deceased wife's sister.*[5] *(Great laughter and cries of Oh, and Hear, hear.)*[f]

Mr. Mill said he [g]had not considered the outs and ins of the question of marriage with a deceased wife's sister[g], but as he did not see any [h]conclusive[h] reason why such marriages should not be permitted, he would vote for freedom in the matter. (*Cheers.*)

[*In reply to Mr. Morrison, an elector of the City of London*] *Mr. Mill said* he would do away with the Irish Church, root and branch. (*Cheers.*)

[*An elector, Mr. Whitely, asked if Mill was in favour of the Permissive Bill.*][6]

[i]*Mr. Mill replied that* this was a question on which it was painful for him to

[5]A recurring question in these years, opposed by strict interpreters of the religious injunctions against marriage within the prohibited degrees of consanguinity. For the most recent legislative attempt, see "A Bill to Render Legal Certain Marriages of Affinity," 25 Victoria (11 Feb., 1862), *PP*, 1862, III, 133–4 (not enacted). The question anticipates the bringing in of "A Bill to Render Legal Marriage with a Deceased Wife's Sister," 29 Victoria (6 Mar., 1866), *PP*, 1866, III, 501–3 (also not enacted).

[6]Another recurrent question, most recently seen in "A Bill to Enable Owners and Occupiers of Property in Certain Districts to Prevent the Common Sale of Intoxicating Liquors within Such Districts," 27 Victoria (10 Mar., 1864), *PP*, 1864, II, 357–64 (not enacted).

[e-e]+DN] Manuscript for the present
[f-f]DN] MS In reply to Mr. Wanold
[g-g]DN did not expect that would be the first question put to him
[h-h]DT sufficient
[i-i]DN] MS *Mr. Mill said* he warmly sympathised with the efforts of the temperance reformers. He believed drunkenness to be the bane of the working classes, and to be one of the greatest obstacles to their political advancement. But he could not violate principle, and did not think that it was right because some persons abused a benefit that others should be deprived of it. He relied mainly on moral means, such as education, for improving the habits of the working classes.] DT On the Permissive Bill and Maine Liquor Law, agreeing as he did with temperance, anti-drunkenness, and almost with total abstinence, on the ground that a twig sometimes required to be bent the wrong way in order to be

touch, because the answer which he was conscientiously compelled to give was one contrary to the opinions of persons for whom he had a sincere respect and sympathy. (*Hear, hear.*) He agreed thoroughly with the teetotallers and the temperance leagues in the objects they had in view, because he believed that the prevalence of drunkenness was one of the greatest obstacles to real national progress. (*Cheers.*) But for all that he could not say that because some persons abused the liberty now given to use intoxicating liquors, others should be deprived of the power of using them temperately. The Permissive Bill gave the power to the majority to coerce the minority in that respect, and therefore he could not assent to such a measure. (*Cheers.*) He trusted to improved education to render all such coercive legislation unnecessary. (*Cheers.*)

Mr. Whitely—I am perfectly satisfied. (Cheers.)[i]

In reply to other questions,

Mr. Mill said he was [j]not opposed to[j] capital punishment in extreme cases—in cases where murder was aggravated by brutality [k]—because, although death by hanging was less painful than death in bed, and was more merciful than imprisonment for life, it had a more deterrent effect on the imagination[k]. He was in favour of the opening of the British Museum and similar institutions on Sundays, under proper regulations.

Mr. Malleson then moved a resolution declaring Mr. Mill a fit and proper person to represent Westminster, and pledging the meeting to make every effort to secure his return. (Cheers.) He announced, amid loud cheers, that the split in the Liberal party was likely, he might say certainly, to be removed, and hoped that the great Liberal party would vote for Mill and Grosvenor.

[*The resolution was supported by Fawcett, Lord Stanley who "appealed to the constituency of Westminster as the 'aristocracy of democracy' to set a good example to the country at large by electing Mr. Mill," Potter, Montague Chambers, and Henry Vincent.*]

[l]*Before the resolution was put, a lady in the body of the room obtained permission to make a speech. Addressing the assemblage as "Gentlemen and ladies," she, in a vigorous and well-finished style of public speaking, said she supposed it would be needless for her to tell them she was not an elector of Westminster—(laughter)—but she had heard as a secret, and as a woman was bound to tell it, that Mr. Mill was in favour of manhood suffrage and womanhood suffrage. (Loud cheers and laughter.) It seemed to her that the complaints against Mr. Mill on that account were not complaints against vice, but against excess of*

---

set straight, still he could not consent to give power to the majority to tyrannise over the minority. He would trust more to improvement of morals and education, of which he believed the promoters of the Permissive Bill were also supporters.

[j-j]DT] MS only in favour of the infliction of

[k-k]+DT

[l-l]+DT

virtue. (Cheers.) The electors of Westminster had been called the aristocracy of democracy. Let then their honour be on the side of virtue. (Cheers.) It was said that men consulted their wives as to whom they should vote for—(laughter, and a voice, That's true)—and she had heard that members of Parliament also who had wives asked them what votes they should give. (Laughter and cheers.) It was a motto of the ancient Spartans that a free man could never be the son of a bond woman. That might be so; but wherever there was intellect, wherever there was character, conscience, responsibility, there ought to be representation, although the sex might be female. (Cheers.)

The lady's remarks were attentively heard, but at this part of her speech the Chairman, finding time was pressing, requested her to postpone further observations until the resolution was put. [l]

[*The resolution was carried unanimously, amidst long-continued cheers, and the meeting ended with a vote of thanks to the Chair.*]

7. The Westminster Election of 1865 [3]

6 JULY, 1865

Daily News, 7 July, 1865, p. 3. Headed: "Westminster." Reported also in the *Daily Telegraph*, 7 July. The evening meeting of the Westminster electors was held in the Regent Music Hall, Regent Street, Vincent Square, which "was densely crowded by an enthusiastic audience" (*Daily Telegraph*). Thomas Hughes took the chair and, alluding to Mill's great practical qualifications, mentioned his advocacy of cooperation and exhorted the electors to vote on Monday or Tuesday. Hughes being obliged to leave the chair, Westerton took his place. Mill, who was "received with loud cheers, the assemblage rising and waving their hats" (*Daily Telegraph*), then spoke.

HE EXPLAINED *in almost precisely the same terms as he used at St. James's-hall*[1] *the reasons that had induced him to come forward and to meet the electors personally. He said that* he accepted the office of candidate on the condition that he should neither solicit nor buy votes. There was an old saying, not altogether true, perhaps, that he who buys will sell, and it was certainly not fair that a candidate who did not intend to sell the votes should be called upon to buy them. This meeting had been called for the purpose of giving what were termed the working classes an opportunity of seeing him and asking him any questions. He did not like the phrase "working classes," because it implied the existence of non-working classes, and nobody in this country had any business to be idle. Indeed there was a growing feeling among those who could afford to be idle that they ought to be

[1]See No. 6.

usefully employed. There was abundant scope for the spread of education among the richer classes as well as among the working men. For his part he never desired to be paid for being idle or for work which he did not do. His sympathies were all with working people. (*Cheers.*) There was a much greater distinction than there ought to be between those who worked with their head and those who worked with their hands. It would probably be better for the head workers if they worked a little more with their hands; it would be better for their health, it would tend to make them more cheerful, and it would lead to increased human fellow feeling and public spirit. It was, perhaps, not generally known that he was one of the first persons in the kingdom who had suggested the adoption of the principles of co-operation in a practical shape. [a]Five years before the Rochdale Pioneers society was established he wrote an article in the *Westminster Review*,[2] the object of which was to show the radical party of the House of Commons, then almost on the eve of dissolution, how it might be reconstructed and rendered more in unison with the radicals out of doors.[a] At that time the radicals in the house did not go for universal suffrage, while those out of doors demanded nothing less, and his object in writing that article was to show the radical party in the house that the best way of getting out of its difficulty was to redress the practical grievances of the working classes, and he then pointed out the fact that by the operation of the then existing law co-operative societies could not be established; when the law was altered,[3] and co-operative societies were established, they went on with surprising rapidity (*hear, hear*), and a way was soon found by which the working classes could raise themselves without pulling down anybody, but, on the contrary, with advantage, not only to themselves, but the country at large. The principle of co-operative societies went on extending itself, and the conviction of the truth of that principle eventually became so strong that it found an advocate [b]of all other places in the world[b] in the pages of the *Quarterly Review* (*oh*).[4] That implied an immense change in public opinion; the working men were in fact emancipated, and their cause was in their own hands. With respect to the extension of the suffrage, he went much further in his views of the concessions which he thought ought to be made to working men than did even those who sympathised warmly with working men, although, on the other hand, some might imagine that he had not gone far

[2]"Reorganization of the Reform Party," *London and Westminster Review*, XXXII (Apr. 1839), 475–508; in *CW*, Vol. VI, pp. 465–95. For the comments on co-operation, see pp. 486–7. The Rochdale Equitable Pioneers' Co-operative store opened in December 1844.

[3]By 15 Victoria, c. 31 (1852).

[4]"Workmen's Benefit Societies," *Quarterly Review*, CXVI (Oct. 1864), 318–50, by Samuel Smiles (1812–1904), the advocate of self-help.

[a-a]DT Five years before 1839, when the Rochdale Pioneers' Society was established, he wrote an article in the *Westminster Review*, the object of which was to show that the law ought so to be altered that these co-operative societies might exist, which at that period they could not.

[b-b]DT] DN even

enough. It could not be a perfect government [c]in which one class of the community could legislate for another which was not represented[c], and he certainly agreed in the opinion that no man who was competent to manage his own affairs ought to be without a vote. He thought the House of Commons ought to be placed in the position of [d]a fair, just, and impartial umpire or[d] arbitrator between contending interests, and that any mode which would secure the return of one-half of the members who were devoted to the interests of the employed, the other half representing landed property, capital and their sympathisers would be in a position to reason justly on any grievance of the working men. Class distinctions should be abolished were it possible to do so; but so long as they existed they ought to be fairly represented in parliament. He would not permit the employer class to be represented in such a way as to be able to outvote the representatives of the employed, while so far as the suffrage itself went, he thought it ought to be given to all persons of age who could read, write, and cypher. [e]But, though he was prepared to give to every man and woman who was of age, and capable of managing his or her affairs, a voice, he was not prepared to give them such an equality that, whether they were right or wrong, they should be able to outvote everybody else. (*Hear, hear.*)[e] [f]Although he had suggested plans of his own to accomplish this,[5] he was quite ready to consider those of any other person. If he was returned to Parliament, he would give his earnest attention to any reform measure which might be proposed, and anything which would bring them nearer to that which they wanted would receive his support, as a compromise; but he would accept nothing which did not increase the influence of the working classes, and give a great many more representatives in Parliament. (*Hear, hear.*)[f]

[g]*A person in the body of the hall put a question, quoting from a placard by the Tories, to this effect: "'The result of observation is borne out by experience in England itself. As soon as any idea of equality enters the mind of an uneducated English working man, his head is turned by it. When he ceases to be servile he becomes insolent.'— Mill's* Principles of Political Economy, *People's Edition, p. 68."*[6]

[5]See *Considerations on Representative Government* (1861), in *CW*, Vol. XIX, pp. 371–577, esp. Chaps. vii and viii.

[6]*Principles of Political Economy* (1848), Bk. I, Chap. vii, Sect. 5 (in *CW*, Vol. II, p. 109); the passage, added in the 3rd ed. (1852), is in the People's Ed. (1865) at p. 68.

[c-c]DT which enabled one class to legislate for its own benefit. (*Applause.*)

[d-d]DT] DN an

[e-e]+DT

[f-f]DT] DN It was not likely that he should be able to bring in a reform bill of his own, but if returned he should give his attention to the plans of others, and he should stand by the principles he had laid down. At the same time he would accept any enlargement of the franchise as a step in the right direction provided they were not called upon to pay the price of a worse distribution. (*Cheers.*)

[g-g]DT] DN *A great many questions were put to the honourable candidate, most of which have been put and answered before, and the proceedings concluded with a resolution to the effect that the meeting considered Mr. Mill to be a fit person to represent Westminster in parliament, which was carried by acclamation.*

Mr. Mill said that he did not want uneducated men voters, and was in favour of an educational test—reading, writing, and simple arithmetic. If the suffrage were not to depend upon that, it would be universal. The honourable candidate then highly praised the conduct of the Lancashire operatives, and expressed his belief that it was owing to their intelligence they knew the cause of their distress.[7] This was mainly owing to the cheap press. (*Loud applause.*) They had seen the discussions respecting the subject, and that they owed to the cheap press. If they had not learnt to read, they could not have benefited by the cheap press, and the press now gave to any man, however humble his circumstances, the means of acquiring the best information respecting political knowledge, written by some of the most able men of the country. (*Cheers.*) To men, therefore, who had the qualification of reading, writing, and arithmetic, he would entrust a share in the management of the destinies of this country, when they had those excellent means of learning the opinions of the ablest men. (*Applause.*) *Respecting the malt tax, Mr. Mill said* a question had been sent up to him, "Will you vote against it?"[8] If that meant, would he advocate free trade in intoxicating drinks, without asking leave of any person in opening a public-house, he would say, "No"—(*hear, hear*)—because public-houses were very often a nuisance, and it was of great importance that nuisances should be out of the way. (*Cheers.*) There must be such things, but they should be out of the way as much as possible consistent with the public convenience. He would have some public authorities whose duty it should be to see that they were not a nuisance. He thought that it was much better to tax stimulants than necessary articles. He would, in the present state of affairs, vote for the Maynooth grant, and was in favour of opening museums on Sundays. The ballot should be an open question. The shopkeepers were much more in need of it than the working classes.

Other questions having been satisfactorily answered, a vote approving of Mr. Mill as a candidate was carried, and the meeting separated. [g]

8. The Westminster Election of 1865 [4]

8 JULY, 1865

Daily Telegraph, 10 July, 1865, p. 2. Headed: "Election Intelligence. / Westminster." Reported fully on the same day in the *Morning Star*; brief summaries appeared also in the *Daily News* and *The Times*. The meeting of electors and non-electors on Saturday evening

[7]The cotton industry collapsed because the Union forces in the U.S. Civil War denied access to the Confederate States' cotton, and great distress resulted in Lancashire, especially in 1862–63. Nonetheless, the operatives expressed support for the North.

[8]"A Bill to Allow the Charging of the Excise Duty on Malt According to the Weight of the Grain Used," 28 Victoria (19 May, 1865), *PP*, 1865, III, 1–6, had been enacted as 28 & 29 Victoria, c. 66 (1865). It was expected that the matter would be raised again.

in the Pimlico Rooms, Winchester Street, was chaired by Charles Westerton. "The room was densely crowded by a most enthusiastic audience" (*Daily Telegraph*).

MR. J.S. MILL, *who upon rising to speak was received with loud cheers, again and again repeated, said that,* as the electors of Westminster must all pretty well know what were the principles upon which he rested his candidature, it was not necessary that he should occupy their time by recapitulating them. But he should like to say a few words upon a most important principle, which was involved in this contest—that this was a protest against the "money power" employed in elections. (*Cheers.*) He was not going to say anything which could possibly offend any party or anybody—nothing about the misuse of money—about using it for the purposes of corruption, giving it to electors to return any particular candidate. If it were stated to candidates that before going to the poll they must spend £2,000, £3,000, £4,000, or any other sum of money, "for the good of the public," things would be pretty much as they now stood, with the important difference, that then the candidate who had to pay this money, as most had, would know that it was used for some other purpose than it was now, *viz.*, the demoralisation of the electors. (*Cheers.*) Did they think it was the right and best thing that the House of Commons should be composed exclusively of rich men, or men with rich connections? (*No.*) There were a good many reasons why this was not desirable, and one was that the rich naturally sympathised with the rich. (*Hear, hear.*) The rich had sympathies enough for the poor when the poor came before them as objects of pity. Their feelings of charity were often highly creditable to their dispositions; and, besides, they had almost universally a kind of patronising and protective sympathy for the poor, such as shepherds had for their flocks—(*laughter and cheers*)—only that was conditional upon the flock always behaving like sheep. (*Renewed laughter, and Hear, hear.*) But if the sheep tried to have a voice in their own affairs, he was afraid that a good many shepherds would be willing to call in the wolves. (*Cheers.*) Now this sympathy of the rich for the rich had manifested itself in a very decided way during the last two or three years, by the extraordinary good wishes of the higher classes of this country for the success of the American slaveholders. He did not make this a matter of reproach against the rich and higher classes of this country, for he was quite ready to let bygones be bygones; but they were not at liberty to renounce the privilege, nay, the duty, of drawing lessons from the very things before their eyes—(*hear, hear*)—and he should like to make a few remarks upon the cause and meaning of the sympathy of the rich for these slaveholders. It was not that they loved slavery; he acquitted them of that. (*Hear, hear.*) But he could not acquit them of not having realised to their own minds by experience or reflection what a dreadful thing slavery really is, and what are the results it produces and gives rise to. It gives a power—whether those who have it use it or not—of torturing human beings to death at their caprice. (*Hear, hear.*) The government which the slaveholders endeavoured to establish, has fortunately been frustrated, or there would have been a kind of reign of evil on the earth. It is this which has given rise to the Bowie knife and the revolver—not the pure government of democracy. (*Hear, hear.*) Our privileged classes did not consider this, or he believed that they would have acted in a different manner from that which they did. They merely saw one thing—a privileged class opposed by those who they thought wanted to take the privilege away; and when they saw that, they said "These (the Southerners) must be gentlemen, with whom gentlemen ought to sympathise." He believed that to be exaggerated. (*Hear, hear.*) The man who nearly murdered Mr. Sumner on the floor of the House of Congress—that man was a gentleman![1] and the wives and daughters of slaveholders, who raised subscriptions to mark their approval of his conduct—they were gentlewomen! but the refined and polished, the highly intellectual society of Massachusetts, the poets, orators, philosophers, the popular preachers, the brightest and best, those who took a lead against these enormities—men such as Channing, Emerson, Theodore Parker, Palfrey, Lowell, Bancroft, Motley, etc.—these were not gentlemen, they were low Radicals and vulgar demagogues.[2] (*Cheers.*) So blind were these people—these privileged ones—on our side of the water, that they did not know or care that the people whom they were thus attacking were those known to all Americans as lovers of England, lovers of English literature, sympathisers with the English people, admirers of us, and ignorant of much that was bad in our institutions. He did not make this a matter of reproach to any one, because when so many joined in it, it would not be right to apportion a share. Many who were well worthy of their respect had yielded to this general perversion of sentiment: and the moral he drew from it was this, that they had here one of the most signal instances, and so recent that it could not be objected to as belonging to olden times, of how far men could be carried away by their bias, unconscious and unintentional bias he was persuaded, but still one that made the rich sympathise with the rich, the privileged with the privileged; and the practical lesson which he deduced from it was this, that it was a very just and proper thing that there should be rich men in Parliament for the purpose of watching over the interests of the rich, but also, if they wanted a similar care to be taken of the poor, they had better not shut the door of the House of Commons upon the poor man. (*Loud cheers.*) The only people they would do well to keep clear of were those kind of poor men who would be glad to use a seat in Parliament to get rich—(*hear, hear*),—or pin themselves to the skirts of those who were rich. They would not suppose that he was one of those.

[1]On 22 May, 1856, Preston Smith Brooks (1819–57), a Congressman from South Carolina, angered by a violent speech attacking Senator A.P. Butler of South Carolina by Charles Sumner (1811–74), Senator from Massachusetts and abolitionist, beat Sumner senseless with a gutta percha cane. Though a vote to expel him from the House of Representatives failed, Brooks resigned, but was unanimously re-elected by his constituents.

[2]For these supporters of the Union position, see App. H.

(*Loud cries of No, no.*) A great writer had said that those who wanted to be well governed should look out for those who did not want to be governors.[3] They knew that he had not thrust himself upon them. (*True.*) If he were as certain of being up to the mark in everything else as he was that he had not sought to force himself upon them, his mind would be quite at ease. Perhaps they might wish him to refer to his general ideas of reform as applied to the Constitution—(*hear*)—and also whether he would be a supporter or non-supporter of the present Ministry. He could not look forward to any time in the history of this country when he should not think any Liberal Ministry preferable to any Conservative Ministry. (*Cheers.*) Whatever the shortcomings of a Liberal party or Government might be, they did not bear in their very names the profession of wishing to keep things as they were.[4] (*Hear, hear.*) Their name implied that they wished to improve them; and although between the least liberal of Liberals and the most liberal of Conservatives there might only be a little difference, a short distance, still it should be ever borne in mind, and seriously remembered, that this least liberal of Liberals was surrounded by those who were far better men than himself, politically speaking, while this most liberal of Conservatives was surrounded by men who, politically speaking, were far worse than himself. (*Loud applause.*) Suppose York was half-way between Edinburgh and London, and two travellers met there from either place, there would be very little, if any, difference in the respective distances they had to go, but that did not decrease in the least the hundreds of miles which London was distant from Edinburgh. (*Hear, hear.*) If he were returned to Parliament, what he should do, and that which he should recommend others to do, would be to vote for any Liberal Government on questions as between them and the Tory Government, but he should not let himself be muddled under the pretence of keeping a Liberal Government in; therefore he would advise the independent Liberals always to vote as they thought best, and to let the Government or Ministry shift for themselves, and take their chances of whatever might be the result of a full and free discussion. As regarded Reform and improvements of details, he thought they might be pretty sure that they would go on under any Government. One of the admirable effects of the reforms and improvements which had already taken place was that the spirit of improvement had penetrated even into the Tory camp—(*hear, hear*)—and he thought that in all the subordinate departments of public affairs the Tories and the Whigs would vie and compete with each other in improvements of that sort. The fact was, they had a difficult problem to solve, let alone how to deal with what were called "proved abuses." There was a general conviction, and one in which he fully shared, that most of the departments of public affairs—almost all the public

[3]Plato (427–347 B.C.), *Republic* (Greek and English), trans. Paul Shorey, 2 vols. (London: Heinemann; Cambridge, Mass.: Harvard University Press, 1946), Vol. I, p. 80 (I, i, 19).

[4]A radical catchphrase, probably deriving from William Godwin (1756–1836), *Things As They Are; or, The Adventures of Caleb Williams* (1794).

business—was either badly done or done not nearly so well as it ought to be done. (*Cheers.*) What they had to do to remedy this—without introducing fresh evils—was to reconcile a skilful management of public affairs by trained and specially qualified people with the preservation and extension of their local liberties and the responsibility of all public functionaries to the people. (*Cheers.*) In short, they wanted a system of administration which should at once be skilful and popular. This was not an easy matter. It would task the best minds, both in and out of Parliament, for a considerable time. But that was what they had to do. He had no doubt that in this some assistance would be rendered by the Conservatives, because, without speaking of such a brilliant exception as Lord Stanley, there were Sir John Pakington, Sir Stafford Northcote,[5] and others, who would be glad to assist in improvements of that sort—(*hear, hear*)—as far as they saw the way, and they often saw a good way. But still, while good service could be got out of such men, the Tories must be looked to as a body, as a party; and as a party they showed what they were, a long way behind the Liberals. The only way in which the Tories could at all distinguish themselves was by actually showing that they were "a little bit worse" than the Liberals. (*Laughter.*) This at least was the best excuse that could be found for them, though recently they had showed that they were a good deal worse than the Liberals, in dealing with such subjects as the church rates and the Catholic Oaths Bill.[6] (*Hear, hear.*) In conclusion Mr. Mill expressed his readiness to answer any questions, *and resumed his seat amidst considerable applause.*

Several of those present availed themselves of the opportunity to examine Mr. Mill respecting certain of his political doctrines.

Question: How do you explain your writing that the upper classes are liars, and the lower classes—the working classes—habitual liars?[7]

Mr. Mill said such was his writing. He thought so, and so did the most intelligent of the working classes themselves, and the passage applied to the natural state of those who were both uneducated and subjected. If they were educated and became free citizens, then he should not be afraid of them. Lying was the vice of slaves, and they would never find slaves who were not liars. It was not a reproach that they were what slavery had made them. But those persons who

[5]John Somerset Pakington (1799–1880), Conservative M.P. for Droitwich, who was a leader in the movement for reform of elementary education, and Stafford Henry Northcote (1818–87), at this time Conservative M.P. for Stamford, who had worked on reorganizing the Board of Trade and the Civil Service.

[6]In the debates and votes on "A Bill for the Commutation of Church Rates," 28 Victoria (21 Feb., 1865), *PP*, 1865, I, 135–54 (not enacted), and "A Bill to Substitute an Oath for the Oath Required to Be Taken by the Statute Passed in the Tenth Year of the Reign of King George the Fourth, for the Relief of His Majesty's Roman Catholic Subjects," 28 Victoria (21 Mar., 1865), *PP*, 1865, IV, 375–8 (not enacted).

[7]Cf. *Thoughts on Parliamentary Reform* (1859), in *CW*, Vol. XIX, p. 338. For Mill's later comment on this exchange, see *Autobiography*, *CW*, Vol. I, pp. 274–5.

quoted this passage were not candid enough to read on. (*Applause.*) He said that he was not speaking of the vices of his countrymen, but of their virtues, and that they were superior to most other countrymen in truthfulness—(*cheers*)—and that the lower classes, though they did lie, were ashamed of lying, which was more than he could venture to say of the same class in any other nation which he knew. (*Hear, hear.*)

[a]*An Elector inquired on what ground Mr. Mill thought the working classes had not the right to have large families as well as the higher classes. (Oh, oh.)*

Mr. Mill said he would have no difficulty in answering the question. For one thing he never had said that the working classes had not as much right as the higher classes, but that they had no more right.[8] Neither had a right to have more children than they could support and educate. The higher classes had no more right than the lower classes to overstock the labour market. If this was a reproach it was a reproach which attached to almost all the writers on political economy during the last half century. Their views on this subject were dictated by the strongest wish for the best interest of the working classes. They felt that as long as wages were as low as they then were, and as they still were, it was not possible to hope for a great political and moral improvement in the country. The interests of the working classes required that their wages should be higher, not only for the obvious reason that they were not sufficient, but because it was a necessary condition of proper education. They felt that wages, though other causes might have helped, were a great deal kept down by excessive competition for employment, and although that excessive competition had been to some extent relieved by emigration, they saw no hope for altering this state of things except by a moral resolution on the part of the labouring classes not to overstock the labour market. Some people said it was absurd to expect this. He said that, on the contrary, all morality was a triumph over some of their natural propensities. The strongest of their natural propensities had been overcome by the various inducements that had been addressed to mankind—by public opinion, by education, by religion, none of which influences had ever been sufficiently or satisfactorily brought to bear on this particular end. Such was his faith in human nature and in the effect of these influences, that when they were brought to bear on the over-multiplication of mankind they would have an influence on all classes of the community. No class who might be called rich had a right to have more sons and daughters than they could provide for, because if they could not leave them well off they might be quartered on the public. (*Cheers.*)[a]

Question (from a person on the platform): How can Mr. Mill reconcile his doctrine with the Scriptural injunction, that we are to increase and multiply?[9] *(Much laughter.)*

[8]Cf. *Principles of Political Economy*, *CW*, Vol. II, p. 358 (II, xii, 2).
[9]Genesis, 1:28.

[a-a]+MS

Mr. Mill: It says we are to eat and drink, but not to over-eat and over-drink ourselves.[10] (*Cheers and laughter.*)

[b]*An Elector asked how Mr. Mill thought the representation of minorities was practicable?*

Mr. Mill said he was sure that the opinion which he had expressed on this point was only not shared by reformers generally because it was not understood. His idea of representation was that not a part only, even if it were a majority, but that everybody should be represented. [c]For instance, if there was a constituency of 5,000, and it had to elect one member, and there were two candidates, and 3,000 voted for one candidate and 2,000 for the other, the man elected would represent the 3,000 voters; but why were the 2,000 to go unrepresented if there could be found another 1,000 to agree with it in returning some other person? The number to be fixed would of course depend on the proportion between the number of representatives and the number of voters; but he would certainly give a member to every 10,000 or 8,000, whatever the number might be, who could agree in electing a representative.[c] This was what they had heard of as Mr. Hare's plan, otherwise the system of personal representation which, instead of being the complicated and unintelligible thing which some people represented, was the simplest thing in the world.[11] Mr. Hare's was the most practical and organising head that he knew, and he believed that they could not carry out the principle of popular representation or democratic government without this plan.[b]

Question: Will you support a bill for purifying the Church of England from Romanising practices and tendencies?

Mr. Mill had often thought that one of the most important uses of a representative constitution was that it caused great questions to be discussed. He was never more sensible of this truth than just now, and this question had given him an opportunity of saying something which he had not been able to do before. The question meant, would he chase out of the Church of England the Tractarian party?[12] That he would not do, because he thought the greatest argument against an

[10]Cf. Ecclesiastes, 2:24.

[11]See No. 4.

[12]A recent move to purge the Church of England of Tractarian (or Puseyite) practices had been made by George Hampden Whalley (1813–78), Liberal M.P., in his Motion on the Church of England, Illegal Usages and Ornaments (23 May, 1865), *PD*, 3rd ser., Vol. 178, cols. 774–5.

[b-b]+MS

[c-c]DT Suppose, for instance, and he took the number at random, that a constituency consisted of 5,000 voters, and these 5,000 voters had to elect one member; and suppose that of these 2,000 were Conservatives, and 3,000 were Liberals, or that 2,000 were Liberals, and the 3,000 Conservatives; in either case it was quite right that the 3,000, the majority, should have the member. But why were the other 2,000 voters to be without a member? They were entitled to one. Well, if these 2,000 could go somewhere else, and find another 1,000 who would agree with them, he would so have it, and give them a representative. (*Hear, hear.*) He would have the number fixed, by simple arithmetic, of those who were entitled to representation, say 5,000, 10,000, 20,000 or any number they liked. Well, if these

Established Church was that it tied up the minds of its clergy. He wanted, within certain bounds, that the clergyman should not have to sign away his mental liberty; that he should have the power, as far as was consistent with an Established Church, of forming his own sincere convictions as to what Christianity was; and although many of the clergy might come to different, and perhaps some to wrong perceptions, he would not turn them out for that, so long as they thought their opinions ought not to turn them out—which some of the Tractarians had done. But if they asked him whether he would leave it in the power of any single clergyman to suppress any of the customary services, or introduce others, he would not give them such power. (*Applause.*) If any body of persons wanted any particular sort of worship, let them have it at their own expense. He did not admit that the clergy had a right to determine what the ceremonials of the Church should be. That ought to rest, if any one had to determine it, with the majority of the parishioners. In short, although in the Church he would have the utmost mental liberty, yet with respect to the ceremonial part, of whatever kind, that ought to rest with the laity, and not with the clergy. For it was not the collective clergy, much more one clergyman, who were the Church, but the clergy and laity. No clergyman, or collective clergy, therefore, ought to have the power of introducing ceremonials into the services against the wishes of the parishioners. (*Hear, hear.*)

Question: How do you reconcile this—to open the museums on Sundays and obey the Divine command to keep the Sabbath day holy?[13] *(Hear, hear.)*

Mr. Mill said that those who were of opinion that this injunction was intended for the Christians, and not for the Jews exclusively, were quite right in not being able to reconcile it. But his opinion was that the Sabbatical institution was an institution for the Jews alone. (*Hear, hear.*) The Christian Sunday appeared to him to be an institution of quite a different character. (*Hear, hear.*)

Question: Has Mr. Mill any confidence in and sympathy with the religion taught by Jesus Christ and his apostles; and does he believe that a State Church is a benefit to this nation or otherwise? (Cries of Don't answer.)

Mr. Mill: He had already declared that he could not consent to answer any questions about his religious creed. (*Loud applause, and "Quite right."*) The question about the State Church was very different, and his opinion was this, that in principle there ought to be no such thing, but he did not think the time had yet arrived when it would be any use to try and abolish it. The thing was not pressing, and at all events the State was more Liberal than the Church, and now the best men in the Church had an opportunity of getting the highest places in it. At present he thought it would be much better to try and improve the Church itself through the State, than to abolish the connection which in principle he objected to; and he had no hesitation in saying that they ought not to be combined.

[13]Exodus, 20:8.

5,000, 10,000 or 20,000 agreed upon a representative, he would give them one. If that were so, there would not be a single person unrepresented.

[d]*Question: What are the disadvantages we labour under in not having a vote, and the advantages we should possess in having one? (Oh.)*[d]

Mr. Mill: The gentleman who had asked that question had asked him in effect to make a speech which would last the rest of the evening. The difference would be this—the man would be a citizen—(*loud cheers*)—and he would feel that he was a citizen. Let them look at America now. Look at the grand display of patriotism; was it not the wonder of the world? Did anybody dream it would be so? Did anybody think that all those millions would be ready to give the blood of their families, and incur a national debt equal to ours—putting it at the lowest—for the nationality of their country? He did not suppose there was a family in New England which had not lost a member. Was it not something to have such a feeling in the whole body of the people? Did they not think that that had something to do with everybody having a vote? (*Hear, hear.*) [e]It seemed to him that the interests of citizenship—an equal right to be heard—to have a share in influencing the affairs of the country—to be consulted, to be spoken to, and to have agreements and considerations turning upon politics addressed to one—tended to elevate and educate the self-respect of the man, and to strengthen his feelings of regard for his fellow-men. (*Cheers.*) These made all the difference between a selfish man and a patriot. (*Hear, hear.*) To give people an interest in politics and in the management of their own affairs was the grand cultivator of mankind. (*Cheers.*)[e] That was one of the reasons why he wanted women to have votes; they needed cultivation as well as men. He could not conceive that a country was what it ought to be without an extension of a share of political right to all. (*Cheers.*) Those left without it seemed a sort of pariahs. Independently of this, there were plenty of practical considerations. There were many, many questions before Parliament in which it was of the greatest consequence that those who had so large an interest in them should be heard on their own behalf, and that in the very place where the questions had to be decided. It was as necessary that they should be heard when they were wrong as when they were right. When such was the case, if a man asked more than he ought, then he had the chance of either being enlightened or shamed out of it. (*Cheers.*)

Question: What are your principles of non-intervention?

Mr. Mill: He did not understand what was meant by "principle" of non-intervention, because that would be a principle of utter selfishness. His opinion was that every nation was much more capable of settling its own affairs than another Power for it. (*Hear, hear.*) But if a Power in trying to establish its own affairs was threatened by a foreign despot, that was another thing, and then it was perfectly legitimate to interfere—not to prevent the first Power from doing that which they thought best for themselves, but to protect them from being persecuted by the despot. (*Cheers.*)

[d-d]MS *Another Elector asked what advantages would be gained by giving the working classes a vote. (Oh, oh, and laughter.)*

[e-e]MS] DT It elevated the self-dignity of a man; it made all the difference between the selfish man and the patriot. (*Cheers.*) Only think of the mental culture it implied.

Question: Is it legitimate for a voter to be told that he must vote for Mr. Smith, or lose custom; or for a person to order a pair of boots and not demand the "exact" price? (Loud cries of Shame! shame!)

Mr. Mill: I think that the feeling of the meeting has sufficiently answered the question already.

Question: What are your opinions respecting primogeniture?

Mr. Mill: Entirely against it, both politically and privately. He thought that the practice of making the oldest son heir by law was in itself unjust. [f]He thought that a man should be allowed to leave what belonged to him to whom he liked, but that in cases of intestacy it should be divided equally among the children.[f]

Question: The ballot?

Mr. Mill did not think it was now necessary, especially to the working classes, and that if it was necessary it was amongst shopkeepers.

[*After other speeches, a resolution was passed by acclamation approving of Mr. Mill as a fit and proper candidate, and pledging the meeting to support his election; the proceedings terminated.*]

9. The Westminster Election of 1865 [5]

10 JULY, 1865

Morning Star, 11 July, 1865, p. 2. Headed: "Westminster." The nomination meeting, at the hustings in front of St. Paul's Church, Covent Garden, at midday, was also reported on the 12th in the *Daily Telegraph*, *The Times*, the *Daily News*, and the *Standard* (the last two in the third person). There was considerable excitement, for this would be "a great political contest such as Westminster had not seen for many years"; by 11:30 nearly 3000 people had assembled, and just before noon they began "to show signs of animation. The quiet which had hitherto prevailed was relaxed, and some good-humoured larking and hustling commenced." (*Morning Star.*) The High Bailiff, H. Scott Turner, the returning officer, appeared, followed by the first of the candidates, Robert Wellesley Grosvenor (1834–1918), a member of the leading Whig family in Westminster and (after an initial period of uncertainty as to his political credentials) Mill's Liberal running mate. He "was received with cheers by his supporters, and yells by the rest of the crowd." Next came Smith, "who received a warm welcome from his supporters," and then Mill arrived, to be "greeted with enthusiastic cheers from his supporters, mingled with yells from the friends of Mr. Smith." Mill occupied the central position, with Smith on his right and Grosvenor on his left. The crier in vain called for silence during the reading of the writ by the high bailiff. "Indeed throughout the whole proceedings, a continuous volley of yells and howls, mingled with cheers for the respective candidates, was kept up. The speeches of neither proposers, seconders, nor candidates could be heard except by those close beside them, and in most cases the speakers wisely addressed their remarks to the reporters, and made them as brief as possible. It is right to state that the uproar came chiefly, not from the respectable portion of

[f-f]+MS

the electors and non-electors, but from bands of ruffianly lads, who seemed to be organised for the purpose." (*Morning Star*.) Grosvenor was proposed and seconded, and then Brewer nominated Mill "amidst great uproar. He alluded to Mr. Mill's high intellectual character and attainments, and to his Liberal and practical and statesmanlike views, and said it would be an honour to Westminster to be represented by such a man." Malleson seconded. Smith, characterized as a man of moderate opinions, was proposed and seconded. Grosvenor was the first of the candidates to speak. Mill then stood forward to address the electors, and "was received with great enthusiasm by his friends in the assemblage. But the shouting and noise still prevailing his remarks could only be heard by those in his immediate vicinity." (The *Daily Telegraph* says he "obtained a much better hearing, though great noise prevailed.")

GENTLEMEN,—It would be entirely useless for me to attempt to make a speech, which it would be impossible that any of you could hear; and I will only therefore attempt to say a few words. (*Noise and cheers*.) I am not here by my own seeking; I am here because a numerous and distinguished body of the electors of Westminster, thinking that that numerous and important portion of this constituency who are advanced Liberals are entitled to a representative (*cheers*), and that my opinions, which have been fully, freely, and unreservedly expressed both in [a]my letters and at very crowded meetings of the electors[a], qualify me to be that representative. They thought also that in electing me you would be asserting a principle which has been honoured in Westminster—the principle of selecting your representatives for some other reason than for their money. (*Cheers*.) It now rests with the electors of Westminster, who have [b]had the means of forming their own[b] opinions on the manner in which the contest has been carried on, to judge whether I have a claim to the votes of the friends of purity of election and of advanced [c]Liberalism as against a Conservative opponent of all Liberalism whatever. I have nothing further to say.[c] (*Cheers from Mr. Mill's supporters*.)

[*Smith spoke, amidst continued uproar. Again silence was ordered, and the high bailiff called for a show of hands.*] [d]*For Captain Grosvenor a considerable number were held up; for Mr. Mill the display of hands was much larger; and for Mr. Smith a great number were held up. As far as could be judged, the numbers in favour of Mr. Smith and Mr. Mill were nearly equal, and there can be no doubt that each of them was larger by three to one than the numbers in favour of Captain Grosvenor. To the surprise, however, of everybody, the high bailiff declared the show of hands to be in favour of Mr. Smith and Captain Grosvenor. We do not know whether this functionary's organs of vision are imperfect, or whether in the*

[a-a]DN private and in public meetings

[b-b]DT] MS the means of expressing their

[c-c]DT] MS Liberals as against a Conservative and an opponent of all Liberalism whatever.] DN liberal as contradistinguished from a conservative opponent, who had declared no liberal opinions whatever. He had nothing further to say.

[d-d]DT *There were but very few for Captain Grosvenor, and about four to five times as many for Mr. Smith and Mr. Mill. Notwithstanding this, however, the Returning Officer declared that the show of hands was for Messrs. Grosvenor and Smith. (Hisses, laughter, and It's a lie.)*

excitement he did not attend sufficiently to the show of hands for each of the candidates but that he made a mistake was manifest to every one who had a view of the assembly.[d] *Mr. Mill's supporters demanded a poll, and the mistake will be of little importance if he and Captain Grosvenor should be placed at the top of the poll.*[1]

[*Smith moved and Grosvenor seconded a vote of thanks to the high bailiff.*]

Each of the candidates, on leaving the hustings, was loudly cheered by his supporters. The assembly, which though noisy and uproarious throughout, was in no way mischievous, then gradually dispersed.

10. The Westminster Election of 1865 [6]

10 JULY, 1865

Daily Telegraph, 11 July, 1865, p. 4. Unheaded; the account comes immediately after the report of Mill's speech at the hustings on the same day (No. 9). The meeting was not reported in other papers. "Last night, at eight o'clock, Mr. John Stuart Mill addressed a meeting at St. Martin's Hall, Long-acre. The large room was densely crowded by a most enthusiastic audience, amongst whom was a large number of ladies. The Count de Paris occupied a seat on the platform."

THE HONOURABLE CANDIDATE, *who was received with great applause, referred to most of the subjects upon which he spoke at the meeting at the Pimlico Rooms on Saturday night, which was fully reported in yesterday's* Daily Telegraph,[1] especially on the purity of election, the great questions between employers and employed, and co-operation. He next noticed the vast improvements which had taken place in the condition of the working classes. Mr. Gladstone had done a great deal for the working classes. (*The name of Mr. Gladstone was received with enthusiastic applause.*) Mr. Gladstone was a statesman who did not hold back his good things till they were wrung from him. He employed his mind in conceiving measures for the benefit of his country, whether they had been demanded or not. That was his (*Mr. Mill's*) idea of a great Minister. (*Applause.*) He believed that the future social condition of the working classes was safe. He hoped some day there would be no such thing as a class distinction; but, while it lasted, they had to take care that the House of Commons should not exercise class legislation. They (the working classes) would not be truly represented unless they had their fair

[1]*The Times*, the *Daily News*, and the *Standard* all agree that the returning officer was mistaken.

---

[1]See No. 8.

share of the voices in the national tribunal. He thought that a Reform Bill would not give the labouring classes an effectual share in and control of the House of Commons, unless they had fully one half of the House of Commons—(*cheers*)—and the remainder of society the other half. *In answer to questions, Mr. Mill said that* he would vote for the opening of the Crystal Palace on Sunday. He did not think it would be a wrong thing to open well-conducted theatres on that day, though he should not be prepared to vote for that at present, as he thought it would be considered an affront to the religious opinions of a large and highly respectable portion of the public. Neither upon this nor any other question would he press his opinion on the Legislature, if he thought the vast majority of the people were not prepared for the proposed change. He did not think that the exercise of the franchise should depend on the payment of rates. The duration of Parliament should be from three to five years. Mr. Hubbard's proposal respecting the income tax was, he thought, a good one.[2] If a *primâ facie* case were made out that it was necessary for convents to be inspected, he would have them inspected; but if there were any such "dreadful mysteries" in the convents,[3] he believed the inmates of those places would be a vast deal too clever for her Majesty's inspectors to find them out. *A variety of other questions were put, and answered to the complete satisfaction of the meeting. A resolution expressive of confidence in Mr. J.S. Mill as a fit and proper candidate was carried amidst great applause. Some other speeches were delivered, and the meeting separated.*

11. The Westminster Election of 1865 [7]

12 JULY, 1865

Morning Star, 13 July, 1865, p. 2. Headed "Westminster." The meeting was also reported in *The Times*, the *Daily News*, and (very briefly and in the third person) in the *Daily Telegraph*. The official declaration of the poll was at the hustings in Covent Garden at 2 p.m. A "dense mass of people" gathered in front of the hustings, crying out such remarks as "Where is Smith now?" A watering cart showered the crowd with cold water, quieting them briefly. The candidates and their friends began to appear on the hustings, Mill being "greeted with loud and long-continued cheers." Grosvenor was also given an enthusiastic reception; Smith did not appear. The poll was declared: Grosvenor at the head with 4534; Mill a very close second with 4525, and Smith with 3824. (The *Daily News* uniquely gives

[2]John Gellibrand Hubbard (1805–89), then M.P. for Buckingham, who proposed a different tax rate for incomes derived from investments and from employment. See his "Draft Report" and "Memorandum" as Chairman in "Report from the Select Committee on Income and Property Tax," *PP*, 1861, VII, 303–18. For Mill's evidence before that Committee, see *CW*, Vol. V, pp. 549–98.

[3]For an example of these words used in the context of Roman Catholicism, see a leading article on convents, *The Times*, 29 Mar., 1854, p. 9.

3224, undoubtedly in error.) Grosvenor spoke first. "Mr. Mill then proceeded to address the assembled crowd. Previous to doing so he was treated to a most enthusiastic ovation. The vast mass of persons present set up a cheer of the most hearty, thrilling character, which was kept up for some minutes, and which certainly must have had rather a startling effect on those who did not take part in it. Mr. Mill looked upon the exciting scene before him with that quiet, benign, and thoughtful expression of countenance for which he is so remarkable under all circumstances, and seemingly not the least moved or discomposed, except what was denoted by a pleasing smile which his intellectual features could not conceal, however desirous their owner may have been to do so. When the enthusiasm had subsided," Mill spoke.

ELECTORS OF WESTMINSTER—not omitting the non-electors, many of whom have worked most vigorously in this cause—you have achieved a great triumph. (*Cheers.*) You have vindicated a principle [a]which has been the glory of[a] Westminster for generations. (*Renewed cheers.*) That principle is that members of Parliament should be elected on public grounds alone (*Hear, hear, and cheers*) and you have done this against all the means, legitimate and illegitimate, which could possibly have been brought to bear to prevent you. (*Cheers.*) This victory of yours illustrates very strongly two things. In the first place, it teaches a lesson which has been renewed from age to age, but which many have found it extremely hard to learn—[b]the power there is in[b] sincere, earnest, and disinterested conviction. All our working was the working of volunteers against opponents who were a disciplined and paid body. (*Hear, hear, and cries of Smith.*) All our friends voluntarily gave their time and their labour, which to most of them is money, and to some of them their [c]means of daily[c] bread, and even many of them gave money in addition for the purpose of defraying expenses rendered necessary by the bad system of carrying on elections which prevails [d], but which they felt, even if necessary, ought to be paid for by any one rather than the candidate himself (*hear, hear*)[d]. All this they have done in the face of much opposition, and they have been successful. (*Cheers.*) Another thing to be learned from this victory is that it may induce persons to consider whether that mode of returning representatives can be good under which [e]the side starting upon principles of electioneering purity is heavily weighted in the race—so heavily weighted, indeed, as to make the contest resemble a race between a man on foot and one on horseback? This simile may be regarded as[e] literally true, because my supporters had to walk to the poll, whilst the supporters of our opponents were carried there in

[a-a]TT,DN] MS glorious to Westminster, a principle which has been glorious to
[b-b]DN] MS a lesson which gives a power based on] TT the power of
[c-c]DN] MS means of] TT daily
[d-d]+TT
[e-e]TT] MS purity of election has to start so heavily weighted in the race as to be something like a man on foot against a man on horseback. (*Hear, hear.*) That is

cabs and carriages not paid for by themselves. (*Hear, hear, and a cry of Why did Grosvenor do it?*) One of the greatest writers and orators which this country has produced, and who was at the head of the Liberal party [f]during the best[f] years of his life—I mean Burke—[g]said, "That system cannot be good which rests upon the heroic virtues."[1] I do[g] say that the mode of election which rendered necessary such heroic exertions as have been made during the last few weeks to maintain purity of election cannot be good. (*Hear, hear.*) There is one more lesson which the electors of Westminster have given by the victory they have achieved. They have shown that whatever differences of opinion may exist amongst the several shades of Liberals, whatever severe criticisms they may occasionally make on each other, they are ready to help and co-operate with one another when the time of need arrives. This has been very provoking to many people. (*A Voice: Yes, to Mr. Smith, and laughter.*) I have often observed that those who are in the wrong think it a great shame when those who are in the right show some degree of common sense, as in the present instance—(*hear, hear*)—and that they entertain the notion that those who are honest must be fools as well. (*Great laughter and cheering.*) But you have proved to these persons that it is possible to be honest, sensible, [h]and patriotic at the same time.[h] The Tories have done their worst. They have exercised all the powers that they could, particularly the force of money power—(*hear*)—but they have received a lesson they will not soon forget, and possibly they will think twice before they repeat it [i]amongst the electors of Westminster[i]. [j](*Loud cheers.*) Gentlemen, I have done. (*Loud and prolonged cheering.*)[j]

This concluded Mr. Mill's remarks. On ceasing to address the assembly the enthusiasm which greeted his first appearance on the hustings was renewed.

On the motion of Dr. Brewer, seconded by Capt. Grosvenor, a vote of thanks was, amidst cries for Smith, who did not put in an appearance, passed to the High Bailiff for the courtesy and efficiency he had displayed in the election.

[1]Edmund Burke (1729–97), *Mr. Burke's Speech in Presenting to the House of Commons . . . a Plan for the Better Security of the Independence of Parliament* (1780), in *Works*, 8 vols. (London: Dodsley [Vols. I-III], Rivington [Vols. IV-VIII], 1792–1827), Vol. II, p. 240.

[f-f]TT] MS for many

[g-g]TT] MS had a saying that that system cannot be good which rests on heroic efforts, and I] DN has a saying that that system cannot be good which rests on the heroic virtues, and I do

[h-h]TT , aye, and practical too. (*Cheers.*)

[i-i]+DN

[j-j]+TT

· · · February to August 1866 · · ·

12. The Cattle Diseases Bill [1]

14 FEBRUARY, 1866

PD, 3rd ser., Vol. 181, cols. 488–92. Reported in *The Times*, 15 February, p. 7, from which the variant and responses are taken. This, Mill's maiden speech in the House of Commons, was delivered in the debate on the second reading of "A Bill to Amend the Law Relating to Contagious or Infectious Diseases in Cattle and Other Animals," 29 Victoria (12 Feb., 1866), *PP*, 1866, I, 423–44. Mill says in his *Autobiography* that the speech "was thought at the time to have helped get rid of a provision in the Government measure which would have given to landholders a second indemnity, after they had already been once indemnified for the loss of some of their cattle by the increased selling price of the remainder" (*CW*, I, 277n).

MR. J. STUART MILL SAID, THAT in the course of the discussion on the Bill many important points had been raised, respecting some of which he was not in a position to form an opinion; and that being the case, he thought it better that he should leave all other topics to Her Majesty's Government, who had the best means of information, and who were responsible for the failure or success of the measures they might introduce. There was one question, however, which it required no agricultural or special knowledge to understand—that of compensation—it was a purely economical question, and upon this part of the Bill alone he thought himself competent to speak. This question had been raised by his honourable Friend the Member for Birmingham,[1] and as his honourable Friend had been rather severely dealt with by the right honourable Gentleman behind him (*Mr. Lowe*),[2] he thought that any one who shared the sentiments of his honourable Friend would be acting unworthily if he did not stand forward and avow them. (*Hear.*) He did not object to the principle of compensation, but he did object, in the highest degree, to the amount proposed in the Bill, and to the manner in which it was proposed to be provided. It was perfectly true, as his right honourable Friend (*Mr. Lowe*) had pointed out, that the farmers were to receive compensation, not for their losses as such, but for what they lost through the interference of the Government.[3] He (*Mr. J.S. Mill*) quite agreed that there could not be a more just

[1]John Bright (1811–89), Speech on the Cattle Diseases Bill (14 Feb., 1866), *PD*, 3rd ser., Vol. 181, cols. 476–80.

[2]Robert Lowe (1811–92), M.P. for Calne, like Bright a Liberal, but increasingly critical of the party's leadership and direction, criticized Bright (*ibid.*, cols. 483–8).

[3]*Ibid.*, col. 484.

claim for compensation than this; and, moreover, the grant of it was expedient on account of the inducement it would give not to evade the provisions of the Act. He quite adopted the conclusion of his right honourable Friend, that the farmers who might be the owners of diseased cattle ought not to be placed under the temptation of concealing the fact. But, on the other hand, the more reason there was for granting compensation, the more necessity was there for taking care that the compensation should not be excessive. If, on the one hand, the owner were not to be compensated at all for his loss, there was a strong inducement for him to do, what it was the very object of this Bill to prevent him from doing—namely, to keep the infected animals as long as possible, and thus to be the means of propagating the infection. If, on the other hand, the compensation were excessive, an inducement would exist to be careless as to the spread of the disease; because if his animals on becoming infected were ordered to be slaughtered, he knew that he should get an exaggerated compensation for them. The compensation provided by the Bill for diseased animals slaughtered was two-thirds of the value, when that sum did not exceed £20. But what were the necessary conditions to render that sum a just compensation? It was that the animal should have two chances out of three of surviving, because if it had a less chance of recovery than this, the owner would be an absolute gainer by the compensation he would receive on its slaughter by authority. The value of an animal in the market was its value in its existing [a]state and with its existing prospects (*murmurs*)[a]; unless, therefore, the marketable value of an animal after infection was two-thirds of its value when healthy, the compensation proposed by the Bill was excessive. Whatever the chances were of the animal's surviving, that would be the measure of compensation which a reasonable person would propose. He came now to another question—in what manner, and at whose expense, the funds for compensation ought to be raised. In order to judge of that, they ought to consider what would be the natural working of economical laws, supposing no compensation were granted at all. If, setting aside merely momentary effects, they took into consideration the ultimate, and indeed speedy, result, there could be no doubt that in whatever proportion the supply of cattle was diminished, in that proportion the price would be enhanced; and, therefore, in the end, the whole burden of the loss would be borne, not by the producer, but the consumer. Farmers and landlords would indeed suffer, but only to the same extent as other members of the community—that is to say, as consumers. As far as it was the whole community which suffered, no class of the community, as a class, had the smallest claim to compensation from the rest. Some, indeed, were less able to bear the loss than others, and it would not have been surprising if a proposal had been made to compensate them; but now, on the contrary, it was proposed to tax them, in order to compensate those who were able

[a-a]TT] PD condition

to bear the loss much better. It appeared to him that the farmers as a class had no claim whatever to compensation, and the only reason for granting compensation at all was, not that the loss fell peculiarly upon the agricultural interest, but because it fell upon that interest with such extreme inequality. He apprehended that in real justice the compensation ought to be paid to the less fortunate by the more fortunate of the class: thus establishing what would be equivalent to a compulsory system of mutual insurance amongst the owners of stock. This Bill did the very contrary—though he did not blame the Government for introducing it, considering the way in which the House was constituted. It compensated a class for the results of a calamity which was borne by the whole community. In justice, the farmers who had not suffered ought to compensate those who had; but the Bill did what it ought not to have done, and it left undone that which it ought to have done,[4] by not equalizing the incidence of the burden upon that class, inasmuch as, from the operation of the local principle adopted, that portion of the agricultural community who had not suffered at all would not have to pay at all, those who suffered little would have to pay little, while those who suffered most would have to pay a great deal. The only argument of any validity which he could anticipate against the opinion he had expressed, was that a portion of our cattle supply is not derived from home production, but from importation; and, as far as that portion was concerned, the compensation which the consumer would pay through the enhanced price of the commodity would not be received by our own agriculturists, but by the importers. This he must admit; but the importation of cattle, though considerable and increasing, bore so very small a proportion to the entire consumption, that it would diminish the indemnity reaped by the home producers only to a very small extent; and this being the case, it would be unworthy of the landed interest to lay any stress upon so small a matter. An aristocracy should have the feelings of an aristocracy, and inasmuch as they enjoyed the highest honours and advantages, they ought to be willing to bear the first brunt of the inconveniences and evils which fell on the country generally. This was the ideal character of an aristocracy; it was the character with which all privileged classes were accustomed to credit themselves; though he was not aware of any aristocracy in history that had fulfilled those requirements. (*Laughter.*) It might also be said that the farmers would derive no benefit from the ultimate high price, because one of the effects of the cattle plague was by making them bring their cattle prematurely to market, temporarily to keep down the price. This, no doubt, was the case, but after the grant of compensation, it would no longer be so, since the inducement to hurry cattle to market would then no longer exist.

[*The Bill was read a second time, and committed for the next day.*]

[4]See the General Confession in the Order for Morning Prayer in the *Book of Common Prayer*.

13. The Cattle Diseases Bill [2]

16 FEBRUARY, 1866

PD, 3rd ser., Vol. 181, cols. 609–10, 620. Reported in *The Times*, 17 February, p. 7, from which the variant readings and responses are taken. Mill's observations were made in Committee on the Cattle Diseases Bill, Clause 31. (For the Bill, see No. 12.) Clause 31 provided, *inter alia*, that "All expenses incurred by a Local Authority in pursuance of this Act, including any Compensation payable by it in respect of Animals slaughtered in pursuance of this Act, shall be defrayed, as to Two-third Parts thereof, out of the Local Rate." Acton Smee Ayrton (1816–86) moved to amend this clause by omitting the words "as to two-third parts thereof," thereby throwing the full cost on the local rate, and made reference to No. 12, saying that he "had been much impressed by the able speech," because he thought that Mill had "given admirable reasons" why a poll-tax to cover one-third of the cost should not be imposed (col. 608). Mill's response immediately follows on Ayrton's conclusion.

MR. J. STUART MILL SAID, the honourable and learned Member for the Tower Hamlets (*Mr. Ayrton*) had referred to some remarks of his with reference to this subject, and as, in all probability through his own (*Mr. Mill's*) fault, the honourable and learned Member had not seized the point of his argument, he hoped he might be allowed, with the permission of the Committee, to repeat the substance of what he then said. The honourable and learned Member had laid down a principle which no one could dispute—namely, that taxation ought not to be partial. On that ground he urged that a particular class ought not to be taxed to defray the expense of compensation for the consequences of a calamity by which they had already suffered to so great an extent. But his (*Mr. Stuart Mill's*) argument[1] was grounded expressly on this—that although they suffered more immediately, they would not ultimately suffer more than the rest of the community who were consumers of food (*no*). It followed that if they were now to tax the whole of the community in order to give a special indemnity to that class for what they suffered, they would, instead of taxing them, tax the rest of the community in order to relieve them. That was his argument, and nothing he had heard had tended to weaken it; and, consequently, that part of the provision for compensation to which the honourable and learned Member objected, the poll tax on cattle, was the only part which he considered sound in principle. (*A laugh.*) It appeared to him that the valid claim for compensation was not for the burden, but for the inequality of the burden, inasmuch as some cattle owners suffered much less than others, and some not at all. The class on whom the calamity had immediately fallen would, as a class, be compensated in the natural course of things, by the increased price of meat consequent on the diminished supply; but the individuals of the class who had not suffered at all, or who had suffered less than their neighbours, should

[1]See No. 12.

contribute for the relief of those who had not been so fortunate. In principle, therefore, the tax, whatever it might be, ought to be a rate on land only. (*Oh!*) Although the clause as it stood was very objectionable, it would be made still more so by the proposal of the honourable and learned Member for the Tower Hamlets.

[*Several members contributed to the discussion, including Lowe (cols. 618–20), who referred to Ayrton's having accepted Mill's arguments. Mill replied:*]

As the arguments of my right honourable Friend (*Mr. Lowe*) derive great weight from his knowledge, his character, and his talents, it seems desirable that anything which can be said in reply should be said as soon as possible, and while the impression of his arguments is still fresh. (*Hear, hear.*) I think what is necessary may be said in a very few sentences. My right honourable Friend thinks it a complete answer to the arguments which I submitted to the notice of the House, to say that the object of the tax is not compensation, but to give a motive to the farmer to declare the disease. Now, Sir, I really think that the motive held out to the farmer to make this disclosure does not depend on the quarter from whence the compensation comes, but on the compensation itself. (*Hear, hear.*) I should like to know whether, if the farmer receives £20 or any other sum for his beast, it makes any difference in the motive held out to him whether it is paid from a cattle tax, or from the county rate, or out of the Consolidated Fund. (*Hear, hear.*) In the next place, my right honourable Friend stated that the scarcity of a commodity does not always raise the price in full proportion to the deficiency in the quantity. Well, Sir, that is very true, but it is also an extremely common thing that the effect should be to raise the price a great deal beyond the proportion of the loss, and the case in which this is peculiarly known to happen is when the article in deficiency is one of food. (*Hear, hear.*) Take, for instance, the commodity which the right honourable Gentleman the Member for Droitwich (*Sir John Pakington*) has brought forward into the prominence which belongs to it, the article of milk.[2] In the case of milk, an article which is of first necessity to even the poorest people in the country, it is hardly conceivable that a scarcity should take place without raising the price immeasurably beyond the proportion of the loss. (*Hear, hear.*) [a]Now, that is an extremely important element in the case.[a] In the next place, my right honourable Friend thought it an extremely unreasonable thing in me to neglect and leave out of sight that portion of the supply of cattle which comes by importation. He said I did not mention it on a former occasion. Sir, I did mention it, and referred to it in a most special manner.[3] (*Hear.*) And the answer which I made then I make now, in the words which my right honourable Friend himself quoted—*de minimis non curat lex* [b]. (*Hear, hear, and laughter.*) It seems to have excited a good deal of

[2]Actually the argument was made by William George Hylton Joliffe (1800–76), M.P. for Petersfield; see *PD*, 3rd ser., Vol. 181, col. 611.

[3]In No. 12.

[a-a]+TT

[b-b]TT] PD , the quantity imported being so small in proportion to the whole supply.

scorn on the other side of the House because I said it was unworthy of the landed interest of this country or of any aristocracy. (*Cries of Oh, oh! in which the conclusion of the sentence was lost.*)[b] There is one more point in my right honourable Friend's speech which I would wish to notice. He asked, "Is it not absurd that because a man or any of his family is not mad, he should object to being taxed for a lunatic asylum?"[4] I ask, is there any economical law by which the patients of a lunatic asylum are compensated for the expense of their maintenance in that asylum? (*Much laughter.*) If there is, the cases are parallel; if not, not.

[*After further debate, Ayrton's amendment was accepted.*]

14. Suspension of Habeas Corpus In Ireland

17 FEBRUARY, 1866

PD, 3rd ser., Vol. 181, cols. 705–6. Not reported in *The Times*. Mill's speech was on Sir George Grey's motion for leave to bring in "A Bill to Empower the Lord Lieutenant or Other Chief Governor of Ireland to Apprehend and Detain until the First Day of March 1867, Such Persons as He or They Shall Suspect of Conspiring against Her Majesty's Person and Government," 29 Victoria (16 Feb., 1866), *PP*, 1866, III, 121–4. Of the speech he says in his *Autobiography*: "In denouncing, on this occasion, the English mode of governing Ireland, I did no more than the general opinion of England now admits to have been just; but the anger against Fenianism was then in all its freshness; any attack on what Fenians attacked was looked upon as an apology for them; and I was so unfavourably received by the House, that more than one of my friends advised me (and my own judgment agreed with the advice) to wait, before speaking again, for the favourable opportunity that would be given by the first great debate on the Reform Bill" (*CW*, I, 277). (For his successful use of that opportunity, see No. 16.)

MR. J. STUART MILL SAID, THAT some asperity had been introduced into this discussion which he should not imitate. The occasion was one for deep grief, not for irritation. He agreed with the honourable Member for Birmingham (*Mr. Bright*) that this Bill was a cause for shame and humiliation to this country.[1] We were present at the collapsing of a great delusion. England had for a considerable number of years been flattering itself that the Irish people had come to their senses; that they were now sensible that they had got Catholic Emancipation and the Incumbered Estates Bill,[2] which were the only things they could possibly want; and had become aware that a nation could not have anything to complain of when it

[4]*PD*, 3rd ser., Vol. 181, col. 620.

[1]Speech on the Habeas Corpus Suspension Bill, Ireland (17 Feb., 1866), *PD*, 3rd ser., Vol. 181, col. 686.

[2]10 George IV, c. 7 (1829), and 12 & 13 Victoria, c. 77 (1849).

was under such beneficent rulers as us, who, if we do but little for them, would so gladly do much if we only knew how. We all knew that in times past England had been unjust to Ireland. Of that national sin this nation had repented; and we were not now conscious of any other feelings towards Ireland than those which were perfectly honest and benevolent, and he did not say this of one party, or of one side of the House only, he said it of all. But we had fallen into the mistake of thinking that good intentions were enough. We had been in the habit of saying pleasant things on this subject in the hearing of foreigners, till, from iteration, foreigners were beginning to believe that Ireland was no longer our weak point—England's vulnerable spot—the portion of our territory where we might perhaps be successfully assailed, and which, in any case, by neutralizing a great portion of our available force, disabled us from doing anything to resist any iniquity which it might be sought to perpetrate in Europe. This pleasing delusion was now at an end. Every foreigner, every continental writer, would believe for many years to come that Ireland was a country constantly on the brink of revolution, held down by an alien nationality, and kept in subjection by brute force. (*No, no!*) He did not mean that he shared that opinion; he disclaimed it. He hardly knew to what to compare the position of England towards Ireland, but some illustration of his meaning might be drawn from the practice of flogging. Flogging in some few cases was probably a necessary abomination, because there were some men and boys whom long persistence in evil had so brutalized and perverted that no other punishment had any chance of doing them good. But when any man in authority—whether he was the captain of a ship or the commander of a regiment, or the master of a school, needed the instrument of flogging to maintain his authority—that man deserved flogging as much as any of those who were flogged by his orders. He was not prepared to vote against granting to Her Majesty's Government the powers which, in the state to which Ireland had been brought, they declared to be absolutely necessary. He was not responsible—they were. They did not bring Ireland into its present state—they found it so, through the misgovernment of centuries and the neglect of half a century. He did not agree with his honourable Friend the Member for Birmingham in thinking that Her Majesty's Ministers, if they could not devise some remedy for the evils of Ireland, were bound to leave their seats on the Treasury Bench and devote themselves to learning statesmanship.[3] From whom were they to learn it? From the Gentlemen opposite, who would be their successors, and who, if they were to propose anything which his honourable Friend or himself would consider as remedies for Irish evils, would not allow them to pass it? The Government had to deal with things as they were, and not with things as they might wish them to be. He did not believe that the power granted to the Government would be strained beyond the necessity of the case. He would not suggest a suspicion that tyranny and oppression would be practised. He

[3]Bright, cols. 689–90.

knew there would be nothing of the kind, at least with their cognizance or connivance. He was not afraid that they would make a Jamaica in Ireland; and, to say truth, the fountains of his indignation had been so drained by what had taken place in that unfortunate island that he had none left for so comparatively small a matter as arbitrary imprisonment. When, however, the immediate end had been effected, he hoped that we should not again go to sleep for fifty years, and that we should not continue to meet every proposal for the benefit of Ireland with that eternal "*non possumus*"[4] which, translated into English, meant, "We don't do it in England." If his honourable and learned Friend the Member for Sheffield thought that nothing was now amiss in Ireland except the Irish Church,[5] he would be likely to hear much more on the subject before long, if he would only listen.

[*The Bill went through all its stages in one day and was finally approved in the Commons by a vote of 354 to 6 (Mill's name is not listed in either lobby).*]

15. Representation of the People [1]

12 APRIL, 1866

Daily Telegraph, 13 April, 1866, p. 6. Headed: "Reform Meeting in Westminster." Reported also on the same day in the *Daily News* (in the third person), the *Morning Star*, and (in brief summary) in *The Times*. (Clippings of all the reports but the last are in the Mill-Taylor Collection.) The evening meeting of Westminster electors, in St. James's Hall, Piccadilly, was in support of the Government's "Bill to Extend the Right of Voting at Elections of Members of Parliament in England and Wales," 29 Victoria (13 Mar., 1866), *PP*, 1866, V, 87–100, which was under discussion in Parliament (see Nos. 16 and 23). Charles Westerton, who chaired the meeting, explained that it could not be held earlier because such a large crowd could not be accommodated anywhere but in St. James's Hall, which had not been available. He said that Mill and Grosvenor were both in the House of Commons, but would appear later. W.T. Mallinson proposed a motion in favour of the Bill; during his speech, Grosvenor arrived, and made a speech in seconding the motion. During that speech, Mill arrived, and after Probyn had spoken in favour of the motion, he rose. Mill, "who upon presenting himself was received with enthusiastic applause," then spoke to the resolution.

I SINCERELY CONGRATULATE my honourable colleague on having been beforehand, and not for the first time. I have had the satisfaction of hearing the excellent speech which he made on the first reading of the Reform Bill.[1] My attendance in

[4]"We cannot." This was the formula for such refusals since Pope Clement VII so responded to Henry VIII's request in 1529 for a divorce from Catherine of Aragon.

[5]John Arthur Roebuck, Speech on the Habeas Corpus Suspension Bill, Ireland, cols. 695–6.

[1]Grosvenor, Speech on the Representation of the People Bill (12 Mar., 1866), *PD*, 3rd ser., Vol. 182, cols. 87–90.

the House of Commons this evening prevented me from hearing more than a part of his speech now, but what I did hear was equally excellent to that which he made in the House of Commons. I think that those who foretold and who calculated that the people of England no longer cared about reform, or if they did that they do not care about this measure, would cease so to think if they could see this present meeting—they would be convinced of their mistake. But, indeed, I think they must be pretty well convinced of that already if the demonstrations that have taken place over the country, and the multitude and quality of the petitions which I have seen this evening presented to the House of Commons—(*cheers*)—can convince them. It must have shown the most incredulous of them that they have made a great mistake. (*Cheers.*) It has been said that the electors don't wish reform—that they don't wish to extend the privilege to other people. Then of the non-electors it was said that they had grown indifferent to politics—that the only questions which occupied their attention were those of wages and co-operation—that they had grown quite Conservative—(*a laugh*)—and that those who did care about reform wanted so much more reform than this bill gave them, and that they would not stop to pick it up. Again, he believed that some members of Parliament thought they would lose their seats if they supported reform, whereas he hoped now that they would lose their seats if they did not support reform. [a](*Cheers.*) This was a very crafty calculation, but there were many things overlooked in it.[a] It was overlooked that in all those constituencies in which the electors were the most numerous, there had been, and always would be, a strong feeling for further reform; secondly, it had been overlooked that there existed such persons as sincere reformers—(*hear, hear*)—reformers in principle, who had faith in a popular Government. Again, some people were foolish and fanatic enough to believe that nothing could be safe which differed from their opinions. It was forgotten that the £10 electors had not been long enough a privileged class to acquire the odious feelings of one. (*Cheers.*) The ten-pounders, as they were fond of calling them, had not grown into an oligarchy just yet, nor did he think they would. (*Hear, hear.*) There was another consideration, and that was that the ten-pounders knew they had but a small portion of power. Land and money now, as always heretofore, were the leading powers in this country. In order to make head against these influences—which are not always salutary—they must be glad to take in you and I to share it with them. (*Hear, hear.*) Now, respecting the non-electors, if there ever was a delusion on the face of the earth I think it is this, because people—the mass of the people—had acquired a degree of education, a degree of cultivation and of knowledge of politics, a degree of familiarity with newspapers and public events, that they never had before, nor anything approaching to it; and because with these things they had acquired powers of intelligence and combination—which excited the admiration even of Conservatives—in the promotion of their own interests, such as co-operation; because these changes and improvements had taken place,

[a-a]+DN

was it true that they had grown less interested in politics—(*No, no*)—less desirous of the good of their country, and less desiring that they themselves should share in its destiny? I think such a delusion is one of the densest that was ever entertained by human beings. (*Cheers.*) Do they wish for more than this? No doubt they do. I do myself. What is more, I believe Mr. Gladstone does. (*Cheers.*) I heard him say this evening that he did not think there would have been any danger in extending the franchise further than this bill; but he said, and said justly, it is the way of this country, a prudent and just way, not to attempt to do everything at once.[2] And I do not think any of us—not even those who desire a much greater change than this bill promises—ever thought that we should step into all that we want at a single stride. But there is one thing that I may remark, and that is that I am very glad to see from all the demonstrations of the unenfranchised classes on this question, that they take this extremely rational view of the matter. We are told continually that the working classes desire this bill only as a stepping-stone to something else.[3] We think it will give us a better Legislature, and it is because we think that it is good in itself that we think it will give us a better Legislature—a Legislature more likely to give us further reform when the time is come for it. Our opponents have thought it best for their interests not to meet the question by a direct negative, but to meet it by what is called a sidewind—by an amendment which merely turned on the order of proceeding, in the expectation that they will be able to add to their minority a certain number of those who habitually vote with the Government.[4] They will—I believe they will—succeed in getting some votes, though not many I think. But it would be a mistake to suppose that all who vote with them on this occasion are insincere reformers, or that they will ultimately vote against the bill. (*Hear, hear.*) I am not speaking of Mr. Horsman[5] or Mr. Lowe. (*Hisses and laughter.*) They are not insincere. There is no duplicity about them. They tell us they want no reform; that they [b]were afraid of it, that they would resist it to the last. (*Loud hisses.*)[b] At least, I know that Mr. Lowe says it, and I believe Mr. Horsman says it.[6] I think we ought to be obliged to them for telling us the worst at once that is in them. (*A laugh.*) Still, I have no doubt that some who will vote for the amendment will ultimately vote for the future stages of the bill. I do not think that this amendment need discourage us in the least. Nobody doubts that the

[2]Gladstone, speech of 12 April, *ibid.*, col. 1139.

[3]E.g., by Lowe, *ibid.* (13 Mar.), col. 149, and by Robert Arthur Talbot Gascoyne Cecil (1830–1903), then M.P. for Stamford, *ibid.*, col. 234.

[4]Hugh Lupus Grosvenor (1825–99), then M.P. for Chester, Motion on the Representation of the People Bill (12 Apr.), *ibid.*, cols. 1152–63.

[5]Edward Horsman (1807–76), then M.P. for Stroud, a nominal Liberal who, like Lowe, was opposed to the reform of parliament proposed by the party's leaders.

[6]See Lowe, Speech on the Representation of the People Bill (13 Mar.), *PD*, 3rd ser., Vol. 182, cols. 141–64; Horsman, *ibid.* (12 Mar.), cols. 90–114.

[b-b]DN] DT detest it.] MS disliked it, and would resist it to the last.

amendment will be defeated, and we shall see the bill carried by increasing instead of diminishing majorities. (*Great cheering.*) I never formed any decided opinion as to which part of reform it would be best to begin with. I could not judge of it so well as those whose duty it is to judge of it; and what is the use of leaders unless we can trust them on a mere matter of tactics? (*Hear, hear.*) This is the first time since 1832 that a Government has pledged itself to stand or fall by a Reform Bill. (*Cheers.*) I confide in the Ministry. [c]Rumours have been current in the back slums of the Tory encampment that some members of the Government are not sincere, and—though I hope it is not for that reason—(*laughter*)—that they will vote and co-operate with the Tory party. They calculate on a possible combination between some members of the Government and themselves. Well, all know how often the wish is father to the thought—(*laughter*)—and how very difficult it is to get some people to believe in the political sincerity and honesty of others. But I shall require[c] [d]something better than the gossip of the Tadpoles and Tapers (as Mr. Disraeli would term it)[d][7] [e]before I shall believe there is any member of the Government who is not sincere in this question. (*Loud cheers.*) There are two members of the Government, however—Earl Russell and Mr. Gladstone—whose sincerity no one ventures to suspect, and that is the reason the Tories are so inveterate against them.[e] Their sincerity and earnestness on this subject is so obvious, so transparent, and so indisputable, that no one for a moment can doubt them. (*Cheers.*) [f]They all know from past history that Earl Russell had the greatest share in giving the people the greatest improvement of modern times—the Reform Bill[8]—[f] to which we owe the next greatest improvement—the repeal of the Corn Laws.[9] [g]What the Tories now reproach Earl Russell with is, after having resisted any further alteration in the representative system,[10] all at once to reopen the question of Reform, which is the highest misdemeanour possible in the eyes of the Tories. (*Laughter.*) But the people know that the question of Reform was never closed. (*Hear, hear.*)[g] Respecting Mr. Gladstone. (*Cheers.*) What was the

[7]Tadpole and Taper are political hacks in Disraeli's *Coningsby*, where they first appear at the end of Chap. i.

[8]Lord John Russell (1792–1878), a perennial Whig leader, had been instrumental in formulating and securing the passage of the First Reform Act, 2 & 3 William IV, c. 45 (1832).

[9]9 & 10 Victoria, c. 22 (1846), repealed 5 & 6 Victoria, Sess. 2, c. 14 (1842).

[10]See Russell, Speech on the Address in Answer to the Queen's Speech (20 Nov., 1837), *PD*, 3rd ser., Vol. 39, col. 70.

[c-c]+MS[*in third person, past tense*]] DN *as* MS . . . sincere upon reform, and that they were consequently fit company for them. The wish was often father to the thought, and it was difficult for some people to believe in the political honesty of other people. But . . . *as* MS

[d-d]+DN] MS very great proof

[e-e]+MS] DN before he believed these rumours. At any rate Mr. Gladstone and Earl Russell were sincere.

[f-f]MS] DT We know the past history of Earl Russell, and the great share which he had in giving us the greatest improvement we have yet had—the Reform Bill

[g-g]+MS

use to speak of him on a question of sincerity? (*Cheers.*) Every year of his official life had been marked by a succession of measures—no year being without them—some great, some small, but all aiming at the public good—to the good of the people of this country, and especially of the poorer classes. These measures were not even suggested to him; they were the offspring of his own mind, will, and purpose—the free gift from him to his countrymen, unprompted, unsuggested. (*Loud cheers.*) And his countrymen would reward him as they had done already. (*Hear, hear, and cheers.*) Mr. Gladstone seems to be the first statesman who has come up to the idea of a great modern statesman: a Minister should be the leader of a free people—not employing his mind only to do that which the people wished, but pointing out to them that which was for their benefit—offering it to them without even being asked—leaving it to them to accept or refuse it—not thinking that it was his business to act only as he was acted upon, and yielding to pressure. What constituted a great statesman was to take the initiative for the good of his fellow-countrymen. Was it not Mr. Gladstone who first broke silence on the subject of reform after the ridiculous failure of 1860?[11] [h]and he was the man who made that celebrated declaration that every human being, inasmuch as he had an interest in good government, had a *primâ facie* cause for admission to the suffrage.[h12] If we do not stand by him as he is doing by our work—if he fails from any defect of ours, from the want of encouragement to go on—the consequence will be that we shall richly deserve to suffer, for we shall not easily find another to serve us in the same way. (*Loud cheers.*)

[*The resolution was carried unanimously. A petition was moved calling for the Commons to pass the Bill without delay, and, after other speeches and demonstrations, the meeting ended.*]

16. Representation of the People [2]

13 APRIL, 1866

Speech of J. Stuart Mill Esq., M.P. for Westminster, upon the Reform Bill, Delivered in the House of Commons, April 13th, 1866. From the "Daily Telegraph." (London: Diprose and Bateman, 1866). (The title page of the penny pamphlet is headed by a quotation from the *Daily Telegraph* of the 14th: "All will read it, and in reading it will learn the views of the boldest, and yet the most sure and measured thinker of the day.") *PD*, 3rd ser., Vol. 182, cols. 1253–63. Reported in *The Times*, 14 April, p. 6, from which variant readings and

[11]"A Bill Further to Amend the Laws Relating to the Representation of the People in England and Wales," 23 Victoria (1 Mar., 1860), *PP*, 1860, V, 597–608 (not enacted).

[12]See Gladstone, Speech on the Borough Franchise Bill (11 May, 1864), *PD*, 3rd ser., Vol. 175, col. 324.

[h-h]+MS

responses are taken. Mill's manuscript draft of the speech (printed in Appendix D) is extant (Harvard); it lacks, of course, Mill's responses to the debate. Another pamphlet version appeared: *Speech of John Stuart Mill, Esq., M.P. for Westminster, During the Debate on the Second Reading of the Representation of the People Bill, in the House of Commons, April 13, 1866. Reprinted from "The Morning Star."* (London: Judd and Glass, [1866]). The copies of the pamphlets in Somerville College have inked corrections that are here accepted; in all cases except the second and the final two, the changes result in the *PD* version: at 62.4, "consequences they" is altered to "consequences—they"; at 62.27, "classes, in" is altered to "classes; on"; at 63.38, "this or" is altered to "this and"; at 65.20, "and most" is altered to "and much"; at 67.1, "interests" is altered to "interest"; at 68.5, "and is honest" is altered to "and honest" (*PD* reads "good, honest"); and at 68.11-12, "(*hear*)—unless I am mistaken. And (it" is altered to "(*hear*).—Unless I am mistaken, (and it)". Mill spoke on the second reading of Gladstone's Reform Bill (see No. 15), specifically on Earl Grosvenor's motion (technically an amendment) on 12 April: "That this House, while ready to consider, with a view to its settlement, the question of Parliamentary Reform, is of opinion that it is inexpedient to discuss a Bill for the reduction of the Franchise in England and Wales, until the House has before it the entire scheme contemplated by the Government, for the amendment of the Representation of the People" (col. 1227).

ALTHOUGH THE QUESTION which will be put from the chair relates ostensibly to the mere order of proceeding, it will hardly be denied, and least of all after the speech of the right honourable baronet,[1] that the question we are really discussing is whether the bill ought to pass. (*Hear, hear.*) Indeed, the noble Lord the member for King's Lynn is the only speaker on the Opposition side who has argued the nominal issue as if he thought that it was the real one, or has even laid any great stress upon it.[2] That noble lord, in a speech marked by all the fairness and candour which were known to be his characteristics, and by even more than the ability—at least by more varied and sustained ability—has said, I think, the most and the best that can be said in favour of the amendment, considered as a substantive motion. He has brought forward considerations well calculated to make an impression, but only on one part of his audience—on those who, though they may be willing to consent to some reform, look with extreme jealousy on the most important part of it, the enfranchisement of a portion of the working classes—who regard this less as a good to be desired, than as a doubtful and perhaps perilous experiment, and tremble lest they should eventually find themselves committed to giving those classes a trifle more representation than they were duly warned of beforehand. (*Cheers.*) What is the very worst extremity of evil with which the noble lord threatens the House, in case it should be so unguarded as to pass this bill without the other measures of Parliamentary Reform by which it is to be succeeded? Why, it is this—that if something happens which it requires the most improbable

[1]Edward George Earle Lytton Bulwer-Lytton (1803–73), then M.P. for Hertfordshire, Speech on the Representation of the People Bill (13 Apr., 1866), *PD*, 3rd ser., Vol. 182, cols. 1237–53.

[2]Stanley, *ibid.*, cols. 1163–76.

concurrence of chances to bring about, something against which neither the personal honour of the Government, nor the inexorable dates fixed by the Registration Acts,[3] nor even the expressed will of Parliament, if Parliament should think fit to express its will, can guarantee us; in this all but impossible case, there may happen—what? That the redistribution of seats may, in spite of all that can be done, possibly devolve upon a House of Commons elected under the enlarged franchise. (*Hear, hear.*) Now, I put it to the noble lord's clear intellect—and impartial because clear—is this an argument which can have any weight with anybody who thinks the enlarged franchise an improvement—(*cheers*)—who thinks it calculated to give us a better Legislature? If the Legislature it gives us is a better one for all other purposes, will it not be a better one for this purpose? (*Hear, hear.*) If it can be trusted to govern us, if it can be trusted to tax us, if it can be trusted to legislate for us, can it not be trusted to revise its own constitution? (*Hear, hear.*) Does experience teach us to expect that this of all things is the work in which legislative bodies in general, and British Parliaments in particular, are likely to be rash, headstrong, precipitate, subversive, revolutionary? (*Loud cheers.*) I think, Sir, that a Parliament which was cautious in nothing else might be depended on for caution in meddling with the conditions of its own power. (*Hear.*) Sir, this formidable one chance in a thousand with which the noble lord threatens us, is only terrific to those in whose eyes the bill is a rash and portentous transfer of power to the working classes. To those who think that the enfranchising provisions are good in themselves, good even if there were no redistribution of seats (*hear, hear*), and still better if there is (*cheers*), this phantom of evil has no terrors. (*Hear, hear.*) And that I believe to be the opinion of the great body of reformers, both in and out of the House. (*Cheers.*) We are, I dare say, as sincerely desirous as the noble mover of the amendment that family and pocket boroughs should be extinguished, and the inordinate political influence of a few noble and opulent families [a]curtailed[a]. (*Cheers and laughter.*) We are, I believe, as anxious to [b]control[b] the power which wealth possesses, of buying its way into the House of Commons, and shutting the door upon other people—as the wealthiest gentleman present. [c](*Hear, hear.*)[c] But though we are quite orthodox on these great points of Conservative Parliamentary Reform—(*hear*)—and look forward with delight to our expected co-operation with gentlemen on the opposite benches in the congenial occupation of converting them from theories into facts—(*hear, hear, and laughter*)—we yet think that a measure of enfranchisement like this bill—moderate, indeed—far more moderate than is desired by the majority of

[3]The dates before which names must be added to the voters' lists are specified in 6 Victoria, c. 18 (1843) (cities and boroughs), 13 & 14 Victoria, c. 69 (1850) (Ireland), 19 & 20 Victoria, c. 58 (1856) (Scotland), and 28 Victoria, c. 36 (1865) (counties).

[a-a]PD abridged] TT curtailed
[b-b]PD curtail] TT abridge
[c-c]TT (*A laugh.*)

reformers, but which does make the working classes a substantial power in this House—is not only a valuable part of a scheme of Parliamentary Reform, but highly valuable even if nothing else were to follow. And as this is the only question among those raised on the present occasion, which seems to me in the smallest degree worth discussing, I shall make no further apology for confining myself to it. (*Cheers.*) Sir, measures may be recommended either by their principle, or by their practical consequences; and if they have either of these recommendations, they usually have both. As far as regards the principle of this measure, there is but little to disagree about; for a measure which goes no further than this, does not raise any of the questions of principle on which the House is divided, and I cannot but think that the right honourable baronet, in intruding these questions into the debate has caused it to deviate somewhat from its proper course. If it were necessary to take into consideration even all the reasonable things which can be said pro and con about democracy [d]—and I fully admit that the right honourable baronet has said things both reasonable and unreasonable on that subject (*laughter*)— [d] the House would have a very different task before it. But this is not a democratic measure. It neither deserves that praise, nor, if honourable members will have it so, that reproach. It is not a corollary from what may be called the numerical theory of representation. It follows from the class theory, which we all know is the Conservative view of the constitution; the favourite doctrine, not only of what are called Conservative reformers, but of Conservative non-reformers as well. (*Hear, hear.*) The opponents of reform are accustomed to say, that the constitution knows nothing of individuals, but only of classes. (*Hear, hear.*) Individuals, they tell us, cannot complain of not being represented, so long as the class they belong to is represented. But if any class is unrepresented, or has not its proper share of representation relatively to others, that is a grievance. Now, all that need be asked at present is that this theory be applied to practice. There is a class which has not yet had the benefit of the theory. While so many classes, comparatively insignificant in numbers, and not supposed to be freer from class partialities or interests than their neighbours (*cheers*), are represented—some of them I venture to say, greatly over-represented, in this House—here is a class, more numerous than all the others, and, therefore, as a mere matter of human feeling, entitled to more consideration—weak as yet, and therefore needing representation the more, but daily becoming stronger, and more capable of making its claims good—and this class is not represented. We claim, then, a large and liberal representation of the working classes, on the Conservative theory of the constitution. (*Cheers.*) We demand that they be represented as a class, if represented they cannot be as human beings; and we call on honourable gentlemen to prove the sincerity of their convictions by extending the benefit of them to the great majority of their countrymen. (*Cheers.*) But, honourable gentlemen say, the working classes are

[d–d]+TT [*in third person, past tense*]

already represented. It has just come to light, to the astonishment of everybody, that these classes actually form 26 per cent. of the borough constituencies.[4] They kept the secret so well—it required so much research to detect their presence on the register—their votes were so devoid of any traceable consequences—they had all this power of shaking the foundations of our institutions, and so obstinately persisted in not doing it—(*loud cheers*)—that honourable gentlemen are quite alarmed, and recoil in terror from the abyss into which they have not fallen. (*Renewed cheers and laughter.*) Well, Sir, it certainly seems that this amount of enfranchisement of the working classes has done no harm. But if it has not done harm, perhaps it has not done much good either; at least not the kind of good which we are talking about. A class may have a great number of votes in every constituency in the kingdom, and yet obtain scarcely any representation in this House. Their right of voting may be only the right of being everywhere outvoted. (*A laugh, and hear.*) If, indeed, the mechanism of our electoral system admitted representation of minorities; if those who are outvoted in one place could join their votes with those who are outvoted in another; then, indeed, a fourth part, even if only of the borough electors, would be a substantial power, for it would mean a fourth of the borough representatives. 26 per cent. concentrated would be a considerable representation; but 26 per cent. diffused is almost the same as none at all. The right honourable baronet [e]who just preceded me has brought forward a very plausible argument on that point. He[e] has said that a class, though but a minority, may by cleverly managing its votes, be master of the situation, and that the tenant farmers in Hertfordshire, [f]though only a third of the constituency[f] can carry an election.[5] They may be able to decide whether a Tory or a Whig shall be elected; they may be masters of so small a situation as that. (*Laughter.*) But what you are afraid of is their carrying points on which their interest as a class is opposed to that of all other classes; on which if they were only a third of the constituency the other two-thirds would be against them. Do you think they would be masters of such a situation as that?—(*cheers*)—Sir, there is no known contrivance by which in the long run a minority can outnumber a majority [g]. What might be done in that way by preternatural contrivance I do not know (*laughter*) but by no natural contrivance can one-third be made to outvote[g] the other two-thirds. (*Renewed laughter and cheers.*) The real share of the working classes in the representation is measured by the number of members they can return—in other words, the number of constituencies in which they are the majority: and even that only marks the extreme limit of the influence which they can exercise, but by no means that which

[4]"Returns of the Total Number of Voters in Every Borough and City in England and Wales," *PP*, 1866, LVII, 747–9.

[5]Bulwer-Lytton, col. 1242.

[e–e]+TT [*in third person, past tense*]

[f–f]–PD,TT

[g–g]TT [*in third person, past tense*)] P —by which one-third of the electors can outnumber

they will. (*Hear, hear.*) Why, Sir, among the recent discoveries, one is, that there are some half-dozen constituencies in which working men are even now a majority;[6] and I put it to honourable gentlemen, would anybody ever have suspected it? At the head of these constituencies is Coventry. Are the members for Coventry generally great sticklers for working-class notions? (*Hear, hear.*) It has, I believe, been observed that these gentlemen usually vote quite correctly on the subject of French ribbons—(*laughter*)—and as that kind of virtue comes most natural to Conservatives—(*renewed laughter*)—the members for Coventry often are Conservative. But probably that would happen much the same if the master manufacturers had all the votes. (*Cheers.*) If, indeed, a tax on power-looms were proposed, and the members for Coventry voted for it, that might be some indication of working class influences; though I believe that the working men, even at Coventry, have far outgrown that kind of absurdities. (*Cheers.*) Even if the franchise were so much enlarged that the working men, by polling their whole strength, could return by small majorities 200 of the 658 members of this House, there would not be 50 of that number who would represent the distinctive feelings and opinions of working men, or would be, in any class sense, their representatives. (*Hear, hear.*) And what if they had the whole 200? Even then, on any subject in which they were concerned as a class, there would be more than two to one against them when they were in the wrong. They could not succeed in anything, even when unanimous, unless they carried with them nearly a third of the representatives of the other classes; and if they did that, there would be, I think, a very strong presumption of their being in the right. (*Hear, hear, and cheers.*) As a matter of principle, then, and not only on liberal principles, but on those of the Conservative party, the case in favour of the bill seems irresistible. (*Loud cheers.*) But it is asked by my right honourable friend the member for Calne, what practical good do we expect?[7] What particular measures do we hope to see carried in a reformed House, which cannot be carried in the present? If I understand my right honourable friend correctly, he thinks we ought to come to the House with a bill of indictment against itself (*a laugh*)—an inventory of wrong things which the House does, and right things which it cannot be induced to do (*hear, hear*)—and when, convinced by our arguments, the House pleads guilty and cries *peccavi*, we have his permission to bring in a Reform Bill. (*Hear, hear, and laughter.*) Sir, my right honourable friend says we should not proceed on *a priori* reasoning, but should be practical. I want to know whether this is his idea of being practical. For my part, I am only sorry it is not possible that in the discussion of this question special applications should be kept entirely out of view: for if we descend to particulars, and point out this and that in the conduct of the House, which we should like to see altered, but which the House, by the very fact that it does not alter

[6]"Returns," pp. 747–9.

[7]Lowe, Speech on the Representation of the People Bill (13 Mar., 1866), *PD*, 3rd ser., Vol. 182, col. 161.

them, does not think require alteration, how can we expect the House to take this as a proof that its constitution needs reform? We should not at all advance our cause, while we should stir up all the most irritating topics in the domain of politics. (*Hear, hear.*) Suppose now—and I purposely choose a small instance to give the less offence—suppose we were to say that if the working classes had been represented, it would not have been found so easy for honourable gentlemen whose cattle were slaughtered by Act of Parliament[8] to get compensated twice over—(*cheers and laughter*)—once by a rate, and again by a rise in price. I use the case only for illustration: I lay no stress on it; but I ask, ought the debate on a Reform Bill to consist of a series of discussions on points similar to this, and a hundred times more irritating than this? Is it desirable to drag into this discussion all the points on which any one may think that the rights or interests of labour are not sufficiently regarded by the House? (*Hear, hear.*) I will ask another question. If the authors of the Reform Bill of 1832[9] had foretold—which they scarcely could have done, since they did not themselves know it—if they had predicted that through it we should abolish the corn laws—that we should abolish the navigation laws—(*cheers*)—that we should grant free trade to all foreigners without reciprocity—(*renewed cheers*)—that we should reduce inland postage to a penny—that we should renounce the exercise of any authority over our colonies—all which things have really happened[10]—does the House think that these announcements would have greatly inclined the Parliament of that day towards passing the bill? (*Loud cheers.*) Whether the practical improvements that will follow a further Parliamentary reform will be equal to these, the future must disclose; but whatever they may be, they are not at the present time regarded as improvements by the House, for if the House thought so, there is nothing to hinder it from adopting them. (*Cheers.*) Sir, there is a better way of persuading possessors of power to give up a part of it: not by telling them that they make a bad use of their power—which, if it were true, they could not be expected to be aware of—but by reminding them of what they are aware of—their own fallibility. Sir, we all of us know that we hold many erroneous opinions, but we do not know which of our opinions these are, for if we did, they would not be our opinions. (*Hear, hear.*) Therefore, reflecting men take precautions beforehand against their own errors, without waiting till they and all other people are agreed about the particular instances; and if there are things which, from their mental habits or their position in life, are in danger of escaping their notice, they are glad to associate themselves with others of different habits and positions which very fact peculiarly qualifies them to see the precise things which they themselves do not see. Believing the House to be composed of reasonable men, this is what we ask them

[8]29 Victoria, c. 2 (1866).

[9]Enacted as 2 & 3 William IV, c. 45.

[10]By, respectively, 9 & 10 Victoria, c. 22 (1846), 12 & 13 Victoria, c. 29 (1849), 23 Victoria, c. 22 (1860), 3 & 4 Victoria, c. 96 (1840), and 28 & 29 Victoria, c. 63 (1865).

to do. (*Hear, hear.*) Every class knows some things not so well known to other people, and every class has interests more or less special to itself, and for which no protection is so effectual as its own. These may be *a priori* doctrines, but so is the doctrine that a straight line is the shortest distance between two points; they are as much truths of common sense and common observation as that is, and persons of common sense act upon them with the same perfect confidence. I claim the benefit of these principles for the working classes. They require it more than any other class. The class of lawyers, or the class of merchants, is amply represented, though there are no constituencies in which lawyers or merchants form the majority; but a successful lawyer or merchant easily gets into Parliament by his wealth or social position, and, once there, is as good a representative of lawyers or merchants as if he had been elected on purpose; but no constituency elects a working man, or a man who looks at questions with working men's eyes. (*Cheers.*) Is there, I wonder, a single member of this House who thoroughly knows the working men's views of trades unions, or of strikes, and could bring these subjects before the House in a manner satisfactory to working men? (*Hear, hear.*) My honourable friend the member for Brighton, if any one;[11] perhaps not even he. Are there many of us who so perfectly understand the subject of apprenticeships, let us say, or of the hours of labour, as to have nothing to learn on the subject from intelligent operatives? I grant that, along with many just ideas and much valuable knowledge, you would sometimes find pressed upon you erroneous opinions—mistaken views of what is for the interest of labour; and I am not prepared to say that if the labouring classes were predominant in the House, attempts might not be made to carry some of these wrong notions into practice. But there is no question at present about making the working classes predominant. (*Hear, hear.*) What is asked is a sufficient representation to ensure that their opinions are fairly placed before the House, and are met by real arguments, addressed to their own reason, by people who can enter into their way of looking at the subjects in which they are concerned. (*Cheers.*) In general, those who attempt to correct the errors of the working classes do it as if they were talking to babies. (*Cheers.*) They think any trivialities sufficient. If they condescend to argue, it is from premises which hardly any working man would admit; they expect that the things which appear self-evident to them will appear self-evident to the working classes; their arguments never reach the mark, never come near what a working man has in his mind, because they do not know what is in his mind. Consequently, when the questions which are near the hearts of the working men are talked about in this House—there is no want of good will to them, I cheerfully admit (*hear, hear*)—but all that it is most necessary to prove to them is taken for granted. Do not suppose that working men would always be unconvincible by such arguments as ought to satisfy them. (*Hear, hear.*) It is

[11]Henry Fawcett (1833–84), economist and politician, a close associate of Mill in and out of the House.

not one of the faults of democracy to be obstinate in error. (*Hear, hear.*) An Englishman who had lived some years in the United States[12] lately summed up his opinion of the Americans by saying, "They are the most teachable people on the face of the earth." Old countries are not as teachable as young countries, but I believe it will be found that the educated artisans, those especially who take interest in politics, are the most teachable of all our classes. They have much to make them so; they are, as a rule, more in earnest than any other class; their opinions are more genuine, less influenced by what so greatly influences some of the other classes—the desire of getting on; their social position is not such as to breed self-conceit. Above all, there is one thing to which, I believe, almost every one will testify who has had much to do with them, and of which even my own limited experience supplies striking examples; there is no class which so well bears to be told of its faults—to be told of them even in harsh terms, if they believe that the person so speaking to them says what he thinks, and has no ends of his own to serve by saying it.[13] (*Cheers.*) I can hardly conceive a nobler course of national education than the debates of this House would become, if the notions, right and wrong, which are fermenting in the minds of the working classes, many of which go down very deep into the foundations of society and government, were fairly stated and genuinely discussed within these walls. (*Hear, hear.*) It has often been noticed how readily, in a free country, people resign themselves even to the refusal of what they ask, when everything which they could have said for themselves has been said by somebody in the course of the discussion. (*Hear, hear.*) The working classes have never yet had this tranquillising assurance. They have always felt that not they themselves, perhaps, but their opinions, were prejudged—were condemned without being listened to. But let them have the same equal opportunities which others have of pleading their own cause—let them feel that the contest is one of reason, and not of power—and if they do not obtain what they desire, they will as readily acquiesce in defeat, or trust to the mere progress of reason for reversing the verdict, as any other portion of the community. (*Cheers.*) And they will, much oftener than at present, obtain what they desire. Let me refer honourable gentlemen to Tocqueville, who is so continually quoted when he says anything uncomplimentary to democracy, that those who have not read him might mistake him for an enemy of it, instead of its discriminating but sincere friend. Tocqueville says that, though the various American legislatures are perpetually making mistakes, they are perpetually correcting them too, and that the evil, such as it is, is far outweighed by the salutary effects of the general tendency of their legislation, which is maintained, in a degree unknown elsewhere, in the direction

[12]Not identified.

[13]Mill is undoubtedly referring to exchanges during his election meetings in 1865; see esp. No. 8.

of the interest of the people.[14] Not that vague abstraction, the good of the country, but the actual, positive well-being of the living human creatures who compose the population. (*Hear, hear.*) But we are told that our own legislation has made great progress in this direction—that the House has repealed the corn laws, removed religious disabilities,[15] and got rid of I know not how many more abominations. Sir, it has; and I am far from disparaging these great reforms, which have probably saved this country from a violent convulsion. As little would I undervalue the good sense and good feeling which have made the governing classes of this country [h](unlike those of some other countries)[h] capable of thus far advancing with the times. But they have their recompense—*habes pretium,* [i]*loris non ureris*[i].[16] Their reward is that they are not hated, as other privileged classes have been. (*Hear.*) And that is the fitting reward for ceasing to do harm—for merely repealing bad laws which Parliament itself had made. (*Cheers.*) But is this all that the Legislature of a country like ours can offer to its people? Is there nothing for us to do, but only to undo the mischief that we or our predecessors have done? Are there not all the miseries of an old and crowded society waiting to be dealt with (*hear, hear*)—the curse of ignorance, the curse of pauperism, the curse of disease, the curse of a whole population born and nurtured in crime? (*Cheers.*) All these things we are just beginning to look at—just touching with the tips of our fingers; and, by the time two or three more generations are dead and gone, we may perhaps have discovered how to keep them alive, and how to make their lives worth having. I must needs think that we should get on much faster with all this—the most important part of the business of government in our days—if those who are the chief sufferers by the great chronic evils of our civilisation had representatives among us to stimulate our zeal, as well as to inform us by their experience. (*Hear, hear.*) Of all great public objects, the one which would be most forwarded by the presence of working people's representatives in this House is the one in which we flatter ourselves we have done most—popular education. And let me here offer to my right honourable friend, the member for Calne, who demands practical arguments, a practical argument which I think ought to come

[14]Charles Alexis Henri Clérel de Tocqueville (1805–59), French politician and social analyst, *De la démocratie en Amérique*, 2 vols. (Paris: Gosselin, 1835), Vol. II, Chaps. v and vi, and, especially in the latter, p. 109.

[15]By 9 George IV, c. 17 (1828), 10 George IV, c. 7 (1829), and 21 & 22 Victoria, c. 49 (1858).

[16]Horace, *Epistles*, in *Satires, Epistles, Ars poetica* (Latin and English), trans. H. Rushton Fairclough (London: Heinemann; New York: Putnam's Sons, 1929), p. 354 (I, xvi, 47). This gives the version in the pamphlet; the concluding clause in *Parliamentary Debates* and *The Times* has not been found.

[h-h]–PD,TT

[i-i]PD,TT *cruci non figeris*

home to him. If those whose children we vote money to instruct had been properly represented in this House, he would not have lost office on the Revised Code.[17] (*Hear, hear, and a laugh.*) The working classes would have seen in him an administrator of a public fund honestly determined that the work for which the public paid should be good and honest work. (*Cheers.*) They are not the people to prefer a greater quantity of sham teaching to a smaller quantity of real teaching at a less expense. Real education is the thing they want, and as it is what he wanted, they would have understood him and upheld him. (*Hear, hear.*) I have myself seen those services remembered to his honour, even at this moment of exasperation, by one of the leaders of the working classes—(*hear*). [j][*Mr. Bright was here understood to say, So have I.*][j]—Unless I am mistaken, (and it is not my opinion alone), very few years of a real working-class representation would have passed over our heads, before there would be in every parish a school-rate, and the school doors freely open to all the world; and in one generation from that time England would be an educated nation. (*Hear, hear.*) Will it ever become so by your present plan, which gives to him that hath, and only to him that hath? Never. If there were no reason for extending the franchise to the working classes except the stimulus it would give to this one alone of the imperial works which the present state of society urgently demands from Parliament, the reason would be more than sufficient. (*Hear.*) These, Sir, are a few of the benefits which I expect from a further Parliamentary Reform; and as they depend altogether upon one feature of it, the effective representation of the working classes, their whole weight is in favour of passing the present bill, without regard to any bill that may follow. I look upon a liberal enfranchisement of the working classes as incomparably the greatest improvement in our representative institutions, which we at present have it in our power to make (*hear*); and as I shall be glad to receive this greatest improvement along with others, so I am perfectly willing to accept it by itself. Such others as we need we shall, no doubt, end by obtaining; and a person must be very simple who imagines that we should have obtained them a day sooner if Ministers had encumbered the subject by binding up any of them with the present bill. (*Loud cheers.*)

Many members, as they passed down the gangway, close to where the honourable member sits, shook hands with him in congratulation for his able address.

[*The debate was later adjourned to 16 April; see No. 17.*]

[17]In 1862, Lowe, then Vice-President of the Committee of Council for Education, introduced the Revised Code (see *PP*, 1862, XLI, 115–62, 167–88); it applied to the capitation grants to elementary schools the principle of "payment by results" (determined by the performance of pupils on examination in the three R's). In 1864 Lowe resigned following a vote of censure in the House of Commons initiated by opponents of the Revised Code and its author (see "Education—Reports of the Inspectors of Schools—Resignation of Mr. Lowe" [18 Apr., 1864], *PD*, 3rd ser., Vol. 174, cols. 1203–11).

[j-j]+TT [TT'*s square brackets*]

17. Representation of the People [3]

16 APRIL, 1866

PD, 3rd ser., Vol. 182, col. 1477. Reported in *The Times*, 17 April, p. 10, from which the response is taken. During the adjourned debate on the second reading of Gladstone's Reform Bill (see Nos. 15 and 16), Mill responded to an interpretation by Hugh Cairns of his remarks in No. 16. Cairns said (cols. 1476–7), "It is saying nothing but what the majority of the House think when I state that, on this point [the whole question of Reform], the speech of the noble Lord the Member for King's Lynn [Lord Stanley] was both unanswerable and has been unanswered. When I say 'unanswered,' I will make one exception. The honourable Member for Westminster did give an answer, and to anybody looking at the question from the same point of view I have no doubt the answer was perfectly satisfactory. The honourable Member said, 'Here is a Bill which will enfranchise 200,000 borough voters. You are apprehensive that possibly 200,000 or 300,000 more may possibly be enfranchised, when the effect of the redistribution of seats is felt, but I am of opinion that the more enfranchised the better.'"

MR. J. STUART MILL: I said nothing of the kind.

Sir Hugh Cairns: I should be sorry to misrepresent anything that fell from the honourable Member, but I understood him to say that every considerable enfranchisement in itself was good.

Mr. J. Stuart Mill: I said that the enfranchisement which this Bill gives is an absolute good; and that if it produced an improved Legislature, that Legislature might be entrusted to make the redistribution of seats. (*Hear, hear.*)

18. The Malt Duty

17 APRIL, 1866

PD, 3rd ser., Vol. 182, cols. 1524–8. Reported in *The Times*, 18 April, p. 6, from which the variants and responses are taken. Mill says in the *Autobiography* that this speech, insisting "on the duty of paying off the National Debt before [the nation's] coal supplies [were] exhausted," following on the success of No. 16, further improved his position in the House (*CW*, I, 277). Fitzroy Kelly (1796–1880), then M.P. for Suffolk, moved "That upon any future remission of indirect taxation, this House will take into consideration the Duty upon Malt with a view to its immediate reduction and ultimate repeal" (*ibid.*, col. 1509). Charles Neate (1806–79), M.P. for Oxford, moved an amendment to substitute: "That in the present state of the taxation and resources of the Country, it is the duty of Parliament to make provision for the systematic reduction of the National Debt, and not to sanction any proposal for any repeal or change of taxes which is likely to be attended with a diminution of the Revenue" (cols. 1523–4). Mill's seconding speech follows on immediately.

IN RISING to second the Amendment of my honourable Friend the Member for Oxford, I hope I shall not be suspected of any disposition to abuse the indulgence which the House has so recently and so kindly extended to me. But I have for some time felt so serious, I may say so solemn a conviction upon the subject which my honourable Friend has brought forward, that it is almost a matter of conscience with me not to let slip an occasion of endeavouring to impress that conviction on some honourable Members of this House. (*Hear.*) Not long ago it might not altogether unreasonably be supposed that the unrivalled growth of this country in every kind of wealth—the limits of which it seemed impossible to define—was an excuse to us, and even a justification, for leaving our pecuniary obligations, without any serious attempt to reduce them, to weigh upon posterity, whom we might reasonably expect to be better able to support them than we ourselves are. This, however, was at no time a conclusive argument or a sound excuse, because future generations will have their own exigencies too; and we have had an example of it in the fact that not many years ago two years of war sufficed to re-add to our National Debt nearly as much as had been subtracted from it by the savings of fifty years.[1] (*Hear, hear.*) But, more recently, facts have been brought to our notice, which have been too much overlooked; showing that the excuse we made to ourselves is not admissible in the case of a nation whose population greatly exceeds that which with the existing resources of science can be supported from its own soil; who are therefore dependent for subsistence on the power of disposing of their goods in foreign markets; and whose command over those markets depends upon the continued possession of an exhaustible material. The termination of our coal supplies, though always certain, has always until lately appeared so distant, that it seeemed quite unnecessary for the present generation to occupy itself with the question. The reason was that all our calculations were grounded upon the existing rate of consumption; but the fact now is that our consumption of coals increases with such extraordinary rapidity from year to year, that the probable exhaustion of our supplies is no longer a question of centuries, but of generations. (*Hear.*) I hope there are many honourable Members in this House who are acquainted with a small volume written by Mr. Stanley Jevons, entitled *The Coal Question.*[2] It appears to me, so far as one not practically conversant with the subject can presume to judge, that Mr. Jevons' treatment of the subject is almost exhaustive. He seems to have anticipated everything which can possibly be said against the conclusion at which he has arrived, and to have answered it; and that conclusion is, that if the consumption of coal continues to increase at the present

[1]See "An Account of Gross Public Revenue and Expenditure from 1851–1857 Inclusive," *PP*, 1857–58, XXXIII, 134, and "An Account of the Expenditure for the Army, Navy, Ordnance, and Militia from 1851–1857 Inclusive," *ibid.*, p. 135.

[2]William Stanley Jevons (1835–82), economist and logician, *The Coal Question: An Enquiry Concerning the Progress of the Nation, and the Probable Exhaustion of Our Coal Mines* (London and Cambridge: Macmillan, 1865).

rate, three generations at the most, very possibly a considerably shorter period, will leave no workable coal nearer to the surface than 4,000 feet in depth; and that the expense of raising it from that depth will entirely put it out of the power of the country to compete in manufactures with the richer coal-fields of other countries. I think that if there be anyone in this House, or out of it, who knows anything which will invalidate these conclusions of Mr. Jevons, it will be right for him to come forward and make it known. I have myself read various attempts to answer Mr. Jevons,[3] but I must say that every one of them, admitting the truth of everything said, has only made out that our supplies will continue a few years longer than the term which Mr. Jevons has assigned. In fact, it has now come to this, that instead of being at liberty to suppose that future generations will be more capable than we are ourselves of paying off the National Debt, it is probable that the present generation and the one or two which will follow, are the only ones which will have the smallest chance of ever being able to pay it off. Now, what is the duty which facts of this sort impose upon this country? Are we going to bequeath our pecuniary obligations undiminished to descendants, to whom we cannot bequeath our assets? Suppose the property of a private individual had come to him deeply mortgaged, and that the bulk of it consisted of a mine, rich indeed, but certain to be exhausted in his lifetime, would he think it honourable to waste the whole proceeds of the mine in riotous living, and leave to his children the [a]payment of the debt out of the residue of the estate[a]? Then what would be vicious and dishonourable in a private individual is not less dishonourable in a nation. We ought to think of these things while it is still time. This country is at present richer and more prosperous than any country we ever knew or read of, and it can without any material inconvenience or privation set aside several millions a year for the discharge of this important duty to our descendants. I do not think we are much to blame as far as we have yet gone. It was perfectly right to get rid of all very bad taxes, all those which produced a greater quantity of incidental mischief than advantage to the revenue from their imposition. Thanks to the progress of opinion, and thanks also to the enlightened and far-sighted Minister who has administered our finances for some years back (*hear, hear*),[4] this work has been nearly performed. There are very few taxes remaining which are utterly unfit to exist. If there are any, they do not yield so large a revenue but that we may hope, without much difficulty, to get rid of them also. The bulk of our revenue is derived from a comparatively small number of

[3]Possibly including anonymous reviews of Jevons in the *Colliery Guardian*, 27 May, 1865, p. 380, and in the *Athenaeum*, 27 May, 1865, pp. 714–15; Joseph Holdsworth, *On the Extension of the English Coal-fields beneath the Secondary Formations of the Midland Counties* (London: Middleton, 1866); and J. Jones, "Our Future Coal Fields," *Intellectual Observer*, VIII (Jan. 1866), 435–9.

[4]I.e., Gladstone.

[a-a]TT duty of paying upon the residue of his estate the interest of heavy mortgages upon what then turned out to be unproductive property

imposts, each yielding a considerable sum, and none of which, I think, is now very seriously objectionable in principle, or greatly mischievous in practice, any further than is inevitably incident on the payment of taxes. I think it is perfectly legitimate to try experiments upon these taxes, if there be any chance, by lowering the amount, to increase the revenue. It is also legitimate to vary the mode of imposing taxes; for example, by levying them at a later stage in the production of the article, by which means we may get rid of objections such as some which have been brought forward by the honourable and learned Member opposite.[5] But if we are to abolish any tax which yields a revenue of £5,000,000 or £6,000,000, merely in order to have the satisfaction of expending the amount in some other way, it will be, as it appears to me, a criminal dereliction of duty. (*Hear, hear.*) If we are able either by increasing our resources or by a retrenchment of our expenditure to dispense with the malt tax, how much wiser and worthier it would be if we were to set apart this tax as a fund for the extinguishment of our Debt. (*Hear, hear.*) I beg permission to press upon the House the duty of taking these things into serious consideration, in the name of that dutiful concern for posterity, which has been strong in every nation which ever did any thing great, and which has never left the mind of any such nation until, as in the case of the Romans under the Empire, it was already falling into decrepitude, and ceasing to be a nation. There are many persons in the world, and there may possibly be some in this House, though I should be sorry to think so, who are not unwilling to ask themselves, in the words of the old jest, "Why should we sacrifice anything for posterity; what has posterity done for us?"[6] They think that posterity has done nothing for them: but that is a great mistake. Whatever has been done for mankind by the idea of posterity; whatever has been done for mankind by philanthropic concern for posterity, by a conscientious sense of duty to posterity, even by the less pure but still noble ambition of being remembered and honoured by posterity; all this we owe to posterity, and all this it is our duty to the best of our limited ability to repay. (*Hear, hear.*) All the great deeds of the founders of nations, and of those second [b]founders[b] of nations, their great reformers—all that has been done for us by the authors of those laws and institutions to which free countries are indebted for their freedom, and well governed countries for their good government; all the heroic lives which have been led, and all the heroic deaths which have been died, in defence of liberty and law against despotism and tyranny, from Marathon and Salamis down to Leipsic and Waterloo; all those traditions of wisdom and of virtue which are enshrined in the history and literature of the past—all the schools and Universities by which the culture of former times has been brought down to us, and

[5]Kelly, Resolution on the Malt Duty, cols. 1512–14.
[6]See Joseph Addison (1672–1719), *The Spectator*, No. 583 (20 Aug., 1714), p. 2.

[b–b]TT fathers

all that culture itself—all that we owe to the great masters of human thought and to the great masters of human emotion—all this is ours because those who preceded us have cared, and have taken thought, for posterity. (*Hear, hear.*) Not owe anything to posterity, Sir! We owe to it Bacon, and Newton, and Locke, [c]and Bentham; aye,[c] and Shakespeare, and Milton, and Wordsworth.[7] I have read of an eminent man—I am almost sure it was Dr. Franklin—who, when he wished to relieve the necessities or assist the occasions of any deserving person by pecuniary help, had a way of his own of doing it, and it was this. He said to them, "I only lend you this; if you are ever able, I expect you to repay it; but not to me: repay it to some other necessitous person, and do it under the same stipulation, that so the stream of benefits may still flow on, as long and as far as human honesty can keep it flowing."[8] (*Hear, hear.*) What Franklin did from beneficence, in order that the greatest possible amount of good might be extracted from a limited fund, our predecessors, to whom we owe so much, have done from the necessities of the case. The debt of gratitude due to them is such as makes it at times almost an oppressive thought that not one tittle of that vast debt can ever be directly repaid to those from whom we have received so much. But, like the objects of Franklin's beneficence, we can indirectly repay it, by paying it to others—to those others whom also they cared for, and for whom, and not merely for us, their labours and sacrifices were undergone. What are we, Sir—we of this generation, or of any other generation, that we should usurp, and expend upon our particular and exclusive uses, what was meant for mankind?[9] It is lent to us, Sir, not given: and it is our duty to pass it on, not merely undiminished, but with interest, to those who are in the same relation to us as we are to those who preceded us. So shall we too deserve, and may in our turn hope to receive, a share of the same gratitude. (*Hear, hear.*)

[*Neate withdrew the amendment, and the motion was defeated 234 to 150, Mill voting with the majority.*]

[7]Francis Bacon (1561–1626), Isaac Newton (1642–1727), John Locke (1632–1704), Jeremy Bentham (1748–1832), William Shakespeare (1564–1616), John Milton (1608–74), and William Wordsworth (1770–1850).

[8]Cf. Benjamin Franklin (1706–90), U.S. founding father, diplomat, and inventor, Letter to Benjamin Webb (22 Apr., 1784), in *The Private Correspondence of Benjamin Franklin* (London: Colburn, 1817), p. 54.

[9]A play on the characterization of Edmund Burke by Oliver Goldsmith (1728–74) as one who "to party gave up, what was meant for mankind" (*Retaliation: A Poem* [London: Kearsly, 1774], p. 7 [l. 32]).

[c–c]–TT

19. Inclosure of Hainault Forest

25 APRIL, 1866

PD, 3rd ser., Vol. 182, col. 2012. Reported in *The Times*, 26 April, p. 6.

MR. J. STUART MILL SAID, he would beg to ask the Secretary of State for the Home Department,[1] Whether the Inclosure Commissioners have finally signed and sealed their award for the Inclosure of the newly-created Common set out for the ratepayers of the parish of Chigwell; if he is aware that the timber on the fifty acres of recreation ground granted by Parliament in 1862[2] for the use of the Metropolitan public is being cut down, thereby destroying the forestal appearance of the spot, which the intention of the Legislature was to keep uninclosed and preserved in its natural wildness; and if the destruction of the timber has been sanctioned by the Inclosure Commissioners?

Sir George Grey: Sir, the Inclosure Commissioners have not finally signed and sealed their award for this inclosure. The appeal meeting was held only on the 17th of this month, and they have not yet received the Report of their Assistant Commissioner on that meeting. With regard to the latter part of the Question of the honourable Member, the Commissioners have no knowledge of the timber on these fifty acres being cut down, and if it is so it is entirely without their sanction. The timber, they believe, belongs to the lady of the manor within which the fifty acres are situated.

20. Representation of the People [4]

26 APRIL, 1866

PD, 3rd ser., Vol. 182, col. 2100. Reported in *The Times*, 27 April, p. 6. During the seventh day of debate on the Second Reading of the Reform Bill (see No. 15), Robert Lowe in a long speech (cols. 2077–99) made repeated attacks on Mill's position concerning representation of the working classes, and concluded by complaining of Mill's "narrowness and illiberality" in "saying that those who differ from [him] must be wrong, and that if it were not for the faulty constitution of this House we should see and judge things in the same narrow manner as he does." Mill immediately rose and, "(*amid loud cries of Order*)" (*The Times*), replied.

I WISH TO CORRECT the last assertion of my right honourable Friend. I never

[1]George Grey (1799–1882), long a leading Liberal, at that time M.P. for Morpeth.
[2]By 25 & 26 Victoria, c. 47 (1862), Sect. 1.

imputed to honourable Gentlemen in this House, or to the landed interest, that they were wilfully wrong.

21. Chichester Fortescue's Land Bill

17 MAY, 1866

Chapters and Speeches on the Irish Land Question (London: Longmans, *et al.*, 1870), 97–107. The speech appears in *PD*, 3rd ser., Vol. 183, cols. 1087–97. Reported in *The Times*, 18 May, pp. 7–8, from which variants and responses are taken. Writing to John Elliot Cairnes on 4 December, 1869, Mill says: "The 'Chapters and Speeches' will be out shortly. The reports of the speeches are taken from Hansard. The first of the two, that of 1866 [i.e., this speech], was printed verbatim from my MS." (*CW*, Vol. XVII, p. 1667.) There are, however, some substantive variants. (For the second speech, see No. 88.) Mill spoke on the second reading of "A Bill Further to Amend the Law Relating to the Tenure and Improvement of Land in Ireland," 29 Victoria (30 Apr., 1866), *PP*, 1866, V, 353–64.

IT WAS IN AN AUSPICIOUS HOUR for the futurity of Ireland, and of the Empire of which Ireland is so important a part, that a British Administration has introduced this Bill into Parliament. I venture to express the opinion that nothing which any Government has yet done, or which any Government has yet attempted to do, for Ireland—not even Catholic Emancipation itself—has shown so true a comprehension of Ireland's real needs, or has aimed so straight at the very heart of Ireland's discontent and of Ireland's misery. It is a fulfilment of the promise held out by the Chancellor of the Exchequer at the beginning of the Session, when, in discharging the painful duty of calling on Parliament to treat Ireland once more—let us hope for the last time—as a disaffected dependency, he declared his purpose, and that of the Government of which he is a Member, to legislate for Ireland according to Irish exigencies, and no longer according to English routine.[1] To have no better guide than routine is not a safe thing in any case; but to make the routine of one country our guide in legislating for another, is a mode of conduct which, unless by a happy accident, cannot lead to good. It is a mistake which this country has often made—not perhaps so much from being more liable to it than other countries, as from having more opportunities of committing it: having been so often called on to legislate, and to frame systems of administration, for dependencies very unlike itself. Sir, it is a problem of this sort which we still have before us when we attempt to legislate for Ireland. Not that Ireland is a dependency—those days are over; she is an integral part of a great self-governing nation: but a part, I venture to say, very unlike the remaining parts. I am not going to talk about natural differences, race

[1]Gladstone, Speech on the Habeas Corpus Suspension Bill, Ireland (17 Feb., 1866), *PD*, 3rd ser., Vol. 181, cols. 721–2.

and the like—the importance of which, I think, is very much exaggerated; but let any honourable gentleman consider what a different history Ireland has had from either England or Scotland, and ask himself whether that history must not have left its impress deeply engraven on Irish character. Consider again how different, even at this day, are the social circumstances of Ireland from those of England or Scotland; and whether such different circumstances must not often require different laws and institutions. (*Hear, hear.*) People often ask—it has been asked this evening[2]—why should that which works well in England not work well in Ireland? or why should anything be needed in Ireland which is not needed in England? Are Irishmen an exception to all the rest of [a]mankind[a], that they cannot bear the institutions and practices which reason and experience point out as the best suited to promote national prosperity? Sir, we were eloquently reminded the other night of that double ignorance against which a great philosopher warned his cotemporaries—ignorance of our being ignorant.[3] But when we insist on applying the same rules in every respect to Ireland and to England, we show another kind of double ignorance, and at the same time disregard a precept older than Socrates—the precept which was inscribed on the front of the Temple of Delphi: we not only do not know those whom we undertake to govern, but we do not know ourselves.[4] (*Cheers.*) No, Sir, Ireland is not an exceptional country; but England is. Irish circumstances and Irish ideas as to social and agricultural economy are the general ideas and circumstances of the human race; it is English circumstances and English ideas that are peculiar. Ireland is in the main stream of human existence and human feeling and opinion; it is England that is in one of the lateral channels. If any honourable gentleman doubts this, I ask, is there any other country on the face of the earth in which, not merely as an occasional fact, but as a general rule, the land is owned in great estates by one class, and farmed by another class of capitalist farmers at money rents fixed by contract, while the actual cultivators of the soil are hired labourers, wholly detached from the soil, and receiving only day wages? (*Cheers.*) Parts of other countries may be pointed out where something like this state of things exists [b]as an exceptional fact[b], but Great Britain is the only country where it is the general rule. In all other places in which the cultivators have emerged from slavery, and from that modified form of slavery, serfage, and have

[2]Lowe, Speech on the Tenure and Improvement of Land Bill, Ireland (17 May), *ibid.*, Vol. 183, col. 1086.

[3]Disraeli, in his Speech on the Redistribution of Seats Bill (14 May), *ibid.*, col. 899, referred to the argument ascribed to Socrates (469-399 B.C.) by Plato; see *Apology*, in *Euthyphro, Apology, Crito, Phaedo, Phaedrus* (Greek and English), trans. H.N. Fowler (London: Heinemann; Cambridge, Mass.: Harvard University Press, 1914), p. 106 (29^b).

[4]Plato, *Protagoras*, in *Laches, Protagoras, Meno, Euthydemus* (Greek and English), trans. W.R.M. Lamb (London: Heinemann; Cambridge, Mass.: Harvard University Press, 1914), p. 196 (343^b).

[a-a]TT the English race
[b-b]PD,TT in an exceptional fashion

not risen into the higher position of owning land in their own right, the labourer holds it, as in Ireland, directly from the landowner, and the intermediate class of well-to-do tenant-farmers has, as a general rule, no existence. Ireland is like the rest of the world, and England is the exceptional country. Then, if we are making rules for the common case, is it reasonable to draw our precedents from the exceptional one? (*Hear.*) If we are to be guided by experience in legislating for Ireland, it is Continental rather than English experience that we ought to consider, for it is on the Continent, and not in England, that we find anything like similarity of circumstances. And this explains why so much has been said in Ireland about tenant-right and fixity of tenure. For what does Continental experience tell us, as a matter of historical fact? It tells us that where this agricultural economy, in which the actual cultivator holds the land directly from the proprietor, has been found consistent with the good cultivation of the land or with the comfort and prosperity of the cultivators, the rent has not been determined, as it is in Ireland, merely by contract, but the occupier has had the protection of some sort of fixed usage. (*Hear, hear.*) The custom of the country has determined more or less precisely the rent which he should pay, and guaranteed the permanence of his tenure as long as he paid it. Such a social and agricultural system as exists in Ireland has never [c], or next to never, [c] succeeded without tenant-right and fixity of tenure. Do I therefore ask you to establish customary rents and fixity of tenure as the rule of occupancy in Ireland? (*Hear, hear.*) Certainly not. It is perhaps a sufficient reason that I know you will not do it (*laughter*); but I am also aware that what may be very wholesome when it grows up as a custom, approved and accepted by all parties, would not necessarily have the same success if, without having ever existed as a custom, it were to be enforced as [d]a law[d]. (*Hear, hear.*) Only I warn you of this. Peasant farming [e], as a rule, [e] never answers [f]anywhere[f] without fixity of tenure. If Ireland is ever to prosper with peasant farming, fixity of tenure is an indispensable condition. But you do not want to perpetuate peasant farming; you want to improve Ireland in another way. You prefer the English agricultural economy, and desire to establish that. The only mode of cultivation which seems to you beneficial is cultivation by well-to-do tenant-farmers and hired labourers. Well, Sir, there is a good deal to be said against this doctrine—it is very disputable, but I am not going to dispute it now. I accept this as the thing you have got to do, and assuming it to be desirable, I ask, how is it to be brought about? This is not the first time that a problem of this sort has been propounded. The French Economists of the eighteenth century—on the whole the most enlightened thinkers of their time—tried to deal with a state of things not unlike what you have to deal with; and they wanted exactly what you want. They had a wretched, down-trodden, half-starved race of peasant cultivators, and they wanted to have, instead of these,

[c-c]−PD,TT
[d-d]TT an act of positive legislation
[e-e]−PD,TT
[f-f]+PD,TT

comfortable farmers. Some of the more enlightened of the great landlords of France adopted the doctrines of the Economists, and would gladly have carried them into practice; but nothing came of it, and the reform of the agricultural economy of France had to wait for a revolution. (*Cheers.*) Now, to what do the best writers attribute the failure of these agricultural reformers? To this—that they aimed at putting farmers in the place of the peasants, when they should have aimed at raising the peasants into farmers. If you are going to succeed where they failed, it can only be by avoiding their error. Instead of bringing in capitalist farmers over the heads of the tenants, you have got to take the best of the present tenants, and elevate them into the comfortable farmers you want to have. You cannot evict a whole nation (*cheers*)—the country would be too hot to hold you and your new tenants if you attempted it. And supposing even that things could be made smooth for the successors of the existing peasantry by means of emigration, are you going to expatriate a whole people? (*Cheers.*) Would any honourable gentleman desire to do that? Would he endure the thought of doing it? Supposing even that you sought to use the right of landed property for such a purpose, is there any human institution which could have such a strain put upon it and not snap? (*Cheers.*) Well, then, how are the present tenantry, or the best of them, to be raised into a superior class of farmers? There is but one way, and this Bill which is before you affords the means. Give them what you can of the encouraging influences of ownership. (*Cheers.*) Give them an interest in improvement. Enable them to be secure of enjoying the fruits of their own labour and outlay. Let their improvements be for their own benefit, and not solely for those whose land they till. There is no parallel problem to be resolved on this side of St. George's Channel. The system of tenancy in England is found to be at least not incompatible with agricultural improvement. In England and Scotland a large proportion of the landowners either give leases to their tenants which afford them sufficient time for reaping the benefit of whatever improvements they may make, or, when there are no leases, there is generally such a degree of confidence and mutual understanding between landlord and tenant, that they make their improvements in concert; or at all events the tenant, as a general rule, has no fear that the landlord will take an unfair advantage of him, and, by accepting a higher offer over his head, will possess himself without compensation of the increased value which the tenant has given to the land. This is the case in England: but how is it in Ireland? The reverse in all respects. (*Oh, oh!*) There are few leases, except old and expiring ones, and no confidence at all between landlords and tenants. [g](*Oh, oh!*) Well, at least one-half[g] of the landlords, or some other proportion of them, do not deserve confidence, and the consequence is that the tenants dare not trust the other half. (*Hear, hear, and laughter.*) If a tenant does trust his landlord, he does not trust, for he does not know, the next heir, or the stranger who may buy the property

[g-g]PD] TT (*Oh, oh!*) Well, at all events, half] CS One-half

in the Landed Estates Court. The extent to which this want of confidence reaches is really one of the most remarkable facts in all history. There have been incontestable proofs of late years that the tenant farmers of Ireland often possess a considerable amount of savings. Where do these savings go to? They go into banks of deposit; they go into the English funds; they go under the thatch; everywhere but to their natural investment, the farm. (*Hear, hear.*) There is something, to my mind, almost tragical in this state of things. For the fact is decidedly honourable to Irish landlords that these savings have been made by their tenants; it exculpates a large proportion of them from the indiscriminate charges often brought against the entire [h]class[h] (*hear, hear*); it proves that a much greater number of them than has often been supposed are neither greedy nor grasping, do not rack-rent their tenants, or take the last farthing in payment of rent; and in spite of this, the tenants are so absolutely without confidence in them, that even the sums which the landlord's forbearance has enabled them to accumulate are sent away everywhere—are employed for any purpose—except the most obvious and natural purpose, the improvement of their farms. (*Hear, hear.*) Now, are you going to let this state of things continue? If we all deplore it—if we all are ashamed of it—what remedy is there but one? Give the tenant compensation, awarded by an impartial tribunal, for whatever increased value—and only for the increased value—he has given to the land. Do not use the fruits of his labour or of his outlay without paying for them, or without giving him assurance of being paid for them. (*Hear.*) The Bill appoints an impartial tribunal. When the parties do not agree, the case is to be adjudged by authorities who even in Ireland deserve and possess the confidence alike of landlords and tenants. Valuers appointed by the Government Board of Works will decide in the first instance, and the assistant barrister, the stipendiary Chairman of Quarter Sessions, is the Judge in appeal.[5] I believe no one doubts that such arbitrators as these would be impartial, and would be trusted by the Irish people. But the right honourable gentleman who spoke last (*Mr. Lowe*) said it was not so much the giving compensation he objected to, as to the fact that improvements might be made under the Bill, to which the consent of the landlord had not been previously obtained.[6] That provision, however, if we consider the matter, is the very essence of the Bill, and is indispensable to its operation. If improvements are only to be made by the landlord's permission, and on his voluntary promise of an indemnity, that can be done now; saving, indeed, some insufficiency in the legal power of a limited owner to bind his successors. But experience proves that when there is a want of confidence between landlords and tenants, improvements which require the previous consent of the landlord are not made at all. The tenant is afraid to serve a notice on his landlord. He is afraid to announce before hand to the

[5]See "A Bill Further to Amend the Law Relating to the Tenure and Improvement of Land in Ireland," pp. 360–2.

[6]Lowe, cols. 1077–8.

[h-h]TT order

landlord that he is in a condition to make improvements, lest, being mostly a tenant-at-will, he should be thought to be also in a condition to pay a higher rent. Or he fears that the landlord will do what some landlords have been known to do—withhold his assent, on the speculation that the tenant may make the improvement notwithstanding, and the landlord may be able to profit by it without paying any indemnity. (*Hear, hear.*) Or he thinks that the landlord may dislike an improving tenant, from a mere wish to keep his tenantry in a state of dependence. And what does the landlord sacrifice by renouncing the condition of previous consent? Nothing whatever but the power of taking for himself the fruits of the labour of others. (*Hear, hear.*) He will still be free to improve the estate himself, if he can and will. But if he does not, and his tenant does, he will be prevented from appropriating the value which the tenant has created, without paying him an equivalent. What he will have to pay, will be determined not by the outlay of the tenant, but by [i]the[i] value actually added to the farm by the tenant's labour or outlay, in the opinion of an impartial tribunal. It is of no consequence how much the tenant may have expended; unless he has made the land worth more money to the landlord for the landlord's uses, he will receive nothing. Even in such a case as that to which the right honourable gentleman alluded, and to which reference was frequently made before the Committee[7]—the case of a landlord wishing to consolidate his farms, and the buildings erected by the tenant not being required when such consolidation takes place—this circumstance would be taken into consideration by the valuer, and the tenant would have to bear the loss. Indeed, in no case would the landlord sustain any pecuniary loss. He would simply have to pay for value received. The objection is what would be called on almost any subject but the present, a purely abstract objection. The Bill is thought to violate a certain abstract right of property in land. I call it an abstract right, meaning that it is of no value to the possessor though it is hurtful to other people. Of what earthly use to any landed proprietor is the right of preventing improvement? (*Hear, hear.*) It is the right of the dog in the manger. Yet, wonderful to relate, even this the Bill does not take away; it leaves to the landlord the power of preventing the tenant's improvements by a previous stipulation. But it does this in the confidence—I believe the well-grounded confidence—that the power will seldom be used, except when there is something to justify it in the special circumstances of the case. The framers of the Bill place a just reliance in the influence of a sound moral principle when once embodied in the law. They know that there is a great difference between requiring the tenant to ask permission from the landlord to make improvements, and throwing the onus on the landlord of prohibiting by anticipation a public benefit (*hear*), which the law, if this Bill passes, will have

[7]Lowe, col. 1083; "Report from the Select Committee on Tenure and Improvement of Land (Ireland) Act" (23 June, 1865), *PP*, 1865, XI, pp. 405 and 509, for example.

[i-i]+PD] TT the fair

declared its purpose of encouraging. I maintain, Sir, that the claim of the improver to the value of his improvements, so far from conflicting with the right of property in land, is a right of the very same description as landed property, and rests on the same foundation. What is the ground and justification of landed property? I am afraid some honourable Members think that I am going to give utterance to some grave heresy on this subject. At least, those honourable gentlemen who have been so obliging as to advertise my writings on an unexampled scale, and entirely free of expense either to myself or [j]to my[j] publisher (*a laugh*), seemed to be much scandalized by some passages they had discovered, to the effect that landed property must be more limited in its nature than other proprietary rights, because no man made the land.[8] Well, Sir, did any man make the land? If not, did any man acquire it by gift, or by bequest, or by inheritance, or by purchase, from the maker of it? These, I apprehend, are the foundations of the right to other property. Then what is the foundation of the right to property in land? The answer commonly made to this question is enough for me, and I agree in it. Though no man made the land, men, by their industry, made the valuable qualities of it; they reclaimed it from the waste, they brought it under cultivation, they made it useful to man, and so acquired as just a title to it as men have to what they have themselves made. Very well: I have nothing to say against this. But why, I ask, is this right, which is acquired by improving the land, to be for ever confined to the person who first improved it? If it requires improving again, and some one does improve it again, does not this new improver acquire a kind of right akin to that of the original improver? Of course I do not pretend that when one person has acquired a right to land by improving it, another, by improving it again, can oust the first man of his right. But neither do I admit that the man who has once improved a piece of land, acquires thereby an indefeasible right to prevent any one else from improving it for the whole remainder of eternity (*hear, hear*); or a right to profit, without cost to himself, by improvements which some one else has made. Landed property in its origin had nothing to rest upon but the moral claim of the improver to the value of his improvement; and unless we recognise on the same ground a kindred claim in the temporary occupier, we give up the moral basis on which landed property rests, and leave it without any justification but that of actual possession—a title which can be pleaded for every possible abuse. We have heard a good deal lately about "thoughtful Reformers" [k]who seemed to be held in some sort of contempt of late (*a laugh*)[k]. It seems there are a great many thoughtful Reformers in this House—some of them very thoughtful ones indeed. I wish there were as many

[8]A phrase used in several places by Mill, but most significantly in his *Principles of Political Economy* (Bk. II, Chap. ii, Sect. 6), *CW*, Vol. II, p. 230. Both his supporters and opponents quoted much from the *Principles* and Mill's other works during his parliamentary career.

[j-j]PD] CS,TT the
[k-k]+TT

thoughtful Conservatives; but I am afraid they keep most of their thoughtfulness for Reform. However, we know there are thoughtful Conservatives, and they cannot be all on this side of the House. Let me remind them of a writer with whose works they must all of them be familiar—the most thoughtful mind that ever tried to give a philosophic basis to English Conservatism—the late Mr. Coleridge. In his second Lay Sermon, this eminent Conservative propounds a theory of property in land, compared with which anything which I ever hinted at is the merest milk and water.[9] (*A laugh.*) His idea of landed property is, that it is a kind of public function—a trust rather than a property—which the owner is morally justified in using for his own advantage, only after certain great social ends, connected with the cultivation of the country and the well-being of its inhabitants, have been amply fulfilled. I am not claiming anything comparable to this. All I ask is, that the improvement of the country and the well-being of the people may be attended to, when they are proved not to be inconsistent with the pecuniary interest of the landowners. This modest demand is the only one I make; because I believe, and because it is believed by those who are better judges of the condition of Ireland than I can pretend to be, that no more than this is necessary to cure the existing evils. Sir, the House has now a golden opportunity. When I think how small a thing it is which is now asked of us, and when I hear, as I have heard, Members of this House, usually classed as of extreme opinions—men who are Irish of the Irish, who have the full confidence of what is called the National party—when such men assure us that the tenantry, who have been scarcely touched by any of the things you have hitherto done for the benefit of Ireland, will, as they hope, and as they think there is ground to believe, be reconciled to their lot (*hear, hear*), and changed from a discontented, if not disloyal, to a hopeful and satisfied part of the nation, by so moderate—I had almost said so minute—a concession as that which is now proposed;[10] I confess I am amazed that those who have suffered so long and so bitterly are able to be conciliated or calmed by so small a gift (*hear*); and deplorable would it indeed be if so small a gift were refused to them. Even if we ourselves had not full confidence in this remedy, there is nothing in it so alarming that we need be afraid to try, as an experiment, what is so ardently wished for by a country to which we owe so much reparation that she ought to be the spoilt child of this country for a generation to come—to be treated not only with justice but with generous indulgence. (*Cheers.*) I am speaking in the presence of many who listened, like myself, to that touching speech which was delivered on the last night

[9]Samuel Taylor Coleridge (1772–1834), *Second Lay Sermon*, in *On the Condition of Church and State, and Lay Sermons* (London: Pickering, 1839), esp. pp. 413–18.

[10]For example, Fulke Southwell Greville Nugent (1821–83), also known as Colonel Greville, M.P. for Longford, Speech on the Tenure and Improvement of Land Bill, Ireland (30 Apr., 1866), *PD*, 3rd ser., Vol. 183, cols. 225–6. Cf. other speeches on the occasion by the Irish members Jonathan Pim (cols. 228–9), John Francis Maguire (cols. 230–1), and Edward Sullivan (col. 230).

of the Reform debate, by the honourable Member for Tralee (*The O'Donoghue*)—when he, who is so well entitled to speak in the name of the Irish people, and of that portion of them of whom we have had the hardest thoughts, and who have had the hardest thoughts of us, held out his hand to us and declared that if there is even one party in this House and in this country who reciprocate the feeling he then showed, and really regard the Irish as fellow-countrymen, they will be fellow-countrymen to us—they will labour and contend by our side, have the same objects with us, look forward to the same and not to a different future, and let the dream of a separate nationality remain a dream.[11] Many, I am sure, must have felt as I felt while I listened to his eloquent and feeling words, that if this House only wills it, that speech is the beginning of a new era. Let us not fling away in want of thought—for it is not want of heart—the reconciliation so frankly tendered. History will not say that we of the present generation are unwilling to [l]govern Ireland as she ought to be governed:—let us not go down to posterity with the contemptible reputation of being unable to do so[l]. Let it not be said of us that, with the best possible intentions towards Ireland, no length of time or abundance of experience could teach us to understand her—whether it is insular narrowness, making us incapable of imagining that Ireland's exigencies could be in any way different from England's; [m]or because the religious respect we cherish for everything which has the smallest savour of a right of property, has degenerated, as is sometimes the case with other religions,[m] into a superstition. Let us show that our principles of government are not a mere generalization from English facts; but that in legislating for Ireland we can take into account Irish circumstances: and that our care for landed property is an intelligent regard for its essentials, and for the ends it fulfils, and not a servile prostration before its mere name. (*Loud cheers.*)

[*After further debate on 25 July the Bill was withdrawn.*]

22. Representation of the People [5]

31 MAY, 1866

PD, 3rd ser., Vol. 183, cols. 1590–2. Reported in *The Times*, 1 June, p. 6, from which the variants and responses are taken. The continued debate was on the motion to go into Committee on the Reform Bill (see No. 15) and "A Bill for the Redistribution of Seats," 29 Victoria (7 May, 1866), *PP*, 1866, V, 33–48. The discussion was on an amendment

[11]Daniel O'Donoghue (d. 1889), then M.P. for Tralee, Speech on the Representation of the People Bill (27 Apr., 1866), *ibid.*, col. 42.

[l-l]TT treat Ireland in a spirit of kindness, fairness, and generosity

[m-m]TT let it not be said that they regarded Irish affairs with the aspect of religious prejudice, for if they viewed them in this light their religion would degenerate

opposing the government's proposal to group boroughs. After considerable debate Pakington spoke, followed by Mill.

HONOURABLE GENTLEMEN OPPOSITE in considerable numbers have shown a very great desire to inform the House, not so much as to their views on the question before us, as with regard to what I have said or written upon the subject, and they have also shown a great desire to know the reasons I have for the course which they suppose I am going to take upon the question.[1] I should be sorry to refuse any honourable Gentleman so very small a request, but I must first of all correct a mistake made by the right honourable Baronet (*Sir John Pakington*) who has just sat down. I did not allow myself to be persuaded not to speak upon the Bill of my honourable Friend the Member for Hull (*Mr. Clay*).[2] I had various reasons for the silence which I observed on that occasion. One of these I have the less hesitation in stating, because I think it is one with which the House will fully sympathize—a decided disinclination for being made a catspaw of. (*Hear, hear.*) What other reasons I had may possibly appear in the very few observations that I am now about to make, for the gratification of those honourable Gentlemen who show so much friendly concern for my consistency. No doubt it is a very flattering thing to find one's writings so much referred to and quoted; but any vanity I might have felt in consequence has been considerably dashed, by observing that honourable Gentlemen's knowledge of my writings is strictly limited to the particular passages which they quote. (*Hear, hear, and laughter.*) I suppose they found the books too dull to read any further. But if they had done me the honour to read on, they would have learnt a little more about my opinions than they seem to know. It may be that I have suggested plurality of votes and various other checks as proper parts of a general system of representation; but I should very much like to know where any Gentleman finds I have stated that checks and safeguards are required against a £7 franchise? (*Laughter.*) The proposals I made had reference to universal suffrage, of which I am a strenuous advocate. It appeared to me that certain things

[1]There had been repeated reference to Mill and his opinions in the debate of 30 May on the Elective Franchise Bill. See the speeches by Robert Montagu (1825–1902), M.P. for Huntingdonshire, who referred (col. 1491) to Mill's describing people lacking participation as a flock of sheep (*Considerations on Representative Government*, *CW*, Vol. XIX, p. 412); James Whiteside (1804–76), M.P. for the University of Dublin, who quoted (cols. 1505–8) several passages from *Thoughts on Parliamentary Reform* (*CW*, Vol. XIX, pp. 323–8); Charles Bowyer Adderley (1814–1905), M.P. for North Staffordshire (col. 1529); John Locke (1805–80), M.P. for Southwark (col. 1532); and Stafford Northcote (col. 1541). Thomas Dyke Acland (1809–98), M.P. for North Devonshire, offered (cols. 1542–3) to surrender the floor to Mill if he would speak; *PD* records that Mill "shook his head."

[2]Pakington quoted (col. 1578) from *Thoughts on Parliamentary Reform* (p. 327), and (col. 1579) from *Representative Government* (p. 450), and asserted (col. 1579) that Mill had been persuaded not to speak on "A Bill to Extend the Elective Franchise for Cities and Boroughs in England and Wales," 29 Victoria (22 Feb., 1866), *PP*, 1866, II, 493–514, brought in by James Clay (1804–73), M.P. for Hull.

were necessary in order to prevent universal suffrage from degenerating into the mere ascendancy of a particular class. Is there any danger that the working class will acquire a numerical ascendancy by the reduction of the franchise qualification to £7? It is ridiculous to suppose such a thing. (*Hear.*) The effect of the present Bill will not be to create the ascendancy of a class, but to weaken and mitigate the ascendancy of a class; and there is no need for the particular checks which I suggested. I must, however, except one of them, which is equally desirable in any representative constitution—the representation of minorities; and I heartily congratulate the right honourable Baronet on the qualified adhesion which he has given to that principle.[3] It is not intended specially as a check on democracy—it is a check upon whatever portion of the community is strongest—on any abuse of power by the class that may chance to be uppermost. Instead of being opposed to democracy, it is actually a corollary from the democratic principle, for on that principle every one would have a vote, and all votes would be of equal value; but without the representation of minorities all votes have not an equal value, for practically nearly one-half of the constituency is disfranchised, for the benefit, it may happen, not even of the majority, but of another minority. Suppose that a House of Commons is elected by a bare majority of the people, and that it afterwards passes laws by a bare majority of itself. The outvoted minority out of doors, and the outvoted minority of the Members of this House who were elected by the majority out of doors, might possibly agree; and thus a little more than one-fourth of the community would actually have defeated the remaining three-fourths. (*Hear, hear.*) On the principle of justice, therefore, and on the principle of democracy above all, the representation of minorities appears to me an absolutely necessary part of any representative constitution which it is intended should permanently work well. If the right honourable Gentleman who has declared in favour of the representation of minorities (*Sir John Pakington*) will bring forward a Motion, in any form which can possibly pass, with a view to engraft that principle upon any Bill, I shall have the greatest pleasure in seconding him. (*Hear, hear.*) I desire to make a brief explanation in reference to a passage which the right honourable Gentleman has quoted from a portion of my writings, and which has some appearance of being less polite than I should wish always to be in speaking of a great party. What I stated was, that the Conservative party was, by the law of its constitution, necessarily the stupidest party.[4] (*Laughter.*) Now, [a]I do not retract this assertion; but I did not mean that Conservatives are generally stupid;[a] I meant, that stupid persons are generally Conservative. (*Laughter and*

[3]Pakington, cols. 1582–3.

[4]Pakington (col. 1574) quoted from *Representative Government* (p. 452n) part of a passage in which Mill had referred favourably to Pakington while criticizing Disraeli; in the key phrase Mill had said: "The Conservatives, as being by the law of their existence the stupidest party," adhered less to their true principles than the Liberals.

[a-a]TT Conservatives are probably stupid, but

cheers.) I believe that to be so obvious and undeniable a fact that I hardly think any honourable Gentleman will question it. Now, if any party, in addition to whatever share it may possess of the ability of the community, has nearly the whole of its stupidity, that party, I apprehend, must by the law of its constitution be the stupidest party. And I do not see why honourable Gentlemen should feel that position at all offensive to them; for it ensures their being always an extremely powerful party. (*Hear, hear.*) I know I am liable to a retort, an obvious one enough, and as I do not intend any honourable Gentleman to have the credit of making it, I make it myself. It may be said that if stupidity has a tendency to Conservatism, sciolism and half-knowledge have a tendency to Liberalism. Well, Sir, something might be said for that—but it is not at all so clear as the other. There is an uncertainty about half-informed people. You cannot count upon them. You cannot tell what their way of thinking may be. It varies from day to day, perhaps with the last book they have read [b], and therefore they are as likely to prove Conservatives as Liberals, and as likely to be Liberals as Conservatives [b]. They are a less numerous class, and also an uncertain class. But there is a dense solid force in sheer stupidity—such, that a few able men, with that force pressing behind them, are assured of victory in many a struggle; and many a victory the Conservative party have owed to that force. (*Laughter.*) I only rose for the purpose of making this personal explanation (*hear, hear*), and I do not intend to enter into the merits of the Amendment, especially as I concur in all that has been said in the admirable speech of my right honourable Friend the Member for London (*Mr. Goschen*).[5] (*Cheers.*)

[*After lengthy debate, there was an adjournment to the following day; another long debate then led to a further adjournment to 4 June, when there was agreement to go into Committee.*]

23. The Ministerial Crisis

23 JUNE, 1866

Daily News, 25 June, 1866, p. 3. Headed: "The Ministerial Crisis. / Westminster." Reported identically in substantives in the *Morning Star*, and the *Daily Telegraph*; the version in *The Times* is a generally compressed rewording with some additions. (Clippings of the *Daily News* and *The Times* reports are in the Mill-Taylor Collection.) The meeting of the electors of Westminster was held on Saturday evening in the Pimlico Rooms, Winchester Street, W.T. Malleson in the chair, "to urge the propriety of dissolving

[5]George Joachim Goschen (1831–1907), Speech on the Representation of the People Bill, and the Redistribution of Seats Bill (31 May), *PD*, 3rd ser., Vol. 183, cols. 1560–72.

[b-b]+TT

Parliament, and voting unabated confidence in the Ministry," following Gladstone's defeat on the Reform Bill (see the debate and votes on 18 June in *PD*, 3rd ser., Vol. 184, cols. 536–643). The room was about half full, and there were only some eight or nine on the platform. Malleson apologized for Grosvenor's unavoidable absence, assuring the audience of his loyalty to the cause. Of Mill he said, "the whole country was proud, and he believed that they would seldom find in the history of the House of Commons any occasion on which a new member had so suddenly risen to so prominent a position, had so rapidly established himself in the House of Commons, and had so soon made a firm place for himself in the hearts of his fellow-countrymen. (Cheers.)" (*Daily Telegraph.*) Probyn moved, Merriman seconding, a resolution expressing confidence in the Ministry. Mill, "on rising, was greeted with tremendous applause, the whole assembly rising and cheering with extraordinary vehemence."

HE SAID they were called together that evening in order that they might ask themselves the question whether or not the people of Westminster cared for reform. That was the question before them, and that was the only question. Who would be the men for whom her Majesty would send to form an administration if she accepted the resignation of her present advisers of course they could not tell, but he could state what her Majesty ought to do, if she followed the old constitutional practice of sending for the leader of the victorious party, and that was to send for Mr. Lowe. (*Hear, hear, and laughter.*) It was he who carried with him the triumphant majority the other night, for although he was the only man amongst the opponents of the present bill who in direct terms declared he was against all reform whatever, yet all who had heard, as he had done, the shouts of rejoicing which greeted every anti-popular sentiment to which Mr. Lowe gave utterance, would know that the whole of the sympathies of the tory party were against any measure of reform, whatever it might be.[1] He believed that there were only two opinions as to what might be the course the conservatives would pursue if they were able to form a ministry—first, whether they would propose a reform bill at all; and second, whether they would propose a reform bill which was not reform. They said that any bill on this subject must be a compromise. Well, the liberal party made a compromise at the commencement of the session, and a very great compromise it was. They gave up the best part of the matter in dispute to the tories, and now after the liberals had given up to them the better half they cried halves for the remainder. (*Laughter.*) The difference was split with them in the first instance, and now they wanted to split the other part. But it was worse even than that, and he was going to tell them something which they had all the means of knowing, but which few had paid much attention to, and a very significant and characteristic process it was. He would tell them what was proposed by one of the best of the tory party. They all knew, perhaps, that a political party had heads and tails. The tails of

[1]Robert Lowe had led the "Adullamites," the Liberals dissenting from parliamentary reform, who had voted with the Conservatives to defeat the Reform Bill. Mill refers specifically to his speeches of 13 March, cols. 141–64, and of 31 May, cols. 1625–50.

the liberal party sometimes thought that the heads were not quite so good as they should be, but the tory heads were unquestionably a great deal better than the tails. One of the best of the tory heads was Sir Stafford Northcote, a gentleman for whom every one ought to entertain a very sincere respect, because it was to him, in conjunction with Sir Charles Trevelyan, that they owed those competitive examinations by which government appointments, instead of being given, as they used to be, to party connexions for political purposes, were given to proved fitness tested by fair examination.[2] Now, when a man agreed that all the spoils of office and all the booty of political life, which unprincipled politicians desired to appropriate for the interests and advancement of their party, should be given up not for the reward of political subserviency, but to persons of whatever class or rank who could prove themselves qualified for public appointments, although they might never have, perhaps, seen the face of a member of parliament, nothing should persuade him that such a man was really a tory, [a]or wished to postpone the interests of the people in order that he might advance the prosperity of his own party. That was what he thought of Sir Stafford Northcote. Well, what did they[a] put Sir Stafford Northcote up to do? They followed out their usual tactics in putting up their best men to do their shabbiest things. All present knew how much had been said about large numbers of working people being admitted to the franchise, and how solemnly parliament had been warned that if they let in many more there might be a majority, who would be induced to let in others, until at length the door was opened so wide that all were let in, and that then Heaven knew what would be the result. Now what did they think Sir Stafford Northcote proposed?[3] If a working man could occupy a 10*l*. house it must in most cases be by letting some part of it, but Sir Stafford Northcote proposed to disfranchise all such persons, unless they were able to show that, after deducting all they received from letting, they paid 10*l*. or 7*l*., or whatever other sum might be agreed upon, to their landlord. [b]Probably he would have spared those who were at present on the register, but he would not consent that any one hereafter should be on the register who did not pay to his landlord that 10*l*. or 7*l*., or other sum. That was a condition which very few working men could fulfil;[b] and if that proposition came from one of the best, most honest, and most liberal members of the conservative party, what might they

[2]Charles Edward Trevelyan (1807–86), who had served with the East India Company, had, while Assistant Secretary to the Treasury, co-authored with Northcote the "Report on the Organisation of the Permanent Civil Service," *PP*, 1854, XXVII, 1–31, which led to Civil Service examinations.

[3]Motion on the Representation of the People Bill (14 June, 1866), *PD*, 3rd ser., Vol. 184, col. 449.

[a-a]TT nor an aristocrat in the ordinary sense of the term. No doubt, Sir Stafford Northcote wanted good government rather than the government of a class; and yet what did they think the tory party had

[b-b]TT He did not wish to do the honourable baronet any injustice, and, therefore, he assumed that it was his intention to spare those already on the register; but so adverse would the plan he proposed be to working men that, if applied to those who occupied 10*l*. houses, it would disfranchise most of them.

expect from the others? (*Hear, hear.*) Now, as to the foreign policy of the tories, he wished all those present could have listened as he had done to the five hours of solemn abuse of the Italians, in which the tories had indulged when the Reform Bill should have been brought under discussion.[4] Liberals, panting to help and defend the noble Italians against the calumnies heaped upon them, were restrained from entering upon the discussion, [c]lest they should have delayed the bill on which the hearts of reformers were set[c]. But now came the question of the present government. All knew the noble manner in which they had held up the banner of the people through the late stormy session. Their political enemies had been taunting them and insulting them day after day, saying that here was a government which started with a clear majority of seventy, and had converted it into a minority of eleven. Well, so they had, and why had they done it? There was a majority of seventy pledged to support a liberal government, and who would have supported them if they had followed out Lord Palmerston's policy of doing nothing, and glossing it off as an excellent joke.[5] The government might have a seven years' undisturbed lease of power if they had adopted a similar course—that is, if they had determined on doing nothing in the way of reform. But they had chosen to resign office, to receive baiting, taunts, and insults, directed against them all; but more particularly against Mr. Gladstone, the greatest parliamentary leader which the country had had in the present century, or, perhaps, since the time of the Stuarts [d], by those who ought to have been in ecstacies of admiration at the way in which he outdid himself and at the beautiful feeling which animated his eloquence. Like Hotspur, he had been nettled and stung by pismires,[6] that annoyance had been inflicted in the hope that either he might be led to give way to something like foolish irritability, or that those eloquent lips, which gave such happy expression to every feeling that became an honest and upright politician, might deny to themselves the utterance of honest indignation[d]. Whatever the speculation might have been, it had been defeated—the hopes of the opponents of the government had not been fulfilled. (*Hear, hear.*) [e]As to dissolution, he, as member for Westminster, was the last who should speak to his constituents of a dissolution; because, perhaps, he was the only member of the House of Commons whose election had cost him nothing. [e] It would appear to him the most natural thing that

[4]Debate on the State of Europe (11 June), *ibid.*, cols. 117–76.

[5]Henry John Temple (1784–1865), Lord Palmerston in the Irish peerage, a member of every administration except those of Peel and Derby from 1807 till his death, Prime Minister 1855–58 and 1859–65, and best known for his control over foreign affairs.

[6]Shakespeare, *Henry IV, Part I*, I, iii, 240; in *The Riverside Shakespeare*, ed. G. Blakemore Evans (Boston: Houghton Mifflin, 1974), p. 853.

[c–c]TT but they did not do so because they knew that the object of the other party was to delay the Reform Bill, and because Mr. Gladstone, in his usual noble manner, said what ought to have been said on the subject

[d–d]+TT

[e–e]+TT

his constituents might not like to incur this great expense twice in the same twelve months. (*Yes, yes.*) It was very natural that they should not wish it, and he should not have the face to ask it for himself. If they thought they could fight this battle more advantageously with any other candidate than himself—any candidate who would bear the expenses that must necessarily be incurred, or part of them—he trusted that no consideration for himself would induce them to refrain from taking that course. [f]So far from thinking himself slighted, he would be the first to condemn them if they lost the seat on the chance of preserving it for him.[f] They had, above all things, to consider how they could carry this bill and support the government, and he most sincerely hoped that no other consideration would induce them to allow that object to be interfered with.

[g]*At the close of the honourable member's speech the meeting with one accord declared that the electors would pay the expenses of his election 50 times, if necessary, and would esteem themselves honoured in having him as their representative. The resolution was then agreed to. In reply to a question from an elector, Mr. Mill said that* Captain Grosvenor had not suffered in the estimation of his political friends by his vote in favour of Sir R. Knightley's amendment for an instruction to the committee to add to the Reform Bill provisions against bribery and corruption.[7] It was a question of tactics. He voted the other way; but, no doubt, Captain Grosvenor thought his vote was in favour of the best policy, and it had not shaken the confidence of the Liberal party in the honourable and gallant gentleman's political honesty.[g]

[*Another resolution in support of the Ministry was moved and accepted unanimously. The meeting concluded, as usual, with a vote of thanks to the chairman.*]

24. The Jamaica Committee

9 JULY, 1866

Daily News, 10 July, p. 3. Headed: "The Jamaica Committee." Reported also in the *Morning Star, The Times*, and (in brief summary) in the *Daily Telegraph*. This special meeting of the Jamaica Committee was held in the evening in Radley's Hotel, Bridge Street, with P.A. Taylor in the chair. The meeting was called because Charles Buxton had published a letter in *The Times*, 30 June, p. 12, and other papers resigning his chairmanship and strongly criticizing the Committee's action. He believed that the Executive Committee had decided by a vote of 11 to 3 to prosecute the ex-Governor of Jamaica, Edward John Eyre

[7]Rainauld Knightley (1819–95), M.P. for Northamptonshire South, made the motion in his Speech on the Representation of the People Bill (28 May, 1866), *PD*, 3rd ser., Vol. 183, cols. 1320–1; Grosvenor's vote is recorded *ibid.*, col. 1345.

[f-f]+TT
[g-g]+TT

(1815–1901), for the murder of George William Gordon 1818–65), a popular Jamaican leader. The meeting opened with a summary of events by Taylor, who condemned the way Buxton had proceeded, his view being that the general opinion at the earlier meeting, not confirmed by a vote, was that the Committee should press the Government to prosecute Eyre for murder, failing which they should give assistance to Gordon's widow to carry on a prosecution. When Buxton defended himself, Bright countered in scathing terms. Ludlow moved "That this committee approves and confirms the resolutions passed by the executive committee on the 26th of June"; Goldwin Smith seconded. T.F. Buxton spoke in support of Charles Buxton's actions, and after further speeches the resolution was passed with one dissenting vote. A motion by Beales that Mill be elected chairman was adopted unanimously. Then Mill spoke.

GENTLEMEN, I thank you for this honour and mark of your confidence. I accept the post you have given me. (*Cheers.*) I do so in the full conviction that the objects of this committee are simply to ascertain whether there exist in this country any means for making a British functionary responsible for blood unlawfully shed—(*applause*)—and whether that be murder or not. I believe it to be murder. (*Hear, hear.*) This committee ought not to rest until it obtains from the legislature the assurance that men like Mr. Eyre will be made responsible for their criminal actions. (*Hear, hear.*)

[*Votes of thanks were passed to Messrs. Gorrie and Payne, solicitors, for their services in Jamaica, and to the chair, and the meeting separated.*]

25. Electoral Franchise for Women

17 JULY, 1866

PD, 3rd ser., Vol. 184, cols. 996–8. Reported in *The Times*, 18 July, p. 8, from which the variant and responses are taken. Mill spoke in moving "for an Address for 'Return of the number of Freeholders, Householders, and others in England and Wales who, fulfilling the conditions of property or rental prescribed by Law as the qualification for the Electoral Franchise, are excluded from the Franchise by reason of their sex.'"

SIR, I rise to make the Motion of which I have given notice.[1] After the petition which I had the honour of presenting a few weeks ago, the House would naturally expect that its attention would be called, however briefly, to the claim preferred in that document.[2] The petition, and the circumstances attendant on its preparation,

[1]See "Parliamentary Intelligence. House of Commons, Friday, June 8," *The Times*, 9 June, 1866, p. 6. (The notice of motion is not recorded in *PD* or the *Journals of the House of Commons*.)

[2]"Petition for Admission of Women to the Electoral Franchise" (7 June, 1866), *Reports of the Select Committee of the House of Commons on Public Petitions, Session 1866*, p. 697. The petition had 1521 signatures, headed by those of Barbara Bodichon, Clementia Taylor, and Emily Davies.

have, to say the least, greatly weakened the chief practical argument which we have been accustomed to hear against any proposal to admit women to the electoral franchise—namely, that few, if any, women desire it. Originating as that petition did entirely with ladies, without the instigation, and, to the best of my belief, without the participation of any person of the male sex in any stage of the proceedings, except the final one of its presentation to Parliament, the [a]amount of response which became manifest, the number of signatures obtained in a very short space of time, not to mention the quality of many of those signatures, may not have been surprising to the ladies who promoted the petition, but was certainly quite unexpected by me[a]. I recognize in it the accustomed sign that the time has arrived when a proposal of a public nature is ripe for being taken into serious consideration—namely, when a word spoken on the subject is found to have been the expression of a silent wish pervading a great number of minds, and a signal given in the hope of rallying a few supporters is unexpectedly answered by many. It is not necessary to offer any justification for the particular Motion which I am about to make. (*Hear, hear.*) When the complaint is made that certain citizens of this nation, fulfilling all the conditions and giving all the guarantees which the Constitution and the law require from those who are admitted to a voice in determining who shall be their rulers, are excluded from that privilege for what appears to them, and for what appears to me, an entirely irrelevant consideration, the least we can do is to ascertain what number of persons are affected by the grievance, and how great an addition would be made to the constituency if this disability were removed. I should not have attempted more than this in the present Session, even if the recent discussions in reference to Reform had not been brought to an abrupt close. Even if the late Government had succeeded in its honourable attempt to effect an amicable compromise of the Reform question, any understanding or any wish which might have existed as to the finality, for a certain period, of that compromise, could not have effected such a proposal as this, the adoption of which would not be, in any sense of the term, a lowering of the franchise, and is not intended to disturb in any degree the distribution of political power among the different classes of society. Indeed, honourable Gentlemen opposite seem to think, and I suppose they are the best judges, that this concession, assuming it to be made, if it had any effect on party politics at all, would be favourable to their side (*hear*); and the right honourable Member for Dublin University, in his humorous manner, advised me on that ground to withdraw this article from my political programme;[3] but I cannot, either in jest or in earnest, adopt his suggestion, for I am bound to consider the permanent benefit of the community before the temporary interest of a party; and I entertain the firmest

[3]James Whiteside, Speech on the Elective Franchise Bill (30 May, 1866), *PD*, 3rd ser., Vol. 183, col. 1509.

[a-a]TT ladies themselves who had originated the petition had been surprised at the great number of signatures it had obtained

conviction that whatever holds out an inducement to one-half of the community to exercise their minds on the great social and political questions which are discussed in Parliament, and whatever causes the great influence they already possess to be exerted under the guidance of greater knowledge, and under a sense of responsibility, cannot be ultimately advantageous to the Conservative or any other cause, except so far as that cause is a good one. And I rejoice in the knowledge that in the estimation of many honourable Gentlemen of the party opposite, the proposal made in the petition is, like many of the most valuable Reforms, as truly Conservative, as I am sure it is truly Liberal. I listened with pleasure and gratitude to the right honourable Gentleman who is now Chancellor of the Exchequer, when in his speech on the second reading of the Reform Bill,[4] he said he saw no reason why women of independent means should not possess the electoral franchise, in a country where they can preside in manorial courts and fill parish offices—to which let me add, and the Throne. (*Hear, hear.*)

[*Spencer Walpole said he would consent to the motion, without pledging himself to any future action, and the motion was agreed to.*]

26. The Disturbances in Jamaica [1]

19 JULY, 1866

PD, 3rd ser., Vol. 184, cols. 1064–6. Reported in *The Times*, 20 July, p. 5.

MR. J. STUART MILL SAID, wishing to spare the House the monotonously painful details contained in the Questions of which he had given notice, he would simply ask the right honourable Gentleman the Chancellor of the Exchequer,[1] Whether any steps had been or would be taken by Her Majesty's Government for bringing to justice those who had been concerned in the commission of various illegal acts in Jamaica?

The Chancellor of the Exchequer: I should prefer, Sir, that the honourable Gentleman should ask the Questions in detail. I think the Questions which the honourable Gentleman has thought proper in his discretion to address to the Executive should be well known to the House, as many honourable Members have not really had an opportunity of making themselves acquainted with them. Under these circumstances, it is due to the House and to the subject that the honourable

[4]Disraeli, Speech on the Representation of the People Bill (27 Apr., 1866), *ibid.*, col. 99.

[1]Benjamin Disraeli.

Gentleman should address himself now to the House, and let them hear what the Questions are. (Hear, hear.)

Mr. J. Stuart Mill: Does the right honourable Gentleman desire me to read the whole?

The Chancellor of the Exchequer: The whole.

Mr. J. Stuart Mill: I beg to ask Mr. Chancellor of the Exchequer, Whether any steps have been or will be taken to bring to trial Lieutenant Adcock,[2] for unlawfully putting to death two men named Mitchell and Hill without trial, and six persons, after alleged trial by Court Martial, on charges not cognizable by a Military Court; for flogging, without trial, John Anderson and others, and authorizing one Henry Ford to flog many men and women without trial, one of whom, named John Mullins, died in consequence: Whether any steps have been or will be taken to bring to trial Captain Hole for hanging one Donaldson without trial; for shooting, and permitting to be shot, various persons without trial; for putting to death by hanging, or shooting, thirty-three persons, after trial by a so-called Military Court, for acts not cognizable by a Military Court, and without observance of the rules prescribed by the Articles of War; for flogging various men and women without trial; and for being accessory, after the fact, to the unlawful putting to death of numerous persons by soldiers under his command: Whether any steps have been or will be taken to bring to trial Lieutenant Oxley, for putting John Burdy to death after a similar unlawful trial, and for permitting the men under his command to fire at unarmed peasants and cause the death of several persons: Whether any steps have been or will be taken to bring to trial Ensign Cullen and Dr. Morris, for putting three men[3] to death without trial, and Dr. Morris for shooting one William Gray: Whether any steps have been or will be taken to bring to trial Stipendiary Magistrate Fyfe, for burning houses of peasantry, putting to death one person without trial,[4] and being accessory to the unlawful putting to death of various others: Whether any steps have been or will be taken to bring to trial Attorney General Heslop, Lieutenant Brand, Captain Luke, and Captain Field, for sitting as presidents or members of alleged Courts Martial, by whom numerous persons were unlawfully put to death: Whether any steps have been or will be taken to bring to trial General O'Connor, for having been accessory before and after the fact to numerous unlawful executions, some of them without trial, and others after the illegal trials already specified: Whether any steps have been or will be taken to bring to trial Colonel Nelson, Brigadier General in Jamaica, for unlawfully causing to be tried, in time of peace, by Military Courts irregularly composed, for acts alleged to have been done before the proclamation or beyond the jurisdiction

[2]For the people named in this question, see App. H. The six hanged by Adcock were John Landran, Dick Hall, John Lawrence, James McKenzie, William Winter, and one whose name is unknown.

[3]Richard Walton, John McCall, and Tommy Miles (*alias* Tom Bell).

[4]Henry Patterson.

of Martial Law, and after such trial to be unlawfully put to death, the following persons:—George William Gordon, Edward Fleming, Samuel Clarke, William Grant, George Macintosh, Henry Lawrence, Letitia Geoghan, and six other women, one of them in a state of pregnancy;[5] Scipio Cowell, Alexander Taylor, Toby Butler, Jasper Hall Livingston, and various other persons who had been previously flogged, and about 180 other alleged rebels; and for authorizing the flogging without trial of Alexander Phillips, Richard Clark, and numerous others: Whether any legal proceedings have been or will be ordered to be taken against Mr. Edward John Eyre, lately Governor of Jamaica, for complicity in all or any of the above acts, and particularly for the illegal trial and execution of Mr. George William Gordon: And, if not, whether Her Majesty's Government are advised that these acts are not offences under the Criminal Law?

[*In response, after expressing his annoyance at the way in which Mill had embodied opinions in his questions, thus "trespassing in some degree upon the liberty and freedom of expression" of the House, Disraeli pointed out that the first nine questions assumed that illegal actions had been taken by individuals, while the tenth asked if the Government was of opinion that the actions were illegal. Not only were the questions put in a form that could lead to great inconvenience, but in substance they were inaccurate. First, Mill ignored the fact that martial law was in force in Jamaica, and so ordinary law was superseded. Second, he ignored the fact that the cases against Cullen and Morris were not proved on the evidence presented, and that further inquiries were being made. Similarly, the statements Mill made against Nelson were not founded on fact. Disraeli then went on to state what had happened: the former Government had—properly in his view—set up a Commission of eminent men whose inquiry led them to recommend the removal of Eyre, and had acted on the Commission's recommendation. The Commission also recommended that the conduct of subordinate officers should be investigated by the Admiralty and the Horse Guards; the former had decided no fresh inquiry was needed, and the latter was still considering the matter. In the circumstances, Mill was quite wrong to be impatient and press for actions that would, if necessary, be taken at the appropriate time. "This being the state of the case," Disraeli concluded, "I am not prepared to offer any further information to the honourable Gentleman."*]

[5]Ellen Dawkins, Judy Edwardes, Mary Ann Francis, Justina Taylor, Mary Ward, and another, unnamed woman who was shot during delivery of a child, according to one witness.

27. The Reform Meeting in Hyde Park [1]

19 JULY, 1866

PD, 3rd ser., Vol. 184, col. 1075. Reported in *The Times*, 20 July, p. 3, from which the variant is taken. P.A. Taylor first asked the Home Secretary, Spencer Walpole (1806–98), then M.P. for Cambridge University, by whose authority, and under what law, the Police Commissioner, Richard Mayne, had issued an order forbidding a public meeting in Hyde Park. Walpole replied that he had himself instructed Mayne, on the grounds that a meeting in a Royal Park would interfere with the recreation of quiet and orderly people. Mill then put his question.

I WISH, SIR, to ask the Secretary of State for the Home Department, Whether we are to understand that the prohibition which he authorized to be issued as to the contemplated public meeting is based only on the circumstance that the meeting was announced to be held in one of the parks? If so—[a]*(Cries of Order, order, which prevented the honourable member from proceeding.)*[a]

Mr. Walpole: I may perhaps be permitted to say that the notice which has been issued is grounded on the circumstance that the meeting was to have been held in Hyde Park; and I may venture to add, as this Question has been put to me, that I hope the notice which I have caused to be issued will not be interpreted as being intended in the least degree to prevent the holding of ordinary public meetings for political discussion, but simply for the preservation of the public peace.

28. W.E. Gladstone [1]

21 JULY, 1866

Daily Telegraph, 23 July, 1866, p. 2. Headed: "The Cobden Club." Reported fully in *The Times*, the *Morning Post*, and (in shorter form) the *Daily News*. (A clipping of the last is in the Mill-Taylor Collection.) The report in the *Daily Telegraph* gives the background to the formation of the Club, mentions its advanced liberalism, and gives a list of the eighty-five members from the Commons, including Mill. The occasion was the inaugural dinner of the Cobden Club, on Saturday evening, at the Star and Garter Hotel, Richmond. A meeting of the Club was held before the dinner, at which fifteen members, including Mill, were appointed as a governing committee. Gladstone presided at the dinner, Mill being one of the vice-chairs. Just before the speeches began, several ladies took seats in a small gallery placed at the side of the room. After the traditional toasts to the Queen and other members of the Royal Family, Gladstone gave the toast of the evening, "To the Revered Memory of Mr. Cobden," in a long speech. The toast was drunk in silence, and then Goldwin Smith, "in a very animated" (but unreported) speech, gave the "Health of Lord Russell," to which

[a-a]TT] PD (*Order, order.*)

Russell replied at length; Russell next proposed the health of Mrs. Cobden. Mill, "who met with the most cordial reception," then spoke.

THERE IS ONE PART of the business of the evening which still remains to be performed; and though I am sensible of my incompetency to do it justice, I cannot but feel some pride in its having been entrusted to me. It is that of tendering our grateful acknowledgments to the distinguished statesman who has done this club the honour of presiding at its inauguratory meeting. (*Loud cheers.*) The nature of this commemoration, which is not of a party, nor even, in the narrower sense of the term, of a political character, [a]discloses[a] to us on this occasion many of the most important topics which are connected in all our minds with Mr. Gladstone's name. (*Hear, hear.*) One thing, however, not only may but ought to be said on such an occasion as the present; that to him of all men belonged the post of honour in a celebration of the great apostle of commercial freedom, being, as he is, the one survivor of the three eminent men by whom, as Ministers, that cause has been most effectually served. (*Cheers.*) If Mr. Huskisson opened the long and arduous campaign; if Sir Robert Peel achieved its most signal and most decisive victory,[1] Mr. Gladstone will be for ever remembered as he who completed the conquest, and who not only made freedom of trade and industry the universal rule of the institutions of our country, but by the brilliant success of his application of it is fast converting the whole of Europe to its principles. (*Cheers.*) There is another thing which this is, perhaps, a suitable opportunity for saying. Veneration for the memory of Mr. Cobden is not confined to any section of the Liberal party, nor even to the Liberal party itself. (*Hear, hear.*) But it has so happened, owing principally to the cast of Mr. Cobden's own political opinions, that an unusual proportion of the original members of this club is composed of gentlemen who would be classed, and who would class themselves, as what are called advanced Liberals. (*Cheers.*) As being one of these, I may say for myself, and I believe they would all join with me in saying, that we claim our fair share, and no more than our fair share, in the great leader of the Liberal party. (*Cheers.*) It is one of the differences between a party of Progress and any Conservative party, that its political sympathies are not restricted to those who conform, or who pretend to conform, to those of a distinctive creed. We have not bound ourselves by any narrow articles of orthodoxy—ours is a broad church. (*A laugh.*) The bond which holds us together is not a political confession of faith, but a common allegiance to the spirit of improvement, which is a greater thing than the particular opinions of any politician or set of politicians. And if there ever was a statesman in whom the spirit of

[1]William Huskisson (1770–1830), advocate of free trade, influential cabinet minister and member of the Board of Trade 1823–27; Robert Peel (1788–1850) during his term as Prime Minister was responsible for the reduction of many duties and worked for the repeal of the corn laws.

[a–a]MP] DT,DN closes] TT recalls

improvement was incarnate—of whose career as a Minister the characteristic feature has been to seek out things which required or admitted of improvement, instead of waiting to be compelled or even to be solicited to it—that honour belongs to [b]the late Chancellor of the Exchequer and leader of the House of Commons[b]. (*Cheers.*) I might stop here; but, fresh as most of us are from listening to that magnificent speech which went forth last night[2] to the furthest extremity of Europe as the utterance, in the noblest language, of what is felt and thought by all the best part of the British nation—(*loud cheers*)—for sympathy with freedom and national independence is not exclusively confined to any section, or even to any party, among us—I should not do justice to the feelings of those present were I to sit down without giving expression to the pride, and more than pride, to the hopefulness with which we are filled when we see the author of that speech standing at the head of the Liberal party to lead it to victory. (*Cheers.*) That speech was not only a splendid specimen of oratory, it was also a good action; for it will [c]cheer[c] those who are struggling and suffering in the cause of freedom and progress; while its value is inestimable in raising—when I remember certain speeches, I might almost say in redeeming—the character of England. I propose "The health of the Right Honourable William Gladstone." (*Loud cheers.*)

[*Gladstone in reply*] *expressed his sincerest thanks to Mr. Mill for the kind way in which he had given the toast, and to the company for the reception they had been pleased to pay it. He was the more grateful to Mr. Mill because he could not forget that he was one of the most distinguished and powerful critics of the day, and, at the same time, possessed the most generous feelings of the heart. (Hear, hear.)* [*He also expressed thanks to Russell and to colleagues in the House for their support. The dinner concluded about eleven o'clock.*]

29. The Reform Meeting in Hyde Park [2]

24 JULY, 1866

PD, 3rd ser., Vol. 184, cols. 1410–12. Reported in *The Times*, 25 July, p. 7, from which the variants and responses are taken. The debate was initiated by a question from Bernal Osborne (cols. 1385–6) to the Home Secretary about the instructions given to Mayne (see No. 27). Ayrton rushed in with other questions in a long speech, in which, after asking what steps Walpole had taken "for disabusing the minds of the people of the erroneous impression that they have a right to use the park for their own purposes" and for preserving the peace of the metropolis, he moved adjournment. Mill joined the ensuing debate.

[2]Gladstone, Speech on Foreign Policy (20 July), *PD*, 3rd ser., Vol. 184, cols. 1241–52.

[b-b]DN,MP,TT] DT Mr. Gladstone
[c-c]TT invigorate

SIR, I have no intention of taking up much of the time of the House, but this is no ordinary occasion, and it seems to me that noble Lords and honourable Gentlemen opposite are by no means aware of the extreme seriousness of it, and of the serious consequences to which it may lead [a]if some steps be not taken, of which at present there appears no promise[a]. (*Hear.*) I am not going to enter into the question of the right of the people to meet in Hyde Park. We know that Her Majesty's Government have the opinion of eminent lawyers to the contrary.[1] We know that they believe they have the right to exclude the people. But lawyers are not unanimous on the subject; there are other distinguished lawyers, who, on legal and high constitutional grounds, have contended that the people have a right to meet there. But I do not desire to lay any stress on this circumstance. I maintain that if the people have not that right now, they ought to have it. (*Hear.*) I maintain further, that if, for reasons unintelligible to me, it was thought necessary for the maintenance of any supposed or nominal right that the people should ask permission to hold a meeting there, that permission ought to have been granted. (*Hear.*) And it ought ten thousand times more to have been granted to them under such circumstances as these, when they believed, erroneously or not, that they had the right; for surely this circumstance, when the people were already in an excited state of mind on another subject, ought to have warned right honourable Gentlemen opposite that the consequences would be such as have actually occurred, and which I believe the people deplore equally with himself. But I maintain that the public ought to have the use of the Park for this purpose, for if not, what other place is there that can suit them? In what other place can they meet where there would be less interruption to recreation? Is there likely to be less interruption to traffic, or to other pursuits or persons, in Trafalgar Square than in Hyde Park? Does a public meeting, if it were held once [b]a month—in the evening, too—[b] cause a thousandth part of the interruption that an ordinary review or meeting of Volunteers in the Park does? If such reasons as these are to exclude the public from meeting in the Parks, which assuredly must be held to belong to the public, for they have been ceded by the Crown to the public for a consideration—like other Crown lands—if these reasons are to prevail to exclude the people, there is no place for which equally strong reasons might not be given for their exclusion. Perhaps this is what honourable Gentlemen opposite wish. I give full credit, indeed, to the assurance which the Home Secretary has given us, that he has no desire to prevent political meetings.[2] I believe in the perfect sincerity of what he said; but I cannot say that it has altogether reassured me. He said he had no objection to open air meetings at proper hours and in the proper places; but he did not tell us what the proper times or the proper places were in his opinion, and

[1]Walpole, Speech on the Reform Meeting in Hyde Park (24 July, 1866), *PD*, 3rd ser., Vol. 184, cols. 1391–8.

[2]*Ibid.*

[a-a]TT from the step which they had taken

[b-b]TT in every two or three years

the newspaper scribes of the Government are already declaring that no open air meeting ought to be tolerated in the metropolis.[3] I advise them to try that. I promise them that they will have to encounter an opposition of a very different kind, and from different persons, to any they have yet encountered. (*Hear, hear, from the Ministerial side of the House.*) Noble Lords and right honourable Gentlemen opposite may be congratulated on having done a job of work last night which will require wiser men than they are, many years to efface the consequences of. (*Hear, hear.*) It has been the anxious wish of all those who understand their age, and are lovers of their country, that the necessary changes in the institutions of the country should be effected with the least possible, and if possible without any, alienation and ill blood between the hitherto governing classes and the mass of the people. Her Majesty's present advisers seem resolved, so far as it depends upon them, that this anxious desire should be frustrated. (*Cries of Oh, oh, and Hear, hear.*) We know that there is a kind of people who can do more mischief in an hour than can be repaired in a lifetime. (*Ministerial cheers.*) I am afraid that the Members of the present Government are animated by the noble ambition of inscribing their names on the illustrious list of those [c]persons[c]. (*Hear.*)

[*The debate was ended by the withdrawal of Osborne's question (col. 1416).*]

30. The Value of Land

25 JULY, 1866

PD, 3rd ser., Vol. 184, col. 1482. Reported in *The Times*, 26 July, p. 6. Mill's intervention came during the second reading of the Tenure and Improvement of Land Bill (see No. 21), after Frederick William Heygate (1822–94), M.P. for Londonderry, had said that Mill had (in No. 21) made an error when comparing rents in England and Ireland without taking the larger Irish acre into account. Mill, however, made no such error, nor, apparently, did anyone else in the debate.

MR. J. STUART MILL EXPLAINED, THAT he had made no comparison of the value of land per acre in England and Ireland. Either, therefore, he must have ill expressed himself, or the honourable Baronet must have attributed to him remarks made by some other Member.

[*The Bill was withdrawn after a few more speeches.*]

[3]See leading articles in *The Times*, 21 July, p. 9, and 24 July, p. 9.

[c-c]TT mischief makers

31. The Reform Meeting in Hyde Park [3]

26 JULY, 1866

PD, 3rd ser., Vol. 184, cols. 1540–1. Reported in *The Times*, 27 July, p. 2, from which the variants and responses are taken. In his *Autobiography* Mill puts great weight on his intervention in this affair: "At this crisis I really believe that I was the means of preventing much mischief. . . . I was invited, with several other Radical members, to a conference with the leading members of the Council of the Reform League; and the task fell chiefly upon myself of persuading them to give up the Hyde Park project, and hold their meeting elsewhere. It was not Mr. Beales and Colonel Dickson who needed persuading; on the contrary, it was evident that those gentlemen had already exerted their influence in the same direction, thus far without success. It was the working men who held out: and so bent were they on their original scheme that I was obliged to have recourse to *les grands moyens*. I told them that a proceeding which would certainly produce a collision with the military, could only be justifiable on two conditions: if the position of affairs had become such that a revolution was desirable, and if they thought themselves able to accomplish one. To this argument after considerable discussion they at last yielded: and I was able to inform Mr. Walpole that their intention was given up. I shall never forget the depth of his relief or the warmth of his expressions of gratitude. . . . I have entered thus particularly into this matter because my conduct on this occasion gave great displeasure to the Tory and Tory-Liberal press, who have charged me ever since with having shewn myself, in the trials of public life, intemperate and passionate. I do not know what they expected from me; but they had reason to be thankful to me if they knew from what I had in all probability preserved them. And I do not believe it could have been done, at that particular juncture, by any one else. No other person, I believe, had at that moment the necessary influence for restraining the working classes, except Mr. Gladstone and Mr. Bright, neither of whom was available: Mr. Gladstone, for obvious reasons; Mr. Bright, because he was out of town." (*CW*, Vol. I, pp. 278–9.) Bernal Osborne having put questions to the Home Secretary concerning his discussions on 25 July about the Reform League's plan to hold a meeting in Hyde Park on the following Monday, Walpole replied that the situation had been much exacerbated by the League's action in announcing that the Government had given permission, when in fact no permission for a meeting in Hyde Park had been or would be given until legal opinion had been received. A meeting could be held on Primrose Hill if the League wished. Mill spoke immediately after Walpole.

SIR, I rise to make a statement [a], with the indulgence of the House,[a] which I believe will give satisfaction to the whole House. I have just had an interview with Mr. Beales[1] and several leading members of the League, including all those who were present at the second interview to which the right honourable Gentleman has referred.[2] I have full authority from them to say this, that so far as they are concerned there is no intention of renewing the attempt to meet in the Park. There

[1]Edmond Beales (1803–81), a barrister, was President of the Reform League.

[2]Walpole, Speech on the Proposed Reform Meeting in Hyde Park (26 July), *PD*, 3rd ser., Vol. 184, col. 1538.

[a-a]+TT

has been no council of the League held, and they are not, therefore, in a position to speak for the League. (*Laughter.*) That ribald laugh might well have been spared. Do honourable Members suppose that Reformers do not mean what they say? I tell them that they do. What I have to say is that these gentlemen regret exceedingly that a misunderstanding should have occurred with regard to the communication made to them by the right honourable Gentleman the Secretary of State for the Home Department. They are perfectly certain that the misunderstanding is in no way imputable to him. The interview left on them the most favourable impression of his feelings, disposition, and character, and there is nothing which they would more regret than to say anything which [b]could in the slightest degree reflect on[b] him. (*Hear, hear.*) That being the case, it is unnecessary to enter into the circumstances, though I might state something that might, perhaps, account for this misunderstanding. But the misunderstanding having taken place, the same motives which induced them to exert themselves last night so as to prevent what they believed would have otherwise resulted in bloodshed, preclude them from taking any advantage of, or in any way acting on, what is now shown to have been a misconception. Whether they will accept the offer of Primrose Hill, or consider that on this occasion it is better to abstain from meeting altogether, I am not authorized to state, and probably they do not consider themselves authorized to decide on that offer without consulting the council of the League. But, so far as their influence goes, nothing will be done that can possibly afford cause for any further [c]disturbance[c]. (*Hear, hear.*)

32. The Reform Meeting in Hyde Park [4]

30 JULY, 1866

Daily News, 31 July, 1866, p. 3. Headed: "The Reform League Demonstration in the Agriculture-Hall." Reported also in *The Times*, the *Daily Telegraph*, the *Morning Star*, and the *Morning Post* (in *The Times* and the *Morning Post* Mill's speech is given in the third person, in the latter case in brief summary). (A clipping of the *Daily News* version is in the Mill-Taylor Collection.) The meeting, held in the Agriculture Hall in Islington at 8 p.m., was chaired by Edmond Beales. Placards had announced that several Members of Parliament would be present, including Mill (who, the *Morning Post* says, "did not seem in good health"). In his *Autobiography*, following his account of his role in the discussions between Walpole and the leaders of the Reform League (see No. 31), Mill says: "After the working men had conceded so much to me, I felt bound to comply with their request that I would attend and speak at their meeting at the Agricultural Hall: the only meeting called by the Reform League which I ever attended." (He dissented from the League's proposals for

[b-b]TT might be offensive to
[c-c]TT collision

manhood suffrage and the ballot.) (*CW*, Vol. I, p. 278.) The enormous building, in which it was very difficult to hear speeches under ideal conditions, was occupied by thousands of working men, and some women. While admission to the body of the hall was free, entrance to the galleries cost 1*s*., while a few reserved seats on and adjacent to the platform were priced at 10*s*. The turbulent and noisy crowd, stimulated by songs (the "Marseillaise" being particularly popular), made it virtually impossible for any of the speakers to be heard; the reporters' table, originally protected by the reserved seats, was eventually exposed to the surges of the crowd, making even less reliable the reports of the speeches. When the platform party arrived, Beales was unable to act in the normal fashion, and had to mount a table to make his opening remarks, which could be heard only after fifteen minutes. His truncated speech was followed by the reading of a resolution: "That the present Government, by assisting to defeat the Bill introduced by the late Government for the amendment of the representation, and by themselves indefinitely postponing the whole question of Reform, and finally by their employing the police to forcibly prevent the working classes from peaceably meeting in Hyde Park on Monday last to complain of the suffrage being withheld from them, have forfeited all claim to the confidence and support of the country." The resolution was seconded, and then Mill rose. "The friends of the honourable member upon the platform were loud in their manifestations of applause when he rose to speak, but those in the body of the hall, even within tolerable hearing distance, were evidently unacquainted with the personal appearance of the honourable member for Westminster, for one of their number, under the full conviction that he had gained an insight into what was coming, led an encouraging cry of 'Bravo, Mills!' The chairman pressed the honourable member to address the meeting, like the other speakers, from the table; but the offer was politely declined. Mr. Mill doubtless felt it to be questionable whether in the universal clamour any advantage of position would enable him to make his utterances audible; certain it is that beyond the reporters' table, and not even to all who were there collected, did his meaning penetrate." (*The Times*.) Mill, "who seemed deeply impressed by the spectacle of the teeming and swaying multitude before him," spoke (according to the *Morning Post*) "in so low a tone that scarcely a word could be gathered."

LADIES AND GENTLEMEN, this [a]vast meeting[a] is a sufficient guarantee that the cause of reform will suffer nothing by your having determined to hold your meeting here instead of repeating the attempt to hold it in the park. (*Cheers.*) But I do not want [b](*so the honourable member was understood*)[b] to talk to you about reform, you do not need to be stimulated by me on that subject. This meeting is a sufficient reply to any one who supposes that you do [c]want to be stimulated. (*Cheers.*) You want to discuss reform.[c] You have been very much attacked for holding such large meetings, on the ground that they are inconsistent with discussion. (*Loud laughter and cheers.*) But discussion is not the only use of public meetings. One of the objects of such gatherings is demonstration. [d](*At this point the address was interrupted for some minutes by a violent lurch of the main*

[a-a]DT] DN building] TT vast multitude assembled in that hall] MS crowded meeting in this vast hall

[b-b]+DT

[c-c]DT] DN not want to discuss reform. (*Hear, hear.*)] MS (*hear, hear*). Neither do you want to discuss reform.

[d-d]TT] DN (*Hear.*)] DT (*Loud cheers.*)] MS (*Hear, hear.*)

body below in the direction of the platform, which seemed in danger of being carried by storm. An appeal from some of the principal members of the League restored order, but not till two or three gentlemen had been propelled bodily to within a few feet of where Mr. Mill was standing.) The honourable member proceeded:[d]—[e]You want to make a display of your strength, and I tell you that the countries where the people are allowed to show their strength are those in which they are not obliged to use it.[e] As regards the parks, your chairman, who is a lawyer, does not doubt your right to meet in them. I am not a lawyer, and know nothing about the matter. But you thought it right to assert your claim, and only to withdraw under protest. Your protest has been made, and you have—I think wisely—determined not to renew it. (*Interruptions.*) You have been promised a fair opportunity of having the question settled by judicial decision, and you have wisely resolved that until that decision is given the question shall remain where it is. [f]*(The soundness of this advice was unquestionable, but just at that moment the crowd manifested a disposition to do anything but remain where they were, for a further and more violent surging in the direction of the platform took place.)*[f] [g]The government, without abandoning what they thought were their legal rights, might have permitted the park for one meeting[g] when permission was asked, and I think it would have been a wise policy and a gracious act to have granted it—(*tremendous cheers*)—but it was refused [h], and the consequence was—(*The meeting was not destined to hear more, for a fresh invasion of the platform took place, and the aspect of affairs at the moment was so threatening that although there were cries of "I will defend you, Mr. Mill," "Our friends will be steady again in a minute," "This is a meeting of men and not of children," etc., the honourable member felt it hopeless to persist in his address and retired at once from the hall.*)[h]

[*After an interval to allow order to be established, the resolution was passed, and Bradlaugh moved a second one, calling for a petition to the House of Commons to establish a committee of inquiry into the conduct of Sir Richard*

[e-e]TT The best way to show strength sometimes was by abstaining from employing it.] DT You wanted . . . *as* DN . . . strength. (*Hear, hear.*) The countries . . . those where the . . . *as* DN . . . it. (*Cheers.*)] MS They tell you you want to make a display of your physical strength. The countries where the people can . . . *as* DT . . . it. (*Hear, hear.*)

[f-f]+TT

[g-g]TT It was true, *the honourable member continued during a momentary lull,* that without abandoning their right the Crown might have permitted the use of the parks for a single meeting.

[h-h]TT] DN [*paragraph*] *At this point the crowd in front of the platform became, from the inevitable effect of pressure, so tumultuous and noisy that it was impossible for the honourable gentleman to proceed so as to make himself audible even to those who were nearest to him, and accordingly he made no attempt to complete his remarks.*] DT (*Cries of Shame.*) [*paragraph*] *At this moment great confusion took place in consequence of the pressure from behind forcing those standing around the reporters' table completely over it. The tressels having given way, the top fell, and seriously endangered those who were using the table. Mr. Mill did not resume his speech.*] MS (*Loud cheers, in the midst of which Mr. Mill retired.*)] MP *The honourable member cut short his address somewhat abruptly, after signifying his assent to the resolution, which was put by the chairman and carried by acclamation.*

Mayne and the police under his command in preventing the meeting in Hyde Park on 23 July and during the next two days. In the course of his remarks he said "Mr. John Stuart Mill has just enunciated a proposition in which I cordially concur. He said if you have not a legal right to meet in the parks you ought to have it. (Loud cheers.)" The resolution was seconded, and passed after another interruption by newly-arrived marchers. Then Colonel Dickson moved a third resolution calling for financial contributions to the Reform League, which after seconding was also passed, and the meeting concluded at 9:30 with the usual vote of thanks to the Chair and three cheers for Bright, Gladstone, and Beales, and then three "For all who strive to preserve the right dearest to England—the right of public meeting." Sectional meetings were held in different parts of the hall. Then the main part of the spectators ("sightseers," The Times *says, for "auditors they could not be called") formed again into processions behind their bands, being joined by the huge crowd outside the hall, and did not finally clear the area until 11 p.m.*]

33. The Disturbances in Jamaica [2]

31 JULY, 1866

"Mr. Mill's Speech on Mr. Buxton's Motion," in *Jamaica Papers, No. III. Statement of the Committee and Other Documents* (London: Jamaica Committee, [1866]), 7–18. A manuscript fragment (Yale University Library, John Stuart Mill Papers, Box 2, MS #350) is printed in full in variant note $^{u-u}$. In *PD*, 3rd ser., Vol. 184, cols. 1797–1806. Published in *The Times*, 1 August, p. 7, from which variants and responses are taken. Charles Buxton (1823–71), M.P. for East Surrey, moved the following Resolutions: "1. That this House deplores the excessive punishments which followed the suppression of the disturbances of October last in the parish of St. Thomas, Jamaica, and especially the unnecessary frequency with which the punishment of death was inflicted. / 2. That this House, while approving the course taken by Her Majesty's Government in dismissing Mr. Eyre from the Governorship of the Island, at the same time concurs in the view expressed by the late Secretary of the Colonies, that 'while any very minute endeavour to punish acts which may now be the subject of regret would not be expedient, still, that great offences ought to be punished;' and that grave excesses of severity on the part of any Civil, Military, or Naval Officers ought not to be passed over with impunity. / 3. That, in the opinion of this House, it is the duty of Her Majesty's Government to award compensation to those whose property was wantonly and cruelly destroyed, and to the families of those who were put to death illegally. / 4. That, since considerably more than 1,000 persons are proved to have been executed or severely flogged on the charge of participating in these disturbances, all further punishment on account of them ought to be remitted." (Col. 1763.) When Buxton had finished his speech, Adderley replied, and then Mill spoke.

THOSE WHO SEEK TO OBTAIN an authoritative condemnation of the transactions in Jamaica, whether they take the milder view of my honourable friend the mover of the resolutions, or the severer one of the body which has been so disrespectfully spoken of, the Jamaica committee, could have desired nothing better for their cause than that the speech which has just been delivered* [a] should go forth to the country as the defence of the Government for not taking any measures to bring those events under the cognisance of a judicial tribunal. I would myself be well content to go to the country on my honourable friend's speech, and that of the right honourable gentleman, without any further discussion. (*Hear, hear.*) But since nothing has [b]yet[b] been said in vindication of the view I take as to the proper course to be pursued, which is different from that recommended by my honourable friend, [c]I shall state to the house what to my mind justifies that course[c]. The honourable mover of the resolution has called upon the house to consider the proceedings of the civil and military authorities in Jamaica, which have been so deservedly but so mildly condemned by her Majesty's commissioners of inquiry,[1] and has invited the house to express an opinion on those proceedings, to the same effect and nearly in the same language as the commissioners. I, also, contend that the acts which have been committed demand the particular attention of the house, not however for the purpose of itself pronouncing any judgment on them, but for the purpose of requiring that they be referred to an authority more competent than this house—the only authority that is competent to pass a binding judgment on such acts—the authority of a judicial tribunal. (*Hear, hear.*) According to the catalogue furnished by the commissioners, 439 of her Majesty's subjects, men and women, have been put to death, not in the field, not in armed resistance to the Government, but unarmed, after having fallen into the hands of the authorities, many after having voluntarily surrendered to them. (*Hear, hear.*) [d]A part[d] were executed without any semblance of a trial; the remainder after what were called trials, by what were called courts-martial.[2] [e]Besides[e] those who were put to death, not fewer than 600 men and women were flogged, partly without trial, and partly by sentence of the same courts-martial; and about 1,000 houses, besides other property, were destroyed by military violence. Now, if after due investigation the Government and the country generally had made up their minds that all these lives were justly and properly taken, and all these floggings and burnings justly and properly inflicted, there would have been no ground on which to require the Government to prosecute the agents and authors, though private individuals would be at liberty to

*[JP] By Mr. Adderley. [Charles Bowyer Adderley (1814–1905), Under-Secretary for the Colonies, M.P. for Staffordshire North, Speech on the Disturbances in Jamaica (31 July), *PD*, 3rd ser., Vol. 184, cols. 1785–97, esp. 1788–9.]

[1]"Report of the Jamaica Royal Commission," *PP*, 1866, XXX, 489–531.

[2]*Ibid.*, p. 515.

[a]PD,TT by the right honourable Gentleman
[b-b]+JP
[c-c]TT therefore he should embody it in an amendment
[d-d]PD,TT Some of these
[e-e]PD,TT In addition to

do so if they pleased. The case, however, is far otherwise. Respecting the degree of culpability of these transactions there is a wide difference of opinion, but that there has been serious culpability no one now disputes. (*Hear, hear.*) The events have undergone a minute inquiry, by commissioners carefully selected, and invested with full power to ascertain the facts, but not, I must remind the right honourable gentleman, empowered to declare what is the character of those facts in the eye of the law. The commissioners have emphatically condemned a large portion of the proceedings.[3] They declare that many more persons have been put to death than ought to have been put to death; some of these on evidence which they declare to have been, so far as it appears on record, wholly insufficient to justify the findings: while in other cases, assuming the evidence to be unimpeachable, the sentences were not justified by the facts deposed to. The floggings they pronounce to have been reckless, and some of them positively barbarous; the flogging of women they reprobate under any circumstances, and in that I am sure the house will not differ from them. The burnings they pronounce wanton and cruel. There is no need to go one step beyond the verdict of the commissioners. I am almost ashamed to speak of such acts with the calmness and in the moderate language which the circumstances require. The house has supped full of horrors throughout the speech of my honourable friend. But we need not go beyond the dry facts of the commissioners' summary. On their showing, the lives of subjects of her Majesty have been wrongfully taken, and the persons of others wrongfully maltreated; and I maintain that when such things have been done, there is a *primâ facie* demand for legal punishment, and that a court of criminal justice can alone determine whether such punishment has been merited, and if merited, what ought to be its amount. The taking of human lives without justification, which in this case is an admitted fact, cannot be condoned by anything short of a criminal tribunal. Neither the Government, nor this house, nor the whole English nation combined, can exercise a pardoning power without previous trial and sentence. I know not for what more important purpose courts of law exist than for the security of human life. [f]It has been the boast of[f] this country [g]that officers of Government must answer for their acts to the same laws and before the same tribunals as any private citizen; and if persons in authority can[g] take the lives of [h]their fellow[h] subjects improperly, [i]as has been confessedly done in this case,[i] without being called to a judicial account, and having the excuses they make for it sifted and adjudicated by the tribunal in that case provided, we are giving up altogether the principle of government by law,

[3]*Ibid.*, p. 531.

[f-f]PD,TT Hitherto in

[g-g]PD,TT the agents of the executive Government have had to answer for themselves in the same Courts of Law as the rest of Her Majesty's subjects. (*Hear.*) But if officers of the Government are to be allowed to [TT *in past tense*]

[h-h]PD,TT the Queen's

[i-i]+PD,TT [TT *in past tense*]

and resigning ourselves to arbitrary power. (*Hear, hear.*) [j]The most proper course, therefore, which could in my opinion be taken by any member[j] of this house, was to attempt to elicit from her Majesty's Government, before the end of the session, some statement of their intentions respecting what, to me and others, appears the solemn duty of bringing the authors of at least the most flagrant of these universally condemned acts before a criminal tribunal. The house knows that this attempt was made,[4] and it knows what was the result. We obtained by it no direct, but a good deal of indirect, information. Since then I have redoubled my efforts to learn, or to divine, what reasons there are against the propriety of a criminal prosecution: and I have arrived at the conclusion that if those I have heard are the best, there will not be much difficulty in resisting any of them. I have been told, for instance (but by whom or on what occasion the rules of the house forbid me to recollect), that to warrant a criminal prosecution for homicide, it is necessary that the act should have been done with malice prepense.[5] But the right honourable the Chancellor of the Exchequer cannot make such a mistake as this; for if not a lawyer himself, he has able lawyers for his advisers, and one need not be a lawyer at all to know that there is such an offence as manslaughter [k](for example)[k] which I have hitherto in my ignorance believed to differ from murder precisely by the absence of malice prepense. The wonder which I felt at this singular specimen of legal knowledge would have been still greater than it was, if I had not just before been told by a very eminent person (but it could not be the right honourable gentleman) that I was grossly inconsistent in assuming through nine questions that certain acts were unlawful, and asking in the tenth whether they were unlawful or not?[6] Now, since what I asked was, whether they were offences under the criminal law, I must conclude that, in the opinion of this eminent person, no actions are unlawful but those which are offences under the criminal law. Did he ever hear, I wonder, of such a thing as an action for damages? which everybody knows will lie in many cases in which a criminal proceeding could not be sustained. And, again, is he not aware of cases in which the law imposes pecuniary penalties, but leaves them to be enforced by anybody who chooses to sue for them by a civil action? [l]Since it

[4]By Mill on 19 July; see No. 26.

[5]By Disraeli, in his Speech on the Outbreak in Jamaica (19 July, 1866), *PD*, 3rd ser., Vol. 184, col. 1069. The act governing this issue is 24 & 25 Victoria, c. 100 (1861). For the rule of the House discouraging references to prior debates, see Thomas Erskine May, *A Treatise on the Law, Privileges, Proceedings and Usage of Parliament* (1844), 14th ed., ed. Gilbert Campion (London: Butterworth, 1946), p. 426.

[6]See No. 26.

[j-j]PD,TT Under these circumstances, it appears to me that the proper course to be adopted by Members [TT *in third person, past tense*]

[k-k]+JP

[l-l]PD Now, as the authority to whom I allude said that no act that could not be the subject of a criminal prosecution is illegal, it follows that, in his opinion, the law awards] TT *as* PD . . . follows that the law awards [*in third person, past tense*]

appears to be the opinion of this high authority that acts which cannot be prosecuted criminally are not unlawful, I presume he thinks that the courts give damages, and the law imposes[l] penalties, for lawful acts. (*Hear, hear.*) [m]I hope the right honourable gentleman will tell us this evening that he disclaims all participation in[m] these peculiar views. I am [n]willing to defer to him[n] as an authority on [o]many[o] subjects, but I shall be quite unable to accept his guidance in any matter of criminal law (*hear*), unless he entirely throws over that other great luminary to whom I have been referring. Then, again, it is asked, how can we think of prosecuting anybody for putting people to death, when we cannot possibly suppose that those who did it believed them to be innocent? Well, very probably they did not, though even this is by no means a thing which it is permissible to take for granted. But admitting the fact, it is an excuse that may be made for actions of still greater atrocity than I claim any right to attribute to these. Did the perpetrators of the massacre of St. Bartholomew think their victims innocent?[7] [p]Did[p] they not firmly believe them to be hateful to God and to all good men? [q]Did[q] the authors of the September massacres—did the French revolutionary tribunals and the Terrorist Government, believe in the innocence of those whom they put to death?[8] Were they not fully persuaded that they were traitors and enemies of their country? I do not want to compare Governor Eyre and his subordinates to Robespierre and Fouquier Tinville, though I confess that their modes of proceeding sometimes remind me very forcibly of some of the minor actors in that great tragedy: but the same sort of excuse may be made for Robespierre and Fouquier Tinville as for them. I dare say that if gentlemen on the other side of the house, and I am afraid some on this side, had had the duty of sitting in judgment on those very vigorous rulers, they would have thought it quite enough to visit them with the penalty with which, for example, Governor Darling has been visited for following his constitutional advisers in an erroneous interpretation of the constitution of Victoria.[9] We should perhaps have been told that the case as respects Robespierre was closed by dismissal from his office as a member of the Committee of Public

[7]The persecution of the Huguenots in France was marked especially by the massacre beginning on St. Bartholomew's Day, 24 August, 1572.

[8]Maximilien François Marie Isidore de Robespierre (1758–94) and Antoine Quentin Fouquier-Tinville (1747–95) were leading prosecutors on behalf of the Committee of Public Safety during the Reign of Terror (1793) in the French Revolution.

[9]Charles Henry Darling (1809–70), Governor of Victoria, 1863–66, was recalled in February 1866 for injudicious comments on petitioners against practices he had permitted; he then resigned from the Colonial Service.

[m-m]PD,TT The right honourable Gentleman the Chancellor of the Exchequer is just now absent from the House, but I trust that in the course of the evening he will utterly repudiate [TT *in third person, past tense*]

[n-n]PD,TT ready to accept the right honourable Gentleman

[o-o]PD,TT some

[p-p]PD,TT On the contrary, did

[q-q]PD,TT Again, did

Safety. As for Fouquier Tinville, it probably would not have been thought advisable, after so many errors of judgment, to re-appoint him to the responsible situation of public prosecutor. We might have been told, in words with which the house is probably familiar, that it would be desirable "to entrust that arduous task to some other person, who may approach it free from all the difficulties inseparable from a participation in the questions raised by the recent troubles," and that by placing the office "in new hands," Government were "taking the course best calculated to allay animosities, to conciliate general confidence, and to establish on firm and solid grounds the future welfare of" France.[10] Again, we are told that in proposing to make the authors of those acts criminally responsible for them, we forget that those acts were done under martial law. Sir, we are not at all likely to forget that (*hear, hear*); we remember it but too well: and we shall remember as long, what it has been declared by the leading member of the Government that martial law is—the total suspension of all law.[11] The right honourable gentleman [r](*Mr. Adderley*)[r] will admit that this is something worth remembering. Well; martial law while it lasts, is the negation of all law; and therefore (such is the conclusion of the right honourable gentleman)[12] it is the negation of all responsibility. Not only, as soon as martial law is proclaimed, the civil and military authorities and their agents may run amuck, if such is their pleasure—may do, as far as any legal restraint is concerned, anything they please; but, if they please to do what is wrong, they cannot be made to account for it afterwards, except to their official superiors, nor to suffer any but the official penalties which those superiors can inflict. If that is our condition, and if any Government or any local administrator that chooses to proclaim martial law can place us under this regimen, we have gained little by our historical struggles, and the blood that has been shed for English liberties has been shed to little purpose. (*Hear, hear.*) But it is not so, sir; it is not so. I do not deny that there is good authority, legal as well as military, for saying that the proclamation of martial law suspends all law so long as it lasts; but I defy any one to produce any respectable authority for the doctrine that persons are not responsible to the laws of their country, both civil and criminal, after martial law has ceased, for acts done under it. The legal opinions, which the right honourable gentleman misunderstands, affirm only this, that martial law is another word for the law of necessity, and that the justification of acts done under that law consists in their necessity. Well, then, we have a right to dispute the necessity. If the right honourable gentleman will consult his legal advisers, he will

[10]Mill is adapting the words of Edward Cardwell (1813–86), Secretary of State for the Colonies, M.P. for Oxford, concerning Governor Eyre, from "Despatch from the Right Hon. Edward Cardwell, M.P., to Lieut.-Gen. Sir H.K. Storks, G.C.B., G.C.M.G.," *PP*, 1866, LI, 143.

[11]Disraeli, speech of 19 July, col. 1067.

[12]Adderley, speech of 31 July, col. 1789.

[r-r]+PD,TT

find that the law is perfectly settled on this point. With the permission of the house I will read a short extract from a law opinion given specifically on the point by two gentlemen, both of them ornaments of their profession, and one of them a member of this house:[13]

> The officers of the crown are justified in any exertion of physical force extending to the destruction of life and property to any extent, and in any manner, that may be required for this purpose. They are not justified in the use of excessive or cruel means, but are liable civilly or criminally for such excess. They are not justified in inflicting punishment after resistance is suppressed, and after the ordinary courts of justice can be reopened. The principle by which their responsibility is measured is well expressed in the case of Wright *v.* Fitzgerald. Mr. Wright was a French master, of Clonmel, who, after the suppression of the Irish rebellion in 1798, brought an action against Mr. Fitzgerald, the sheriff of Tipperary, for having cruelly flogged him without due inquiry. Martial law was in full force at that time, and an act of indemnity had been passed to excuse all breaches of the law committed in the suppression of the rebellion. In summing-up, Justice Chamberlain, with whom Lord Yelverton agreed, said: "The jury were not to imagine that the legislature, by enabling magistrates to justify under the indemnity bill,[14] had released them from the feelings of humanity, or permitted them wantonly to exercise power, even though it were to put down rebellion. They expected that in all cases there should be a grave and serious examination into the conduct of the supposed criminal, and every act should show a mind intent to discover guilt, not to inflict torture. By examination or trial he did not mean that sort of examination and trial which they were now engaged in, but such examination and trial the best the nature of the case and existing circumstances would allow of. That this must have been the intention of the legislature was manifest from the expression 'magistrates and all other persons,' which provides that as every man, whether magistrate or not, was authorised to suppress rebellion, and was to be justified by that law for his acts, it is required that he should not exceed the necessity which gave him the power, and that he should show in his justification that he had used every possible means to ascertain the guilt which he had punished; and, above all, no deviation from the common principles of humanity should appear in his conduct." Mr. Wright recovered £500 damages; and when Mr. Fitzgerald applied to the Irish parliament for an indemnity, he could not get one.[15]

In the year 1866, thirty-four years after the passing of the Reform Act, we have to reaffirm the principle of this judgment, and reassert the responsibility of all officers of the executive to the tribunals, in order that in our regard for law and liberty we may be on a level with the Orange Government and the Orange Parliament of Ireland in the most tyrannical period of modern Irish history, the rebellion of 1798. (*Hear, hear.*) And great cause is there why we should assert this responsibility. If martial law indeed is what it is asserted to be, arbitrary power—the rule of force, subject to no legal limits—then, indeed, the legal

[13]James Fitzjames Stephen (1829–94), barrister, and Edward James (1807–67), M.P. for Manchester.

[14]38 George III, c. 19 (1798), Irish Statutes.

[15]Mill is quoting from the legal opinion obtained for the Jamaica Committee; cf. "The Jamaica Committee," *The Times*, 16 Jan., 1866, p. 3, where much of the material appears. The quoted judgment is found in Thomas Bayley Howell, *A Complete Collection of State Trials*, 34 vols. (London: Longman, *et al.*, 1809–28), Vol. XXVII, col. 765.

responsibility of those who administer it, instead of being lightened, requires to be enormously aggravated. So long as the power of inflicting death is restricted by laws, by rules, by forms devised for the security of innocence, by settled usage, by a long series of precedents—these laws, these forms, these usages and precedents, are a protection to those who are judged; but they are also eminently a protection to those who judge. If a law is prescribed for their observance, and they observe the law, they are, in general, safe from [s]further[s] responsibility. The less we leave to their discretion, the less necessity is there, in the interest of the general safety, for making them personally accountable. But if men are let loose from all law, from all precedents, from all forms—are left to try people for their lives in any way they please, take evidence as they please, refuse evidence as they please, give facilities to the defence or withhold those facilities as they think fit, and after that pass any sentences they please, and irrevocably execute those sentences, with no bounds to their discretion but their own judgment of what is necessary for the suppression of a rebellion—a judgment which not only may be, but in a vast proportion of cases is sure to be, an exasperated man's judgment, or a frightened man's judgment of necessity (*hear, hear*); when there is absolutely no guarantee against any extremity of tyrannical violence, but the responsibility which can be afterwards exacted from the tyrant—then, sir, it is indeed indispensable that he who takes the lives of others under this discretion should know that he risks his own. (*Cheers.*) I do not wonder that there are conscientious military men who shrink from so vast a responsibility, and prefer any view whatever of martial law to that which we are given to understand is the true one. I hold in my hand a letter written to me by a retired general officer,[16] which, after saying that the intelligent officers of the army feel bewildered at the very idea of martial law, from the absence of all precise instructions on the subject, goes on to say,

> I had fully made up my mind how I should act if ever called upon to enforce martial law. I had resolved, as the only safe and prudent plan, to consider martial law as simply military law extended to civilians, feeling convinced that a fixed or written code was indispensable, and that what was sufficient to curb soldiers in war was surely sufficient to restrain civilians in revolt.

He adds:

> Taken fighting with arms in their hands should alone justify the summary execution of rebels; whilst the composition and powers of the courts-martial on rebels should follow the articles of war, which are amply sufficient to cover all cases that could ever arise under martial law. (*Hear, hear.*)

We are now informed that neither the Articles of War nor the Mutiny Act[17] are

[16]Not identified.

[17]The Articles of War, published annually, codify the military law for governing and

[s-s]TT all penal

in force at all during the proclamation of a martial law, and that the courts-martial are not bound by their provisions. But the oath which is administered to the members of every court-martial, and which was taken by all the members of the courts-martial in Jamaica, begins with these words: "You shall duly administer justice according to the rules and articles for the better government of her Majesty's forces, and according to an act now in force for the punishment of mutiny and desertion."[18] This is what they swore to do: nobody pretends that they did it; and [t]the Government now justifies them[t] by saying that they were not bound by their oath. Sir, I have stated to the house the principles on which I am acting, and on which those act with whom on this subject I am co-operating. We want to know—as the noble lord, the secretary for India, said on a not more important occasion[19]—we want to know who are to be our masters: her Majesty's judges and a jury of our countrymen, administering the laws of England, or three naval and military officers, two of them boys, administering, as the Chancellor of the Exchequer tells us, no law at all.[20] This we want to know; and this, if it be humanly possible, we mean to [u]know. It remains to be seen whether the people of [v]this country will sustain[v] us in the attempt to [w]procure a[u] solemn reassertion of the principle, that whoever takes human life without justification must account for it to the law[w]. This great public duty may be discharged without help from the Government, but without help from the people it cannot. It is their cause; and we will not be wanting to them if they are not wanting to us. (*Hear, hear.*)

[*Eventually the first resolution was accepted, and the others were withdrawn following Governmental concessions (cols. 1839–40).*]

---

disciplining troops for lesser offences. Offences punishable by death are covered by Mutiny Acts; the one here referred to is 28 Victoria, c. 11 (1865).

[18]The oath, still in use, was included in the Mutiny Acts up to 1858; see, e.g., 19 Victoria, c. 10 (1856).

[19]Robert Arthur Talbot Gascoyne Cecil (1830–1903), Lord Cranborne, M.P. for Stamford, Speech on Electoral Statistics (23 Mar., 1866), *PD*, 3rd ser., Vol. 182, col. 876.

[20]Disraeli, speech of 19 July, col. 1067.

[t-t]PD they are now justified

[u-u]Manuscript know. We stand here to assert the authority and majesty of law. That cause we will not desert or compromise, neither from a weak pity for Governor Eyre because he is a public functionary and a gentleman while those whom he hanged and shot were coloured people and peasants—nor from an idle fear of being called vindictive. It would be well, perhaps, if people were a little more vindictive, for other people's wrongs, than they are. Vindictiveness of that kind had formerly another name, it was called the love of justice—and used to be strong in Englishmen. I wish I did not think that while we have improved in so many other respects, we have gone back somewhat in this; but I hope there is enough of it left to give us the support without which our efforts must be unavailing. It now remains to be seen whether the British people will sustain us in the attempt to procure a [*the manuscript fragment contains only this passage*]

[v-v]PD,TT England will support [TT *in past tense*]

[w-w]PD,TT assert the great principle of the responsibility of all agents of the Executive to the laws, civil and criminal, for taking human life without justification

34. The Reform Meeting in Hyde Park [5]

2 AUGUST, 1866

PD, 3rd ser., Vol. 184, col. 1905. Reported in *The Times*, 3 August, p. 4, from which the variants and response are taken. For the meeting alluded to, see No. 31.

MR. J. STUART MILL presented the petition adopted at the meeting in the Agricultural Hall, complaining of the exclusion of the public from Hyde Park on Monday week, and praying the House to institute an inquiry into the conduct of the Chief Commissioner of Police,[1] and of the Police generally.

Major Stuart Knox[2] *said, he would beg to ask the honourable Gentleman,* [a]*who he understood was connected with the Reform League,*[a] *Whether a letter which appeared in that morning's paper from Mr. Beales was genuine;*[3] *and, if so, whether he can inform the House who the "*[b]*public*[b] *leaders" mentioned in it were?*

Mr. J. Stuart Mill: Sir, [c]I can assure the honourable and gallant Gentleman that I have not the slightest objection to give him any information which I can command in reply to his queston.[c] Sir, I am not in the least degree authorized to make any communication to the House on behalf of the Reform League, of which I am not even a member; and I beg to refer the honourable and gallant Gentleman to those who are members, and particularly to Mr. Beales himself. (*A laugh.*)

35. Public Health

2 AUGUST, 1866

PD, 3rd ser., Vol. 184, col. 1908. Not reported in *The Times*. Mill's interjection came in the debate on the third reading of "A Bill [as Amended by the Select Committee . . .] to Amend the Law Relating to the Public Health," 29 Victoria (29 June, 1866), *PP*, 1866, IV, 425–48, Clause 39. This clause, concerning proof that inmates of a house or part thereof were family members, put the onus of proof on the claimants. Ayrton moved (unsuccessfully) to strike out this clause. He was followed by Thomas Chambers, who said "nothing

[1]Richard Mayne (1796–1868).

[2]William Stuart Knox (1826–1900), Conservative M.P. for Dungannon.

[3]A letter purporting to be from Beales to the committee of the Athenaeum, whose property had been damaged during the commotion, was published in *The Times*, 2 Aug., p. 5; on 3 August (the day this debate was reported), a letter of 2 August from Beales to the editor repudiated the earlier letter as a hoax (*The Times*, 3 Aug., p. 3).

[a–a]+TT

[b–b]TT popular

[c–c]+TT [*in the third person, past tense*]

could be easier than for the parties charged to show that they were one family, while it would be an impossibility for the police to prove the negative." Mill replied.

MR. J. STUART MILL SAID, the only proof that would be required would be repute.

36. The Extradition Treaties Act [1]

3 AUGUST, 1866

PD, 3rd ser., Vol. 184, cols. 2023–6. Reported in *The Times*, 4 August, p. 7, from which the variants and reponses are taken. Mill spoke in the debate on the second reading of "A Bill Intituled An Act for the Amendment of the Law Relating to Treaties of Extradition," 29 & 30 Victoria (26 July, 1866), *PP*, 1866, III, 39–42. The Bill eventually passed (see No. 39), though Mill says in the *Autobiography* that he "joined with several other independent Liberals in defeating an Extradition Bill, introduced at the very end of the session of 1866 and by which, though surrender avowedly for political offences was not authorised, political refugees, if charged by a foreign government with acts which are necessarily incident to all attempts at insurrection, would have been surrendered to be dealt with by the criminal courts of the government against which they had rebelled: thus making the British Government an accomplice in the vengeance of foreign despotisms" (*CW*, Vol. I, pp. 282–3). He may have in mind that his proposal to limit the duration of the Act to one year had later been accepted (No. 39). In any case, as he says further: "The defeat of this proposal led to the appointment of a Select Committee (in which I was included) to examine and report on the whole subject of Extradition Treaties; and the result was that in the Extradition Act, which passed through Parliament after I had ceased to be a member, opportunity is given to any one whose extradition is demanded, of being heard before an English Court of justice to prove that the offence with which he is charged is really political. The cause of European freedom has thus been saved from a serious misfortune, and our own country from a great iniquity." (*Ibid.*, p. 283.) For Mill's part in the Select Committee, see App. B.

SIR, I do not mean to say anything against the French Government, but I think it is neither in any way improper nor at all impertinent to the question to say something about the French law, and particularly those parts of it which are thought most defective by the best Judges in France itself. There are many things in that law which are worthy of great praise, and many from which we in this country have a great deal to learn; but I never met with any enlightened Frenchman who did not think that the worst part of the French law is the law of criminal procedure, and that the mode in which the preliminary evidence is taken is the worst part even of that.[1] The depositions which are taken preparatory to a criminal trial in France by the *juge d'instruction* are taken in secret. They are not taken in the presence of the

[1]Code d'instruction criminelle, Bull. 214 *bis* (17 Nov.–16 Dec., 1808), *Bulletin des lois de l'empire français*, 4th ser., Livre I, Chap. vi, Sect. iii, Arts. 71–3.

accused; he is not confronted with the witnesses, much less has he any opportunity of cross-examination. It is, therefore, the easiest thing in the world to get up a false charge against a person, if on the part of any other person there is the slightest disposition to do so. I have, indeed, much confidence in the love of justice and the integrity and dignity of the French Judges, who, very often, when the trial comes on, are able to prevent these great defects in the preliminary proceedings from issuing in final injustice [a], but with this final trial the House has nothing to do, for[a] we are now called upon to surrender the accused persons upon the original depositions only. (*Hear.*) Now, we are told[2]—and it is true—that the committing magistrate has the power, and is bound, to consider whether the evidence is such as would in his own opinion establish a *primâ facie* case against the accused, sufficient to warrant a committal for trial. But there is great danger lest the magistrate, not being fully aware of the differences between French and English criminal procedure, might be led, unless something is put in this Bill to guard against it, to attach the same weight, or nearly the same weight, to those depositions as if they had been taken in his presence. It would be very desirable if the magistrate is to have the power of ordering the extradition of an accused person, that something should be done in the way of directing him how to exercise it. When even so experienced a magistrate as the Chief Magistrate at Bow Street, appears to have laboured under some misapprehension in this respect,[3] it appears to me important that magistrates should receive warning from their superiors not to attach more than the due weight to those depositions. If, however, they attach no more than the due weight to those depositions, the effect desired will not be produced. Consequently, either the French Government will have to waive the point of honour which they are said to entertain,[4] or the new Act will be as much a dead letter as was the old one.[5] We are told by high authorities, in a place not far from this, that the old Act was an entirely dead letter;[6] and it has been said by every one who has spoken in favour of the Bill that the objection to it is equally an

[2]Just before Mill spoke, by the Attorney General, Hugh MacCalmont Cairns (1819–85), M.P. for Belfast, in his Speech on the Extradition Treaties Act Amendment Bill (3 Aug.), *PD*, 3rd ser., Vol. 184, col. 2022.

[3]Thomas James Hall (1788–1876) had been Chief Magistrate at Bow Street from 1839 to July 1864. For his misapprehension, see Frederick Thesiger (1794–1878), Baron Chelmsford, the Lord Chancellor, Speech on the Extradition Treaties Bill (19 July), *ibid.*, col. 1055.

[4]Cf. *ibid.*, col. 1056.

[5]The new Act, resulting from the Bill under debate, 29 & 30 Victoria, c. 121, was given royal assent on 10 Aug., 1866. The old Act, 6 & 7 Victoria, c. 75 (1843), was accompanied by a facilitating Act, 8 & 9 Victoria, c. 120 (1845).

[6]In the House of Lords, by Thesiger, speech of 19 July, cols. 1054–5, and by George William Frederick Villiers (1800–70), Lord Clarendon, who had served as Foreign Secretary for many years, on the same occasion, cols. 1058–9.

[a–a]TT [*in the past tense*]] PD . But

objection to the law as it stands, under which we are subject to the same obligations as are now sought to be imposed on us. I admit that nothing can be more harmless in appearance than this Bill. No substantial alteration, it is argued, is proposed in the law, and therefore nobody can possibly object to the Bill. But it unfortunately happens that although nominally there is no alteration, practically there is the greatest alteration in the world. [b]The old Act, we are told, has not been acted upon at all—nobody has been surrendered under that Act—and it is precisely in order to call the Extradition Treaty[7] out of the condition of a dead letter into that of a practical fact, that this Bill is brought in. If it does not do this, it answers no purpose. Therefore, if the Bill passes, one of two things must ensue: either our magistrates will give up offenders, on evidence which would be in great danger of being insufficient, or it will be necessary to come to us again on some other occasion to reinforce this Bill and make it still more easy to effect the extradition of accused persons. I can conceive that in the case of ordinary offences it may not be necessary to insist upon these considerations. But as soon as an application is made for the extradition of a political offender, we shall find the strongest reasons for hesitating on the question. If the laws of any country afford facilities for getting up a false case, that false case is very much more likely to be got up where political offences are concerned. Political offences *eo nomine* are not, it is true, included in the Extradition Treaty, but acts really political often come within the definition of offences which are so included. Apply this observation to the case of the French Emperor at Boulogne,[8] and you will perceive—as doubtless the Emperor himself would perceive—the force of what I am advancing.[b] The noble Lord who has introduced this Bill (*Lord Stanley*) has expressed his willingness, if it be possible, to exempt offences really political from being made the grounds for extradition, under the name of murder, or attempt to murder.[9] This declaration is worthy of the noble Lord, and is such as might be expected from his character. I perfectly sympathize in the difficulties he feels. His difficulty is the case of political

[7]"Convention between Her Majesty and the King of the French, for the Mutual Surrender, in Certain Cases, of Persons Fugitive from Justice" (13 Mar., 1843), *PP*, 1867–68, VII, 257.

[8]In 1840 at Boulogne, Napoleon III (1808–73), then Louis Napoleon, with fifty-six followers, failed to instigate a rebellion in the 42nd Regiment, with the aim of establishing himself Emperor of France. For an account mentioning his shooting the sentinel referred to in the variant note, see "Enterprise of Prince Louis Napoleon," *The Times*, 10 Aug., 1840, pp. 4–5. (He was elected President in December 1848 and, after a successful coup in December 1851, became Emperor in 1852.)

[9]Edward Henry Stanley, Motion on the Extradition Treaties Act Amendment Bill (3 Aug.), *PD*, 3rd ser., Vol. 184, cols. 2007–8.

[b-b]TT It was, however, because the French Government wished to call the treaty out of its present condition of being a dead letter that the present Bill was brought in. The French Government, in fact, wished to have such a law as would have compelled the English Government to give up the present Emperor of the French for shooting the sentinel at Boulogne. (*Hear, hear.*)

assassination. I do not pretend, if the only question were with reference to persons who had really done these things, that I should have much to say against it. People who do such things ought to make up their minds to sacrifice their lives; and if they have any honest feeling in the matter they generally do. (*Hear, hear.*) When there has been an actual attempt at political assassination, it is not perhaps difficult, in most cases, to distinguish between a false charge and a true one. But it is often uncommonly so in the case of complicity in such an attempt; and these are precisely the cases in which there is most danger of a false charge. It is a thing which may happen any day, our being called upon to deliver up some person charged with complicity in such an offence; and this charge may be the most false imaginable, and yet such as is extremely likely to be entertained. If I may offer, merely by way of illustration, a case fresh in the memory of every Member of this House, I will say that Governor Eyre felt convinced that Mr. Gordon was an instigator of the insurrection in Jamaica,[10] and on that ground Mr. Gordon was put to death, although the evidence has been pronounced by those who have examined it judicially—one of them expressed himself very strongly on the point in this House[11]—utterly insufficient to establish this charge. Well, we have heard no end of testimony from both sides of the House as to what a good man, a clever man, and a blameless man Mr. Eyre was. Well, then, let Mr. Eyre be all this: it follows, that let a man be as good, and wise, and blameless as it is possible for a man to be, he may yet make this mistake; and, if a Governor may make it, a King or an Emperor may make it. We cannot doubt that in such cases depositions will always be forthcoming, and that, if undue weight were attached to these depositions, it would be extremely difficult to resist the extradition of anyone charged with complicity in an attempt on the life of any foreign Sovereign or statesman. The great majority of people, especially people in power, are ready to believe almost anything against their political enemies, especially those who have said or published things tending to excite disapprobation of their conduct; as witness the case of Mr. Gordon. I am not contending for the impunity of these persons. Even those who look with the least horror on political assassination do not doubt that it ought to be punished as murder [c]. The least the Government of this country could demand in such cases is that the foreign Government should send over here the same evidence that would be necessary to put the man on his trial in the country that shelters him. (*Hear, hear.*) I cannot approve a Bill under which our magistrates will be called upon to surrender prisoners upon depositions taken in secret, and under no circumstances ought an extradition treaty to deal with political offenders. (*Hear, hear.*)[c]

[10]Eyre, "Despatch to the Rt. Hon. Edward Cardwell, M.P." (20 Oct., 1865), *PP*, 1866, LI, 151–60, Sect. 48.

[11]Russell Gurney (1804–78), M.P. for Southampton, Speech on the Disturbances in Jamaica (31 July, 1866), *PD*, 3rd ser., Vol. 184, cols. 1833–4.

[c–c]TT [*in the third person, past tense*]] PD ; but if the case be genuine, the foreign Power should take the trouble to send over the evidence, and the accused should be tried here.

37. The Extradition Treaties Act [2]

4 AUGUST, 1866

PD, 3rd ser., Vol. 184, cols. 2056–7. Not reported in *The Times*. A motion had been made to take the Extradition Treaties Act Amendment Bill (see No. 36) into Committee.

MR. J. STUART MILL appealed to the Government to postpone the further consideration of this Bill, on the ground of the absence of his honourable Friend the Member for Reading (*Sir Francis Goldsmid*), who had an Amendment on the paper, to which he attached great importance.[1] His honourable Friend was obliged to leave the House yesterday before the division, and was probably unaware of the intention of the Government to have a sitting of the House that day, in order to pass that as well as other measures on the paper through their remaining stages.

Mr. Walpole asked, whether the honourable Member for Westminster was not prepared to move the Amendment?

Mr. J. Stuart Mill doubted whether he should be able to do justice to the subject, as he had come to the House totally unprepared to undertake the task.

[*The Committee was deferred until the 6th.*]

38. The Naval Dockyards

4 AUGUST, 1866

PD, 3rd ser., Vol. 184, col. 2067. Reported in *The Times*, 6 August, p. 6, from which the variant is taken. Adjournment had been moved by John Pakington (cols. 2057–60) so that the House could discuss allegations of extravagance by officials in the Royal Dockyards.

MR. J. STUART MILL thought the conclusion to be drawn from this discussion was, that a great improvement had been attempted in the mode of conducting public business, but that, as is often the case with first attempts, it had not proved very successful. Every one must feel the great advantage it would be to this House and the public if the facts in any matter relating to public expenditure could be authenticated and agreed upon on both sides [a]by previous inquiry[a] before the question founded on those facts was brought before the House. His honourable Friend the Member for Lincoln (*Mr. Seely*), with great credit to himself, applied

[1]Francis Henry Goldsmid (1808–78) made his motion on 6 August (*PD*, 3rd ser., Vol. 184, cols. 2108–12), proposing that political offenders be exempt from the provisions of the Act. (See No. 39.)

[a-a]+TT

to be allowed to ascertain his facts in the best possible way, and with the assistance of those best qualified to help him:[1] and the Admiralty consented to that arrangement,[2] though they did not appear to have persevered in that laudable intention to the end. The misunderstanding which appeared to have arisen was to be regretted, as they all knew how much more information could be obtained on a complicated matter across a table than across this House, and how much more complete and intelligible that information was likely to be when asked for in a friendly than in a hostile manner.

39. The Extradition Treaties Act [3]

6 AUGUST, 1866

PD, 3rd ser., Vol. 184, cols. 2115–18. Reported in *The Times*, 7 August, p. 7, from which the variant and response are taken. Goldsmid, now being in the House (see No. 37), moved his amendment to the Bill (see No. 36 for it and the related Acts), to add a clause: "That nothing in this Act, nor in any previous Act relating to Treaties of Extradition, shall be construed to authorize the extradition of any person in whose case there shall be reasonable grounds for belief that his offence, if any, had for its motive or purpose the promotion or prevention of any political object, nor to authorize the extradition of any person the requisition for the delivery of whom shall not contain an undertaking on the part of the Sovereign or Government making such requisition, that such person shall not be proceeded against or punished on account of any offence which he shall have committed before he shall be delivered up, other than the offence specified in the requisition." Mill spoke after Lord Stanley.

MR. J. STUART MILL FELT THAT many of the sentiments which they had just heard from the noble Lord[1] were of a very reassuring character, and if the noble Lord were always to be Foreign Secretary, he should not require much further security; but since the country was not likely to be always so far favoured, he could not help regretting that the deliberations of the noble Lord had not led him to frame some other clause, if that already proposed did not meet with his approbation. It should be remembered that if a person charged with political assassination were not given

[1]Charles Seely (1803–87), in his Speech on Supply—Navy Estimates (1 Mar., 1866), *PD*, 3rd ser., Vol. 181, cols. 1361–2, had asked that his assistants be allowed to confer with the Admiralty's staff, and that points of dispute be submitted to a professional accountant.

[2]Clarence Edward Paget (1811–95), M.P. for Sandwich, Secretary to the Admiralty, indicated (*ibid.*, col. 1366) willingness to explore the issues with Seely. In the event, the Government did not act on Seely's request.

---

[1]Stanley, Speech on the Extradition Treaties Act Amendment Bill (6 Aug.), *PD*, 3rd ser., Vol. 184, col. 2114.

up, he would not necessarily escape punishment; for he might still be prosecuted in the country where he had sought refuge. Nobody wished that political should enjoy any more impunity than any other kind of assassination; but if we had only the alternative of trying in this country persons charged with political offences, or of giving up everybody charged with homicide of a political character, he (*Mr. Stuart Mill*) should prefer the former. At the same time, he did not think it impossible to define political offences. Various attempts at definition had, to his knowledge, been communicated to the noble Lord. [a]One of them, suggested by a learned Gentleman, he would mention. It was,[a] "Any offence committed in the course or in furtherance of any civil war, insurrection, or political movement."[2] That he thought would not include political assassination. It appeared to him that this matter required much more consideration than it had yet received; the more one examined into it the worse it looked. There was at the present moment the utmost uncertainty as to the nature of the inquiry which an English magistrate was bound to make, previous to delivering up any person charged with a political offence. He found in the papers before the House two entirely different views of the law of this country. The Extradition Act said—

> It shall be lawful for any justice of the peace, having power to commit for trial, to examine upon oath any person or persons touching the truth of such charge, and upon such evidence as according to the law of that part of Her Majesty's dominions would justify the apprehension and committal of the person accused if the crime had been there committed, it shall be lawful for the magistrate to commit the prisoner into the custody of the officers of the Power so demanding him.[3]

Now, it was stated in the able and excellent letter of Lord Clarendon to Lord Cowley, that a magistrate, when called upon in this country to commit any person for trial, was authorized to examine into the truth of the charge; that, according to our practice, when a person has made oath that another person has committed a certain crime, a warrant is issued for his apprehension; and that the next step is to bring the accused person before a magistrate, when the accuser must appear with his witnesses and be confronted with him in open court, and it must be proved to the satisfaction of the magistrate, before committing the prisoner for trial, that there was sufficient *primâ facie* ground for believing, first, that the crime had been committed, and next, that the prisoner was the party who had committed it.[4] According to this view of the law, it would be in the power of the person accused,

[2]The originator has not been identified. Edward George Clarke (1841–1931), *A Treatise on the Law of Extradition* (London: Stevens and Haynes, 1867 [1866]), p. 6, quotes this definition, and attributes it to Mill.

[3]6 & 7 Victoria, c. 75, Sect. 1.

[4]"The Earl of Clarendon to Earl Cowley" (10 Jan., 1866), in "Correspondence Respecting the Extradition Treaty with France," *PP*, 1866, LXXVI, 375–8. Henry Richard Wellesley (1804–84), 1st Earl Cowley, was Ambassador to France.

[a-a]TT He would suggest something like this:—

before the order is passed for delivering him up, to produce witnesses and have them examined. By the treaty now entered into, the prisoner might be delivered up on the production of written depositions. But he had always understood that, although the depositions might be received in evidence, yet conformably with our practice it would be open to the prisoner to produce counter evidence in contradiction to them, which might show them to be untrustworthy. But now look at the memorandum of the Conference at the Foreign Office on the 8th of February. It was there stated that an impression prevailed in France that the English magistrate actually tried the case; and that that impression was unfounded.[5] Of course it was, because there was a great deal of difference between the inquiry previous to committal and the actual trial. But, then, the memorandum went on to say, that when the prisoner was brought before the magistrate he would be entitled to have the depositions read in his presence; but that he would not be allowed to controvert the truth of those depositions, or to produce counter evidence, except as to his identity. Could there be a more flagrant case of contradiction between theory and practice? They were entitled to ask Government whether the law laid down in the Act or the practice laid down in the Foreign Office memorandum was right. If the practice were to prevail over the law, a law should be made to legalize it; but it ought to be considered whether such a law would not be an absolute enormity. Could it be dreamt of that even in respect to an ordinary offence, depositions taken unknown to the person charged—which he had no opportunity of disputing—with reference to which he was not permitted to cross-examine his accusers, should be sufficient to require his surrender?[6] Were these depositions, produced in evidence in a court in this country, to be made the grounds for delivering up a person to be tried in the country in which the depositions were made, on the sole condition that he was not shown to be the person named in the warrant? If he really were the person charged, was he not to be allowed to tender any evidence to show that the depositions did not establish a case against him? That was a subject on which the noble Lord the Secretary of State should tell them his mind. Then they had been led to think that there was an understanding with foreign Powers, including the Government of France, that political prisoners should not be delivered up. It now appeared, however, that there was no such understanding, but it was assumed that the French Government would not ask them to deliver up such persons. If that was the case, it was extremely honourable to the French Government, or to our own, perhaps to both—honourable to the French Government if they did not desire to have such persons delivered up, honourable to the reputation of our own Government in foreign countries, if the absence of the demand was grounded on a conviction that it would not be complied with. They had the noble Lord's assurance that he would not deliver up such persons, but they ought to have some

[5]"Memorandum of the Conference at the Foreign Office" (8 Feb., 1866), *ibid.*, p. 390.
[6]As in the French Code d'instruction criminelle, Livre I, Chap. vi, Sect. iii, Arts. 71–3.

more complete security. Was that intention grounded on an understanding that the treaty did not require us to give up persons charged with political murder, or on a belief that, although the treaty did bind us to deliver them up, the demand would not be made? Surely it would have been better to have some words inserted in the Act showing that it was not the intention of Parliament that the Act should authorize the extradition of political offenders. It was admitted that the Act in terms admitted the extradition of political offenders, but we were told that the right was not exercised. That might be the case with regard to a particular Sovereign, but what security had they for the conduct of his successors. It seemed now that there had not been even a verbal understanding, and that absence of any demands from which it had been sought to infer one, might have arisen only from the circumstance that during the period which had elapsed there had not been a sufficiently strong desire for the surrender of any person included in the class referred to, to induce the French Government to demand his extradition. It was said that we could get rid of the treaty in six months, but that could not or would not be done until something irrevocable had taken place, until, perhaps, some illustrious exile had been delivered up, whose surrender would cover this country with ignominy. He entreated the noble Lord to apply his mind to the subject, and see if it were possible to insert words that would show at least the will and intention of Parliament that the extradition should not extend to political cases, so that there might be something to be relied upon by the Secretary of State in justification of the course he might have to take. This Act was an experiment which they were going to try for the first time, and surely it would be worth while to try it avowedly as an experiment. Would the noble Lord limit the duration of the Act to twelve months? At the expiration of that time they would perhaps have better means of judging than they had now, and might be able to renew the Act from time to time for a longer period. (*Hear, hear.*)

[*Later in the debate Kinglake suggested acceding to Mill's suggestion of limiting the duration of the act to one year, so that the House could consider the matter more carefully; Goldsmid's amendment was withdrawn, and Kinglake's clause added (col. 2124). The Bill thus amended passed its third reading.*]

40. The Disturbances in Jamaica [3]

10 AUGUST, 1866

PD, 3rd ser., Vol. 184, col. 2160. Reported in *The Times*, 11 August, p. 6.

MR. J. STUART MILL SAID, he wished to ask the Under Secretary of State for the Colonies, Whether any further information has been received as to the apprehensions which he stated to be entertained by the authorities in Jamaica of a new outbreak in the Colony;[1] and whether he has any objection to state more particularly to the House the information which had previously been received on that subject?

Mr. Adderley said, in answer to the honourable Member's question, he must beg to state that just before the recent debate on the subject of Jamaica despatches were received, from which it appeared that disturbances were apprehended by the Custos of the parish of Metcalfe, a Member of the Colonial Government, as likely to take place in his district during the present month of August. Her Majesty's Government immediately took such precautions as they deemed fully adequate to secure the peace of the colony, and they ascertained from the Admiralty that a considerable naval force was about the island, and available for any emergency which might arise. The Governor, Sir Henry Storks, felt no distrust in the powers which he possessed to meet any such disturbances as were apprehended. No further information had been received since the arrival of those despatches, but he had laid papers on the table that day which gave the despatches in extenso, *together with the fullest information up to the most recent period respecting the late lamentable occurrences.*

41. The Lord Chief Baron

10 AUGUST, 1866

PD, 3rd ser., Vol. 184, col. 2165. Reported in *The Times*, 11 August, p. 6.

MR. J. STUART MILL SAID, he rose to move for an Address for Copies of all the Correspondence which has taken place between Members of the Government and Mr. Rigby Wason in relation to the appointment of Sir FitzRoy Kelly to be Lord Chief Baron of the Exchequer;[1] and of any Correspondence between the Members of Government and Sir FitzRoy Kelly upon the same subject.

Mr. Walpole said, he had no objection to the first part of the Motion; but as the

[1]Adderley, speech of 31 July, col. 1787.

---

[1]Peter Rigby Wason (1798–1875) had been M.P. for Ipswich 1832–37, during which time he had been opposed in elections by Fitzroy Kelly. Three decades later, when Kelly's appointment was announced, Wason wrote to Walpole, the Home Secretary, and to the Prime Minister, objecting on the grounds that Kelly had lied to the election committee that had unseated him after he defeated Wason in 1835. Wason succeeded in bringing the matter before the Lords in the next session, by which time Kelly had responded (*PD*, 3rd ser., Vol. 185, cols. 257–73).

second part related to communications made to him by the Lord Chief Baron which were of a private character, he (Mr. Walpole) could not assent to their production. There might be an investigation into the matter in another Session, and in that case he thought that the Lord Chief Baron should have an opportunity of considering what answer he should make.

[*Mill's motion, which came on the last day of the Session, was not acted upon.*]

· · · February to August 1867 · · ·

42. Political Progress

4 FEBRUARY, 1867

Manchester Examiner and Times, 5 February, 1867, p. 6. Headed: "Opening of the Manchester Reform Club." (A clipping of this version is in the Mill-Taylor Collection.) The speech was reported in London on the 6th in the *Daily News* and the *Morning Star*. Mill had travelled down from St. Andrews, where on 1 February he had delivered his Inaugural Address as Rector (see *CW*, Vol. XXI, pp. 215–57), to attend the inaugural luncheon meeting of the Manchester Reform Club at Spring Gardens. Hugh Mason presided. In addition to Mill, Goldwin Smith was present as a guest (see No. 43 for Mill's speech in his honour later the same day). After the formal business of the meeting was concluded, toasts were offered, including one by Thomas Bayley Potter (1817–98), M.P. for Rochdale, who proposed "Political progress, the only safeguard of civil liberty," with which he coupled the names of Mill and Smith. "Mill, on being called upon to respond," then spoke.

MR. CHAIRMAN AND GENTLEMEN, you have done me the honour of associating my name with the words of "political progress." It is with you, it is with the men of Lancashire, that that idea should be more particularly connected. We of the south are accustomed to look to you—to the north—as invariably leading the van, not only in the industrial and the commercial progress, but in the political progress of this country. And in doing so you have only confirmed the idea which we have heard from our childhood, which is admitted and even asserted as a general principle by Conservative as well as Liberal thinkers, that manufacturing and commercial populations are always the leaders on the side of progress—(*hear*),—and that agricultural populations, and particularly the territorial aristocracy and the great landowners, have a different function in the community—a function sometimes necessary, although often it has become excessive—the Conservative function, the function of keeping that which is good, and I am afraid sometimes that which is bad too. [a](*Cheers and laughter.*) But to you it particularly belongs—to[a] the manufacturing and commercial communities of the world, and to the manufacturing and commercial part of mixed communities, belongs the lead in improvement, both in ideas and above all in the application of those ideas to practice. It is natural that it should be so, because those who are constantly employed in devising more and more new contrivances for making the laws of nature [b]available[b] for the increase of the national wealth, and for attaining

[a-a]DN,MS] MET To
[b-b]DN,MS applicable

all the objects that are pursued in the economical department of things with ever-increasing facility; those of us, a very large proportion of whom are always men who have made their own position and their own fortunes, who are always rising, a succession of them rising from inferior to higher positions—those are the persons whose practice and whose whole course in life naturally ought to make them, and very generally does make them, habitual improvers and reformers [c]. (*Hear, hear.*) Those are the industries[c] which turn men's minds to improvement in all departments of things as well as in their own. I wish it were not, unfortunately, to be set down to the general infirmities of human nature, that even these very men, after they have raised themselves, their fortune completely made, they and their descendants [d]very often cherish[d] the rather low ambition of passing over to the class of territorial magnates—(*hear, and cheers*), and from that time [e]we[e] rather see their influence employed on the Conservative side—often, wholesomely, sometimes perhaps not quite so wholesomely, than on the side on which they have themselves made their position. (*Cheers.*) Still, it is to them, it is to this class that we must look in all great national movements for political improvement, and it is to them we look mainly for [f]success for the future[f] in the great battle in which we are now engaging against what remains of privilege in this country. (*Cheers.*) The sentiment which has been given by my friend Mr. Potter [g]associates[g] political progress, with civil liberty, as being the sole condition of it; and I think no person who uses the smallest reflection can doubt that this is true, for [h]our history and our principles together combine[h] in showing, in the first place, that the nation which is not going forward always goes back; the nation which is not constantly employed in improving whatever it has both of [i]physical and moral good,[i] and also of spiritual good, which is not constantly engaged in improving, gets into a state of stagnation [j], and actual indolence and indifference[j], the sure consequence of which is decline [k]in these things, and with decline in these things, with decline either in mental prosperity, in mental or moral culture,[k] comes necessarily—where a people has been free—the gradual loss of liberty. (*Hear, hear.*) Consequently it is not to be expected that any country should long retain its liberty which is not engaged in political progress, which does not keep political progress constantly going. And more than this, there is a point which more especially tempts and invites our attention at this present moment, namely, the question of how a country—in the [l]new[l] state of the world—is to protect, not only

[c-c]DN,MS ; these are the antecedents
[d-d]DN,MS] MET often try
[e-e]DN,MS they would
[f-f]DN,MS victory
[g-g]DN,MS] MET asserts
[h-h]DN,MS] MET all the history of all principles together combines
[i-i]DN,MS material
[j-j]DN,MS and mental indolence
[k-k]DN,MS . And we have declined to those things. We have declined either in material prosperity, or in mental and moral culture, and with that decline
[l-l]DN,MS] MET now

its liberty, but its national independence, against foreign countries. Look at the armed hosts that are rising up all over the world just now. Look at the immense extent to which the governments of Europe—all the more powerful governments—are devoting their resources,—the whole, almost we may say, of their population,—to the maintenance of enormous armies, and not merely defensive but aggressive armies. (*Hear, hear.*) Is not that menacing to this country? Does anybody suppose that these governments look with pleasure on the degree of freedom that we enjoy, or upon the contrast whereby, in many respects, our position offers to that of their subjects, [m]in all this[m] freedom? Not at all. Yet what position are we in? We, with our small army, and I hope we shall never have a large and an aggressive army—we actually cannot keep it up, we cannot get recruits, because—and this is the point to which the most attention, I think, should be turned, as being one of the most remarkable signs of the times—the people of this country, and, indeed, of other countries, but especially of this country, will no longer fight for a cause that is not their own. Men will not be soldiers as a mere profession, or at least the number is constantly diminishing, who will hire themselves out to shed the blood of others when it is not for the protection of their own freedom and laws. And we have a noble example of what a people will do—how a people will fight—when it is for themselves, for their own cause, for their own liberty, or for moral principles which they regard equally with their liberty. We have seen that in the late heroic and glorious struggle of the United States. (*Loud cheers.*) We have seen there a million of men in arms for their own freedom, but chiefly for the freedom of others, chiefly for the general cause of liberty; a million of men in arms—every family in the country almost had some one of its members in that force, and scarcely a family in the [n]country, or in the free states, is not[n] in mourning in consequence of that war. Nevertheless they fought on until they had triumphed. They have triumphed, and they have gone back to their ploughs and to their looms, and have resumed the pursuits of civil life, no more thinking to continue a military life, or to make [o]any invidious encroachments[o] on their neighbours, or to engage in any war but such a one as they have carried so nobly to a conclusion—(*hear, hear*)—any more than if they had never handled a musket. (*Hear, hear.*) That is the defensive army which we require—(*loud cheers*)—it is the defensive force we seek—(*cheers*)—and we ought with the utmost vigour to oppose any attempt to increase it so as to give us an aggressive force. What we want is a defensive force; what we want is that the people shall be a disciplined people, shall be an armed people, shall be ready to fight, and to go forth as the Americans did, in their own cause, [p]or in any cause in which they feel a disinterested concern;[p] that it shall be for themselves and not for others—and that they shall offer the highest places in that force not to those who

[m-m]DN,MS owing to our
[n-n]DN,MS Free States that is not now
[o-o]DN an invasion or encroachment] MS any invasion or encroachment
[p-p]DN,MS] MET but not in any cause in which their interest is not concerned—

have bought, or who are born to it, but to those who [q]can show[q] that they have earned it, and that they deserve it. (*Loud applause.*)

[*Goldwin Smith also responded, and after several more toasts and replies the meeting ended.*]

43. Goldwin Smith

4 FEBRUARY, 1867

Manchester Examiner and Times, 5 February, 1867. Headed: "Mr. Goldwin Smith's Lectures. / William Pitt." (A clipping of the report is in the Mill-Taylor Collection.) No other report has been located. Mill's second public appearance on this day (see No. 42) was in the evening at the Assembly Room of the Free Trade Hall. Mill, who was in the Chair, "received a very enthusiastic reception from the audience." His speech introduced Goldwin Smith (1823–1910), Regius Professor of Modern History at Oxford, who was to deliver the last of his four lectures on the Political History of England, which were given to raise funds for the Jamaica Committee.

LADIES AND GENTLEMEN, if Mr. Goldwin Smith were a stranger here, there are many things which it would be my duty, and still more my pleasure, to have said respecting him; but he was no stranger here before he delivered the lectures which have been so well received here, and which have so well deserved it; and he is still less a stranger after them. I therefore need not tell you who or what Mr. Goldwin Smith is. I will only say this, that what makes him, in my estimation, a perfectly invaluable man at this period in this country, is not his talents, not his acquirements, not even his courage—rare as that quality is, which ought to be the commonest of all public virtues—but it is that these talents, and those acquirements, and that courage have been, above all, exercised and called forth in defence of outraged moral principles. (*Applause.*) Whenever there is a high moral principle to be asserted against the insolence of power, or against the prevailing opinion of the powerful classes, there Mr. Goldwin Smith is to be found. (*Hear.*) You all know two of the most conspicuous instances—the stand which he made against the sympathy with the worst of all rebellions, the slaveholders' rebellion,[1] and that which he is now making against the outrages in Jamaica.[2] Above all, when any outrage is committed against those united principles, principles which never were dissevered in the best times of our history, and never ought to be dissevered—liberty and law—it is then that we most need the services and the aid,

[1]See, e.g., his "England and America," *Daily News*, 27 Nov., 1862, p. 5.

[2]I.e., in this lecture series. For reports, see *The Times*, 16 Jan., p. 12, 22 Jan., p. 9, 29 Jan., p. 7, and 5 Feb., p. 6.

[q-q]DN,MS have shewn

the championship of a man in whom those two ideas are for ever united—ideas which are now so separated in the minds of the powerful that the most lawless outrages are condoned by the proper and authorised defenders of law, provided they are perpetrated against liberty. (*Applause.*)

[*After Smith's address, the meeting's thanks to Smith for the series were moved. The motion was carried by acclamation, and Smith responded, commenting that when it was first suggested to him that his friend Mill should preside, he had said that "it would be rather like drawing a champagne cork with a steam engine. (Laughter.) But the steam engine was so kind and unconscious of its own magnitude that it came. (Hear, and laughter.)" Jacob Bright then took the Chair, so that T.B. Potter could move a vote of thanks to Mill. Bright, in putting the motion, remarked that when Mill entered the House of Commons, he "found himself much too large to be a Tory—(laughter)—he was too generous and had too much courage to be a Whig, and he gave his great powers unsought to the cause of the people, which was the cause of humanity. (Cheers.)" After the vote was approved with loud applause, Mill rose again.*]

Mr. Mill said: Ladies and gentlemen, I am most sincerely and deeply grateful for the kind feelings with which you have received me, and for the kind vote of thanks you have been pleased to pass, though I do not feel that I at all deserve it, for having come here to give myself the opportunity of hearing the noble address which has kept us all in such a state of delight from beginning to end, and the opportunity also of giving, so far as the case admits of it, my adhesion to the whole tone and tenour of that discourse, and to nearly all the sentiments and statements which it contains. I say nearly all, because it is impossible that, in any address of that length, there should not be some things on which differences of opinion might arise, and if I could wish to suggest any difference of opinion from this noble discourse it would be to put in a word for the poor French Revolutionists. (*Applause.*) Unfortunately, there is too much of what Mr. Goldwin Smith has brought against them which can neither be denied nor palliated; but I should be very sorry, and I have no doubt Mr. Goldwin Smith himself would be very sorry, that you should suppose that there is not another side to the question—that there is nothing whatever to be said for them. On the contrary, in many of what seem their most exceptionable acts, there were circumstantial justifications of detail which, if they were stated, would very often, in my opinion, justify, and always excuse their conduct. I am speaking of the comparatively good period of the revolution. I would not, any more than the best revolutionists did then, and their greatest admirers have done since, palliate for one instant either the massacre of September or the excesses of the reign of terror. There were many bad men among them, and there were many bad acts; but there were also men of the purest virtue, some of the most heroic characters that ever existed, many of whom gave their lives, not only for their principles, but to preserve the purity and the fame of those principles by preventing, as far as could be, the atrocities with which they were stained, and rather sacrificed their own lives when they could have saved them, than tacitly connive at, or appear to be any parties to those iniquities. For what there was—and there was very much—for which no excuse can be offered, the greatest share of the blame rests where Mr. Goldwin Smith placed it, upon the odious system under which they had hitherto lived, the oppressions under which they had suffered, and the entire failure of their governing classes to establish any claim whatever on their forbearance. But even among those governing classes there were exceptions—a minority of the *noblesse* in the first States General, the minority which first joined with the people, consisting of about forty-five, among which there is not one name that was not eminent. Those 45 men, or thereabouts, I take to be about as heroic a body of men as ever existed, Lafayette being at their head.[3] (*Applause.*) However, this is not the occasion on which it would be suitable to go any further into this subject. I have only entered upon it at all because I thought that possibly, without any intention on the part of the lecturer, a more unfavourable impression than he intended might be given to some of those who had not studied the history of the period; and I could not help saying what little depends upon myself to reduce this too heavy catalogue of just accusations against the French revolutionists within its legitimate bounds. (*Hear.*) I cannot sufficiently congratulate this assembly and this city upon what Mr. Brodrick[4] has so well called the union between Oxford and Manchester—that is, between the best part of Oxford and Manchester—(*laughter and applause*)—which is inaugurated, I hope, by Mr. Goldwin Smith's presence here. (*Applause.*) Mr. Goldwin Smith is one of that band of reformers who have made Oxford so different from what it was not long ago. (*Hear.*) There was a time not very distant when it seemed as if the University of Oxford existed for the purpose of preventing all which a university is supposed to exist in order to create. That time has gone by. There is abundant need for reform in Oxford still; but there is abundance of good there. There is a race of men now rising in Oxford in whom the spirit of improvement is as strong and as enlightened as in any other class or body of men who can be found in this country—(*applause*), who are taking the lead in all Liberal improvements—not only in politics, but in all that with which Oxford is more particularly connected—in ecclesiastical matters. We have an example of this in the two Fellows[5] of an illustrious college at Oxford who have appeared among you on this occasion, and uttered sentiments which all present will appreciate. They also form part of this noble band of men from whose exertions England will yet reap admirable fruits, and fruits which will doubtless

[3]Marie Joseph Gilbert du Motier, marquis de Lafayette (1757–1834), French aristocrat who distinguished himself in the U.S. War of Independence and then on the popular side in the French Revolution.

[4]George Charles Brodrick (1831–1903), a lawyer and leader writer for *The Times*, and a Fellow of Merton College, had spoken before Mill.

[5]In addition to Brodrick, Charles Saville Roundell (1827–1906), a lawyer who had been Secretary to the Jamaica Inquiry, was a Fellow of Merton.

increase year after year. The improvements which are taking place, and which will take place, are being prepared and will be forwarded and carried into effect in a great degree, as I fully believe, by them all, such men as they are. I am sure that my friend, Mr. Goldwin Smith, may well leave this city with the feelings of satisfaction, of pleasure, and of thankfulness which he has expressed. (*Hear.*) And I am sure that no less those whom I am addressing sincerely feel the thanks which they have voted to Mr. Goldwin Smith. I am sure that from the lectures he has delivered, and of which I have only had the satisfaction of hearing one, but, if the others were like it, I know what I must have lost—you must be quite aware how much you have yet to look to from him. (*Applause.*) How he can possibly suppose that his sole means of usefulness is his pen, I know not, and I think the statement must have surprised all of you as much as it surprised me. But I have no doubt that the faculty which appears to have been a secret to himself, but which he has manifested in so remarkable a manner to us, will be yet exercised in many other ways and on many other occasions, equally with his very active pen, for the service, not only of parliamentary reform, but of all other public improvements. (*Applause.*)

[*The meeting then terminated.*]

44. The Royal Commission on Trades' Unions

15 FEBRUARY, 1867

Morning Star, 16 February, 1867, p. 5. Headed: "The Trades' Unions Commission. / Deputation to the Home Secretary." Reprinted without substantive variants in *Report of the Various Proceedings Taken by the London Trades' Council and the Conference of Amalgamated Trades, in Reference to the Royal Commission on Trades' Unions, and Other Subjects in Connection Therewith* (London: Kenny, 1867), pp. 33–4. The deputation of representative working men called on Spencer Walpole at the Home Office. Mill introduced them and, after others exchanged comments, spoke.

I HAVE NO DOUBT the commission will examine every person that may be produced, and that any person the working classes wish to represent them will get a fair hearing, but if I understand the matter rightly the difficulty was not that witnesses will not get opportunities of giving all the evidence they consider desirable, but that some persons in the interests of the trades' unions, and properly understanding their working, should be present to answer any charge that may be made affecting the character of any one of the trades. I believe what is desired is, that some persons having practical acquaintance with trades' unions should be put in position to contradict anything that may be said, through, perhaps, ignorance, damaging to the character of these societies, or to put such questions as would have the effect of enabling the commission to form a better and more impartial opinion than perhaps they otherwise could have done. Very likely Mr. Harrison may do it well,[1] but Mr. Harrison with a working man may be able to do it better. If the commission had the power to do what the trades' unions desired with regard to the attendance of persons to watch the interests of each trade as questions affecting that trade came up for inquiry, no doubt it would be better.

Mr. Walpole: I think the commission can do so, but I should not like to interfere any further.

Mr. Mill then thanked Mr. Walpole for the courteousness of his reception, and the delegation withdrew.

45. The Metropolitan Poor Bill [1]

8 MARCH, 1867

Saint Stephen's Chronicle, Vol. II, p. 148. Not in *PD*. *The Times*, 9 March, p. 6, summarizes Mill's intervention in a clause. On 7 March (*PD*, 3rd ser., Vol. 185, col. 1510) Gathorne Gathorne-Hardy (1814–1906), M.P. for the University of Oxford and President of the Poor Law Board, moved that the House go into Committee *pro forma* on "A Bill for the Establishment in the Metropolis of Asylums for the Sick, Insane, and Other Classes of the Poor, and of Dispensaries; and for the Distribution over the Metropolis of Portions of the Charge for Poor Relief; and for Other Purposes Relating to Poor Relief in the Metropolis," 30 Victoria (7 Mar., 1867), *PP*, 1867, IV, 283–324 (as amended). He proposed that the discussion proper should begin on the next day, and Mill spoke at the beginning of that session, concerning the scheduling of the Bill. In reply to a question, Gathorne-Hardy said that he intended to proceed with the Committee on the Metropolitan Poor Bill that evening, and Mill intervened.

THE BILL with the amendments of the right honourable gentleman is not yet in the hands of honourable members, and they are therefore hardly in a position to go into committee upon it.

[*Sir Thomas Chambers (1814–91), M.P. for Marylebone, agreed with Mill, but Gathorne-Hardy concluded the discussion by saying that the importance of the matter entailed continuing immediately, and that the amended version would soon be in members' hands. For the ensuing discussion, see Nos. 47–9.*]

[1]Frederic Harrison (1831–1923), positivist man of letters, known as friendly to working-class aspirations.

46. The Straits Settlements

8 MARCH, 1867

PD, 3rd ser., Vol. 185, cols. 1606–7. Reported in *The Times*, 9 March, p. 7. Myles William O'Reilly, M.P. for Longford, asked questions of Adderley, the Colonial Secretary, concerning the treatment of officers as a result of the transfer of the Settlement from the India to the Colonial Office. Adderley replied, saying in part that the Colonial Office did not communicate with the superseded officers because it dealt only with its own appointees, not those of the Indian Department. Mill then spoke.

MR. J. STUART MILL SAID, he knew nothing of these particular cases, but he did know something of the Straits Settlements. He hoped that the general proceedings of the Colonial Office were not such as they appeared to have been in this instance. The reason why Parliament desired to transfer the Straits Settlements from the India to the Colonial Office was, he apprehended, because those settlements were totally different from India, in a totally different state of society, and had always been under a totally different system of government. There was no natural connection between the Straits Settlements and India; but as soon as the transfer was made it was thought necessary by the Colonial Office that the officers, who had been conducting the affairs of the Settlements, as seemed to be implied, upon the Indian system, should be superseded by others who would conduct them upon the colonial system. He wanted to know what the colonial system was. He hoped and trusted that there was no such thing. How could there be one system for the government of Demerara, Mauritius, the Cape of Good Hope, Ceylon, and Canada? What was the special fitness of a gentleman who had been employed in the administration of the affairs of one of those colonies, for the government of another of which he knew nothing, and in regard to which his experience in other places could supply him with no knowledge? What qualifications had such a man, that should render it necessary to appoint him to transact business of which he knew nothing, in the place of gentlemen who did understand it, and who had been carrying it on, not certainly upon the Indian system, and he believed upon no system whatever but the Straits Settlements system? He did not know upon what principle the government of the Straits Settlements was to be carried on by the Colonial Office; but he did know that the principle upon which such trusts were administered by the old East India Company was that of retaining a man in the position the duties of which he understood, and they would never have thought of removing a man from an office of which he understood all the details, and replacing him by one who knew nothing about them. He knew nothing of the gentlemen who had administered the government of the Straits Settlements. He was not even aware whether they desired to retain their offices: but he was sure that if they did, it would have been for the public advantage that they should be allowed to keep them. At all events, if they were to be removed, they ought to have been informed of that intention by some Department of the Government, and ought not to have been allowed to learn it from reading in a newspaper that their successors had been appointed.[1] That that should have occurred was very discreditable to somebody; and for his own part he should have thought that it was the duty of the Colonial Office to communicate with these gentlemen, because they were still serving in a territory which had been transferred to that Department, and were not then acting under the India Office. They must, indeed, until they ceased to exercise their functions, have been in communication with the Colonial Office upon a hundred other subjects, and it was curious that the only topic upon which the Colonial Department did not think it necessary to intimate its sentiments to them, was that of their removal from their posts, and the appointment of their successors.

47. The Metropolitan Poor Bill [2]

8 MARCH, 1867

PD, 3rd ser., Vol. 185, cols. 1608–10, 1616. Reported in *The Times*, 9 March, p. 7, from which the variant and responses are taken. Mill indicated in a letter of 9 March to Chadwick that his comments were "imperfectly reported," though the account in the *Morning Star*—which Hansard would have used in his collation—was "the best" (*LL*, *CW*, Vol. XVI, pp. 1254–5). Mill spoke during Committee consideration of the Metropolitan Poor Bill (for which, see No. 45). Clause 5, on which Mill first spoke, and which was approved, read: "Asylums to be supported and managed according to the provisions of this Act may be provided under this Act for Reception and Relief of the Sick, Insane, or Infirm, or other Class or Classes of the Poor Chargeable in Unions and Parishes in the Metropolis." Mill's second intervention came on Clause 9—"the Managers shall . . . be partly elective and partly nominated"—immediately after speeches by Chambers and Torrens that are summarized in the text below. (Chambers's amendment was defeated.)

MR. J. STUART MILL SAID, he was too much alive to the extreme difficulty of carrying any measure for the improvement of the law or its administration to be over critical in regard to the present Bill, as it was brought forward with a real desire to improve the administration of the Poor Law,[1] and really did so in many important particulars. But he wished to make a few observations, chiefly for the purpose of eliciting the views of the right honourable Gentleman (*Mr. Gathorne-Hardy*), and of entering a caveat in respect to principles of administration which

[1]See *The Times*, 6 Feb., 1867, p. 8, quoting from the *London Gazette* of 5 February.

---

[1]4 & 5 William IV, c. 76 (1834).

seemed to him true and just, but which that measure was very far from carrying out to the extent which he was persuaded the House and the country would come in time to think desirable. He wished to ask the reason why the Bill, in the new system which it originated, preserved so much of the fractional character of the old system. Why was it necessary, for example, that there should be one set of managers for asylums, and a different set for dispensaries? Why were asylums to be provided according to districts marked out by the Poor Law Board, while dispensaries were to be provided according to parishes and unions? Both of those institutions, being kindred institutions, must be managed in a certain degree on the same principles, and those who were capable of managing the one must be capable of managing the other. Why was it thought necessary that the management of every separate asylum should be under a separate body, and that every separate dispensary should be under a separate management? No doubt, the right honourable Gentleman meant that there should be the same system of administration for them, and trusted to the powers reserved for the Poor Law Board for establishing it.[2] But it was a sound rule that the administration of the same kind of things ought to be, as far as possible, on a large scale, and under the same management. A Central Board would be under the eye of the public, who would know and think more about it than about local Boards. It would act under a much greater sense of responsibility. The number of persons capable of adequately performing the duties in question was necessarily limited, and such persons would be more easily induced to undertake duties on a large scale than on a small one. It was probable that a considerable number of powers now reserved to the Poor Law Board might safely be exercised by such a Central Board; which would, to that extent, preserve the principle of the administration of the local affairs of the people by their own representatives. (*Hear.*) He was not one of those who desired to weaken the power of the Poor Law Board to guide local authorities, and supersede them when they failed in their duty, for Poor Law administration is not a local but a national concern. But there was much force in what was said by some local authorities, who did not object to the main principles of this Bill, who admitted that its proposals were necessary, who applauded the right honourable Gentleman for making them, yet had fair ground for urging that they ought to have the opportunity of themselves doing what was required, and that interference should take place only when they had failed. With a view to future legislation it would be well worth considering whether the administration of the relief of the sick poor for the whole of London should not be placed under central instead of local management, the Central Board to be constituted by election, or partly by election and partly by nomination. He did not wonder that the right honourable Gentleman (*Mr. Gathorne-Hardy*) had not chosen to leave the sick poor in the hands of the vestries.

[2]Gathorne-Hardy spoke on introducing the Bill on 8 February (*PD*, 3rd ser., Vol. 185, cols. 150–75), and on moving its second reading on 21 February (*ibid.*, cols. 771–80).

Vestry government was hole and corner government, and he hoped the time was coming when they would not tolerate hole and corner administration for any purpose whatever. He hoped, before long, to have the opportunity of bringing this matter before the House in connection with the general subject of metropolitan local government. Of course, some of the vestries had suffered wrongfully for the deficiencies of those who had done worse; but it was in the essence of hole and corner government to be comparatively irresponsible, inefficient, jobbing, and carried on by inferior persons—objections which would not apply to a Central Board. With a Central Board in existence, the duties of the vestries would be those of superintendence rather than of execution. A numerically large Board was unfit for executive or administrative duties, but admirably fitted for looking after those who were intrusted with such duties. Administrative duties were best intrusted to a single hand, which should be responsible, and, if possible, paid (*hear, hear*); and the executive administration of the Poor Laws should principally devolve on paid officers, who would be watched in the districts by the vestries, which would consist of ready-made critics superintending others with a vigilance with which they did not like others to superintend them. (*Hear, hear.*) [a]In this way an addition might be made to the provisions of this Bill for securing appropriate superintendents.[a] The proposal to make the asylums medical schools, and thus to secure to them a high degree of publicity and the constant supervision of skilled persons, did the greatest credit to whoever suggested it, and was a proof of a real capacity for practical legislation.[3] (*Hear, hear.*)

[*In the discussion of Clause 9, Thomas Chambers moved an amendment to the effect that all the managers should be elected. McCullagh Torrens, while expressing great anxiety that the Bill should pass, argued in favour of the amendment, asserting that opinion outside the House was unanimous that control should not be taken out of the ratepayers' hands.*[4]]

Mr. J. Stuart Mill said, he agreed with the honourable Gentleman, and did not see any reason for the provisions in the Bill by which the Poor Law Board were empowered to appoint a certain number of guardians.[5] According to his view, the guardians were, or ought to be, quite competent to perform their duties without any assistance from the Government of any kind; but in the case of the appointment of a manager, in whom special skill was required, popular election might not be altogether so satisfactory as the appointment of a responsible functionary. He was therefore fully disposed to support this particular clause, although he should oppose, with his honourable Friend the Member for Finsbury, that part of the Bill which left the nomination of the guardians in the hands of the Poor Law Board.

[3]By Clause 29 of the Bill as amended.

[4]William Torrens McCullagh Torrens (1813–94), M.P. for Finsbury, Speech on the Metropolitan Poor Bill (8 Mar.), *PD*, 3rd ser., Vol. 185, cols. 1615–16.

[5]By Clause 79 of the Bill as amended.

[a-a]+TT

48. The Metropolitan Poor Bill [3]

11 MARCH, 1867

PD, 3rd ser., Vol. 185, cols. 1678–9, 1680, 1685, and 1696. Reported in *The Times*, 12 March, p. 7, from which the variant and response are taken. Mill wrote to Chadwick on the 12th to say that his remarks were "better reported this time than last [see No. 47], though briefly" (*LL*, *CW*, Vol. XVI, p. 1256). The Committee consideration of the Metropolitan Poor Bill (see No. 45) continued, with Mill speaking on Clause 45, which provided that the District Medical Officers for the Unions and Parishes should be appointed by the Dispensary Committee, subject to the rules and orders of the Poor Law Board, except that those in employment when the Dispensary Committee was first set up should continue in office under such modifications of their duties and remuneration as should be made by the Poor Law Board.

MR. J. STUART MILL SAID, he had ventured on a former clause to make some suggestions which had been received very courteously,[1] and he was now going to make two other suggestions, which were not new, but had been frequently made by, perhaps, the highest authority on the subject, Mr. Chadwick, the only surviving member of the Royal Commission which drew up the Poor Law.[2] That Commission was one of the most enlightened and able that ever sat, and so long ago as 1834 proposed principles on the subject of education, which, Parliament being afraid of doing too many good deeds at once, left for adoption by generations to come. He regretted Mr. Chadwick was not himself a Member of that House; there was scarcely any one whose services would be more valuable on many points of administrative improvement. (*Hear.*) The first suggestion he had to offer was this—if they wished the poor to be effectually taken care of, the medical officers appointed should not be in private practice.[3] It was not to be expected in the ordinary run of human affairs that public duty would not be neglected for private practice. It was eminently honourable to the profession that public duties were so well attended to as they were; but medical officers should be under no temptation to postpone their public duties to private practice. Could any one suppose that in a time of epidemic and disorder, when their services would be most required by the poor, that they would not be under the temptation of postponing their public duties for their private practice? One had heard of people advertising for perfection in a schoolmaster for £40 a year, which they were just as likely to get as a Board of

[1]For Mill's speech, see No. 47; it was received courteously by Gathorne-Hardy, Speech on the Metropolitan Poor Bill (8 Mar.), *PD*, 3rd ser., Vol. 185, cols. 1610–11.

[2]"Report from His Majesty's Commissioners for Inquiring into the Administration and Practical Operation of the Poor Laws" (21 Feb., 1834), *PP*, 1834, XXVII, 1–263; the brief reference to education is on p. 209. The Report resulted in 4 & 5 William IV, c. 76 (1834). See also No. 147, n8.

[3]"Report on the Sanitary Condition of the Labouring Population of Great Britain," *PP*, 1843, XII, 602.

Guardians were likely to get a competent medical officer for £100 a year. The other point was as to the mode of the appointment of the medical officers. He thought we might well adopt the practice of the hospitals of Paris, which were the best managed in Europe, where the medical officers were appointed by a medical board after examination; and he would suggest whether it would not be in the power of the College of Physicians and the College of Surgeons, in combination with the Civil Service Commissioners, to have a system of competitive examinations in order to test the capacity of those medical officers who were appointed.[4] It was clear that the House was not at present prepared to adopt this suggestion; but he laid it before the House and the right honourable Gentleman, in the hope that it might be taken into consideration on some future occasion.

[a]*In reply to the Chairman,*

Mr. Mill said[a] He did not move any Amendment on the subject.

[*Gathorne-Hardy replied (cols. 1679–80) that it would not be possible to employ officers if they were prohibited from engaging also in private practice. As to Mill's suggestion of competitive examinations, he had no experience of them in such cases, and thought that such a system would lessen the responsibility of those appointing the officers. In fact, the present checks were sufficient. Gathorne-Hardy was followed by John Brady, F.R.S., M.P. for Leitrim, who expressed surprise that Mill, "so well informed on subjects in general," should argue a case on which he knew nothing. Were he to visit the hospitals, he would find eminent men attending without any salary; if private practice were denied, the officers would be drawn from inexperienced men who would give up the post for private practice as soon as they were qualified. Further, the present examinations for physicians and even more for surgeons were sufficiently severe.*]

Mr. J. Stuart Mill said, that as the suggestion which he ventured to make was an administrative, not a medical, suggestion, he did not see why he should be prevented from making it, though he was not a medical man. As to the question of remuneration, he had said before what he now repeated, that if his suggestions were agreed to, the remuneration to medical officers must be considerably raised. Whatever money was spent in this direction was most usefully employed, because they ought to have the best medical assistance that could be obtained for the poor.

[*Clause 45 was agreed.*]

Mr. J. Stuart Mill said, the clause,[5] as he understood it, would empower the Poor Law Board to dismiss the officers of any Poor Law district, on grant of compensation at their discretion, though those gentlemen had hitherto held office

[4]*Ibid.*, pp. 590, 592.

[5]Clause 59, which provided for the Poor Law Board's determining and varying as necessary existing contracts with resident workhouse medical officers.

[a-a]+TT

for life, except in case of misconduct. Whatever the confidence which those officers felt in the right honourable Gentleman (*Mr. Gathorne-Hardy*), they did not like to be in the power absolutely of an unlimited line of his successors. They would accordingly be very glad if the right honourable Gentleman would either sanction an appeal or a reference to arbitration, so that they might not be at the mercy or discretion of a single officer.

[*Gathorne-Hardy responded negatively (cols. 1685–6). The Clause was agreed.*]

Mr. J. Stuart Mill said, he wished to ask if it were worth while risking the popularity of the measure for the sake of the clause.[6] Boards of Guardians, who had hardly any power left, except in relation to the outdoor poor, would be quite as fit to inspect asylums, etc., without nominee guardians as with them.

[*The Clause was approved, amended to limit such nominees to one-third of the total number.*]

49. The Metropolitan Poor Bill [4]

14 MARCH, 1867

PD, 3rd ser., Vol. 185, cols. 1861–2. Reported in *The Times*, 15 March, p. 5, from which the variants and response are taken. Mill was the first speaker in debate on the third reading of the Bill (see No. 45).

I WISH TO MAKE only one or two observations. This Bill effects a great improvement in the existing state of things, and the chief thing to be regretted is that it does not go further. (*Hear, hear.*) The right honourable Gentleman (*Mr. Gathorne-Hardy*) has reserved to himself[1] the decision of a point which he was urged by several deputations to decide by the Bill itself—namely, the extent and boundaries of the districts, each of which is to have an asylum to itself.[2] I wish to urge upon the right honourable Gentleman the importance of making these districts large; as large as the present or future Parliamentary districts. Less than this will not answer the purpose; and I hope the right honourable Gentleman will give us this evening some idea of what are his purposes on this subject. Another point of

[6]Clause 79, which provided for the addition of nominated members to the Boards of Guardians.

[1]By Clause 6 of the Bill.

[2]See, e.g., "The Metropolitan Poor Bill," *The Times*, 7 Mar., 1867, p. 6, which reports the views of the deputation from the vestry of St. James in Mill's constituency.

more importance is, that there should be created, to stand between the Poor Law Board and the local Boards, an intermediate representative body, which might be intrusted with the [a]execution of those rules and principles which concerned[a] the metropolis as a whole, and which, although elected, might have the exercise delegated to it of some of the functions now reserved to the Poor Law Board. I much regret that the right honourable Gentleman has not taken powers to establish such an authority, for we know that he is himself favourable for it.[3] The value of large bodies representing large constituencies, as compared with small bodies representing small districts, is indisputable. I will at present confine myself to suggesting one or two practical cases in which it will be found of importance. Take the case of an epidemic likely to affect the whole metropolis, but for the present confined to a single district. In that case the resources of the entire metropolis could, through the administration of the general Board, be applied to the district in which they were wanted. Something like this was done lately in apprehension of a visit of the cholera, by the establishment of a central committee sitting at the Mansion House.[4] That committee centralized the charity of the whole of London. Again, there is the case of [b]severe[b] destitution confined to certain districts. In these cases the buildings and beds in some parts of the metropolis are empty, while in the districts suffering the distress they are crowded. The value of a central or intermediate Board between the Poor Law Board and the local bodies, to superintend the application of the resources of the whole metropolis to the immediate exigencies of the distressed districts, is in such cases obvious. This function might well be discharged by a Central Board composed partly of the ratepayers' nominees, and partly of persons selected by the Commissioners. Another most important consideration is that referring to the providing of food, medicine, and other necessaries for the hospitals. In many cases, also, relief is most advantageously given in kind, which makes it very important that provision should be made for obtaining the best articles possible. To make contracts for the supply of these things is an operation for which no local or small body can be by many degrees so fit as is a central body either in point of efficiency or economy. Jobbing, which is inseparable from hole-and-corner proceedings, need not be apprehended in the case of a body representing the whole metropolis, making purchases on a large scale, and entering into large contracts competed for by opulent firms, for these transactions, being of a public nature, would be carried on under the eyes of the world, and subject to public criticism. No one can dispute, and the right honourable Gentleman must be perfectly aware, that efficiency and

[3]See Gathorne-Hardy's speech of 8 Mar., cols. 1610–11.
[4]See "The Distress of East London," *The Times*, 21 Jan., 1867, p. 4.

[a–a]TT] PD administration of the law concerning
[b–b]+TT

economy in contracts are better secured when the body which makes them must do so with publicity—when it stands conspicuous in the public eye. To any one disposed to object to the suggestion for creating an intermediate or central elected Board, like the one I am speaking of, that it is a step on the road to centralization, I would say that if the establishment of such an intermediate body be denied, the denial of it would be a far greater step towards centralization. The powers which such a body is best qualified to exercise have become indispensable. They will therefore be necessarily assumed by a purely Government Board, without any elected body at all—by the Poor Law Board. These are the suggestions I offer to the right honourable Gentleman, and the reasons by which I support them.

[*After a few more observations, including Gathorne-Hardy's that they might institute such a Board if the need for new powers became apparent in the next year and a half (cols. 1864–5), the Bill was given third reading.*]

50. The Reform Bill [1]

8 APRIL, 1867

PD, 3rd ser., Vol. 186, col. 1321. Not reported in *The Times*. Under Public Business, the House was discussing the scheduling of debate on "A Bill Further to Amend the Laws Relating to the Representation of the People in England and Wales," 30 Victoria (18 Mar., 1867), *PP*, 1867, V, 521–46 (the Second Reform Bill), and on "A Bill to Provide for the More Effectual Prevention of Corrupt Practices and Undue Influence at Parliamentary Elections," 30 Victoria (9 Apr., 1867), *ibid.*, II, 213–32. Mill followed Ayrton, who suggested putting the Reform Bill first, and deciding when it had got into Committee whether or not to proceed with the Bribery and Corrupt Practices Bill.

MR. J. STUART MILL SAID, there was a great deal of inconvenience in leaving a matter of so much importance in vagueness and uncertainty. He spoke feelingly on the subject, as he had a Motion on the paper which would be the first Amendment on the Reform Bill when they got into Committee,[1] and he was naturally anxious therefore to know whether the Bill would come on on Thursday. He was perfectly ready to bring forward his Motion on that day, or later if the House thought fit; but it was extremely important that he should know on what day he would be called upon to bring it forward.

[*Disraeli followed immediately on Mill's speech (cols. 1321–2), and accepted Ayrton's proposal.*]

[1]See No. 55.

51. Trades Unions

10 APRIL, 1867

PD, 3rd ser., Vol. 186, cols. 1452–3. Reported in *The Times*, 11 April, p. 6. The variant reading is taken from the *St. Stephen's Chronicle*, Vol. III, p. 112. Moving the second reading of "A Bill to Exempt Associations of Workmen from Certain Disabilities for a Limited Time," 30 Victoria (14 Feb., 1867), *PP*, 1867, I, 129–30, Charles Neate, M.P. for Oxford, said its main aim was to restore to trade societies the right of summary process against defaulting treasurers that they had enjoyed prior to a recent judgment in the Court of Queen's Bench. The Government's contention was that the second reading should not be proceeded with, because the Bill proposed to give sanction to what had just been declared illegal; the societies should change their constitutions to avoid the illegality, and then they would enjoy the protection of the Friendly Societies Act. Mill spoke after two further interventions.

MR. J. STUART MILL SAID, THAT if he were a party man he should be enchanted at the course taken by the Government on this subject; since what they were now doing took away all the grace from the concession they had made in granting an inquiry into the subject of trades unions.[1] As far as mere words went, nothing could sound fairer than to say to the unions—Set yourselves right before the law, and we will then see what can be done for you. But, what was the fact? The law which they were said to have violated was a mine sprung under them.[2] No one dreamt of it until the recent decision of the Court of Queen's Bench.[3] Under the power which our law allowed the Judges to assume, of declaring that whatever was in restraint of trade was illegal, anything might be made law; but when a law was made in this way, it was to all intents and purposes a new law. As the law which these societies were said to have violated was a law of which they and everybody else had been entirely ignorant, the only rational course was to preserve the *status quo* until the whole subject had been reconsidered, which would only be done by legalizing provisionally the course which the societies had pursued, and allowing them to continue in that course until a final settlement was come to. It was a highly demoralizing practice to attempt to prevent people from doing what it was desired they should not do, not by punishing them, but by enabling any scoundrel to plunder them—by granting him complete immunity for acts which in any other case would be severely punished. The Legislature should not employ the vices of mankind, but their virtues, to carry out its intentions. It would have been infinitely

[1]Resulting in "Reports of the Commissioners Appointed to Inquire into the Organization and Rules of Trades Unions and Other Associations," *PP*, 1867, XXXII, 1–396.

[2]18 & 19 Victoria, c. 63 (1855).

[3]Hornby *v*. Close, 2 Queen's B 153–60 (1867), ruling that Trades' Unions did not fall under the provisions of Sect. 24 of 18 & 19 Victoria, c. 63, which gave protection to Friendly Societies, because such associations acted in restraint of trade.

better [a]that these societies, or their officers, should have been punished long ago for violating the law, than that they should now be put in the position they were placed in by the recent decisions[a].

[*Following an argument that the Bill should be withdrawn, the debate adjourned, and the Bill was not proceeded with.*]

52. The Reform Bill [2]

11 APRIL, 1867

PD, 3rd ser., Vol. 186, cols. 1492–3. Reported in *The Times*, 12 April, p. 4, from which the variant and response are taken. Hugh Lupus Grosvenor (Earl Grosvenor) having moved adjournment with the aim of postponing consideration of Reform until after the Easter holidays, the discussion turned on whether Mill's or Gladstone's amendments should be first given consideration. For Mill's amendment, see No. 55. *The Times* reported that, "Mr. Mill and Mr. Henley having risen at the same time, loud calls arose for Mr. Henley; but Mr. Mill, declining to give way," proceeded to speak.

SIR, I confess I attach the highest importance to the Amendment [a] which stands on the paper in my name. Nevertheless, I shall waive my right to proceed with it now, entertaining as I do a confident hope that the House, on both sides of which that proposition has most distinguished supporters and sympathizers, will with one consent allow me at some early period an opportunity for a full discussion upon a proposal which I can assure honourable Gentlemen is a most serious one, and is becoming every day more serious from the number as well as the quality of its supporters. I should not for a moment think of interposing this Motion in the way of anything so important as the Amendment of my right honourable Friend the Member for South Lancashire,[1] upon which the House is desirous, no doubt, of coming to a decisive judgment before we either adjourn or are dissolved. I am sure that the House is not so eager for its own amusement as not to be willing, if necessary, to sit through a part of next week. (*Hear, hear.*) To think that the House would rather leave the question as it is than submit to this minute sacrifice of its pleasure or recreation would be so disgraceful to its character, that I cannot think of entertaining so uncourteous a supposition.

[*After a long discussion, Grosvenor's motion was withdrawn, and the House went into Committee, where eventually Gladstone's amendment was considered (col. 1525); it was defeated the next day (col. 1699).*]

[1]Gladstone's amendment proposed the elimination of the distinction in Clause 3 between direct rate payers and compounders (*PD*, 3rd ser., Vol. 186, cols. 1509–25).

[a–a]SSC] PD for these societies to have punished their officers criminally, than to put the societies themselves out of the protection of the law

[a]TT (*proposing to give the franchise to women*)

53. The Reform Bill [3]

9 MAY, 1867

PD, 3rd ser., Vol. 187, cols. 280–4. Reported in *The Times*, 10 May, p. 7, from which the variants and responses are taken. The *St. Stephen's Chronicle*, Vol. III, pp. 336–7 agrees with *The Times* in the variants. In Committee on the Reform Bill, when considering Clause 3, dealing with qualifications for voting in boroughs, Disraeli had proposed inserting the italicized words in the third qualification: "Has during the Time of such Occupation been rated *as an ordinary occupier* in respect of the Premises so occupied by him within the Borough to all Rates (if any) made for the Relief of the Poor in respect of such Premises . . ." (cols. 15–19). *The Times* reported that Mill "spoke in a low and at times inaudible tone."

IT MUST BE ADMITTED that the Government, by the last concession which they have made, have abated one of the most obvious objections to the most objectionable of all the provisions of the Bill. The compound-householders are not to be burdened with any fine. They are to pay it, but they will be allowed to deduct it from their rent, and will thus be subject to one disadvantage the less. So much has been said about this single disadvantage—so great stress has been laid on what is called the fine—that attention has not been sufficiently directed to the many other impediments which will remain. The honourable Member (*Mr. Hibbert*) has called the Amendment a great improvement.[1] He should rather have called it a real, but a small improvement. Not only will the voter have to keep money by him for a quarterly payment, instead of a weekly payment which gives no trouble, being confounded with his rent; not only will he have to lie out of his money until he has recovered it—perhaps by weekly instalments; but another most essential condition is requisite, on which the honourable Member has justly laid much stress—his landlord must consent.[2] And who is his landlord? One of that powerful class, destined henceforward to be more powerful than ever—not a popular class either with this House or with the public—the owners of small tenements: every one of whom, if his solvent tenants take advantage of the Bill, will lose, to say the least, a profitable contract. Let honourable Gentlemen realize to themselves what an obstacle this is, and then say whether it is likely that in the face of it, the Bill will give more than a very limited amount of honest enfranchisement. But I might be better inclined to accept it as an instalment, if it did no worse; if it was satisfied with keeping almost every small householder out, and did not let anybody in by unfair means. But [a]what will happen?[a] If the Bill becomes law in its present shape, no sooner will it have passed than the scramble will begin for the 465,000

[1]John Tomlinson Hibbert (1824–1908), M.P. for Oldham, Speech on the Representation of the People Bill (9 May), *PD*, 3rd ser., Vol. 187, col. 267.

[2]*Ibid.*, cols. 270–1.

[a-a]TT,SSC the proposal would have, also, quite a contrary effect.

compound-householders. It is safe to say that whichever party can put the greatest number of these people on the register, and, what is of still greater consequence, can keep them there, will have a tolerably secure tenure of power for some time to come. Now, success in this will be principally a question of money. We need not necessarily suppose any direct bribery, any payment of rates, anything distinctly illegal. But there will have to be, and there will be, a perpetual organized canvass of the 465,000. Organizations will be formed for hunting up the small householders who are not rated, and inducing them to come on the rate book. The owners of small tenements must be canvassed too, that they may give their tenants leave to register. Every motive that can be brought to bear on either class will be plied to the utmost. Perpetual stimulus will be applied to the political feelings of those who have any, and to the personal interests of all. Both sides in politics will be prompted to this conduct by the strongest possible motive—by that which makes so many men, not wholly dishonourable or without a conscience, connive at bribery—the conviction that the other party will practise it, and that unless they do the same, their side, which is the right, will be at an unfair disadvantage. Now, this annual, or rather perennial, rating and registering campaign among the small householders, will cost much money. I hope that honourable Gentlemen on this side of the House, who, loving household suffrage not wisely but too well,[3] have brought matters to this state, intend to come down handsomely to the registration societies in their own neighbourhoods; for the registration societies are destined henceforth to be one of the great institutions of the country. I wonder if any one, possessed of the necessary pecuniary statistics, has estimated how much will be added to the already enormous expenses of our electoral system when this Bill has passed. The Chancellor of the Exchequer knows perfectly well which side is likely to carry off the prize when it comes to a contest of purses (*Hear, hear, and Oh!*); though, after the profound contempt which I was happy to hear that he entertains for all such considerations,[4] it would be uncourteous to suppose that he is in any way influenced by them. But this serviceable piece of knowledge, though the right honourable Gentleman is indifferent to it, is one which I should like to impress upon the clever Gentlemen who are going to outwit the Chancellor of the Exchequer, and make his Bill bring forth pure and simple household suffrage, contrary to the intentions of everybody except themselves who will vote for it. Now, if the Conservatives do, what without doubt the right honourable Gentleman intends they should—namely, by dint of money, bring everybody on the register who is dependent on them, or who they think for any reason is likely to vote with them; what is it expected that the Radicals will do? Every creature must fight with its own natural weapons: honourable Gentlemen opposite carry theirs in their pockets (*Oh, oh!*): the natural weapon of the Radicals is political agitation. In

[3]Shakespeare, *Othello*, V, ii, 344; in *The Riverside Shakespeare*, p. 1240.
[4]Disraeli, Speech on the Representation of the People Bill (6 May), cols. 43–5.

mere self-defence they will be compelled to be greater agitators than ever, more vehement in their appeals to Radical feeling, more strenuous in counter-working the voter's personal interest by exalting to the highest pitch every political passion incident to his position in life. This is what will happen even if we make the chimerical assumption, that the money expended in making voters will all be expended in modes which are conventionally innocent—that there will be nothing scandalous, nothing absolutely illegal; not even that decent form of bribery, payment of rates. But is any one so simple as to believe that this will be the case? Encouraged by the brilliant success of your bribery laws,[5] you are going to make payment of rates for political purposes an offence against those laws:[6] and your reward will be, that whereas you do now and then detect a case of bribery, it is questionable if there will ever be a single conviction for the other offence. You find it difficult enough to prove bribery, committed where all eyes are watching for it, amidst the heat and publicity of a contested election. Will it be an easy matter, think you, to prove judicially that the non-rated householder, who a month or two before the registration, goes quietly to the parochial officer and pays his full, not his composition rate, has had it put into his hands a few days previous, when no one but the registration agent was thinking about him? And if you could prove it, whom could you convict? Not the candidate; at the time of the registration there is no candidate. The offender is a society of gentlemen in the neighbourhood. If you can convict any one, it will be some needy agent, some man of straw, unauthorized by anybody, beyond general instructions to do the best he can for the Conservative or the Liberal interest. I just now called what would take place a scramble for the compound-householders. I might have called it an auction. Except under the impulse of strong political excitement, we may expect that the small householders who will get on the register will generally get there at some other person's expense. And the work which begins in this way will not end with it. Once paid for his vote, the integrity of the elector is gone. (*Hear, hear.*) Many a one will go further, and take payment in a grosser and more shameless form. This is the futurity which the Government Reform Bill provides for us. There was but one thing wanting to complete the picture, and that one thing has been vouchsafed to us. It is, that the Minister who is in this way sowing bribery broadcast with one hand, should hold a Bill for the better prevention of bribery in the other.[7] That Bribery Bill completes the irony of the situation. (*Laughter.*) Sir, the point on which we are now deliberating is, in the judgment of this side of the House, the most important of all the points which we shall have to decide. I sincerely hope, in spite of what was said

[5]5 & 6 Victoria, c. 102 (1842), and 17 & 18 Victoria, c. 102 (1854).

[6]By Clause 36 of the Reform Bill (*PP*, 1867, V, 536).

[7]"A Bill to Provide for the More Effectual Prevention of Corrupt Practices and Undue Influence at Parliamentary Elections," 30 Victoria (9 Apr., 1867), *PP*, 1867, II, 213–32.

by the honourable and learned Gentleman who spoke last,[8] that it is not so in the eyes of the Government. No one now wants to throw out the Bill. (*Hear, hear, and Oh, oh.*) If it is wrecked it will be by its authors; nobody can wreck it but themselves. The Bill, however, has now come out in its true colours, as a Bill which restricts the suffrage. Of course, I do not mean that it does nothing else. But if it passes, it will make the franchise more difficult of access to a considerable portion of those who are by the present law entitled to it. As regards the new electors, the right honourable Gentleman the Chancellor of the Exchequer has framed his measure very skilfully to effect the greatest apparent, and the smallest real, enfranchisement of independent voters (*No, no, and Hear, hear*), and the greatest, both apparent and real, enfranchisement of the bribeable and the dependent. Perhaps the House thinks I mean this as a reproach to the right honourable Gentleman, as if there were something tricky and insincere in it. But I am bound to say that the right honourable Gentleman, from as long ago as I remember, has seemed to me remarkably constant to a certain political ideal, which may be defined, an ostensibly large and wide democracy, led and guided by the landed interest. (*Laughter.*) He has always aimed at shaping our institutions after this type, whenever he has meddled with them, either as a theoretical or a practical politician; and there need be no doubt that he sincerely thinks it the best form of Government. But that is no reason why we should follow him, who like neither his end nor his means. (*Hear, hear.*) I am afraid that this Bill, so far as it relates to compound-householders, will make ten electors with other people's money, for other people's purposes, for every one who will make himself an elector by the exercise of the social virtues: and will greatly increase, instead of diminishing, the influence of money in returning Members to Parliament. I believe that in consequence, instead of attaining the end to which so many honourable Members are willing to sacrifice everything, that of putting the question to sleep, and giving a long truce to agitation, this Bill, if it passes with its present provisions, will achieve the unrivalled feat of making a redoublement of agitation both inevitable and indispensable. Thinking these things, I must resist to the utmost these parts of the Bill; and must vote for [b]the Amendment of the honourable member for Oldham (*Mr. Hibbert*), and for every other[b] Amendment (*Ministerial cheers*) which tends to diminish, either in a great or in a small degree, the obstructions, removeable by money, which the Bill throws in the way of a small householder's acquisition of the suffrage. (*Hear, hear.*)

[*After a long debate Disraeli's amendment was carried, Mill voting in the negative.*]

[8]William Balliol Brett (1817–99), Conservative M.P. for Helston, Speech on the Representation of the People Bill (9 May), *PD*, 3rd ser., Vol. 187, col. 280.

[b-b]TT,SSC] PD any

54. The Reform Bill [4]

17 MAY, 1867

PD, 3rd ser., Vol. 187, cols. 738–9. Reported in *The Times*, 18 May, p. 7, from which the responses are taken. Continued discussion in Committee of the Reform Bill had moved to consideration of an amendment to Clause 3 (see No. 53) proposed by Grosvenor Hodgkinson (1818–81), M.P. for Newark, that would have the effect of removing the issue of compound householders by having all householders pay rates directly (cols. 708–12).

IT APPEARS TO ME that the Chancellor of the Exchequer has held out to us a great and splendid concession,[1] which it has been the whole occupation of those of his supporters, who have since spoken, to explain away.[2] (*Hear, hear.*) In the opinion of some of them, we cannot have the complete embodiment of the principle of the honourable Member (*Mr. Hodgkinson*); and it appears to be the opinion of the Attorney General that we cannot have that embodiment this year at all. That is to say, we are called upon to pass a Reform Bill this year, and to wait until next year for the measure that is necessary to render that Bill tolerable. In what position will the House be placed if they give way to that? A General Election may occur in the meantime, with all the evils which have induced us to oppose that part of the Bill which relates to the compound-householders. We ought to have some security against that. (*Hear.*) We could have some security, but it must consist in something more than mere general words, which, however sincere they may be, are not to be acted upon until after an indefinite time, and in an indefinite way. No one can be more eager or anxious than I am that the arrangement which the Chancellor of the Exchequer has offered to us should be fairly and honourably carried into effect. I am sure we are all most sincere in that. At the same time, it is absolutely necessary that we should not proceed with the clauses relating to compound-householders as preparatory to doing away with compound-householders altogether. The country feel a great deal more doubt about the sincerity of the House than the Chancellor of the Exchequer seems to think, and I do not think the country will believe that we intend to do away with the compound-householders if we pass the Bill this year, and postpone till next the measure for the abolition of compound-householders. As to the difficulties anticipated by the honourable and learned Member (*Mr. Ayrton*),[3] and by the last speaker,[4] I will not undertake to say what reality there may be in them; but the

[1]Disraeli, cols. 720–6.

[2]Francis Sharp Powell (1827–1911), M.P. for Cambridge (cols. 730–2); John Rolt (1804–71), the Attorney General, M.P. for West Gloucestershire (cols. 735–6); and Brett (cols. 737–8).

[3]Ayrton referred to the enormous complexity of the matter, necessitating, if a bill were contemplated, a select committee and its attendant delay (cols. 727–9).

[4]Brett argued that the views of parishes and towns should be consulted, and that a select committee was needed (cols. 737–8).

greater the practical difficulties in the way of carrying out the principle of my honourable Friend the Member for Newark, the more important and absolutely essential it is that the House should see the Bill by which these things are to be done before they commit themselves to the Bill of the Chancellor of the Exchequer. (*Hear, hear.*) There is no need to lose time, because there is a great portion of the Bill which does not relate to the borough franchise, and with that we can go on. If we are only assured by the Chancellor of the Exchequer that he will bring in a Bill to give effect to his undertaking, and that we shall see that Bill before we part company with the present one, it would, in my opinion, be the best course to suspend further action upon the borough franchise clauses, and proceed with the other clauses, and only resume the borough franchise clauses when we have seen the promised Bill. At all events, I think we ought not to read the present Bill a third time until we have read the promised Bill a second time. (*Hear, hear.*)

55. The Admission of Women to the Electoral Franchise

20 MAY, 1867

Speech of John Stuart Mill, M.P. on the Admission of Women to the Electoral Franchise. Spoken in the House of Commons, May 20th, 1867 (London: Trübner, 1867), and *PD*, 3rd ser., Vol. 187, cols. 842–3. The text of the pamphlet is reproduced *ibid.*, cols. 817–29, Mill having instructed Trübner to send a copy to Hansard; see *CW*, Vol. XVI, p. 1277. That Hansard used that text is indicated by the asterisk in *PD*. (There are no substantive differences except two misprints in *PD*: "Nor, Sir" for "Now, Sir" at 152.6, and "indirect" for "in direct" at 157.27.) Reported in *The Times*, 21 May, p. 9, from which variants and responses are taken; the variants are all supported by the report in the *St. Stephen's Chronicle*, Vol. III, pp. 475–81. The copies in SC have no corrections or emendations.

I RISE, SIR, to propose an extension of the suffrage which can excite no party or class feeling in this House; which can give no umbrage to the keenest assertor of the claims either of property or of numbers; an extension which has not the smallest tendency to disturb what we have heard so much about lately, the balance of political power; which cannot afflict the most timid alarmist with revolutionary terrors, or offend the most jealous democrat as an infringement of popular rights (*hear, hear*), or a privilege granted to one class of society at the expense of another. There is nothing to distract our attention from the simple question, whether there is any adequate justification for continuing to exclude an entire half of the community, not only from admission, but from the capability of being ever admitted within the pale of the Constitution, though they may fulfil all the conditions legally and constitutionally sufficient in every case but theirs. Sir, within the limits of our Constitution this is a solitary case. There is no other example of an exclusion which is absolute. If the law denied a vote to all but the possessors of £5000 a year, the poorest man in the nation might—and now and then would—acquire the suffrage; but neither birth, nor fortune, nor merit, nor exertion, nor intellect, nor even that great disposer of human affairs, accident, can ever enable any woman to have her voice counted in those national affairs which touch her and hers as nearly as any other [a]person in the nation[a]. (*Hear, hear.*)

Now, Sir, before going any further, allow me to say, that a *primâ facie* case is already made out. It is not just to make distinctions, in rights and privileges, without a positive reason. I do not mean that the electoral franchise, or any other public function, is an abstract right, and that to withhold it from any one, on sufficient grounds of expediency, is a personal wrong; it is a complete misunderstanding of the principle I maintain, to confound this with it; my argument is entirely one of expediency. But there are different orders of expediency; all expediencies are not exactly on the same level; there is an important branch of expediency called justice; and justice, though it does not necessarily require that we should confer political functions on every one, does require that we should not, capriciously and without cause, withhold from one what we give to another. As was most truly said by my right honourable friend the Member for South Lancashire, in the most misunderstood and misrepresented speech I ever remember;[1] to lay a ground for refusing the suffrage to any one, it is necessary to allege either personal unfitness or public danger. Now, can either of these be alleged in the present case? Can it be pretended that women who manage an estate or conduct a business,—who pay rates and taxes, often to a large amount, and frequently from their own earnings,—many of whom are responsible heads of families, and some of whom, in the capacity of schoolmistresses, teach much more than a great number of the male electors have ever learnt,—are not capable of a function of which every male householder is capable? (*Hear, hear.*) Or is it feared that if they were admitted to the suffrage they would revolutionize the State,—would deprive us of any of our valued institutions, or that we should have worse laws, or be in any way whatever worse governed, through the effect of their suffrages? No one, Sir, believes anything of the kind.

And it is not only the general principles of justice that are infringed, or at least set aside, by the exclusion of women, merely as women, from any share in the representation; that exclusion is also repugnant to the particular principles of the British Constitution. It violates one of the oldest [b]and most cherished[b] of our constitutional maxims—a doctrine dear to reformers, and theoretically acknowledged by most Conservatives—that taxation and representation should be co-extensive. Do not women pay taxes? Does not every woman who is *sui juris* contribute exactly as much to the revenue as a man who has the same electoral

[1]Gladstone, speech of 11 May, 1864, cols. 312–27, specifically, col. 324.

[a-a]TT,SSC member of the community
[b-b]+TT,SSC

qualification? If a stake in the country means anything,[2] the owner of freehold or leasehold property has the same stake, whether it is owned by a man or a woman. There is evidence in our constitutional records that women have voted, in counties and in some boroughs, at former, though certainly distant, periods of our history.

The House, however, will doubtless expect that I should not rest my case solely on the general principles either of justice or of the Constitution, but should produce what are called practical arguments. Now, there is one practical argument of great weight, which, I frankly confess, is entirely wanting in the case of women; they do not hold great meetings in the parks, or demonstrations at Islington.[3] (*Oh!*) How far this omission may be considered to invalidate their claim, I will not undertake to decide; but other practical arguments, practical in the most restricted meaning of the term, are not wanting; and I am prepared to state them, if I may be permitted first to ask, what are the practical objections? The difficulty which most people feel on this subject, is not a practical objection; there is nothing practical about it; it is a mere feeling—a feeling of strangeness; the proposal is so new; at least they think so, though this is a mistake; it is a very old proposal. Well, Sir, strangeness is a thing which wears off; some things were strange enough to many of us three months ago which are not at all so now; and many are strange now, which will not be strange to the same persons a few years hence, or even, perhaps, a few months. And as for novelty, we live in a world of novelties; the despotism of custom is on the wane; we are not now satisfied with knowing what a thing is, we ask whether it ought to be; and in this House at least, I am bound to believe that an appeal lies from custom to a higher tribunal, in which reason is judge. Now, the reasons which custom is in the habit of giving for itself on this subject are usually very brief. That, indeed, is one of my difficulties; it is not easy to refute an interjection; interjections, however, are the only arguments among those we usually hear on this subject, which it seems to me at all difficult to refute. The others mostly present themselves in such aphorisms as these: Politics are not women's business, and would distract them from their proper duties: Women do not desire the suffrage, but would rather be without it: Women are sufficiently represented by the representation of their male relatives and connexions: Women have power enough already. (*Laughter.*) I shall probably be thought to have done enough in the way of answering, if I answer all this; and it may, perhaps, instigate any honourable gentleman who takes the trouble of replying to me, to produce something more recondite.

Politics, it is said, are not a woman's business. Well, Sir, I rather think that politics are not a man's business either; unless he is one of the few who are selected and paid to devote their time to the public service, or is a member of this or of the other House. The vast majority of male electors have each his own business, which

[2]For the phrase, see William Windham (1750–1810), Speech on Defence of the Country (22 July, 1807; Commons), *PD*, 1st ser., Vol. 9, col. 897.

[3]For the former, see Nos. 27, 29, 31, 32, and 34; for the latter, No. 32.

absorbs nearly the whole of his time; but I have not heard that the few hours occupied, once in a few years, in attending at a polling booth, even if we throw in the time spent in reading newspapers and political treatises, ever causes them to neglect their shops or their counting-houses. I have never understood that those who have votes are worse merchants, or worse lawyers, or worse physicians, or even worse clergymen than other people. One would almost suppose that the British Constitution denied a vote to every one who could not give the greater part of his time to politics: if this were the case, we should have a very limited constituency. But allow me to ask, what is the meaning of political freedom? Is it anything but the control of those who do make their business of politics, by those who do not? Is it not the very essence of constitutional liberty, that men come from their looms and their forges to decide, and decide well, whether they are properly governed, and whom they will be governed by? And the nations which prize this privilege the most, and exercise it most fully, are invariably those who excel the most in the common concerns of life. The ordinary occupations of most women are, and are likely to remain, principally domestic; but the notion that these occupations are incompatible with the keenest interest in national affairs, and in all the great interests of humanity, is as utterly futile as the apprehension, once sincerely entertained, that artisans would desert their workshops and their factories if they were taught to read. I know there is an obscure feeling—a feeling which is ashamed to express itself openly—as if women had no right to care about anything, except how they may be the most useful and devoted servants of some man. But as I am convinced that there is not a single member of this House, whose conscience accuses him of so mean a feeling, I may say without offence, that this claim to confiscate the whole existence of one half of the species for the supposed convenience of the other, appears to me, independently of its injustice, particularly silly. For who that has had ordinary experience of human affairs, and ordinary capacity of profiting by that experience, fancies that those do their own work best who understand nothing else? A man has lived to little purpose who has not learnt that without general mental cultivation, no particular work that requires understanding is ever done in the best manner. It requires brains to use practical experience; and brains, even without practical experience, go further than any amount of practical experience without brains. But perhaps it is thought that the ordinary occupations of women are more antagonistic than those of men are to the comprehension of public affairs. It is thought, perhaps, that those who are principally charged with the moral education of the future generations of men, cannot be fit to form an opinion about the moral and educational interests of a people: and that those whose chief daily business is the judicious laying-out of money, so as to produce the greatest results with the smallest means, cannot possibly give any lessons to right honourable gentlemen on the other side of the House or on this, who contrive to produce such singularly small results with such vast means. (*Ironical cheers.*)

I feel a degree of confidence, Sir, on this subject, which I could not feel, if the political change, in itself not great or formidable, which I advocate, were not grounded, as beneficent and salutary political changes almost always are, upon a previous social change. The notion of a hard and fast line of separation between women's occupations and men's—of forbidding women to take interest in the things which interest men—belongs to a gone-by state of society, which is receding further and further into the past. We talk of political revolutions, but we do not sufficiently attend to the fact that there has taken place around us a [c]silent[c] domestic revolution: women and men are, for the first time in history, really each other's companions. Our traditions respecting the proper relations between them have descended from a time when their lives were apart—when they were separate in their thoughts, because they were separate equally in their amusements and in their serious occupations. In former days a man passed his life among men; all his friendships, all his real intimacies, were with men; with men alone did he consult on any serious business; the wife was either a plaything, or an upper servant. All this, among the educated classes, is now changed. The man no longer gives his spare hours to violent outdoor exercises and boisterous conviviality with male associates: the two sexes now pass their lives together; the women of a man's family are his habitual society; the wife is his chief associate, his most confidential friend, and often his most trusted adviser. Now, does a man wish to have for his nearest companion, so closely linked with him, and whose wishes and preferences have so strong a claim on him, one whose thoughts are alien to those which occupy his own mind—one who can neither be a help, a comfort, nor a support, to his noblest feelings and purposes? Is this close and almost exclusive companionship compatible with women's being warned off all large subjects—being taught that they ought not to care for what it is men's duty to care for, and that to have any serious interests outside the household is stepping beyond their province? Is it good for a man to live in complete communion of thoughts and feelings with one who is studiously kept inferior to himself, whose earthly interests are forcibly confined within four walls, and who cultivates, as a grace of character, ignorance and indifference about the most inspiring subjects, those among which his highest duties are cast? Does any one suppose that this can happen without detriment to the man's own character? Sir, the time is now come when, unless women are raised to the level of men, men will be pulled down to theirs. The women of a man's family are either a stimulus and a support to his highest aspirations, or a drag upon them. You may keep them ignorant of politics, but you cannot prevent them from concerning themselves with the least respectable part of politics—its personalities; if they do not understand and cannot enter into the man's feelings of public duty, they do care about his personal interest, and that is the scale into which their weight will certainly be thrown. They will be an influence always at hand,

[c-c]TT,SSC social and

co-operating with the man's selfish promptings, lying in wait for his moments of moral irresolution, and doubling the strength of every temptation. Even if they maintain a modest forbearance, the mere absence of their sympathy will hang a dead-weight on his moral energies, making him unwilling to make sacrifices which they will feel, and to forego social advantages and successes in which they would share, for objects which they cannot appreciate. Supposing him fortunate enough to escape any actual sacrifice of conscience, the indirect effect on the higher parts of his own character is still deplorable. Under an idle notion that the beauties of character of the two sexes are mutually incompatible, men are afraid of manly women; but those who have considered the nature and power of social influences well know, that unless there are manly women, there will not much longer be manly men. When men and women are really companions, if women are frivolous, men will be frivolous; if women care for nothing but personal interest and idle vanities, men in general will care for little else: the two sexes must now rise or sink together. It may be said that women may take interest in great public questions without having votes; they may, certainly; but how many of them will? Education and society have exhausted their power in inculcating on women that their proper rule of conduct is what society expects from them; and the denial of the vote is a proclamation intelligible to every one, that whatever else society may expect, it does not expect that they should concern themselves with public interests. Why, the whole of a girl's thoughts and feelings are toned down by it from her schooldays; she does not take the interest even in national history which her brothers do, because it is to be no business of hers when she grows up. If there are women—and now happily there are many—who do interest themselves in these subjects, and do study them, it is because the force within is strong enough to bear up against the worst kind of discouragement, that which acts not by interposing obstacles, which may be struggled against, but by deadening the spirit which faces and conquers obstacles.

We are told, Sir, that women do not wish for the suffrage. If the fact were so, it would only prove that all women are still under this deadening influence; that the opiate still benumbs their mind and conscience. But great numbers of women do desire the suffrage, and have asked for it by petitions to this House. How do we know how many more thousands there may be, who have not asked for what they do not hope to get; or for fear of what may be thought of them by men, or by other women; or from the feeling, so sedulously cultivated in them by their education—aversion to make themselves conspicuous? Men must have a rare power of self-delusion, if they suppose that leading questions put to the ladies of their family or of their acquaintance will elicit their real sentiments, or will be answered with complete sincerity by one woman in ten thousand. No one is so well schooled as most women are in making a virtue of necessity; it costs little to disclaim caring for what is not offered; and frankness in the expression of sentiments which may be unpleasing and may be thought uncomplimentary to their nearest connections, is not one of the virtues which a woman's education tends to cultivate, and is, moreover, a virtue attended with sufficient risk, to induce prudent women usually to reserve its exercise for cases in which there is a nearer and a more personal interest at stake. However this may be, those who do not care for the suffrage will not use it; either they will not register, or if they do, they will vote as their male relatives advise: by which, as the advantage will probably be about equally shared among all classes, no harm will be done. Those, be they few or many, who do value the privilege, will exercise it, and will receive that stimulus to their faculties, and that widening and liberalizing influence over their feelings and sympathies, which the suffrage seldom fails to produce on those who are admitted to it. Meanwhile an unworthy stigma would be removed from the whole sex. The law would cease to declare them incapable of serious things; would cease to proclaim that their opinions and wishes are unworthy of regard, on things which concern them equally with men, and on many things which concern them much more than men. They would no longer be classed with children, idiots, and lunatics, as incapable of taking care of either themselves or others, and needing that everything should be done for them, without asking their consent. If only one woman in twenty thousand used the suffrage, to be declared capable of it would be a boon to all women. Even that theoretical enfranchisement would remove a weight from the expansion of their faculties, the real mischief of which is much greater than the apparent.

Then it is said, that women do not need direct power, having so much indirect, through their influence over their male relatives and connections. I should like to carry this argument a little further. Rich people have a great deal of indirect influence. Is this a reason for refusing them votes? Does any one propose a rating qualification the wrong way, or bring in a Reform Bill to disfranchise all who live in a £500 house, or pay £100 a year in direct taxes? Unless this rule for distributing the franchise is to be reserved for the exclusive benefit of women, it would follow that persons of more than a certain fortune should be allowed to bribe, but should not be allowed to vote. Sir, it is true that women have great power. It is part of my case that they have great power; but they have it under the worst possible conditions, because it is indirect, and therefore irresponsible. I want to make this great power a responsible power. I want to make the woman feel her conscience interested in its honest exercise. I want her to feel that it is not given to her as a mere means of personal ascendency. I want to make her influence work by a manly interchange of opinion, and not by cajolery. I want to awaken in her the political point of honour. Many a woman already influences greatly the political conduct of the men connected with her, and sometimes, by force of will, actually governs it; but she is never supposed to have anything to do with it; the man whom she influences, and perhaps misleads, is alone responsible; her power is like the back-stairs influence of a favourite. Sir, I demand that all who exercise power should have the burthen laid on them of knowing something about the things they have power over. With the acknowledged right to a voice, would come a sense of the corresponding duty. Women are not usually inferior in tenderness of conscience to men. Make the woman a moral agent in these matters: show that you expect from her a political conscience: and when she has learnt to understand the transcendent importance of these things, she will know why it is wrong to sacrifice political convictions to personal interest or vanity; she will understand that political integrity is not a foolish personal crotchet, which a man is bound, for the sake of his family, to give up, but a solemn duty: and the men whom she can influence will be better men in all public matters, and not, as they often are now, worse men by the whole amount of her influence.

But at least, it will be said, women do not suffer any practical inconvenience, as women, by not having a vote. The interests of all women are safe in the hands of their fathers, husbands, and brothers, who have the same interest with them, and not only know, far better than they do, what is good for them, but care much more for them than they care for themselves. Sir, this is exactly what is said of all unrepresented classes. The operatives, for instance: are they not virtually represented by the representation of their employers? Are not the interest of the employers and that of the employed, when properly understood, the same? To insinuate the contrary, is it not the horrible crime of setting class against class? Is not the farmer equally interested with the labourer in the prosperity of agriculture,—the cotton manufacturer equally with his workmen in the high price of calicoes? Are they not both interested alike in taking off taxes? And, generally, have not employers and employed a common interest against all outsiders, just as husband and wife have against all outside the family? And what is more, are not all employers good, kind, benevolent men, who love their workpeople, and always desire to do what is most for their good? All these assertions are as true, and as much to the purpose, as the corresponding assertions respecting men and women. Sir, we do not live in Arcadia, but, as we were lately reminded, *in faece Romuli*:[4] and in that region workmen need other protection than that of their employers, and women other protection than that of their men. I should like to have a return laid before this House of the number of women who are annually beaten to death, kicked to death, or trampled to death by their male protectors: and, in an opposite column, the amount of the sentences passed, in those cases in which the dastardly criminals did not get off altogether. I should also like to have, in a third column, the amount of property, the unlawful taking of which was, at the same sessions or assizes, by the same judge, thought worthy of the same amount of punishment. We should then have an arithmetical estimate of the value set by a male legislature and

[4]Cicero (106–43 B.C.), *Letters to Atticus* (Latin and English), trans. E.O. Winstedt, 3 vols. (London: Heinemann; New York: Macmillan, 1912), Vol. I, p. 108 (II, i): "the dregs of humanity collected by Romulus" rather than the inhabitants of Plato's Republic (Arcadia).

male tribunals on the murder of a woman, often by torture continued through years, which, if there is any shame in us, would make us hang our heads. Sir, before it is affirmed that women do not suffer in their interests, as women, by the denial of a vote, it should be considered whether women have no grievances; whether the laws, and those practices which laws can reach, are in every way as favourable to women as to men. Now, how stands the fact? In the matter of education, for instance. We continually hear that the most important part of national education is that of mothers, because they educate the future men. Is this importance really attached to it? Are there many fathers who care as much, or are willing to expend as much, for the education of their daughters as of their sons? Where are the Universities, where the High Schools, or the schools of any high description, for them? If it be said that girls are better educated at home, where are the training-schools for governesses? What has become of the endowments which the bounty of our ancestors destined for the education, not of one sex only, but of both indiscriminately? I am told by one of the highest authorities on the subject, that in the majority of the endowments the provision made is not for boys, but for education generally; in one great endowment, Christ's Hospital, it is expressly for both: that institution now maintains and educates 1100 boys, and exactly 26 girls.[5] And when they attain womanhood, how does it fare with that great and increasing portion of the sex, who, sprung from the educated classes, have not inherited a provision, and not having obtained one by marriage, or disdaining to marry merely for a provision, depend on their exertions for subsistence? Hardly any decent educated occupation, save one, is open to them. They are either governesses or nothing. A fact has recently occurred, well worthy of commemoration in connection with this subject. A young lady, Miss Garrett, from no pressure of necessity, but from an honourable desire to employ her activity in alleviating human suffering, studied the medical profession.[6] Having duly qualified herself, she, with an energy and perseverance which cannot be too highly praised, knocked successively at all the doors through which, by law, access is obtained into the medical profession. Having found all other doors fast shut, she fortunately discovered one which had accidentally been left ajar. The Society of Apothecaries, it seems, had forgotten to shut out those who they never thought would attempt to come in, and through this narrow entrance this young lady found her way into this profession. But so objectionable did it appear to this learned body that women should be the medical attendants even of women, that the narrow wicket through which Miss Garrett entered has been closed after her, and no second Miss Garrett

[5]Sarah Emily Davies (1830–1921), *On the Application of Funds to the Education of Girls* (London: Longman, *et al.*, 1865). (Originally a paper read before the Education Department of the National Association for the Promotion of Social Science, 3 May, 1865.)

[6]Elizabeth Garrett (1836–1917), later Anderson.

will be allowed to pass through it.[7] And this is *instar omnium*.[8] No sooner do women show themselves capable of competing with men in any career, than that career, if it be lucrative or honourable, is closed to them. A short time ago, women might be Associates of the Royal Academy; but they were so distinguishing themselves, they were assuming so honourable a place in their art, that this privilege also has been withdrawn.[9] This is the sort of care taken of women's interests by the men who so faithfully represent them. This is the way we treat unmarried women. And how is it with the married? They, it may be said, are not interested in this motion; and they are not directly interested; but it interests, even directly, many who have been married, as well as others who will be. Now, by the common law of England, all that a wife has, belongs absolutely to the husband; he may tear it all from her, squander every penny of it in debauchery, leave her to support by her labour herself and her children, and if by heroic exertion and self-sacrifice she is able to put by something for their future wants, unless she is judicially separated from him he can pounce down upon her savings, and leave her penniless. And such cases are of quite common occurrence. Sir, if we were besotted enough to think these things right, there would be more excuse for us; but we know better. The richer classes take care to exempt their own daughters from the consequences of this abominable state of the law. By the contrivance of marriage settlements, they are able in each case to make a private law for themselves, and they invariably do so. Why do we not provide that justice for the daughters of the poor, which we take care to provide for our own daughters? Why is not that which is done in every case that we personally care for, made the law of the land, so that a poor man's child, whose parents could not afford the expense of a settlement, may retain a right to any little property that may devolve on her, and may have a voice in the disposal of her own earnings, which, in the case of many husbands, are the best and only reliable part of the incomings of the family? I am

[7]Three young women had followed Elizabeth Garrett's path, but they and any further potential candidates were made ineligible for certification by a ruling that public lectures (from which women were barred) were a requirement. See "Female Candidates at Apothecaries' Hall," *Medical Times and Gazette*, 2 Mar., 1867, p. 229, and "Ladies Not Admitted," *British Medical Journal*, 9 Mar., 1867, p. 269.

[8]Pliny the Elder (ca. 23–79 A.D.), *Natural History* (Latin and English), trans. H. Rackham, *et al.*, 10 vols. (London: Heinemann; Cambridge, Mass.: Harvard University Press, 1938–62), Vol. IV, p. 64 (XII, 87).

[9]The reference to Associates of the Royal Academy is puzzling. When the Academy was founded in 1768, two women, Angelica Kauffmann and Mary Moser, had been made Associates, but no more were elected until the twentieth century. Women had regularly, however, been exhibitors at the annual exhibitions, and since 1861 had been admitted in limited numbers as students, the first, Laura Anne Herford, perhaps being allowed entry because she signed her submission only with her initials. Some of these students, including Louisa Starr, distinguished themselves, and consequently there was an effective limit placed on their numbers.

sometimes asked what practical grievances I propose to remedy by giving women a vote. I propose, for one thing, to remedy this. I give these instances to prove that women are not the petted children of society which many people seem to think they are—that they have not the over-abundance, the superfluity of power that is ascribed to them, and are not sufficiently represented by the representation of the men who have not had the heart to do for them this simple and obvious piece of justice. (*Hear, hear.*) Sir, grievances of less magnitude than the law of the property of married women, when suffered by parties less inured to passive submission, have provoked revolutions. We ought not to take advantage of the security we feel against any such consequence in the present case, to withhold from a limited number of women that moderate amount of participation in the enactment and improvement of our laws, which this motion solicits for them, and which would enable the general feelings of women to be heard in this House through a few male representatives. We ought not to deny to them, what we are conceding to everybody else—a right to be consulted [d]in the choice of a representative[d]; the ordinary chance of placing in the great Council of the nation a few organs of their sentiments—of having, what every petty trade or profession has, a few members who feel specially called on to attend to their interests, and to point out how those interests are affected by the law, or by any proposed changes in it. No more is asked by this motion; and when the time comes, as it certainly will come, when this will be granted, I feel the firmest conviction that you will never repent of the concession.

[*At the end of his speech, Mill moved his amendment to substitute the word* person *for the word* man *"(hear, hear)" in Clause 4 of the Reform Bill, which dealt with the occupation qualifications for voters in counties. Following seven other speakers, Mill concluded the debate.*]

I will merely say, in answer to the noble Lord who requested me to withdraw the Motion,[10] that I am a great deal too well pleased with the speeches that have been made against it—his own included—to think of withdrawing it. There is nothing that has pleased me more in those speeches than to find that every one who has attempted to argue at all, has argued against something which is not before the House (*hear, hear*): they have argued against the admission of married women, which is not in the Motion; or they have argued against the admission of women as Members of this House; or again, as the honourable Member for the Wick boroughs (*Mr. Laing*) has done, they have argued against allowing women to be generals and officers in the army;[11] a question which I need scarcely say is not before the House. I certainly do think that when we come to universal suffrage, as

[10]George Edward Arundell Monckton-Arundell, Viscount Galway (1805–76), M.P. for East Retford, cols. 841–2.

[11]Samuel Laing (1812–97), col. 840.

[d-d]+TT,SSC

some time or other we probably shall come (*oh, oh!*)—if we extend the vote to all men, we should extend it to all women also. So long, however, as you maintain a property qualification, I do not propose to extend the suffrage to any women but those who have the qualification. If, as is surmised by one of the speakers,[12] young ladies should attach so much value to the suffrage that they should be unwilling to divest themselves of it in order to marry, I can only say that if they will not marry without it, they will probably be allowed to retain it. (*Hear, and a laugh.*) As to any question that may arise in reference to the removal of any other disabilities of women, it is not before the House. There are evidently many arguments and many considerations that cannot be overlooked in dealing with these larger questions, but which do not arise on the present Motion, and on which, therefore, it is not necessary that I should comment. I will only say that if we should in the progress of experience—especially after experience of the effect of granting the suffrage—come to the decision that married women ought to have the suffrage, or that women should be admitted to any employment or occupation which they are not now admitted to—if it should become the general opinion that they ought to have it, they will have it.

[*After Mill's speech, the question was put, and the amendment lost, 196 to 73, Mill being a teller.*]

56. The Municipal Corporations Bill

21 MAY, 1867

PD, 3rd ser., Vol. 187, cols. 882–5, 891. Reported in *The Times*, 22 May, p. 7, from which the variant and response are taken. Mill spoke in moving for leave to introduce "A Bill for the Establishment of Municipal Corporations within the Metropolis," 30 Victoria (21 May, 1867), *PP*, 1867, IV, 447–66.

MR. J. STUART MILL SAID, he did not do so in any spirit of hostility to the Report of the Committee relative to the Local Government of the Metropolis, of which Committee he had the honour of being a Member.[1] It was true he had disagreed from the majority of the Committee on several of their Resolutions, but as a whole their Report had his general concurrence, and he considered it a great step in the

[12]John Burgess Karslake (1821–81), M.P. for Andover, cols. 829–30.

---

[1]"First" and "Second Reports from the Select Committee on Metropolitan Local Government" (16 Apr. and 30 July, 1866), *PP*, 1866, XIII, 171–628. For Mill's part in the Committee, see App. B.

progress of this question. The Committee, in the first place, freely acknowledged existing defects; and, in the second place, it recognised the general principles upon which, in his opinion, a reform of those defects should proceed. It recognised that good municipal institutions for the metropolis must consist of two parts—namely, local bodies representing districts, and a general body representing the metropolis at large—the latter to take the place of the present Board of Works. Neither was his Motion framed in hostility to the Board of Works. It might at least be said for the Board that it had been appointed to perform a great and laborious work,[2] and that it had actually done that work. The Report proposed increased powers and an improved mode of election for the general Board; and with regard to the local district bodies, the Report considered the present districts to be too small, and virtually recommended the abolition of hole-and-corner local government. The Report might be considered in that and other respects as an outline of what municipal reformers desired; and the Bill he proposed to introduce would do something towards filling up that outline with regard to the local bodies only. He had given notice of his intention to ask for leave to bring in a Bill for the establishment of a central federal municipality for the whole of the metropolis,[3] but he was not yet prepared with that Bill, and he should not ask the House to read the present Bill a second time until he was able to lay before them the entire plan. The plan he was now about to propose was not his own, but originated with one of the most important vestries in Westminster,[4] and it had obtained the warm support of many of the leading vestrymen of the metropolis. He had no hostility to the vestries. Our parochial institutions, with all their defects, had done great things for the country. They had carried down to comparatively low grades of society a familiar acquaintance with the forms of public business and the modes of carrying it on, and in consequence this country possessed an advantage which, perhaps, no other country (except the United States) enjoyed—namely, that when circumstances call for the expression of an opinion by a collective body of citizens, there are numerous persons who know how that opinion should be collected and expressed. These merits could not be denied to our local system; but that system, as established in the metropolis, appeared to him to be on too small a scale. The Report of the Committee did not recognise that fact to so great an extent as he could have wished, and therefore he ventured to propose his plan. The Committee said

[2]By Sect. 31 of 18 & 19 Victoria, c. 120 (1855).

[3]Eventually brought in as "A Bill for the Better Government of the Metropolis," 30 & 31 Victoria (6 Aug., 1867), *PP*, 1867, IV, 215–56 (see No. 82).

[4]See "Memorial to the Home Secretary, from the Vestry of St. James," App. 1 in "Second Report from the Select Committee on Metropolis Local Taxation" (24 June, 1861), *PP*, 1861, VIII, 321–2; and "A Bill Intituled 'An Act for the Establishment of Municipal Corporations within the Metropolis,'" App. 9 in "Second Report from the Select Committee on Metropolitan Government," pp. 619–28.

that the districts of the metropolis were too small and inconvenient in some cases.[5] He (*Mr. Stuart Mill*) believed they were too small in all cases, and that the municipal boroughs of the metropolis ought to be conterminous with the Parliamentary boroughs. He thought it necessary that the municipal districts should be of considerable extent, and highly desirable that they should also be units in themselves. Unless the districts were considerable they were always more or less a kind of hole-and-corner government. It was a common fallacy, now going the round of Europe, but still a fallacy, that the mere circumstance of a body being popularly chosen was a guarantee that it would conduct its proceedings on popular principles. His faith in popular governments did not depend on their being popularly elected. The real value of popular institutions consisted in the popular power of correcting mistakes, and enforcing responsibility to the people. Owing to this responsibility, it would not be possible for any body long to retain its position if it habitually exercised its powers contrary to the public interest as generally understood. Another point was that the greatest attainable publicity should be secured to the business transacted by these bodies; but when the business was on a very small scale it did not excite much attention. The check was not effectual unless the business was of such a nature that the public eye would be fixed on it. It was further desirable, for the sake of greater publicity, that not only should the district be of considerable magnitude and the business important, but that the districts should, if possible, be natural units in themselves, or at least, should be units for other purposes than this special one. The importance of this was, that it would tend to induce a higher class of men to enter these bodies. Three of the metropolitan boroughs (the City, Westminster, and Southwark) were, if not natural, at least historical units; the other districts, though of more recent origin, were gradually acquiring an *esprit de corps*, and a sense of common interest. It had been at first thought desirable that an additional district should be created out of parts of Marylebone and Finsbury. The great importance, however, of making the municipal and Parliamentary boundaries coincide, had led to the abandonment of this idea, except so far as regarded the formation of a new police district, there being at present no police-office between Marlborough Street and Worship Street in the extreme east. The Bill provided for the division of the Tower Hamlets; but this would be dealt with by the Bill for the Representation of the People. [a]There

[5]For such views, see "Third Report from the Select Committee on Metropolis Local Taxation with the Proceedings of the Committee" (26 July, 1861), *PP*, 1861, VIII, 383. From the context, it would seem that Mill is referring to the two Reports on Metropolitan Local Government cited in n1 above; though neither contains such statements by the Committee, Mill himself voices them in his questions (see below, App. B, Questions 1866–71 and 2163 ff.)

[a-a]+TT

would also be a district for Kensington and Chelsea.[a6] He should not ask the House to read the Bill a second time till he had introduced the remainder of the plan of which it formed a part. Whatever merit the plan had, and that merit appeared to him to be considerable, it belonged entirely to his constituents who originated the plan. He himself had no part in it except that, at his own special request, he was permitted to introduce it to the House. (*Hear, hear.*) He now begged to move for leave to bring in a Bill to establish Municipal Corporations within the Metropolis.

[*Mill was followed,* inter alia, *by Ayrton, who had chaired the committee on the Metropolis that Mill refers to, and Locke, who had served on the committee; Gathorne-Hardy said the Government would not oppose the introduction of the Bill, but indicated hesitation over such a complex matter, on which the Metropolitan members were not themselves agreed. Mill's concluding sentence follows on Gathorne-Hardy's remarks.*]

Mr. J. Stuart Mill, in reply, observed, that he believed the Bill would be approved of by the City when its provisions became known.

[*The Bill was given first reading.*]

57. The Fenian Convicts

25 MAY, 1867

Morning Star, 27 May, 1867, p. 6. Headed: "The Fenian Convicts. Important Deputation to Lord Derby." Reported in the *Evening Star* (identically with the *Morning Star*), the *Daily Telegraph*, the *Daily News*, and *The Times* (an abbreviated summary of Mill's remarks). (Clippings of the *Morning Star* and *Daily News* reports are in the Mill-Taylor Collection.) On Saturday, 25 May, in the afternoon, a deputation of about sixty people, mainly Members of Parliament, called on the Prime Minister, Edward George Geoffrey Smith Stanley (1799–1869), 14th Earl of Derby, at his residence, to ask for a Royal pardon for "General" Thomas Francis Bourke, or Burke (b. 1840), who, having been found guilty of high treason for his part in the March uprising in Tipperary, had been sentenced to be hanged on 29 May. The delegation would have been larger, had some Members not gone by mistake to the Prime Minister's official residence in Downing Street. Mill, who was "sensibly . . . moved by the affecting nature of the task," spoke second.

MY LORD, we have come here without distinction of party. (*Loud cries of Hear.*) We come here with as deep and earnest a feeling as it is possible for human beings to have, to implore your lordship not to erect the scaffold in this

[6]30 & 31 Victoria, c. 102, in Sect. 19 provided that Chelsea should return two members (under Schedule B, Kensington was included as a parish of Chelsea), and in Sect. 21 Tower Hamlets was given two members for each of the two divisions.

country for political offences. It is not, my lord, for the sake of these unfortunate men we say it.[1] Heaven knows the punishment of failure, under the desperateness of these cases, is as painful a measure of punishment as almost any. The punishment to which, at all events, those men have subjected themselves, should their lives not be taken, for the rest of their existence, may be supposed to be quite sufficient to vindicate the law, and deter persons—as we all admit they ought to be deterred—from attempting a revolution when there is not a feeling in the country which would enable them to succeed. We most seriously apprehend that the effect of executing these men will be to make them heroes and martyrs. You must remember that the cause of Irish nationality has not yet had [a]its[a] martyrs. Irish wrongs have had martyrs, but long since this has been put an end to as far as we are concerned. Emmett and Fitzgerald were not martyrs to Irish nationality;[2] but the execution of these unhappy men will give a sanctity to the cause in which they embarked which must bring about results most unhappy for Ireland and for this country. We ought to think a little of what will be thought in foreign countries if these men are executed. We know what the feeling of foreign countries is on nationalities. They do not know the actual state of Ireland. They do not know with what a deep and sincere desire we have tried to make Ireland prosperous, and give her no cause to regret her union with us. They know nothing of this. They only know that there is one oppressed nationality which is ruled by another nationality, as they think, by force. [b]I think that state of things can only be remedied when a country can be induced to forget, as Scotland has forgotten, what is past.[b] In this view, therefore, I think it would be the most fatal thing in the world to put these men to death. The punishment of death, God knows, is not the most severe punishment, but it is a punishment which excites most sympathy. If these men be executed they will be dearly remembered, their memory will be held sacred by the Irish people, and their example will bring hundreds of their fellow-countrymen to their ruin. (*Hear, hear.*) There is another point in this matter which is not unworthy the consideration of a statesman, and it is this: It is much to be feared that there must be an impression among the American people that when, with respect to the invaders of Canada,[3] many persons desired that the severest punishment should be resorted to, yet with a correct morality—for it was a correct morality to

[1]In fact the cases of John McCafferty and John McClure, the other accused Fenians, were not yet under consideration. Their sentences were eventually commuted to life imprisonment, and they were deported in 1871 after four years in jail.

[2]Robert Emmett (1778–1803) was hanged for his part in an uprising in 1803 that aimed at the capture of Dublin Castle and resulted in the death of Lord Kilwarden. Edward Fitzgerald (1763–98) died from a wound received in the United Irishmen rebellion of 1798.

[3]On 1 June, 1866, 800 Fenians crossed the Niagara River and captured Fort Erie. They were defeated at Ridgeway by the Canadians, and the remainder surrendered to U.S. forces on 3 June.

[a-a]+DT,DN
[b-b]+DT,DN

condemn people to penal servitude instead of death—the execution of these men did not take place, that that was done because her Majesty's Government thought the lives of the men could not be taken with safety. There are many other gentlemen on the deputation anxious to address your lordship, and I will not therefore further detain you.

[*Mill was followed by a dozen other speakers before Derby replied at length, explaining that while the Government had considered the case for mercy most carefully before rejecting it, he would be willing to place before Cabinet that afternoon any document they might prepare. The deputation, after thanking the Prime Minister for his attention and courtesy, assembled in Derby's drawing room and prepared a document, signed by them all, and given to Derby, saying: "We the undersigned members of the House of Commons, very respectfully beg to express the hope that the extreme sentence of capital punishment in the case of the convict Burke may be commuted."*]

58. Reform of Parliament

25 MAY, 1867

Daily News, 27 May, 1867, p. 2. Headed: "Reform Meeting at St. James's-Hall." Reported in the *Daily Telegraph*, the *Morning Star* (identically in the *Evening Star*), and the *Morning Post* (all of these with similar texts of Mill's speech), *The Times* and the *Evening Mail* (these two with similar reports that rearrange and summarize the speeches and events), the *Morning Post* (a condensed version of the *Daily News* text), and the *Standard*. (Clippings of the *Daily News*, *Daily Telegraph*, and *Evening Mail* reports are in the Mill-Taylor Collection.) This second meeting of the National Reform Union (with many members of the Reform League present) was held on Saturday evening at 7 p.m., chaired by Samuel Morley, who had also chaired the first meeting on Wednesday, 15 May, at which Mill was on the platform though he did not speak. It might have been expected that fewer would attend than at the first, but "such was not exactly the case; for although there was not so much pressure as to put the physical endurance of a large part of the audience to a severe trial, yet every available place, whether for sitting or standing, was occupied; while an ardour, not to say enthusiasm, prevailed, which rivalled the demonstrativeness of the former meeting. Doubtless owing to the fact that Mr. Stuart Mill was announced as the leading orator of the evening, the fair sex was more fully represented than on the previous occasion; many of them, we will not say invading the platform, but occupying places there." (*Daily Telegraph*.) After preliminaries by the Chair, a resolution congratulating the reformers of the country on having won from the Government concessions in favour of household suffrage was moved and seconded. Mill "rose to support the resolution, and was received with loud and prolonged cheering, the audience rising in a body and waving hats and handkerchiefs."

BROTHER AND SISTER REFORMERS—(*laughter and cheers*)—since I had the satisfaction last week of looking from this platform upon you or other reformers, equally numerous and equally [a]earnest[a], many things have happened. At the beginning of the week it really seemed as if the greatest of the objects for which you are agitating had actually been attained.[1] It seemed as if we had got household suffrage, real, honest household suffrage, and that there was very little for us to do but to sit down and congratulate one another. (*Laughter.*) It is very fortunate that you did not think so, and that you stood to your guns, for here is our friend the compound-householder up again, and as strong as ever. (*Laughter.*) We have the whole battle to fight over again from the beginning. (*Hear, hear.*) We hope that we shall fight it out successfully (*hear, hear*), and we shall have you to thank for it. I will explain how this matter stands. It is not we who object to the compound householder. We do not object to householders compounding for their rates. It is a very great convenience, and it is very desirable that we should have the whole subject properly discussed without any reference to political questions, which ought to have nothing to do with it. [b](*Hear, hear.*) It is the government that has forced this upon us; because the government—as it would not quite do to say there was no principle at all in their bill, and as they did not see that they had a very firm hold on any other—somehow attached all their self-consequence to sticking to this little principle. (*Laughter.*) I am very glad it is not a greater. (*Laughter and Hear, hear.*) For it seems they would insist[b] to the very last—the principle that no one should compound and vote too. (*Laughter and cheers.*) There is no reason in the nature of things why a person should not compound and vote too. Compounding may be a good thing, and I am sure voting is a good thing, and I do not see any incompatibility between them. (*Hear, hear.*) However, the government do (*laughter*), and they appear determined that you shall not give every householder a vote unless you prevent him from compounding. Mr. Hodgkinson proposed that, and we thought they had conceded it. (*Laughter.*) But what have they done? They say, it is very true, that everybody shall be rated unless he objects himself, but if the landlord and he apply to compound they may be allowed to compound, and then he shall lose his vote. Well, that does not suit us. (*Laughter and cheers.*) [c]It is not only that we want every householder to have a

[1]I.e., after Disraeli's Speech on the Representation of the People Bill (17 May), *PD*, 3rd ser., Vol. 187, cols. 720–6, which gave the impression that the Government would accept the abolition of compounding householders as proposed in the amendment of Hodgkinson on the same day (*ibid.*, cols. 708–12).

[a-a]S,MP honest

[b-b]DT] DN It is a government that has forced this upon us because it would not quite do to say there was no principle at all in their bill—(*a laugh*)—and as they did not feel that they had got a very firm hold of any other, they seem to have attached all their self-consequence to sticking to their little principle—I am very glad it is not a greater—which it seems they will insist upon] MS *as* DT . . . Government who has . . . us—(*hear, hear*)—because . . . did not feel they had got a . . . other—they somehow . . . to this. (*A laugh.*) This little principle—I am . . . greater—but this little principle they would insist upon

[c-c]DT,MS] DN We want every householder to have a vote,] MP *as* DT,MS . . . vote,

vote, as we do;[c] [d]that is not all. See what would happen[d]. If the Chancellor of the Exchequer's clause pass, the householder's having a vote will depend upon his landlord.[2] (*Hear, hear.*) Now that is what we have been afraid of all along (*hear, hear*), because it is the landlord's interest that he should not have a vote if he cannot have a vote and compound too. It is the landlord's interest, and it is the interest of vestries, local boards, and [e]other authorities in parishes[e], that he should compound, and therefore it is their interest that he should not have a vote unless he can compound too. Well, if that is the case, observe what would happen. The landlord, it being his interest that such householders should not have a vote, and his consent being necessary, he will not consent unless it is made worth his while; and we know what that means. (*Laughter and cheers.*) It means that if the landlord wants the votes of his tenants for a political purpose, or if anybody else [f]can make it worth his while to want their votes for a political purpose, they will have the vote; and if not, not[f]. (*Laughter and cheers.*) That is not what we want, and we are not disposed to stand it. (*Loud cheers.*) We know very well that if we once get household suffrage, though we may be obliged to give up the convenience of compounding, when all these small householders have got votes, if they want to compound, if it is for their interest, convenience, and advantage to compound they will soon alter the law so that they may compound without the monstrous political consequences wanted to be attached to the act. (*Cheers.*) This is very like all that has been going on ever since the beginning of these reform discussions. It has been a succession—I will not say of tricks, because I do not like to use hard words, especially when I cannot prove them (*laughter*), but of what is called in the vernacular, trying it on. (*Great cheering and laughter.*) The object is just to see what you will bear, and anything that you will bear you shall have to bear (*laughter*), but if you show that you will not bear it, then perhaps it may not be required of you. (*Renewed laughter and cheers.*) I dare say that it is thought by the people who do it, and by many others, to be fair political strategy. Well, if the government were our enemies, I mean the enemies of our objects, if we are trying to get the most parliamentary reform that we can, and they are trying to give us the least, if we are openly attempting to take every advantage that we can against one another, these things may be fair enough. If that is the case they should tell us so. (*Hear, hear, and a laugh.*) But they do not, they leave us to find it out. (*Loud*

[2]Disraeli, in his Answer to a Question on the Business of the House (23 May), *ibid.*, cols. 941–2, had said the Government would bring forward a Clause amending Clause 34 to allow compounding with the joint consent of the owner and occupier (see *ibid.*, col. 1180).

[d-d]MS] DN but that is not all.] DT but see what would happen.

[e-e]DN of all the important people about] MS of the rich and important people about] S,MP church-wardens

[f-f]DT] DN should make it worth the landlord's while to secure the votes, the tenants will find their names on the register] MS *as* DN . . . while to want their vote for political purposes, they will register, and . . . *as* DT

laughter.) I must say that Mr. Disraeli cannot be charged with having broken faith with us. Men of his ability seldom do [g]break faith with anybody[g]. (*Laughter.*) He has been very careful [h]and guarded, indeed[h], and no one can say he has deceived us; but I think he has encouraged us a good deal to deceive ourselves. (*Laughter.*) I ought, perhaps, to be ashamed to make the confession, but he certainly succeeded with me this time. (*Loud laughter.*) I certainly thought when Mr. Disraeli came forward in the house, and with that bland and conciliatory, and frank and open manner—(*cheers and laughter*)—which he always exhibits when he chooses (*laughter*)—and during this session he has often so chosen, except towards our great leader, Mr. Gladstone—[i](*shame*)[i]—when he came forward in this way, as soon as Mr. Hodgkinson asked for the abolition of the compound household, [j]in order that we might not disfranchise the small householders,[j] he claimed that idea as his own—(*laughter*)—as what he had wanted from the beginning, what he had not only no objection to, but what he positively loved.[3] (*Laughter.*) When he did this I really thought we were going to have real household suffrage. But he has taught me a lesson—(*cheers and laughter*)—which I did not think I needed; but I did—(*laughter*)—and that is, to be a precious great distance out of the wood before I holloa in future. (*Laughter and cheers.*) This may not be so [k]bad as it looks. Some of our friends—some of the liberal members—[k] place a deal of trust, I am sorry to say, not in the Chancellor of the Exchequer's virtues, but in the bad opinion they have of him, for they think that in all this that looks a little equivocal in his conduct, as if he is going both ways, he is trying to impose upon his own party. I do not know that he is trying to impose upon anybody. If I thought he was I should think at least if he was going to impose on anybody it was not so likely to be on his friends as on his foes. (*Laughter.*) I think rather that if he were disposed to impose on anybody it is likely to be upon us. I hope we shall be mistaken, and that on Monday next, when the subject comes up again, we shall really get the household suffrage that we want. (*Loud cheers.*) If we get that we can afford to smile when Mr. Disraeli gets up in an exulting tone—whether we have beaten him or he us, it is all the same to him—he always thinks it his victory—(*laughter*)—and we can smile when he tells us that we have all come over to him. He tells us that with the gravest face in the [l]world[l]. But we are not quite so patient, and ought not to be so, when he gibes at those to whom we really owe all this, when he [m]calls them "blunderers,"[m] talks of their "blundering hands,"[4] and gives it to

[3]Disraeli, speech of 17 May, cols. 720 and 724.
[4]*Ibid.*, col. 726.

[g-g]+MS] DN,DT so] MP *as* MS . . . faith
[h-h]MS] DN indeed] DT,S,MP and guarded
[i-i]DT (*Loud cheers.*)] MS —(*groans and hisses*)—] MP —(*hear, hear*)—
[j-j]+DT,MS
[k-k]DT] DN,MP , but so it looks to some of our friends, some of the liberal members who] MS *as* DT . . . looks. There are some of ... *as* DN
[l-l]DT,MS House of Commons
[m-m]+DT,MS,MP

be understood that they have not been able to carry reform and he can, and that it is not their measure. He is quite satisfied if he can say to Mr. Gladstone, "You did not do it." But Mr. Gladstone did do it. (*Loud and long-continued cheering.*) He could not carry his measure last year[5] because Mr. Disraeli and his friends opposed it; Mr. Disraeli can carry his Reform Bill because Mr. Gladstone will not oppose anything but that which is not real reform, and will support to the utmost that which is. (*Cheers.*) I have no objection to thank everybody for their part in it when once we have got it, but I will always thank most those to whom we really owe it. (*Cheers.*) The people of England know that but for the late government this government would have gone one hundred miles [n]out of their way[n] before they would have brought in any Reform [o]Bill at all. (*Hear, hear.*) And[o] every good thing we have got in this bill, even that which seems to be more than Mr. Gladstone was prepared to give, has only been given for the purpose of outbidding Mr. Gladstone. (*Hear, hear.*) [p]I have nothing more to say on this subject, but I should like to say something on another. I am reminded by my friend on my right (*Mr. Gilpin*)[6]—one of the most thorough and determined reformers in the House of Commons—that I had the gratification of being along with him in the[p] deputation to Earl Derby [q]which he mentioned to you[q], to endeavour to save the life of a poor convict. We do not know what the result will be.[7] [r]We met under very great disadvantages.[r] The deputation was arranged last night when the house was very thin, and when the news that [s]these poor men were[s][8] to be executed came upon us like a clap of thunder. (*Cries of Shame.*) [t]We had to hunt up all the members of Parliament we could, many of them as it was the night before (*Friday*) were out of town, or were going out, having formed engagements, and under the circumstances we got[t] together some 50 or 60 English, Scotch, and Irish members, including some of the most honoured names in the house [u]—(*cheers*)—and saw the Prime Minister[u]. We do not know what the result is. I myself, from Lord Derby's tone, felt a good deal discouraged; but some of my friends, [v]who know

[5]For the measure, see No. 15.

[6]Charles Gilpin (1815–74), M.P. for Northampton, the only other M.P. on the platform, had spoken before Mill.

[7]Thomas Francis Bourke (see No. 57), in the event, had his death sentence commuted to penal servitude for life, but he was released after seven years.

[8]For the others, see No. 57.

[n-n]DT] DN,MS,MP off

[o-o]DT] DN Bill; and

[p-p]DT] DN,MP Today I had the gratification of being with a] MS *as* DT . . . another which was referred to by . . . right, one . . . House. (*Cheers.*) I . . . *as* DT

[q-q]+DT

[r-r]+DT,MS

[s-s]DT,MS] DN,MP this poor man was

[t-t]DT] DN Under the circumstances it is a wonder that we were able to get] MS We got together as many members of Parliament as we could. Many members had gone out of town, and under the circumstances it is a wonder that we got

[u-u]+DT

[v-v]+DT

more of him, and[v] who are much better judges than I am, think there is a great deal of hope. As long as there is a chance of this hope being gratified, I would not say a word to mar the grace of the concession. I am willing to give the most hearty thanks to her Majesty's government if they change the resolution which they are understood to have come to [w]only[w] by a majority, in which some of the most eminent members of the government did not join. (*Hear, hear.*) I do not wish to say anything that could excite any hostile feeling against the government, since I hope it will appear that they have not deserved it. But I should like to elicit a little feeling from you. (*Cheers.*) I should like to know, first, whether you think that we have any right to hold Ireland in subjection unless we can make Ireland contented with our government. (*Cries of No, no.*) That expression of your sentiment will resound through Ireland, and win the hearts of her people to you. (*Cheers.*) Let me ask you now: Do you think the Irish people are contented with our government?[9] (*Cries of No, no.*) Is that your fault? (*No, no.*) Do you think those men who have been driven desperate by the continuance of what they think misgovernment—although it is not so intentionally, if it was once; the reason we govern Ireland badly is because the ruling classes do not know how to do it better—do you think that these poor men, who do not understand the English people, and do not understand that you are determined to do them justice, and do not know that you are going soon to be strong enough to do it—(*cheers*)—and because they do not know this, their patience is worn out, and in most desperate circumstances they endeavour to get rid of what they think misgovernment at the risk of their lives—do you think, I say, that those men are not fit to live for that reason? [x](*Cries of No.*)[x] It is necessary to punish them. (*Hear, hear.*) It is necessary to punish any unsuccessful revolutionists (*Oh, oh*); because no man has a right to endanger the lives of his fellow-creatures, to raise civil war in the country, unless the event proves that there was such a feeling in the country at the time [y], and that the circumstances were altogether such[y] that he had reasonable prospect of success.[10] (*Hear, hear.*) If people did not risk anything by making

[9]In *England and Ireland* Mill refers to this meeting and quotes from this passage: "The question was put, some six months ago, to one of the largest and most enthusiastic public meetings ever assembled in London under one roof—'Do you think that England has a right to rule over Ireland if she cannot make the Irish people content with her rule?' and the shouts of 'No!' which burst from every part of that great assemblage, will not soon be forgotten by those who heard them" (*CW*, Vol. VI, p. 521). Cf. his letter of 16 November, 1867, to J.H. Bridges, where he again gives the circumstances and the quotation, saying in this case that the audience was "composed in great part of working men," and that the "enthusiastic shout of 'NO' . . . might have been heard, I think, outside the building" (*CW*, Vol. XVI, p. 1328).

[10]Questioned by G.W. Sharp as to the accuracy of the report of this passage, Mill said it was correct, adding: "And I do not know how anyone could express himself otherwise who

[w-w]DT,MS,S,MP] DN finally
[x-x]+MS] DT (*Loud and unanimous cries of Yes.*)
[y-y]+DT

these attempts we should have them made upon all sorts of absurd grounds by small minorities. It is necessary, then, to punish these people, but it is not necessary to hang them. (*Cheers.*) It is important that the world should know that you, the people of England, abhor the idea of staining the soil with the blood of political [z]offenders[z]. (*Loud cheers, and a cry of Hang the Government.*) I hope that we shall not have to reproach any one for this. But if it is done, I hope that you will show that it is not your doing—that you do not sympathise, that it is not you who want to hang the poor men who aimed to obtain the liberty of their country even by the [a]most mistaken means[a]. (*Hear, hear.*) Political malcontents are very seldom bad men; they are generally better than the average. They very often do wrong things; but the man who will risk his life and all that is dear to him for a public object is generally a better man than the common—he is an object of pity, and not of hatred. (*Cheers.*) If he is not successful, his failure will itself be a terrible blow to him. [b](*Some person in the body of the hall here asked*[b] *"How would you punish them?"*) I assume that it is unnecessary to punish all. It is only necessary to punish the leaders, and I would punish them by imprisonment, but not for life. They should not be treated like the scum of the earth; and we would always hope that the time would come, and we would do our utmost to make the time come, when an amnesty would let them all out of prison. (*Cheers.*) These things are done even in some of the most despotic countries of Europe, and I am sure that the people of England will not bear that their government should be the only one except those of Spain and Russia, which does such things. (*Cheers.*) If the government were so unfortunate as to hang these men, they would have the sympathy of none but Marshall Narvaez and General Mouravieff.[11] [c](*Cheers.*)[c] I could not help addressing you on this subject. (*Cheers.*) Many of us who went up to Lord Derby feel deeply that it will be a most fatal thing for the honour of this country, for its estimation in the eyes of all other countries, for its future prosperity, for the future good feeling between class and class, and, above all, for

---

believes, as all Englishmen do, that insurrections and revolutions are sometimes justifiable." He mentions the cases of the English Civil War and Glorious Revolution, the Polish insurrections, and Garibaldi's revolutions, and continues: "I did not mean that all insurrections, if successful, stand exculpated; the rebellion of the American slaveholders would have been equally guilty and even more detestable if it had succeeded. What I was arguing for was that even those revolutionists who deserve our sympathy, ought yet for the general good, to be subject to legal punishment if they fail." (*CW*, Vol. XVI, p. 1275 [1 June, 1867].)

[11]Ramon Maria Narvaez (1800–68), duque de Valencia, field marshall, and at that time authoritarian prime minister of Spain, and Mikhail Nikolaevich Mouravieff (1796–1866), military governor, who savagely repressed uprisings in Lithuania and Belorussia in 1863.

[z-z]S martyrs
[a-a]MP perilous resort to arms
[b-b]MP] DN,S (*A voice:*
[c-c]+MS] MP,S (*A Voice: Is this a Fenian meeting?*)

the future good feeling between Ireland and England, which was so precious to them all, if the government should persevere in the [d]calamitous[d] resolution to which they have come, but from which many of our friends feel [e]confident, and I feel[e] considerable hope, that they will virtuously abstain. (*Loud and continued cheering.*)

[f]*On the honourable gentleman resuming his seat the vast audience rose* en masse, *and gave three vigorous cheers in his honour.*[f]

[*The resolution was passed unanimously, and then Thomas Mason Jones moved a second one, condemning the government's "breach of faith" over compounding. In his speech Jones said, "as an Irishman," he must thank "the most illustrious philosopher in Europe—(loud cheers)—for the speech . . . worthy of even the great reputation of John Stuart Mill"* (Morning Star). *Later in his speech, Jones referred to a conversation in which Mill indicated that though he had been opposed to the ballot, he "was so convinced of the dangerous state of things in Ireland, that he was willing the ballot should be tried in that part of the kingdom—(great cheering)—that, if the experiment were to be tried at all, that was the place to try it"* (Morning Star). *When Jones finished, Mill rose again.*]

[g]*Mr. J.S. Mill:* My friend who has just addressed the meeting, and whose enthusiasm has led him greatly to overrate my merits, has misunderstood in some degree the communication which took place between him and me on the subject of the ballot. I have never concealed from you any opinion which you dislike. (*Hear, hear.*) I did not do so at my election, and you won't expect me to do so now. I am not in favour of the ballot. I think there are great objections to it, and that we are getting strong enough to do without it. (*Hear, hear.*) I was not able to say so much of the unfortunate Irish. I said, and I say again, if the ballot is to be tried, try it first in Ireland. (*Cheers.*)[g]

[*After the unanimous passing of this and another resolution, and thanks to the Chair, the meeting agreed to send a memorial to the Queen, praying that she spare the lives of the Fenian convicts. Morley's response to the vote of thanks closed the meeting proper, as the "vast assemblage" of some 3,000 separated. A few of those most involved, including Mill, then gathered in a smaller room to draw up the memorial concerning the Fenian prisoners, of which the substantial clause read: "We, your Majesty's humble memorialists, beg earnestly to pray your Majesty to exercise your Royal prerogative of mercy in sparing the lives of our unhappy countrymen in Ireland now lying under sentence of death for high treason." It was sent with a covering letter by Morley to Gathorne-Hardy, recently appointed Home Secretary.*]

[d-d]+MS
[e-e]DT , if I do not feel,
[f-f]+DT
[g-g]+MS

59. The Reform Bill [5]

27 MAY, 1867

PD, 3rd ser., Vol. 187, cols. 1142–3, 1185, 1188. Reported in *The Times*, 28 May, p. 9, from which the responses are taken. In the renewed discussion in Committee of Clause 4 of the Reform Bill, Disraeli made an extended defence of the Government's intentions, in the course of which he referred to Mill's having attended a meeting (see No. 58) and "if not [moving] at least [supporting] or sanction[ing] a resolution to the effect that I, representing Her Majesty's Government, had committed a breach of faith with the House of Commons on this matter" (col. 1139). Mill's first intervention is in response to that accusation.

I HOPE the Committee will kindly indulge me for a few minutes. No one, so far as I am aware, on the occasion to which the right honourable Gentleman has alluded, charged him with having broken faith with the House or with the country on the subject of the compound-householder. I most explictly acquitted him of having done so. If such a charge has been made I most willingly admit, and justice would compel me to admit, that he has most clearly and satisfactorily answered it. (*Cheers.*) I was well aware that the shaft with which he had transfixed us was taken from our own quiver. (*Hear.*) When the Amendment of the honourable Member for Pontefract (*Mr. Childers*) was announced,[1] I felt, and said, that if it were carried it would entirely destroy us (*hear, hear*)—that we should be obliged to begin again at the beginning and fight the whole battle over again. If that Amendment had proceeded from this part of the House I should have opposed it, and I shall oppose it now. I had not in my mind that my honourable Friend the Member for Newark (*Mr. Hodgkinson*) had expressed concurrence in that Motion. I now remember that he did concur in it. But the Committee know that he withdrew that concurrence by placing a fresh Amendment of an entirely different character on the Paper. As the right honourable Gentleman has done me the honour to attend to what I said in another place, he no doubt is well aware of the reasons why I think the 3rd and 4th clauses are entirely inadmissible. I have said this to set myself right with the right honourable Gentleman, against whom I have always endeavoured to avoid saying anything personally offensive. On the occasion referred to, I spoke with studied moderation.

[*The Committee moved from Clause 4 to Clause 34, also bearing on the issue of compound-householders; Mill's second intervention, on an amendment by Ayrton (col. 1183) that would have the effect of making landlords liable for payments not made by short-term occupiers who had been rated in order to gain the franchise, came after Gathorne-Hardy had indicated that the basis of the Government's*

[1]Hugh Culling Eardley Childers (1827–96), anticipating that Hodgkinson's amendment (see No. 54) would be defeated, had intimated that he would move an amendment to make compounding optional in all boroughs; when Disraeli had apparently accepted Hodgkinson's proposal, Childers (20 May, col. 780) declared he would not proceed.

objection to payment of compounded rates through the landlord was "that men would get on the register without paying the full rate, and that persons therefore paying unequal rates would be equally entitled to the franchise" (col. 1185).]

Mr. J. Stuart Mill said, that in addition to the objection mentioned by the right honourable Gentleman, the Amendment would place the weekly tenant of a dwelling-house in a worse position than the weekly tenant of a lodging who would not have to pay any poor rate.

[*Ayrton also moved that where "the dwelling-house or tenement shall be wholly let out in separate apartments or lodgings, the owner of such dwelling-house or tenement shall be rated in respect thereof to the poor rate" (col. 1186); Mill's subsequent motion came after some discussion of the matter.*]

Mr. J. Stuart Mill moved the omission of the words "separate apartments or" in the Amendment.

[*The amendment was withdrawn so that a substitute amendment using the words "apartments or lodgings not separately rated" could be agreed to.*]

60. Personal Representation

30 MAY, 1867

Personal Representation. Speech of John Stuart Mill, Esq., M.P. Delivered in the House of Commons, May 29th [sic], *1867. With an Appendix Containing Notices of Reports, Discussions, and Publications on the System in France, Geneva, Germany, Belgium, Denmark, Sweden, the Australian Colonies, and the United States*, 2nd ed. (London: Henderson, *et al.*, 1867), and *PD*, 3rd ser., Vol. 187, col. 1362. Reported in *The Times*, 31 May, pp. 7–8, from which variants and the responses are taken; the report in the *St. Stephen's Chronicle*, Vol. IV, pp. 44–7, supports the readings in *The Times*, but may derive from a common source. The first and main part of the speech is given in *PD*, 3rd ser., Vol. 187, cols. 1343–56. The incomplete listing in Mill's bibliography reads "Speech in the House of Commons on 1867, in moving for the adoption of Mr. Hare's system of representation: reprinted in a pamphlet with other writings on Mr. Hare's plan entitled " (MacMinn, p. 97). The copy in Mill's library, Somerville College, has no corrections or emendations. He spoke first.

[a]SIR,[a] the proposal to which I am about to call the attention of the House, and which I move as an amendment to the redistribution clauses,[1] because if it were adopted it would itself constitute a complete system of redistribution, has been

[1]At the end of his speech, Mill moved that "From and after the passing of the present bill, every local constituency shall, subject to the provisions hereinafter contained, return one member for every quota of its registered electors actually voting at that election, such quota

[a-a]–P1,P2

framed for the purpose of embodying a principle which has not yet been introduced into our discussions—a principle which is overlooked in the practical machinery of our constitution, and disregarded in most of the projects of constitutional reformers, but which I hold, nevertheless, to be most important to the beneficial working of representative government; and if while we are making great changes in our system of representation we omit to engraft this principle upon it, the advantages we obtain by our changes will be very much lessened, and whatever dangers they may be thought to threaten us with will be far greater and more real than they otherwise [b]need[b] be; and this I think I can establish by reasons so clear and conclusive, that, though I cannot expect to obtain at once the assent of the House, I do confidently hope to induce many members of it to take the subject into serious consideration. I cannot, indeed, hold out as an inducement that the principle I contend for is fitted to be a weapon of attack or defence for any political party. It is neither democratic nor aristocratic—neither Tory, Whig, nor Radical; or, let me rather say, it is all these at once: it is a principle of fair play to all parties and opinions without distinction: it helps no one party or section to bear down others, but is for the benefit of whoever is in danger of being borne down. It is therefore a principle in which all parties [c]might[c] concur, if they prefer permanent justice to a temporary victory; and I believe that what chiefly hinders them is that, as the principle has not yet found its way into the commonplaces of political controversy, many have never heard of it, and many others have heard just enough about it to misunderstand it. In bringing this subject before the House I am bound to prove two things: first, that there is a serious practical evil requiring remedy; and then, that the remedy I propose is practicable, and would be efficacious. I will first speak of the evil. It is a great evil; it is one which exists not only in our own, but in every other representative constitution; we are all aware of it; we all feel and acknowledge it in particular cases; it enters into all our calculations, and bears with a heavy weight upon us all. But as we have always been used to think of it as incurable, we think of it as little as we can; and are hardly aware how greatly it affects the whole course of our affairs, and how prodigious would be the gain to our policy, to our morality, to our civilization itself, if the evil were susceptible of

---

being a number equal to the quotient obtained by dividing by 658 the total number of votes polled throughout the kingdom at the same election, and if such quotient be fractional, the integral number next less. Provided always, that where the number of votes given by the constituency shall not be equal to such quota, the quota may be completed by means of votes given by persons duly qualified as electors in any other part of the United Kingdom; and the candidate who shall have obtained such quota may notwithstanding be returned as member for the said constituency if he shall have obtained a majority of the votes given therein as hereinafter mentioned." For the remainder of his amendments on the Order Paper, see *PD*, 3rd ser., Vol. 187, cols. 1343–4.

[b-b]PD,P1 would
[c-c]PD,P1 may

a remedy. This House and the country are now anxiously engaged, and certainly not a day too soon, in considering what can be done for the unrepresented. We are all discussing how many non-electors deserve to be represented, and in what mode to give them representation. But my complaint is that the electors are not represented. The representation which they seem to have, and which we have been quarrelling about the extension of, is a most imperfect and insufficient representation; and this imperfect and insufficient representation is what we are offering to the new classes of voters whom we are creating. Just consider. In every Parliament there is an enormous fraction of the whole body of electors who are without any direct representation, consisting of the aggregate of the minorities in all the contested elections, together with we know not what minorities in those which, from the hopelessness of success, have not even been contested. All these electors are as completely blotted out from the constituency, for the duration of that Parliament, as if they were legally disqualified; most of them, indeed, are blotted out indefinitely, for in the majority of cases those who are defeated once are likely to be defeated again. Here, therefore, is a large portion of those whom the constitution intends to be represented, a portion which cannot average less than a third, and may approximate to a half, who are virtually in the position of non-electors. But the local majorities, are they truly represented? In a certain rough way they are. They have a member or members who are on the same side with themselves in party politics; if they are Conservatives, they have a professed Conservative; if Liberals, a professed Liberal. This is something; it is a great deal, even; but is it everything? Is it of no consequence to an elector who it is that sits in Parliament as his representative, if only he does not sit on the wrong side of the House? Sir, we need more than this. We all desire not only that there should be a sufficient number of Conservatives or of Liberals in the House, but that these should, as far as possible, be the best men of their respective parties; and the elector, for himself, desires to be represented by the man who has most of his confidence in all things, and not merely on the single point of fidelity to a party. Now, this is so entirely unattainable under the present system, that it seems like a dream even to think of it [d]. As a rule, the[d] only choice offered to the elector is between the two great parties. There are only as many candidates of each party as there are seats to be filled; to start any others would divide the party, and in most cases ensure its defeat. And what determines who these candidates are to be? Sometimes the mere accident of being first in the field. Sometimes the fact of having stood and been defeated on some previous occasion, when the sensible men of the party did not engage in the contest, because they knew it to be hopeless. In general, half a dozen local leaders, who may be honest politicians, but who may be jobbing intriguers, select the candidate: and whether they are of the one kind or the other, their conduct is much the same—they select the gentleman who will spend

[d–d]P1 as a rule. The [*printer's error?*]

most money (*Oh!*); or, when this indispensable qualification is equally balanced, it answers best to propose somebody who has no opinions but the party ones; for every opinion which he has of his own, and is not willing to abnegate, will probably lose him some votes, and give the opposite party a chance. How many electors are there, I wonder, in the United Kingdom, who are represented by the person whom, if they had a free choice, they would have themselves selected to represent them? In many constituencies, probably not one. [e]There might be a single exception.[e] I am inclined to think that almost the only electors who are represented exactly as they would wish to be, are those who were bribed (*a laugh*); for they really have got for their [f]member the gentleman[f] who bribed highest. Sometimes, perhaps, the successful candidate's own tenants would have voted for him in preference to any one else, however wide a choice had been open to them. But in most cases the selection is the result of a compromise, even the leaders not proposing the man they would have liked best, but being obliged to concede something to the prejudices of other members of the party. Having thus, as I think, made out a sufficient case of evil requiring remedy, let me at once state the remedy I propose. My proposal, then, is this: That votes should be received in every locality, for others than the local candidates. An elector who declines to vote for any of the three or four persons who offer themselves for his own locality, should be allowed to bestow his vote on any one who is a candidate anywhere, whether put up by himself or by others. (*Laughter, and Hear, hear.*) If the elector avails himself of this privilege, he will naturally vote for the person he most prefers—the one person, among all that are willing to serve, who would represent him best; and if there are found in the whole kingdom other electors, in the proper number, who fix their choice on the same person, that person should be declared duly elected. Some number of electors there must be who may be considered entitled to one representative: what that number is, depends on the numbers of the House, compared with the total number of electors in the country. Suppose that there is one member for every 5,000 registered electors, or one for every 3,000 actual voters: then every candidate who receives 3,000 votes would be returned to this House, in whatever parts of the country his voters might happen to live. (*Laughter, and some cries of Hear, hear.*) This is the whole of my proposal, as far as its substance is concerned. To give it effect, some subsidiary arrangements are necessary, which I shall immediately state. But I must first notice an objection which presents itself on the threshold, and has so formidable an appearance that it prevents many persons from giving any further consideration to the subject. It is objected, that the plan destroys the local character of the representation. (*Hear, hear.*) Every constituency, it is said, is a group having certain interests and feelings in common, and if you disperse these groups by allowing the electors to

[e-e]+TT,SSC
[f-f]P1 members the gentlemen

group themselves in other combinations, those interests and feelings will be deprived of their representation. Now I fully admit that the interests and feelings of localities ought to be represented: and I add that they always will be represented; because those interests and feelings exist in the minds of the electors; and as the plan I propose has no effect but to give the freest and fullest play to the individual elector's own preferences, his local preferences are certain to exercise their proper amount of influence. I do not know what better guardian of a feeling can be wanted than the man who feels it, or how it is possible for a man to have a vote, and not carry his interests and feelings, local as well as general, with him to the polling booth. Indeed, it may be set down as certain that the majority of voters in every locality will generally prefer to be represented by one of themselves, or one connected with the place by some special tie. It is chiefly those who know themselves to be locally in a minority, and unable to elect a local representative of their opinions, who would avail themselves of the liberty of voting on the new principle. As far as the majority were concerned, the only effect would be that their local leaders would have a greatly increased motive to find out and bring forward the best local candidate that could be had, because the electors, having the power of transferring their votes elsewhere, would demand a candidate whom they would feel it a credit to vote for. The average quality of the local representation would consequently be improved, but local interests and feelings would still be represented, as they cannot possibly fail to be, as long as every elector resides in a locality. If, however, the House attaches any weight to this chimerical danger, I would most gladly accept by way of experiment a limited application of the new principle. Let every elector have the option of registering himself either as a local or as a general voter. Let the elections for every county or borough take place on the local registry, as they do at present. But let those who choose to register themselves as members of a national constituency, have representatives allowed to them in proportion to their number; and let these representatives, and no others, be voted for on the new principle. I will now state the additional, but very simple arrangements, required to enable the plan to work. Supposing 3,000 voters to be the number fixed upon as giving a claim to a representative: it is necessary that no more than this minimum number should be counted for any candidate; for otherwise a few very eminent or very popular names might engross nearly all the votes, and no other person might obtain the required number, or any number that would justify his return. No more votes, then, being counted for any candidate than the number necessary for his election, the remainder of those who voted for him would lose their vote, unless they were allowed to put on their voting paper a second name, for whom the vote could be used if it was not wanted by the candidate who stood first. In case this second candidate also should not need the vote, the voter might add a third, or any greater number, in the order of his preference. This is absolutely all that the elector would have to do, more than he does at present; and I think it must be admitted that this is not a difficult idea to master, and not beyond the comprehension of the simplest elector. The only persons on whom anything more troublesome would devolve are the scrutineers, who would have to sort the voting papers, and see for which of the names written in it each of them ought to be counted. A few simple rules would be necessary to guide the scrutineers in this process. My amendment entrusts the duty of drawing up those rules to the judgment and experience of the right honourable gentleman who presides over our deliberations; subject [g], as in other cases,[g] to the approbation of the House. (*Hear, hear, and a laugh.*) Let me now ask honourable members—is there anything in all this, either incomprehensible or insuperably difficult of execution! I can assure the House that I have not concealed any difficulty. I have given a complete, though a brief, account of what most honourable members must have heard of, but few, I am afraid, know much about—the system of personal representation proposed by my eminent friend, Mr. Hare[2]—a man distinguished by that union of large and enlightened general principles, with an organizing intellect and a rare fertility of practical contrivance, which together constitute a genius for legislation. (*Hear, hear.*) People who have merely heard of Mr. Hare's plan have taken it into their heads that it is particularly hard to understand and difficult to execute. But the difficulty is altogether imaginary: to the elector there is no difficulty at all; to the scrutineers, only that of performing correctly an almost mechanical operation. Mr. Hare, anxious to leave nothing vague or uncertain, has taken the trouble to discuss in his book the whole detail of the mode of sorting the voting papers. People glance at this, and because they cannot take it all in at a glance, it seems to them very mysterious. But when was there any act of Parliament that could be understood at a glance? (*Hear, hear, and a laugh*) and how can gentlemen expect to understand the details of a plan, unless they first possess themselves of its principle? If we were to read a description, for example, of the mode in which letters are sorted at the Post-office, would it not seem to us very complicated? Yet, among so vast a number of letters, how seldom is any mistake made. Is it beyond the compass of human ability to ascertain that the first and second names on a voting paper have been already voted for by the necessary quota, and that the vote must be counted for the third? And does it transcend the capacity of the agents of the candidates, the chief registrar, or a committee of this House, to find out whether this simple operation has been honestly and correctly performed? If these are not insuperable difficulties, I can assure the House that they will find there are no others. Many will think that I greatly over-estimate the importance of securing to every elector a direct representation, because those who are not represented directly are represented indirectly. If Conservatives are not represented in the Tower Hamlets, or Liberals in West Kent, there are plenty of Conservatives and Liberals returned elsewhere;

[2]In his *Treatise on the Election of Representatives* (1859); see No. 4.

[g-g]+P2

and those who are defeated may console themselves by the knowledge that their party is victorious in many other places. Their [h]party, yes[h]: but is that all we have to look to? Is representation of parties all we have a right to demand from our representative system? If that were so, we might as well put up three flags inscribed with the words, Tory, Whig, and Radical, and let the electors make their choice among the flags, and when they have voted, let the leaders of the winning party select the particular persons who are to represent it. (*A laugh.*) In this way we should have, I venture to say, an admirable representation of the three parties: all the seats which fell to the lot of each party would be filled by its steadiest and ablest adherents, by those who would not only serve the party best in the House, but do it most credit with the country. All political parties, merely as such, would be far better represented than they are now, when accidents of personal position have so great a share in determining who shall be the Liberal or who the Conservative member for each place. Why is it, then, that such a system of representation would be intolerable to us? Sir, it is because we look beyond parties; because we care for something besides parties; because we know that the constitution does not exist for the benefit of parties, but of citizens; and we do not choose that all the opinions, feelings, and interests of all the members of the community should be merged in the single consideration of which party shall predominate. We require a House of Commons which shall be a fitting representative of all the feelings of the people, and not merely of their party feelings. We want all the sincere opinions and public purposes which are shared by a reasonable number of electors to be fairly represented here; and not only their opinions, but that they should be able to give effect by their vote to their confidence in particular men. Then why, because it is a novelty, refuse to entertain the only mode in which it is possible to obtain this complete reflection in the House of the convictions and preferences existing in the constituent body [i]—to make the House, what we are so often told that it ought to be, the express image of the nation[i]? By the plan I propose, every elector would have the option of voting for the one British subject who best represented his opinions, and to whom he was most willing to entrust the power of judging for him on subjects on which his opinions were not yet formed. Sir, I have already made the remark, that this proposal is not specially liberal, nor specially conservative, but is, in the highest degree, both liberal and conservative; and I will substantiate this by showing that it is a legitimate corollary from the distinctive doctrines of both parties. Let me first address myself to Conservatives. What is it that persons of conservative feelings specially deprecate in a plan of parliamentary reform? It is the danger that some classes in the nation may be swamped by other classes. What is it that we are warned against, as the chief among the dangers of democracy? not untruly, as democracy is vulgarly conceived and practised. It is that the single class of manual labourers would, by dint of numbers, outvote all other classes, and

[h-h]P1 party. Yes
[i-i]+P2

monopolize the whole of the legislature. But by the plan I propose, no such thing could happen; no considerable minority could possibly be swamped; no interest, no feeling, no opinion which numbered in the whole country a few thousand adherents, need be without a representation in due proportion to its numbers. It is true that by this plan a minority would not be equivalent to a majority; a third of the electors could not outvote two-thirds, and obtain a majority of seats; but a third of the electors could always obtain a third of the seats; and these would probably be filled by men above the average in the influence which depends on personal qualities, for the voters who were outnumbered locally would range the whole country for the best candidate, and would elect him without reference to anything but their personal confidence in him; the representatives of the minorities would, therefore, include many men whose opinion would carry weight even with the opposite party. Then, again, it is always urged by Conservatives, and is one of the best parts of their creed, that the legislators of a nation should not all be men of the same stamp—a variety of feelings, interests, and prepossessions should be found in this House—and it should contain persons capable of giving information and guidance on every topic of importance that is likely to arise. This advantage, we are often assured, has really been enjoyed under our present institutions, by which almost every separate class or interest which exists in the country is somehow represented, with one great exception, which we are now occupied in removing—that of manual labour. And this advantage many Conservatives think that we are now in danger of losing. But the plan I propose ensures this variegated character of the representation in a degree never yet obtained, and guarantees its preservation under any possible extension of the franchise. Even universal suffrage, even the handing over of political predominance to the numerical majority of the whole people, would not then extinguish minorities. Every dissentient opinion would have the opportunity of making itself heard, and heard through the very best and most effective organs it was able to procure. We should not find the rich or the cultivated classes retiring from politics, as we are so often told they do in America, because they cannot present themselves to any body of electors with a chance of being returned. Such of them as were known and respected out of their immediate neighbourhood would be elected in considerable numbers, if not by a local majority, yet by a union of local minorities; and instead of being deterred from offering themselves, it would be the pride and glory of such men to serve in Parliament; for what more inspiring position can there be for any man, than to be selected to fight the uphill battle of unpopular opinions, in a public arena, against superior numbers? (*Cries of Agreed, agreed.*) All, therefore, which the best Conservatives chiefly dread in the complete ascendancy of democracy would be, if not wholly removed, at least diminished in a very great degree. These are the recommendations of the plan when looked at on its conservative side. Let us now look at it in its democratic aspect. (*Agreed, agreed.*) I claim for it the support of all democrats, as being the only true realization of their political principles. What is the principle of democracy? Is it not that everybody should be represented, and that everybody should be represented equally? Am I represented by a member against whom I have voted, and am ready to vote again? Have all the voters an equal voice, when nearly half of them have had their representative chosen for them by the larger half? In the present mode of taking the suffrages nobody is represented but the majority. But that is not the meaning of democracy. Honest democracy does not mean the displacement of one privileged class, and the instalment of another in a similar privilege because it is a more numerous or a poorer class. That would be a mere pretence of democratic equality. That is not what the working classes want. The working classes demand to be represented, not because they are poor, but because they are human. No working man with whom I have conversed desires that the richer classes should be unrepresented, but only that their representation should not exceed what is due to their numbers; that all classes should have, man for man, an equal amount of representation. He does not desire that the majority should be alone represented. He desires that the majority should be represented by a majority, and the minority by a minority, and [j]he only needs to have it shown to him[j] how this can be done. But I will go further. It is not only justice to the minorities that is here concerned. Unless minorities are counted, the majority which prevails may be but a sham majority. Suppose that on taking a division in this House you compelled a large minority to step aside, and counted no votes but those of the majority; whatever vote you then took would be decided by the majority of that majority. Does not every one see that this would often be deciding it by a minority? (*Laughter and cries of Agreed, agreed.*) The mere majority of a majority may be a minority of the whole. Now, what I have been hypothetically supposing to be done in this House, the present system actually does in the nation. It first excludes the minorities at all the elections. Not a man of them has any voice at all in determining the proceedings of Parliament. Well, now, if the members whom the majorities returned were always unanimous, we should be certain that the majority in the nation had its way. But if the majorities, and the members representing them, are ever divided, the power that decides is but the majority of a majority. Two-fifths of the electors, let us suppose, have failed to obtain any representation. The representatives of the other three-fifths are returned to Parliament, and decide an important question by two to one. Supposing the representatives to express the mind of their constituents, the question has been decided by a bare two-fifths of the nation, instead of a majority of it. Thus the present system is no more just to majorities than to minorities. It gives no guarantee that it is really the majority that preponderates. A minority of the nation, if it [k]be[k] a majority in the prevailing party, may outnumber and prevail over a real majority in the nation. Majorities are never sure of outnumbering minorities,

[j-j]PD,P1 they only need to have it shown to them
[k-k]PD,P1 is

unless every elector is counted—unless every man's vote is as effective as any other man's in returning a representative. No system but that which I am submitting to the House effects this, because it is the only system under which every vote tells, and every constituency is unanimous. This system, therefore, is equally required by the Conservative and by the Radical creeds. In practice, its chief operation would be in favour of the weakest—of those who were most liable to be outnumbered and oppressed. Under the present suffrage it would operate in favour of the working classes. Those classes form the majority in very few of the constituencies, [l]but they are a large minority in many, and if they amount, say to a third of the whole electoral body, this system would enable them to obtain a third of the representation[l]. Under any suffrage approaching to universal, it would operate in favour of the propertied and of the most educated classes; and though it would not enable them to outvote the others, it would [m]secure[m] to them and to the interests they represent, a hearing, and a just share in the representation. I am firmly persuaded, Sir, that all parties in this House and in the country, if they could but be induced to give their minds to the consideration of this proposal, would end by being convinced, not only that it is entirely consistent with their distinctive principles, but that it affords the only means by which all that is best in those principles can be practically carried out. It would be a healing, a reconciling measure; softening all political transitions; securing that every opinion, instead of conquering or being conquered by starts and shocks, and passing suddenly from having no power at all in Parliament to having too much, or the contrary, should wax or wane in political power in exact proportion to its growth or decline in the general mind of the country. So perfectly does this system realize the idea of what a representative government ought to be, that its perfection stands in its way, and is the great obstacle to its success. There is a natural prejudice against everything which professes much; men are unwilling to think that any plan which promises a great improvement in human affairs has not something quackish about it. I cannot much wonder at this prejudice, when I remember that no single number of a daily paper is published whose advertising columns do not contain a score of panaceas for all human ills; when, in addition to all the pamphlets which load our tables, every member of this House, I suppose, daily receives private communications of plans by which the whole of mankind may at one stroke be made rich and prosperous, generally, I believe, by means of paper money. But if this age is fertile in new nonsense, and in new forms of old nonsense, it is an age in which many great improvements in human affairs have really been made. It is also an age in which, whether we will or not, we are entering on new paths; we are surrounded by circumstances wholly without example in history; and the wonder would be if exigencies so new could be dealt with in a completely satisfactory manner by the

[l-l]TT,SSC although they were in a considerable majority in the nation
[m-m]P1 leave

old means. We should therefore ill discharge our duty if we obstinately refused to look into new proposals. This, Sir, is not the mere crotchet of an individual. It has been very few years before the world, but already, by the mere force of reason, it has made important converts among the foremost public writers and public men in Germany, in France, in Switzerland, in Italy, in our Australian colonies, and in the United States. In one illustrious though small commonwealth, that of Geneva, a powerful association has been organized and is at work, under the presidency of one of the most eminent men in the Swiss federation, agitating for the reform of the constitution on this basis.[3] And what in our own country? Why, Sir, almost every thinking person I know who has studied this plan, or to whom it has been sufficiently explained, is for giving it at least a trial. Various modes have been suggested of trying it on a limited scale. With regard to the practical machinery proposed, neither I nor the distinguished author of the plan are wedded to its details, if any better can be devised. (*Hear.*) If the principle of the plan were admitted, a committee or a royal commission could be appointed to consider and report on the best means of providing for the direct representation of every qualified voter, and we should have a chance of knowing if the end we have in view could be attained by any better means than those which we suggest. But without some plan of the kind it is impossible to have a representative system really adequate to the exigencies of modern society. In all states of civilization, and in all representative systems, personal representation would be a great improvement; but, at present, political power is passing, or is supposed to be in danger of passing, to the side of the most numerous and poorest class. Against this class predominance, as against all other class predominance, the personal representation of every voter, and therefore the full representation of every minority, is the most valuable of all protections. Those who are anxious for safeguards against the evils they expect from democracy should not neglect the safeguard which is to be found in the principles of democracy itself. It is not only the best safeguard but the surest and most lasting: because it combats the evils and dangers of false democracy by means of the true, and because every democrat who understands his own principles must see and feel its strict and impartial justice.

[*Viscount Cranborne followed Mill, dissenting from the measure as impracticable, but arguing that it should be given a full hearing, as the evil Mill described was a real one. After other speeches, Mill concluded the debate.*]

Mr. J. Stuart Mill said, he would obey what appeared to be the general wish of the House, and would not press his Amendment to a division; but there were many things which he might have said in reply if the temper of the House had permitted. He must, however, follow his honourable Friend behind him[4] in thanking the

[3]L'Association Réformiste of Geneva, founded in 1865, was headed by Jules Ernest Naville (1816–1909), Christian philosopher and prolific author.

[4]Mountstuart Elphinstone Grant Duff (1829–1906), M.P. for Elgin Burghs, cols. 1361–2.

noble Lord the Member for Stamford (*Viscount Cranborne*) for his able speech, and for the conviction he had expressed that statesmen must make up their minds to think upon this subject as the only way of getting over a difficulty that must be got over.[5] He must also express his warm acknowledgments to the Chancellor of the Exchequer for the manner in which he had dealt with the question.[6]

[*The amendment was withdrawn.*]

61. The Bankruptcy Acts Repeal Bill

4 JUNE, 1867

PD, 3rd ser., Vol. 187, col. 1572. Reported in *The Times*, 5 June, p. 7. Mill spoke in the debate on going into Committee on "A Bill to Repeal Enactments Relating to Bankruptcy in England, and to Matters Connected Therewith," 30 Victoria (14 Mar., 1867), *PP*, 1867, I, 377–80.

THE LAWS OF THIS COUNTRY on the subject of debt have passed, not suddenly, but by a succession of steps, from one bad extreme to another. After having continued the old savage treatment of debtors far into an advanced state of civilization, we have now gradually lapsed into such a state that the debtor may be guilty of any kind of misconduct, short of actual fraud, and escape with practical impunity. Last year, for nearly the whole of the Session, I had a Notice on the Paper for an Instruction to the Committee, that it have power to remedy this evil by introducing provisions for the punishment of such debtors as might be shown on inquiry to have, with culpable temerity, risked and lost property which belonged to their creditors.[1] The Bill of last year[2] never reached such a stage that I could move that Instruction. The present Bill has passed the stage when a similar Instruction could be proposed. Under these circumstances I shall give my best support to the Amendments to be proposed by the honourable and learned Member for Cambridge (*Mr. Selwyn*),[3] and I shall move other clauses going further in the same direction.

[*The discussion concluded with a deferment of the Committee until 7 June, when*

[5]Cecil (Lord Cranbourne), cols. 1357–9.

[6]Disraeli, col. 1362.

---

[1]Mill's Notice of Motion appears on the Order Paper on 10 May and 25 June, 1866, *Journals of the House of Commons*, 1866, pp. 602, 1075.

[2]"A Bill to Amend and Consolidate the Law Relating to Bankruptcy in England, and to Abolish Imprisonment for Debt in Final Process," 29 Victoria (16 Apr., 1866), *PP*, 1866, I, 103–236.

[3]Charles Jasper Selwyn (1813–69), M.P. for Cambridge, cols. 1565–6, proposed that after-acquired property of insolvents be chargeable for debts.

*it was again put off. Mill indicated to Helen Taylor on 10 June that he hoped to speak again on the matter (*CW*, Vol. XVI, p. 1281), but the Bill was withdrawn without discussion on 11 July.*]

62. Petition Concerning the Fenians

14 JUNE, 1867

PD, 3rd ser., Vol. 187, cols. 1894–5. Reported in *The Times*, 15 June, p. 9, from which variants and responses are taken. On 3 May, John Bright had submitted a petition, signed by Edward Truelove, Richard Congreve, Frederic Harrison, and eight others, condemning Fenianism because of its secrecy and premature dedication to violence, but nonetheless asserting the political nature of the offences, and asking that the sentences already assigned to prisoners be revised, that they be segregated from common criminals, that moderation be shown in applying the law in Ireland, and that Fenian prisoners be treated well before trial, and judged and sentenced leniently (Petition 8687, *Reports from the Select Committee of the House of Commons on Public Petitions*, 1867–68; the wording is in App. 530, pp. 223–4). The *Report* now having been printed, Augustus Henry Archibald Anson (1835–77), M.P. for Lichfield, moved (cols. 1886–90) that the petition itself be "discharged" and that its wording in the Appendix be "cancelled," on the grounds that its aim was to encourage Fenianism and insult the British army. He referred to criticisms made in the House by Perronet Thompson in 1858 concerning the army's reaction to the Indian Mutiny.

I RISE, not for the purpose of discussing the question raised upon the Motion submitted to us, which I cannot imagine, especially after the opposition made to it by the Chairman of the Committee on Petitions,[1] that the House will think of adopting. I rise, moved by a feeling of self-respect, to say that if the honourable and gallant Gentleman thought it his duty to move that the petition be expelled from the House, he should go further, and move that I be expelled from it, for there is not a single sentiment in the petition [a], as far as I am aware,[a] which I do not adopt. (*Oh, oh!*) I will not say that I adhere to every word in it, but to every sentiment in it I most implicitly do, and I thank my honourable Friend who presented it for having given utterance for once in this House to a feeling which nearly all [b]Europe and the civilized world entertain, respecting certain acts done

[1]Charles Forster (1815–91), M.P. for Walsall, pointed out that the Committee on Petitions had no power to object to a petition on the grounds of substance.

[a-a]+TT [*in third person, past tense*]
[b-b]TT [*in past tense*]] PD England and all the world entertain

in the dependencies of this country[b].[2] The honourable and gallant Gentleman is mistaken in supposing that utterance to be an attack on his profession. I have been infinitely more disgusted in reference to the Indian transactions referred to, by the inhuman and ferocious displays of feeling made by unmilitary persons, persons in civil life, who were safe at home, and who, it seems to me, were far more culpable than those who committed excesses under such provocation as there is no denying was given in the case of India. Even the deeds there done of inhuman and indiscriminate massacre, the seizing of persons in all parts of the country and putting them to death without trial, and then boasting of it in a manner almost disgraceful to humanity, [c]as was the case in innumerable instances which were described at the time,[c] were by no means confined to the army. I have no doubt that in many cases the habitual discipline of the army, and their professional feelings, prevented them from being guilty of such deeds. I could tell the House of gentlemen who resigned their commissions and left the army because they could not bear the deeds which they not only saw done, but were compelled by their orders to do. (*Name, name!*) I decline to name them, and by naming them to expose them to attacks (*Oh, and Hear*) like those which have been made to-night against a well-known public man, formerly a Member of this House, for the vindication of whom I return my sincerest thanks to the honourable Member for Bradford.[3] With respect to the sentiments contained in the petition [d]and its alleged palliation of the conduct of[d] the Fenians, I beg to point out that it contains a very decided and strong condemnation of their conduct. All it said was that it was conduct [e]such as honourable but mistaken men might be capable of[e]. That cannot be denied. It cannot be denied that such men as Wolfe Tone,[4] Emmett, and Lord Edward Fitzgerald, however wrongly they may have acted, were the very stuff of which patriot heroes are made. The errors of the Fenians may be more blameable than theirs. Do I exculpate their conduct? Certainly not. It was greatly culpable, because it was contrary to the general interests of society and of their country. Still, errors of this character are not errors which evince a vulgar mind—certainly not a mind likely to be guilty of ordinary crime and vice—rather a mind capable of heroic actions and lofty virtue. Such acts have been committed by the most

[2]John Bright, Speech on Presenting a Petition on Fenianism (3 May, 1867), *PD*, 3rd ser., Vol. 186, cols. 1929–31.

[3]William Edward Forster (1818–86), M.P. for Bradford, cols. 1891–2, defended Perronet Thompson (1783–1869), formerly M.P. for Bradford, for the remarks in Thompson's Speech on India (16 Feb., 1858), *ibid.*, Vol. 148, cols. 1539–42.

[4]Theobald Wolfe Tone (1763–98), a founder of the United Irish Society, who joined in the French invasion of Ireland in 1798, was captured, condemned to death, and committed suicide. For Emmett and Fitzgerald, see No. 57.

[c–c]+TT
[d–d]TT] PD relating to
[e–e]TT] PD of which men of honour might have been capable

self-devoted and admirable persons. [f]How far that is so in the present instance I am unable to say, because, not knowing the antecedents of those whose conduct was implicated, I cannot form an accurate judgment upon the point. I feel, at the same time, sure that the acts for which they have been made amenable to the law, and which the good of society demands should be punished with severity, do not brand them as detestable, but only as pitiable.[f] (*Hear.*)

[*After further debate, Anson's motion was lost.*]

63. The Sunday Lectures Bill

19 JUNE, 1867

PD, 3rd ser., Vol. 188, cols. 99–103. Reported in *The Times*, 20 June, p. 8, from which variants and responses are taken. In moving the second reading of "A Bill to Amend the Act of the 21st Year of George III, c. 49, intitled 'An Act for Preventing Certain Abuses and Profanations on the Lord's Day, called Sunday,'" 30 Victoria (2 Apr., 1867), *PP*, 1867, VI, 367–70, John Russell, Viscount Amberley (1842–76), M.P. for Nottingham, pointed out (cols. 89–95) that the Bill affected only lectures and speeches to which admission was charged; it did not apply to amusements, or even to performances of sacred music. Immediately before Mill spoke, Alexander James Beresford Hope (1820–87), M.P. for Stoke-upon-Trent, suggested (cols. 97–9) that a Select Committee should look thoroughly into the whole subject.

THERE IS MUCH GOOD SENSE and good feeling in the speech of the honourable Member for Stoke-upon-Trent (*Mr. Beresford Hope*). I agree that it is desirable that this question and others should be dealt with in a much broader way than they usually are by the House. But whose fault is it that they are not? Not my noble Friend's.[1] If I may be permitted to say so, it is the fault of the House, which never will look at any subject except by fractions, and will not consent to legislate otherwise than bit by bit. If it would, there would be many things different in our laws and in our discussions. (*Hear.*) My noble Friend professes wider views on the subject than correspond with the breadth of the measure he has proposed. In his Bill he has dealt with a small portion, a corner of the subject upon which he thinks it hardly possible that there can be a difference of opinion among reasonable persons. (*A laugh.*) He gives the House credit for being capable of stopping where it likes, and deciding how far it will or will not go. He thinks that wherever the line

[1]I.e., Amberley's.

[f-f]TT [*in third person, past tense*]] PD I know nothing of those particular men which can enable me to judge whether this be the case with them or not; but the conduct by which they have made themselves amenable to the law, and for which they must be punished, does not stamp them as objects of detestation, but rather of pity.

ought to be drawn, it ought not to be drawn where it is now; and that there is something to be done in the way of promoting useful and instructive amusements, to call them nothing more, on a Sunday, in place of mere sensualities. I am not going to say anything, although much might be said, about the value of the instruction and recreation which these lectures afford. I am going to put it on the lowest ground, and ask whether you will have these or the public-house. (*Hear, hear*.) It is true that the honourable Member for Chichester (*Mr. J.A. Smith*) has proposed, and probably will receive much support in proposing, to take away even this from the working man, and leave him nothing whatever to do on Sunday but to go to church, if he should be so disposed.[2] But there is no incompatibility between going to church and going to these lectures also. If you are not able to make the churches so attractive to the class of persons who are most in need of moralizing influences as to induce them to go there, you will, if you induce them not to go to the public-house, be doing some good. I refer to the question of closing the public-houses on Sunday, because that is a remedy which probably many gentlemen would propose. They would say, "You have not to choose between scientific lectures and the public-house, because you may close the public-house, and shut up the working people in their homes," such as those are. There are two ways of keeping people out of what is considered to be mischief. One is to exclude them from what is regarded as hurtful indulgence, without giving them any other. The other is to facilitate their obtaining indulgences, amusements, recreations, to use no higher term, which if possible may be beneficial, and which certainly cannot be noxious. The latter plan appears to me the better, not only for the interests of society, but for the interests of religion itself. If you prevent any but a strictly religious employment of the Sunday, the only leisure day which is possessed by the mass of working men, what happens? You compel mankind, made as they are of flesh and blood, and needing a great deal which is not provided for by the church service—you compel them to look to the church service, and to their religious observances, not merely for spiritual instruction or spiritual edification, but also for all their excitement, and even for all their amusement. And this has two consequences equally serious and equally mischievous, and certainly equally undesirable in the eyes of [a]rationally[a] religious people. One is to make the churches places of display, places of amusement and levity. The other is to make them places of boundless fanaticism. (*Hear.*) Both the love of lighter and the love of serious and grave excitement seek their gratification in this way, when others are denied them. The consequence is, that you are very likely to have, under cover of religious observances, all sorts of worldly feelings and worldly excitement, or else bigotry and fanaticism raised to their highest point. Speaking, therefore, in the

[2]John Abel Smith, Motion on the Sale of Liquors on Sunday Bill (27 March, 1867), *PD*, Vol. 186, col. 666.

[a-a]+TT

interests of religion, it is not desirable that all places but churches should be closed on the only day of leisure which the mass of the community enjoy. Then as to the mode in which Sunday is to be employed [b]after a certain portion of it is left open for religious observances, other employments being allowed[b], I would ask any reasonable religious person whether, if he cannot have all that he would think best, he ought not to desire to have what is next best—and which he thinks nearest to religion: science, or sensuality? (*Hear, hear.*) With regard to the question of taking money at the doors for admission to these exhibitions, services, or whatever they are called, I understood my honourable Friend the Member for Perth (*Mr. Kinnaird*) [c]—for whom I entertain a degree of respect with which nothing I shall say will be in the slightest degree inconsistent—[c] to say that those who are anxious to give interesting instruction to the people may do it if they choose to defray the expenses themselves; but that it shall not be allowed that those who seek it shall themselves pay the expenses.[3] That may be very well for once, twice, or thrice, but can it be expected to last? Is it to be desired that this instruction should be denied to the working classes unless others are willing to do what they themselves are not allowed to do—namely, to keep up a constant succession of these lectures, at the expense of others, and not at the expense of those who are able and willing to pay for them? Surely that is not what would be thought just and desirable in any other case. But perhaps my honourable Friend is of the opinion which seemed to be entertained by the right honourable Gentleman the Home Secretary (*Mr. Gathorne-Hardy*) on another occasion, when, with a degree of irascibility which I have not seen him exhibit upon any other subject, he spoke of "miserable philosophers" who are never willing to sacrifice anything for their opinions;[4] not perhaps sufficiently considering that "miserable philosophers" have not always the means of making great endowments (*hear, hear*), and that there seems to be no very strong reason why the promulgation of opinions should be left exclusively to those who are able to provide such endowments. As to the evil consequences which my honourable Friend expects to follow if money is taken at the door on these occasions, which, he appears to think, would necessarily lead to the licensing of all sorts of amusements on Sunday, he does not appear to have sufficient confidence in the legislative capacity of the House, or to believe that it is capable of defining what shall be permitted and what shall not. I may, however, observe to my honourable Friend that this Bill actually does draw a line. My honourable Friend says that he once attended these lectures, and that the great attraction was the sacred music. But the Bill of my noble Friend does not include music. He has purposely excluded it, and therefore, also, the paid singers. With regard to that

[3]Arthur Fitzgerald Kinnaird (1814–87), moved the rejection of the Bill, col. 96.

[4]Gathorne-Hardy, Speech on the Uniformity Act Amendment Bill (29 May, 1867), *ibid.*, Vol. 187, col. 1275.

[b-b]+TT [*in past tense*]

[c-c]+TT [*in third person, past tense*]

invidious expression, "paid singers,"[5] are not the singers at our cathedrals paid? Is there anything necessarily unedifying in sacred music, because those who even thus humbly minister to the altar live by the altar? (*Hear.*) With reference to my honourable Friend's fear that if music were allowed dancing must be allowed also, he cannot be indifferent to, or unaware of, the difference between sacred and other music. Is it not the distinctive characteristic of sacred music that its effect upon the mind is at the same time calming and elevating? and therefore I suppose the best preparation for any desirable and good form of religious sentiment. I am not aware that there is any such thing as sacred dancing (*a laugh*), at least according to our notions, although there is according to the ideas of other nations. Therefore there is no ground for the apprehensions of my honourable Friend. I apprehend that in this matter it is perfectly possible to draw a line of distinction if we choose to do so; to say what modes of amusement—if we put it only upon that ground—we consider to be, if not absolutely edifying, not inconsistent with edification, and what we think it desirable to put under restraint for one reason or another. As to these reasons, and the extent to which they would carry restraint, probably no two persons in this House are agreed. There is therefore—not that I apprehend there could be any reasonable objection to passing my noble Friend's Bill—ground for assenting to the proposal of the honourable Member for Stoke, and referring the question to a Select Committee. I concur with him as to the desirability of considering these questions in the broadest possible way, and deciding what are the modes of amusement to which there is no objection, and what are those which, from their more suspicious and more dangerous character, require restraint. It is probable that if a Select Committee be appointed, it will extend rather than restrict the scope of my noble Friend's Bill, and will find that on no broad principle that can be laid down will it be necessary to restrict the measure so much as my noble Friend has done. If the Bill is read a second time I shall be willing, as I presume from what he said my noble Friend will be, to consent to its being referred to a Select Committee, which will probably receive a great deal of valuable evidence—throw some light upon the subject, and I hope remove some prejudices. (*Hear, hear.*)

[*The Bill was lost (col. 116).*]

64. The Libel Bill

25 JUNE, 1867

PD, 3rd ser., Vol. 188, col. 546. Reported in *The Times*, 26 June, p. 7. In Committee on "A Bill to Amend the Law of Libel, and Thereby to Secure More Effectually the Liberty of the Press," 30 Victoria (8 Feb., 1867), *PP*, 1867, III, 391–4, Colman Michael O'Loghlen

[5]Kinnaird, col. 96.

(1819–77), M.P. for County Clare, moved to add a new clause: "No action or prosecution shall be maintainable for the publication of any defamatory matter contained in any report, paper, votes, or proceedings of either House of Parliament, which either House of Parliament shall have ordered to be published; nor shall any action or prosecution be maintainable against a printer or publisher for the publication of any defamatory matter in any periodical or other publication, if such defamatory matter shall be a true and fair report of the proceedings of either House of Parliament" (col. 544).

MR. J. STUART MILL SAID, the first part of the clause provided that there should be no remedy for any defamatory matter contained in any document ordered by the House to be printed. Remembering the multifarious sources of the documents which the House ordered to be printed, he could not help thinking that if there was to be no remedy against the public, as there could be none against the House, for the circulation of any defamatory matter, the House could not do less than appoint some person to look carefully over all documents and see that no defamatory matter was needlessly introduced.

[*Eventually the clause was withdrawn (col. 547).*]

65. The Reform Bill [6]

27 JUNE, 1867

PD, 3rd ser., Vol. 188, cols. 635–8. Reported in *The Times*, 28 June, p. 7, from which the variant and responses are taken. In a further Committee on the Reform Bill (see No. 50), Disraeli moved a new Clause A to provide for increased polling places (cols. 616–17). To an amendment putting the expenses of elections on the local rates, a sub-amendment was attached, requiring the payment of £50 (boroughs) and £100 (counties) by anyone demanding a poll (col. 627). Joseph Warner Henley (1793–1884), M.P. for Oxfordshire, spoke before Mill, pointing out that in county towns a factious candidate might gain nomination by a show of hands; then the other candidate would have to demand and so be put to the expense of a poll; at present, each candidate put down a deposit.

THE RIGHT HONOURABLE GENTLEMAN who has just addressed the House appears to me to have raised a difficulty which is, in fact, no difficulty at all, and which he himself pointed out the means of removing. The obvious remedy against relieving the sham candidate, who might have the show of hands, at the cost of the *bonâ fide* candidate, with a chance of election, was to require deposits from all. But I cannot help thinking that a great deal too much is said of the danger of sham candidates. The expense of the hustings, or the returning officer's expenses, are not only a very small part of the expense of elections as they now are; but I am afraid bear a very small proportion to the expense which it is impossible to prevent. Though a great amount of expense, which, though not corrupt, is very noxious, ought to be, and can be, prevented, it is impossible to prevent, or defray out of a public fund, such expenses as those of advertisements, printing, public meetings to address the electors. The candidates of whom all seem so much afraid, and who have no chance of being elected, cannot present themselves to the electors without incurring a certain amount of these expenses, and if they cannot pay these it is obvious nobody need care for their candidature. The honourable and learned Member for the Tower Hamlets (*Mr. Ayrton*) has said that if this sham candidature is kept up, the counties or the other candidates may be put to expense.[1] But I have no doubt the general opinion would so strongly condemn this, that it would be hardly possible for anyone who cares for the opinion of the constituency, and wishes to make himself favourably known to them, to present himself in this capacity. It may happen, perhaps, or the public may be led to think, that under this horror of sham candidates there is concealed a greater fear of real candidates. This is, as was well observed by the honourable Member for Stoke-upon-Trent (*Mr. Beresford Hope*),[2] part of a much greater question, that of election expenses generally, with which, in all its parts, this House must necessarily have to deal; and I hope it will see the necessity of dealing with it soon. (*Hear, hear.*) But this particular expense, though a small part of the total cost of elections, is a part which it is really in the power of the House to control. It is a necessary part of the expenditure of the country, like any other portion of the public charges. If a foreigner asked how this country provided for that part of its expenditure which attends the election of its representatives, would he not be astonished to hear that it was done by a tax on candidates? (*Hear, hear.*) Of all sorts of taxation, was there ever such a partial and unjust specimen as that would be? But it is really a great deal worse. I can compare it to nothing short of requiring a Judge to pay large sums towards the cost of the administration of justice. It is true that you make men pay for commissions in the army, but you do not apply the price of these commissions towards defraying the expense of the army. Does this House, in any other case, arrange to defray any part of the necessary expenses of the country by a special tax on the individuals who carry on its service? The honourable Member for Stoke-upon-Trent (*Mr. Beresford Hope*), though he has fears of the consequences of the constitutional change we are making, which I by no means share, has expressed an anxiety in which, I think, we must all participate—a sense of the duty under which this House and the country now lie, to provide for educating, in the morality of politics, that large class who are now for the first time to be admitted to the electoral suffrage. What sort of a lesson are we giving them—what sort of instructions do we offer—when we lead them to believe that the great trust of legislating for this country is a thing to be paid for, that it is worth while paying for it, and that men can be made to pay for it? What more natural than that they should

[1]Cols. 633–4.
[2]Cols. 630–1.

think it might as well be paid for directly to those who confer it? The noble Lord who spoke earlier in the debate (*Lord Hotham*)[3] seems to consider that the law of demand and supply should be left to regulate these matters, so that, in fact, those who are willing to pay money should have a clear field, and that the representation should be knocked down to the highest bidder. That is, perhaps, to a certain extent, done already (*a laugh*); but the House ought not to extend and perpetuate the practice. There is in this country a large and growing class of persons who have suddenly and rapidly acquired wealth, and to whom it is worth any sacrifice of money to obtain social position. The less they have to recommend them in any other respect—the less chance they have of obtaining a place in what is called good society—esteem, either by qualities useful or ornamental—the more sure they are to resort, if they can, to the only infallible and ready means of gaining their end, the obtaining a seat in this House. This is a growing evil which ought to be guarded against. (*Hear.*) I hope the Government will deal with this subject in all its parts, as it is certainly highly needful to do; but we have now an opportunity of dealing with one part which is entirely in our control, and which forms an element of the question we are now discussing. We can deal with that small part of election expenses which is an unavoidable part of the expense of governing the country, and which, though the right honourable Gentleman the Member for Oxfordshire (*Mr. Henley*) said it would be extremely shabby to throw on the constituencies,[4] I think it would be a monstrous deal more shabby to throw on the candidates. (*Hear, hear, and a laugh.*) When a man has no personal object of his own to gain by obtaining a seat in this House, it is not for the House to require that he should pay the expense which the country and the electors incur by his election: if he has any such object, we ought to do everything in our power, and to throw every obstacle in his way, to prevent him from obtaining it by money. Above all, it is our duty to show to the new electors, and that large portion of the old who, I am sorry to say, still need the lesson, that the business of election is a thing far removed from aught of buying and selling; that the business of a Member of this House is a laborious and onerous task, and when not sought from personal motives, one which it requires a high sense of public duty to undertake, and that the burthen, therefore, ought not to be increased by throwing any part of the expense on the candidate. [a]If members, indeed, are not to be paid for undertaking the business of legislation, they certainly ought not to be made to pay for leave to govern the country.[a] (*Cheers and laughter.*) We ought, above all things, to show the electors that they are doing what we and the world consider disgraceful, if they put the candidate to any expense, and thus tempt him to use his seat for his personal advantage. (*Hear.*)

[*Both the sub-amendment and the amendment were defeated.*]

[3]Beaumont Hotham (1794–1870), an Irish peer, M.P. for the East Riding of Yorkshire, col. 632.

[4]Col. 635.

[a-a]+TT [*in past tense*]

66. Redistribution

28 JUNE, 1867

Morning Star, 29 June, 1867, p. 6. Headed: "National Reform Union. Meeting Last Evening." An identical report is in the *Evening Star*; *The Times* has a full report in the third person; shorter reports appeared in the *Daily News*, the *Daily Telegraph*, and the *Morning Post*. (Clippings of the *Morning Star* and *The Times* are in the Mill-Taylor Collection.) The evening meeting, under the auspices of the National Reform Union, was held in St. James's Hall, to protest against the government's redistribution scheme, on the grounds that it discriminated against the large boroughs. The Chair was taken by Jacob Bright, and Mill ("who was received with prolonged cheering" [*Daily News*]), was in the platform party. After Bright spoke, a resolution regretting the government's refusal to introduce an Irish Reform Bill in the present session was moved, seconded, and passed. A second resolution condemning the government's redistribution plan was passed, as was one (seconded by Beales, who also praised Mill), endorsing continued action by the National Reform Union. Then, at 11:10 p.m., in response to repeated calls, the Chair called upon Mill. "The immense audience at once rose *en masse*, and hats and handkerchiefs were set waving, and the cheering lasted for several minutes."

THERE IS NOT THE SMALLEST NEED that I should address you this evening, for you have already heard many excellent speeches, and there is nothing which I have to say, or that I think it useful to say on this subject on this occasion which has not already been anticipated by some speaker. I had hoped, therefore, that you would have excused me; but as you may wish to hear my view of this question—(*cheers*)—and as possibly there may be many of my constituents present to-night who have a right to hear what my sentiments are, I will [a]therefore at this late hour very[a] briefly explain them. (*Hear, hear.*) I think that Reformers will only do their duty if they continue to agitate until they obtain a bill far better than the present one in the essential point of the redistribution of seats,[1] and, above all, I think no Reformers ought to be satisfied unless the large towns obtain, not a third member here and there, but a great number of additional members—(*cheers*)—and when I speak of the large towns, I include amongst them the metropolitan districts, which [b]are eminently entitled to a large representation—(*hear, hear*)—and I say this ought to be the case even from what our opponents admit.[b] Mr. Disraeli has, from the beginning, proclaimed and declared with frequent iteration that the counties must have a larger representation than they have at present, because if you take the whole numbers of their population they are more populous than the towns.[2] Now,

[1]Clauses 8–16 of the Reform Bill (for which see No. 50).

[2]E.g., in his Speech on the Representation of the People Bill (24 June), *PD*, 3rd ser., Vol. 188, cols. 467–8.

[a–a]+TT [*in the past tense*]

[b–b]TT , even upon the single ground of population, were entitled to a large increase in representation. But all the large towns were entitled to an increased representation, not only upon the principles advocated by the Liberals but upon the principles even of their opponents, for if this argument is good for the counties it is good for the great towns; and the great towns are far more populous than some of the counties. In this metropolis you have over 3,000,000 in population, and if you allow to the counties 12,000,000,[3] which is exceeding Mr. Disraeli's calculation, it follows that London ought to have one-fourth of the amount of representation which the counties have—(*hear, hear*)—and at that rate London would be entitled to forty or fifty members—(*cheers*)—and the other large towns of the country would have to have a proportionately large increase [c], this increase, of course, being at the expense of the representation of the small towns [c]. But let us look a little more closely into this question of the counties. Now what is the population of which these 11,000,000 are composed? First of all there are the landlords, and then there are the farmers. Well, they do not count 11,000,000. Then there are the small shopkeepers and professional men [d]living in the small unrepresented towns[d], and we do not know how many of these will have votes, but theirs is a fair claim as far as it goes. But how is the remainder of the 11,000,000 made up? Why, it is made up by counting the agricultural labourers. (*Cheers.*) Now, I should like to know whether these gentlemen will have the face to stand up in the House of Commons or anywhere else and say that [e]the landlords as county members[e] represent the agricultural labourers. (*Cheers.*) Why, [f]those are precisely the only people that the agricultural labourers ever have any dispute or quarrel with. But let them look at the subject in another point of view. These[f] agricultural labourers have not even votes, and this bill is not going to give them any—(*hear, hear*)—and they are not to have votes either in the counties or in the boroughs [g]; but if they possess no votes the Conservatives have no right to count that portion of the population as forming a part of the county constituencies[g]. But it may be said that if they are not represented directly, they are represented indirectly. Well, sometimes those who are not represented directly are represented indirectly by those who have the same interest as themselves. But I want to know, has the agricultural labourer the same interest as the landlords and the farmers? (*Cheers.*) It is very well to say that the interests of all classes of the nation are much the same in the long run. I am not going to say anything against that, but mankind are much more governed by their immediate than their ultimate interests [h], and if I had any immediate interest to be settled I should much prefer that the man who has to decide the matter should not be chosen from persons who have opposite interests to my own[h]. (*Hear, hear.*)

[3]Mill uses the higher figure for easy calculation; he then uses 11,000,000 as a rounded lower figure for what was calculated to be a county population of 11,428,632.

[c-c]+TT
[d-d]+TT
[e-e]TT] MS they
[f-f]TT [*in the past tense*]] MS the
[g-g]+TT [*in the past tense*]
[h-h]+TT [*in the third person, past tense*]

Now if there are any persons in the community that the agricultural labourers would not wish to be represented by, I should say it is the landlords. (*Hear, hear.*) Why, the town members represent them better. (*Hear, hear.*) We town representatives have no disputes with them. (*Hear, hear.*) We are not their masters, and people do not like to be represented by their masters. (*Hear, hear.*) We are not their employers, and we never have any dispute with them about wages as the farmers have, and moreover we want to educate them, and farmers generally, I think, do not want to do that. (*Cheers.*) They think, in the first place, that education makes the labourers too independent; and, in the next place, they want them to make them labour a great deal too early so as to render it impossible for them to remain at school. I do not say this of the landlords. I am now referring to the farmers. Many of the landlords are desirous that the agricultural labourers should be educated, and perhaps things would get on much better if it was not for that accursed subject—game. (*Cheers.*) Now, we town representatives never have any quarrels with the agricultural labourer on that subject. (*Hear, hear.*) But such is the state of things and feeling on the subject of game, which has taken possession of the landed interest, that I cannot conceive that any agricultural labourer, if he had his choice, would like to be represented by any man who kept a gamekeeper. (*Laughter and cheers.*) I am told by persons who live in the country that it is a fixed belief with agricultural labourers that a bench of magistrates think that the word of a gamekeeper is law, and that whenever a gamekeeper charges a person with an offence against the game laws, that person is sure to have to go to prison. (*Hear, hear.*) Now, I do not know whether this is true or not, but so it is asserted, and it is a great pity that every now and then something happens which gives a great deal of colour to this assertion. (*Cheers.*) Many present may have noticed a recent case, which is very striking in its features, and we should have known nothing of it had it not been for a noble-hearted clergyman who brought the facts before the public.[4] A gamekeeper who had had the satisfaction or accident to make a mistake before in charging a person wrongfully, made oaths that two persons had been seen by him in the act of poaching. The father and mother of each of these two supposed delinquents gave positive evidence that these two young men were in their respective houses on the night in question. The gamekeeper, however, was believed by the magistrates, and the two young men were sent to prison. One was sent for a short period, which he served. While the other was still in prison, two persons who had really committed the offence came forward and confessed that they had done so. Now, what would you suppose this circumstance

[4]Richard Payne (1810–90), Vicar of Downton and Rural Dean of Wilton, wrote a letter to the *Daily News*, published on 11 June, 1867, in which he outlined the case. George Pilgrim, a gamekeeper, had accused Henry Fulford and Mark Wellstead of poaching, before Edward Hinxman (b. 1810), a Wiltshire magistrate. The two who later confessed were Stephen Deer and Charles Moody. See "The Game Laws and County Representation," *Spectator*, 15 June, 1867, pp. 658–9. See also No. 72.

would have inspired in the minds of the magistrates? One would have thought at least a doubt respecting the testimony of the gamekeeper. (*Hear, hear.*) Not so, however, because they did not see their way to letting the confined man out of prison—(*cries of Shame*)—and he would have remained in prison to the end of his sentence had it not been for this clergyman who gave publicity to the affair, and after considerable delay and consideration the Home Secretary[5] let the man out. (*Cheers.*) [i]As to any atonement being made to the man, such a thing was never to be dreamt of. Nay, more, after all, the man, though innocent, was held to bail.[i] Now, I believe that these things do not often happen, but one such thing in a year is quite enough to reveal the difference of feeling between a country gentleman and an agricultural labourer. (*Cheers.*) And it makes it not at all probable that agricultural labourers, if they had any choice, would choose landlords to be their representatives. (*Cheers.*) I say, therefore, whatever claims the counties may have for representation, those claims should not at all events be put forward as regards the agricultural labourers, who, as I have already said, are better represented by the town members. (*Cheers.*) [j]It is said that these labourers have no votes; but that is not strictly correct, for some of them have votes. I may be asked where. Why, in the towns and, still more, in those petty sham counties—that is to say, in those places hardly better than villages which have large landed districts attached to them. All the agricultural labourers will have votes, but these will count as town votes, and, therefore, as I have said before, the town representatives are the more real representatives of the agricultural labourers than the landlords. Well, it being assumed that the great towns ought to have more representatives, the question, then, to be considered is where are those additional members to come from. I would call attention in respect to this point to those small sham counties of which I have spoken. They are Cricklade, Aylesbury, and Shoreham. By the disfranchisement of other boroughs these have had the surrounding districts added to them, and ought, therefore, to be counted among the county representatives. By the Reform Bill of 1832 many of these boroughs were created. A Conservative member of the House of Commons the other day gave the history of Wenlock, which covered 75 square miles, while the town was not larger than a village, and yet it returned two members to Parliament.[6] I should like to know where they could find a better place than this for disfranchisement, which would give them two members to be

[5]Gathorne-Hardy.

[6]Richard Dyott (1808–91), M.P. for Lichfield, Speech on the Representation of the People Bill (25 June, 1867), *PD*, 3rd ser., Vol. 188, col. 532.

[i-i]+TT

[j-j]TT [*in the third person, past tense*]] MS *The honourable gentleman then briefly spoke of the unsatisfactory character of the redistribution bill of the Government, and concluded amidst great cheering.*] DT As for the redistribution, there are many towns where one member has been returned by the patron and one by the town. Which of these two is to be given up? (*Cheers.*) I am afraid the people will lose theirs and the patron retain his. (*Cheers.*)

disposed of elsewhere. There are other places of a similar description, such as Thetford, Tavistock, and Totnes, all of which return two members, the plan generally being that the patron returns one member, and the people the other member. Some of these places are to be deprived of one of their members, and the question is who will be the loser, the patron or the people? (*Cheers.*) Where there is no member to be disposed of I fear the patron will be stronger than the people, but all such ought to be considered county representations. I will give the Government what credit may be due to them for giving additional members to the metropolis, and also a member to the London University; but while they have added largely to the representation of the counties they will not grant any additional member to the great towns. (*Cheers.*)[j]

[*The meeting concluded towards midnight with the customary vote of thanks to the Chair, during which Harriet Law (whom the* Daily News, *not knowing her name, identified as "a lady in a sailor's hat"), who "had shortly before taken her seat by the side of Mr. Mill," made "a long oration on the subject of women's political rights. She called for a show of hands in favour of Mr. Mill's proposition to admit women to the suffrage, and the meeting, which had half dwindled away, cordially answered the appeal"* (Morning Post).]

67. William Lloyd Garrison

29 JUNE, 1867

Proceedings at the Public Breakfast Held in Honour of William Lloyd Garrison, Esq., of Boston, Massachusetts, in St. James's Hall, London, on Saturday, June 29th, 1867. Revised by the Speakers; with an Introduction by F.W. Chesson, and Opinions of the Press (London: Tweedie, 1868), pp. 33–5. Reported in full in the *Morning Star*, and much compressed in the *Daily News*; the *Daily Telegraph* gives only a one-sentence summary of Mill's remarks. Some 300–400 people, including a large number of women, sat down to breakfast, with John Bright in the Chair. After letters were read from the American Ambassador and the Comte de Paris, regretting their inability to attend, Bright gave a lengthy eulogy of William Lloyd Garrison (1805–79), the prominent anti-slavery advocate and pacifist. Then George Douglas Campbell (1823–1900), Duke of Argyll, read an address to Garrison composed by Goldwin Smith. Argyll was followed by Lord Russell; then Mill spoke.

MR. CHAIRMAN, LADIES, AND GENTLEMEN,—The speakers who have preceded me have, with an eloquence far beyond anything which I can command, laid before our honoured guest the homage of admiration and gratitude which we all feel is due to his heroic life. Instead of idly expatiating upon things which have been far better said than I could say them, I would rather endeavour to recall one or two lessons applicable to ourselves, which may be drawn from his career. A noble work nobly done always contains in itself, not one, but many lessons; and in the case of him whose character and deeds we are here to commemorate, two may be singled out specially deserving to be laid to heart by all who would wish to leave the world better than they found it.

The first lesson is,—Aim at something great; aim at things which are difficult; and there is no great thing which is not difficult. (*Hear, hear.*) [a]Do not pare down your undertaking to what you can hope to see successful in the next few years, or in the years of your own life.[a] Fear not the reproach of Quixotism [b]and impracticability, or to be pointed at as the knight-errants of an idea. (*Hear, hear, and a laugh.*) After[b] you have well weighed what you undertake, if you see your way clearly, and are convinced that you are right, go forward, even though you, like Mr. Garrison, do it at the risk of being torn to pieces by the very men through whose changed hearts your purpose will one day be accomplished. (*Cheers.*) [c]Fight on with all your strength against whatever odds, and with however small a[c] band of supporters. (*Hear, hear.*) If you are right, the time will come when that small band will swell into a multitude: you will at least lay the foundations of something memorable, and you may, like Mr. Garrison—though you ought not to need or expect so great a reward—be spared to see that work completed which, when you began it, you only hoped it might be given to you to help forward a few stages on its way. (*Cheers.*)

The other lesson which it appears to me important to enforce, amongst the many that may be drawn from our friend's life, is this: if you aim at something noble and succeed in it, you will generally find that you have succeeded not in that alone. A hundred other good and noble things which you never dreamed of will have been accomplished by the way, and the more certainly, the sharper and more agonizing has been the struggle which preceded the victory. The heart and mind of a nation are never stirred from their foundations without manifold good fruits. In the case of the great American contest, these fruits have been already great, and are daily becoming greater. The prejudices which [d]beset every form of society[d]—and of which there was a plentiful crop in America—are rapidly melting away. The chains of prescription have been broken; it is not only the slave who has been freed[1]—the mind of America has been emancipated. (*Loud cheers.*) The whole intellect of the country has been set thinking about the fundamental questions of society and government; and the new problems which have to be solved, and the

[1]Abraham Lincoln (1809–65), *Emancipation Proclamation* (Washington: n.p., 1863); it came into effect on 1 January, 1863.

[a–a]MS Let the world sneer or censure as it will, do not pare down your endeavours to the level of those who would seek to disparage them.
[b–b]MS] P or of fanaticism; but after
[c–c]MS He did all his work at great odds, with none to help but a small though heroic-minded
[d–d]MS gather round the frame of society like rust

new difficulties which have to be encountered, [e]are calling forth new activity of thought, and that great nation is saved[e], probably for a long time to come, from the most formidable danger of a completely settled state of society and opinion—intellectual and moral stagnation. (*Hear, hear.*) This, then, is an additional item of the debt which America and mankind owe to Mr. Garrison and his noble associates; and it is well calculated to deepen our sense of the truth which his whole career most strikingly illustrates—that though our best directed efforts may often seem wasted and lost, nothing coming of them that can be pointed to and distinctly identified as a definite gain to humanity; though this may happen ninety-nine times in every hundred, the hundredth time the result may be so great and dazzling that we had never dared to hope for it, and should have regarded him who had predicted it to us as sanguine beyond the bounds of mental sanity. So has it been with Mr. Garrison. (*Loud cheers.*)

[*The address was passed unanimously, and Garrison spoke to great applause. Other speeches followed, and the meeting concluded with the customary vote of thanks to the Chair.*]

68. Martial Law

2 JULY, 1867

PD, 3rd ser., Vol. 188, cols. 912–14. Reported in *The Times*, 3 July, p. 7, from which the variants and response are taken. The debate was on a motion (col. 903), based on a charge by the Lord Chief Justice to the Grand Jury at the Central Criminal Court on 10 April, 1867, that would make it clear that martial law could not be invoked in the United Kingdom.

THERE APPEARS TO BE, as far as the discussion has gone on both sides of the House, a real disposition to consider this question with reference to the future rather than the past. Certainly it is most desirable that when we are considering what is essentially a question of legislation, we should not allow ourselves to be diverted to the consideration of past transactions any further than they throw light upon questions which may exist or arise in the future. At the same time it appears to me that certain considerations of great importance have not yet been touched upon, and which I think it is particularly necessary should not remain unstated when we see an obvious desire to explain away and get rid of the effect of the Charge of the Lord Chief Justice of England.[1] I do not mean to say that what has been stated by

[1]Alexander James Edmund Cockburn (1802–80), *Charge of the Lord Chief Justice of England to the Grand Jury at the Central Criminal Court, in the Case of the Queen against Nelson and Brand*, ed. Frederick Cockburn (London: Ridgway, 1867).

[e–e]MS have raised up the faculties of the people to corresponding activity, so that they have been freed

the right honourable Gentleman the Home Secretary in diminution of the validity, in a legal point of view, of this Charge is unfounded.[2] We know, on the contrary, that it is well founded. We know that the Charge to the Grand Jury is not law, because it has not undergone the preliminary processes necessary to make it law. At the same time there can be no doubt that such a declaration as this Charge contains, supported by such a *catena* of authorities [a]from the very earliest period of our history[a], and coming from a Judge of such high character and reputation, so elaborately produced and bearing the marks it does of most diligent and careful study, is, at all events, an exceedingly strong corroboration of that view of this subject which some of us have taken from the beginning, and which I will briefly state. Our opinion has been [b]—and it has been confirmed by this charge—[b] that the law is what I shall now venture to state, and that if it has not been so, it ought to be made so. Our opinion was, that there is not, properly speaking, as regards non-military persons, such a thing as martial law, and that it has no existence except for military [c]purposes[c]. Of course, Parliament can give it existence, because Parliament can make any law, however inexpedient or unjust. But the Crown, being only one branch of Legislature, cannot [d]make that to be law which is not law[d]. We have thought that, although there was no such thing as martial law, except for military purposes, there was a law of necessity. There may be a public necessity in case of rebellion, requiring that certain acts not justified by the ordinary law of the country should be done; but these acts should be acts of suppression and not of punishment. Now, a point which has not been noticed, and to which I attach the highest importance, is this—that in a case of public necessity, as in any analogous case of private necessity, those who act upon it, and do under the supposed necessity that which they would not ordinarily be justified in doing, should be amenable to the laws of their country for so doing. As in the case of killing any person in self-defence, so in the case of putting any person to death in defence of the country, the person who does it ought to have the *onus* thrown upon him of satisfying the ordinary tribunals of the country that this necessity existed. What, therefore, we say does not exist, and ought not to exist, and which if it does exist we should do our utmost to put an end to, is, the idea that any proceeding, such as a declaration of martial law, can or ought to exempt those who act upon it from amenability to the laws of their country. We contend that the law of necessity, of which nobody denies the existence, would justify the Executive in doing these things if no such thing as martial law had ever been heard of, and that by using the term martial law you ought not to be able to get rid of all responsibility. We demand that the officers of the Government of this country

[2]Gathorne-Hardy, col. 910.

[a-a]+TT
[b-b]+TT
[c-c]TT persons
[d-d]TT] PD do this

should not be able to escape or get out of the region and jurisdiction of the law; but, that whatever they do, if it be against the law, they should be compelled to justify. They must show the necessity which existed, not to the satisfaction of a court martial merely, but of the regular tribunals of the country. When it is said by the right honourable Gentleman the Home Secretary that it is much better that the officers who intend to assume this power, and act on this supposed necessity, should declare beforehand their intention of doing so,[3] by all means let them do so; but do not let them, or any one else, think that by using the term martial law, or by announcing that they mean to make a military tribunal one of the instruments by which they will exercise their power of superseding the law, they will clear themselves from all responsibility. (*Hear, hear.*)

[*The motion was withdrawn (col. 918).*]

69. The Reform Bill [7]

4 JULY, 1867

PD, 3rd ser., Vol. 188, cols. 1024, 1026, 1029. Reported in *The Times*, 5 July, p. 7, from which the response is taken. The variants are taken from the report in the *St. Stephen's Chronicle*, Vol. IV, pp. 426–7. The discussion in Committee of the Reform Bill (see No. 50) turned to a new clause: "That no committee of any candidate . . . shall sit, or hold any meeting, or transact any business . . . in any hotel, tavern, public-house, or other building licensed . . . for the sale or consumption of wine, spirits, beer, porter, or other intoxicating liquors; and if any such candidate shall, by himself or his agents, cause or permit any breach of this enactment, the Return of such candidate shall be null and void, and no expenses incurred by such committee [in these circumstances] . . . shall be recoverable by law from such committee . . . or from any such candidate . . ." (col. 1019). Mill spoke on an amendment by Joseph Henley (cols. 1023–4) to change "of any candidate" to "appointed by any candidate," immediately after Gabriel Goldney (1813–1900), M.P. for Chippenham, had pointed out that people quite unknown to the candidate could constitute themselves a committee and call a meeting in a public house.

MR. J. STUART MILL SAID, he thought the object which the honourable Gentleman who had just sat down, as well as that the right honourable Gentleman the Member for Oxfordshire had in view, was a legitimate one. He would suggest that if some such word as "sanction" were substituted for the word "permit," the clause would be made efficient for its purpose.

[*Mill's second intervention came after Gathorne-Hardy had commented (col.*

[3]*Ibid.*, col. 909.

1026) that it was preposterous to make candidates liable for practices over which they often had no control.]

Mr. J. Stuart Mill said, he would remind the right honourable Gentleman that the first part of the clause did not touch the candidate. (*Hear, hear.*) He also proposed to insert the word "sanction" instead of "permit," as to the second part [a]making the election void only if the expense were sanctioned or permitted by the candidate[a].

[*Henley's amendment was successful; it was then moved to insert "or on behalf of" after "appointed by" (col. 1026), and the Attorney General suggested "no committee appointed by or with the consent of any candidate" as a better alternative; Mill's third intervention was in reply.*]

Mr. J. Stuart Mill said, that in that case the committee might be appointed first and sanctioned afterwards. [b]He thought that "recognized by" was much more satisfactory than "with the consent of."[b]

[*That amendment being lost, another was offered, to insert "acting on behalf of and with the consent of" (col. 1029), prompting Mill's fourth comment, which was not acted upon.*]

Mr. J. Stuart Mill said, he would suggest the addition of the words "recognized by."

[*Eventually the whole clause was rejected.*]

70. Tancred's Charity Bill

4 JULY, 1867

Saint Stephen's Chronicle, Vol. IV, p. 432. Not in *PD*. Reported in *The Times*, 5 July, p. 8, from which the variant is taken. The debate was on Shaw Lefevre's motion to go into Committee on "A Bill [as Amended by the Select Committee] for Continuing a Scheme of the Charity Commissioners for the Several Charities Founded by the Settlement and Will of Christopher Tancred of Whixley in the County of York, Esquire, Deceased," 30 & 31 Victoria (25 June, 1867), *PP*, 1867, VI, 381–4. Mill spoke immediately after Lefevre.

MR. J.S. MILL SAID this was a question of considerable importance, and he trusted, therefore, that the noble lord[1] would not press the Bill forward at so late an hour (*a*

[1]Lord Robert Montagu.

[a–a]+SSC
[b–b]+SSC

quarter to 1 o'clock) [a]as there were various amendments on the paper, all of them worthy of discussion. (*Hear, hear.*)[a]

[*After Montagu replied and Ayrton spoke, the House went into Committee.*]

71. The Reform Bill [8]

5 JULY, 1867

PD, 3rd ser., Vol. 188, cols. 1102–7. Reported in *The Times*, 6 July, p. 8, from which one variant and the responses are taken. The concluding sentence is taken from the report in the *St. Stephen's Chronicle*, Vol. IV, pp. 442–4. The discussion in Committee of the Reform Bill (see No. 50) turned to a new clause proposed by Robert Lowe (M.P. for Calne): "At any contested Election for a County or Borough represented by more than two Members, and having more than one seat vacant, every voter shall be entitled to a number of votes equal to the number of vacant seats, and may give all such votes to one candidate or may distribute them among the candidates as he thinks fit" (col. 1068). John Bright (M.P. for Birmingham) had argued (cols. 1090–7) that he had always invited the House "to march along the ancient paths of the Constitution," while Lowe's plan would put an end to contests for representation.

I HOPE my honourable Friend the Member for Birmingham will forgive me if the highly Conservative speech which he has delivered, almost the first which I ever heard him deliver with which I could not sympathize, has not converted me from the eminently democratic opinions which I have held for a great number of years. (*A laugh.*) I am very glad that my honourable Friend stated so candidly the extremely Conservative vein of thought and tone of feeling which is the foundation of his political feelings. It is true that it is almost as opposite a frame of mind from my own as it is possible to conceive; but, fortunately, in the case of most of the practical questions that we have to decide we draw nearly the same conclusions from our so different premises. Nevertheless, I am extremely glad that my honourable Friend has shown that it is upon the principle of standing by old things, and resisting new-fangled notions, that his antipathy to the proposal of my right honourable Friend the Member for Calne, which I most strongly support, has been derived. It is the less necessary that I should address the House at any length upon this question, because on a previous occasion I expressed myself strongly in favour of the principles upon some of which this Motion rests,[1] and expressed my strong sense of the necessity for a change in our mode of election, directed in some degree to the same ends as those pointed out by this almost insignificant makeshift—a makeshift not, however, without considerable real efficacy, and resting in part upon the same principles upon which Mr. Hare's system of personal representation

[1]"Personal Representation" (30 May), No. 60 above.

[a–a]+TT

is founded. There are two principles which we must mainly regard. In the first place, it appears to me that any body of persons who are united by any ties, either of interest or of opinion, should have, or should be able to have, if they desire it, influence and power in this House proportionate to that which they exercise out of it. This, of course, excludes the idea of applying such a system as this to constituencies having only two Members, because in that case its application would render a minority of one-third equal to a majority. The other principle upon which I support the representation of minorities is because I wish—although this may surprise some honourable Members—that the majority should govern. We heard a great deal formerly about the tyranny of the majority, but it appears to me that many honourable Gentlemen on both sides of the House are now reconciled to that tyranny, and are disposed to defend and maintain it against us democrats.[2] My own opinion is, that any plan for the representation of minorities must operate in a very great degree to diminish and counteract the tyranny of majorities. I wish to maintain the just ascendancy of majorities, but this cannot be done unless minorities are represented. The majority in this House is got at by the elimination of two minorities. You first eliminate at the election the minority out of the House, and then upon a division you eliminate the minority in the House. Now, it may very well happen that those combined minorities would greatly out-number the majority which prevails in this House, and consequently that the majority does not now govern. The true majority can only be maintained if all minorities are counted; if they are counted there is only one process of elimination, and only one minority left out. Perhaps I may be allowed to answer one or two objections which have been made to the proposal of my right honourable Friend.[3] The right honourable Gentleman the Under Secretary for the Colonies urged that, according to our constitution, representation should be by communities, and upon that subject he said several things with which it is impossible not to agree.[4] But it seems to me that this is one of many remarkable proofs now offering themselves, that honourable Gentlemen opposite, not content with coming to our opinions, are now adopting our arguments. For instance, the right honourable Gentleman insisted upon the greatness of the mistake of supposing that the country was divided into a majority and a minority, instead of into majorities and minorities. I have said that myself I should think at least 500 times. The right honourable Gentleman said one thing that perfectly amazed me. He said, as we all admit, that it was wrong that the representative of any community should represent it only in a single aspect, should represent only one interest—only its Tory or its Liberal opinions; and he added that, at present, this was not the case, but that such a state of things would be produced by the adoption of this proposal. I apprehend that then, even more than

[2]E.g., Robert Montagu, Speech on the Representation of the People Bill (13 Apr., 1866), *PD*, 3rd ser., Vol. 182, cols. 1282–93, and Samuel Laing, *ibid.*, cols. 1306–21.

[3]I.e., Lowe (cols. 1036–42).

[4]Charles Adderley, cols. 1082–5.

now, each party would desire to be represented, and would feel the importance of getting itself represented by those men who would be most acceptable to the general body of the constituency; and therefore on all other points, except that of being Liberals or Tories, those Members would represent the constituencies fully as much, if not more, than they do now. The right honourable Gentleman thinks that the local communities ought to be represented as units,[5] but that is not my opinion. For example, the right honourable Gentleman would contend that if a Member were elected by two-thirds of a constituency he ought to sit in that House as representing the whole. If that were the case they would evidently pass for what they are not. I have no idea of Members sitting in this House as the representatives of mere names of places, or bricks and mortar, or some particular part of the terrestrial globe, in different localities. What we want is the representation of the inhabitants of those places. If there should be a place in which two-thirds of the constituency are Conservative, and one-third Liberal, it is a falsehood to contend that the Conservative Member represents the Liberals of that place. On the other hand, if there were three Members for such a place, two of whom represented the majority, and the third the minority, there would be a full representation of the constituency, and certainly a far more accurate representation than if a man returned by a simple majority assumed to represent the whole constituency. Another objection made and insisted upon by my honourable Friend below me, in one of the most eloquent parts of his speech,[6] and in the spirit of which I quite agree, is that the effect of this system will be to put an end to contests at elections, and to all the instruction they afford, and all the public spirit and interest in public affairs which they excite. This appears to me to be an opinion, which only the extreme dislike that my honourable Friend professes for everything new in politics prevents him from seeing to be an entire mistake. The fault which my honourable Friend and others find with the proposed mode of election is one that is in an eminent degree attributable to the existing system; because under that system wherever it is known from the state of the registration [a]or from previous elections[a] that one side is able to return all the Members, the other side now take little or no interest in the election, and therefore it will be evident that if those persons who cannot be represented in their own locality cannot obtain a representation elsewhere, representation, so far as they are concerned, will be a perfectly effete institution. What is it that induces people when they are once beaten at an election to try again? Is it not the belief that possibly a change has taken place in the opinions of at least some of the electors, or that, at all events, there has been such a change in the general feeling of the constituency that there is some chance of their being returned, and therefore there is a sufficient motive to induce them to try

[5]Adderley, col. 1083.
[6]Bright, col. 1094.

[a-a]+TT

again? But that motive never can exist under the present system where there is so great a discrepancy between the parties as two-thirds and one-third, because in no case can one-third of the constituency ever hope to convert itself into a majority. What motive, then, is there for trying? But under the new system, suppose the minority obtains one Member out of three, the minority can always try for the second seat, and precisely the same motive will exist if the parties should be nearly equal. Indeed, in such a case, the motive would be all the stronger, because then the majority will try to get all the members. What will be the case where there are three Members to be returned? The majority of two-thirds will only have two of the Members, and if any change in opinion takes place favourable to the minority they will always be in a position to bid for the third seat; so that I apprehend the healthy excitement of contest in an election, which follows from the existence of the motives which will induce persons to embark in the struggle, will be more certainly guaranteed by the more perfect representation of the constituency. It has been argued by my honourable Friend below me, and it has been several times insisted on by the Chancellor of the Exchequer, that the Executive will be rendered very weak by the adoption of this principle,[7] and I must own that there is some truth and justice in that argument. But the House cannot fail to perceive that so long as you give to the minority the same power as is possessed by the majority, it is perfectly clear that there may be a large majority of the constituency in favour of the Government, while there may be no majority in the House. At the present moment we do not care what majority the Government may have in the country; all that we want is to prevent it having a large majority in the House. No one is more opposed to such a state of things than I am; but the practical application is, that we wish to prevent the Government having a large majority in the House, with a small majority in the country. That is the case in Australia, as was very strongly exemplified on the question of Free Trade and protection, and also in the United States, where there is a moderate difference in the constituencies between one party, and the other, but a very much greater difference in the House of Representatives. (*Hear, hear.*) When the right honourable Gentleman says that this system will make a weak Government, my answer is that it is not desirable that a Government should be a strong one, if it rests on a small majority of the constituencies; nor is it desirable that a Government should be lured on and deceived by a great majority in the House; because a very small change in the constituencies would be sufficient to deprive them of that majority, and it is not desirable that the policy of the Government should be tumbled about from one extreme to the other (*hear, hear*) when the opinion of the constituency is almost equally divided between the two parties. I quite agree with my honourable Friend

[7]Bright, col. 1093; Disraeli, Speech on the Representation of the People Bill (31 May, 1867), Vol. 187, cols. 1419–20.

the Member for Birmingham, that in revolutionary times it is necessary that a party should be as strong as possible while the fight lasts, since the sooner the fighting is over the better.[8] But although in such a case there should be a decisive predominance, such times are exceptional, and circumstances do not apply which apply in ordinary and peaceful times. They are times for which we cannot legislate or adapt our ordinary institutions. Under such circumstances men may be obliged to dispense with all law, and, if necessary, to have a dictatorship in the hands of one man, but that is altogether an exceptional case. I am extremely anxious that the feeling should not get abroad, from the circumstance of the right honourable Member for Calne having brought forward this proposal, and from its being so largely supported by Gentlemen on the other side of the House, that this is essentially a Conservative "move," and is intended solely for the purpose of doing away as far as possible with the effect of the Reform Bill now before us. I have always entertained these opinions, long before the introduction of this Reform Bill, and although I never supposed that I should see such a Reform as this adopted in my life, I have protested and reprobated oppression of this kind, on whichever side it has been practised. The only reason why it can be said that it is brought forward as a Conservative measure, and in aid of Conservatives, is that it really operates in favour of those who are likely to be weakest; it is those who are in danger of being outnumbered and subjected to the tyranny of a majority who are protected. I have always been afraid that the Conservative party would not see the necessity of these things until they actually saw that it is their interest, and that they would not see it until the power has passed away to the other side. Had they taken up the question four or five years ago they might by this time have made it the general opinion of the country, and have led the masses of the people to be more just when their time came than they have been to them. (*Hear, hear.*) Their eyes are not so soon opened to those things which appear to be against them as they are to those that are in their favour; but there are minds on the other side of the House quite capable of seeing the value and importance of the principle, and of representing it with such effect that ultimately the principle of the representation of minorities will be generally adopted. [b]Upon the understanding that it is not to be supposed that those opinions with reference to the proposed system of voting are not peculiarly applicable to the circumstances of the Reform Bill, no one will more heartily and cordially welcome the opinions of honourable Gentlemen opposite than I will.[b]

[*Mill was a teller for the "Ayes," who were defeated, 173 to 314.*]

[8]Bright, col. 1093.

[b-b]+SSC

72. The Case of Fulford and Wellstead

5 JULY, 1867

PD, 3rd ser., Vol. 188, cols. 1157–8. Reported in *The Times*, 6 July, p. 10, from which variants and responses are taken. P.A. Taylor (1819–91), M.P. for Leicester, moved an address for a copy of the deposition that had led in the preceding March to the conviction by the Salisbury Bench of County Magistrates of Henry Fulford and Mark Wellstead for poaching. (See No. 66, n4, for details.) Taylor implied that their conviction, based on the evidence of a gamekeeper that was controverted by relatives and other witnesses, was unjust. Mill spoke immediately after Gathorne-Hardy (cols. 1153–7) had attacked Taylor's views.

MR. J. STUART MILL SAID, THAT since he had the honour of being a Member of that House he had never heard so unjustifiable an attack made upon any Member of it (*loud cries of Oh!*), as that which had been made on his honourable Friend by so high a functionary as the right honourable Gentleman. That right honourable Gentleman had not shaken a single word of the statement which had been made. The right honourable Gentleman had only misstated what his honourable Friend had said, being too angry to attend to him. (*Oh, oh.*) The right honourable Gentleman said the magistrates believed the evidence given before them to be true;[1] but the whole strength of the case was that the tendency of magistrates was always to believe the evidence of gamekeepers. (*Oh, oh.*) Whether that was so or not, it was the general opinion, and this was an extraordinary and emphatic corroboration of that opinion. It was not denied that Pilgrim had made an unfortunate mistake as to identity before, and that on his evidence this person was found guilty, notwithstanding the other evidence and that the error was not corrected until evidence had been produced in addition—namely, the self-crimination of other persons. One would think it was the imperative duty of the magistrates to sift the matter to the very bottom, and to take care that the whole should be perfectly understood, so that they might be sure that they were not continuing to perpetrate a great injustice. As to appealing to Quarter Sessions, [a]our unfortunate labouring classes[a] in the rural districts were not likely to appeal from magistrates to magistrates; they were [b]infinitely[b] too much afraid, and too much cowed to do that (*Oh, oh!*); and, besides, they had not the pecuniary means. The only other thing they had heard, was that one of these magistrates was likely to be appointed chairman of Quarter Sessions, in which office he would have to perform some of the most important judicial functions that could devolve on any person in these dominions, with the least amount of responsibility. They might be

[1]Gathorne-Hardy, col. 1155.

[a–a]TT] PD persons in the labouring class
[b–b]+TT

honourable men; but honourable men were sometimes singularly prejudiced, singularly unjudicial, and singularly disposed to believe [c]on exceedingly insufficient evidence the particular acts charged against persons who had no means of defending themselves[c].

[*Gathorne-Hardy replied that there was no formal deposition, as it had been a summary conviction. Taylor's motion was then defeated (col. 1162).*]

73. The Reform Bill [9]

15 JULY, 1867

PD, 3rd ser., Vol. 188, col. 1579. Not reported in *The Times*. The debate was now on the third reading of the Reform Bill (see No. 50) as amended in Committee, introduced on 9 July (*PP*, 1867, V, 547–80). Mill's interjection was prompted by the attack on John Bright by Francis Wemyss-Charteris-Douglas (1818–1914), Lord Elcho, M.P. for Haddingtonshire, who had just said, "if the honourable Member were present . . . " when Mill intervened.

HE has spoken.[1]

[*The riposte (col. 1579) was that Bright "has rather a habit of speaking and then leaving the House. . . .*"]

74. Commodore Wiseman and the Turkish Navy [1]

16 JULY, 1867

PD, 3rd ser., Vol. 188, cols. 1621, 1622. Reported in *The Times*, 17 July, p. 6.

MR. J. STUART MILL SAID, he would beg to ask the Secretary of State for Foreign Affairs, Whether it is true that Commodore Sir William Wiseman[1] has been appointed head of the Naval Council to the Turkish Government, for the purpose of re-organizing the Turkish navy; if so, whether that Officer has previously retired from Her Majesty's service; and, if not, whether the lending of British Officers to

[1]For Bright's speech, see cols. 1550–4.

---

[1]William Saltonstall Wiseman (1814–74), K.C.B., had spent his full career in the Royal Navy.

[c–c]TT] PD in the sufficiency of evidence in a particular kind of charge

the Porte for such a purpose, in the very crisis of the Cretan insurrection,[2] is, in the opinion of Her Majesty's Government, consistent with their declared principle of non-intervention?[3]

Lord Stanley: In answer to the Question of the honourable Member I beg to state that when the sanction of Her Majesty's Government was given to a British officer being employed to assist in the re-organization of the Turkish navy—following a course for which there are various precedents—it was my belief that long before that appointment could take effect this Cretan business would have been settled one way or the other. As that is not the case, I have since that time agreed with my right honourable Friend at the head of the Admiralty and the Turkish Government that this appointment should not be cancelled, but suspended for a time.

Mr. J. Stuart Mill: Am I to understand from the noble Lord's Answer that Sir William Wiseman will not proceed to Turkey and will not take any charge in this business as long as the hostilities continue?

Lord Stanley: At any rate he will not proceed at present. The appointment has been suspended.

75. Commodore Wiseman and the Turkish Navy [2]

22 JULY, 1867

PD, 3rd ser., Vol. 188, col. 1873. Reported in *The Times*, 23 July, p. 8. Mill had found unsatisfactory Stanley's answer to his previous question (see No. 74, and *CW*, Vol. XVI, p. 1290).

MR. J. STUART MILL SAID, he would beg to ask the Secretary of State for Foreign Affairs, Whether he will undertake that, unless in the event of a complete cessation of hostilities in Crete, Sir William Wiseman will not proceed to Turkey or take up his appointment until the House has had an opportunity of expressing an opinion on the subject?

Lord Stanley said, he had no objection to give the House the intimation to which the Question of the honourable Gentleman pointed. Indeed, he thought he had implied as much in the answer he had given on the same subject a few nights before.

[2]In 1866 an insurrection in Crete against the Turkish rulers had broken out over long-standing issues of equality between Christians and Muslims. The Turks were engaged in a prolonged attempt to put down the rebellion, and the Sultan had arrived in England on 12 July, presumably seeking British support.

[3]See Stanley, Speech on Turkey and Crete (28 Mar., 1867), *PD*, 3rd ser., Vol. 186, col. 724.

76. Meetings in Royal Parks [1]

22 JULY, 1867

PD, 3rd ser., Vol. 188, cols. 1890–3. Reported in *The Times*, 23 July, p. 8, from which the response is taken. In the debate on the second reading of "A Bill for the Better and More Effectually Securing the Use of Certain Royal Parks and Gardens for the Enjoyment and Recreation of Her Majesty's Subjects," 30 Victoria (3 May, 1867), *PP*, 1867, IV, 63–6, Mill had seconded (col. 1888) P.A. Taylor's amendment that would have had the effect of aborting the Bill.

MR. J. STUART MILL SAID, among the many, to me, regrettable things which were said by my honourable and learned Friend the Member for Oxford (*Mr. Neate*),[1] there was one with which I entirely agree: that this question is entirely a political question. It is only as a political question that I care about it. I see no reason why we should at present discuss all the purposes for which the Parks should or should not be allowed to be used. All I am anxious about is that political meetings should be allowed to be held there. And why do I desire this? Because it has been for centuries the pride of this country, and one of its most valued distinctions from the despotically-governed countries of the Continent, that a man has a right to speak his mind, on politics or on any other subject, to those who would listen to him, when and where he will. (*Cries of No.*) He has not a right to force himself upon anyone; he has not a right to intrude upon private property; but wheresoever he has a right to be, there, according to the Constitution of this country, he has a right to talk politics, to one, to fifty, or to 50,000 persons. I stand up for the right of doing this in the Parks. I am not going to discuss this matter as an affair of technical law. We are not here as lawyers, but as legislators. We are not now considering what is the interpretation of the existing law; we are considering what the law ought to be. We are told that the Parks belong to the Crown, but the Crown means Her Majesty's Government. Her Majesty's Government of course have power over the Parks; they have power over all thoroughfares, all public places, but they have it for purposes strictly defined. It is not, I believe, even pretended that the Parks are the property of the Sovereign in the same manner as Balmoral and Osborne are her property. They are part of the hereditary property of the Crown, which the Sovereign at her accession gave up to the nation in exchange for the Civil List;[2] and the right honourable Gentleman would find some difficulty in showing that the surrender was accompanied with any condition as to the particular uses to which the Parks should be applied—any stipulation confining their use to walking and riding, or, as it is called, recreation. As long as the compact with Her Majesty exists, so long, I contend, the Parks are public property, to be managed for public

[1]Charles Neate, cols. 1882–4.
[2]By 1 Victoria, c. 2 (1837).

uses at the public expense, and to be applied to all uses conducive to the public interest. If a technical right of exclusion has been allowed to be kept up, it is for police purposes—for the safety of the public property and the maintenance of the public peace—and not for the restriction of the freedom of public speaking. On what principle is the House asked to curtail this inherited freedom of speech, and make it penal for the people to use that freedom in large numbers, in the only places now left in the metropolis where large numbers can conveniently be assembled? On no principle can this be done, except that of the most repressive acts of the Governments most jealous of public freedom. The French Emperor says that twenty-one people shall not meet and talk politics in a drawing-room without his license.[3] Her Majesty's Government only says that 100,000 people shall not meet for a similar purpose in the Parks without theirs. This is a wide difference in degree. It is much better to have our lips sealed in the Parks than in our own houses—better that free speech should be limited to a few thousands or hundreds than to tens; but the principle is the same, and if once it is admitted, a violation has commenced of the traditional liberties of the country, and the extent to which such violation may afterwards be carried becomes a mere question of detail. But what is the justification alleged for introducing arbitrary restrictions by which the holding of a great open-air meeting in London without the previous consent of the Government will be made impossible? The excuses which profess to be founded on public convenience do not deserve an answer, even if they had not been already answered a hundred times; the fact is, no one believes them to be serious. There is no decent argument for the interdiction of political meetings in the Park, which does not proceed on the assumption that political meetings are not a legitimate purpose to apply a public place to, and that it is, on the whole, a desirable thing to discourage them. I wish honourable Gentlemen to be aware what it is they are asked to vote for; what doctrine respecting the constitutional liberties of this country they will give their adhesion to if they support the Bill. The opinion they will pledge themselves to is something like this—unfortunately the people of this country are so foolish that they *will* have the right of holding large political meetings, and it is impossible to take it from them by law; but that right, though necessary, is a necessary evil, and it is a point gained to render its exercise more rare by throwing impediments in its way. If honourable Gentlemen opposite would be candid, I am persuaded they would confess that this is a fair statement of what is really in their minds. It is proved by the arguments they use. They say that these multitudinous meetings are not held for the purpose of discussion, but for intimidation. Sir, I believe public meetings, multitudinous or not, seldom are intended for discussion. That is not their function. They are a public manifestation of the strength of those who are of a certain opinion. It is easy to give this a bad

[3]By the Code pénal, Bull. 277 *bis*, Nos. 1–7 (1810), *Bulletin des lois de l'empire français*, 4th ser., numéros *bis*, Art. 291.

name; but it is one of the recognized springs of our Constitution. Let us not be intimidated by the word "intimidation." Will any one say that the numbers and enthusiasm of those who join in asking anything from Parliament, are not one of the elements which a Statesman ought to have before him, and which a wise Statesman will take into consideration in deciding whether to grant or to refuse the request? We are told that threatening language is used at these meetings. In a time of excitement there are always persons who use threatening language. But we can bear a great deal of that sort of thing, without being the worse for it, in a country which has inherited from its ancestors the right of political demonstration. It cannot be borne quite so well by countries which do not possess this right. Then, the discontent, which cannot exhale itself in public meetings, bursts forth in insurrections, which, whether successful or repressed, always leave behind them a long train of calamitous consequences. But it is said that it is not meant to put down these public meetings, or to prevent them from being held. No; but you mean to render them more difficult; you mean to impose conditions on them, other than that of keeping the public peace. Now, any condition whatever imposed on political meetings, over and above those by which every transaction of any of Her Majesty's subjects is necessarily bound—and any restriction of place or time imposed on political speech, which is not imposed on other speech—involves the same vicious and unconstitutional principle. Sir, I contend that all open spaces belonging to the public, in which large numbers can congregate without doing mischief, should be freely open for the purpose of public meetings, subject to the precautions necessary for the preservation of the peace. A great meeting cannot possibly be called together in London without the Government knowing of it beforehand, and having ample warning to have a sufficient force of police at hand to meet any exigency, however improbable. I must therefore oppose this Bill to the utmost.

[*The amendment was lost, but the Bill was not enacted.*]

77. Public Education

29 JULY, 1867

PD, 3rd ser., Vol. 189, cols. 373–4. Reported in *The Times*, 30 July, p. 6. The variant is taken from the report in the *St. Stephen's Chronicle*, Vol. IV, p. 749. Robert Montagu, in Committee of Supply, when moving the Education Vote, had surveyed the measures achieved and contemplated, including those for technical education (cols. 353–61).

MR. J. STUART MILL SAID, he wished to express a hope that the noble Lord (*Lord Robert Montagu*) might be able soon to lay before them the Minute of the Council of Education,[1] laying down some definite rule for carrying into effect the very great—that inestimable improvement which he had announced in the educational arrangements. He meant not merely the introduction of technical education, which was in itself an important addition to our present arrangements, but above all the adoption of the plan which had been found so useful in many foreign countries—that of making the advantages of technical education a reward for the good use of the advantages of elementary education—holding out an inducement to the pupils of elementary education to distinguish themselves so as to obtain the benefits of technical education. He could not conceive anything more calculated to alleviate a great deficiency in our present system—namely, the strong inducement to take children away from the schools before there had been imparted to the pupils all that those schools were intended to teach. It was true that it was not only the clever and apt pupils who had to be thought of; but that it ought also to be a great object to retain those who did not attain such proficiency as would entitle them to the reward he had referred to. Consequently, the proposal could not be regarded as one that would remove the whole difficulty. But it was judicious and well judged, and, he believed, was likely to be an effectual measure for removing the difficulty in part. He congratulated the noble Lord [a]and his department[a] on what would be so important an improvement.

78. The Courts-Martial in Jamaica

1 AUGUST, 1867

PD, 3rd ser., Vol. 189, cols. 598–9. Reported in *The Times*, 2 August, p. 7.

MR. J. STUART MILL SAID, he wished to ask Mr. Attorney General,[1] Whether he has taken into consideration the evidence produced at the trials by Court-Martial lately held in Jamaica on Ensign Cullen and Staff Assistant-Surgeon Morris;[2] and whether it is his intention to institute proceedings against those Officers in the ordinary tribunals of this country? He understood Mr. Morris was now in this country.

[1]See "Copy of the Minutes of the Lords of the Committee of Council on Education Relating to Scientific Instruction," *PP*, 1867–68, LIV, 17–22.

---

[1]John Burgess Karslake.

[2]See "Copy of the Proceedings of the Courts Martial Recently Held in Jamaica upon Ensign Cullen and Assistant-Surgeon Morris of Her Majesty's Service" (29 Mar., 1867), *PP*, 1867, XLII, 31–342.

[a–a]+SSC

The Attorney General: In answer, Sir, to the Question of the honourable Member, I may say, that since this Question was put on the Paper, I have, as far as possible, mastered the details of the evidence and the proceedings of those courts-martial held in Jamaica, and it is not my intention to advise Her Majesty's Government to take any proceedings against those officers before the ordinary tribunals of this country.

79. Meeting in the Tea-Room of the House of Commons

2 AUGUST, 1867

PD, 3rd ser., Vol. 189, cols. 768–9, 769. Reported in *The Times*, 3 August, p. 7, from which the variant and responses are taken. A series of questions had been put in the House concerning a meeting in the Tea-room on 29 July, attended by members of the public. It was reported that when the Deputy Sergeant-at-Arms had been informed of this irregularity, he had proceeded to the room, and the meeting terminated.

AS ONE OF THE MEMBERS who was present in the Tea-room on the occasion in question, I desire to express my regret for having unwittingly been guilty of an irregularity against the forms of this House, an irregularity of which I was not aware at the time. (*Hear, hear.*) In order to set one point right, I desire to say that the conference in question was not in the nature of a public meeting. It was really a deputation to consult with certain Members of Parliament, [a]most of us were seated,[a] and nothing in the way of speech-making was done which is not usually done at deputations. (*Cries of Oh!*)

Colonel Stuart Knox: I would ask the honourable Member whether it is not a fact that members of the Reform League at that meeting in the Tea-room held out a threat that unless honourable Members voted in support of their views those Members need not put themselves forward again as candidates for metropolitan constituencies?

Mr. J. Stuart Mill: I heard no such statement from any person present, whether a member of the Reform League or not.

[a-a]+TT

80. England's Danger through the Suppression of Her Maritime Power

5 AUGUST, 1867

Views of Mr. John Stuart Mill on England's Danger through the Suppression of Her Maritime Power. Speech Delivered at the House of Commons, August 5, 1867 (London: *Diplomatic Review* Office, 1874). This version is identified as "From the revised copy communicated by Mr. John Stuart Mill to the *Diplomatic Review* of February 5, 1868" (p. 2). In *PD*, 3rd ser., Vol. 189, cols. 876–84. Reported in *The Times*, 6 August, p. 7, from which some variants and responses are taken. The report in the *St. Stephen's Chronicle*, Vol. IV, pp. 796–800, has been used as a check. For other comments by him on the issues, see *CW*, Vol. XVI, pp. 1199, and 1315. Mill was speaking on the motion to go into Committee of Supply.

I RISE, SIR, to ask the attention of the House to a subject more germane to the business of a Committee of Supply, than most of those which the Motion to go into committee gives occasion for bringing before the House. The immense burthen of our naval and military expenditure would of itself give ample reason for reconsidering the position in which this country has been placed by the abandonment of its maritime rights eleven years ago.[1] Of these eleven nearly ten have been years of profound peace, in which international commerce, which we had always believed to be our truest guarantee against war, has increased to an extent previously unexampled; while the doctrines and practice of free trade have been spreading through the different countries of Europe, and those protectionist theories which have so often made commerce a provocative to war instead of a deterrent from it, have lost their hold on all the leading minds of the Continent. Yet, during this period, we have been engaged, not as might have been expected, in diminishing, but in enormously increasing our naval and military establishments, until our total expenses exceed by about twenty millions a year, not what economists like Mr. Hume used to maintain that they ought to be,[2] but what they actually have been in the life of the present generation. Why has this happened? What has been our inducement for maintaining those "bloated armaments"?[3] To protect ourselves against the bloated armaments of our European neighbours. Other Powers, as much perhaps for internal as for external purposes, are keeping

[1]See the "Declaration of Paris," an agreement amongst Great Britain, Austria, France, Prussia, Russia, Sardinia, and Turkey, printed as "Declaration Respecting Maritime Law" (16 Apr., 1856), *PP*, 1856, LXI, 153–8.

[2]Joseph Hume (1777–1855), radical politician and advocate of financial retrenchment; see, e.g., his Speech on Spain—Report on the Address (5 Feb., 1836), *PD*, 3rd ser., Vol. 31, col. 127.

[3]Disraeli, Speech on the Customs and Inland Revenue Bill (8 May, 1862), *PD*, 3rd ser., Vol. 166, col. 1426.

up gigantic and ruinous military establishments, the existence of which we justly feel to be a danger to us. But why is it a danger? What obliges us, an insular people, to measure our necessities by the wild extravagances of the military rulers of the Continent?—extravagances which, let us do as we will, we cannot compete with; for if our wealth is equal to the effort, the numbers of our population are not. Why, then, do we find ourselves engaging deeper [a] in this [b]mean[b] rivalry? Because we have put away the natural weapon of a maritime nation, because we have abandoned the right recognised by international law, and legitimated, as much as the consent of nations can legitimate anything, of warring against the commerce of our enemies. We have made this sacrifice, receiving a merely nominal equivalent. We have given up our main defence; but the other Powers who are parties to the transaction have not given up theirs; they have divested themselves not of their special means of warfare, but of ours; they have with a good grace, consented not to use the weapons in which they are inferior, but to confine themselves to those in which the advantage is on their side. The greatest naval Power after ourselves[4] has been far too wise to join in so unequal a compact. Unless by resuming our natural and indispensable weapon we place ourselves again on an equality with our possible enemies, we shall be burthened with these enormous establishments and these onerous budgets for a permanency; and, in spite of it all, we shall be for ever in danger, for ever in alarm, cowed before any Power, or combination of Powers, capable of invading any part of our widely-spread possessions. We shall be condemned to see, what we have seen, and worse than we have yet seen, great international iniquities perpetrated before our eyes, and our expressions of deprecation, even of reprobation, passed over with civil, or scarcely civil contempt—(*hear, hear*)—until our most patriotic advisers feel obliged to recommend to us, as the only rule for our conduct, that which despots prescribe to their subjects, "Hold your peace. Keep your moral disapprobation within your own breasts: for as you cannot back it by the only argument which the wicked and the oppressor can [c]put[c], you only bring yourselves and your just indignation into contempt." Thus it will be while we abstain from that which once made a war with England a formidable thing, even to the united strength of all Europe. Sir, I venture to call the renunciation of the right of seizing enemy's property at sea a national blunder. Happily it is not an irretrievable one. The Declaration of 1856 is not a Treaty, [d]it has never been ratified[d]. The authority on which it was entered into was but the private letter of a Minister.[5] It is not a permanent engagement between

[4]The United States of America.

[5]Lord Clarendon drafted the principles in a letter to Lord Palmerston of 6 April, 1856; the letter was circulated to Cabinet, but was not published, and there was no official approval.

[a]PD,SSC and deeper

[b–b]PD mad] SSC man [*printer's error for either* mean *or* mad]

[c–c]PD feel] SSC *as* P

[d–d]TT which we had no power to revoke] SSC *as* P

nations, it is but a joint declaration of present intention; binding us, I admit, until we finally withdraw from it; for a nation is bound by all things done in its name, unless by a national act it disowns them. Why did not the Parliament and people of the country protest at the time? Some of them did; among the rest several of the most important members of the present Government.[6] [e]*The bulk of the Liberal party acquiesced silently or approvingly; and therein, I confess, we showed less knowledge of the subject, less understanding of the situation, than the Conservative Leaders.*[e] (*Hear, hear.*) There is much to be said in excuse for us. Nearly the whole world shared [f]in our[f] error. The world was fresh from the recent triumph of free trade, fresh from the great Exhibition of 1851, which was to unite all nations, and inaugurate the universal [g]substitution[g] of commerce for war. The first enthusiastic days of peace congresses had scarcely passed; the short episode of the Crimean war had not shaken the belief that great European wars were drawing to a close. We were mistaken; but the light which led us astray was light from heaven.[7] (*Cheers.*) We have since had opportunities of learning a sadder wisdom. We had not then seen wars of conquest and annexation renewed on a great scale, and fresh wars of the kind continually impending over Europe; we had not seen the Continental Powers outvying one another in converting all the flower of their youth into standing armies, ready at any moment to draw the sword, not only in defence, but in aggression. We had not seen what is to my mind a still more warning sight. Some twenty years ago a great French thinker, by way of showing how alien a thing war is to the modern spirit, remarked that though destruction is incomparably the easiest of the works to which human ingenuity applies itself, the science and art of destruction had remained greatly in arrear of the arts of production, and might almost be said to have been passed over by the inventive genius of later generations.[8] What would this philosopher see now? He would see inventive genius, with all the lights of modern science, and all the resources of modern [h]industry[h], girding itself to the work of destruction as its principal task, and bringing forth every year more and more terrific engines for blasting hosts of human beings into atoms, together with the defences by which they vainly seek to shelter themselves. While this work is going on all around us, is there nothing for us to do but to exhaust our invention and our finances in striving to provide ourselves with engines still more destructive—engines which other nations will

[6]Most notably the Prime Minister, Lord Derby, Speech on the Treaty of Paris (22 May, 1856), *PD*, 3rd ser., Vol. 142, cols. 521–39.

[7]Robert Burns (1759–96), *The Vision* (1786), Duan Second, xviii, in *Works*, new ed., 2 pts. (London: Tegg, *et al.*, 1824), Vol. II, p. 56.

[8]Mill probably has in mind Auguste Comte (1798–1857): cf. *Cours de philosophie positive*, 6 vols. (Paris: Bachelier, 1830–42), Vol. IV (1839), pp. 569–70 (Leçon 51).

[e-e]PD,SSC [*not in italics*]
[f-f]SSC] P in an] PD our
[g-g]PD] P,SSC institution
[h-h]PD] P,SSC history

instantly adopt, when their superiority has been proved, unless they in the meanwhile contrive for themselves others yet more murderous? Sir, we have a better resource; to shake off the chains which we have forged for ourselves, and resume that natural weapon which has been the main bulwark of our power and safety in past national emergencies, and without which neither ironclads nor fortified harbours will suffice for our security in those which may be yet to come. Sir, great almost beyond calculation as are the British interests depending on this issue, it is on no narrow grounds of [i]purely[i] British patriotism that I now raise it. I should be ashamed to claim anything for my country which I believed to be a damage and an injury to the common interests of civilisation and of mankind. I will not even urge, though the feelings of the *élite* of Europe would bear me out if I did, that the safety, and even the power of England, are valuable to the freedom of the world, and therefore to the greatest and most permanent interests of every civilised people. No, Sir; my argument shall not have even a tinge of nationality about it. It is on the broadest cosmopolitan and humanitarian principles that I rest the case. I maintain it to be for the general interest of the world, if there is to be fighting, that every Power should fight with its natural weapons, and with its best strength, that so there may be the greatest possible division of force, and no one Power may be able to [j]disturb[j] the world, nor any two or three Powers to divide it among them. Above all it is for the interests of the world that the naval Powers should not be weakened, for whatever is taken from them is given to the great military Powers, and it is from these alone that the freedom and independence of nations has anything to fear. Naval power is as essentially defensive as military is aggressive. It is by armies, not by fleets, that wars of conquest can be carried on; and naval Powers, both in ancient and in modern times, have ever been the cradle and the home of liberty. Take away the naval Powers of the world at this moment, and where would be the main defence of the minor European States? Two or three military monarchies could, in a few years, parcel out all Europe, and everything else on this side of the Atlantic, among them; and after they had done so, would probably desolate the earth by fighting for a re-division. Happily, the naval Powers exist, and long may they exist; but short will be the duration of their existence if they disarm themselves of their most powerful weapon; if they leave the entire navies of their enemies free to convey troops to their shores, being no longer required to protect the enemy's commerce; if they, who can be invaded, but who cannot successfully invade, abandon the chief means they possess of doing their enemies substantial damage, and wearying them of the war. There is another consideration of vital importance to the subject. Those who approve of the Declaration of Paris mostly think that we ought to go still further; that private property at sea (except contraband of war) should be exempt from seizure in all

[i-i]PD,SSC merely
[j-j]PD bestride] SSC *as* P

cases, not only in the ships of neutral but in those of the belligerent nations. This doctrine was maintained with ability and earnestness in this House during the last session of Parliament,[9] and it will probably be brought forward again, for there is great force in the arguments on which it rests. Suppose that we were at war with any Power which is a party to the Declaration of Paris: if our cargoes would be safe in neutral bottoms, [k]but unsafe in our own,[k] then, if the war was of any duration, our whole import and export trade would pass to the neutral flags—(*hear, hear*)—most of our merchant shipping would be thrown out of employment, and would be sold to neutral countries, as happened to so much of the shipping of the United States from the pressure of two or three—it might almost be said of a single cruiser. Our sailors would naturally follow our ships, and it is by no means certain we should regain them even after the war was over. Where would then be your naval reserve? Where your means of recruiting the royal navy? A protracted war on such terms must end in national disaster. It will thus become an actual necessity for us to take the second step, and obtain the exemption of all private property at sea from the contingencies of war. But are we sure that we shall be able to do so? Our own consent is not all that is required. Will other Powers, having got us at this disadvantage, consent to relieve us from it? And if they would, what a spectacle should we then behold? Nations at war with nations, but their merchants and shipowners at peace; our own merchants driving a roaring trade with the enemies whose resources we were endeavouring to cripple, and contributing, perhaps, a great part of their revenue. Some persons think that this would be a great improvement, that it would be a gain to humanity if war were confined to what they call a duel between Governments—(*hear, hear*)—a strange gain to humanity if the merchants, manufacturers, and agriculturists of the world lost nothing by a state of war, and had no pecuniary interest in preventing it except the increase of their taxes—a motive which never yet kept a prosperous people out of war—a burthen which such a people is often but too ready to take upon itself for mere excitement, much more from the smallest motive of national self-assertion or desire of aggrandisement. How war is to be humanised by shooting at men's bodies instead of taking their property, I confess surprises me. (*Hear, hear, and a laugh.*) [l]The result of such a system would be that the merchants, the manufacturers, and even agriculturists would have nothing to lose by a state of war, and therefore would have no motive to abstain from it except an increase of taxation, a burden which people were often only too ready to inflict upon themselves from the smallest motive of national self-assertion.[l] The result would

[9]E.g., by William Henry Gregory (1817–92), M.P. for Galway County, Speech on International Maritime Law (2 Mar., 1866), *PD*, 3rd ser., Vol. 181, cols. 1407–20, and in the same debate by McCullagh Torrens, cols. 1433–7, Charles Buxton, cols. 1437–43, and Samuel Laing, cols. 1448–55.

[k-k]+PD] TT and not in our own] SSC *as* P
[l-l]+TT

be, that as long as the taxpayers were willing, or could be compelled by their Governments to pay the cost of the game, nations would go on massacring one another until the carnage was stopped by sheer impossibility of getting any more soldiers to enlist, or of enforcing a conscription. That would be the amount of gain to humanity. Those fine notions of making war by deputy may go down for a while, so long as a nation fancies itself safe from invasion; but let an enemy ever touch our shores, and I think we should regret that we had not, by making war on his imports and exports, kept him at a distance from our hearths—that we had not [m]prepared[m] to defend ourselves by our cruisers rather than by our rifle volunteers. Many who do not like to secede from the Declaration of Paris are quite aware of its dangers [n]; but they think that the evil is irreparably done, and that we cannot withdraw from it, for fear of embroiling ourselves[n] with France and America. Sir, if the Declaration of Paris has brought us to such a pass that we can neither stand still nor move, our national independence is as good as gone; our being yoked to the car of some great military potentate is a mere question of time. But this [o]apprehended[o] danger from France and America seems to me to have little reality in it. France, though a great military, is also a naval Power, and is historically identified almost as much as ourselves with what is called the Right of Search.[10] She has always asserted it for herself, except when she has waived it during a particular war by express engagement with some particular country. The first Napoleon, it is true, while carrying on the war against British commerce to extremities never before practised or justified, thought it suited his purpose of the moment to declaim pompously against what he called our tyranny of the seas.[11] [p]*But the interests of France in this matter are greatly changed. The immunity of neutral bottoms could be of service to her, if at all, only if her enemy were England or the United States, and even then the benefit would not be without alloy; but if the calamity should occur, of a war between France and any other great Power, it is more likely that her antagonist* [q]*will*[q] *be either Germany or Russia, and against either of these the right of seizure would be so important to France, would be so powerful a weapon in her hands, that she could not dispense with it for herself.*[p] The noble Lord the Foreign Secretary must think so; for, in the important correspondence which has gained for him the distinguished honour of averting a European war (*hear, hear*), the noble Lord urged upon the Prussian Government the certain extinction of the maritime commerce of Germany in case of a war with

[10]The much disputed view that a belligerent had the right to stop all vessels in international waters to search for enemy goods or contraband.

[11]Décret impérial (17 Dec., 1807), *Gazette Nationale, ou Le Moniteur Universel*, 25 Dec., 1807, p. 1387.

[m-m]PD preferred] SSC *as* P
[n-n]+PD
[o-o]PD,TT] P,SSC approaching
[p-p]PD,SSC [*not in italics*]
[q-q]SSC [*not in italics*]] PD,TT,P would

France, exactly as if the Declaration of Paris had never existed.[12] (*Hear.*) As for America, she is not even a party to the Declaration of Paris; and I greatly doubt if she ever will be. She is herself one of the great Powers of the sea, and in case of war the destruction of her enemy's commerce will be her most potent weapon. Many are misled by vague and inaccurate notions of the American war of 1812. It is asserted far too positively that the war was provoked by our stoppage of the neutral navigation. People forget that the United States had a far more serious quarrel with us through our unjustifiable pretension to impress American citizens on board American ships, when they were, or even were falsely said to be, natives of any British possession—(*hear, hear*)—a pretension which we did not even renounce at the peace, but which it is earnestly to be hoped we shall never revive; if we were wise, we should even come forward unasked and surrender it. Such a grievance is quite sufficient to account for the war, even had there been no other subject of quarrel. But there was another equally independent of the right now under consideration—our paper blockades, which were a new practice, not authorised, as the Right of Search was so fully authorised, by the law and practice of nations. I believe it will be found, by examining the diplomatic correspondence of the time,[13] that our differences with America about the Right of Search were capable of being made up, and would almost [r]certainly[r] have been made up, but for those additional grievances. Before I conclude I am obliged to speak of a notion which I am afraid is rather common among us, but which I am almost ashamed to mention—that, dangerous as is the position we should be placed in by adhering to the Declaration of Paris, it is of no practical consequence, because if war comes the Declaration is sure to be treated as waste paper. Sir, I should indeed be humiliated in my feelings as an Englishman if I thought that these were the maxims by which my countrymen were content to guide themselves, or on which they would allow their rulers to act. (*Hear, hear.*) No, Sir; let us either disown this obligation or fulfil it. (*Cheers.*) Let us disclaim it like honest men in the face of the world, openly and on principle, and not hypocritically profess one doctrine up to the very moment when an immediate interest would be promoted by exchanging it for another. If England should choose that moment for announcing a change of opinion, she would justify the most prejudiced of her foreign revilers in the accusation which they are [s]in the habit[s] of bringing against her of national selfishness and perfidy. It is not when the emergency has come, but before it comes, that we have to form our resolution on this most momentous subject, and not only to form our resolution but to declare it. And I implore every honourable

[12]See especially Stanley's letter to Lord Loftus (17 Apr., 1867), in "Correspondence Respecting the Grand Duchy of Luxemburg," *PP*, 1867, LXXIV, 457.

[13]See "Papers, Presented to the House of Commons, Relating to the Correspondence with America, on Certain Orders in Council" (1 Feb., 1809), *PP*, 1809, IX, 375–430.

[r-r]PD] P,SSC entirely
[s-s]PD never tired] SSC *as* P

member, and especially those who have now or may have hereafter a share in the direction of public affairs, to consider these things well before they commit themselves any deeper than they may be already committed, to persistence in a course to which they are so likely to repent that they ever, even by their silence, allowed themselves to be committed at all. (*Cheers.*)

81. The Extradition Treaties Act [4]

6 AUGUST, 1867

PD, 3rd ser., Vol. 189, cols. 983–6, 991. Reported in *The Times*, 7 August, p. 3, from which the variant and response are taken. During the debate on going into Committee on "A Bill to Continue Various Expiring Laws," 30 & 31 Victoria (26 July, 1867), *PP*, 1867, II, 733–6, discussion had turned to the Extradition Treaties Act (see No. 36). Mill spoke after Edward William Watkin (1819–1901), M.P. for Stockport, had asserted (cols. 982–3) the importance to society of malefactors receiving their proper punishment, even if a few might be given up under cover of criminal accusations when they really were political dissidents.

MR. J. STUART MILL SAID, THAT the argument of his honourable Friend (*Mr. Watkin*) carried out to its logical conclusion would carry him much farther than to giving up mere criminals; it would induce the House to connive at the most tyrannical exercise of power on the part of a Government. It was very important, no doubt, that malefactors should be given up, and that peaceably disposed persons should be able to walk about in security; but he did not think that anybody in that House would be found to agree in such an argument as that made use of by the honourable Member for Stockport, which was an argument that had always been made use of in defence of tyranny. If they restrained tyranny, if they restricted the abuse of power, if they did anything which had a tendency to weaken the hands of those who conducted the administration of the country, it did not follow that they were disposed to throw aside all the advantages which society derived from the existence of law and government. That argument, therefore, might be put out of the question. No doubt it was very important that malefactors should not be able to fly from one country to another. Other countries as well as this felt the importance of delivering up ordinary malefactors. But every country did not think it right to surrender persons who were only charged as criminals, because they were deemed to be political offenders; and to make such a concession would stamp any free country with disgrace. Was the House prepared to entertain the doctrine that we ought to have such unbounded confidence in every Government with which we had diplomatic relations that we ought to rely upon the honour of that Government that it would not demand the extradition of political offenders, instead of taking proper precautions against the abuse of the treaty by foreign Governments? The honourable Member had referred to the circumstances of the Lamirande case.[1] Everyone was aware that the extradition of that person had been obtained by a fraudulent proceeding, but at the same time everyone was aware that Lamirande was a scoundrel, and probably the consciousness of that fact went far to prevent any prolonged discussion upon the subject of the treaty, such as would have taken place had it been the case of the extradition of a political offender. The honourable Member for Southwark (*Mr. Layard*) had alluded to the difference between the French and English procedure in criminal cases, stating that here we always presumed a man to be innocent till he was proved guilty, whereas in France a man was presumed to be guilty till he had proved himself to be innocent.[2] No doubt this did not necessarily imply a failure of justice in foreign countries; because the tribunals were bound to act precisely on the same abstract principles of truth and justice as were presumed to be acted upon by our Courts of Justice. It was true, however, that in this country the tribunals considered themselves simply bound to hear the case, and if justice was defeated the fault was with the parties, the Judge being impartial; while abroad—in France for instance—the Judge acted to a certain extent as an officer of police as well as of justice; he thought it his business to hold an inquisition—not, of course, of the nature of the Spanish Inquisition—into the case, and felt bound to discover by whom the offence had been committed. He was as little disposed as any Member of the House to flatter his countrymen at the expense of other nations; but in this respect the feelings and opinions of our Courts were much better than those of most foreign countries, and in his opinion we ought not to give up any portion of the advantage which we derived from that difference. With their feelings in this respect, it was exceedingly natural that the French tribunals, and still more the subordinates of the French tribunals, should take very much the same view as the honourable Member for Stockport, and should think that everything was fair by means of which a person accused of a crime could be brought before a tribunal. This it was that was so strikingly illustrated by the case of Lamirande, which placed in a very strong light indeed the impolicy and injustice of that confidence which his honourable and learned Friend the Member for Oxford was willing to place in the Governments and officers of foreign countries.[3] It showed that it would not do for us to abandon the right that we had always exercised, of examining, before we delivered up an alleged criminal, whether there was such

[1]Sureau Lamirande, a cashier of the Bank of France, accused of forgery, had been committed to jail in Montreal in August 1866, and then handed over to a French inspector of police, and taken back to France. In fact a judge, believing the transaction was contrary to law, issued a writ of *habeas corpus* on 25 August, but the prisoner had already sailed. (See "Extraordinary Case of Extradition," *The Times*, 17 Sept., 1866, p. 10.)

[2]Austen Henry Layard (1817–94), col. 978.

[3]Charles Neate, cols. 978–80.

evidence as appeared to our tribunals to be sufficient to justify his being placed upon his trial. When, last year, the noble Lord (*Lord Stanley*), [a]yielding to their arguments and not to their numbers, consented to limit the duration of this measure till[a] the 1st of September,[4] the general expectation was that the interval would be employed in placing the matter upon a more satisfactory footing, either by means of negotiation, or, as he (*Mr. Mill*) should prefer, by laying down some principle which should apply to all extradition treaties. They left the matter willingly in the hands of the noble Lord. He hoped that the noble Lord would be able to say that something of the sort had been done. Unless the noble Lord could make out some very strong case as to the extreme difficulty of dealing with this subject, he did not see how he could ask for a longer prolongation of the statute than that which was granted last year. The demand indeed reminded him of the story of Hiero and Simonides.[5] Hiero asked Simonides to define the Godhead. Simonides asked for a day; at the expiration of that time he asked for two, and at the expiration of the two he asked for four, explaining that the more he considered the subject the more difficult he found it. The Government first asked them for a year and now, having had it, for what amounted to two years. An honourable and learned Friend of his,[6] who was not in his place, contemplated proposing that, instead of prolonging the Act until the end of the Session of 1869, the endurance of the measure should be limited till the 15th July next, in order that the question might be thoroughly discussed in a full House. If the noble Lord was not prepared to assent to that Amendment he hoped that the noble Lord, when he rose to reply, would be able to assure the House that the time that had elapsed had been usefully employed, and that some plan had been drawn up, or that negotiations had been entered into with foreign Governments that would lead to a satisfactory result being arrived at with reference to this important question. (*Hear, hear.*)

[*Following Mill, Stanley said,* inter alia, *that Mill had mistaken him if he thought a specific pledge had been given that a general inquiry should be made following passage of the Extradition Treaties Act; the Government would not object if someone wanted to move a Committee on the matter (cols. 986–9). He then reiterated the latter statement.*]

Mr. J. Stuart Mill said, he had never intended to say that the noble Lord had

[4]Edward Henry Stanley, Speech on the Extradition Treaties Act Amendment Bill (6 Aug., 1866), *PD*, 3rd ser., Vol. 184, col. 2124.

[5]Cicero, *De natura deorum* (I, xxii), in *De natura deorum, Academica* (Latin and English), trans. H. Rackham (London: Heinemann; New York: Putnam's Sons, 1933), p. 58. The story concerns Heiron I, tyrant of Syracuse 478–467/6 B.C., and Simonides of Ceos (ca. 557–468/7 B.C.), poet and man of learning.

[6]Not identified.

[a–a]TT , as he understood, last year to the voice of the majority of the House, had only asked for the extension of the Bill until

broken any pledge. If the noble Lord had given any pledge, doubtless he would have kept it. He had only said that there had been an expectation and a hope in the House that the question would be discussed.

[*Stanley again indicated the Government's willingness to have a Committee (col. 991).*]

82. The Metropolitan Government Bill

7 AUGUST, 1867

PD, 3rd ser., Vol. 189, cols. 1040–1. Not reported in *The Times*. Mill here brings forward "A Bill for the Better Government of the Metropolis," 30 & 31 Victoria (6 Aug., 1867), *PP*, 1867, IV, 215–56.

MR. J. STUART MILL SAID, he moved for leave to introduce a Bill for the better Municipal Government of the Metropolis. The Bill embodied the remainder of the plan, part of which he had introduced in another Bill at an earlier period of the Session.[1] It could not be expected that the Bill could pass into law this Session, and his object was simply to have it printed so that it might be laid before the public with a view to its being considered next Session. It provided for a central municipal government, as the other Bill provided local district municipalities. The Bill borrowed from a variety of sources; from the recommendations of a Royal Commission some years ago;[2] from those of the Committee recently presided over by his honourable and learned Friend the Member for the Tower Hamlets (*Mr. Ayrton*);[3] and from the views which had been brought before the House on various occasions by the honourable and learned Member for Southwark (*Mr. Locke*).[4] The Bill did not make a *tabula rasa*[5] of the old system, but made use of the existing materials. The Bill proposed that the present corporation of the City of London should be enlarged by absorbing the Board of Works. The object of the Bill was to enlarge the corporation into a municipality for the whole of London, leaving behind in the City as much power as was necessary for purely local administration,

[1]"A Bill for the Establishment of Municipal Corporations within the Metropolis" (see No. 56).

[2]"Report of the Commissioners Appointed to Inquire into the Existing State of the Corporation of the City of London," *PP*, 1854, XXVI, 1–1098.

[3]"Reports from the Select Committee on Metropolitan Local Government," *PP*, 1866, XIII, 171–628.

[4]E.g., John Locke, Speech on the Metropolis Local Management Acts Amendment Bill (26 Feb., 1862), *PD*, 3rd ser., Vol. 165, cols. 747–9.

[5]The phrase evidently originated with Robert South (1634–1716), *A Sermon Preached at the Cathedral Church of St. Paul* (Oxford: Robinson, 1663), p. 10.

which under the other Bill all the other districts of the municipality would also have. The Lord Mayor, under this Bill, would grow into a Lord Mayor for all London, and the Common Council would be converted into a Common Council for all London. That Common Council would consist of the Lord Mayor, aldermen, and common councilmen, but the aldermen would not be a separate body, but, with the Common Council, would be elected by the ratepayers. It was proposed by the Bill that the present aldermen of the City should retain their offices for life, but that no vacancy amongst them should be filled up until their number was reduced to six, which would be double the number of aldermen for other districts of the Metropolis. There would be two aldermen in the Common Council for each district, they being those among the successful candidates for the district councillorships who had obtained the greatest number of votes. The corporation property would pass into the possession of this larger municipality. The City, it was right to say, had not given its assent to this transfer, but from what was known of the state of opinion in the City, there was ground to hope that there would be no corporate opposition to it. In consideration of the surrender of the corporation property, it was proposed to make certain concessions to the City in return, which he thought would not be considered more than a fair equivalent. It was proposed that the City should have twice the number of representatives in the Common Council that its population would justify. It was further proposed that the Deputy Mayor, who would represent the Lord Mayor in his absence or fill his place in case of his dying in office, should always be one of the aldermen of the City. There were a few other arrangements which would be sufficiently shown by the Bill itself. The county of the City of London would become the county of all London, and would have one Commission of Peace, of which all the aldermen would be members. As a temporary measure it was proposed that the Board of Works and all the present aldermen should be added to the Council, Sir John Thwaites[6] being appointed Chairman of the standing Committees at his present salary, provided that he was willing to accept the office.

83. The Reform Bill [10]

8 AUGUST, 1867

PD, 3rd ser., Vol. 189, col. 1192. Reported in *The Times*, 9 August, p. 8, from which variants and responses are taken. One variant is taken from the report in the *St. Stephen's Chronicle*, Vol. IV, pp. 843–4. The discussion is on a new Clause C introduced into the Reform Bill (see No. 50) by the Lords: "Any Voter for a County or Borough may, in

[6]John Thwaites (1815–70) was Chairman of the Metropolitan Board of Works from 1855 until his death.

compliance with the Provisions herein-after contained, give his Vote by a Voting Paper instead of personally."

IT [a]IS SCARCELY POSSIBLE that the House will be induced to pass, or that the Government will attempt to force upon the House, this really monstrous proposal[a]. (*Oh! and laughter.*) The vast mass of fraud to which it would give birth has been shown, but it will produce effects worse than even that mass of fraud. If the House have the smallest desire to diminish bribery and intimidation—if they do not wish to increase it to an enormous extent, they will refuse to assent to this Amendment. If it passes, every tenant may be taken to the drawing-room of his landlord and there compelled to sign his voting paper [b]in accordance with the party interest of his landlord[b]. (*Oh! and laughter.*) Do not we know what electioneering agents will do? Will they not take the voter before the magistrate who has the greatest power over him? This will become the general rule of the country. (*Oh! oh!*) I do not say that bribery will be as universal as intimidation. But the voting papers are to be signed before a magistrate, and, recollect, Mr. Churchward is a magistrate.[1] (*Oh! oh! and laughter.*) When I heard that the Upper House had adopted this [c]in principle but not in detail,[c2] I did expect something decent would be done to place checks and restraints on its consequences. I could not have believed that any serious person pretending to the character of a politician would have brought forward such a set of rules, which are apparently constructed to aggravate instead of diminishing the mischievous operation of the system. (*Loud cries of Oh! and Divide.*) I should prefer that no Reform Bill should be passed, rather than that this monstrous scheme should be carried into effect. (*Oh! and laughter.*)

[*The Clause was rejected.*]

[1]Joseph George Churchward, a magistrate for Dover, in 1853 had been convicted of election bribery by a Committee of the House of Commons, and had been scrutinized by another Committee in 1859 for his role in the Dover election. On 19 March, 1867, P.A. Taylor had moved to have Churchward removed from his office.

[2]On 5 August (*PD*, 3rd ser., Vol. 189, cols. 638–42). In the current debate Disraeli had signalled the Government's favourable view of the amendment (cols. 1111–12).

[a–a]TT appeared to him almost incredible that the House of Lords could have adopted this monstrous proposition

[b–b]+TT

[c–c]SSC] PD,TT principle

84. East India Revenue

12 AUGUST, 1867

PD, 3rd ser., Vol. 189, cols. 1382–7. Reported in *The Times*, 13 August, p. 5, from which variants and responses are taken. In the debate on going into Committee, Ayrton moved as an amendment resolutions on conducting business in India (cols. 1340–55).

MR. J. STUART MILL SAID, THAT as the House, notwithstanding the deprecation of the Minister for India,[1] had drifted into a debate on general policy, and as the right honourable Gentleman would be expected next year to bring forward a measure which might effect changes in the machinery of government, he could not help expressing his fear lest some of the changes which had been recommended would make the administration of India worse than it was at present. The use and importance of Councils had, in particular, been undervalued. No doubt it was a most important principle of representation that responsibility should rest as far as possible on one person, and that that person should not be screened by a Board or Council.[2] But he apprehended that this principle applied only to one department of the Government—the Executive. Now, the work of Government was twofold; it was executive and deliberative: and in the Indian Government the deliberative was quite as extensive as the executive work, and even more important. As was stated by the honourable Member for Wick, there was no place in the world where so much depended on the personal qualities of the particular officer who was intrusted with power in all the important appointments.[3] Upon the person who was at the head of the administration in any one district of India the prosperity of that district, to a very large extent, depended. But it did not follow that you had only to choose the best man, and then leave him to do as he liked. You should not rely solely upon the policy of one man, and that a man who filled office only for a brief period. Before any important act was done in India, there should be a full and complete statement, as far as possible, of the different sides of the question; the *pros* and *cons* should be brought forward by different people, and not solely by the particular officer concerned. Especially should this be so in the case of the Governor General. He perfectly agreed in the opinion that those who were entrusted with the chief power in India should not in general be persons who had passed their lives there. India ought to furnish knowledge of detail; but knowledge of principles and general statesmanship should be found more easily and in greater abundance in England, and here it should be sought. But when this officer went out

[1]Stafford Northcote, col. 1358.

[2]For the image, see Jeremy Bentham, *Letters to Lord Grenville* (1807), in *Works*, ed. John Bowring, 11 vols. (Edinburgh: Tait, 1838–43), Vol. V, p. 17.

[3]Samuel Laing, col. 1370.

to India, however able he might be, he rarely knew anything of his business. No doubt an able man would learn his business quicker than another man; but meanwhile he must be more or less dependent on the opinion of other people. That opinion, if he had not a well-chosen and sufficiently numerous Council, must be the opinion of the executive officers under him. Such opinions were often very valuable, but those who gave them were under no responsibility for the advice thus given. Now, if there was one thing more than another to which the great success of our Indian administration was due—for notwithstanding many defects it was on the whole a successful administration—it was to the fact that the Government had, to so large an extent, been carried on in writing; that no important act had been done the reasons for which had not been fully stated on paper, so that those at a distance were able to study them, and to decide upon the validity of the arguments by which the responsible officers justified their acts. It was not enough to trust to one despatch from the one officer who was so responsible; there should be a substantial discussion in the place itself, so that if different opinions were held on the subject, all of them should be placed before the functionary who was to decide in the last resort. It was this necessity which justified not only the existence of Councils, but of numerous Councils. He did not agree with his honourable and learned Friend (*Mr. Ayrton*) that the Government of Bengal had been a Government of inefficient, superannuated people.[4] He did not wish to say anything of Sir Cecil Beadon,[5] whose conduct had been so much canvassed of late, because he did not know much of that gentleman; but those who preceded him were, first, Mr. Halliday, and then Sir J.P. Grant,[6] and two more efficient, enlightened administrators than those gentlemen were, it would be difficult to find in any service. Like all the great officers in India, these men were over-worked; and this was the great excuse for their shortcomings. The Governor of Bengal had never had the benefit of a Council. He (*Mr. Stuart Mill*) thought it was desirable that he should have one. If that Governor had had the benefit of an efficient Council, perhaps that great calamity which had lately occurred in a particular district of India would have been averted.[7] One reason the more for a Council in Bengal would be supplied if it were determined that a member of the Civil Service should not be at the head of this Government, and that Bengal should be put on the same footing in this respect as Bombay and Madras. In that case it would be all the more necessary that the Governor should have some members of the Civil Service

[4]Ayrton, cols. 1349–50.

[5]Cecil Beadon (1816–81), Lieutenant-Governor of Bengal 1862–67.

[6]Frederick James Halliday (1806–91), Lieutenant-Governor of Bengal 1854–59, and his successor 1859–62, John Peter Grant (1807–93).

[7]The Orissa famine of 1866, in which one-quarter of the population perished. Beadon's failure to take decisive action led to the questioning of his competence. Writing to John Plummer on 15 August, Mill referred to the present speech, but said he had not taken part in the debate on Orissa (2 August) because he thought it "a good rule not to speak where there are other people capable and desirous of saying what one wishes should be said" (*CW*, Vol. XVI, p. 1307).

to assist him. He believed that such a Council would have been created in Bengal if it had not been for the expense. It was from motives of economy that a Council had not hitherto been appointed. As the Governor General and his Council were nearer to the Lieutenant Governor of Bengal than to the Governments of Bombay and Madras, it was thought that in Bengal a local Council could be dispensed with. But he was afraid that this would be found, and had, indeed, been found, a mistake. In appointing to the great office of Governor General or Viceroy, it might be said with truth that every Government had, as a general rule, chosen one of the best of themselves—a man who might aspire to a high or even to the highest office in this country. In that respect there had been no failure of duty, though mistakes had now and then been made. But his experience did not tell him that the same care and conscientiousness had been shown in England in choosing men to be the Governors of the minor Presidencies.[8] He had known stupid men, careless, frivolous men, idle men, appointed to both the minor Presidencies (*hear*)—men so little fitted for the business of government that if it had not been for their Councils he did not know how the government of those Presidencies would have gone on. (*Hear, hear.*) It seemed to him, therefore, that if instead of a Lieutenant Governor there was to be a Governor of Bengal and a Governor of the North-Western Provinces, it was more important than ever that each of them should have a Council. One word now as to the Council of India in this country. The difficulty raised by the noble Lord opposite was real, and required serious consideration.[9] On the one hand, it was of the highest importance to have a Council which should be a check upon the Secretary of State in matters of expense. On the other hand, it was true, as the noble Lord said, that the Secretary of State was in some degree compelled to bear a responsibility which might not be his own. How this difficulty should be overcome—if it could be overcome—was a matter well deserving the consideration of the House. But with regard to the necessity of a Council, and even of a numerous Council, not only to prevent the waste of the money of India, but also for the purpose of enlightening the Secretary of State on the general affairs of India, it appeared to him (*Mr. Stuart Mill*) to be clearer than many honourable Gentlemen seemed to think. He believed that many persons looked at it as if the question was, whether the Secretary of State should prevail or the Council, overlooking the fact that the Council would most probably not be all of one mind. The great advantage of a Council was that it represented many minds, that it embodied many of the opinions existing among public men. This was the case in the Court of Directors of the East India Company. They comprised permanent settlement men, village settlement men, and Ryotwar men: and again, in judicial matters, men who were for the regulation system, men who were for the non-regulation system, and men who were for the Native system. Indeed, every variety of Indian policy was there represented. There was no leading variety of

[8]I.e., those of Bombay and Madras.
[9]Robert Cecil, Lord Cranborne, cols. 1380–2.

Indian policy, the reasons for and against which were not certain to be stated very strongly by persons who had studied the subject, and were capable of urging the best arguments in favour of the views they advocated. It was surely an advantage to the Secretary of State, who could seldom know much about India when he took office for the first time, to obtain on the best authority that various knowledge which the great diversities of people and civilization rendered necessary. When he (*Mr. Stuart Mill*) was concerned, in a subordinate capacity, in the administration of India, he found that those who were at the centre of government in England really knew India, as a whole, better than those who were in India. Gentlemen knew their own Presidencies, and those who were concerned in the administration of one had more or less of prejudice against the system which prevailed in another. Those who were resident in Bengal knew less of Madras and Bombay, and *vice versâ*, than those who had access to the records of all the Presidencies and were accustomed to deliberate upon and discuss them, and to write about them; and so with regard to each of the Presidencies. He believed that a [a]larger view of Indian affairs, less coloured by imperfect information and prejudice,[a] would be found in a Council than in any one of the local Governments, or even in the Governor General, if he were not acting with a Central Board. He thought that no Secretary of State who was aware of the imperfection of his own knowledge when he entered office, would wish to deprive himself of the advantage which he was likely to derive from an experienced Council. It was, however, another question whether the members of that Council should hold their office for life. It would be better, in his opinion, that they should give up office at intervals; but, nevertheless, he thought that they should be eligible for re-election; [b]not in order that they might habitually be re-elected, but in order that, by the votes of the other members and the Secretary of State, the department might still retain the services of[b] any member who was still in the vigour of his intellect and capable of rendering good service to the country. Those were the observations he was desirous of making.

[*Shortly after Mill's speech, the amendment was withdrawn.*]

85. Meetings in Royal Parks [2]

13 AUGUST, 1867

PD, 3rd ser., Vol. 189, cols. 1482–4. Reported in *The Times*, 14 August, p. 7, from which the variants and the response are taken. The Bill on the use of Royal Parks (see No. 76), now recommitted, was to be considered in Committee. P.A. Taylor moved that the Chairman leave the chair—i.e., that the Committee not sit (col. 1453).

[a-a]TT] PD much more unprejudiced view of Indian affairs

[b-b]TT] PD and therefore power should be given to the Council to re-elect and to the Crown to re-appoint

MR. J. STUART MILL, *who spoke amid much confusion and cries for a division, said,* he was anxious to state to the House what he and those who agreed with him claimed, and what they thought the working classes of London were entitled to, on this subject. They had heard a great deal about the necessity of legislating for the Parks. Well, he had no objection to any legislation which could properly partake of the nature of police. He did not suppose that any of them would have the least objection to the suppression in the Parks of anything, the toleration of which in any public place was a questionable matter, such as the gaming and betting of which they had heard so much. What they stood up for was that there should be some place open for the purpose of holding great public meetings. He had no objection to preventing meetings being held in such of the Parks as were manifestly unfit for that purpose. No one would think of claiming the right of holding a public meeting in St. James' Park, because, in the first place, there was not room for such a meeting, and, in the second place, it could not be attempted without [a]destroying the ornamental character of the place[a]. (*Hear.*) The question at issue concerned none of the parks except Hyde Park, and the reason why it concerned Hyde Park was that it was the only great open space in the neighbourhood of London on which it was possible to hold a multitudinous open-air meeting. He could perfectly understand those Gentlemen who said that there ought to be no public meeting of that character at all; but such was not the opinion of the Chancellor of the Exchequer, and he should be surprised if the right honourable Gentleman continued to give his support to this Bill, because in his speech on the second reading of the Bill—a speech that was most moderate in its tone, although not equally so in substance—he admitted that there were cases in which it might be desirable that a multitudinous meeting, a meeting larger than could be contained in any public building, should be held.[1] But if such a meeting were to be held, he (*Mr. Stuart Mill*) did not know any place except Hyde Park, in which it could be held with so little disturbance to the convenience of any class. It was true that the right honourable Gentleman did tell the working classes of London that they might meet on Primrose Hill or on Hampstead Heath,[2] and he was sure that this advice must have been accompanied with a twinkle of the right honourable Gentleman's eye, which he (*Mr. Stuart Mill*) wished he had been near enough to have seen. He thought that nobody who had ever seen Hampstead Heath or Primrose Hill would say that they were places in any way suitable for the holding of public meetings. There was scarcely a spot of level ground on either of them, and no place could possibly be less convenient. Did anybody who had seen these public meetings in Hyde Park think that they had been accompanied with inconvenience to any class? It might, indeed, be said that inconvenience was caused, not by the meeting itself,

[1]Disraeli, Speech on the Parks Regulation Bill (29 July, 1867), *PD*, 3rd ser., Vol. 189, col. 396.

[2]*Ibid.*, col. 397.

[a-a]TT the destruction of a great deal of public property

but by the processions to and from the meeting. That was an argument for those who thought there ought to be no great public meetings at all; but, unfortunately, it was an argument which, if applicable to Hyde Park, was quite as applicable to a meeting held at any of the places where the Chancellor of the Exchequer had said that they might be held. It seemed to him that no person who admitted, as the Chancellor of the Exchequer had done, that there may be certain cases in which it was desirable and right that great multitudinous meetings should take place, could contend that they ought to be held in a corner or at a great distance. He did not think it was in the interest of either order or liberty to choose this time—at the close of the Session—with only a small number of Members present—for carrying a measure of which no opportunity had been given for discussion at a proper period. (*Cries for a division.*) Assent had been given to a second reading of the Bill, because many honourable Members on that side of the House were not unfavourable to the principle of legislating in some way upon this matter. The Bill had been since much altered, and it appeared to him an unjustifiable exercise of power to proceed at this period of the Session with the Bill, in the absence of so many Members. There were other most important Bills on the Paper, which could not be passed if the Government persisted in going on with this Bill. One of these was the Hours of Labour Regulation Bill,[3] than which there was no measure more creditable to the Government, and it was most important that it should be passed this Session [b], and another was the Artisans' and Labourers' Dwelling Bill[b];[4] but if the Government were determined to press on the Parks Bill,[5] the House would not have made one step nearer to the useful legislation involved in the measure of which he spoke. (*Divide, divide.*) [c]He hoped the Bill would be withdrawn.[c]

[*The honourable Member resumed his seat amid continued interruption and cries for a division. These manifestations of impatience were continued to the end of the debate, which was, consequently, very little heard.*]

[3]"A Bill for Regulating the Hours of Labour for Children, Young Persons, and Women Employed in Workshops," 30 Victoria (1 Mar., 1867), *PP*, 1867, III, 121–32 (enacted as 30 & 31 Victoria, c. 146 [1867]).

[4]"A Bill to Provide Better Dwellings for Artizans and Labourers," 31 Victoria (20 Nov., 1867), *PP*, 1867-68, I, 21-42.

[5]The Bill continued in Committee on 15 August, but, that being the final day of the session, it died on the order paper.

[b-b]+TT
[c-c]+TT

· · · February to November 1868 · · ·

86. Proportional Representation and Redistribution

29 FEBRUARY, 1868

Morning Star, 2 March, 1868, p. 2. Headed: "The Redistribution of Seats. / Conference at the Reform League Rooms." Reported also in the *Daily News* (in the third person); *The Times* and the *Pall Mall Gazette* summarize Mill's remarks in one sentence. The conference, attended by about fifty people, with Beales in the Chair, was held on Saturday afternoon in the League's rooms, Adelphi Terrace. The meeting was occasioned by a suggestion by Hare (in a letter to the *Daily News*) that the League engage in a discussion of his system (see Nos. 4, 60, and 71). Hare opened the discussion, which included several substantial speeches, as well as shorter comments and "conversational" exchanges. Mill was the last to comment.

I ONLY WISH, SIR, that when I may have the good fortune to address another assembly[1] on this subject I may have the further good fortune of hearing as intelligent a discussion on it as it has been my pleasure to listen to this afternoon. Although, judging from the past, I have not any great expectations on the subject, I cannot but think that if the question is discussed in that other assembly on as good grounds, and with as much knowledge of the subject as has been showed to-day, we shall be very near carrying Mr. Hare's plan. (*Cheers.*) I should not have risen probably on this occasion but for the objections which have just been made by my friend Mr. Boyd Kinnear.[2] Those objections are of a quality which render it imperative they should be met. The difficulties which Mr. Kinnear feels are difficulties that require to be faced, and they have been faced by Mr. Hare. With regard to Mr. Kinnear's first objection, there has been much discussion as to the best mode of procedure in rejecting surplus votes given for a popular candidate, and several suggestions have been made with the view of securing fairness, and preventing a possibility of partiality being exercised. If there can be no better plan suggested, why not draw lots? That would secure fairness, and ensure a beneficial working of the plan. [a]Mr. Hare himself has given an extremely long and careful attention to this part of the subject; so have many others who support the plan.

[1]I.e., the House of Commons.

[2]John Boyd Kinnear (1828–1920), a radical barrister and author, had spoken at length earlier in the meeting.

[a–a]DN [*in past tense*]] MS There have, as I said, been many suggestions made, any one of which would probably prevent the difficulty which Mr. Kinnear feels from being fatal to the plan.

Several different modes have been suggested, any one of which will probably suffice to prevent the difficulty being fatal to the plan. However, if nothing better can be found, fairness will at least be attained by a resort to the lot, and perhaps some mode may be invented which will meet the difficulty in a manner that will provide for a better representation of the general sense of the electors.[a] I apprehend that the communication between a member and his constituents, to which Mr. Kinnear attaches some importance, would take place under Mr. Hare's plan in a somewhat different but still as effectual a manner as now. The majority of the members—the celebrities being the exceptions—would be returned from particular localities, and so far as regards them the difficulty would not exist [b], because if a member goes down to a place where he knows he has been voted for by a great number of persons, and holds a public meeting, he has the opportunity of discussion with a large portion of his constituents, can answer questions, and give publicity to his sentiments. But if a great number of persons scattered over the country vote for some candidate, it may be safely concluded that every one of them feels a special interest in that candidate, because they have selected him from the whole country, and not because of his fitness for representing or connexions with any particular neighbourhood. I, however, fear one of the difficulties will be the active correspondence that will go on between the candidate and the electors. (*Laughter.*) Although not, perhaps, in such a public way as we are accustomed to, mutual explanations will yet take place in a very close and perfect manner[b]. Or a voter could write to one of the newspapers and request the member to reply through the same channel, by which means all the new member's voters would be put into possession of his opinions upon particular points. The spirit of modern civilization is substituting more and more communication by writing for that which was the only mode of communication in former days—I mean word of mouth—and by this means a member's responsibility to his constituents will be to the full as great as Mr. Boyd Kinnear so justly considers it desirable it should. (*Hear, hear.*) With regard to what Mr. Kinnear said in reference to Mr. Cobden's plan,[3] I don't think Mr. Hare's scheme requires more intelligence in the voter than we may reasonably presume will be possessed by the large body who are now called to be electors of this country. Nobody of ordinary intelligence would feel any difficulty after the first election or two. All that would have to be explained to him would be that his vote would only be recorded for one person, and that if the first person on his list did not require the vote it would be taken by the second, and so on. [c]It is therefore

[3]Richard Cobden outlined his plan to divide large boroughs into electoral wards, with one member to a ward, so as to represent the different classes more accurately, in a speech at Rochdale on 18 August, 1859 (*The Times*, 19 Aug., p. 7).

[b-b]DN [*in third person, past tense*]] MS ; while with reference to the others the communication could be by epistolarly correspondence

[c-c]+DN [*in past tense*]

desirable the voter should put down a few more names in order that somebody else may have the probability of being elected. When the voter has once seized this idea, which is not at all an obscure one, there will be no difficulty again.[c]

Mr. Kinnear: I did not mean intelligence so far as the mere sending in of the voting paper is concerned, but the intelligence that would be required to enable a man to make out a considerable list of persons.

Mr. Mill: No doubt in this, as in all systems of election now and always, whether the systems work well or ill, there must be some organisation; and wherever there is concert there is a certain amount of power given to wire-pullers, and I don't think the power will be greater under this plan than under any other. There is no doubt that persons agreeing in any common set of opinions would send out lists of candidates holding those opinions; but it does not follow that the voter would blindly and implicitly follow those opinions. He would probably put down first on his list the names of the people he preferred, and follow them with the names selected from the list sent out by those with whom, as a party, he agreed most closely. Inasmuch as everybody agrees with a great many other people in most things, voters would vote for the candidate who in a general sense agrees with them, and by this means I apprehend that the influence of the wire-pullers would be less noxious than it would in any other way. The benefit of having leaders would be that they would try to find out good candidates, and it would be their interest to put on their list not merely the names of men who are the strongest party men, but those of men who would recommend themselves by their general character and knowledge of other things, because by this means they would secure some votes from people not members of their party. I look upon this as one of the ways in which Mr. Hare's system would work most excellently. Some say that by this plan all the "isms," all the crotchets of obstinate people, would be represented; and others say that the electors would implicitly follow the leaders of parties. I think these two objections might well pair off together. The suppositions on which the two rest are entirely opposite; but nevertheless they both deserve consideration, for the reason that, working against each other, they would produce a better House than we should otherwise get. Take, for instance, the teetotallers, who are a type of the sectarian sort of persons—they would be supposed to elect none but teetotallers; but the contrary would be the case, because, so anxious would they be to make their own opinions prevail, and knowing they are not in a majority themselves, they would have the strongest possible interest in putting on their list not only people who are teetotallers, but people who are so distinguished in other respects that they would on these other grounds be voted for by electors who are not teetotallers. Look how this would operate. The two great parties would, because they are in an enormous majority in the country, get—as indeed they would be entitled to—a large proportion of the votes, but they would have, in order to lay themselves out for votes, to put on their lists a number of people who, apart from party, would represent what I may describe as the various "isms." (*Hear, hear.*) [d]Now, we know very well that only three or four candidates put up for the representation. The[d] candidates are frequently such men as no reasonable man would care to vote for, but, being compelled to vote there, or leave it alone, a great number of the electors vote simply for the Liberal or the Conservative, without reference to anything else, the candidates being the greatest noodles, who, having offended nobody, are what is known as respectable men, and, in the majority of cases, possess plenty of money. (*Hear, hear, and laughter.*) [e]Under Mr. Hare's plan things will be different, because people's interests will be different, and their object will be to put upon their lists not only the best party men, but those who best represent ability and virtue all over the country. Liberals and Conservatives will then be represented by their best men, instead of, as frequently now, by their silliest, or by men of mediocre order. (*Cheers.*) The suggestion of Mr. Morrison,[4] to introduce Mr. Hare's plan on a small scale, such as in counties, or in a large district in the metropolis, will very likely be adopted some day, because things are never carried except by successive steps in this country; and a thing so new as this people will naturally wish to see tried on a small scale first. At the same time it is necessary to bear in mind that a trial like that will be by no means a fair trial of the scheme. Even if London were chosen, the whole merits of the plan would not be brought out as it is conceived by Mr. Hare, because the quota of votes of a candidate would be confined to London, instead of being spread all over the country. Nevertheless, it would be a trial to some extent of the practicability of the machinery, and as it will be a difficult thing to beget confidence in it without some such trial, it is very likely some day it will be attempted, and it will be an exceedingly good thing if it is.[e] (*Cheers.*)

[*The conference was then adjourned until the next Saturday at 3 p.m.*]

87. The *Alabama* Claims

6 MARCH, 1868

PD, 3rd ser., Vol. 190, cols. 1190–5. Reported in *The Times*, 7 March, p. 7, from which the variant and responses are taken. In the debate on going into Committee, George John

[4]Walter Morrison (1836–1921), M.P. for Plymouth, had made the suggestion in a speech preceding Mill's.

[d-d]DN [*in past tense*]] MS Under the present system, the

[e-e]DN [*in past tense*]] MS All this would be reversed by Mr. Hare's plan, which would give the elector an opportunity of voting for the best men in the whole of the country. I think Mr. Morrison's suggestion, or something of the kind, will probably be adopted, because things are never carried except by degrees, and with a proposal so novel as this of Mr. Hare, the Government and the people would be naturally desirous to see it tried on a small scale before making it universal.

Shaw-Lefevre (1831–1928), M.P. for Reading, moved for "Papers Relative to the Negotiations with the United States Government for Arbitration of the *Alabama* Claims" (col. 1167).

I THINK, SIR, that no one can have listened to this debate without being ready to admit that it has elicited statements of a singularly gratifying and satisfactory nature, and it might have been hoped that we were approaching to a very great degree of unanimity upon the essentials of the question, had it not been for the two speeches of the honourable Gentlemen who have just preceded me, and who have revived points of International Law in connection with this dispute in a manner that would almost lead one to suppose they had not read very attentively the discussions which have previously taken place on the subject.[1] I say this, with the more regret, because no fault can be found with the tone or feeling of either of those honourable Gentlemen; and in the case of the honourable Gentleman opposite (*Mr. Sandford*) an amount of good feeling towards America has been displayed which may perhaps surprise some who sit on this side of the House, but which does not surprise me. It seems to me that, in reviving these questions, those honourable Gentlemen have ignored the distinction which has been the fundamental and grand point on which the discussion has turned—I allude to the broad distinction which writers on International Law recognize between trade in contraband of war, and the use of a neutral country as a base of military and naval operations. (*Hear, hear.*) It is true, and has not been denied, that a ship-of-war might be exported from England to one of two belligerents with no more objection or violation of International Law than there would be in the case of exporting military stores; but in that case there was this condition—that the ship ought to go direct to the port of the belligerent for whom she is intended, without any intermediate hostile operations, and thence might go forth to carry devastation and destruction among the ships and commerce of the other belligerent. But what has been done in the case of the *Alabama* was very different from this. An emissary was sent by the Confederate States to make arrangements for the fitting out in this country of a naval expedition to levy war against the commerce of the North.[2] The honourable and learned Member for Dundalk (*Sir George Bowyer*) appeared to think that that would be fair if both parties were allowed to be equally benefited;[3] but practically both parties never can be equally benefited, for although the liberty may ostensibly be the same to each, the fact generally is that only one party needs it, and is benefited, while the other is not benefited. Again, if a neutral country allows its territory to be made the basis from which a hostile expedition can be fitted out, it

[1]George Bowyer (1811–83), M.P. for Dundalk, cols. 1183–8, and George Montagu Warren Sandford (1821–79), M.P. for Maldon, cols. 1188–90.

[2]James Dunwoody Bulloch (1823–1901) had the responsibility for equipping and dispatching the Confederate cruising ships from Britain.

[3]Cols. 1184–5.

permits this to be done in a place which the opposite party is not permitted to go to for the purpose of obstructing the operation. Suppose the *Alabama* had been fitted out in a Confederate port, it would have been in the power of the North, on receiving intelligence of this being the case, to have cut the vessel out of the harbour, or intercepted its departure, or to have bombarded and destroyed the dockyard in which it was under construction. But they could not do that in a neutral country, and consequently such a country, in permitting such a proceeding, would voluntarily have committed a breach of neutrality, by giving the benefit of its protection to a portion of the naval force of one belligerent against the other. (*Hear.*) As to the question whether this country can be required by a foreign country to enforce its own municipal laws, the honourable Member for Maldon (*Mr. Sandford*) has gone so far as to attach blame to the noble Lord the Secretary for Foreign Affairs for allowing that question to be referred to an arbitrator.[4] But I apprehend the noble Lord has assented to nothing of the kind. The question is not whether we have permitted a violation of our municipal law—with which foreign countries have nothing to do; the question is, whether foreign countries have a right to require of us the fulfilment of our international duties? It is on the ground of international duty, and on that ground only, that they can bring any complaint against us. The question is simply this—are we bound by International Law to prevent certain things from being done, and being so bound, did we do all we could to fulfil that duty? It may have been that we were under obligations to make fresh municipal laws if those in existence were not sufficient to enable us to fulfil our international duties. Without going any further into this question of International Law, I congratulate the House and the country on the fact, now so obvious, that the point at issue is an extremely small one. But if a very small point prevents the settlement of a very great question, the smaller that point the greater the reason for lamentation, and possibly for blame. I do not think there is much room in the present case for blame in any quarter, because this discussion, as well as the correspondence—and especially this discussion—has brought out evidence that the two parties to the correspondence have not thoroughly understood one another.[5] (*Hear.*) The noble Lord (*Lord Stanley*) [a]as it seems,[a] has not thoroughly understood what the United States demanded;[6] and, on the other hand, the United States Government has not thoroughly understood what the noble Lord refused. I apprehend that the United States have never demanded that the question whether we were premature in recognizing the belligerent rights of the Confederates, should be referred to the arbitrator. I do not think they have ever claimed that,

[4]For Sandford's criticism of Stanley, see col. 1189.
[5]"Correspondence Respecting British and American Claims Arising out of the Late Civil War in the United States," *PP*, 1867, LXXIV, 1–48, and "Further Correspondence," *PP*, 1867–68, LXXIII, 1–10.
[6]Cf. Stanley, cols. 1168–78.

[a-a]+TT

or possibly could claim it, because they have never maintained that our recognition, even if premature, was a violation of International Law. I have seen it admitted again and again in strongly written statements of American writers, and even, I believe, in the writings of Mr. Seward himself, that our recognition of belligerent rights was a thing about the time of which we had by International Law a right to decide for ourselves.[7] It was urged that what we did was unfriendly, precipitate, and even unprecedented in its precipitation; but I am not aware that it has ever been contended that by our act, unfriendly, precipitate, and unprecedented though it might have been, we committed any violation of International Law for which we owed them reparation. It has been observed by my honourable Friend the Member for Reading (*Mr. Shaw-Lefevre*), in his very able and conclusive speech, and it has also been repeated in the very valuable remarks of my honourable Friend the Member for Bradford (*Mr. W.E. Forster*), that what the Americans claim is that they should be allowed to use this early recognition as an argument to convince the arbitrator that the depredations of the *Alabama* would probably not have taken place at all, or not to so great an extent, if it had not been for this unfriendly act on our part.[8] They contend that, inasmuch as they have a right to reparation on different grounds, they have a right to show that this conduct on our part has made the evil worse than it would otherwise have been. Whether this would be a good argument or not I will not say; but if it is a relevant one, they ought to be allowed to use it; and, if it is not relevant, why should you stipulate for its exclusion? If you are to stipulate for the exclusion of every frivolous or irrelevant argument, I fear that you will have a very long list of such stipulations. Surely anyone who is competent to arbitrate between two great States is competent to decide also what are relevant and what are frivolous arguments. I cannot help thinking that no impartial person would have any difficulty in allowing either side full liberty to introduce what argument it pleased, and that we might safely allow him to listen to this or to anything else that might be urged in aggravation of the claim against us for damages. Would it be worth while to exclude one fallacious argument when we cannot exclude all? We must leave some latitude, limited only by the check which the good sense and forbearance of the disputants on either side would impose upon them. The United States might stipulate on their part that we should not use irrelevant arguments, but they have not done so. (*Hear, hear.*) This, however, is only a part of the case; and perhaps I should not have risen if I had not wished to say how cordially I welcome those hints which have been thrown out by the noble Lord (*Lord Stanley*), and the observations which have been made by my honourable Friend (*Mr. W.E. Forster*) as to the possibility of our settling this question in some

[7]William Henry Seward (1801–72), then U.S. Secretary of State, "Despatch to Mr. Adams" (27 Aug., 1866), in "Correspondence Respecting British and American Claims," p. 4.

[8]Shaw-Lefevre, cols. 1163–5, and Forster, *ibid.*, col. 1182.

other way than by arbitration.[9] Indeed, I do not very clearly see what arbitration is specially required for. The case is this—I believe there are few in this country now, and but for the last two speakers,[10] I might have said I should hope there were none in this House—whatever might have been the case formerly—who were disposed to deny that we owed reparation of some sort, or in some degree, to the United States—it is quite clear that the noble Lord thinks so—and therefore this is not a case where we want arbitration. If we owe anything we must pay it, and what we want is some one to say, not whether we ought to pay, but how much. This would be best decided, not by an arbitrator, but by a mixed Commission. (*Hear, hear.*) The principal duty which this mixed Commission would have to discharge would be to investigate each particular claim, and to say what might be rejected altogether, and what had nothing particular to do with the depredations of the *Alabama*. It would have in fact to ascertain the real damage which the commerce of the United States had received from this act of negligence on our part in letting the *Alabama* leave our ports. I cannot but think that there is a great increase of good and friendly feeling on both sides. The noble Lord admits that the Americans are coming to more reasonable views, and with the great change of opinion which has taken place in this country I venture to think that there are now few people who do not believe that the arbitrator would decide against us, and that it would be extremely for the interests of the country that he should so decide. (*Hear, hear.*) In this state of things if some person—I will not say my honourable Friend the Member for Birmingham (*Mr. Bright*), but if any person not unacceptable to the Americans, were sent to them, and negotiations re-opened, if those negotiations began with an admission that we owed them reparation, and that the object was merely to ascertain what was the amount that was reasonably due from us, I cannot believe that there would be any serious difficulty in arriving at a settlement without going beyond the two disputants. I most earnestly hope that something of this sort was intended in the hint which Mr. Seward has thrown out.[11] It is, besides, not unworthy of consideration, that the grand point is the settlement of what is to be henceforth the law of nations; and that question is settled, so far as we are concerned, the moment we admit that reparation is due from us. If we admit that we owe reparation for the depredations which the *Alabama*, without any bad intention on our part, was enabled to commit, then I apprehend that a question of International Law which was much disputed, and which may again be the subject of quarrel, will, so far as this country and the United States are concerned, be for ever settled. (*Cheers.*)

[*The motion was withdrawn (col. 1198).*]

[9]Stanley, col. 1178; Forster, cols. 1182–3.
[10]Bowyer and Sandford.
[11]"Despatch," pp. 3–4.

88. The State of Ireland

12 MARCH, 1868

"Speech on Mr. Maguire's Motion on the State of Ireland, March 12, 1868," in *Chapters and Speeches on the Irish Land Question* (London: Longmans, *et al.*, 1870), pp. 108–25. In *PD*, 3rd ser., Vol. 190, cols. 1516–32. Reported in *The Times*, 13 March, p. 7, from which variants and responses are taken. Writing to John Elliot Cairnes on 4 December, 1869, Mill mentions the impending publication of *Chapters and Speeches*, and says that the text is taken from *Parliamentary Debates*, but that "not being a written speech," this one "could not be given so exactly [as No. 21, *q.v.*], but the newspaper report was carefully corrected for Hansard by myself, and is tolerably adequate" (*CW*, Vol. XVII, p. 1668). He nonetheless made some minor alterations, recorded here in the variant notes. On 10 March, John Francis Maguire had moved "That this House will immediately resolve itself into a Committee, with the view of taking into consideration the condition and circumstances of Ireland" (col. 1314), thus occasioning this debate.

IT WAS WITH A FEELING, I will not say of disappointment—because there can be no disappointment where there has not previously been hope—but of regret, that I witnessed the "beggarly account of empty boxes"[1] which the Government has laid before us, instead of an Irish policy. My dissatisfaction was not so much with what they did, or what they refused to do, on the subject of the land—although I look upon that question as outweighing all the rest put together, and I believe that without a satisfactory dealing with it, nothing can be done which will be at all effectual. I am afraid the time is far distant when it would be fair to expect that a Government, and especially a Conservative Government, should be found in advance of public opinion—which I cannot deny that the present Government would be, if they were to propose such a measure on the Irish Land question as I conceive would alone be effectual to settle it. But what we have a right to expect even from a Conservative Government, at all events from a Conservative Government which professes a Liberal policy—even with the qualifying adjunct, "truly Liberal"—is that they shall be on a level with the opinion of the people: and this they most assuredly are not, on the subject of the Irish Church. If there ever was a question on which I might say the whole human race has made up its mind, it is this. I concur in every word that was said, and every feeling that was expressed, by my right honourable friend the Member for Calne (*Mr. Lowe*) on this subject:[2] and I thank him from my heart for his manly and outspoken declaration in reference to that great scandal and iniquity, which was so well described by the right honourable gentleman now at the head of the Government (*Mr. Disraeli*), in a speech which, although last year he endeavoured to explain away, I am not aware

[1]Shakespeare, *Romeo and Juliet*, V, i, 46; in *The Riverside Shakespeare*, p. 1088.
[2]Lowe, cols. 1501–3.

that he has ever disavowed.[3] It is an institution which could not be submitted to by any country, except at the point of the sword. Now, on this subject the Government have not shown themselves altogether inflexible. The noble Lord the Chief Secretary for Ireland has expressed his willingness in some degree to entertain the principle of religious equality,[4] and I thank him for it; but, as has been remarked by my honourable friend the Member for Manchester (*Mr. Jacob Bright*), he proposed to do it—if at all—by levelling up instead of levelling down.[5] The noble Lord is willing that every valley [a]shall[a] be exalted; but he does not go on to the succeeding clause, and say that every mountain and hill shall be laid low.[6] (*Hear, hear, and laughter.*) So long as the national property which is administered by the Episcopal Church of Ireland is not diverted from its present purpose, the noble Lord has no objection at all to this country's saddling itself with the endowment of another great hierarchy, which, if effected on the principle of religious equality, would be a great deal more costly than even that which now exists. (*Hear, hear.*) Does the noble Lord really think it possible that the people of England will submit to this? I may be permitted, as one who, in common with many of my betters, have been subjected to the charge of being Utopian, to congratulate the Government on having joined that goodly company. It is, perhaps, too complimentary to call them Utopians, they ought rather to be called dys-topians, or cacotopians. What is commonly called Utopian is something too good to be practicable; but what they appear to favour is too bad to be practicable. Not only would England and Scotland never submit to it, but the Roman Catholic clergy of Ireland refuse it. They will not take your bribe. (*Hear, hear.*) As in many other things I differ from the honourable and learned Member for Oxford (*Mr. Neate*), who moved the Amendment,[7] so my opinion on the subject of Irish remedies is directly contrary to his. Whereas the honourable and learned Member thinks that the real obstacle to the peace and prosperity of Ireland is the proposal of extravagant and impossible remedies, my opinion, on the contrary, is that the real obstacle is not the proposal of extravagant and impossible remedies, but the persistent unwillingness of the House even to look at any remedy which they have pre-judged to be extravagant and impossible. (*Hear, hear.*) When a country has been so long in possession of full power over another, as this country has over

[3]On 26 July, 1867, Disraeli, in a speech on Ireland (*PD*, 3rd ser., Vol. 189, cols. 201–9), attempted to explain his remarks on Ireland on 16 February, 1844 (*ibid.*, Vol. 72, cols. 1007–17).

[4]Richard Southwell Bourke (1822–72), Lord Naas, M.P. for Cockermouth, Speech on the State of Ireland (10 Mar., 1868), *ibid.*, Vol. 190, cols. 1387–91.

[5]Jacob Bright (1821–99), M.P. for Manchester, and brother of John Bright, col. 1514.

[6]Isaiah, 40:4.

[7]Neate, Motion on the State of Ireland (10 Mar., 1868), *PD*, 3rd ser., Vol. 190, col. 1323.

[a-a]PD] CS,TT should

Ireland, and still leaves it in the state of feeling which now exists in Ireland, there is a strong presumption that the remedy required must be much stronger and more drastic than any which has yet been applied. (*Hear, hear.*) All the presumption is in favour of the necessity of some great change. Great and obstinate evils require great remedies. If the House does not think so—if it still has faith in small remedies, I exhort it to make haste and adopt them. It has already lost a great deal of time. Counting from 1829, which was the time when this country first began to govern Ireland, or even to profess to govern Ireland, for the sake of Ireland,[8] thirty-nine years have elapsed, and during that time, although there may have been some material progress, as there has been everywhere else, moral progress, in reconciling Ireland to our Government, and to the Union with us, has not been made, and does not seem likely soon to be made, unless we change our policy. Honourable gentlemen prefer to soothe themselves with statistics, flattering themselves with the idea that Ireland is improving, and that the evil was greater at some former time than it is now. My right honourable friend the Member for Calne has told us that we have no occasion to care for Fenianism, and that it is [b]not[b] of any consequence.[9] I do not suppose my right honourable friend thinks that the remedies proposed by me or any one else for the benefit of Ireland are intended to conciliate the Fenians. I know very little of the Fenians. I do not pretend to know what their opinions are, nor do I believe my right honourable friend knows them a bit better. (*A laugh.*) We do know, however, that they desire what I greatly deprecate—a violent separation of Ireland from this country; and they desire this with such bitterness and animosity that there is no chance of conciliating them [c]by any of the remedies proposed by himself or others[c]. But the peculiar and growing danger in the state of Ireland is this—that there is nearly universal discontent, and very general disaffection. Honourable gentlemen need not flatter themselves that this is an evil which can be safely disregarded. Ireland has had rebellions before. As a rebellion this recent one is nothing—it is contemptible. A great deal has been said about the circumstance that no person of consequence, personally or socially, has put himself at the head of it. It was not likely that any one who had anything to lose would do so. Is it within the range of possibility that an insurrection could be successful in Ireland at this particular time? (*Hear, hear, from the Ministerial benches.*) What does Mitchel himself say of it?[10] This is the reason why every one who has something to lose (and every one who is an occupant of land has something to lose) will not, until he sees a greater chance of success, countenance

[8]I.e., after Catholic Emancipation (by 10 George IV, c. 7 [1829]).
[9]Lowe, cols. 1484–5.
[10]*The History of Ireland, from the Treaty of Limerick to the Present Time* (New York: Sadlier, 1868), p. 609, by John Mitchel (1815–75), Fenian leader, at this time publishing the *Irish Citizen* in New York,

[b–b]PD nothing
[c–c]+TT

rebellion, or throw any other difficulty in the way of suppressing it than by sheltering from the police those who are involved in it. That is not the danger. The danger is one of which there is the strongest evidence. My own information is derived from many trustworthy persons, not of extreme opinions, persons whose idea of remedial measures for Ireland falls far short of mine, but who are unanimously of opinion that the state of Ireland is more dangerous at this moment than at any former period, and that the feeling of the people is one of general discontent and wide disaffection. (*Cries of Name.*) Gentlemen who hold land in Ireland do not think so; but they would be the last persons to find it out. Persons in possession of power are usually the last to find out what is thought of them by their inferiors. They [d] awake from their dream and find it out when they little expect it. There are two circumstances which make the disaffection more alarming at this time than at any former period since the rebellion of 1798. One is a circumstance which has never existed before. For the first time, the discontent in Ireland rests on a background of several millions of Irish across the Atlantic. This is a fact which is not likely to diminish. The number of Irish in America is constantly increasing. Their power to influence the political conduct of the United States is increasing, and will daily increase; and is there any probability that the American-Irish will come to hate this country less than they do at the present moment? The noble Lord the Chief Secretary for Ireland said truly that many Irish go to our colonies, and that they remain loyal.[11] But why? The Irish who go to those colonies find everything [e]there which[e] they seek in vain here. (*Hear.*) They have the land; they have no [f]sectarian[f] church; they have even a separate Legislature. All this they have under the British Crown and the British flag. If you gave all this to Ireland the people would be tranquil enough there. They will be so with much less than that; but those who go to America, on the contrary, [g]associate England with the deprivation of their rights, and[g] will be loyal only to the American Government, while their feeling towards England is, and must be, directly opposite to that of the Irish who go to Australia and the other English Colonies. That is one most serious cause of danger in Ireland. Another is that the disaffection has become, more than at any former period, one of nationality. The Irish were taught that feeling by Englishmen. England has only even professed to treat the Irish people as part of the same nation with ourselves, since 1800.[12] How did we treat them before that time? I will not go into the subject of the penal laws, [h]because it may be said that those laws affected the Irish not as Irish but as Catholics[h].[13] I will only mention the

[11]Bourke (Lord Naas), col. 1354.

[12]By the Act of Union, 39 & 40 George III, c. 67 (1800).

[13]E.g., by the two Test Acts, 25 Charles II, c. 2 (1672) and 30 Charles II, Second Session, c. 1 (1677), and by 7 & 8 William III, c. 27 (1696).

[d]PD , however,

[e-e]+CS

[f-f]TT Established

[g-g]+TT [*in past tense*]

[h-h]TT or the horrible oppression exercised towards the Roman Catholics

manner in which they were treated merely as Irish. I grant that, for these things, no man now living has any share of the blame; we are all ashamed of them; but "the evil that men do lives after them."[14] First of all, this House declared the importation of Irish cattle a public nuisance.[15] When we refused to receive Irish cattle, the Irish thought they would slaughter and salt them, to try whether we would receive them in that shape. But that was not allowed.[16] Then they thought that if they could not send the cattle or the flesh, they might send the hides in the form of leather. No; that was not allowed either.[17] Being thus denied admission for cattle in any shape, they tried if they [i]might[i] be allowed to do anything with respect to sheep; and they commenced exporting wool to this country. No; we would not take their wool.[18] Then they began to manufacture it, and tried if we would take the manufactured article. This was worst of all, and we compelled our deliverer, William III, of "pious and immortal memory,"[19] to promise his Parliament that he would put down the Irish woollen manufacture.[20] (*Hear, hear.*) This was not, I think, a brotherly course, or at all like treating Ireland as a part of the same nation. If we had been determined to impress upon Ireland in the strongest manner that she was regarded as a totally different and hostile nation, that was exactly the course to pursue. In fact, Ireland was treated in that thoroughly heathenish manner in which it was then customary for nations to treat other nations whom they had conquered [j]or were afraid of[j]—with the feeling that the dependent nation had no rights which the superior nation was bound to respect. It is unjust, however, to call that feeling heathenish, since it belonged only to the worst times of heathenism, before the Stoic philosophy—before the great, the immortal Marcus Antoninus proclaimed the kinship of all mankind.[21] From the year 1800, these things began to change; but down to 1829 it may be said that though in some sense we treated Ireland as a sister, it was as sister Cinderella. Dust and ashes were good enough for her; purple and fine linen were reserved for her sisters. (*A laugh.*) From 1829, however, we ceased to govern Ireland in that way. From that time there has been no feeling in this country with respect to Ireland, but a continuance

[14]Shakespeare, *Julius Caesar*, III, ii, 75; in *The Riverside Shakespeare*, p. 1121.

[15]18 Charles II, c. 2 (1666), Sect. 2.

[16]*Ibid.*

[17]Mill may be thinking of the duty imposed by 8 & 9 William III, c. 21 (1697).

[18]By 1 William and Mary, c. 32 (1688), Parliament had made it difficult, but not impossible, for the Irish to export wool to Britain.

[19]Part of the traditional Whig toast, celebrating William III (1650–1702), called from Holland to replace James II at the time of the English Revolution; cf. *Whig Club, Instituted in May, 1784, by John Bellamy* (London: n.p., 1786).

[20]As was done by 10 & 11 William III, c. 10 (1699).

[21]Marcus Aurelius Antoninus (121–180), Roman Emperor and philosopher, *Communings with Himself* [*Meditations*] (Greek and English), trans. C.R. Haines (London: Heinemann; New York: Putnam's Sons, 1930), pp. 70–1 (IV, 4).

[i-i]PD should
[j-j]+TT

of the really sisterly feeling which then commenced. Since that time it has been the sincere desire of all parties in England to govern Ireland for her good (*hear*); but we have grievously failed in knowing how to set about it, and [k]been very slow in learning the lesson[k]. Let me take a brief review of the things done for Ireland during that time. They may be easily counted. First, we made the landlord the tithe-proctor.[22] That was a right thing to do; it prevented a great deal of bloodshed, and an enormous amount of annoyance and disaffection. I only wish it had been done before it had become practically impossible to collect the tithes in the old way. But, after all, this was merely changing the mode of taking something from the Irish people: it was not taking less. Next, we gave to Ireland a really unsectarian education.[23] Ireland, long before England, received from us an elementary education which came down to the lowest grade of the people; and by degrees she also obtained unsectarian education in the higher branches. This is the most solid, and by far the greatest benefit we have yet conferred upon Ireland: and this, if the proposal of the Government is adopted, we are going in a great measure to give up.[24] In your difficulties, this is what you are going to throw over. You are going, in a great measure, to sacrifice the best thing you have done for Ireland, to save the bad things. (*Hear, hear.*) The third thing did more credit to our kindness and generosity than to our wisdom. It was the £8,000,000—ultimately amounting to £10,000,000—that we gave at the time of the Irish famine, for the relief of the destitution in that country.[25] Nobody will say that it was not right to give it; but I do not think that a people ever laid out £8,000,000 or £10,000,000 to meet an immediate emergency, in a manner calculated to do so very minute a quantity of permanent good. We were lavish in the amount that we expended. We certainly saved many lives—though there were probably a greater number that we could not save—and for that we are entitled to all credit. In a case of desperate distress there is in this country no grudging of money. All parties are united in that respect. But when circumstances obliged us to lay out this great sum, we had an opportunity of doing permanent good, by reclaiming the waste lands of Ireland for the benefit of the people of Ireland; and if we had done that, we should probably never have heard anything about fixity of tenure in the shape in which we hear of it now. At that time there was a sufficient quantity of waste land in Ireland to have enabled us

[22]By 1 & 2 Victoria, c. 109 (1838), which substituted charges on rent for composition for tithes.

[23]In 1831; see "Copy of a Letter from the Chief Secretary for Ireland, to His Grace the Duke of Leinster, on the Formation of a Board of Commissioners for Education in Ireland," *PP*, 1831–32, XXIX, 757–60.

[24]Bourke, in his Speech on the State of Ireland (10 Mar., 1868), *PD*, 3rd ser., Vol. 190, cols. 1384–6, had proposed the founding of a Catholic university in Ireland.

[25]See "An Account of Loans Advanced by the Imperial Treasury for Public Works in Ireland" (which includes other expenditures since 1800), *PP*, 1847, LIV, 91–282.

[k-k]+TT

to establish a large portion of the Irish population, by their own labour, in the condition of peasant proprietors of the land which they would themselves have reclaimed. We lost that opportunity, and we lost it for ever: because since that time fully one half of all the reclaimable waste land which existed at the time of Sir Richard Griffith's survey has been reclaimed;[26] that is, it has been got hold of by the landlords; it has been reclaimed for the landlords, mainly, or very largely, by the aid of public money lent to them for the purpose. Therefore, it is no longer possible to produce these great results in Ireland merely by reclaiming the waste lands. The opportunity lost never can be regained; and now, therefore, you are asked to do much larger, and, as it appears to you, much more revolutionary things. There is only one more thing that we have done which is worth mentioning, and that is the Encumbered Estates Act.[27] The Encumbered Estates Act was a statesmanlike measure; it was a measure admirably conceived, and excellent, provided it had been combined with other measures. Even as it was, it was in many respects a very valuable measure. In the first place, it effected a very great simplification of title. In the next, it to a great extent liberated Ireland from the great evil of needy landlords. But there is another side to the matter. The Act has had another effect, which was not, I believe, anticipated by anybody, at least to the extent to which it has been realized. It has shown to Ireland that there might be a still greater evil than needy landlords—namely, grasping landlords. Those who have bought estates under the Act are, I believe, in the great majority of cases, much harder landlords than their predecessors; and naturally so, because they had no previous connexion with the localities in which the estates they have purchased are situated. They were strangers—I do not mean to Ireland—but to the neighbourhood of their new properties. Many of them came from the towns. At all events, they had no connexion with the tenants, and did not feel that the tenants had any moral claim upon them, beyond the claim—a claim they ought to have recognised—which all who are dependent on us have upon us. They bought the land as a mere pecuniary speculation, and have very generally administered it as a mere speculation. Not unfrequently the first step they took was to raise the rents to the utmost possible amount, and in many cases they have ejected tenants because they could not pay those rents. These, then, are the things that we have done, since we began to do the best we could, the best we knew how to do, for Ireland; and I do not think they are [l] well calculated to remove from the minds of the Irish people the bitterness which had been produced by our previous mode of government. If you say that there was nothing better to be done, you confess your incompetency to

[26]Richard Griffith (1784–1878), "Return of the Probable Extent of Waste Lands in Each County in Ireland," in "Report from Her Majesty's Commissioners of Inquiry into the State of the Law and Practice in Respect to the Occupation of Land in Ireland," *PP*, 1845, XIX, 48–52.

[27]12 & 13 Victoria, c. 77 (1849).

[l]PD very

govern Ireland. I maintain that there is no country under heaven which it is not possible to govern, and to govern in such a way that it shall be contented. If there was anything better to be done, and you would not do it, your confession is still worse. But I do you more justice than you do yourselves. I believe that if [m]small[m] measures would have sufficed you would have granted them; and it is because [n]small[n] measures will not suffice, because you must have large measures, because you must look at the thing on a much larger scale than you now do, because you must be willing to take into consideration what you think extravagant proposals—it is because of that, and not from any want of good intentions, that you have failed. The present state of Ireland is, I hope, gradually convincing you, if it does not do so all at once, that you must do something on a much larger scale than you have ever acted upon before, whether the particular things proposed to you are the right things or not. It is under this conviction that I have thought it my duty not to keep back three-fourths of what I believe to be the truth in regard to Ireland, for fear of prejudicing minor measures which the very people who propose them do not expect to produce any very large results. As to the plan which I have proposed—and whether honourable gentlemen think that it is right or wrong, surely they will admit that it is good to have it discussed—as to that plan, it seems necessary that I should in the first place state what it is; for it does not appear to have been at all correctly understood by most of those who have attacked it, and least of all by the noble Lord the Chief Secretary for Ireland.[28] When I listened to his speech, I did not [o]recognise[o] my own plan. It is evident that the arduous duties of his important position had not left him time to read my pamphlet,[29] and that he had been compelled to trust to the representation of some one who had given him a very unfaithful account of it. The noble Lord seemed to think that my plan was that the State should buy the land from the present proprietors, and re-sell or re-let it to the tenants. Now, I have said nothing whatever about buying the land. I should think it extremely objectionable to make that a part of the plan. I do not want the rent-charge to be bought up by the tenants, because that would absorb the capital which I hope to see them employ in the improvement of the land. There is another mistake which seems to have been made pretty generally. Those who have objected to my proposal have always argued as if I was going to force perpetuity of tenure on unwilling tenants. I propose nothing of the sort. There are at present in Ireland a very great number of tenants who do not pay a full rent. The most improving landlords are precisely those who are the most moderate in their exactions. Now, it is an indispensable part of my plan that perpetuity should only be granted at a full rent—a fair rent, not an excessive, but still a full rent; and

[28]Bourke, col. 1369.

[29]*England and Ireland* (London: Longmans, *et al.*, 1868); in *CW*, Vol. VI, pp. 505–32.

[m-m]PD smaller

[n-n]PD smaller

[o-o]PD,TT know

probably, therefore, many of these tenants will prefer to remain as they are. They might not do so if they were never to have another chance of gaining a perpetuity; but as according to my plan they would retain the power of claiming a perpetuity at any future time, on a valuation to be then made, I think it extremely likely that many would wish to go on as they are. Many landlords, too, might prefer to arrange amicably with their tenants at something less than a full rent, in order to retain the present relations with them: and these, I believe, would be the best landlords, the most improving landlords, those who are on the best terms with their tenants, and whom it is most important to retain in the country. Many practical objections have been raised to the plan, to all of which I believe that I have answers; but there is a preliminary question that I should like to ask. Does the House really wish that these difficulties should be met? Because it is very possible that in the minds of honourable gentlemen the question may be concluded and closed by [p]a preliminary objection; such, for instance, as[p] that it is an interference with the rights of property. If honourable gentlemen are determined by this single circumstance—if this is enough to make them absolutely resist and condemn the plan—it is probable that they would be rather sorry than glad if it is possible to answer the practical objections, and show that the plan would work; and in that case I cannot expect to have a very favourable or very unprejudiced audience when I attempt to answer them. And then there is another sort of preliminary objection: that which was made by my right honourable friend the Member for Calne, in the name of political economy.[30] In my right honourable friend's mind political economy appears to stand for a [q]particular[q] set of practical maxims. To him it is not a science, it is not an exposition, not a theory of the manner in which causes produce effects: it is a set of practical rules, and these practical rules are indefeasible. My right honourable friend thinks that a maxim of political economy if good in England must be good in Ireland. (*Hear, and a laugh.*) But that is like saying that because there is but one science of astronomy, and the same law of gravitation holds for the earth and the planets, therefore the earth and the planets do not move in different orbits. So far from being a set of maxims and rules, to be applied without regard to times, places, and circumstances, the function of political economy is to enable us to find the rules which ought to govern any state of circumstances with which we have to deal—circumstances which are never the same in any two cases. I do not know in political economy more than I know in any other art [r]or science[r], a single practical rule that must be applicable to all cases; and I am sure that no one is at all capable of determining what is the right political economy for any country until he knows its circumstances. My right honourable friend perhaps thinks that what is good political economy for England must be

[30]Lowe, cols. 1494–7.

[p-p]TT the primary objection
[q-q]+CS
[r-r]+PD

good for India—or perhaps for the savages in the back woods of America. My right honourable friend has been very plain spoken,[31] and I will be plain spoken too. Political economy has a great many enemies; but its worst enemies are some of its friends, and I do not know that it has a more dangerous enemy than my right honourable friend. It is such modes of argument as he is in the habit of employing that have made political economy so thoroughly unpopular with a large and not the least philanthropic portion of the people of England. In my right honourable friend's mind, political economy seems to exist as a bar even to the consideration of anything that is proposed for the benefit of the economic condition of any people in any but the old ways: as if science was a thing not to guide our judgment, but to stand in its place—a thing which [s]can[s] dispense with the necessity of studying the particular case, and determining how a given cause will operate under its circumstances. Political economy has never in my eyes possessed this character. Political economy in my eyes is a science by means of which we are enabled to form a judgment as to what each particular case requires; but it does not supply us with a ready-made judgment upon any case, and there cannot be a greater enemy to political economy than he who represents it in that light. (*The honourable member was here interrupted by expressions of impatience from several members.*) [t]I presume that the House will not be unwilling to allow me to state my answer to the attack which has been made upon me by the right honourable gentleman. (*Hear.*) A good deal has been said about the sacredness of property. Now, this regard for the sacredness of property is connected with[t] a feeling which I respect. (*Ironical cheers and laughter.*) But the sacredness of property is not violated by taking away property for the public good, if full compensation is given; and the interference that I propose is not more an interference, it is not even so much an interference, with property, as taking land for public improvements. Then, too, a man's right to his property is sacred [u]unless that property is required for public purposes[u]; but is not a man's right to his person still more sacred? And yet no man is allowed to dispose of his person—in marriage, for instance—except in such way as the law provides (*great laughter*); nor will it allow him to relieve himself from the contract, except on very special grounds, to be decided on by a Court of Justice. To those honourable gentlemen who are fond of applying the term confiscation to the plan that I propose,[32] I will say that I recal them to the English language. I assure them that it is possible to argue against any proposition, if need be, and to refute what we think wrong, without altering the meaning of words, by doing which

[31]*Ibid.*, esp. col. 1493.

[32]E.g., Frederick Snowdon Corrance (1822–1906), M.P. for East Suffolk, col. 1479, and Lowe, col. 1497.

[s-s]PD may

[t-t]TT [*in third person, past tense*]] CS,PD I will presume, therefore, that the House will not be unwilling to allow me to state what answer I can make to the practical objections to my plan. First, there is the objection founded upon the sacredness of property. That is

[u-u]+TT [*in past tense*]

people only succeed in imposing upon themselves and others. How can that be confiscation in which the "fisc" instead of receiving anything, has only to pay; by which no individual will be the poorer, but many, I hope, a good deal richer? (*Oh!*) It may be objectionable, but that is a matter of argument; it may be undesirable, because the case may not be deemed strong enough to require it; but let us fight against opinions from which we differ without extending the war to the English language. I recommend to honourable gentlemen to be always strictly conservative of the English tongue. (*Oh!*) I will now come to arguments of a more practical kind. (*Ironical cheers and laughter.*) I will first mention the strongest argument I have ever heard, either in this House or elsewhere, against my plan—namely, that if we substitute the Government in the place of the present proprietors, we shall expose the Government to great difficulties, and make it still more unpopular than it has ever yet been.[33] I have two answers to make to this objection, and if honourable gentlemen are not impressed by the one they may perhaps be convinced by the other. Undoubtedly, if the proposal is not received by the tenants as a great boon—if they do not think that perpetuity of tenure on the terms I have suggested is a gift worth accepting, then I admit that there is nothing to say in favour of my plan; it would be idle to propose it. If, when we offer to the tenantry of Ireland that which they desire more than anything else in the world—a perfect security of tenure—the certainty that they will never have more to pay than they pay at first—that everything which their industry produces shall belong to them alone—if they do not think that a boon worth having, I have nothing more to say. But this is a most improbable supposition. A similar prediction was made about the serfs of Russia. Many people said and believed that the emancipated serfs would never consent to pay rent, especially to the Government, for land which they had been accustomed to receive gratis when in their servile condition. That was the general prediction; but we do not hear that the prediction has been fulfilled. Everything seems to be going on smoothly, and the serfs, as far as is known, pay their rents regularly. This, then, is one answer. I have another which is more decisive. If it is thought that it will not do to make the Government a substitute for the landlord, I answer that this is an objection affecting only [v]the smallest[v] part of my plan—an additional provision, not for the benefit of the tenant, but for the convenience and consolation of the landlords (*laughter*)—that they should be allowed to receive their rents from the public Treasury [w]or in Consols[w]. If, after the rent is converted into a rent-charge, it be thought that the landlords should, like other rent-chargers, be left to the ordinary law of the country to collect their dues, by all means leave them to the ordinary legal remedies. If it be thought injurious to the public interest to give [x]the proposed[x] consolation to the landlords, then do not

[33]Again Corrance, col. 1479, and Lowe, cols. 1494–6.

[v-v]PD a
[w-w]+TT
[x-x]PD this

give it. So falls to the ground a full half of the dissertation of the right honourable Member for Calne on the fatal consequences of the plan. But I must say that I do not believe the landlords as a body would wish to exchange their present condition for that of being mere receivers of dividends from the State. I observe that those who argue against any plan supposed to be contrary to the interest of landlords, invariably assume that the landlords are destitute of every spark of patriotic feeling. I do not think so. I believe that a large proportion of the landlords would prefer to retain their [y]connexion with the land[y]; that they would make private arrangements with their tenants on terms more favourable to them than my plan would give, and that so Ireland would retain a large proportion of the best class of landlords [z], while the tenants, knowing that if they choose they can obtain a perpetual tenure, will feel themselves in perfect security[z]. Another objection made against my plan is, that many of the holdings are too small.[34] But Lord Dufferin states in his pamphlet that the consolidation of small holdings has ceased—that the number of separate holdings has not diminished in the last fifteen years.[35] We may conclude from this that the holdings, generally speaking, are as large as is required by the present state of the industry and capital of Ireland; because, if that were not so, I cannot but believe that the movement of consolidation would still be going on. I perfectly admit that a great many tenants hold smaller holdings than could be desired. But if the holdings are so small that the tenants cannot live on them, and, at the same time, pay the amount of rent that would be required, they will soon fall into arrears; and, if they fall into arrears, it is a necessary part of my plan that they should be ejected. (*Hear, hear.*) This would enable the landlord, if he thought fit, in every case of eviction, to consolidate farms; and whether he did so or not, the consequence would be the substitution of a better class of tenants. It is part of my plan that the landlord, if the holding were forfeited by non-payment of the rent-charge, should choose the tenant's successor, and that the consent of the landlord should be necessary to any sale of the occupier's interest. Another objection which has been urged is, that in Ireland lands held on long leases are always the worst farmed. Now, these are almost always old leases, granted to middlemen. These middlemen hold the farms at low rents; but I never heard that they granted leases at low rents to the sub-tenants; and who on earth would or could improve under competition rents? What interest has a man in improving, who has promised a rent he can never pay, and who therefore knows that, lease or no lease, he may be turned out at any moment? If the farmers have undertaken to pay a rent equal to double what they make from the land, is it likely that they will exert themselves to double the produce, merely for the benefit of the landlord? One of

[34]Horsman, col. 1475, and Lowe, col. 1494.

[35]Frederick Temple Hamilton Temple Blackwood (1826–1902), Lord Dufferin, *Mr. Mill's Plan for the Pacification of Ireland Examined* (London: Murray, 1868), p. 32.

[y-y]PD present position

[z-z]+TT [*in past tense*]

the most extraordinary circumstances connected with the attack made on my plan by my right honourable friend the Member for Calne, is that he went on ascribing all manner of evil effects to peasant proprietorship,[36] and yet from the beginning to the end of his speech he never made allusion to any of the arguments in its favour. One would have thought that he had never heard the common and principal argument, that the sentiment of property, the certainty that [a]the fruits of a man's labour are to be his own[a] is the most powerful of all incentives to labour and frugality. (*Hear, hear.*) This is the universal experience of every country where peasant proprietorship exists. And this brings me to the noble Lord the Chief Secretary for Ireland, who gave three reasons why peasant proprietorship is not desirable.[37] These reasons were, that it does not prevent revolution, that it does not obviate famine, and that it leads to great indebtedness on the part of the holders. In regard to the first of these reasons, the case which the noble Lord appealed to, that of France, is certainly not in his favour; for in France the revolutions have not been made by the peasant proprietors, but by the artizans [b]in the towns[b] (*hear, hear*); all that the peasant proprietors have had to do with them being to put them down. (*Hear, hear.*) Whether it was right or wrong—whether it was for good or evil—to substitute the present Government of France for the Republic, it was the peasant proprietors who did it. As to the co-existence of great famines and small properties, the noble Lord was rather unhappy in the instance he gave of East Prussia, for it so happens that East Prussia is not a country of peasant proprietors, there being next to no small properties there. It is the Rhine Provinces of Prussia that are a country of small proprietors, and the noble Lord did not tell us of any famine there. With reference to the argument as to the indebtedness of the small proprietors, I rather think the noble Lord is indebted to me for one instance he gave—that of the canton of Zurich;[38] but in adducing that instance he omitted to mention the testimony given, by the same author, to the "superhuman" industry of the peasant proprietors there.[39] If we take the instance generally appealed to on this subject, that of France; M. Léonce de Lavergne stated some ten years ago that the mortgages on the landed property of France did not on the average exceed 10 per cent of its value, and on the rural property did not exceed 5 per cent; and he estimated the burthen of interest at 10 per cent of the income.[40] He added that these

[36]Lowe, cols. 1489–99.

[37]Bourke, cols. 1370–4.

[38]Bourke referred to the citation in Mill's *Principles of Political Economy*, II, vi, 2, of the description by Gerold Meyer von Knonau (see *CW*, Vol. II, p. 258n).

[39]The reference is actually to Eduard Im Thurn, another Swiss author; see *ibid.*, II, vii, 1 (Vol. II, p. 278).

[40]Louis Gabriel Léonce Guilhaud de Lavergne (1809–80), *Economie rurale de la France depuis 1789* (1860), 2nd ed. (Paris: Guillaumin, 1861), pp. 453–4 (cf. *CW*, Vol. II, p. 436).

[a-a]TT [*in past tense*]] CS,PD that they are working for themselves
[b-b]+TT

burthens were not increasing, but diminishing. It is true that this average is taken from all the landed properties in France, and not solely from the small properties; but the large proprietors must be very unlike other large landed proprietors if their estates are not generally burthened to at least this extent, so that the average is probably fairly applicable to the small properties. With regard to the danger of sub-letting, what [c]should a man who has received a perpetuity sub-let it for[c]? He could only sub-let at the rent he himself paid, unless he had in the meantime improved his holding, and if he had done so he would have a good right to be allowed to realize his improvements, if he pleased, by sub-letting at an increased rent. [d]But if he had not improved the land he would be no gainer by sub-letting.[d] It is thought that even if he did not sub-let, he would subdivide. But to suppose that subdivision would be general, is to ignore altogether one of the strongest motives that can operate on the mind. There is nothing like the possession of a property in the land by the actual cultivator, for inspiring him with industry and a desire to accumulate. It is not necessary to suppose that this influence would operate on the whole body of tenant proprietors. If it acted only on one-half, a great deal would be gained. Let honourable gentlemen consider what an accumulation of savings there is in the hands of Irish farmers. I must say that it reflects great credit on the landlords of Ireland, taken as a body, that the tenants should have been able to accumulate such almost incredible sums as it is admitted that they have. Well, what is done with these savings? The farmer carries them anywhere but to the farm. (*Hear, hear.*) They are invested in everything but the improvement of his holding; [e]and this is a most striking circumstance,[e] showing that the very landlords through whose forbearance these sums have been accumulated, are not trusted by the tenants; or, if they trust the landlord himself, they do not trust his heir, whom they do not know, or his creditor who may come into possession, or the stranger to whom he may be obliged to sell. But under the small proprietary system, these sums would be brought out and applied to the farms, and there is enough of them to make all Ireland blossom like the rose.[41] Tenants who had given such proof of forethought would be more likely to provide for their younger sons by buying more land than by subdividing their own holdings. Moreover, it must be remembered that a bridge has now been built to America, over which the younger sons might cross. According to the testimony of Lord Dufferin, marriages are already less early in Ireland than they used to be, and many farmers have become sensible of the disadvantage of subdividing the small holdings.[42] It may be thought that owing to the competition which exists for land, [f]those who hold at a full rent

[41]Cf. Isaiah, 35:1.
[42]Blackwood, p. 27.

[c-c]TT [*in past tense*]] CS,PD motive would a tenant have to sub-let
[d-d]+TT
[e-e]+TT [*in past tense*]
[f]PD even

might [g] sub-let at an increase, [h]even if they could not[h] sell their interest for a large sum of money. But even if this worst result should happen, the purchaser would, even then, be in as good a condition as the Ulster tenant would be in, if the tenant right, which he enjoys by a precarious custom, were secured to him by law: and this tenant right, even while resting only on custom, has been found to give a considerable feeling of security, and some encouragement to improvement. Then I am asked, what my scheme would do for the agricultural labourers of Ireland?[43] It would give to them what is found most valuable in all countries possessing peasant proprietors—the hope of acquiring landed property. This hope is what animates the wonderful industry of the peasantry of Flanders, most of whom have only short leases, but who, because they may hope, by exertion, to become owners of land, set an example of industry and thrift to all Europe. (*Hear, hear.*) My plan is called an extreme one, but if its principle were accepted, the extent of its application would be in the hands of the House. Let the House look at the question in a large way, and admit that rights of property, subject to just compensation, must give way to the public interest. If the Commission which I propose[44] were appointed, it would soon find out what [i]conditions and limitations[i] might be applied in practice. I could myself suggest many [j]such[j]. I would not undertake that I myself would support them, but the House might. For instance, if it were thought that the holdings were too small, the holders of all farms below a certain extent might receive, not a perpetuity at once, but only the hope of it. Leases might be given to them, and the claim to a perpetuity might be made dependent on their, in the meantime, improving the land. Again, such a change as I propose is less required in the case of grazing than of arable land: confine it then, if you choose, in the first instance, to arable land, dealing with the purely grazing farms on some other plan, such as that of buying up such of them as might advantageously be converted into arable, and re-selling them in smaller lots. It is not an essential part of the scheme that every tenant should have an actual perpetuity, but only that every tenant who actually tills the soil should have the power of obtaining a perpetuity on an impartial valuation. I believe that as the plan comes to be more considered, its difficulties will, in a great measure, disappear, and the House will be more inclined to view it with favour than at present. (*Hear, hear.*)

[*The debate continued on Maguire's motion on 13 and 16 March, when it was withdrawn (col. 1792).*]

[43]Neate, cols. 1317–18.
[44]*England and Ireland*, *CW*, Vol. VI, p. 527.

[g]PD be able to
[h-h]PD or
[i-i]TT] CS,PD temperaments
[j-j]+PD

89. Election Petitions and Corrupt Practices at Elections [1]

26 MARCH, 1868

PD, 3rd ser., Vol. 191, cols. 308–11. Reported in *The Times*, 27 March, p. 7, from which variants and responses are taken. In preparation for the debate on "A Bill for Amending the Laws Relating to Election Petitions, and Providing More Effectually for the Prevention of Corrupt Practices at Elections," 31 Victoria (13 Feb., 1868), *PP*, 1867–68, II, 267–86, Mill wrote on 27 January to Edwin Chadwick asking him for a summary of his recommendations for a bill against electoral corruption. The debate in which he spoke was on the Bill as amended in Committee (*ibid.*, pp. 291–307). After the debate, he wrote to William Dougal Christie to say that he had "broke[n] ground on the subject of the two or three most important of your [Christie's] suggestions respecting a bribery bill" (*CW*, Vol. XVII, pp. 1355, 1380).

SIR, if the question were solely between the Bill of Her Majesty's Government and the Amendment,[1] I should have no hesitation in at once deciding for the Bill. Not that it corresponds or comes up in all respects to my notion of what such a Bill should be. Nor do I believe that by any one expedient—and there is only one expedient in this Bill—we can hope to put down corrupt practices. If the House are in earnest in their desire to put down corrupt practices at elections—and I am bound to believe that they are, however little credit they receive for such earnestness out of doors—I apprehend they will be obliged to have recourse, not to one, but to several expedients. Nevertheless, I think favourably of the Bill, because though it does in reality only one thing, that thing is a vigorous one, and shows an adequate sense of the emergency. It shows a sense that, in order to put down this great evil, it is necessary to go out of the common path. The truth is that, however possible it may be for Committees of this House to be impartial on the question to whom the seat shall be given—and I do not deny that they are often impartial in that respect, nor is it hopeless that they might be always so—nobody out of this House, and I think I may almost add in it, believes that so long as the jurisdiction remains in this House the penalties against the giver of the bribe will ever be seriously enforced. There are several reasons for this, some of which, perhaps, had better be understood than expressed. (*A laugh.*) To confine myself to what may be said with safety; any tribunal that acts only occasionally as a tribunal, still more any person called for the first time so to act, as is often the case with Members of Parliament, has naturally a very strong indisposition to convict: and still more is this the case when those who have to decide are men of the same class, and the same general cast of feelings, and subject to the same temptations as the

[1]Alexander Mitchell (1831–73), M.P. for Berwick, moved an amendment to reserve the trial of election petitions to the Commons (cols. 296–8).

accused, and men of whom it must be said that hitherto they have been disposed to consider a scrape of this sort as much more a misfortune than a crime. (*Hear.*) I think that there is, after all, something in the objection to the proposal for giving the ultimate decision to a Judge not appointed by the House. There is some reason against their handing over their jurisdiction at once and for ever to a functionary appointed solely by the Crown (*hear*); but there is an easy mode of getting rid of that objection—namely, by making the Act temporary. (*Hear.*) I am not sure that it should not be annual—that it ought not, like the Mutiny Act, to be renewed every year, so that there should never be any long time during which evil consequences need be suffered. And although I do not myself think that any evil consequences are likely to follow, still, as where there is a bare possibility there is always apprehension, I hope that, if the House adopts the Bill, the Government will see the propriety of introducing some limitation such as I have suggested. There is another point on which I wish to say something. Great objections appear to be felt to turning over these inquiries to the Judges of the land. Would it not be a suitable way of meeting these objections if this tribunal were to be only a tribunal of appeal? Indeed, even if the House should not choose to adopt this tribunal—if they should keep these matters in the hands of a Committee of their own Members presided over by a legal assessor—and few, I think, will now deny that there must at least be a legal assessor—whether the House adopt this way, or whether they adopt the proposal of the Government—there are very strong reasons for making the tribunal only a tribunal of appeal. It is only by inquiry diligently made on the spot, that the truth in such matters can be discovered. I will make one suggestion, which will be found in a pamphlet which has attracted a good deal of attention, and has been read, I know, by Members of the Government.[2] It is written by Mr. W.D. Christie, formerly a Member of this House, and who I hope may be so again. (*Hear.*) It is that there should be a local inquiry by a person of competent legal qualifications after every Parliamentary election, whether there is a petition or not. (*Laughter, and cries of Oh, oh!*) Notwithstanding the dissent with which this proposition seems to be met, much may be said in its favour; for the very worst cases are invariably those in which petitions are either not presented (*hear, hear*), or, having been presented, are afterwards withdrawn [a]by a compromise[a], because it is found that an inquiry would be equally damaging to the case of the petitioner, both parties being tarred with the same brush [b], and, however certain it is that the seat has been obtained by bribery, the losing party are afraid to prosecute the petition for fear of the disclosures, which would bring discredit upon themselves[b]. These are such flagrant cases that I am sure it must be admitted that, unless

[2]*Electoral Corruption and Its Remedies* (London: National Association for the Promotion of Social Science, 1864), by William Dougal Christie, who had been M.P. for Weymouth 1842–47, and failed in attempts at election in 1865 and 1868.

[a-a]+TT
[b-b]+TT [*in past tense*]

they are in some manner provided for, it will be impossible effectually to put down bribery. The officer whom I suppose to be appointed would proceed after every election to the spot, and there sit in public to receive any complaints that may be made. Of course it is a necessary consequence that this officer should have the power, where the complaints are frivolous, of throwing the expense on the complainant. And whatever expenses would not thus be met, should be defrayed by the locality—should be, in fact, a public charge. There is the more reason for appointing such an officer, as it is indispensably necessary that there should be an inquiry, not only into Parliamentary, but into municipal elections, which are the nurseries of Parliamentary bribery. (*Hear.*) Mr. Philip Rose, a Conservative solicitor, well known to many honourable Members opposite, has expressed an opinion on this subject which is well entitled to attention. Mr. Rose says, in his evidence before a Committee of the House of Lords, that in a vast number of places, illegal practices are carried on at municipal elections by a regular machinery, which is also made use of at Parliamentary elections.[3] (*Hear.*) He adds that great pressure is brought to bear upon Members of Parliament to contribute towards the expenses of municipal contests (*hear*), because it is held out to them that £10 spent upon one of these is better than £100 spent in a Parliamentary contest (*hear, hear*); and that it is an axiom among agents—"We were able to return our municipal candidate, and we shall therefore be able to return our Parliamentary candidate."[4] After such testimony, coming from such a quarter, it is plain that, if you really wish to put down bribery and corruption at Parliamentary elections, you must extend your interference to municipal elections also. (*Cheers.*) In addition to the duties which I have suggested that the Commissioners of Inquiry should perform after each election, there are a number of other duties which might well be performed by those functionaries. They would naturally act as election auditors; and, in places from which no petition proceeds, their principal business will probably consist in scrutinizing the accounts which Members are already obliged to render, and which ought to be required from them with greater accuracy and completeness. Belonging to the same class from which revising barristers are taken, there will be an obvious propriety in their acting also in that capacity; and they might even fulfil the duties of returning officers. (*Oh, oh!*) Whatever functionaries of this description may be appointed, no fear need be entertained that there will be any want of work for them. If you feel that the control of all these matters ought not to pass out of your own hands, you might leave the nomination of these functionaries in the hands of the Speaker; but any difficulty on that score will best be got rid of by making the legal authority proposed by the Bill of Her Majesty's Government the tribunal of appeal.[5] These are the suggestions which I

[3]See the evidence of Philip Rose (1816–83), "Report from the Select Committee of the Lords," *Sessional Papers*, 1860, I, 129.

[4]*Ibid.*, p. 130.

[5]By Clause 10.

have felt it my duty to offer in reference to the measure brought forward by the right honourable Gentleman the Head of the Administration.[6] The reasons in support of them will be found at length in the very able pamphlet to which I have referred. (*Hear, hear.*)

[*Mitchell's amendment was defeated (col. 321).*]

90. Election Petitions and Corrupt Practices at Elections [2]

2 APRIL, 1868

PD, 3rd ser., Vol. 191, col. 702. Reported in *The Times*, 3 April, p. 5. Writing the next day to William Dougal Christie, his close ally in this matter, Mill said, "Mr. Disraeli's answer to my question was civil but in no degree satisfactory" (*CW*, Vol. XVI, p. 1383).

MR. J. STUART MILL SAID, he would beg to ask the First Lord of the Treasury, Whether it is his intention to propose any measure, either separately or as a provision in the Election Petitions and Corrupt Practices at Elections Bill,[1] for the prevention of bribery at Municipal Elections?

Mr. Disraeli: Sir, the subject to which the Question of the honourable Member relates is one of very great importance, but I am not prepared to deal with it in the manner he suggests. I shall make every possible effort to carry the Bill which refers to Parliamentary Elections before the dissolution. I think that that is a matter of the greatest moment; but I do not contemplate mixing it up with the subject referred to by the honourable Member.

91. Procedure in the House: Amendments

21 APRIL, 1868

PD, 3rd ser., Vol. 191, col. 1030. Reported (in one sentence) in *The Times*, 22 April, p. 6. Mill spoke during an extensive discussion in Committee of Supply on Ayrton's motion to amend a resolution of the House dating from 1858, "That when it has been proposed to omit or reduce items in a Vote the Question shall be afterwards put upon the original Vote or upon the reduced Vote, as the case may be, without amendment," by replacing the final two

[6]Disraeli introduced the Bill on 13 February (*PD*, 3rd ser., Vol. 190, cols. 693–702).

[1]See No. 89.

words with "unless an Amendment be moved for a reduction of the whole Vote" (col. 1025).

MR. J. STUART MILL SAID, THAT as it appeared likely that this matter would go back for re-consideration, he might be permitted to suggest a further point. The Motion of his honourable and learned Friend was on a very important and very valuable subject, and formed part of the largest questions. The rules which, in the course of centuries, had been elaborated in this House for the conduct of the Business had been most deservedly admired. But difficulties might arise when the House could only have one Amendment on the same point; because, as soon as one Amendment had been rejected, it had resolved that the original Motion should be put unamended. It might be well for the House to examine this point. According to the rule of the French Chamber, whatever number of Amendments there might be moved, the question of precedency was decided in this way:—The Amendment which was farthest from the original Motion was put first, and if this were lost, the others were put in succession. Might it not be as well to adopt the plan here?

[*The matter was resolved by a Government resolution on 28 April that provided for a final vote on the original or amended motion (cols. 1464–6).*]

92. Capital Punishment

21 APRIL, 1868

PD, 3rd ser., Vol. 191, cols. 1047–55. Reported in *The Times*, 22 April, p. 6, from which the variant and responses are taken. Mill spoke during second reading of "A Bill to Provide for Carrying out of Capital Punishment within Prisons," 31 Victoria (20 Feb., 1868), *PP*, 1867–68, I, 261–6 (enacted as 31 Victoria, c. 24 [1868]). Mill (according to *The Times*) "rose amid loud cries of 'Divide!'"

IT WOULD BE a great satisfaction to me if I were able to support this Motion.[1] It is always a matter of regret to me to find myself, on a public question, opposed to those who are called—sometimes in the way of honour, and sometimes in what is intended for ridicule—the philanthropists. (*A laugh.*) Of all persons who take part in public affairs, they are those for whom, on the whole, I feel the greatest amount of respect; for their characteristic is, that they devote their time, their labour, and much of their money to objects purely public, with a less admixture of either personal or class selfishness, than any other class of politicians whatever. On almost all the great questions, scarcely any politicians are so steadily and almost uniformly to be found on the side of right; and they seldom err, but by an

[1]Gilpin had moved an amendment to abolish capital punishment (col. 1041).

exaggerated application of some just and highly important principle. On the very subject that is now occupying us we all know what signal service they have rendered. It is through their efforts that our criminal laws—which within my memory hanged people for stealing in a dwelling house to the value of 40*s.*[2]—laws by virtue of which rows of human beings might be seen suspended in front of Newgate by those who ascended or descended Ludgate Hill—have so greatly relaxed their most revolting and most impolitic ferocity, that aggravated murder is now practically the only crime which is punished with death by any of our lawful tribunals; and we are even now deliberating whether the extreme penalty should be retained in that solitary case. This vast gain, not only to humanity, but to the ends of penal justice, we owe to the philanthropists; and if they are mistaken, as I cannot but think they are, in the present instance, it is only in not perceiving the right time and place for stopping in a career hitherto so eminently beneficial. (*Hear, hear.*) Sir, there is a point at which, I conceive, that career ought to stop. When there has been brought home to any one, by conclusive evidence, the greatest crime known to the law; and when the attendant circumstances suggest no palliation of the guilt, no hope that the culprit may even yet not be unworthy to live among mankind, nothing to make it probable that the crime was an exception to his general character rather than a consequence of it, then I confess it appears to me that to deprive the criminal of the life of which he has proved himself to be unworthy—solemnly to blot him out from the fellowship of mankind and from the catalogue of the living—is the most appropriate, as it is certainly the most impressive, mode in which society can attach to so great a crime the penal consequences which for the security of life it is indispensable to annex to it. I defend this penalty, when confined to atrocious cases, on the very ground on which it is commonly attacked—on that of humanity to the criminal; as beyond comparison the least cruel mode in which it is possible adequately to deter from the crime. If, in our horror of inflicting death, we endeavour to devise some punishment for the living criminal which shall act on the human mind with a deterrent force at all comparable to that of death, we are driven to inflictions less severe indeed in appearance, and therefore less efficacious, but far more cruel in reality. Few, I think, would venture to propose, as a punishment for aggravated murder, less than imprisonment with hard labour for life; that is the fate to which a murderer would be consigned by the mercy which shrinks from putting him to death. But has it been sufficiently considered what sort of a mercy this is, and what kind of life it leaves to him? If, indeed, the punishment is not really inflicted—if it becomes the sham which a few years ago such punishments were rapidly becoming—then, indeed, its adoption would be almost tantamount to giving up the attempt to repress murder altogether. But if it really is what it professes to be,

[2]Until the enactment of 2 & 3 William IV, c. 62 (1832), though in fact the death penalty was seldom applied in such cases, as Mill indicates below.

and if it is realized in all its rigour by the popular imagination, as it very probably would not be, but as it must be if it is to be efficacious, it will be so shocking that when the memory of the crime is no longer fresh, there will be almost insuperable difficulty in executing it. What comparison can there really be, in point of severity, between consigning a man to the short pang of a rapid death, and immuring him in a living tomb, there to linger out what may be a long life in the hardest and most monotonous toil, without any of its alleviations or rewards—debarred from all pleasant sights and sounds, and cut off from all earthly hope, except a slight mitigation of bodily restraint, or a small improvement of diet? Yet even such a lot as this, because there is no one moment at which the suffering is of terrifying intensity, and, above all, because it does not contain the element, so imposing to the imagination, of the unknown, is universally reputed a milder punishment than death—stands in all codes as a mitigation of the capital penalty, and is thankfully accepted as such. For it is characteristic of all punishments which depend on duration for their efficacy—all, therefore, which are not corporal or pecuniary—that they are more rigorous than they seem; while it is, on the contrary, one of the strongest recommendations a punishment can have, that it should seem more rigorous than it is; for its practical power depends far less on what it is than on what it seems. There is not, I should think, any human infliction which makes an impression on the imagination so entirely out of proportion to its real severity as the punishment of death. The punishment must be mild indeed which does not add more to the sum of human misery than is necessarily or directly added by the execution of a criminal. As my honourable Friend the Member for Northampton (*Mr. Gilpin*) has himself remarked, the most that human laws can do to anyone in the matter of death is to hasten it;[3] the man would have died at any rate; not so very much later, and on the average, I fear, with a considerably greater amount of bodily suffering. Society is asked, then, to denude itself of an instrument of punishment which, in the grave cases to which alone it is suitable, effects its purpose at a less cost of human suffering than any other; which, while it inspires more terror, is less cruel in actual fact than any punishment that we should think of substituting for it. My honourable Friend says that it does not inspire terror, and that experience proves it to be a failure.[4] But the influence of a punishment is not to be estimated by its effect on hardened criminals. Those whose habitual way of life keeps them, so to speak, at all times within sight of the gallows, do grow to care less about it; as, to compare good things with bad, an old soldier is not much affected by the chance of dying in battle. I can afford to admit all that is often said about the indifference of professional criminals to the gallows. Though of that indifference one-third is probably bravado and another third confidence that they shall have the luck to escape, it is quite probable that the remaining third is real.

[3]Gilpin, cols. 1040–1.
[4]*Ibid.*, col. 1034.

But the efficacy of a punishment which acts principally through the imagination, is chiefly to be measured by the impression it makes on those who are still innocent: by the horror with which it surrounds the first promptings of guilt; the restraining influence it exercises over the beginning of the thought which, if indulged, would become a temptation; the check which it exerts over the gradual declension towards the state—never suddenly attained—in which crime no longer revolts, and punishment no longer terrifies. (*Hear, hear.*) As for what is called the failure of death punishment, who is able to judge of that? We partly know who those are whom it has not deterred; but who is there who knows whom it has deterred, or how many human beings it has saved who would have lived to be murderers if that awful association had not been thrown round the idea of murder from their earliest infancy? Let us not forget that the most imposing fact loses its power over the imagination if it is made too cheap. When a punishment fit only for the most atrocious crimes is lavished on small offences until human feeling recoils from it, then, indeed, it ceases to intimidate, because it ceases to be believed in. The failure of capital punishment in cases of theft is easily accounted for: the thief did not believe that it would be inflicted. He had learnt by experience that jurors would perjure themselves rather than find him guilty; that Judges would seize any excuse for not sentencing him to death, or for recommending him to mercy; and that if neither jurors nor Judges were merciful, there were still hopes from an authority above both. When things had come to this pass it was high time to give up the vain attempt. When it is impossible to inflict a punishment, or when its infliction becomes a public scandal, the idle threat cannot too soon disappear from the statute book. And in the case of the host of offences which were formerly capital, I heartily rejoice that it did become impracticable to execute the law. If the same state of public feeling comes to exist in the case of murder; if the time comes when jurors refuse to find a murderer guilty; when Judges will not sentence him to death, or will recommend him to mercy; or when, if juries and Judges do not flinch from their duty, Home Secretaries, under pressure of deputations and memorials, shrink from theirs, and the threat becomes, as it became in the other cases, a mere *brutum fulmen*;[5] then, indeed, it may become necessary to do in this case what has been done in those—to abrogate the penalty. That time may come—my honourable Friend thinks that it has nearly come.[6] I hardly know whether he lamented it or boasted of it; but he and his Friends are entitled to the boast: for if it comes it will be their doing, and they will have gained what I cannot but call a fatal victory, for they will have achieved it by bringing about, if they will forgive me for saying so, an enervation, an effeminacy, in the general mind of the country. (*Hear, hear.*) For what else than effeminacy is it to be so much more shocked by taking a man's life

[5]This term for a vain menace comes from Pliny, *Natural History*, Vol. I, p. 254 (II, xliii, 113).

[6]Gilpin, cols. 1037–8.

than by depriving him of all that makes life desirable or valuable? Is death, then, the greatest of all earthly ills? *Usque adeone mori miserum est*?[7] Is it, indeed, so dreadful a thing to die? Has it not been from of old one chief part of a manly education to make us despise death—teaching us to account it, if an evil at all, by no means high in the list of evils; at all events, as an inevitable one, and to hold, as it were, our lives in our hands, ready to be given or risked at any moment, for a sufficiently worthy object? I am sure that my honourable Friends know all this as well, and have as much of all these feelings as any of the rest of us; possibly more. But I cannot think that this is likely to be the effect of their teaching on the general mind. I cannot think that the cultivating of a peculiar sensitiveness of conscience on this one point, over and above what results from the general cultivation of the moral sentiments, is permanently consistent with assigning in our own minds to the fact of death no more than the degree of relative importance which belongs to it among the other incidents of our humanity. The men of old cared too little about death, and gave their own lives or took those of others [a]with equal recklessness. Our danger is of the opposite kind, lest we should be so much shocked by death, in general and in the abstract, as to care too much about it in individual cases, both those of other people and our own, which call for its being risked[a]. And I am not putting things at the worst, for it is proved by the experience of other countries that horror of the executioner by no means necessarily implies horror of the assassin. The stronghold, as we all know, of hired assassination in the eighteenth century was Italy; yet it is said that in some of the Italian populations the infliction of death by sentence of law was in the highest degree offensive and revolting to popular feeling. Much has been said of the sanctity of human life, and the absurdity of supposing that we can teach respect for life by ourselves destroying it. But I am surprised at the employment of this argument, for it is one which might be brought against any punishment whatever. It is not human life only, not human life as such, that ought to be sacred to us, but human feelings. The human capacity of suffering is what we should cause to be respected, not the mere capacity of existing. And we may imagine somebody asking how we can teach people not to inflict suffering by ourselves inflicting it? But to this I should answer—all of us would answer—that to deter by suffering from inflicting suffering is not only possible, but the very purpose of penal justice. Does fining a criminal show want of respect for property, or imprisoning him, for personal freedom? Just as unreasonable is it to think that to take the life of a man who has taken that of another is to show want of regard for human life. We show, on the contrary, most emphatically our regard for it, by the adoption of a rule that he who violates that right in another forfeits it for himself, and that while no other crime that he can commit deprives him of his right to live,

[7]Virgil, *Aeneid*, Vol. II, p. 342 (XII, 646).

[a-a]TT without adequate reason; but, on the other hand, many persons of the present day appeared likely to fall into the other extreme, and be ready to deprive the law of its last punishment

this shall. There is one argument against capital punishment, even in extreme cases, which I cannot deny to have weight—on which my honourable Friend justly laid great stress, and which never can be entirely got rid of. It is this—that if by an error of justice an innocent person is put to death, the mistake can never be corrected; all compensation, all reparation for the wrong is impossible. This would be indeed a serious objection if these miserable mistakes—among the most tragical occurrences in the whole round of human affairs—could not be made extremely rare. The argument is invincible where the mode of criminal procedure is dangerous to the innocent, or where the Courts of Justice are not trusted. And this probably is the reason why the objection to an irreparable punishment began (as I believe it did) earlier, and is more intense and more widely diffused, in some parts of the Continent of Europe than it is here. There are on the Continent great and enlightened countries, in which the criminal procedure is not so favourable to innocence, does not afford the same security against erroneous conviction, as it does among us; countries where the Courts of Justice seem to think they fail in their duty unless they find somebody guilty; and in their really laudable desire to hunt guilt from its hiding-places, expose themselves to a serious danger of condemning the innocent. If our own procedure and Courts of Justice afforded ground for similar apprehension, I should be the first to join in withdrawing the power of inflicting irreparable punishment from such tribunals. But we all know that the defects of our procedure are the very opposite. Our rules of evidence are even too favourable to the prisoner: and juries and Judges carry out the maxim, "It is better that ten guilty should escape than that one innocent person should suffer,"[8] not only to the letter, but beyond the letter. Judges are most anxious to point out, and juries to allow for, the barest possibility of the prisoner's innocence. No human judgment is infallible: such sad cases as my honourable Friend cited will sometimes occur;[9] but in so grave a case as that of murder, the accused, in our system, has always the benefit of the merest shadow of a doubt. And this suggests another consideration very germane to the question. The very fact that death punishment is more shocking than any other to the imagination, necessarily renders the Courts of Justice more scrupulous in requiring the fullest evidence of guilt. Even that which is the greatest objection to capital punishment, the impossibility of correcting an error once committed, must make, and does make, juries and Judges more careful in forming their opinion, and more jealous in their scrutiny of the evidence. If the substitution of penal servitude for death in cases of murder should cause any relaxation in this conscientious scrupulosity, there would be a great evil to set against the real, but I hope rare, advantage of being able to make reparation to a condemned person who was afterwards discovered to be

[8]William Blackstone (1723–80), *Commentaries on the Laws of England*, 4 vols. (Oxford: Clarendon Press, 1765–69), Vol. IV, p. 352.

[9]Gilpin, cols. 1037–9.

innocent. In order that the possibility of correction may be kept open wherever the chance of this sad contingency is more than infinitesimal, it is quite right that the Judge should recommend to the Crown a commutation of the sentence, not solely when the proof of guilt is open to the smallest suspicion, but whenever there remains anything unexplained and mysterious in the case, raising a desire for more light, or making it likely that further information may at some future time be obtained. I would also suggest that whenever the sentence is commuted the grounds of the commutation should, in some authentic form, be made known to the public. (*Hear, hear.*) Thus much I willingly concede to my honourable Friend; but on the question of total abolition I am inclined to hope that the feeling of the country is not with him (*hear, hear*), and that the limitation of death punishment to the cases referred to in the Bill of last year will be generally considered sufficient.[10] The mania which existed a short time ago for paring down all our punishments seems to have reached its limits, and not before it was time. (*Hear, hear.*) We were in danger of being left without any effectual punishment, except for small offences. What was formerly our chief secondary punishment—transportation—before it was abolished,[11] had become almost a reward. Penal servitude, the substitute for it, was becoming, to the classes who were principally subject to it, almost nominal, so comfortable did we make our prisons, and so easy had it become to get quickly out of them. Flogging—a most objectionable punishment in ordinary cases, but a particularly appropriate one for crimes of brutality, especially crimes against women (*cheers*)—we would not hear of, except, to be sure, in the case of garotters, for whose peculiar benefit we re-established it in a hurry, immediately after a Member of Parliament had been garotted.[12] (*Hear, and laughter.*) With this exception, offences, even of an atrocious kind, against the person, as my honourable and learned Friend the Member for Oxford (*Mr. Neate*) well remarked, not only were, but still are, visited with penalties so ludicrously inadequate, as to be almost an encouragement to the crime.[13] I think, Sir, that in the case of most offences, except those against property, there is more need of strengthening our punishments than of weakening them: and that severer sentences, with an apportionment of them to the different kinds of offences which shall approve itself better than at present to the moral sentiments of the community, are the kind of reform of which our penal system now stands in need. I shall therefore vote against the Amendment.

[*The amendment was defeated.*]

[10]"A Bill to Provide for the Carrying into Effect Capital Punishments within Prisons," 30 Victoria (14 Feb., 1867), *PP*, 1867, I, 521–4 (not enacted).

[11]By 16 & 17 Victoria, c. 99 (1853).

[12]Flogging for garotters, abolished by 24 & 25 Victoria, c. 100 (1861), Sect. 43, had been reinstituted by 26 & 27 Victoria, c. 44 (1863), Sect. 1, consequent upon the non-fatal garotting of James Pilkington (1804–90), M.P. for Blackburn, in London on 16 July, 1862 (see *The Times*, 18 July, p. 5).

[13]Cf. Neate, col. 1047.

93. The Municipal Corporations (Metropolis) Bill [1]

5 MAY, 1868

PD, 3rd ser., Vol. 191, cols. 1859–63. Reported in *The Times*, 6 May, p. 10, from which the variants and responses are taken. Mill spoke in moving for leave to introduce both "A Bill for the Creation of a Corporation of London," 31 Victoria (7 May, 1868), *PP*, 1867–68, I, 347–96, and "A Bill to Provide for the Establishment of Municipal Corporations within the Metropolis," *ibid.*, III, 515–36.

MR. J. STUART MILL OBSERVED THAT both were substantially the same as those which the House permitted him last year to lay on the table.[1] The alterations were extremely slight. He was quite aware that no private Member could expect to carry through such measures. In order that they might succeed Government must take them up; but the Government had not shown any disposition to take up the subject, and in the present year, considering all the circumstances of the case, he could not blame them. No Government was likely to embarrass itself with such a subject until much discussion had taken place, and public opinion had been called forth to give them a sufficient degree of support. The introduction of the Bills had already produced considerable effect. This was shown by the number of petitions, which were almost all in favour of the Bills.[2] The opposition to the Bills had chiefly proceeded from persons connected with the present local administrative bodies, who were not likely to be wholly unprejudiced on the subject of their own mode of administration. The passing of the Reform Bill last Session had paved the way for such legislation.[3] One marked feature of the political movement, of which the passing of the Reform Act was a part, is a demand on the part of the people, he would not say for more government, but for more administration. It is not only sanitary measures, properly so called, but control over the dwellings provided for the working classes, [a]arrangement of the streets in such a way as would promote the comfort, convenience, and health of the community,[a] and a hundred similar arrangements, which are now required at the hands of Government; and the effecting of these things has been again and again prevented by the want of any sufficient local authority. When much has to be done for society, it cannot be all done by the central Government, and there was in this country great jealousy of intrusting too much to that authority. It was a national principle that a great part of our administration should be local, and the constitutional mode of giving local government to different parts of the country, especially to towns, was by means of

[1]See Nos. 56 and 82.

[2]Mill himself brought a large number of petitions before the House on that day (see *The Times*, 6 May, p. 8), having brought in others on 23 and 24 April (see App. C).

[3]Enacted on 15 August, 1867, as 30 & 31 Victoria, c. 102.

[a-a]+TT

municipalities. Now, London had only the benefit of a municipality in that which was originally the whole of its extent—the City proper. With that exception the local government of the metropolis was a parish government. What other town in the kingdom would be satisfied with a parish administration extending over the greater portion of its area? (*Hear, hear.*) The government of London by means of vestries had endured long enough. To show the magnitude of the questions which were involved in the local administration of the metropolis, he might mention that in the year 1840 London was rated upon an annual value of £6,000,000 sterling. In 1861 the annual value of property had risen to £12,500,000, and in 1866 to nearly £14,500,000. The expenditure of the metropolis was growing, and now amounted to nearly £3,000,000 a year. The Metropolitan Board had during the twelve years of its existence raised by rates [b]£2,182,000[b], and by loans £5,581,000. The vestries collectively expended £2,784,000 per annum, while to show the quantity of legislation required to deal with local questions arising within the metropolis, Lord Brougham, so long ago as 1837, stated that the Acts relating to the parish of Marylebone alone, passed since the year 1795, filled a volume of 480 pages,[4] being much greater in size, he would not say than the *Code Napoleon*, but certainly than the *Code Civil*.[5] Parliament had attempted, and did attempt, to provide for this local legislation; but Parliament could not possibly do it, and it only continued the attempt because there were no local authorities in whom Parliament or the country sufficiently confided to turn over to them this important business. What had occurred with reference to the Dwellings of Artizans and Labourers Bill, introduced by his honourable Friend the Member for Finsbury (*Mr. M'Cullagh Torrens*) was an illustration of the want of some more satisfactory authorities than at present existed in the metropolis. As originally introduced, the [c]duty it imposed of providing that such of these habitations as were not fit for human habitations should be removed and others substituted for them was[c] entrusted to the vestries; but the Select Committee would not trust the vestries, and gave the powers to the Metropolitan Board of Works.[6] The Metropolitan Board itself was, however, regarded with great distrust; and he had received many letters urging him to oppose that part of the measure which empowered that Board to levy any rates in addition to those which they were already authorized to raise. If there were municipalities in the different metropolitan boroughs, with a general central

[4]Henry Peter, Lord Brougham (1778–1868), Speech on the Business of Parliament (5 June, 1837), *PD*, 3rd ser., Vol. 38, col. 1176.

[5]The Code civil des Français (Paris: Imprimerie de la république, 1804) was incorporated into the even larger Code Napoléon (3 Sept., 1807), *Bulletin des lois de l'empire français*, 4th ser., Numéros bis.

[6]The provision in Sect. 4 of "A Bill to Provide Better Dwellings for Artizans and Labourers," 29 Victoria (20 Feb., 1866), *PP*, 1866, I, 43–52, was removed in the version amended by the Select Committee (see its First Schedule, Table A), *ibid.*, pp. 53–72.

[b-b]TT £2,180,000

[c-c]TT] PD powers conferred by that Bill were

municipality, there would be authorities upon whom Parliament could confer the many powers of local administration and local regulation which at present it was necessary to provide for by separate Acts. The difference between London and other cities, arising mainly from the great size of the metropolis, was, that while for provincial cities a single corporation sufficed, in London it was necessary to have a double system. There would in London be too much for a single body to do; and any single body which was so constituted as to be able to do the work, would be so powerful that it would excite the jealousy of the other civil authorities of the country. What was proposed by the Bill which he had been requested to introduce, but of which he was not the author, although he approved of all its provisions, was, that there should be for all the Parliamentary boroughs of which the metropolis was composed, separate municipalities grouped round the City municipality, which would be the type of all; that these municipalities should discharge all such duties as did not require that the whole of London should be taken into consideration at once; and that in addition there should be a central municipality, which should deal with those questions in the decision of which the interests and wants of the whole metropolis were involved. The first of these proposals was strongly recommended by the Commission which was presided over by the late Sir George Lewis.[7] But there was also a necessity for a general municipal government of the metropolis, and this necessity was so strongly felt that, without intending to create a municipality, Parliament had created one in the Metropolitan Board of Works.[8] The purpose for which that Board had been called into existence—namely, the Main Drainage—was now nearly completed. But the necessity for a general government was such that, almost as soon as the Board was created, other new and important duties began to be intrusted to it. But when Parliament was creating this body, was it aware that it was establishing a municipal body for the whole of London? Did it take that large subject into consideration, and examine whether this was the best way of providing for the municipal government of a great capital? Certainly not. The Board was created for a limited and temporary purpose, and it had gradually become a central municipality, without due consideration whether it had been constituted in the way best calculated to perform the duties of such. He did not propose to supersede this body, but to leave it standing, and also to leave standing the Corporation of the City of London; but to make such changes in its constitution as would render it an adequate municipal constitution for the whole metropolis. The first Bill proposed to give municipal institutions to the different Parliamentary boroughs in London; and the second, to create a central body into which the Board of Works would be absorbed: to constitute this central body in such a way as Parliament might think best, and to define its duties and powers,

[7]"Report of the Commissioners Appointed to Inquire into the Existing State of the Corporation of the City of London," *PP*, 1854, XXVI, 35. The Commission was presided over by George Cornewall Lewis (1806–63), author and politician.

[8]By Sect. 31 of 18 & 19 Victoria, c. 120 (1855).

marking them off from those of the municipal bodies. He would conclude with a saying of Lord Coke—that no good measure of legislation was ever proposed from which, in the end, some amount of good did not result.[9] Though in the present Session he could not hope to carry the Bills, and though great modifications might be made in them before they were carried, still he was doing that from which, according to Lord Coke's maxim, good must eventually result. (*Hear, hear.*) The honourable Gentleman moved for leave to introduce the first Bill.

[*The Government indicated that it would not oppose the introduction of the Bill. Sir George Bowyer pointed to a major difficulty, the reconciliation of the powers of the Corporation of the City of London with those of the Metropolitan Board of Works. He opposed the abolition of the municipality of the City of London, the Lord Mayor and the Corporation being "the only representative body" existing that could "do the public honours on great occasions."*]

[d]*Leave was given.*

Mr. Mill, in moving for leave to introduce a Bill for the creation of a Corporation of London, said that on the second reading he would be prepared to meet the objections which had been taken to the measure by the honourable baronet.

Leave was given.[d]

94. The Established Church in Ireland

7 MAY, 1868

PD, 3rd ser., Vol. 191, cols. 1928–9. Reported in *The Times*, 8 May, p. 7, from which the response is taken. In Committee to discuss the Acts pertaining to the Established Church in Ireland, the House was considering a Resolution by Roger Sinclair Aytoun (b. 1823), M.P. for Kirkcaldy, that would have discontinued the Maynooth Grant and the Regium Donum if and when the Church was disestablished in Ireland, and would also have precluded the expenditure of any of the secularized funds thus obtained from being used for the Roman Catholic religion or Roman Catholic schools (cols. 1902–5). There being some question in the mind of the Chairman, John George Dodson (1825-97), about the jurisdiction of the House over the last matter (col. 1924), an amendment to delete it was proposed, whereupon Aytoun offered to alter his own resolution to make the last provision apply to any religious bodies and any denominational schools. It was ruled that he could not do so, as there was already an amendment on the floor. The vote referred to by Mill was on a motion to let the original wording stand; it failed. Just before Mill, Charles Newdigate Newdegate (1816–87), M.P. for North Warwickshire, said that by leaving out half of Aytoun's resolution, they reserved a power of spending every shilling obtained by disendowment for Catholic purposes (col. 1928).

[9]This comment by Edward Coke (1552–1634), parliamentarian, judge, and legal authority, has not been located.

[d-d]+TT

THE HONOURABLE MEMBER for North Warwickshire (*Mr. Newdegate*) has stated that we, who sit on this side of the House, have by the vote we have just given, declared that we intend to retain the power of bestowing the whole or part of the property taken from the Irish Church upon the Roman Catholic body. For myself, and I know for a great portion of those who surround me, I utterly deny that statement. (*Cheers.*) I will resist to the utmost of my power any proposal for giving one farthing of the property to the Roman Catholic or to any other religious body in any shape whatever. I had no motive whatever in voting against the Motion of the honourable Member for Kirkcaldy (*Mr. Aytoun*), except that it had been declared by you, Sir, not properly to come within the spirit of the Reference to the Committee; and also because it had been declared to be contrary to the Orders of the House—very strangely, I think—for the honourable Gentleman to alter his Resolution from a form in which I could not vote for it, to one in which I could have done so.

[*Eventually, after further refinement, the amendment to delete the resolution was accepted.*]

95. Local Charges on Real Property

12 MAY, 1868

PD, 3rd ser., Vol. 192, cols. 152–4. Reported in *The Times*, 13 May, p. 7, from which the variant is taken. The debate, in Committee, was on a resolution by Lopes Massey Lopes (1818–1908), M.P. for Westbury: "That, inasmuch as the Local Charges on Real Property have of late years much increased and are annually increasing, it is neither just nor politic that all these burdens should be levied exclusively from this description of property" (col. 145).

MR. J. STUART MILL SAID, the honourable Baronet who had introduced the Motion (*Sir Massey Lopes*) had rendered a real service to the House and the country, for no one who had considered the subject could doubt that it required a much more systematic and deliberate consideration than it had yet received, not only on account of its great importance and the amount of taxation it involved, but because its importance was constantly increasing. In the natural progress of things more and more duties were continually being imposed on the Government, which duties would be almost always best performed by the localities, and at the same time, as the taxation of localities must constantly increase in order to meet increasing expenses, if there was any injustice in this taxation it must be an increasing injustice. The honourable Baronet, and those who took his view, thought that the local taxation was entirely borne by real property; but he (*Mr. Stuart Mill*) conceived that although real property bore an extra proportion of that taxation, it by no means bore the whole. The local charges consisted of two parts, one of which was proportional to the rent of land, and was therefore equivalent to a tax on land, the other was proportional to the rent of houses, and equivalent to a house tax. Now, a house tax did not fall on the owner, but on the occupier, and within moderate bounds was one of the fairest of all possible taxes, and one of those that came nearest to a perfectly fair income tax. Indeed, the house rent a person was able to pay was probably a better measure of what he could afford to spend, than could be afforded by the mere numerical amount in pounds sterling of his income. So far as the house tax fell on the ground rent it was a charge on property; but the ground rent bore only a small proportion to the whole rent of a house, except in cases of peculiar eligibility of situation, which favourable situations were a kind of wealth having a constant tendency to increase without any labour or outlay on the part of the owner, and therefore a fair subject for some degree of special taxation. He admitted that in most of the rural districts the burden was mainly on the rent of land; but he did not think the grievance so great as had been represented, because the prescriptive, and what might almost be called the constitutional mode of levying local taxation was to levy it on rental, and property had generally been acquired by inheritance or purchase, subject to that peculiar burden. If the burdens on land had a tendency to increase by the progress of [a]population, wealth, and civilization[a], so had the income from land, and income derived from real property was nearly the only one which increased by the effects of the industry, outlay, privation, and frugality of other persons than the owners; and inasmuch as the value of land did constantly increase from generation to generation, and the income from it increased independently of exertion or outlay on the part of the owners, this made it fair to regard it as in some degree a proper subject for increasing taxation. No one could doubt that the time had come when the whole subject of local taxation must be more fully considered. If they considered that portion of taxation which he thought fair in principle—namely, the house tax—they would find that this had become so heavy in many localities that the difficulty of increasing it had become a serious obstacle to any new outlay for general improvements. How it was possible to raise the additional sums that might be required in a manner less burdensome, because more equal and just, would have to be more and more seriously considered, and the different modes by which this could be accomplished would have to be well meditated. One mode, which had been partially adopted in this country, deserved consideration as one of the possible modes—namely, that of placing a certain proportion of some of these burdens on the general taxation of the country; for when this was done in the way of a fixed proportion it did not destroy, although it might weaken, those motives to economical legislation which so strongly recommended making these expenses local rather than general. There were great difficulties in adjusting the amounts of

[a-a]TT] PD society

taxation on the various descriptions of property, and these questions would probably occupy their minds for a long time to come. He was glad that the honourable Baronet had introduced this subject to the House, and no doubt it would be seriously considered by the new Parliament. In the excellent speech of the honourable Member for Edinburgh (*Mr. M'Laren*) there was one principle which, if adopted, would involve an injustice—it was that of taxing terminable incomes, he did not mean at a lower rate than permanent ones, for that he entirely approved of, but of taxing them only according to their capitalized value.[1] That would be a great injustice; but this was not the time for further discussing that principle.

[*The motion was withdrawn (col. 161).*]

96. Election Petitions and Corrupt Practices at Elections [3]

21 MAY, 1868

PD, 3rd ser., Vol. 192, cols. 685–6, 691. Reported in *The Times*, 22 May, p. 8, from which the variants and response are taken. Mill was moving an amendment to Clause 5 of the Bill (see No. 89). He proposed to add "or of general or extensive prevalence of corrupt practices in an Election" after the words "to serve in Parliament" in the preamble to the Clause: "From and after the next Dissolution of Parliament a petition complaining of an undue Return or undue Election of a Member to serve in Parliament for a County or Borough may be presented to the Court of Common Pleas by any one or more of the following persons. . . ." After some discussion of the general question of corruption, Mill's second speech closed the debate. For William Dougal Christie's involvement in Mill's tactics, see *CW*, Vol. XVI, pp. 1381, 1397–1400, 1403 (a specific reference to the fate of this amendment), 1403–4, 1421, and 1425.

MR. J. STUART MILL SAID, he had to move an Amendment to the clause, which was the first of a series of Amendments, of which he had given Notice.[1] The Bill, as it stood, was very incomplete; but, at the same time, he thought it, in the main, very creditable to the Government; and therefore he was glad that this Bill was not to be part of the baggage to be thrown overboard, for the purpose of lightening the ship on its last voyage. Incomplete as it was, the Bill was a bold attempt to grapple with an acknowledged political and moral evil; and the Government had not feared to ask the House to do what it greatly disliked—to make a sacrifice of its own jurisdiction. He now asked the Prime Minister to complete his own work—to help

[1]Duncan McLaren (1800–86), M.P. for Edinburgh, col. 147.

[1]The proposed amendments are in *Notices of Motion, and Orders of the Day* for 7, 11, and 19 May, pp. 733, 739–40, 754–5, 759–60, and 882–4.

those who were trying to help him, and lend the aid of his ingenious and contriving mind, and the able legal assistance with which he was provided, to make this really an efficacious and complete measure. It was no party measure, and no party were interested in passing it, except the party of honesty. They desired to diminish the number of men in this House, who came in, not for the purpose of maintaining any political opinions whatever, but solely for the purpose, by a lavish expenditure, of acquiring the social position which attended a seat in this House, and which, perhaps, was not otherwise to be attained by them. They were not more attached to one side than to the other, except that they were generally to be found on the gaining side. They were the political counterparts of those who were contemptuously described by Dante as "neither for God nor the enemies of God, but for themselves only."[2] Unfortunately, it was not possible in this case to follow the poet's advice, "Speak not of them, but look and pass on!"[3] [a]They were men whom the House must endeavour to keep out from among them. (*Hear.*)[a] The Bill proceeded on the theory that the law was to be put in motion by the defeated candidate alone. This was contrary to the very idea of criminal law [b], and he wished to supply the deficiency[b]. When the law intended to confer a pardoning power on an individual, it did not grant a criminal process at all, but only an action for damages. The immediate object of the present Amendment was the following: the Bill, if passed, would repeal the 5 & 6 Victoria, c. 102;[4] but Section 4 of that Act contained an important provision—namely, that where a Petition complained of general or extensive bribery, and the Committee reported that there was reasonable and probable ground for the allegations, the Committee should have power to order that the costs of the petitioners should be borne by the public. If the House was in earnest such a provision was indispensable; and he therefore intended to propose Amendments, the effect of which would be to restore it in the present Bill.

Mr. J. Stuart Mill said, his object was that an inquiry into general corrupt practices should be instituted with the same promptitude and before the same tribunal as the inquiry concerning a claim to the seats. He did not mean, however, as the Solicitor General seemed to infer, that the sitting Member should be at the expense of eliciting such a general inquiry.[5] That matter was provided for in his subsequent Amendments.

[*The amendment was defeated (col. 691).*]

[2]Dante Alighieri, *Inferno*, Canto III, ll. 37–9; cf. the prose translation by John A. Carlyle, *Dante's Divine Comedy: The Inferno* (Italian and English) (London: Chapman and Hall, 1849), p. 28.

[3]*Ibid.*, Canto III, l. 51 (p. 29).

[4]Of 1842.

[5]Brett, col. 690.

[a-a]+TT

[b-b]+TT

97. Representation of the People (Scotland) [1]

28 MAY, 1868

PD, 3rd ser., Vol. 192, cols. 965–6, 979. Reported in *The Times*, 29 May, p. 7, from which the responses are taken. The House was in Committee on "A Bill for the Amendment of the Representation of the People in Scotland," 31 Victoria (17 Feb., 1868), *PP*, 1867–68, IV, 583–616. During consideration of Clause 9 (as earlier amended), "the City of Glasgow, until otherwise directed by Parliament, shall comprise the Places mentioned in Schedule (A.) hereto annexed" (i.e., the city of Glasgow and the towns of Govan and Partick), giving three members to the combined constituency, William Graham (1817–85), M.P. for Glasgow, moved to insert after Glasgow, "shall be divided into three districts, each of which shall return one Member of Parliament" (col. 959).

MR. J. STUART MILL SAID, the honourable Member for Nottingham (*Mr. Osborne*) had called on Gentlemen on that side to support the Motion of the honourable Member for Glasgow (*Mr. Graham*), holding out to them the inducement of getting rid of the principle of the representation of minorities.[1] That was the strongest possible reason why those who were in favour of the representation of minorities—not as being a Conservative measure, but as a measure of justice (*hear*)—should vote against the present Motion. Nothing could be more unfair than to speak of the representation of those persons who happen to be in a minority, whatever might be their political opinions, in any constituency, as being in any exclusive sense a Conservative principle. On the contrary, it was not only the most democratic of all principles, but it was the only true democratic principle of representation, and they could not have a complete system of representation without it. (*Hear, hear, and a laugh.*) Man for man, those who happened to be in a minority had just as much claim to be represented as the majority.

[*The amendment was lost, Mill voting with the majority. After some further discussion, a motion was made to replace from after "comprise the" to the end of the clause with "existing Parliamentary boundaries." Mill spoke on this amendment.*]

Mr. J. Stuart Mill said, Glasgow having grown to so great an extent, it was not unreasonable that its boundaries should be revised and extended, provided its representation were extended also. He apprehended that its fair proportion of Members, in reference to its population and wealth, would be not less than six. (*Oh!*) The arguments of the Government would be extremely good then; but as the vast population of Glasgow was represented by an inadequate number of Members, he could not admit that in order to admit an additional number of persons to share in that inadequate representation, a large proportion of them should be deprived of their county vote, which was really valuable to them.

[1]Ralph Bernal Osborne (1811–82), col. 964.

[*Finally the Chairman, breaking a tie, voted to leave the Clause unamended, so allowing further discussion on another occasion (col. 981).*]

98. Representation of the People (Scotland) [2]

8 JUNE, 1868

PD, 3rd ser., Vol. 192, cols. 1241, 1242, 1243, 1252. Reported in *The Times*, 9 June, p. 7, from which the variant is taken. In Committee on the Reform Bill for Scotland (see No. 97), consideration turned to Clause O (Clause S in the Bill as amended), into which Mill moved the addition of the italicized words: "All the Provisions of an Act passed in the 24th and 25th Years of the Reign of Her present Majesty, intituled 'An Act to provide that Votes at Elections for the Universities may be recorded by means of Voting Papers,' *except so much of the said Act as requires that the voting paper shall be personally delivered by a Member of Council who shall make attestation of his personal acquaintance with the voter, and his knowledge of the signature,* shall apply to every Election of a Member for the Universities of Edinburgh and Saint Andrews, and for the Universities of Glasgow and Aberdeen. . . ." His remarks followed immediately after his motion.

IF THE TERMS of the English Act upon this point were adopted in the Scotch Reform Bill, half, if not more than half, of those who formed the University constituency would be disfranchised. There was always a large number of residents at the English Universities who could authenticate the signatures to the voting papers; but in the Scotch Universities undergraduates did not form such intimate acquaintance with each other as in this country, and in most instances towards the end of the year they were scattered all over the British Empire. The voters would be virtually confined to a small number of residents, unless some such alteration as he proposed were made.

[*The Lord Advocate, Edward Strathearn Gordon (1814–79), then M.P. for Thetford, in replying, said that while he was willing to give up the requirement of personal acquaintance, he thought voting papers should be personally delivered and attested by a Member of Council (col. 1241).*]

Mr. J. Stuart Mill asked, whether the delivery of the voting paper by a Member of Council would not involve a considerable additional expense?

[*Several Members pointed to the dangers of fraud if there were no means of attestation.*]

Mr. J. Stuart Mill said, that many operations took place on the same security—namely, that if persons committed frauds they would be prosecuted.

[*Mill then withdrew his amendment, and the following words, as suggested by the Lord Advocate, were inserted in the same place: "except so much of the said*

Act as requires that the person delivering the voting paper shall make attestation of his personal acquaintance with the voter" (col. 1242), and the Clause was accepted. After other discussion, attention moved to Schedule A, concerning the boundaries of the city of Glasgow, and James Fergusson (1832–1907), M.P. for Ayrshire, asserted that the working people of Partick and Govan were eager to be annexed to Glasgow (col. 1252); other speakers denied this assertion.]

Mr. J. Stuart Mill said, that if this argument was correct the suburbs of Glasgow ought to have a representative to themselves. But because they did not choose to give to the population of these considerable places a representative in this House, to which they were justly entitled, were they to deprive those who were county electors of a vote which they valued [a]and be merged in a large constituency[a] in order to give to others a vote which would scarcely be of any value?

[*Eventually Schedule A was defeated, so that the constituency of Glasgow was not enlarged to include Partick and Govan.*]

99. Married Women's Property

10 JUNE, 1868

Speeches of Mr. Jacob Bright, M.P., Mr. Robert Lowe, M.P., Mr. J.S. Mill, M.P., and Mr. G. Shaw Lefevre, M.P., in the Debate on the Second Reading of "The Bill to Amend the Law with Respect to the Property of Married Women" (Manchester: Ireland, 1868), pp. 9–11. Based on *PD*, 3rd ser., Vol. 192, cols. 1370–2. Reported in *The Times*, 11 June, p. 6, from which the responses are taken. Mill presented petitions in favour of the Bill (31 Victoria [21 Apr., 1868], *PP*, 1867–68, III, 375–8) on 9 and 10 June. On the day he spoke, Mill wrote to a correspondent (possibly Isabella Tod, of Belfast) to say that the Bill had passed its second reading, "(after an interesting debate of which all the honours were on our side) by the casting vote of the Speaker, and is to be referred to a Select Committee" (*CW*, Vol. XVI, p. 1413).

[a]PERHAPS, SIR, those[a] who, like myself, [b]think that women can never hope that the laws and customs of society will do them full justice unless they are admitted to participate in political rights, ought, perhaps, to wish that the House would reject[b] this Bill, because [c]it is quite certain that[c] its rejection would give a most extraordinary impulse to the movement, which has lately made so much progress, for giving the suffrage to women. (*Hear, hear.*) I wish, however, that my sex

[a-a]+TT

[a-a]PD] P Those
[b-b]PD support the extension of political rights to women, should desire the rejection of
[c-c]+PD

should have the credit of giving up unjust [d]and impolitic privileges before they are brought under the influence of other motives than their own good feelings[d]. The debate has produced many gratifying expressions of opinion—the able and persuasive speech of my honourable friend the member for Manchester for example, and the logical and high-principled address of my right honourable friend the member for Calne.[1] (*Hear, hear.*) The honourable and learned member for Colchester[2] [e]has very truly said that his honourable friend the member for Reading[3] is not the author of the Bill, but has adopted it from others, who, he seems to think, must be persons strongly prejudiced against the existing institutions of society[e]. I regret that the learned gentleman has left the House, as I could have told him who some of those persons were. I do not think the learned gentleman can have been aware that among [f]the persons whom he was condemning[f] were those eminent socialists and revolutionists the present Secretaries of State for Foreign Affairs and for War.[4] The noble lord (*Lord Stanley*), along with that eminent judge Sir Lawrence Peel,[5] was a member of the committee of the Social Science Association which drew up the Bill, similar to this, formerly introduced by Sir Erskine Perry;[6] and the right honourable baronet (*Sir J.S. Pakington*) took the chair at a public meeting for the same purpose.[7] The learned gentleman is aware that [g]he has against him the right honourable Recorder of London,[8] but attributes his absence to not being hearty in the cause. I wonder the learned gentleman does not know that the recorder is prevented from being present

[1]Jacob Bright, cols. 1360–4, and Robert Lowe, cols. 1364–7.

[2]Edward Kent Karslake (1820–92), cols. 1355–8.

[3]Shaw-Lefevre, who had introduced the Bill, and later (cols. 1373–6) spoke to it.

[4]Stanley and Pakington.

[5]Lawrence Peel (1799–1884) had been Chief Justice of Calcutta (1842–55) and a Director of the East India Company (from 1857) when Mill was Chief Examiner.

[6]Thomas Erskine Perry (1806–82), then M.P. for Devonport, Speech on the Married Women's Property Bill (14 May, 1857), *PD*, 3rd ser., Vol. 145, cols. 266–74, introducing "A Bill to Amend the Law with Respect to the Property of Married Women," 20 Victoria (14 May, 1857), *PP*, 1857, III.ii, 243–8 (not enacted).

[7]On 31 May, 1856; see "Property of Married Women," *The Times*, 2 June, p. 5.

[8]Russell Gurney, like Mill, was a sponsor of the Bill.

[d-d]PD] P privileges voluntarily

[e-e]PD said with great truth that the real authors of the Bill are not present, and he seemed to think they must be persons in whose eyes any change in existing institutions must be an improvement

[f-f]PD] P them

[g-g]PD the right honourable Recorder of London (*Mr. Russell Gurney*) is a supporter of the Bill, because his name is on the back of it; but he seems to think that Gentleman's absence intentional, though, as a lawyer, it is strange he should not have known that the Recorder's absence is caused by his presiding in his Court. That conscientious and feeling judge was very desirous of being present, and would, from his judicial experience, have put the House in possession of the real effects of the present law, and afforded to the Attorney General and the honourable Member for Colchester some information as to the true working of that power in the Divorce Act to which allusion has been made. It is only in cases of desertion that this power comes into exercise, and that the magistrate has power to make orders of protection; but cases are continually happening,

by the discharge of his judicial duties. His feelings on the subject are very strong, and, had he been present, he would probably have given the House his experience of the manner in which the law affects the women of the humbler classes. That conscientious and feeling judge might also have given the Attorney-General[9] an insight into the working of the provisions of the Divorce Act,[10] and how unreal and nominal an amount of protection has been given by that Act to the women of the humbler class. It does, indeed, allow married women to apply to the magistrate for protection to their earnings, but only in cases of desertion. Cases are, however, constantly occurring[g] [h], some within my own knowledge,[h] in which the husband just avoids the amount of desertion which would justify the magistrate in giving protection to the wife. He stays away for a sufficient time to enable her to accumulate a small sum, and then he lives with her just long enough to squander it. As, however, the Attorney-General has expressed a willingness to extend and improve the operation of that Act,[11] I trust that he will himself introduce a Bill on the subject. (*Hear, hear.*) There has been, indeed, on the part of the Legislature a wonderful overlooking of the need of some similar protection. Even in cases where the words "to her separate use"[12] are introduced by the Court of Chancery for the wife's protection, the sole effect of the words is that the trustees cannot pay the income of the settled property except upon the wife's receipt. That is a perfect protection if the wife be living away from her husband, but if she be living with him the money immediately becomes the husband's income, and he has a right to take it from her the moment she receives it. (*Hear, hear.*) [i]A large portion of the inhabitants of this country are now in the anomalous position of having imposed on them, without their having done anything to deserve it, what we inflict as a penalty on the worst criminals. Like felons they are incapable of holding property. And the class of women who are in that position are married women, whom we profess a desire to surround with marks of honour and dignity.[i] [j]Many people seem to think it impossible that two persons can live together in harmony[j] unless one of them has absolute power over the other. This [k]may have been the case in savage times, but we are advanced beyond the savage state; and I believe it is not found that civilized men or women cannot live with their brothers or with their sisters except on such terms, or that business cannot be successfully carried on unless one partner has the

[9]John Burgess Karslake.

[10]20 & 21 Victoria, c. 85 (1857).

[11]Karslake, col. 1369.

[12]See Sect. 25 of 20 & 21 Victoria, c. 85.

[h-h]+PD

[i-i]+PD

[j-j]PD It seems to be the opinion of those who oppose the measure that it is impossible for society to exist on a harmonious footing between two persons

[k-k]PD] P might be true whilst people were savages; but civilized men are able to live with their brothers, women with their sisters, and men with their sisters, without any such absolute power, and why not men with their wives? I am quite aware that men may suffer from bad wives, as well as women from bad husbands

absolute mastery over the other. The family offers a type and a school of the relation of superiors and inferiors, exemplified in parents and children; it should also offer a type and a school of the relation of equality, exemplified in husband and wife. I am not insensible to the evils which husbands suffer from bad and unprincipled wives[k]. Happily, the [l]evils[l] of slavery [m](and I do not use the word in an invidious sense)[m] extend to the slave-master as well as to the slave. But if we were endeavouring to invent a mode of giving to the wife the strongest possible motive to strain to the utmost her claims [n]against the property of her husband, what step more effectual for this object could be taken than to enact that she should have no rights of her own, and should be entirely dependent upon what she can extract from the husband?[n] It is only by doing justice to women that we can hope to give them any moral feeling against encroaching on the rights of others. [o]It is by remedying the injustice that married women now suffer that real harmony is to be introduced into the married state.[o] [p]Would the honourable Member for Colchester accept for himself exclusion from all rights of property, on condition that some one else should pay his debts, and make atonement for his wrongs?[p] The Attorney-General adverted to what is certainly the weakest part of the Bill when he pointed out that, if the rights of husband and wife are to be equal, their obligations ought also to be equal, and if the Bill should go into committee it will be necessary to alter the clauses so as to establish an obligation equally on both parties.[13] The Bill will no doubt require a great deal of consideration in committee, not so much with a view to the omission of some clauses as to the addition of others. No doubt it is true that many other [q]alterations of the law will be necessary; for when the law is founded on a bad principle much re-adjustment is necessitated by the adoption of a good one. But if it should please the House to refer the Bill to a Select Committee, there are honourable and learned Gentlemen on both sides of the House quite[q] capable of proposing such [r]additions as would[r] make the Bill work smoothly. (*Hear.*)

[*The division on second reading was tied, and the Speaker voted "Aye" to allow further discussion (cols. 1376–8).*]

[13]Karslake, col. 1369.

[l-l]PD sufferings
[m-m]+P
[n-n]PD] P over her husband, it would be by giving her no rights of her own.
[o-o]+P
[p-p]+PD
[q-q]PD] P parts of the law, having been adjusted to a bad principle, will require modification, in order to accommodate them to a good one. But a select committee, comprising able lawyers, will be perfectly
[r-r]PD alterations as will

100. Registration of Publications

12 JUNE, 1868

PD, 3rd ser., Vol. 192, col. 1514. Reported in *The Times*, 13 June, p. 7, from which the variant and response are taken. During the debate on going into Committee, attention was called to the law requiring newspapers to give a deposit as security against blasphemous and seditious libels. It was pointed out by Thomas Milner Gibson (1806–84), M.P. for Ashton-under-Lyne (cols. 1512–14) that the fault lay not with the officials of the Board of Inland Revenue, but with the laws themselves.

MR. J. STUART MILL SAID, he was glad the right honourable Gentleman had endeavoured to impress upon the Government the propriety of putting an end to all the difficulties to which reference had been made, by repealing the Acts in question, which inflicted a punishment upon the whole body of the Press because some of its members might possibly be guilty of a violation of the law.[1] What would be said if every physician were bound to give security that he would not poison his patients? (*Hear, hear, and a laugh.*) Surely it was sufficient to punish him if he did poison them [a], without placing restrictions like those complained of upon the innocent[a]. His purpose in rising was to express a hope that if the Government could not bring in a measure of the kind proposed this Session, they would at least suspend all prosecutions under these Acts, which were generally condemned by public opinion, which it had been found impossible to enforce impartially, and which, therefore, operated most unjustly upon those who were prosecuted under them; often by individuals without the concurrence of the Attorney General and of the Board of Inland Revenue.

101. Representation of the People (Ireland)

15 JUNE, 1868

PD, 3rd ser., Vol. 192, col. 1592. Reported in *The Times*, 16 June, p. 7, from which the responses are taken. Mill spoke in Committee on "A Bill to Amend the Representation of the People in Ireland," 31 Victoria (19 Mar., 1868), *PP*, 1867–68, IV, 549–64. Under consideration was Clause 18: "It shall not be lawful for any Candidate, or any One on his Behalf, at any Election for any City, Town, or Borough, to pay any Money on account of

[1]See particularly 60 George III and 1 George IV, c. 9 (1819).

[a-a]+TT

the Conveyance of any Voter to the Poll, either to the Voter himself or to any other Person; and if any such Candidate, or any Person on his Behalf, shall pay any Money on account of the Conveyance of any Voter to the Poll, such Payment shall be deemed to be an illegal Payment within the Meaning of 'The Corrupt Practices Prevention Act, 1854.'" An amendment was proposed to exempt Carrickfergus, Cork, Drogheda, Galway, Kilkenny, Limerick, and Waterford, on the ground that these towns included rural districts where homes were far from the polling places. Mill spoke after some discussion of whether people would walk five miles to vote.

MR. J. STUART MILL SAID, he thought that if the House was in earnest on this subject of Parliamentary Reform in Ireland there ought to be no hesitation in dealing with the question now before the Committee. (*Hear, hear.*) If they decided upon granting the suffrage to the Irish people, they ought to give all possible facilities for the exercise of the voting power. Those facilities ought not, however, to be provided at the expense of the candidates, but of the public; and even if carriages were necessary for the conveyance of voters to the poll, these also ought to be provided at the public cost. (*Hear, hear.*) Additional polling places were provided in the English Reform Bill,[1] and if, being necessary in Ireland, they were not provided by the Legislature, what would the Irish Reform Bill be worth after all? There were numbers of places in England much larger than those in Ireland for which exemptions were now sought, and, in his opinion, exceptions ought only to be made in extreme cases.

[*After Drogheda, Kilkenny, and Waterford had been deleted from the amendment, it was accepted.*]

102. The Government of India Bill [1]

15 JUNE, 1868

PD, 3rd ser., Vol. 192, col. 1599. Reported in *The Times*, 16 June, p. 7, from which the variant is taken. Mill spoke during the second reading of "A Bill to Amend in Certain Respects the Act for the Better Government of India," 31 Victoria (23 Apr., 1868), *PP*, 1867–68, II, 479–82, following Ayrton, who suggested that twelve years was too long a term for members of the Council (col. 1598).

MR. J. STUART MILL SAID, he agreed with his honourable Friend in thinking that seven years was a sufficiently long period for the tenure of office in the case of members of the Council; but he would suggest that there should be a power of re-appointment, because, while it was desirable to bring in those whose

[1]I.e., the Reform Act, 30 & 31 Victoria, c. 102 (1867).

information was fresh, it would often be a great disadvantage to the Council to lose the services of some particular Member. [a]That condition might be satisfied by providing that, instead[a] of two members being obliged to retire every year, one of the two might be eligible for re-appointment.

[*After further brief debate, the second reading was agreed.*]

103. Lodger Registration

15 JUNE, 1868

PD, 3rd ser., Vol. 192, cols. 1611–12. Reported in *The Times*, 16 June, p. 8. Mill spoke during the second reading of "A Bill to Amend the Law of Registration so far as Relates to the Year 1868, and for Other Purposes Relating Thereto," 31 Victoria (11 June, 1868), *PP*, 1867–68, IV, 395–406. Reference had been made to the disabilities of lodgers who were not served notice of objections to their registration.

MR. J. STUART MILL SAID, he thought the point relating to lodgers a very serious one. Unless the lodger franchise was to be merely nominal, the law ought to require that notices should be served upon them when their right to vote was objected to; for otherwise, though the greater portion of them would be poor men, they would have to attend the Court from the very beginning of the revision to the end, in order to know whether they were objected to or not. Knowing this, very few of them would register at all. The obstacles in the way of the lodger were much greater than in the way of any other class, for instead of being put on the register by the overseers he had to make his own claim, and to repeat it every year. He ought not, then, to be liable to unknown objections at an unknown time.

[*After other objections had been raised, the Bill was given second reading.*]

104. Public Schools [1]

16 JUNE, 1868

PD, 3rd ser., Vol. 192, cols. 1650, 1655. Reported in *The Times*, 17 June, p. 9, from which the responses are taken. Mill spoke in Committee on the recommitted "Bill [as Amended in Committee and by the Select Committee] to Make Further Provision for the Good Government and Extension of Certain Public Schools in England," 31 Victoria (22 May, 1868), *PP*, 1867–68, IV, 317–36. His first intervention concerned Clause 2, which, *inter*

[a-a]TT] PD Instead

alia, defined "school" as including, "in the Case of Eton and Winchester, Eton College and Winchester College." On 31 March, Mill had written to Chadwick to say that, though he could not write or open a debate on the issue, he would probably speak on it (*CW*, Vol. XVI, p. 1381).

MR. J. STUART MILL SAID, he understood that the Fellows of Eton College had very little to do with the school, except to usurp to themselves the greater portion of the endowments. (*Hear, hear.*) He thought that the Head master rather than the Provost should be the head of the governing body. (*Loud cheers.*)

[*The Clause was accepted.*]

[*To Clause 3, which defined the existing "Governing Body," with particular mention of various public schools, Henry Du Pré Labouchere (1831–1912) had moved (col. 1654) to include the Head Masters in such bodies.*]

Mr. J. Stuart Mill hoped the right honourable Gentleman who had charge of the Bill[1] would take into serious consideration the Amendment of his honourable Friend the Member for Middlesex (*Mr. Labouchere*). The object which they all had in view was to improve the schools. The Provost and Head master had the most to do in the management of the schools, and as the good government of those institutions was what should be steadily aimed at, that object could not be better promoted than by including the Provost and Head master in the governing body.

[*Labouchere withdrew his amendment after assurance that the matter would be attended to.*]

105. The Municipal Corporations (Metropolis) Bill [2]

17 JUNE, 1868

PD, 3rd ser., Vol. 192, cols. 1730–5. Reported in *The Times*, 18 June, p. 6, from which the variants and responses are taken. Mill was moving the second reading of one of the Bills he had introduced on 5 May (see No. 93). As he indicates, he had been prevented from proceeding with the other, establishing a Corporation of London.

THE HOUSE IS AWARE that this Bill is only one of two which have some claim to be considered as one, inasmuch as they are parts of a combined plan for the local government of the metropolis. The most important of them, as the House is also aware, I have been unexpectedly prevented from proceeding with. It has been

[1]Spencer Walpole, then Minister without Portfolio.

decided to be a violation of the Standing Orders.[1] It appears to me a subject well worthy the consideration of the House under what circumstances this difficulty has arisen, and that I should have been unable to propose to the House a plan for the general municipal government of the metropolis because due notice has not been given to the Corporation of the City of London. The Bill is not of private, but of public interest; the Corporation is solely interested in it by reason of the property it holds for public purposes; the City of London is perfectly aware of all that is proposed, and has made no complaint of not having received notice. The promoters of the measure do not expect to make money by it, but may have a great deal to spend in carrying out its objects; and it appears to me worthy of consideration whether the forms required by the Standing Orders were ever intended for such a case as this, and whether the promoters of the Bill ought to be required to spend several hundreds of pounds out of their own pockets to give formal notice to the Corporation. Since the House did me the honour of permitting me to introduce the former measure,[2] a great change has taken place in the situation of this country as respects its institutions. [a]The great measure of last Session has been passed,[3] and our Constitution has been materially altered in a democratic direction. This new state of things imposes new duties; it requires the House, on the one hand, to do more than it was previously obliged to do; and, on the other, to consider the inconveniences, whether great or small, that may be created by the new direction in which we are proceeding, and to guard against them as far as possible.[a] It is well understood what is the special danger of democratic institutions: it is the absence of skilled administration; and I strongly recommend to the consideration of the honourable Member for Whitehaven (*Mr. Bentinck*), who I believe intends to move the rejection of the Bill,[4] that the great political problem of the future, not only for this country, but for all others, is to obtain the combination of democratic institutions with skilled administration. It is extremely desirable that this House without either idle regret for the past or vain confidence in the future should apply itself to find out how these two things may best be united. I am anxious to impress on the House the importance of reviewing our institutions in

[1]The Bill had been referred to the Examiners of Petitions for Private Bills, who passed it on to the Committee on Standing Orders, noting that it violated Standing Orders because insufficient attention had been paid to publicity of its provisions to all affected by it. The Committee then ruled that the Standing Orders should not be dispensed with, and so the Bill could not proceed. (*Journals of the House of Commons*, Vol. 123 [1867–68], pp. 158, 188, and 211.)

[2]In its earlier form; see No. 56.

[3]The Reform Act, 30 & 31 Victoria, c. 102 (1867).

[4]George Augustus Frederick Cavendish Bentinck (1821–91) spoke against the Bill after Mill's speech (cols. 1735–7).

[a-a]TT By passing the Reform Act the House had given a pledge that it would inquire into and revise all the local institutions of the country.

this particular point of view, and to induce the friends of democracy to appreciate the advantages of skilled administration, and the admirers of skilled administration to appreciate the merits of democratic institutions. As regards the general principle on which municipal institutions should be founded, the established practice with us is that all the ratepayers should have a voice in the expenditure. In the democratic direction, nothing further than this can be desired. But in the matter of skilled administration there is much to be altered. All the defects of democratic institutions are great in proportion as the area is small; and if you wish to work them well, I do not know any rule more important than that you should never have a popular representative assembly on a small area, for if you do, it will be impossible to have skilled administration. There will be much less choice of persons; a much smaller number, and those less competent for the task, will be willing to undertake the conduct of public affairs. And here I must direct attention to a principle of great importance. The value of a popular administrative body—I might say of any popular body—is measured by the value of the permanent officers. When a popular body knows what it is fit for and what it is unfit for, it will more and more understand that it is not its business to administer, but that it is its business to see that the administration is done by proper persons, and to keep them to their duties. I hope it will be more and more felt that the duty of this House is to put the right persons on that Bench opposite, and when there to keep them to their work. Even in legislative business it is the chief duty—it is most consistent with the capacity of a popular assembly to see that the business is transacted by the most competent persons; confining its own direct intervention to the enforcement of real discussion and publicity of the reasons offered *pro* and *con*; the offering of suggestions to those who do the work, and the imposition of a check upon them if they are disposed to do anything wrong. People will more value the importance of this principle the longer they have experience of it. This principle, when applied to local popular administration, shows itself in a very strong light indeed. A popular assembly that has only a little work to do in a little area, tries to do it itself, and to transact public business by making speeches—the most ineffective way in which public business can be done. In proportion as the local body approaches to the position of a great assembly like the present—though at a great distance—and has to represent a large area, and has a great deal of various work to do, in that proportion it will feel that its business is not to do the work itself; its business is to set the right people to do it, and to use for the purpose of controlling them all the lights which the collision of opinion amongst their own members may produce, but not to take the work out of the hands of the administrators. The adoption of that principle absolutely requires that the popular democratic representative bodies, such as those by which our local administration is carried on, should not be on the small scale of a local board, but should be on a larger scale—as large a scale as is consistent with unity of interest in the body whose affairs they have to administer.

The local business of the metropolis is now divided, in kind, amongst a variety of administrative bodies, and is likewise divided, in a most minute manner, geographically. The various parishes carry on their business by means of vestries and local boards, and there are duties besides, that do not belong to the vestries, which are of the most multifarious description possible. There are 37 districts for the registration of births, 56 for the purposes of the Building Act, 19 divisions for police purposes, 30 County Court districts, and 15 Militia districts.[5] There should be for the administration of all this business a consolidation of those very small districts. Among the advantages to be derived from consolidation would be greater efficiency and economy. Nothing can surprise me more than to find any petition presented against this Bill on the ground that its effects will be to raise the rates; that is not only impossible, but it must have the contrary effect, because in proportion as the present divisions approach the size they would all reach when combined under the plan I propose, economy has been effected. Compare the two districts, for example, of Marylebone and Westminster, which are about equal in population. Marylebone is all one parish under one local government, and is an approximation to the system I would establish, and its administrative expenses amount to £8,000 a year. Westminster is divided amongst five boards, and the five boards cost £20,000 a year. Probably not more than a third of the number of officers employed in Westminster is employed in Marylebone. In fact, the more an area is divided into independent districts, the more paid officers there must be, and the less skilled they will be. The small districts cannot afford to pay for the greatest skill, and the smallness of the districts prevents the officers from acquiring it. Add to this the expense now arising from quarrels and litigation, which, of course, would not exist if these boards were fused into one. I find that no less than 4,000 persons are engaged, in some capacity or other, in the local government of the metropolis. I cannot help asking, would any person now think of establishing the present system of administration in the metropolis if it did not already exist? Would it exist at all except for the accidental growing up of arrangements that have never been reviewed? In a great metropolis, who cares about his parish, except for its church? and, as we are going to get rid of church rates, the parish will have no common interest at all in future. If we are to have a body that can do the work well, the first condition must be unlimited publicity—publicity which must not be theoretic, but real. It is not only that the people should have a right to know what is done; but that they should really and actually know what is being done. You must get them to give their attention to it; and that is not accomplished on the present system, because the area of administration being on so small a scale, the public

[5]For statutes bearing on these matters, see, respectively, 6 & 7 William IV, c. 86 (1836) (registration); 18 & 19 Victoria, c. 122 (1855) (building); 10 George IV, c. 44 (1829) (police; the divisions were an administrative responsibility); 9 & 10 Victoria, c. 95 (1846) (county courts); and 15 Victoria, c. 50 (1852) (militia).

does not take sufficient interest in the subject to inquire into what is being done. [b]No one troubles himself either to be a candidate for a seat in the vestry or to read the debates. But, while the ratepayers will not look after their own interests, the power of those who take a part in parish affairs from private and interested motives is increased, because they have an opportunity of promoting their ends by unseen modes.[b] Except in a large parish, no light is thrown on what is going on. I am far from undervaluing what the local institutions, imperfect as they are, have done; but they are doing much less every day, as the conditions on which they were established become less adapted to existing circumstances. It is very generally believed that it is an extremely frequent thing for persons who sit in vestries of the metropolis to be landlords of small tenements utterly unfit for human habitations (*hear, hear*), men whose interest—I do not say they always yield to that interest—is not to promote those sanitary arrangements for the improvement of the dwelling places of the great mass of the community which it should be our object to promote. (*Hear.*) In the Bill of my honourable Friend the Member for Finsbury (*Mr. M'Cullagh Torrens*)—the Labourers' and Artizans' Dwellings Bill—it was desired to give greater powers in dealing with that class of property,[6] but no authority could be found that was deemed fit to exercise those powers. [c]The Bill proposed to give powers to the vestries, but this was struck out in Committee, on the ground that they were not bodies of sufficient importance, and that they could not be trusted. But when the Metropolitan Board of Works was substituted[7] and the Bill came on for discussion in the House, objection was taken to the Metropolitan Board as not being a sufficiently representative and popular body[c];[8] and I have received repeated applications to oppose the Bill on that ground. It may be said that, acting on the principles I have enunciated, I ought to have proposed one municipal government for the whole metropolis. There is a good deal to be said for such a course. But on the other hand, it might shock settled ideas to propose at once

[6]Torrens introduced the latest version of his "Bill to Provide Better Dwellings for Artizans and Labourers," 31 Victoria, *PP*, 1867–68, I, 21–42, on 20 November (*PD*, 3rd ser., Vol. 190, col. 103). The first version, to which Mill here refers, is 29 Victoria (20 Feb., 1866), *PP*, 1866, I, 43–52; see Clause 4 for the powers of the vestries. (Cf. No. 93.)

[7]See the second version of the Bill, as amended by the Select Committee, *ibid.*, pp. 53–72 (18 June, 1866), First Schedule, Table A. The Bill was withdrawn on 31 July without debate. As reintroduced in the next session, 30 Victoria (12 Feb., 1867), *PP*, 1867, I, 109–28, this third version retains the provision of the second version. It was withdrawn on 4 August. For the Board of Works, see 18 & 19 Victoria, c. 120 (1855).

[8]The objection came in the debate on the second reading, from John Harvey Lewis (1814–88), M.P. for Marylebone, Speech on the Artizans' and Labourers' Dwellings Bill (27 Mar., 1867), *PD*, 3rd ser., Vol. 186, cols. 697–8.

[b-b]+TT [*in past tense*]

[c-c]TT] PD At first the Bill intrusted those powers to the vestries; but the vestries were not trusted, and the Select Committee preferred intrusting them to the Metropolitan Board of Works: and then it appeared that the Board of Works was not trusted either

to entrust the whole local government of so vast an area, with about 3,000,000 of inhabitants, to one local body. The business to be intrusted to their management would, moreover, be too great, and it would give them the control of too large an amount of revenue; and it would have been useless to attempt to obtain the consent of the House to such a measure. Probably it is better to have local municipal bodies for the different Parliamentary boroughs, and that the central Board should not be troubled with any business but such as is common to the whole metropolis. The Parliamentary boroughs offer a medium between the contemptibly small size of an ordinary parish and the inordinate size of the whole metropolis; and in them there has grown up, from the circumstance of their being Parliamentary boroughs, a certain feeling of local connection amongst the whole of the inhabitants. This feeling exists in a very great degree in the old Parliamentary districts, the City of London, Westminster, and Southwark; and some amount of it has grown up even in those which were created by the Act of 1832.[9] I therefore propose by the Bill which I ask you to read a second time, to create municipalities for the Parliamentary districts, which shall exercise the powers of the municipalities under the Municipal Corporations Act,[10] and also those of the vestries and local boards of the metropolis, except so far as Parliament shall otherwise dispose. It may be said that the Metropolitan Board of Works meets the idea of a central Board. The Metropolitan Board is a clumsy creation, arising from the felt want of some body to represent the whole metropolis. It was at first called into existence to [d]execute the great work of main drainage[d] which is now nearly completed, and its existence would in consequence have soon expired, but that Parliament in the meantime found out the necessity of some such central body, and threw upon it a great variety of duties, which originally were not contemplated [e], down even to the naming of the streets[e]. It never was intended that the Board should be a municipality for the whole of London; and I cannot conceive that that body can continue to discharge those duties without its construction being at least greatly modified. (*Hear, hear.*) I could not expect that this Bill would pass at this period of the Session, even if the Government were to adopt it; but I think it is right to remind the House of this question, and to prepare the public mind for a more mature consideration of it. On these grounds I beg to move that the Bill be now read a second time. (*Hear, hear.*)

[*After some debate the matter was adjourned until 30 June when, after more discussion, the Bill was lost.*]

[9]The constituencies of Finsbury, Greenwich, Lambeth, Marylebone, and Tower Hamlets were created by the first Reform Act, 2 & 3 William IV, c. 45 (1832).

[10]5 & 6 William IV, c. 76 (1835).

[d-d]TT] PD carry out a great sanitary improvement

[e-e]+TT

106. The Government of India Bill [2]

22 JUNE, 1868

PD, 3rd ser., Vol. 192, cols. 1876–7. Reported in *The Times*, 23 June, p. 7, from which the variants and responses are taken. For the Bill, see No. 102. In the debate on going into Committee, Lord William Montagu Hay (1826–1911), M.P. for Taunton, had opened the discussion of the Bill's main provision, that Council membership should be for twelve years rather than life, by suggesting that Council's power of overruling the Secretary of State on matters of expenditure should be curtailed. He suggested that expenses should be submitted to Parliament in the estimates. (Cols. 1870–6.)

MR. J. STUART MILL SAID, he agreed with the noble Lord that it was most important that India should be governed in India, and that there was a great tendency in the change of circumstances which had rendered communication with India so much easier to lead to over-interference on the part of the Home Government.[1] But, after all, they could not altogether abdicate their control, though the best way in which that control could be exercised would be to send out men to represent us who could be relied upon to perform their duty well. (*Hear, hear.*) Since there must be a controlling power here, the question was between placing it in the Secretary of State alone or in the Secretary of State and the Council. On that point he did not think the noble Lord had said anything which tended to show that it was better to place that control in the Secretary of State alone rather than in the Secretary of State and a Council which had an effective power. The noble Lord had admitted the absolute necessity of the Secretary of State being assisted by persons who had acquired a knowledge of India [a], and who should hold a more responsible position than that of being a mere consultative body[a].[2] About that there could be no difference of opinion between the noble Lord and himself. But if the Council did not possess some substantive power, if they were made a consultative body only, they never would have that degree of weight which they ought to possess; they would be [b]a mere superfluous wheel in the machinery[b]. If they had only the power of giving their opinions they would never be so powerful with the Secretary of State as his own subordinates in Office. (*Hear, hear.*) If the House did not think that the Council as at present constituted was the best controlling body, they could try to improve it; and various modes of doing so had been suggested, some of which he thought were improvements. Perhaps it would be an improvement if a portion of them were allowed to sit in that House. He confessed he was surprised, however, when the noble Lord said that if the present powers of the Council were

[1]Hay, cols. 1870–1.
[2]Hay, col. 1872.

[a-a]+TT
[b-b]TT mere superfoetation

continued he would be against its Members being admitted to seats in that House; but if their powers were taken away then he thought it would be of advantage that they should have seats.[3] Now, such an expression of opinion appeared to him at variance with the whole course of the noble Lord's argument, because he had contended that the Council were irresponsible, and that the Secretary of State was the only one who had any responsibility.[4] But what responsibility had the Secretary of State? It was that he could be called to account in that House, and if he did not succeed in defending his measures he could be turned out of Office. But the same thing would happen to the Council. They could be turned out (*No*) after a period of trial, because the proposal of this Bill was to make the duration of Office as a matter of course shorter. But of all the surprising things in the speech of the noble Lord that which had surprised him most was that the noble Lord should have brought forward the tendency of this country to throw all expenditure, when any excuse could be found, on the people of India, as a reason for asking the consent of England, not India, when such expenditure was in question.[5] (*Hear.*) If there was one thing which might be held absolutely certain, it was that the majority of a body constituted like the Council would in such matters be on the side of India. The Court of Directors had always been so, and many a battle to his knowledge had been fought by them with the Board of Control, in order to prevent such expenditure from being thrown upon India; and they often succeeded, but, he was sorry to say, still oftener failed. Now, if the power of sanctioning expenditure were taken away from the Council, which represented India, and given to that House, which did not represent India; and which seldom troubled itself about India at all, but which did care about England and its burthens, and if the noble Lord believed that the House would be actuated in such matters by a generous and chivalrous spirit and would take the burden from India to throw it upon their own constituents, he must say that the noble Lord had a far higher opinion of the virtue of that House than his (*Mr. Stuart Mill's*) experience had taught him to have of that or perhaps any other public body in similar circumstances. (*Hear.*)

[*The House went into Committee on the Bill.*]

107. Public Schools [2]

23 JUNE, 1868

PD, 3rd ser., Vol. 192, cols. 1928–9, 1931–2. Reported (first part) in *The Times*, 24 June, p. 6. For the Bill, see No. 104. Mill spoke in Committee on Clause 6, concerning the power

[3]Hay, col. 1875.
[4]Hay, col. 1873.
[5]Hay, cols. 1874–5.

of the governing bodies to make statutes under certain restrictions. James Lowther (1840–1904), M.P. for York, had proposed an amendment to leave out the section: "With respect to the privileges and number of boys who, under any Statute or Benefaction, may be entitled to any rights to education or maintenance" (col. 1926).

MR. J. STUART MILL earnestly hoped that the Committee would not adopt the Amendment proposed by the honourable Member for York. One of the most scandalous abuses connected with endowed schools was that the endowments intended for the education of children of parents who could not afford to pay for their education, had been in fact confiscated for the benefit of those who could afford to pay for it. Whether this was a case of the kind he did not know; but it appeared that the choristers and the sons of the tenants of the Dean and Chapter had some rights by virtue of the old endowment. The clause did not define their rights, or state whether such rights existed; it merely gave the governing body the power to consider whether such rights existed, and to take measures with respect to them. The subject had attracted the attention of the working classes themselves. To his own knowledge there had been formed in the North of England an association of the working classes to obtain a restoration of their rights—he would not say in Westminster School particularly—but in endowed schools generally. Unless means were taken to deal with this question by a measure of wider extent, the feeling amongst the working classes would grow much stronger, and the House might expect to hear a great deal more of it. It was not merely that there were rights, but the rights were known by the persons for whose benefit they were created. The House would do well to give to the authorities who were to make the new statutes the power of considering this matter amongst others.

[*The amendment was defeated (col. 1930). Mill's second intervention was on Clause 6 as a whole.*]

Mr. J. Stuart Mill said, he wished to impress upon the right honourable Member for the University of Cambridge (*Mr. Walpole*), who had charge of the Bill, the importance of the suggestion that had been made by the honourable Member for North Devon (*Mr. Acland*).[1] The schools whose case they were considering differed from schools generally, in that they were schools intended for the purpose of imparting the highest class of education; and no one supposed that this either ought to, or need be given to the whole of the children of the working or lower middle classes. But, on the other hand, the *élite* of those classes had a right to claim that that sort of education should be afforded to them. To those who are most proficient in the lower grades of education, the next highest ought to be opened at the expense of the magnificent endowments for educational purposes in this country. As this was a matter of great importance, requiring to be carefully considered, not so much by the House as by the body the House was about to

[1]Cols. 1929–30.

create, he hoped the Committee would not predetermine that no part of those great endowments should be appropriated to the purpose of providing the higher kinds of education for such persons as those to which he had referred.

[*Acland's suggestion, not being an amendment, was not voted on; the Clause was accepted (col. 1932).*]

108. The Sea-Fisheries (Ireland) Bill

24 JUNE, 1868

PD, 3rd ser., Vol. 192, cols. 2021–2. Reported in *The Times*, 25 June, p. 6, from which the responses are taken. Mill spoke during the second reading of "A Bill to Amend the Laws Relative to the Coast and Deep Sea Fisheries of Ireland," 31 Victoria (30 Apr., 1868), *PP*, 1867–68, V, 205–20, following Shaw-Lefevre (col. 2021).

MR. J. STUART MILL SAID, the main objection of his honourable Friend who had just sat down to the granting of loans to the Irish fishermen was that if this were done for Ireland it should be done for Scotland and England. His answer was that Ireland was a more backward country than either Scotland or England. Government might very properly undertake to do things for a country which was industrially backward, which no one could expect from them in the case of a country which was in a more advanced and prosperous condition. (*Hear, hear.*) This consideration was of all the more weight when it was remembered that the industrial backwardness of Ireland was, in a great measure, attributable to the past legislation of this country. For a long period English legislators, without distinction of party, employed themselves in crushing this and most other branches of Irish enterprize. It was therefore incumbent on us, now that we were wiser and able to look upon our past conduct with shame, to legislate in an opposite direction, and even to risk if necessary the loss of small sums of money to advance that industry which we had formerly endeavoured to retard. (*Hear, hear.*)

[*The Bill was given a second reading.*]

109. Election Petitions and Corrupt Practices at Elections [4]

25 JUNE, 1868

PD, 3rd ser., Vol. 192, cols. 2180–1. Reported in *The Times*, 26 June, p. 9, from which the response is taken. For the Bill, see No. 89. Mill spoke in Committee on Clause 5: "From and after the next Dissolution of Parliament a Petition complaining of an undue Return or undue Election of a Member to serve in Parliament for a County or Borough may be presented to the Court of Common Pleas by any One or more" of certain designated people. Edward Henry John Crauford (1816–87), M.P. for Ayr, had moved an amendment to replace "Court of Common Pleas" by "House of Commons" (col. 2173).

MR. J. STUART MILL SAID, THAT, in the course of the rather severe criticisms which had been made upon the Bill, it seemed to have been forgotten that, whatever might be its defects, it provided one of the most important remedies for bribery and corruption—a local investigation. (*Hear, hear.*) His own opinion was that the worst plan which involved such an investigation would be better than the best plan without it. But if there were a local investigation the jurisdiction must be altered; and the question was whether a tribunal should be constituted composed of one of the Judges of the land as proposed in the Government plan, or of a Judge sitting with a jury as suggested by the right honourable Gentleman the Member for Kilmarnock (*Mr. Bouverie*)?[1] However that might be he was anxious to impress on the House that any such tribunal would be only fit to be a tribunal of appeal, and that it would be necessary to have besides a tribunal of investigation. The best plan, therefore, to adopt, seemed to him that of which he had given Notice, and which he had drawn up with the assistance of Mr. Serjeant Pulling,[2] providing that the Revising Barrister, an officer conversant with elections, and having a considerable acquaintance with the locality, should be the person to hold the investigation in the first instance. The investigation should take place before the return of the writ, and there should be a scrutiny. They must endeavour to put an end to excessive expenditure; and he thought the expense of the preliminary investigation should be borne by the public, either out of the borough rate or be charged on the Consolidated Fund. If the Amendment were pressed to a division he should vote for the provision in the Bill as against the Amendment.

[*The amendment failed (col. 2189).*]

110. The Municipal Corporations (Metropolis) Bill [3]

30 JUNE, 1868

PD, 3rd ser., Vol. 193, col. 419. Reported in *The Times*, 1 July, p. 8. For the Bill, see No. 93. Mill opened the adjourned debate on the second reading.

MR. J. STUART MILL appealed to the Secretary of State for India, by whom the ad-

[1]Edward Pleydell Bouverie (1818–89), Speech on the Election Petitions and Corrupt Practices at Elections Bill (21 May, 1868), *PD*, 3rd ser., Vol. 192, cols. 682–5.

[2]Alexander Pulling (1813–95), legal author, municipal reformer, an active member of the National Association for the Promotion of Social Science.

journment of the debate had been moved on the former occasion,[1] to proceed with his argument.

Sir Stafford Northcote said, that at that late hour he did not feel justified in launching the House upon a fresh discussion.

Mr. J. Stuart Mill then briefly replied to some of the arguments advanced in the course of the debate a few days since upon this Bill,[2] expressing his regret that the measure, instead of being met with a direct negative by a private Member,[3] had not been left for the consideration of the Government.

[*The Bill was put off for three months, i.e., abandoned.*]

111. Election Petitions and Corrupt Practices at Elections [5]

6 JULY, 1868

PD, 3rd ser., Vol. 193, cols. 734–5, 742, 744, 746. Reported in *The Times*, 7 July, p. 7, from which the responses are taken. For the Bill, see No. 89. Mill spoke in Committee again on Clause 5 (see No. 109), following a proposal by Bouverie (cols. 722–8) that jurisdiction be given to tribunals of Members of Parliament presided over by Judges from the Superior Courts. Writing to W.D. Christie on 7 July, Mill says: "When you read the Bribery debate of last night, do not suppose that I have abandoned, even temporarily, the advocacy of *our* plan of a jurisdiction. I told the House (though this is not reported) that I should bring that forward before Clause 10 is disposed of: and it will come on at the beginning of the next discussion." (*CW*, Vol. XVI, p. 1421.)

MR. J. STUART MILL SAID, he thought it was desirable that the discussion should not be complicated by a reference to all the various plans which had been suggested; and he should therefore address himself to the Amendment of his right honourable Friend the Member for Kilmarnock (*Mr. Bouverie*) as compared with the provisions of the Bill. His right honourable Friend contended that Committees of the House, as at present constituted, gave their decisions in Election cases with great impartiality, and he was not prepared to deny that such was the fact as far as the decision with respect to the seat and the existence of corrupt practices was concerned. Did a Committee of that House, however, he should like to know, ever find a Member guilty of bribery? (*Cries of Yes.*) Not once in fifty years. But if

[1]Northcote, Motion on the Municipal Corporations (Metropolis) Bill (17 June, 1868), *PD*, 3rd ser., Vol. 192, col. 1740.

[2]E.g., by John Harvey Lewis (*ibid.*, cols. 1737–8), and James Macnaughton McGaul Hogg (1823–90), then M.P. for Bath (*ibid.*, cols. 1738–9).

[3]I.e., Bentinck, who spoke against the Bill and moved that it be put off for three months (*ibid.*, cols. 1735–7).

it were proved that a candidate had deposited a large sum at his bankers, that he made no inquiry as to how it was expended, and that his recognized agents had laid out portions of it in bribing, would not any tribunal, except one composed of Members of the same class as himself, and who were liable to the same temptations, find him guilty of some kind of corruption? (*Hear, hear.*) What he desired to see was a tribunal which would consider bribery which was tolerated by a candidate as if it had been committed by him, and that would not be done, he believed, so long as the decision rested with the House itself. The Amendment of his right honourable Friend would be an improvement on the existing state of things, but it failed in the essential condition of providing a local inquiry, and one that could be pursued when Parliament was not sitting. By means of a local inquiry the commission of offences could be much more easily detected than if the investigation were conducted at a distance. If local inquiry was of no advantage, what was the use of the Judges going circuit? The cases were precisely analogous. Although he thought that the plan of the Government possessed a great advantage over that of his right honourable Friend, yet he was far from being disposed to place implicit confidence in the Judges. He could not forget that they had been politicians, and that they were sometimes thought to be politicians still. There was reason to believe that a recent charge in the Court of Queen's Bench would cost the Government several votes on the present Bill, though it would not cost them his.[1] If, however, the Bill were passed as it stood, it would not be in the power of the House—as they had been reminded at an earlier stage of the debate by the right honourable Member for Oxfordshire (*Mr. Henley*)[2]—after trying the experiment, to discontinue it without the consent of the other branch of the Legislature. Now, he thought it very important that the House should be able to put a stop to the experiment without any consent but its own, and he should therefore suggest that the operation of the Act be limited to two years. Under ordinary circumstances he should say five years, but having regard to the experience which they would at once have of the working of the Act, he thought two years sufficient. In the meantime we should have a most important General Election, and there would, in all probability, be a sufficient number of Election Petitions to give an ample trial of the experiment. (*Hear, hear.*)

---

[1]Colin Blackburn (1813–96), Charge to the Westminster Grand Jury in the Case of Governor Eyre, in "Ex-Governor Eyre," *The Times*, 3 June, 1868, pp. 9–10. Blackburn's Charge found that the proclamation of martial law in Jamaica by Governor Eyre had been consistent with statutes previously adopted by the Jamaican assembly. Mill's allusion implies that the response of several anti-Eyre members of the House to the central provisions of the Elections Bill might be adversely affected by Blackburn's handling of the case.

[2]Henley, Speech on the Election Petitions and Corrupt Practices at Elections Bill (13 Feb., 1868), *PD*, 3rd ser., Vol. 190, cols. 714–15.

[*The Clause was agreed, and discussion turned to Clause 6, dealing with regulations as to presentation of petitions. Karslake, the Attorney General, announced that he would introduce a clause (col. 741) which would meet all the objections made.*]

Mr. J. Stuart Mill stated that as his three Amendments on this clause had been virtually disposed of, he did not propose to move them.[3]

[*Clause 6 was agreed (col. 744). In the discussion of Clause 7, dealing with the manner in which a recognizance might be objected to, Mill proposed an amendment to add,*] "And the respondent making any such objection shall be required to serve notice of it, precisely describing the ground of it, on the Petitioner, or on all the Petitioners, if more than one, within the said prescribed time, not exceeding five days."

They ought not to discourage, but rather to facilitate the presentation of Petitions, and petitioners ought to have such warning of any objection taken to their sureties as would enable them, if any mistakes had been made, to rectify them.

[*The Attorney General said, the present practice in that matter worked very well, and he thought the use of the word* precisely *in the Amendment would not add much to its efficacy, while it might raise numerous questions in regard to every one of the notices served.*]

Mr. J. Stuart Mill said, he had no objection to omit from his Amendment the words "precisely decribing the ground of it," but he thought that notice of objection ought to be given.

[*George Denman (1819–96), the chief commentator on Mill's amendment, remarked on the number of vexatious petitioners who preyed on honest candidates (col. 745).*]

Mr. J. Stuart Mill said, he was fully aware of the evil to which his honourable and learned Friend the Member for Tiverton (*Mr. Denman*) referred. He believed that there were nearly as many dishonest Petitions as there were corrupt elections. But the remedy for this evil must be taught independently, and not by rendering *bonâ fide* Petitions expensive and difficult.

[*The amendment was lost, and the Clause agreed (col. 746).*]

[3]For Mill's amendments, notice of which was given on 7 May, see *Notices of Motions, and Orders of the Day*, 1868, p. 739.

112. Public Schools [3]

7 JULY, 1868

PD, 3rd ser., Vol. 193, col. 823. Reported in *The Times*, 8 July, p. 7, from which the variants are taken. For the Bill, see No. 104. Mill spoke in Committee on a Clause introduced by Lowe: "That all boys educated at the seven Schools mentioned in this Act shall be examined once a year, by one of the Inspectors of the Committee of Council on Education, in reading, writing from dictation, arithmetic, including vulgar fractions, practice, and the rule of three, geography, English grammar and history, and the results of such examination and the Report of the examining Inspectors shall be laid before Parliament" (col. 819). Some speakers objected that outside examinations involved a degradation of the schools and some that government should not interfere; one suggested an entrance examination.

MR. J. STUART MILL SAID, the remedy which was now proposed was that the scholars should be examined, not in [a]those higher branches of learning which[a] the schools professed to teach, but in what every boy should know before he went. To examine them in what any boy should know at a National School might be an extremely good joke [b]against the schools; but he hoped no one would vote for it seriously[b]. The examination should be in those subjects the cultivation of which was the purpose of the schools. But he quite agreed that the examination provided by the clause might be applied as an entrance examination.

[*Finally the Clause was withdrawn.*]

113. Supply—Post Office

7 JULY, 1868

PD, 3rd ser., Vol. 193, col. 833. Reported in *The Times*, 8 July, p. 7. In Committee of Supply, considering the Post Office estimates, McLaren had suggested that the Post Office could easily carry such printed materials as election circulars for 1/2*d*. instead of 1*d*. (cols. 832–3).

MR. J. STUART MILL SAID, THAT with reference to the matter so ably advocated by his honourable Friend, he could not help suggesting to the Chancellor of the Exchequer that it would be very proper to carry *bonâ fide* election circulars through

[a-a]TT] PD what

[b-b]TT at the expense of Harrow and Eton, but he hoped it was not meant seriously to press it to a division

the Post Office free.[1] If that were done it might come to pass that candidates would address their constituents much more by circulars than by speeches. Election expenses were increased much more than honourable Gentlemen were aware by the charges for the delivery of election circulars.

114. The Government of India Bill [3]

8 JULY, 1868

PD, 3rd ser., Vol. 193, cols. 859–60, 861–2. Reported in *The Times*, 9 July, p. 6, from which the variant and responses are taken. For the Bill, see No. 102. Mill spoke in Committee on Clause 2, which provided yearly salaries for future Members of the India Council of £1500, but ruled out retiring pensions for them. An amendment had been offered that would have had the effect of treating continuing Members in the same way, and the debate turned on the issue of whether those appointed under the India Act of 1858 had legitimately expected a choice between continuing for life or retiring after ten years with a pension. Ayrton argued that Parliament had the right to reconsider the arrangements of the Act of 1858; it was better, he asserted, that such Members should serve another ten years at £1500 than to fix no limit at all, and in any case most of them already had a pension from their Indian service (col. 859).

MR. J. STUART MILL SAID, THAT his honourable and learned Friend the Member for the Tower Hamlets (*Mr. Ayrton*) had forgotten one matter—namely, that the pensions from India were bought, being derived from stoppages from pay. He (*Mr. Stuart Mill*) quite agreed that an ample salary rendered a retiring pension unnecessary. But there would be a hardship if, when the expectation of pensions had been held out to the existing Councillors, they were deprived of pensions in the end. If an increase of salary were to be given instead, that increase should range over a fresh series of ten years. But the reason which induced the House to limit the service of future Councillors should prevent it from continuing the old for another ten years. He, therefore, recommended the Committee to agree to give the old members an opportunity of serving for another five years at the increased salary, or else to grant them a pension at the end of the ten years.

[*After a short discussion, Stafford Northcote said that Mill's suggestion could best be dealt with in a new clause, which he would consider carefully; he recommended that the amendment be withdrawn (col. 860).*]

Mr. J. Stuart Mill said, he would be happy to bring up a new clause.

[*The amendment was withdrawn, and another offered to reduce the salary to £1200.*]

[1]George Ward Hunt (1825–77), M.P. for Northamptonshire, the Chancellor, replied to both McLaren and Mill at col. 834.

Mr. J. Stuart Mill said, that if it was not for the Council the Government of India would be left wholly to the Secretary of State—who before his appointment was [a]generally[a] ignorant of Indian affairs—and to such irresponsible persons as he might choose to consult, who if he had a pre-conceived opinion would be likely to share it. The Secretary of State would be left with no regular assistance but that of the subordinates in his office. Of the latter, having himself been included in the number, he entertained, generally speaking, a very high opinion; but he did not think Parliament and the country would approve of handing over the government of India entirely to them. It was absolutely necessary that there should be associated with them some men of standing, of professional knowledge, and practical acquaintance with India, whose names and character were known to the public. (*Hear, hear.*) It was also necessary that such salaries should be given them as would induce them to continue in their offices. Although yielding to no one in his desire for economy, he did not think that retrenchment was judicious when it took the form of stinting the remuneration for the best and most difficult work. (*Hear, hear.*) It was possible they might get very much the same class of men for £1,200 as for £1,500; but, in the absence of a pension, he did not think the latter amount excessive.

[*The Bill was withdrawn on 27 July because there was insufficient time for its discussion (col. 1871).*]

115. Election Petitions and Corrupt Practices at Elections [6]

10 JULY, 1868

PD, 3rd ser., Vol. 193, cols. 1015–16, 1020. Reported in *The Times*, 11 July, p. 6. For the Bill, see No. 89. Mill spoke in Committee first on Clause 14, dealing with the trial of election petitions.

MR. J. STUART MILL SAID, he had intended, before the clause was finally agreed to, to make some observations in vindication of a plan which was embodied in three pages of Amendments that stood on the Notice Paper in his name.[1] As the Committee had, however, already virtually decided against his plan, he would not now press his Amendments.

---

[1]For the amendments, notice of which was given on 19 May, see *Notices of Motions, and Orders of the Day*, 1868, pp. 882–4.

[a-a]TT , perhaps,

[*Mill's second intervention came during the discussion of Clause 17, dealing with the judge's report as to corrupt practices.*]

Mr. J. Stuart Mill said, that as he had an important Amendment to propose,[2] and there was not time for the discussion, he would beg to move that the Committee report Progress.

116. Election Petitions and Corrupt Practices at Elections [7]

14 JULY, 1868

PD, 3rd ser., Vol. 193, cols. 1166–8, 1169, 1176–7, 1177, 1178. Reported in *The Times*, 15 July, pp. 6–7. For the Bill, see No. 89. Mill spoke in Committee on discussion of Clause 17 (see No. 115).

THE ADDITION which I propose to this clause is one of great importance, since it raises the question of providing better security against corrupt practices in municipal, as well as Parliamentary elections. No one is likely to deny that bribery in municipal elections deserves repression as much, and is as unfit to be tolerated or indulged, as bribery in Parliamentary elections; and the special reason why it should be dealt with in this Bill is that, as we are told by all who know anything about the matter, municipal bribery is the great school of Parliamentary bribery. Honourable Members of this House have on a former occasion testified to this fact from their personal knowledge, and I shall quote only two authorities for it. One is that eminent Conservative solicitor, Mr. Philip Rose, formerly as intimately known to honourable Gentlemen opposite as his partner, Mr. Spofforth, now is.[1] Mr. Rose, before the Select Committee of this House on Corrupt Practices, in 1860, expressed himself in these words—

> My strong opinion is, that all the efforts which are now being made to check bribery at Parliamentary elections will fail, for this reason, that you do not attempt to strike at the root of the offence. The real nursery for the evil is the municipal contests; and those oft-recurring contests have led to the establishment of what I might almost term an organized system of corruption in the municipal boroughs throughout the kingdom, which provides a machinery ready made to hand, available when the Parliamentary contest arrives.[2]

[2]See No. 116.

---

[1]For Philip Rose, see No. 89. Markham Spofforth (b. ca. 1824), a lawyer, assisted Rose as a Conservative party agent, and then took over the position of Principal Agent in 1859.

[2]"Evidence Taken before the Select Committee on the Corrupt Practices Prevention Act," *PP*, 1860, X, 112.

My next authority is the Committee itself, before whom this evidence was given, and who reported—

> That it has been proved to the satisfaction of your Committee, that an intimate connection exists between bribery at municipal and Parliamentary elections, and it is expedient that the provisions as to punishments and forfeitures for the offences of bribery at each such election should be assimilated as far as possible.[3]

Notwithstanding this recommendation of the Select Committee, which I hope that the next House of Commons will see the propriety of adopting in its integrity, I have not ventured to propose that the present Bill should provide a machinery for the investigation and punishment of corrupt practices at municipal elections. But I do propose, by the present Amendment, and by an additional clause which will follow in due course,[4] that when the machinery which the Bill does provide for the investigation of corrupt practices at Parliamentary elections is actually set in motion, the inquiry may extend to municipal as well as to Parliamentary corruption. If the House adopt my Amendment, the Special Commission, which is already empowered to inquire into Parliamentary elections previous to that which caused the issue of the Commission, will have the power conferred on it of inquiring, to exactly the same extent, into previous municipal elections. By the additional clause, the Judge who tries an Election Petition, may take evidence to prove that an elector who voted at the Parliamentary election had been guilty of corrupt practices at any municipal election within two years previous, for the purpose, of course, of showing that his vote was corruptly influenced at the Parliamentary election. The period of two years is selected with reference to the term fixed by the 56th clause of the Municipal Corporations Act;[5] and I confidently claim, both for the Amendment and for the new clause, the support of all honourable Members who really desire to lay the axe at the root of electoral corruption. The honourable Member moved to add at the end of the clause the following words—

> And it shall be competent for any such Commission to inquire into corrupt practices at previous municipal Elections within the county or borough as fully as into corrupt practices at previous Parliamentary Elections.

[*John George Dodson, Chairman of the Committee of Ways and Means, expressed opinion that the amendment, because it dealt with municipal elections, was not sufficiently relevant to be considered (col. 1168).*]

Mr. J. Stuart Mill observed that he had so altered his Amendment as to obviate the difficulty started by the Chairman. He proposed it should run thus—

> And it shall be competent for any such Commission to inquire how far corrupt practices at

[3]"Report from the Select Committee on the Corrupt Practices Prevention Act," *ibid.*, p. 6.

[4]See No. 123.

[5]5 & 6 William IV, c. 76 (1835).

any previous municipal Election may have conduced to corrupt practices at the Parliamentary Election.

[*Even in this form, the Chairman said, the amendment went beyond the proper limits of the Bill, and suggested that, at the Report stage, Mill bring up a clause to that effect (col. 1169).*]

Mr. J. Stuart Mill said, he would avail himself of that suggestion.

[*The amendment was withdrawn.*]

[*Mill's third intervention came at the beginning of discussion of Clause 43, which was designed to throw costs of a petition fully on the petitioner or petitioners.*]

Mr. J. Stuart Mill proposed, in page 14, line 11, to insert after "on the whole successful" the words—

> And in the case of any such Petition where any corrupt practice is charged to have taken place, and where the court or judge has decided that any corrupt practice has been proved, the court or judge shall have power to order any portion or the whole of the costs, charges, and expenses to be defrayed by any party or parties who may have been proved guilty of corrupt practices, or by the county or borough, in the same manner as expenses incurred in the registration of voters for the county or borough, regard being had to the importance of securing the best efforts of the county or borough for repression of corrupt practices.
>
> In the case of any Petition complaining of general or extensive prevalence of corrupt practices, if the court or judge shall be of opinion that there was reasonable and probable ground for its allegations, the petitioner or petitioners shall be relieved of all costs, charges, and expenses incurred in and about the inquiry, and it shall be in the power of the court or judge to distribute the said costs, charges, and expenses in such proportions as it or he may think fit between parties who shall have been found guilty of corrupt practices, or who shall have caused expense by vexatious conduct, unfounded allegations, or unfounded objections, and the county or borough, as the case may be, the expenses charged on the county or borough to be defrayed in the same manner as expenses incurred in the registration of voters for the county or borough.

The principle of this Amendment is that to bring to light, and prosecute to conviction, acts of bribery, or other corruption at elections, is a public service; and that, being a public service, those who are judicially decided to have performed that service ought not to be required to pay the expenses of it from their private purse. It is enough that they take upon themselves the risk of failing to establish the charge, which, we all know, may easily, and does frequently, happen when it is perfectly notorious that the charge is true. But when it has been proved true, and is judicially declared to be so proved, I maintain that the Petitioners have a clear moral right to be indemnified for the expense. Their first claim, no doubt, is upon the parties who, through their instrumentality, have been found guilty; but the Judge may not always think fit to inflict even upon proved corruption, so heavy a penalty as the entire expenses of the Petition; and it will often happen that the parties have not the means of paying it. I propose, therefore, that the Judge should have the power of apportioning the expense in whatever manner he deems most just, between the persons convicted of corrupt practices, and the county or borough.

[*After some objections, Karslake, the Attorney General, asserted that the amendment would allow anyone to assert that a bribe had been offered, without the person accused having a chance of defence (col. 1177).*]

Mr. J. Stuart Mill asked, whether since Judges could be trusted to decide cases of political importance, the Attorney General believed they could not be trusted to exercise proper caution in awarding costs?

[*The amendment was defeated, and the clause agreed.*]

[*Mill proposed his last amendment to Clause 45, dealing with punishment of candidates found guilty of bribery: their election would be declared void, and they would be ineligible for reelection for seven years.*]

Mr. J. Stuart Mill moved, in page 14, line 35, to leave out the word "bribery," in order to insert the words "corrupt practice" in its stead. "Corrupt practice" were the words used generally throughout the Bill as a description of the offence with which the measure dealt. His object was to extend the operation of the clause to persons guilty of treating or of intimidation.

[*It was argued that the amendment would place too heavy a punishment on mere treating or intimidation, and the amendment was lost (col. 1178).*]

117. The Fenian Prisoners [1]

16 JULY, 1868

PD, 3rd ser., Vol. 193, cols. 1282–3. Reported in *The Times*, 17 July, p. 7.

MR. J. STUART MILL SAID, he wished to ask the Chief Secretary for Ireland,[1] If Her Majesty's Government will take into favourable consideration the question whether the time is arrived when the very heavy sentences passed on Warren and Costello, the only two persons of the crew of the *Jackmell* who have not been released, may be remitted or mitigated?[2]

[1]Richard Southwell Bourke, 6th Earl of Mayo.

[2]The *Jackmell* (renamed *Erin's Hope*) had sailed from the U.S.A. with forty-eight Fenians, to support the rebellion in Ireland of March 1867. Arriving after it had ended, they cruised the coast until 1 June, when in desperation they landed and were arrested, arms being discovered on board. They were tried in November 1867, and convicted, but most

The Earl of Mayo, in reply, said, he was glad the honourable Member put the Question, because considerable misapprehension seemed to exist upon the subject. The two prisoners referred to were convicted for coming to Ireland in an armed vessel, and cruizing along the coast in order to raise an armed insurrection against the Queen. The only evidence given against them of their proceedings in the United States of America—was that they were members of the Fenian Brotherhood previous to the 5th of March, 1867, the date of overt acts connected with the rising in which their brother conspirators were engaged. That evidence was necessary to connect them with the Fenian society, and in accordance with the terms of the Treason Felony Act that brought them within the jurisdiction of this country, so that in reality their case did not differ in any considerable degree from those of the great mass of the Fenian prisoners tried and convicted in Ireland. He was afraid the time was hardly yet come when it would be possible to enter into anything like a general consideration of the sentences passed upon the Fenian prisoners with a view either to a commutation or a remission of their sentences, and, therefore, he did not see any exception in the case of these two prisoners.

118. Election Petitions and Corrupt Practices at Elections [8]

17 JULY, 1868

PD, 3rd ser., Vol. 193, cols. 1370, 1373, 1381. Reported in *The Times*, 18 July, p. 7. For the Bill, see No. 89. Mill spoke in Committee first on Clause 46, which voided election of anyone found guilty of employing corrupt agents. Amberley moved an amendment to add the penalty of disqualification from election for three years (col. 1370). Mill's comment was prompted by an objection that an innocent might unwittingly fall into the hands of a corrupt agent.

MR. J. STUART MILL SAID, the Amendment would only apply to a candidate who knowingly employed a corrupt agent.

[*The amendment was defeated, and the clause agreed (col. 1373).*]

[*Mill's second intervention came during discussion of Clause 47, providing that people, other than the candidate, found guilty of bribery should lose their votes.*]

Mr. J. Stuart Mill moved, in page 15, line 16, after "voting at any," insert

---

were released on 6 May, 1868. John Warren and Augustine Costello, both Irish-born U.S. citizens, were released in 1869, when they lectured in Ireland against the government, and then returned to the U.S.A.

"Parliamentary and municipal," the object being to extend penalties to bribery at municipal Elections.

[*Brett, the Solicitor General, argued that at this time in the session, and in this Bill, they should confine themselves to Parliamentary elections (col. 1373).*]

Mr. J. Stuart Mill said, that his proposition was simply that a person convicted of bribery at a Parliamentary Election should be disqualified from voting at future municipal as well as Parliamentary Elections.

[*Disraeli objected that municipal elections would have to be considered later; Mill withdrew his amendment, and the clause was agreed (col. 1373).*]

[*Mill's third intervention followed the introduction of a new Clause by the Solicitor General, providing for Commissions of Inquiry into corrupt practices (col. 1380).*]

Mr. J. Stuart Mill said, he wished to express his acknowledgments to the Government for the great improvement which had been effected in the Bill.

119. Poor Relief [1]

17 JULY, 1868

PD, 3rd ser., Vol. 193, cols. 1424–5. Reported in *The Times*, 18 July, p. 8, from which the response is taken. Mill spoke in Committee on "A Bill to Make Further Amendments in the Laws for the Relief of the Poor," 31 Victoria (23 June, 1868), *PP*, 1867–68, IV, 167–78. The discussion was of Clause 3, which allowed the Poor Law Board to appoint officers if the Guardians failed to do so.

MR. J. STUART MILL SAID, THAT the grand principle of improvement in Poor Law administration was not to strengthen the power of the guardians but of the Poor Law Board. (*Hear.*) The guardians frequently refused to perform their obvious local duties, to the injury of the sick, the poor, and the lunatics, and to the oppression of the medical profession, which performed the most important duties to these suffering and unprotected persons. In all these matters the central authority was more to be depended upon than the local Boards. He preferred the Amendment of his honourable Friend (*Mr. P.A. Taylor*),[1] but, as the Committee had negatived it, he should give his strong support to the clause.

[1]Taylor's amendment (col. 1421) provided that the Board should not insist on the appointment of a chaplain if the duties of that officer could be secured without payment. For its defeat, see col. 1423.

120. Election Petitions and Corrupt Practices at Elections [9]

18 JULY, 1868

PD, 3rd ser., Vol. 193, cols. 1449, 1451, 1456. Reported in *The Times*, 20 July, p. 6, from which the variants and response are taken. For the Bill, see No. 89. The discussion in Committee was on an additional Clause proposed by Fawcett, which provided that the expenses of returning officers be paid out of the rates, and required a deposit on behalf of every candidate of £100, such monies, in the case of candidates receiving less than 10% of the votes received by the least successful of the successful candidates, to be used to help defray expenses (cols. 1443–4). After some discussion, including the assertion that candidates' paying of returning officers was not a corrupt practice, the case was raised of Members who, having accepted office, had to stand for re-election: Should the rates cover their expenses?

[a]IS IT FAIR OR REASONABLE to take advantage of a technical difficulty in order to leave a question of this sort undecided until after the next election? If in a purely legal point of view it does not belong to the subject of corrupt practices, yet it belongs to a system of measures of which that relating to corrupt practices is the completion. Unless it be agreed to, the system will be left incomplete, and the Reform Act will, in some important respects, actually deteriorate the representation, for its practical effect will be to bring us nearer to a plutocracy than we ever have been before.[a] I would most earnestly appeal to the honourable Member for Suffolk (*Mr. Corrance*), who has made so excellent a speech in favour of the proposition,[1] to put for the present in abeyance his objections to any additional burthen on the local rates—objections in which, as I have stated on a former occasion,[2] I in part agree, and which will certainly, with the whole subject of the incidence of rates, come under the early consideration of the new Parliament. I beg him to trust the fairness and sense of justice of the future House of Commons, and not to resist a provision required for the beneficial working of our political institutions, because it involves a very small, and probably temporary, addition to the local expenditure. (*Hear, hear.*)

[*There was still objection to the requirement that £100 be deposited.*]

Mr. J. Stuart Mill said, the House would be glad to learn that anyone could be

[1]Cols. 1445–6.

[2]See No. 95 (12 May, 1868).

[a–a]TT Even supposing that logically or properly this clause has nothing to do with corrupt practices, would the House make use of a technical difficulty in the way of inserting in what might be called the completion of the measures of Reform a clause which would go far to show the people that Parliament did not mean, under the guise of a wide scheme of enfranchisement, to impose on the country a scheme which would enable parties to make the representation a plutocracy?

nominated and elected who was not in possession of £100, but whose friends were willing to put down £100 for him.

[*Discussion continued on the question of the deposit, and that proviso was removed from the Clause, which was then approved. Then the debate turned to a further Clause that candidates be required to subscribe to a declaration of honesty. It was objected that such declarations would not prevent lying.*]

Mr. J. Stuart Mill said, it was no great compliment to the House to represent that it consisted of persons whom a declaration upon honour would not bind. He himself thought a declaration on honour would bind the Members of the House, provided it was imposed with a serious intention of doing so. It had been too much the fashion to regard these declarations as mere forms; but they were so only when the engagement which they made was one which opinion did not really desire to enforce. The object should be to impress upon Members that the House was really in earnest and meant the declaration to be a sincere one. That object was sought to be obtained by the penalty of £500, and he thought this would be a means of enforcing the declaration.

[*After further discussion,*]

[b]*Mr. Mill said that* many of the amendments undisposed of were of considerable importance. Four of them were at least as important as those which had been discussed already. He doubted whether it would not be better to go on with the discussion than postpone it till the fag end of the evening.[b]

[*After Disraeli said that he would bring the Bill on as the first order of the day on Wednesday, the Clause was negatived.*]

121. Imprisonment for Costs on a Dismissed Charge [1]

21 JULY, 1868

PD, 3rd ser., Vol. 193, cols. 1553–4. Reported in *The Times*, 22 July, p. 6. See No. 131 for a further question on the case.

MR. J. STUART MILL SAID, he would beg to ask the Secretary of State for the Home Department, If his attention has been called to the case of Mr. William Castle, of Melton Mowbray, recently sentenced by a bench of magistrates to fourteen days' imprisonment with hard labour, for non-payment of twelve shillings imposed on him as costs on account of a dismissed charge, he being sixty-three years old, and, as he states, unable to pay that sum; and whether Her Majesty's Government will

[b–b]+TT

adopt any measure to prevent imprisonment, imposed in lieu of a pecuniary payment, from being accompanied by the penal infliction of hard labour?

Mr. Gathorne-Hardy replied, that he had not heard of this case till it was mentioned by the honourable Gentleman yesterday;[1] *but he had taken steps to obtain information. When he was fully informed on the subject he would state his impression as to whether there was any necessity for further legislation.*

122. The Fenian Prisoners [2]

21 JULY, 1868

PD, 3rd ser., Vol. 193, cols. 1556–7. Reported in *The Times*, 22 July, p. 6, from which the variants are taken. See No. 117. John Vance (d. 1875), then M.P. for Armagh, asked Mill "Whether it is true, as reported in the *Irishman* newspaper, 14th July 1868, that he wrote a letter to Mr. Nevin, dated the 2nd July, in which he objected to ask a Question concerning the convicts Warren and Costello, because he 'thought that asking the Question publicly could do the prisoners no good, and would only enable the Government to claim and obtain credit for clemency'" (*The Times*). Mill had written a letter on 2 July, 1868, to George Francis Train (1829–1904), a U.S. merchant and author, who was in the U.K. working on behalf of the imprisoned Fenians (*CW*, Vol. XVII, p. 2015). The letter, which contains the passage quoted by Vance, was published in "George Francis Train's Levees," *The Irishman*, 18 July, 1868, p. 37. "Mr. Nevin" was a fictitious character invented by Train.

I BELIEVE, Sir, I am under no obligation to answer the honourable Member's Question, but I have not the smallest objection to do so. I have not seen the article in the *Irishman*, nor have I ever corresponded on any subject with that paper; nor, so far as I am aware, with Mr. Nevin. But I did write a letter to a friend of the two prisoners in question, which contained some words bearing some resemblance to those here quoted. Having been asked by a friend of the prisoners to put a Question concerning them, I thought it right before doing so to lay the case before the friends of the prisoners, in order that they might consider whether, from the point of view of the prisoners themselves, it was desirable or not that this Question should be [a]asked[a]. What words I used I cannot exactly remember; but the statement quoted conveys in two important particulars an extremely inaccurate notion of my sentiments. In the first place, it represents me as having been unwilling to ask the Question. I never was in the smallest degree unwilling, and, as the House is aware, I did ask the Question. Secondly, it represents me as unwilling that the Government should claim or obtain any credit [b]for clemency[b]. I desire extremely

[1]I.e., when he saw Mill's Notice of Motion (reported in *The Times*, 21 July, p. 9).

[a-a]TT] PD answered
[b-b]+TT

that the Government should both claim and obtain credit for everything meritorious that they have done.

123. Election Petitions and Corrupt Practices at Elections [10]

22 JULY, 1868

PD, 3rd ser., Vol. 193, cols. 1623, 1639, 1640–1, 1643, 1646, 1647–8, 1650. Reported in *The Times*, 23 July, p. 4. For the Bill, see No. 89. Consideration was being given to the Bill as amended, with indignation being expressed at the Government's now introducing new amendments and wishing to reconsider the Clause Fawcett had successfully moved on 18 July (see No. 120).

MR. J. STUART MILL SAID, the Solicitor General had misunderstood what it was the Opposition considered unfair conduct on the part of the Government.[1] No one dreamt of imputing unfairness to the Government in proposing to re-consider the decision of Saturday last;[2] but what was complained of was that so short a Notice should have been given of their intention to rescind that decision. It was utterly impossible, when it became known long after post hour, to communicate with absent Members in time for them to attend in their places. He thought, after the indignant display of virtue on the part of the right honourable Gentleman at the Head of the Government, when the question of his honourable Friend the Member for Bradford (*Mr. W.E. Forster*) was asked on Monday,[3] they had a right to complain of the unfairness of the Notice given by the Government.

[*After several amendments and new clauses were considered, Mill brought in his first motion.*]

Mr. J. Stuart Mill moved the following clause:

At the trial of an Election Petition under this Act the judge shall have power to receive evidence of corrupt practices which any elector who shall have voted at the Parliamentary Election to which the Petition refers may have committed at any Municipal Election within the same county or borough within two years before the presentation of the Petition, with the object of proving that the voter was corruptly influenced in voting at the said Parliamentary

[1]Brett, cols. 1622–3.

[2]I.e., the approval of Fawcett's amendment (*PD*, 3rd ser., Vol. 193, col. 1554).

[3]For Forster's question on 20 July, 1868, concerning the Government's intentions with reference to Fawcett's amendment, and Disraeli's reply, see *The Times*, 21 July, p. 7 (*PD* does not report the exchange).

Election; and any special Commission appointed to inquire into the existence of corrupt practices shall have power to inquire into corrupt practices at Municipal Elections to the same extent and in the same manner as into corrupt practices at Parliamentary Elections.

As he had expressed his sentiments on the subject of the clause on a former occasion he would not again trouble the House with any observations upon it.[4]

[*The Solicitor General objected, as he and others had to Mill's earlier amendments involving municipal elections (see Nos. 116 and 118), that they were a separate matter. The Clause was rejected.*]

[*Mill then introduced his second motion.*]

Mr. J. Stuart Mill: Sir, I rise to move a clause declaring illegal the employment of paid canvassers, or paid agents other than the one appointed under the Corrupt Practices Prevention Act.[5] The clause is directed against the greatest of all the sources of undue expense at elections, especially in counties and large towns. It is well-known that when a candidate presents himself to a large constituency, determined to carry all before him by dint of money, a great part of his outlay consists in hiring canvassers, and they are hired by hundreds, very often without any real intention that they should canvass, and many of them never do canvass. Up to last year, under pretence of payment for canvassing, any number of electors might, without any breach of law, be paid for their votes. A clause, however, in the Reform Act, which the country is indebted to an honourable Member near me for proposing, and to the Government for accepting, has struck a blow at this mode of bribery, by enacting that no one in the actual pay of a candidate shall be allowed to vote.[6] Hereafter, therefore, a man can no longer be paid in this manner for his own vote. But he can still be paid for the vote of his father, or his brother, or his wife's father or brother; and, besides, there is such a thing as collective bribery—bribery of a whole constituency, by spending money freely in the place. Every petty tradesman in the town is virtually bribed by a man who flings money about lavishly on all sides, most of which comes back almost immediately to be spent at their shops. All expenditure by which electors profit is a kind of bribery; and, though it may not be feasible to put a stop to all forms of it, still, if there be a form which answers no useful purpose whatever—unless confining the representation to millionaires be a useful purpose—this at least ought surely to be put a stop to. Now, what useful purpose, at this time of day, is promoted by personal canvassing? A seat in this House ought no more to be obtained by private solicitation than by money payment. The use of canvassing, when there was a use,

[4]See No. 116 (14 July, 1868).

[5]17 & 18 Victoria, c. 102 (1854).

[6]Sect. 11 of 30 & 31 Victoria, c. 102 (1867), proposed by John Candlish (1816–74), M.P. for Sunderland, on 1 July, 1867 (*PD*, 3rd ser., Vol. 188, cols. 795–8), and accepted (*ibid.*, col. 811).

was to make the candidate and his pretensions known to the constituency; but this is now done by addressing them in a body, through the Press or at public meetings. It is from the candidate's public addresses, or from the newspapers, that the electors even now learn all that they ever do learn about the candidate; they do not want canvassers to tell them. If there is to be canvassing, it ought to be done by volunteers. Everybody who has any business to be a candidate has a sufficient number of zealous supporters to do all the canvassing that can be needful. Acquaintances may talk to acquaintances, and neighbours to neighbours, and win them over by persuasion and moral influence; but what moral influence has a man who is paid for his persuasiveness? And what would the electors lose if they could only be talked to by somebody who believes what he says, and cares enough about it to say it gratis?

[*The Solicitor General replied that there was nothing corrupt about employing ordinary paid canvassers. After some expressions of agreement with Mill, the Clause was lost (col. 1643).*]

Mr. J. Stuart Mill said, it would be useless, after the division which had just been taken, for him to move the next clause of which he had given Notice, which was a supplement to the one just rejected.[7]

[*Ayrton moved a new Clause to allow the Speaker to appoint attorneys for the House of Commons (cols. 1644–5).*]

Mr. J. Stuart Mill said, that the only fault which he found with the Amendment of his honourable and learned Friend the Member for the Tower Hamlets (*Mr. Ayrton*) was, that it did not go far enough. His (*Mr. Stuart Mill's*) opinion was, that if they desired to put an end to corrupt practices they must provide a public prosecutor, and not rely upon the private interest of candidates and their supporters for proceeding against suspected individuals. They would never get rid of corrupt practices, unless they made it the duty of some particular person to inquire, not into compromises only, but into all matters connected with corrupt practices, and to institute prosecutions where evidences of corruption were found to exist. The proposed clause, however, was a good one as far as it went, and he should therefore give it his support. He hoped the Government would accept the clause.

[*Ayrton's Clause was rejected.*]

Mr. J. Stuart Mill said, he rose to move the following clause:

(Provision for expenses of trials and inquiries.)

The expenses of all trials or inquiries held under the present Act, except such expenses as are hereinbefore provided for, and except such part as the court or judge shall impose by way of penalty upon either the Petitioner or the Respondent, shall be defrayed in the case of

[7]For the amendment, see *Notices of Motions, and Orders of the Day*, 1868, pp. 2089–90.

any county from the county rate, and in the case of any borough, out of the monies, and in the manner and proportions mentioned in the Act of the sixth year of the reign of Victoria, chapter eighteen, section fifty-five, with respect to the expenses of carrying into effect the provisions of that Act; and the account of such expenses shall be made, allowed, and paid in the manner provided in the said Act, unless the court or judge shall certify that there is reason to believe that corrupt practices do not generally or extensively prevail in the constituency, in which case the said expenses shall be charged upon the Consolidated Fund.

He desired to carry into effect what he considered was a true and sound principle—namely, to throw the expenses of all inquiries into corrupt practices upon the community who were implicated. He left to the tribunal to determine what portion of these expenses should in any case be laid, to the relief of the ratepayers, upon the persons who had been proved to be guilty of corrupt practices, or upon those who were shown to have brought frivolous and improper accusations.

[*The Attorney General objected, saying that costs should fall on the defeated party. The Clause was lost.*]

[*After some further discussion, it was moved that the forthcoming municipal elections be postponed for a month, to prevent bribery during them from affecting the imminent parliamentary elections. It was argued that the motion would upset the extensive arrangements already made for the municipal elections, although it was admitted that municipal corruption sometimes affected parliamentary elections.*]

Mr. J. Stuart Mill said, he could conceive nothing more stultifying than for the House, after having passed stringent measures for putting down corruption at Parliamentary Elections, to allow perfect freedom of corruption in the case of municipal Elections. There could be no greater facility given to bribery at the Parliamentary Elections than to have the municipal Elections taking place just before them.

[*The motion was lost (col. 1650).*]

124. The Westminster Election of 1868 [1]

22 JULY, 1868

Morning Star, 23 July, 1868, p. 3. Headed: "The Members for Westminster and Their Constituents. / Meeting in St. James's Hall Last Night." In a letter to Edwin Chadwick of 28 July, Mill says: "The correct and complete report of my speech at St. James's Hall is that of the Star" (*CW*, Vol. XVI, p. 1426). Reprinted in *Addresses of the Hon. R.W. Grosvenor and J.S. Mill, Esq., Delivered at a Public Meeting of Their Constituents, Held at St. James's Hall, on the 22nd July, 1868* (London: Grosvenor and Mill Committee, Sept.,

1868), pp. 5–8. The full report in the *Daily Telegraph* (also in the first person) is so close in wording to that in the *Morning Star* as to suggest a common source; that in the *Daily News* is less full, and *The Times* merely summarizes Mill's speech. At the evening meeting the Chair was taken by Brewer; a large number of non-electors, including many women, attended. Brewer introduced the Members, and (as usual) Grosvenor spoke first, summarizing the history of the parliament from 1865. Mill "was received with the most enthusiastic applause, the whole meeting rising and joining in prolonged cheers" (*Daily Telegraph*).

LADIES AND GENTLEMEN, my honourable colleague in his able address has given you a very interesting review of the past, and no man was better entitled to do so, for during the three years in which he has been your representative his conduct has been in complete conformity with the opinions and sentiments which you have heard from his lips. (*Cheers.*) [a]We have been fellow-soldiers in one cause, and although we may perhaps represent, in some degree, different shades of the great Liberal party, and although some electors might, if there were a question between us, like my honourable colleague best, and some perhaps would prefer to be represented by me, I hope there is no one calling himself a Liberal who would not prefer either of us to a Tory. [b](*Loud applause and laughter.*)[b] I hope my friends, to whom alone I have a right to speak a few words, will consider the two Liberal candidates as one man.[a] (*Cheers.*) Ladies and gentlemen, as I have observed, my honourable colleague has dealt chiefly with the past, I will deal chiefly with the future. (*Hear, hear.*) We are assembled here under new circumstances. A great change has been made in our representative institutions, and the constituencies greatly enlarged in mere numbers, and still more improved by including in them portions of the community hitherto almost unrepresented, are now about to be asked what use they are going to make of their new power. Do they mean that the great addition which has been made to the strength of the popular element in our institutions shall bring forth fruit? Are they determined that the great alteration in the structure of our Government shall be attended with a corresponding improvement in its administration? The masses of the community have obtained, what they never had before, an influential voice in the conduct of the Legislature and of the executive. Is it their purpose that their interests, moral and material, shall be more and better attended to by the Legislature and the executive than has hitherto been the case? It depends on themselves. If they are indifferent to their own interests, they may be certain that other people will be indifferent too; but, if not—if they mean that the Government under which we are hereafter to live, shall be a good Government for the whole people, willing and able to cope with those great social difficulties which are pressing in upon us, and which we have got to conquer, or else they will conquer us—then it is time for them to bestir themselves, and as the first step in bestirring themselves, it is time for them to

[a-a]P [*in italic*]
[b-b]DT] MS,P (*Loud cheers.*)

bethink themselves, and see how they can best use their electoral suffrage to bring this about. (*Applause.*) The nation has now to a considerable extent a new task before it, and one which demands different qualities in those who have it to perform. There are two kinds of improvements: one kind which, to enable them to be accomplished, only requires that the nation shall make up their mind that it shall be done. Nothing is wanted but the will; where there is the will there is no difficulty about the way. When once the nation had decided that the corn laws ought not to exist, it had only to say to the Parliament, "repeal them." Anybody could do it. When it was once determined that it had to be done it only required a few lines of an Act of Parliament.[1] In the same manner the Irish Church, when the nation has determined, as I believe it has determined—(*loud applause*)—that it will no longer commit the great injustice of endowing with national property the Church of a small minority, and when it has also recognised that, in getting rid of this old iniquity, respect ought to be paid to life interests, it has only to make known its determination. The thing can be done almost as easily as said. (*Laughter.*) But the statesmanship of the country has much more to do nowadays than merely to abolish bad institutions. It has to make good laws for a state of society which never existed in the world before. We have to deal with a richer, a more struggling, and a more overcrowded society than our ancestors could have formed any conception of. A vast manufacturing and commercial industry has built itself up—no, not built itself, for there has been no building capacity, no constructive talent or foresight in the whole affair; neither can I say it has grown up, for growth supposes an internal principle of organisation and order, and there has been nothing of the kind—I can only say a vast manufacturing and commercial industry has thrown itself up—(*loud laughter and applause*)—by great energies, of which accident has almost alone determined the application; and from the necessities of the case, a hundred evils have sprung up along with it, which philanthropists are toiling after, with some, but with very imperfect, success. Now those evils are not of the kind respecting which the nation can say to its rulers "Do this," and they do it.[2] There are now many things to be done which demand long and patient thought—more thought than the public of any rank or class are able to bestow. What the public have to do is to find men capable of doing these things—(*applause*)—and to send them to Parliament. (*Loud cheers.*) For instance, let us take the question which is in every one's mind at present—the proper relations between capital and labour. (*Applause.*) As I said, this question is in everybody's thoughts; yet how far has the public mind advanced on the subject? It has got thus far: that the old relation between workmen and employers is out of joint; that probably good laws would help to make things straight; but that there are many things which laws had better not attempt, as the result would probably be a break-down and a miscarriage. This,

[1]By 9 & 10 Victoria, c. 22 (1846).
[2]Cf. Luke, 7:8, and Matthew, 8:9.

then, is not a case in which the people can tell Parliament what to do; it has got to be found out what to do; and the business of the public is to send men to Parliament who can find it out. [c] Next, let me speak of our pauperism and our system of poor relief. We know the vices of the system, we know that vast sums are levied, and that those who most deserve and most need public charity are badly relieved. We know that the nursing of the sick, the care of the aged and helpless, the education of the young, are often, we do not know how often, a cruel mockery. (*Loud cheers.*) But what is the cause of this? Because these things are not so organised that the persons concerned are compelled to do their duty. And we shall never cure the evil by merely crying out when some very flagrant case is found out and published. What is wanted is to put into the important positions men of organising minds, who know how to make people do their duty, and who know how to give due and adequate relief to destitution without encouraging those to claim it who can do without it. Then, as to the state of our town populations. The poorer quarters of our great cities are nests of disease and vice for want of proper sanitary arrangements, and from the bad construction and wretched overcrowding of the dwellings of the poor. (*Applause.*) How are these things to be remedied? For I do not suppose any of you think that it is to be done by rebuilding these quarters out of the taxes, and inviting the poor to come and live in them rent free. (*Laughter.*) It is a matter for thought and study, and one which will tax to the utmost the highest legislative and administrative ability. Next, as to education. We are all determined that a good education the people shall have, cost what it may. (*Loud applause.*) About that I think we are all agreed, and if it could be done by mere good will, we should not have long to wait. But look at the schools we already have. Those for the higher and middle classes, still more than the elementary schools. There are enough of them, and they have funds enough, to give a good education to the whole nation, yet all classes, from the highest to the lowest, are wretchedly ill-taught. (*Hear, hear.*) Why is this? Because the teachers are unfit for their work, or, at all events, do not do it. (*Applause.*) And why do they not? Because those whose duty it was to appoint good schoolmasters appointed bad ones; because those whose duty it was to look after the teaching left it to take care of itself; and because parents did not take the trouble to ascertain whether their children were taught anything or nothing. Well, then, how are good schoolmasters to be obtained? And how are they to be kept to their duty? Unless we place national education in the hands of men who can do both these things, the end will be that we shall spend a great deal more money, and be no better taught than we are at present. Now turn to the great subject of administrative reform—how to obtain the most effective government at the smallest cost. We might have our persons and property far better protected than at present, paying much less for protection, but paying to competent persons for good service what is now jobbed away or wasted. We might have a defensive force

[c]P [*paragraph*]

much more effective than at present, for a fraction of what our army and navy cost us; but can it be had by merely willing it? No; it requires men with planning heads, organising and contriving minds, who, with a large theoretical and practical knowledge of the particular subjects, have also the art of governing men, and of managing bodies of men. Unless the nation find out and lift into the posts of favour and command men of this quality, our military and naval systems will remain failures for national purposes, and successes only for those who profit by them. In every branch of our government the great want is of capable men; and in order that the most capable men may be in office, it is necessary that the House of Commons, which decides who shall be in office, should be rich in capable men. (*Hear, hear.*) The people of England have an opportunity such as they have not had since the days of the Commonwealth. The present leader of the popular party sincerely desires to do for the people in these and on many other subjects the best that can be done—(*great cheering*)—if they will only put it in his power. But if the electors want this done, they must not think it enough to send men to Parliament who will support Mr. Gladstone; they must send men who can help Mr. Gladstone. (*Loud applause.*) One man cannot suffice for everything; whatever Mr. Gladstone can do by himself is incomparably well done; but what has now to be performed requires many eminent men, instead of one. A vote for a member of Parliament is always a grave moral responsibility. When one has a voice in deciding whether the well-being of this empire, and all the great things thereon dependent, shall be entrusted to a man who is fit or to a man who is unfit, nothing can excuse the elector who, for purposes of his own, or from indifference to the public good, votes for the wrong man and against the right. (*Applause.*) But on this occasion there is a peculiar obligation on the electors to search the country for the very best men that can be found, for the course of history for a whole generation may depend on it. I am not advising them to discard their present members when these have served them faithfully and intelligently, but there are many members who retire; many seats may be gained from Tories; and there is a considerable number of new constituencies.[d] I hope we shall re-elect all our Liberal members who are good for anything; but I hope we shall reinforce them by others who will carry with them into the House of Commons some better furniture than money-bags and pledges. (*Loud cheers.*) I hope the electors will be wiser than to elect men of whom they have no opinion; whom they dare not trust to examine and think for themselves, and whom they therefore send to the House with tied hands, under promise to do exactly as they are bid. For my part, I am not ashamed to say that both in public and in private affairs I desire to be represented by somebody who can tell me what ought to be done instead of my telling him, for I well know that I shall never be able to instruct him in half the things which he will have to decide; so that, unless I choose somebody who can inquire and judge for himself, my affairs will be

[d]P [*paragraph*]

ill-managed. The electors are responsible to posterity; they are responsible to the unrepresented; they are responsible to the innumerable inhabitants of England's foreign dependencies, and they are responsible to their own consciences for sending to the next Parliament thoughtful men, and men with talents for government; and unless they rise to the height of this duty, the great benefits which we are entitled to expect from the reform in our institutions will be reaped much more slowly, and for a long time more imperfectly, than we would willingly hope. (*Mr. Mill resumed his seat amidst loud and continued cheering.*)

An Elector wished to know what the honourable members thought about the question of equalization of poor rates in the metropolis. [*Grosvenor said to cheers that he was in favour of equalization of rates.*]

Mr. Mill thought that every community was entitled to one administration of the poor laws. (*Cheers.*)

In answer to another Elector,

Mr. Mill said [e]he would induce guardians to perform their duties both by reorganisation and by means of a controlling authority. The principles of a good poor law are to give relief to unavoidable destitution in such a manner that those who can support themselves shall have no chance of obtaining, and no motive for claiming, it[e]. (*Cheers.*) He might be compelled to accept a division of the metropolis with reference to the administration of the poor law, but he thought the rates should be the same throughout the whole of the metropolis because its inhabitants suffered from each other's sickness and poverty. (*Cheers.*)

Mr. Webber wished to know what steps the honourable members had taken to reduce our enormous national expenditure.

Captain Grosvenor said that, with the view of reducing that expenditure, he would endeavour to place Mr. Gladstone on the Treasury Bench. (*Cheers.*)

Mr. Mill said his honourable colleague had given exactly the answer which he himself should have given.

In answer to another Elector, [*Grosvenor said he favoured opening museums on Sunday, but would not pledge himself; unquestionably he was not in favour of opening places of amusement on Sundays.*]

Mr. Mill said he should be willing, without hesitation, to vote for the opening of any place of instructive amusement. As to theatres and similar places they might, he believed, be made places of instructive amusement, but he believed they were very seldom such. Whether they were or not, the opening of them in the present state of the public mind would shock the feelings of many good people [f], and he advised those who wish to open such places as those referred to on Sunday, to limit themselves to the more useful kind (*hear, hear*)[f].

[e-e]DT] MS the principles of a good poor law were the giving of relief to unavoidable destitution in such a manner that those should have no chance of obtaining relief who could support themselves by their labour

[f-f]+DT

In answer to another Elector, [*Grosvenor said that probably some of the funds taken from the Church in Ireland would be applied to all the religions professed in Ireland.*]

Mr. Mill [g]*said* while there was agreement between himself and his honourable colleague on the great principle of religious equality, there was some difference between them in its application. He opposed the application of any of the property of the Irish Church to the support of any clergy or any sectarian denomination[g]. (*Cheers, and cries of Bravo.*)

[*Probyn moved, Beal seconding, approbation of the Members, and full support of them jointly, sinking "all minor differences." An amendment was moved by B.B. Sapwell, to "expressions of disapprobation," that the unsatisfactory views expressed by the Members disqualified them as representatives for Westminster. "The speaker went on to make some remarks in support of his amendment, but the storm of groans, hisses, and other discordant sounds was so great that what he said was inaudible." But "on the interposition of Mr. Mill, Mr. Mason Jones, and the chairman"* (Daily Telegraph), *he was allowed to complete his remarks, and Ross rose to second the amendment, bringing on another round of disturbance; the amendment was defeated. Harriet Law then spoke, to loud cheers, in favour of the motion and of suffrage for women. The motion being passed (the Chair having ruled against the proposal of a "lady near the platform" that the names of the Members be put separately), the customary vote of thanks to the Chair was moved, and then Fawcett arrived; in seconding the motion, he described Mill's "assiduous attention to his duties, and remarked that his defeat—which he could not believe possible—would be an injury to the House of Commons, a loss to the Liberal party, and a blow from which the great cause of democracy throughout the world would not recover for years"* (Daily Telegraph). *The vote of thanks was carried, and the meeting ended.*]

125. Election Petitions and Corrupt Practices at Elections [11]

23 JULY, 1868

PD, 3rd ser., Vol. 193, cols. 1676, 1678, 1685, 1691. Reported in *The Times*, 24 July, p. 6. For the Bill, see No. 89. The debate was on a new Clause: "Whenever any person or persons shall have been reported by the Judges to have been guilty of corrupt practices, the Attorney General shall institute against such persons or person such proceedings as the law will allow" (col. 1676).

[g-g]DT] MS objected to any portion of those funds being appropriated to the support of any clergy or sectarian body

MR. J. STUART MILL thought it very important that some official person should be charged with the duty of considering whether a prosecution was necessary or not.

[*The Clause was negatived.*]

[*Then Lowther moved to amend Clause 43 (see No. 116) to make repeated corruption a misdemeanour. This modification the Attorney General thought too harsh: an agent who had already been punished for corruption, if he got another appointment within seven years, would be liable to two years' imprisonment.*]

Mr. J. Stuart Mill said, he hoped the House would divide, as the country would like to see the names of the honourable Members who thought it was too severe a course to punish an agent or canvasser who, having been guilty of corrupt practices in one election, procured similar employment in a subsequent election.

[*The amendment was lost.*]

[*The debate then returned to Clause 53 (Fawcett's clause; see No. 120). Various amendments were moved concerning a deposit to be used for election costs if the candidate failed to poll certain percentages of the vote. Wentworth Blackett Beaumont (1829–1907), M.P. for Northumberland, proposed that the percentage should be one-fifth of the votes cast, the failed candidate being liable for his share of the costs, and after some discussion added that the proposer and seconder of such a candidate should be liable for that share (cols. 1681–2). George Leeman (1809–82), M.P. for York, proposed an amendment retaining the one-fifth provision, but calling for a deposit of £100 in boroughs and £200 in counties.*]

Mr. J. Stuart Mill thought the object which the honourable Member for York had in view would be sufficiently attained by the proposal of the honourable Member for Northumberland.

[*Leeman withdrew his amendment, and then the proposal of Beaumont was defeated. The Government continued to try to subvert Fawcett's Clause 53; the Solicitor General moved to leave it out (cols. 1687–8), saying in defence of his motion that the obscure and intricate machinery of rating would make the Clause impracticable.*]

Mr. J. Stuart Mill: If the Government were aware of the profound feeling of satisfaction that went forth through the country on learning that the Amendment of the honourable Member for Brighton was carried, they would, instead of imposing any technical objection in the way of the passing of the clause, introduce a Bill, if necessary, for the purpose of giving it effect, and pass it through both Houses, as they could easily do, within a week. The representative of an extensive constituency remarked to me that the adoption of the clause marked the commencement of a purer era, and would bring forward more eligible candidates.

[*In the event, Clause 53 was struck out of the Bill.*]

126. Election Petitions and Corrupt Practices at Elections [12]

24 JULY, 1868

PD, 3rd ser., Vol. 193, cols. 1729–30. Reported in *The Times*, 25 July, p. 7, from which the response is taken. For the Bill, see No. 89. As the third reading began, Fawcett moved an amendment to recommit the Bill to consider the question of providing for election officers' expenses out of the rates (col. 1716). Mill spoke after Clare Sewell Read (1826–1905), then M.P. for Norfolk East (col. 1729). Writing to W.D. Christie on 27 July, 1868, Mill says: "You will have seen that after many days and nights of hard fighting, all our efforts to improve the Bribery Bill have been defeated, even Fawcett's clause being at last negatived. Good however has been done by the discussion, and a foundation laid for future success, as even the Saturday Review acknowledges. The Bill has, as you see, been extended to Scotland and Ireland. But its good effects, as it stands at present, will not be very great." (*CW*, Vol. XVI, p. 1425.) For a later reference to the matter, see his letter to C.W. Dilke on 14 February, 1872 (*CW*, Vol. XVII, pp. 1871–2).

THE HONOURABLE GENTLEMAN who has just sat down seems to think that unexpensiveness and purity of election is a matter which affects the electors only, and that the non-electors have no interest in the matter—a view in which I confess I do not share. I do not propose to revive the question of how far the Government has treated us fairly in regard to this matter. We must accept the statement of the First Minister of the Crown that at the time when he replied to the question of the honourable Member for Bradford (*Mr. W.E. Forster*) the Government had no intention of opposing this clause.[1] But when the right honourable Gentleman proceeds to give a history—the correctness of which is countersigned by the right honourable Member for Oxfordshire (*Mr. Henley*)[2]—of what has passed, and says that the House have rejected as ineffectual all propositions to reconcile the scheme of the honourable Member for Brighton (*Mr. Fawcett*)[3] with the desirableness of giving security against vexatious contests, I cannot assent to the correctness of his statement. There was not one of the proposals made which would not, in the opinion of the supporters of the clause, have proved perfectly effectual. The objections did not turn on the efficacy of the proposals, but on which of them was most likely to pass the House. They were overthrown by the action of the Government, but the right honourable Gentleman has not shown that there would be any difficulty in working them. The course pursued fully illustrates the old proverb "None so deaf as those who won't hear." Does anyone think that if the right honourable Gentleman applied his mind to the subject every difficulty would not quickly vanish? We have an apt illustration of the mountain-like magnitude

[1]For Forster's question and Disraeli's response on 20 July, 1868, see *The Times*, 21 July, p. 7.

[2]Cols. 1727–8.

[3]Fawcett, motion of 18 July, cols. 1443–4.

that molehill objections may assume, in the argument of one honourable Gentleman—that if a little more money than enough is taken from the county rate for the purpose of paying election expenses it will be impossible to know what to do with the balance.[4] We have heard of lions in the path,[5] but difficulties such as these are snails or earwigs in the path, and not lions. Were the Government aware of the feeling of satisfaction that went through the country along with the news that the clause of the honourable Member for Brighton was carried, they would, I think, instead of throwing technical difficulties in the way of its adoption, rather bring it in in the form of a separate Bill than lose the chance of its passing. I hope, therefore, that the Motion to re-commit the Bill will be carried. (*Divide, divide!*)

[*Fawcett's amendment was lost, and the Bill received its third reading (col. 1732).*]

127. Smoking in Railway Carriages [1]

24 JULY, 1868

PD, 3rd ser., Vol. 193, col. 1736. Reported in *The Times*, 25 July, p. 7. In Committee on "A Bill Intituled An Act to Amend the Law Relating to Railways," 31 Victoria (28 May, 1868), *PP*, 1867–68, IV, 513–30, the discussion was on a motion to insert after Clause 17 the following clause: "And all Railway Companies shall, from and after the passing of this Act, in every passenger train, provide smoking compartments for each class of passengers" (col. 1735). It being objected that some trains having so few carriages, or even only one, such a policy was impracticable, Mill made his first intervention.

MR. J. STUART MILL SUGGESTED THAT the provision should be made to apply only to trains of a certain length. The abuse of smoking had become so great, and the violation of the companies' by-laws so frequent, that the smoking in trains had become a positive nuisance. Scarcely a railway carriage could be entered in which smoking was not going on, or which was not tainted with stale tobacco.

[*It was remarked that the issue should be settled by public opinion.*]

Mr. J. Stuart Mill said, public opinion in this instance was swayed by a majority of smokers. It was a case of oppression by a majority of a minority.

[4]John Floyer (1811–87), M.P. for Dorset, col. 1723.
[5]Proverbs, 26:13.

128. The Westminster Election of 1868 [2]

24 JULY, 1868

Daily Telegraph, 25 July, 1868, p. 5. Headed: "Election Intelligence. / Westminster." The report of Mill's speech in the *Daily News* agrees so closely with that in the *Daily Telegraph* as to suggest that they were taken from a single report, or that Mill supplied copy to both papers. *The Times* has only a brief summary of the proceedings; its account, however, provides an introductory topic linking Mill's speech to the conclusion of Grosvenor's, and gives more of the substance of the question period than does the *Daily Telegraph*. The *Morning Star* gives only Gladstone's letter. This election speech, like No. 124, was delivered while Parliament was still in session. Mill and Grosvenor addressed their constituents in an evening public meeting, chaired by Dr. Brewer, in the Pimlico Rooms, Warwick Street. Brewer opened the proceedings by reading a letter from Gladstone which lightly touched on the undesirability of W.H. Smith's representing Westminster, and then briefly praised Grosvenor before saying: "Of Mr. Mill, who has obtained a world-wide fame, it would almost be impertinent in me to speak the language of eulogy. Yet I will venture on two assertions, both having exclusive reference to his Parliamentary career. Firm in the maintenance of his own opinions, Mr. Mill has ever exhibited the largest indulgence for those of others; and with this liberal tolerance of differences he has shown, in the most remarkable manner, how to reconcile on the one hand a thorough independence, and on the other an enlightened sense of the value and power of that kind of union which is designated by the name of political party. More than this, Mr. Mill has set us all a rare example of forgiving temper, of forgetfulness of self, of absolute devotion to public duty; and I do not hesitate to express my deliberate opinion that his presence in the House of Commons has materially helped to raise and sustain its moral tone." Grosvenor as usual spoke before Mill, alluding to Smith's candidature (and thereby provoking an interruption that led, against Mill's and the Chair's wishes, to an ejection), and reviewing the Government's record. He closed with an attack on the Metropolitan Cattle Market measure, and then Mill, who "met with an enthusiastic reception," rose.

[a]MR. MILL THEN ADDRESSED THE MEETING. He spoke in strong terms against the Metropolitan Cattle Markets Bill, which he said would have his most strenuous opposition.[a1] He said that during the last two or three weeks he and his colleague had been engaged several days in each week, and latterly two or three days in succession, in endeavouring to prevent the electors of Westminster and throughout the country being given over into the hands of millionaires, and they had failed. (*A Voice: More's the pity.*) He said, more was the shame. (*Hear, hear.*) When the present Government introduced the Bribery Bill,[2] he really was in hopes that there was something like an intention to suppress, if possible, the bad practices prevailing at our elections. The Government took one rather bold step—they

[1]"A Bill for the Establishment of a Foreign Cattle Market for the Metropolis," 31 Victoria (5 Dec., 1867), *PP*, 1867–68, III, 387–94 (not enacted).
[2]See No. 89.

[a-a]+TT

asked the House of Commons, tenacious as that assembly was of its privileges, to give up the power of judging as to the extent to which corruption might have prevailed at elections. That power had hitherto been in the hands of the committees of the House of Commons, and the Government asked Parliament to transfer it to the judges of the land. They thought, and he thought, those judges were not so likely to sympathise with the offenders as the very class from which the offenders were drawn, and who were therefore placed in the same circumstances of temptation as themselves; and besides the change of tribunal, the Government proposed to increase the penalties upon the offenders. This gave him hopes. He thought there was coming from the Tories something substantial for the prevention of corruption. The meeting were not to think him credulous. It was very possible for Tories to be sincere in what might favour their cause at elections. (*Laughter.*) In the terrible struggle which had been going on for some weeks, almost from day to day, to endeavour to introduce into the bill precautions against corruption at elections, and to prevent that improper expense which made it impossible for any but rich men to gain a seat in Parliament, no persons stood more consistently by those who promoted the effort, and more honourably, than ten or a dozen Tories—high-minded honourable men, who would not owe a seat in Parliament to corruption. (*Cheers.*) That very day he had listened to a speech which had done his heart good—he meant the speech of Mr. Corrance, the Tory member for Suffolk.[3] Mr. Corrance complained of the great increase of rates, and the disproportionate degree in which, in his opinion, those rates would fall upon landed property; but notwithstanding, when he was told that purity of election, inexpensiveness of election, would be secured by so much as even a farthing or half a farthing increase of rates, he scorned the circumstance, and said that he and all the best agriculturists would much rather pay higher rates, if by that they could obtain better and more capable members of Parliament. (*Cheers.*) This was said in the language and tone which was irresistibly and unmistakeably characteristic of an honest man. He could name several other Tories who, not only by their votes, but by motions and speeches did what they could. But it was all in vain. After the Ministers had carried their own original proposition for a change of jurisdiction, not one single improvement would they allow to be made in the bill. One after another, Liberal and honest Tory members moved resolution after resolution, and amendment after amendment, and pressed these to a division, every one of which had for its object to make elections purer and cheaper. But not one of them would the Government suffer to be carried. Many Liberal members had gone into the country, to which they generally rushed at this period of the session—and he was sorry to say it was the period at which all tricks were perpetrated—(*hear, hear*)—and by this combination of causes those who promoted improvement had been defeated. As far as concerned the present Government, electors were now delivered into the

[3]*PD*, 3rd ser., Vol. 193, cols. 1730–2.

hands of millionaires. Two instances he would mention as peculiarly remarkable in this way. He then referred to the result of Professor Fawcett's amendment and that of Mr. Schreiber.[4] Continuing, he said he gave credit to the Government for a slight preference for honesty when they introduced the bill, but he had no doubt [b]that[b] Mr. Spofforth, who managed the elections for the Tory party, who knew all that was going on everywhere, and in every constituency in the Tory camp as well as any man living—he had no doubt this individual told his friends in the Cabinet they must not, at this election at least, put these practices at an end; if they acted too rigidly it was very much to be feared some of their members would not get in. (*Laughter.*)

The honourable gentleman resumed his seat amid loud applause, excusing himself for not further detaining the meeting by his anxiety to be present at the division on the Foreign Cattle Markets Bill. Both he and Captain Grosvenor were catechised as usual. [c]*In reply to an Elector, he said that* he had been in favour of the ballot, but was not in favour of it now. He thought that it rested with the electors themselves, who, if they were to band together after the manner of trades unions, might check electoral bribery and intimidation.[c]

[d]*Another Elector asked what the opinions of the members for Westminster were as to the reform of the House of Lords, and whether Bishops would not be better turned out.* [*Grosvenor said he had not thought about the matter, but such a change was not imminent.*]

Mr. Mill, in reply, said that he had his opinions on the matter, and they could be obtained by any elector for 18*d.* in the form of a book.[5] He thought that the better House of Commons they got the better Bishops they would have.[d]

[e]*As to the game laws, Grosvenor expressed himself in favour of some equitable arrangement between landlord and tenant; and Mr. Mill said that* he should like the game to belong to him who fed it.[6]

[4]For Fawcett's amendment, see Nos. 120, 123, and 125. Charles Schreiber (1826–84), M.P. for Cheltenham and Poole, on 22 July moved that municipal elections be postponed until after the parliamentary elections (*PD*, 3rd ser., Vol. 193, cols. 1649–50).

[5]The People's Edition of *Considerations on Representative Government* (London: Longman, *et al.*, 1865), pp. 100–1 (*CW*, Vol. XIX, pp. 517–19).

[6]The Game Law of 1831 (1 & 2 William IV, c. 32) allowed all to hunt who possessed a licence, but trespass was forbidden; the abiding dispute was over the right to hunt on leased land.

[b-b]+DN

[c-c]+TT

[d-d]TT] DT *In reply to one question as to the propriety of bishops having seats in the Lords, Mr. Mill said* he did not think they were a very valuable element in that assembly. But until we took the whole subject of the proper constitution and proper position of the Church of England into consideration, as he supposed we some day should—*laying sarcastic emphasis upon the words*—he did not suppose we should get better bishops unless we got better ministers.

[e-e]TT] DT,DN *A vote, pledging the meeting to support the honourable candidates, closed the proceedings.*

An Elector having put a question as to the duration of Parliaments, the Honourable Mr. Grosvenor said that the average duration of Parliaments at present was three, four, and five years, and he thought that quite short enough.

Mr. Mill said that that was also his opinion.

In reply to another Elector, Mr. Mill expressed himself favourable to the Abyssinian war. It had been treated as a necessary evil, and carried out with every sentiment of honour and of justice.[7]

A resolution was then passed, pledging the meeting to support the two speakers in the forthcoming contest; and a vote of thanks to the chairman brought the proceedings to a close.[e]

129. The Metropolitan Foreign Cattle Market

25 JULY, 1868

PD, 3rd ser., Vol. 193, col. 1780. Reported in *The Times*, 27 July, p. 6, from which the variant is taken. The Government had announced the previous night that it was withdrawing the Bill (for which, see No. 128), so on the order for Committee on its re-commitment, Montagu moved that the order be discharged (col. 1775). Nonetheless Members, including Mill, offered opinions on the measure.

MR. J. STUART MILL wished only to make one suggestion, which he was sure the noble Lord (*Lord Robert Montagu*) would take in good part—that if he drew up a new Bill, its provisions should be confined [a]not to cattle from infected countries, which should be entirely excluded, but[a] to cattle from suspected countries. If this were done there would very soon be no suspected countries. The two principal countries suspected were Holland and Prussia, both of which had a very valuable trade with us in their own cattle; and if they found that this trade was stopped because they allowed cattle from infected countries to pass through them, they would soon see the expediency of ceasing to do so. The proposed new market would then be superfluous, or could be made supplementary to the present market.

[7]In December of 1863, Theodore, King of Abyssinia, unhappy with the refusal of the British government to respond favourably to his diplomatic overtures, took captive the British Consul and a number of missionaries. Non-military efforts to secure their release having failed, an expedition was launched in the summer of 1867 under Robert Cornelis Napier (1810–90); it was quickly successful in freeing the captives, and Theodore committed suicide. When Napier was created Baron Napier of Magdala in recognition of his triumph, Mill submitted a petition in objection from a group in Macclesfield; he explained his action as being simply in accord with his view that citizens' positions should be known. The questioner here was undoubtedly prompted by Conservative efforts to portray Mill as unpatriotic.

[a-a]+TT

130. Smoking in Railway Carriages [2]

25 JULY, 1868

PD, 3rd ser., Vol. 193, cols. 1789–90. Reported in *The Times*, 27 July, p. 6. On consideration of the Regulation of Railways Bill (see No. 127), Mill spoke during the discussion of a proposed Clause: "And all Railway Companies shall, from and after the passing of this Act, in every passenger train where there are more carriages than one of each class, provide smoking compartments for each class of passengers" (col. 1787).

MR. J. STUART MILL THOUGHT THAT the permission sought to be given to smokers travelling by railways, by the proposal before the House, was right and proper; and, for the reasons which had been already urged by honourable Members who had preceded him, he thought that the permission was especially desirous in the case of passengers going long journeys; but he thought that smoking compartments should be in connection with the hindermost carriages.

[*The Clause in slightly amended form was accepted, and the Bill was approved.*]

131. Imprisonment for Costs on a Dismissed Charge [2]

27 JULY, 1868

PD, 3rd ser., Vol. 193, col. 1826. Not reported in *The Times*. See No. 121.

MR. J. STUART MILL SAID, he would beg to ask the Secretary of State for the Home Department, Whether he is now in possession of any information respecting the circumstances under which Mr. Castle, of Melton Mowbray, was sentenced to imprisonment and hard labour for non-payment of costs?

Mr. Gathorne-Hardy: Sir, I have received some information on the subject, from which it appears that Mr. Castle had taken proceedings against a man for using threatening and abusive language. The summons was dismissed, and Mr. Castle was ordered to pay the costs, or to be imprisoned with hard labour. I may mention that the Act, commonly known as Jervis's Act,[1] *gives the magistrate discretionary power to impose imprisonment with or without hard labour. Mr. Castle, it further appears, has been several times imprisoned for non-payment of costs, or things of that sort. On this occasion, however, somebody, to prevent his going to prison, came forward and paid the costs for him, and therefore he was not*

[1]11 & 12 Victoria, c. 43 (1848), associated with John Jervis (1802–56), M.P. for Chester until he became Lord Chief Justice of Common Pleas in 1850.

imprisoned at all, nor was he put to the slightest inconvenience, though he protested loudly against the interference of his friends, and professed himself very desirous of undergoing imprisonment.

132. Poor Relief [2]

27 JULY, 1868

PD, 3rd ser., Vol. 193, cols. 1885–6. Reported in *The Times*, 28 July, p. 6, from which the variant is taken. In Committee on the Poor Relief Bill (see No. 119), discussion was on a Clause proposed by John Harvey Lewis to the effect that lands and buildings acquired and used under the Poor Law Acts be exempted from increased assessment (col. 1885).

MR. J. STUART MILL SAID, he had given Notice of a clause of similar effect, though not going so far as that proposed by the honourable Member for Marylebone (*Mr. Harvey Lewis*). No injustice would be done to any locality by the adoption of the clause of which he had given notice.[1] Its principle was that asylums, hospitals, and other buildings, and all land used or occupied therewith for the purposes of the Metropolis Poor Act, 1867,[2] should be assessed for rates upon the annual value of the site, and any buildings on it at the time of the purchase.

[*The Clause was negatived (col. 1886).*]

[a]*Mr. Mill next moved* a clause regulating assessment on asylums, etc., used for the purposes of the Metropolis Poor Act, 1867.

[*The Clause was negatived without a division, and after two more clauses were negatived,*] *Mr. Mill* again brought up the proposal which had been negatived in an altered form, which he contended made a new clause of it, *but it was negatived without a discussion.*[a]

133. The Westminster Election of 1868 [3]

2 NOVEMBER, 1868

Daily Telegraph, 3 November, 1868, p. 2. Headed: "Election Movements. / Westminster." Reported in slightly less full form in *The Times* and the *Morning Star* (both in the third

[1]For the proposed amendment, see *Notices of Motions, and Orders of the Day*, 1868, p. 2007.

[2]30 Victoria, c. 6 (1867), Sects. 31, 32, and 55.

[a–a]+TT

person); the report of Mill's remarks in the *Daily News* is shorter. In a letter to Edwin Chadwick on 7 November, Mill says, "the papers have given only the most trumpery reports of any of my speeches except the first [on 2 November], which was comparatively commonplace; and of that, the only good report that I saw was in the Telegraph. All have been immensely successful." (*CW*, Vol. XVI, p. 1481.) The meeting of Mill and Grosvenor with their constituents was held at 8 p.m. in the Regent Music Hall, Regent Street, Vauxhall Bridge Road, with Dr. Lankester in the chair. The large room was densely crowded, many women being in attendance. Lankester, in introducing the Members, reminded the audience that he had presided over the meeting when Mill had first addressed the electors in 1865 (5 July; see No. 6). Grosvenor again spoke first. Mill rose "amid the loud cheers of the audience."

ELECTORS OF WESTMINSTER—I need hardly now add non-electors, for I believe and hope that by far the greater part of those whom I have now the honour to address, if they were not electors formerly, are so now. If they are not electors now, they will be as soon as the obstacles thrown in the way shall have been removed as far as possible, as I trust they will be, by the new Parliament. I therefore need not say electors and non-electors—but I will say old electors and new electors of Westminster—the question, the issue, which is presented to you at this general election I take to be as simple an issue as ever came before an electoral body. You have not got to decide between one Liberal and another, or between one school or one shade of Liberalism and another. There are constituencies that have this choice to make, and I can conceive that when they have this choice to make there may be difficulties and grounds for much discussion and difference of opinion; and I hope that the constituencies that may find themselves in this position will come to some clear decision and understanding before it comes to the day of polling [a], and thereby destroy all hope of Tory candidates being returned at the head of the poll[a] —(*hear, hear*)—and I speak this disinterestedly. The example which has just now been set in the great new borough of Chelsea—that example is well worthy of imitation by Liberals of all shades. I deeply regret that Mr. Odger—(*cheers*)—has been under the necessity—as a man of honour, and as a man who preferred his cause to himself, Liberalism and the good of his country to his personal feelings or vanity, or even his own opinions—to retire from the candidature for the representation of Chelsea.[1] I applaud Mr. Odger. I highly appreciate his conduct, and I deeply regret that he is the candidate who has had to retire. (*Interruption.*) I hope that those who supported him in his candidature will support the Liberal cause [b], and that they will be united, Liberals of all shades of opinion, in the grand and paramount object of keeping out a Tory[b]. In this city you

[1]George Odger (1820–77), trade unionist, Secretary of the London Trades Council, having failed to gain election in Staffordshire, had put his name forward in Chelsea, but had retired to avoid splitting the left-Liberal vote (Dilke was elected).

[a-a]+TT
[b-b]+TT [*in past tense*]

have no such choice to make. It is not between Liberal and Liberal, or even between professed Liberal and professed Liberal. It is between Liberals and Tories, or rather a Tory. [c]I am not aware that the gentleman who has presented himself—as he did before—to oppose your present members claims your suffrages on any other grounds than that of being a Tory. [c2] I am not aware that he gives you any other reason to support him, excepting that he will support a Tory Ministry. The question before you is the simplest possible. It is whether you, who have got a Reform Bill, will have as the fruits of that Reform Bill a Tory Administration? (*No, no.*) Will you have a popular and Liberal representative system and a Tory Government? (*No, no.*) It would be peculiarly out of place if you were to have any hesitation on this subject. (*Interruption.*)

The Chairman hoped that the meeting would keep quiet, as they would then be able to hear Mr. Mill.

It would be peculiarly out of place if any Liberal—more especially any advanced Liberal—were to have any hesitation on this subject, when the Liberal party has such a chief as I venture to say it has not had for centuries. (*Cheers.*) I do not believe that any one here will contradict me when I say that the one statesman in this country who, perhaps, more than any other within living memory has the confidence of the people, is Mr. Gladstone—(*loud cheers*)—who has the confidence of the mass of the people. The public believe that he is one who plans measures for the public good, who invites public support, who does not wait until there is a cry raised outside, not merely for something, but for the precise measure he brings forward; but he employs his own mind, his time, and thought to devise measures for the public good, and endeavours to put in practice the means of successfully carrying them. (*Cheers.*) With such a man at the head of the Liberal party, [d]who is, in my opinion, the only possible chief of the Liberal party at the present day, [d] I think any Liberal, of any shade whatever, would prove himself to be false to his principles if he were—I won't say to vote for a Tory against persons who would support Mr. Gladstone, but if he failed to vote for those who would support Mr. Gladstone. When the choice is between persons who would support Mr. Gladstone and those who would vote against him, the choice, as I say, is extremely simple. (*Cheers.*) There are some persons, whose Liberalism is not insincere, [e]who flatter themselves with what appears to me an extremely false and misapplied notion, [e] who fancy it is not of much importance who is Minister, and who think there is perhaps some advantage in having the Tories in place, because

[2]W.H. Smith, who had been defeated by Grosvenor and Mill in 1865.

[c-c]DN The gentleman who was now before them as a supporter of the present government did not base his claims upon anything other than the fact that he would vote with Mr. Disraeli, and it was well known that no measures of reform were proposed by that right honourable gentleman of his own free will. (*Cheers.*)] MS The more opponents Mr. Disraeli had the better measures he would give. He (*Mr. Mill*) did not think the Tory candidate would compel Mr. Disraeli; he possibly might follow him.

[d-d]+TT [*in third person, past tense*]

[e-e]+TT [*in third person, past tense*]

when they are in place you can force them to pass Liberal measures, which, if they were out of place, they would oppose. (*Oh.*) According to this you are to give them place and office in order that you may make them the instruments of carrying things against their convictions. Now, I do not mean to say anything about the morality of this. Your own minds will say whether it is a good thing to hold out inducements to make people, in the greatest of matters, act against their convictions? (*Hear, hear.*) I won't enter into this at all, but what I will say is this—you have no occasion to do it. If you return a sufficient majority to the House of Commons you are sure to carry any measure which you deliberately say you ought to have. (*Cheers.*) We are told you can carry measures through the House of Commons, but that the Tories are masters of the House of Lords, and that if you turn out the Tories they won't let Mr. Gladstone's measures pass through the House of Lords. (*A cry,—Do away with them, then.*) We will see what this comes to. This would be making the House of Lords determine who should form the Government of this country. (*Hear, hear.*) That was a power which the House of Lords never had before, and which they never claimed. The House of Lords has the power to prevent the passing of laws, or rather, I should say, of delaying them for some years. (*A laugh.*) The power of refusing to pass laws has gone by, or you would never have had the Reform Bill. (*Hear, hear.*) Of all the great measures which have made this country so improved as it is from what it was in Tory times, there is not one which the House of Lords has not resisted as long as it could. If they had succeeded, you would neither have had Parliamentary Reform nor measures so comparatively unimportant as the abolition of church rates[3] or the admission of Jews to equal power with other people.[4] Great or small, the House of Lords has shown its desire to prevent good legislation. In order to bribe them to get laws passed a little sooner than you could by a strong administration of your own, you are to give them the power of framing those bills and drawing them up. You know that their drawing up would be as far from your wishes as the Reform Bill brought in by the present Government was like the Reform Bill that passed the House. (*Hear, hear.*) You are asked to give them the power of framing bills in order that effect may be given to your political purposes. You are to give them a power of enjoying a government which was not their right even under the old constitution before the constitution was reformed. The House of Lords never claimed the power to say what should be the Government. Now you are to give the Lords power to cover the bench with Tory justices. They have covered half the bench with Tories during the two years they have been in power already. You are to give them power to cover the bench of bishops with Tories. You are to give them the power to appoint governors and viceroys. They are not so bad as to make all Tories, for they have done something better than that; their power in that direction

[3]By 31 & 32 Victoria, c. 109 (1868).

[4]Initially by 21 & 22 Victoria, c. 49 (1858), and then by 29 Victoria, c. 19 (1866).

is limited, but unlimited is the evil of holding out a prospect to ambitious people throughout the country to induce them to become Tories in order to gratify their ambition. The wavering man, the active lawyer, the active and rising clergyman, and the military man, or the civil servant of the Crown, who would like to have a governorship—all these are things to tempt a Tory Government to remain in power. But if these principles were acted upon, personal interest would be so placed against public duty that you could only rely on those few who would prefer their duty to their interest. I do not think we can do without people who used, during the time of Oliver Cromwell, to be called self-seekers.[5] It would not do to put them against us. There are always enemies enough to good. Let us suppose that you really would get better measures from the Tories than you could by displacing them for Mr. Gladstone and the Liberal party. I am far from thinking it is so; but supposing it is, how do you get them? It will be by compulsion. Their business will be to get into Parliament people who will not compel them. Your business is to get in people who will. If we want to get in a Tory Government for the purpose of extracting Radical measures from them, as has been sometimes done before now—(*cheers*)—the way to do it is to put in as many men as you can who won't let them stay there unless they do pass these measures. (*Cheers.*) So that, whether you expect to get good measures from a Liberal Government or a Tory Government, your course must be to send Liberal men to Parliament. The more supporters you send to Mr. Gladstone the better measures he will give. Mr. Disraeli will give better measures the more opponents you send. I do not think that the gentleman started in the Tory interest in this great city is likely to compel Mr. Disraeli to grant Liberal measures. It is possible that he might be willing to follow him. (*Laughter.*) That is not what we want. That is not what Mr. Disraeli wants. He wants people who will be Tories with him; or, if he turns Radical, will be Radical with him. (*Laughter.*) If you want him to turn Liberal you must send Liberals there. (*Hear, hear.*) I do not like to charge anybody with, or to suspect anybody of insincerity. Suppose the Tories, from Mr. Disraeli through the Cabinet down to those who voted with him on Reform, are perfectly sincere, and that they are glad they passed it—I do not think this true of them all—(*laughter*)—I am not sure it is true of any—(*laughter*)—but suppose it is—suppose they really rejoiced in the Reform Bill, and thought it would be a good thing. If they thought it would be a good thing—why, it must be because they thought it would bring forth fruits for them. Now what sort of fruits must it produce for them to be pleased at? (*Laughter.*) I like to believe what people say whenever I can. I think there is no time when we can more believe what a man says of himself than when it is to his

[5]Oliver Cromwell (1599–1658), a member of parliament from 1628, and Lord Protector 1653–58. For the term, see Edward Symmons (fl. 1640s), Royalist divine, *The First Sermon, Entitled "The Ecclesiastical Selfe-seeking"* (1632), in *Four Sermons* (London: Crooke, 1642).

own disadvantage; and when Mr. Disraeli says he is a Tory I believe him. (*Laughter.*) If Mr. Disraeli be a Tory and supports Tories, and they think the Reform Bill an excellent measure, what must be the consequence? They must expect the consequence to be Tory measures and Tory administration. If they do think so I do not think you would thank them for it. (*Laughter.*) If they are sincere they must think that you, who are new electors below ten pounds, are Tories at heart; but, unless you are so, I hope you will show them the contrary. (*Hear, hear.*) That is one thing they may say; or they may think you are not Tories, but that you are more subject than other electors to intimidation—that you can be forced to vote against your convictions. Well, I hope you will show them you won't do that. I dare say there are some who are good enough to think you are more bribeable than others. I am quite certain you will fling that imputation in their faces, at all events. (*Hear, hear.*) Did they give you a Reform Bill because they were afraid of Hyde Park meetings, or did they believe it to be a good measure? If they thought so, they must think the new electors would vote for them, and that the new electors want Tory measures and a Government more Tory than it is. The people who think that, think that you are bribeable, or can be forced into voting against your consciences. Europe and America have their eyes on this country at this moment. They want to see whether the masses of this country who have received the franchise are worthy of it or not. They want to see whether the working classes of this country, who have never before had any participation in the franchise, have got opinions of their own, and will insist upon having such men as they believe will exercise their minds upon such legislation as will give them a full share of the social advantages which they think, and to a great degree reasonably, that they have not yet had. (*Cheers.*) I do not think that is what the Tories mean. It is a simple question you have to decide. You have to decide whether your interests are better served by the Liberals than by the Tories. If by the Liberals, then vote for the Liberals. If you can get a better Liberal than I am, I will give way to him at once. (*Hear, hear.*) Only I think it is not fair to ask you to dismiss me for a Tory. I do not think he will serve you better. I have nothing further to say, except that I shall be happy to answer any question and to listen to any gentleman who has any remarks to make or any objections to offer, or suggestions for the future. Such meetings as these are the proper occasions for putting questions to representatives or candidates, and for asking them to explain anything that requires explanation. I shall be happy to listen to any objections, and to answer to the best of my ability.

[*The Chair announced a question about the candidates' willingness to admit local decisions in parishes and townships to prohibit by a 2/3 majority the sale of intoxicating liquors.*]

The Honourable Mr. Grosvenor: The only answer I can give is this, that if 999 people out of 1,000 were to combine to prevent the other unit from doing the thing which he had a perfect right to do, they should have no assistance from me. (Loud cheers.)

Mr. Mill: My colleague has expressly stated my views. (*Cheers.*) I will not weaken his words, but will simply give my adhesion. (*Cheers.*)

[*Mr. Anderson, a City Missionary, expressed great regret at these answers, and asked, amidst much interruption, whether the Members would vote for the Permissive Bill.*[6]]

Mr. Grosvenor said that the gentleman who had put the question had stated that the poor man ought to have the same law as the rich man. He would ask how that was to be, if the rich man could enter his place of refreshment and amusement, if need be, at any time on the Sunday, and yet the poor man was not to have any similar privilege. (Cheers.)

Mr. Mill thought it might be said further, that one effect of closing these places on Sundays would be to increase houses for "tippling"—(*hear, hear*)—and intoxication would be much less under control than it was at present.[7]

An Elector: It is reported that Mr. Mill is opposed to the equalisation of rates.

Mr. Mill: I am in favour of the equalisation of poor-rates in one town or city, however large, but not for the nation.

[*A question was asked about the funds of the Irish Church; Grosvenor indicated no answer was as yet possible.*]

Mr. Mill: Without being able to say with precision exactly the way in which the funds should be distributed, I think there are certain facts which must be observed.[8] They must be used for Irish purposes. They are Irish. They come from Irish land and Irish produce. They must not be given for the endowment, wholly or partially, of any religious body whatever—(*cheers*)—nor to any exclusive denominational system of education; but that they shall be applied to the more pressing social needs of Ireland—by preference, perhaps, to unsectarian and undenominational education.

In answer to other questions,

[f]As regarded the ballot he (*Mill*) desired to say that he was as much against it as ever—(*hear, hear*)—because he considered that what was a trust for the public ought to be exercised in the eye of the public, and if the working classes would only stand by one another as in the case of trades unions, he felt they would be able to prevent their being compelled to vote against their consciences. (*Cheers.*)[f]

[6]A constantly reintroduced measure, the next version of which was "A Bill to Enable Owners and Occupiers of Property in Certain Districts to Prevent the Common Sale of Intoxicating Liquors within Such Districts," 32 Victoria (22 Feb., 1869), *PP*, 1868–69, IV, 285–90.

[7]For Mill's response to an elector who objected to these answers, see *CW*, Vol. XVI, p. 1480.

[8]The reference is to the Liberal proposals that would eventually be incorporated in "A Bill to Put an End to the Establishment of the Church of Ireland, and to Make Provision

[f–f]DN] DT *Mr. Mill stated his reasons for disliking the ballot.* He thought a public trust should be exercised in a public manner.

Respecting the bill for giving legal security to the funds of trades' unions,[9] [*Grosvenor said while some protection should be given, he could not pledge himself to the details of any present measure.*]

Mr. Mill could not pretend that he had examined the provisions of the bill drawn up on behalf of trades' unions, but he was perfectly clear about two things—that it ought not to be in the power of any one to rob them, and, as long as people were members, they should be liable for their subscriptions.

[*Lyulph Stanley moved approval of the two Members, attacking Smith, referring to rumours that had "passed in Mr. Mill's absence," and declaring his own adherence to Mill's position concerning Governor Eyre. Mr. B. White referred favourably to Mill's correspondence with Bouverie. "Some people said that this correspondence would cost Mr. Mill hundreds of votes, and even his seat. (Loud cries of No, no.) He was sure that, so far from this being the case, the constituency would rally round Mr. Mill, and support him the more." The resolution was passed unanimously, and Grosvenor and Mill moved thanks to the Chair, and the meeting concluded.*]

134. The Westminster Election of 1868 [4]

4 NOVEMBER, 1868

Morning Star, 5 November, 1868, p. 2. Headed: "Election Intelligence. Westminster." The report in the *Daily Telegraph*, though shorter, contains some details not in the *Morning Star*. The brief account in the *Daily News* contains no additional matter. In a letter to John Plummer on 5 November, Mill commented that he had said "a good deal at the meeting yesterday" about "the expense of elections and the difficulty of getting working men's candidates into Parliament," but "it was not reported" in the newspapers (*LL*, *CW*, Vol. XVI, p. 1479; cf. *ibid.*, p. 1484). Mill and Grosvenor again addressed their constituents in an evening public meeting, chaired by J.F. Pratt, in Caldwell's Assembly Rooms, Dean Street, Soho, where in "the gallery and front seats were a good many ladies." Grosvenor, speaking first, alluded to his record and attacked that of the Government, saying it would be necessary to reform the Reform Bill in the next Parliament. Mentioning that he favoured the ballot, he referred to Mill's dissent on this issue, the only point of discord between them, and said (to applause) that the electors should not turn from Mill on this one point. After dealing with other questions of the day, Grosvenor concluded, and Mill rose, and was "accorded a reception of quite a remarkable character. All present stood up and for some time waved their hats and handkerchiefs, and cheered with much genuine enthusiasm."

---

in Respect of the Temporalities Thereof, and in Respect of the Royal College of Maynooth" (1 Mar., 1869), *PP*, 1868–69, III, 85–116; enacted as 32 & 33 Victoria, c. 42 (1869).

[9]It was known that in the next session there would be introduced "A Bill to Amend the Law Relating to Trade Combinations and Trade Unions," 32 Victoria (9 Apr., 1869), *PP*, 1868–69, V, 323–8.

MR. MILL REMARKED THAT it was now three years since the electors of Westminster were last called upon to select their representatives in the House of Commons. He was one of those in whom they reposed their confidence on that occasion, and he came now before them to seek for their verdict as to the manner in which he had discharged that trust; and, if they approved of his conduct, to ask for a renewal of their confidence. (*Cheers.*) But they had something more important to do than to express their judgment on the merits or demerits of any one individual. They had important public issues to effect. An expression of opinion by a large and important place like the city of Westminster exercised a good deal of influence, and it therefore depended upon them, to a great extent, as to how other districts would vote and decide. They had to decide, to some extent, whether the new Parliament should be under a Liberal or a Tory Administration. (*Cries of Liberal, and cheers.*) That was to say, whether the important work that remained to be done was to be accomplished by persons whose hearts were in the work—(*hear, hear*)—or whether it was to be continued to be entrusted to persons who would do it only by compulsion. (*Hear, hear.*) He did not mean to say that the Tories were opposed to all sorts of improvement—indeed, in the present day no political body of men could exist for any length of time that would be entirely opposed to improvement; but he thought he was justified in saying that the Tories were not in general distinguished by having the spirit of improvement exceedingly strong in them. (*Laughter.*) He therefore thought that they would not be satisfied to entrust the important work that remained to be accomplished in the hands of people who would not perform it unless they were driven to it. (*Hear, hear, Hyde Park, and cheers.*) He had heard a good deal about intimidation. (*Hear, hear.*) Carrying on the business of the country by intimidating the Government was a thing he was not fond of. That was the strange system by which legislation on the Reform question had been accomplished. [a]The adhesion of the Tories to change was only to be got by persuading them that it was more dangerous to refuse than to make improvements. (*Hear, hear.*) These were not the qualities of the rulers of the country; and he did not think the electors would entrust improvements to those who had to be frightened into making them. (*Loud cheers.*) He was no more favourable to government by intimidation than to voting by intimidation; but he thought, like Burke, that such acts of pressure were the occasional medicine of the Constitution, and ought not to be its daily bread. (*Hear, hear.*)[a1] Such a system was troublesome and expensive, and was, besides, not creditable to the country. (*Hear, hear.*) On the whole, he thought it was much better to put the work into the hands of those who did not want to be whipped into doing it. (*Hear, hear.*) Mr. Mill then proceeded to touch upon the proceedings in Parliament during the past session, particularly the efforts that were made to reduce election expenses,

[1]*Reflections on the Revolution in France* (1790), in *Works*, Vol. III, p. 95.

[a-a]+DT

and to take them out of the public purse of the district in which the election takes place instead of out of the purses of the candidates. It had been said that this would be shabby. He asked would it be shabby to defray the election expenses of such a man as Mr. Odger—(*cheers*)—who had come forward for Chelsea, and had conducted his candidature with an amount of straightforwardness and honour that might well be emulated by some of his betters; or the election expenses of Mr. Edmond Beales—(*great cheering*)—who had been mulcted some thousands of pounds on account of openly expressing his views on political affairs?[2] (*Hear, hear, and cheers.*) On the contrary, he thought it would be shabby to ask these gentlemen to defray the cost of their election. (*Hear, hear.*) [b]In support of his opinion, Mr. Mill referred to the action of the Tory party on Professor Fawcett's proposal[3] to throw the expenses of the returning officers at elections on the public, and Mr. Schreiber's motion to postpone the municipal elections till after the Parliamentary elections, which were made during last session.[4 b] As for bribery at elections, the attempt made to do away with that disgraceful practice he attached little importance to. He believed that before they could successfully put an end to bribery at parliamentary elections they must first of all check effectually bribery at municipal elections. He fully agreed with the evidence given on this point by the solicitor of the late Governor Eyre.[5] (*Hisses, cries of Hang him, and general commotion.*) That evidence was, in effect, that the corruption at municipal elections was the school and nursery of the bribery at parliamentary elections. (*Hear, hear, and cheers.*) It happened that municipal elections occurred this year immediately before the parliamentary elections, so that the opportunities and inducements for corruption became much enhanced. An endeavour was made to have the municipal elections this year postponed until after the general election; but notwithstanding what had been stated by the Tory authority to whom he had alluded, the postponement would not be granted. What object the Government had in opposing the postponement of the municipal elections he would leave to his hearers to judge. He would not undertake to say that the majority of the Tory party thought it would be serviceable to them to have a little corruption this one time more—(*a laugh*)—but they at all events opposed the separation of the two elections. (*Shame.*) Whatever the motives of the Tories were, he thought the carrying out of the Reform Bill and those other great questions in which they were all alike interested, ought not to be left in such hands. (*We don't mean it, and Hear, hear.*) *After repeating some matters in connection with his conduct in*

[2]Beales had been a Revising Barrister in Middlesex from 1862 to 1866 when, because of his political agitation, he was refused reappointment.

[3]See No. 120.

[4]See No. 128.

[5]Mill apparently confuses Philip Rose, the Conservative agent who gave the evidence referred to (see No. 116), with James Anderson Rose (1819–90), Eyre's solicitor.

[b-b]+DT

Parliament, which have been already published, Mr. Mill went on to say that he was ready and desirous to answer any questions which they wished to have answered. [c]*He said that,* being anxious to give opportunity for the asking of questions, he would not allude to other subjects, except that of which Captain Grosvenor had spoken. He regretted to find himself conscientiously opposed to many of the Liberal party, though not in principle, upon the ballot question. He abominated intimidation even more than bribery. Of two bad things, he disliked less the inducing people to do wrong by doing good for them than compelling them to do wrong by taking something from them. (*Laughter and cheers.*) He would not sacrifice permanent principles to temporary advantage; and the ballot would give a temporary advantage, because the cause of democracy was growing too strong to tolerate intimidation much longer—if all men would stand by each other as the members of the trades' unions did—while it was a permanent principle that a public duty should be performed in public. (*Cheers.*) He stood by his opinions. (*Loud cheers.*) If he was wrong, he would be beaten in the end; so they could afford to let him have his way. (*Laughter and cheers.*)[c]

An Elector wished to know the candidates' opinions on the Permissive Bill.[6]

Captain Grosvenor: I am against the Permissive Bill. (Cheers.)

Mr. Mill: I am against allowing the majority in any place to make laws regulating the tastes and morality of the minority. (*Cheers.*)

[*Following the question period after Mill's speech, a resolution of support for the Members was spoken to by Fawcett, who also received enthusiastic applause; he described Mill as "that great statesman, that good man, that illustrious thinker, and that eminent philosopher." The meeting ended with "Cheers for Gladstone and the two sitting members for Westminster and Professor Fawcett," the proceedings being "throughout of a remarkably earnest and enthusiastic character."*]

135. The Westminster Election of 1868 [5]

6 NOVEMBER, 1868

Morning Star, 7 November, 1868, p. 2. Headed: "Election Intelligence. / Westminster." Reported also in summary in the *Daily Telegraph*; the *Daily News* has only a one-sentence comment. In a letter to Chadwick of 7 November, Mill says: "I had already addressed one of my meetings on election expenses [see No. 134], and in compliance with your suggestion I

[6]See No. 133, n6.

[c-c]DT] MS (*A voice: The ballot.*) As he had before fully explained, he was on principle opposed to the ballot, and he was not prepared to give up that principle. By that principle he meant to stand. If, however, he was wrong, he was sure to be beaten in the end, so that they need not be afraid to let him have his way in this particular.

did so again last evening" (*CW*, Vol. XVI, p. 1481), but, as he goes on to complain, the newspapers were not reporting his remarks in full. He repeats the complaint in a letter to Chadwick on 10 November, saying: "The newspapers have not reported what I said about election expenses and I have no note of it" (*ibid.*, p. 1484). The public meeting of the electors of St. George's Without and Knightsbridge was held in the evening in the Pimlico Rooms, Warwick Street, Mr. West in the Chair. Most of the "leading inhabitants of Pimlico" were on the platform. Grosvenor spoke first; being interrupted by the Chair with the warning that pickpockets were about, he commented that he did not see the connection between pickpockets and the Irish Church. Mill was greeted with enthusiastic cheers.

MR. MILL IMPRESSED ON THE ELECTORS THE FACT THAT they had something more important to decide than the merits of their representatives. As a part of the electoral body of the United Kingdom, they had to decide whether they would be governed by a Conservative Administration or not. [a]"Conservative" was an extremely pleasant term; and it would be time for a Conservative Government when there was nothing else to be done. (*Laughter and cheers.*) When everybody was perfectly happy and comfortable, there would be a state of things worth conserving; but the world was not just yet happy enough for anybody to be conservative in it. (*Loud laughter.*) If they wanted it made better they had better trust to earnest Liberals. (*Cheers.*) It would be unjust to say all Tories were the enemies of improvement; but it was so uncommonly difficult to make them perceive that there was anything to improve, or that anything could be safely improved. (*Laughter.*) When an improvement was made, and evidently successful, they very often would accept it and be glad of it; but, on the whole, they were not people who could be expected to do much in that way of their own accord. (*Hear, hear.*)[a] [b]This had been, and was likely to continue to be, the character of the Tory party, because if any man arose amongst them possessed by the spirit of improvement, he was sure to become a Liberal and to throw off the Tory party, as Mr. Gladstone had done; or the Tory party would throw him off, as they did with Sir Robert Peel. (*Cheers.*) Therefore[b] there could be no surprise that the residuum of that party should not be depended upon for making great improvements—(*hear, hear*)—and there could also be no surprise that the remaining members of that party should require a great deal of educating. (*Laughter.*) The Tory party had now got a very able man to lead them who would make us believe that he had educated the party to which he was supposed to be attached. [c]Mr. Disraeli had professed to educate his party,[1] as the Irishman did his pig when he tied a string to its hind leg, and took it into Limerick[c] backwards. The Irishman was asked the

[1]Disraeli, Speech at the Corn Exchange, Edinburgh (29 Oct., 1867), reported in *The Times*, 30 Oct., p. 5.

[a-a]+DT

[b-b]DT] MS As the Tory party was constantly losing its best and greatest men, either because it rejected them or they rejected it,

[c-c]DT] MS Mr. Disraeli's education of the Tory party reminded him (*Mr. Mill*) of the story of the Irishman who managed to get his pig into the town of Limerick by making it walk

meaning of his getting his pig to walk backwards, and replied in what is known in Ireland as a "pig's whisper:" "Hush! The pig must not suspect where I'm taking it to; walking this way it does not see where I'm taking it to; the pig thinks it's going home; I couldn't get it into Limerick otherwise." (*Laughter.*) Mr. Disraeli had also taken his party into Limerick. There was, however, this difference between the Irishman and his pig, and Mr. Disraeli and his party. The Irishman made his pig go forward by making it fancy it was going backward, but Mr. Disraeli made his party believe they were going backward when they were really going forward. (*Laughter.*) But this was a thing that could happen only once. Mr. Disraeli could not make his party go into Limerick a second time in a similar way. (*Hear, hear, and laughter.*) But he (*Mr. Mill*) did not believe that Mr. Disraeli was entitled to the credit which that gentleman took to himself of educating his party. Besides, he believed that even Mr. Disraeli himself had undergone a process of education. (*Laughter.*) [d]He believed that Mr. Edmond Beales—(*cheers*)—had had much more to do with the educating of the Tory party than Mr. Disraeli, and he believed also that the same popular gentleman had a hand in educating Mr. Disraeli himself.[d] But he (*Mr. Mill*) did not think that this educating of the leaders of the great parties was a thing that could answer in the long run. (*Hear, hear.*) [e]But driving one's leader was uphill work, and the country had better send men to Parliament to support the most earnest Minister of the day in doing these things. (*Cheers.*) To get rid of the ratepaying clauses of the Reform Act, to secure purity and freedom of election, to remove the real and heavy grievances of Ireland, to secure a fair and equal management of charities for the welfare of the poor, and to accomplish similar needed reforms, Mr. Gladstone and a Liberal Government must be substituted for Mr. Disraeli and a Tory Government. (*Loud cheers.*)[e]

[*Grosvenor answered questions about the Prince of Wales's allowance, primogeniture, working-class representation, and payment of members.*]

Mr. Mill, replying to questions, thought that £60,000 a year ought to be enough for the Prince of Wales[2]—(*Hear, hear, and cheers*)—but he thought the question might be left in the hands of Mr. Gladstone. He should vote for the abolition of the law of primogeniture.[3] (*Cheers.*) He thought it was of great

[2]Albert Edward (1841–1910), Prince of Wales, later Edward VII.

[3]"A Bill for the Better Settling the Real Estates of Intestates," 29 Victoria (13 Mar., 1866), *PP*, 1866, V, 29–32, had been defeated; a bill with the same title was to be introduced in the next session, 32 Victoria (11 Mar., 1869), *PP*, 1868–69, V, 29–30.

[d-d]DT Mr. Disraeli had not been so clever or so unprincipled as he represented; for he had been himself educated, with his party, by the ancient goddess Necessity, whose high priest on this occasion had been Mr. Beales. (*Cheers.*)

[e-e]DT] MS *Mr. Mill then proceeded* to review the various measures—among them the settlement of the Reform, Church and land, and trade-union questions—which he considered necessary to be passed as soon as possible, so as to improve the physical and moral condition of the working classes, and which he believed would never be done by the Tory party unless the people of London and Mr. Beales did as they had done before. (*Cheers.*) Mr. Gladstone was, he believed, the most likely person to be able to carry those measures. (*Loud cheering.*)

importance that working men, who could be considered good representative men, should be in Parliament. (*Cheers.*) He was not in favour of paying members of Parliament. He would vote against the three-cornered constituencies.[4] He did not think, however, that those constituencies would injure the Liberal cause at the forthcoming elections. On the contrary, he believed that the Liberals would gain in the counties, and in Liverpool. It was a question to him whether they would lose anywhere by the introduction of that principle.

[*A resolution supporting Grosvenor and Mill was moved, seconded, and passed with three dissenting votes, and the meeting concluded.*]

136. The Westminster Election of 1868 [6]

9 NOVEMBER, 1868

Morning Star, 10 November, 1868, p. 3. Headed: "Election Intelligence. / Westminster." A summary report also appeared in the *Daily Telegraph*. The evening meeting of the electors of St. Margaret's was held in the Regent Music Hall, Regent Street, Vauxhall Bridge Road, Serjeant Tozer in the Chair. The meeting was well attended, with the stage boxes being "filled with ladies." Grosvenor, speaking first, was enthusiastically received. He referred to his difference of opinion with Mill over the ballot, saying that every time he heard Mill express his views he was "horribly afraid" that Mill might be right, but having read W.H. Smith and being reminded of how Tory employers treated their employees, he would stick with his views. Mill, "on rising to address the meeting, was greeted with several rounds of enthusiastic cheering."

HE SAID THAT he was present, like his honourable colleague, for the purpose of giving an account of his political opinions; but it would be more agreeable to himself if, before addressing them, any person present who might have reason to find fault with him or his conduct as the representative of Westminster would get up and give his reasons for doing so. (*Cheers.*) He thought that persons who entertained unfavourable opinions respecting him should not content themselves with merely calling out something in the body of a large meeting like this, and in such a way that nobody could understand them. (*Hear, hear.*) If anybody present had anything to say against him he therefore hoped that they would get up at once like men and Englishmen, and tell what was the cause of complaint. [a]*A man, attired in a white smock, at the back of the gallery, here called out, in a stentorian*

[4]The Reform Act of 1867 had given some boroughs three members, the electors voting for only two, with the intention of facilitating representation of minorities.

[a-a]DT] MS (*Cheers; some noisy demonstrations in the gallery, and a cry, "Some of Smith's lambs."*) [*paragraph*] *The Chairman said he was quite sure that the request of Mr. Mill would not be disregarded. (More interruptions and symptoms of opposition in the gallery.)*

voice, that he was a working man and a Constitutional man, and came forward to ask the candidates why they had not done as much as the "Constitutional candidate," Mr. Smith?

This question elicited loud groans from the meeting and considerable uproar. The Chairman in vain tried to obtain a hearing, but in a few minutes the "Constitution man" disappeared, and silence was restored.[a]

Mr. Mill went on to say that his friends would render him a great service if they would allow any person who wished to question him to do so. He had heard that plenty of things had already been said against him, and many more things which he dared say he had never heard. (*Laughter.*) It was of importance that he should fully know all that his opponents had to say of him. He had been told, for instance, that Mr. Smith's committee had put forth numerous placards with reference to him (*Mr. Mill*), but he had not seen them—not from any disregard of them, but because he did not reside in Westminster, and therefore they had not met his eye. Whatever those persons desired to say against him, he wished they would say it at a meeting like this. (*Hear, hear.*) [b]It was very little use talking with those who agreed with one; he liked to talk to those who differed from him, in order that he might hear them, and say what he could in reply. And so strongly did he feel this, that it would give him the greatest pleasure if the Westminster Conservatives would call a meeting of their own—they might pack it by tickets if they liked, so long as they admitted reporters—and although he went without a single friend, he was ready to go among them, and to[b] answer every question they might choose to bring forward—(*great cheering*)—and he trusted that such an opportunity would be afforded him; but he felt that here, where he had so many friends, no proper opportunity was given his opponents to criticise his conduct, and he was anxious that they should have fair play. (*Enthusiastic cheers.*) He would be better able to speak if gentlemen would point out to him any particular points upon which they desired information. (*Hear, hear.*) If there were any gentlemen present who desired to at once put to him any questions respecting his political conduct or his political opinions, he begged they would now at once come forward.

[c]*The honourable gentleman resumed his seat, but, as no one attempted to address the meeting, the Chairman, after a pause, requested him to continue his speech.*[c]

The honourable gentleman then proceeded to state his opinions on the leading topics of the day, the substance of which have been several times before the public within the past eight or ten days. He particularly dwelt upon the questions of

[b-b]DT] MS It was very easy to talk to people who agreed with one, but he wished to speak to those who differed from him. It would therefore give him great pleasure if the Conservatives of Westminster would call a meeting of their friends and invite him to it. He should be most happy to respond to such an invitation, provided the representatives of the press were allowed to be present at such a meeting. (*Cheers.*) He was ready to go among the Conservatives of Westminster, and

[c-c]DT] MS (*Mr. Mill then sat down, and remained so for a short time, but there was no response to his invitation.*) [*no paragraph*]

education and taxation. With regard to the former he reiterated the statement he made on previous occasions, to the effect that there existed enormous funds which were intended originally for the promotion of popular education, and which, if properly applied, were sufficient, in the opinion of those knowing most of the matter, to go very near giving education to every one in the community who needed it. (*Cheers.*) It was not advisable that the education should be given absolutely gratuitously to all. Those who could afford to pay for it ought to be obliged to pay for it; but education should be provided for all. (*Hear, hear.*) This need not at all interfere with individual action or Government assistance. Individual action might be made available to supply the religious education desired by the several denominations, and the secular education could be left until the other general means would be available. And it was not merely elementary education that could be given by means of these funds, but [d]education of a higher and less immediately necessary character[d]. (*Hear, hear.*) He thought they would admit that they had had quite enough of the present mode of giving public assistance for education. The system seemed to be to give to those who had got some assistance already and were becoming well to do, and to withhold from those who had nothing in the way of assistance, and were therefore in a state of helplessness. (*Hear, hear.*) But now that persons of position were beginning to take the matter into consideration, he had hopes that some more satisfactory system would soon be established in England. He believed that they were nearer the improved state of things which he desired than they were aware of. It, he believed, only remained for the people to back up Mr. Gladstone. (*Cheers.*) If they did so, he believed that before many years were over their heads they would see the beginning of a new and much better system of education in this country. (*Cheers.*) Respecting the questions affecting the inhabitants of London, in his opinion the whole of the metropolis ought to be one union for the purpose of rating, particularly for the purpose of rating for the relief of the poor. [e]This would remedy the injustice to the poor under the present arrangement, which naturally arose from the tendency of the rich to live in parts of the town entirely distinct from those occupied by the poor. With one management for the metropolis in respect to rating, something effectual might be done with regard to the extreme poverty in the East-end.[e] He should like to see something done for the poor of the East-end of London, similar to what was done for Lancashire during the cotton famine.[1] [f]In this way useful public works would be executed, and the country would not lose a valuable part of its population by emigration.[f] (*Hear, hear, and cheers.*) He also thought that the metropolis should be governed by municipalities such as were

[1]By 25 & 26 Victoria, c. 110 (1862).

[d-d]DT a much higher education for those scholars who showed great efficiency in particular branches while in the elementary schools

[e-e]+DT

[f-f]+DT

sketched in the bill which he introduced into Parliament last session,[2] and which, if returned, he would again bring in next session. He hoped the new Parliament would give his propositions on that head a more favourable consideration than the one just dying out. (*Cheers.*) After again expressing his desire to be questioned on any point on which there was a difference of opinion, *Mr. Mill resumed his seat amid much cheering.*

The candidates were asked no questions.

[*It was moved that the meeting approve the Members, and pledge continued support. A working man supported the resolution, talking of the "schoolmaster of the House of Commons," who was at the moment indulging in the "characteristic twaddle" he had uttered at the Mansion House;*[3] *the motion was passed and the meeting concluded.*]

137. Fawcett for Brighton

10 NOVEMBER, 1868

Brighton Guardian, 11 November, 1868, p. 8. Headed: "Great Meeting of Liberals,—Last Night." The *Brighton Examiner*, a weekly, also covered the meeting at length on 17 November, while *The Times* gave a shorter report, including only Mill's speech in abbreviated form, on 13 November. James White (1809–83) and Henry Fawcett, the two sitting Liberal members for Brighton, met their constituents in an evening public meeting at the Corn Exchange, Brighton. In opening the meeting the Chair called special attention to Mill's presence. White spoke first, followed by Fawcett, and then Mill was called upon.

HE SAID THAT some advanced Liberals who live in other parts of the kingdom and who either have no contested election of their own or are not completely absorbed in it, so as to prevent them from looking round and watching with the deepest interest the prospects of the general election at this crisis of our history, had been startled from their propriety by hearing that there is an opposition made here to the re-election of his friend, Professor Fawcett. (*Hear, hear.*) Not by the Tories only. It is nothing new for the Tories to court defeat; they are now courting it in several hundred constituencies throughout the country; and the electors of Brighton might have been safely left to deal with them at this juncture. But what had astonished the advanced Liberals of whom he spoke was that the opposition to Mr. Fawcett's re-election was made by a gentleman of the very same political opinions, speaking in a general way, and who can only recommend himself by the same opinions to the electors who had hitherto preferred, and it was to be hoped would still prefer,

[2]See No. 93.

[3]The reference is evidently to Disraeli's Speech at the Mansion House (29 July, 1868), reported in *The Times*, 30 July, p. 7.

Mr. Fawcett.[1] (*Cheers.*) If there was any member of the late Parliament who should not have been opposed by any man who calls himself an advanced Liberal it is Mr. Fawcett. (*Cheers.*) They were accustomed in the House of Commons to consider Mr. Fawcett as about the most rising man on the whole Liberal side of the house. Entering the house under disadvantages which to many men would have been insuperable,[2]—and which must have been so to any one of less courage, consistency, and energy than Mr. Fawcett possessed,—he had succeeded not only in gaining the ear of the House, whether of his political friends or of his political opponents, but he had established a position in the House such as had rarely been acquired by a young man in so short a space of time after his election. (*Loud cheers.*) Mr. Fawcett had been found on all occasions ready not only to give his vote and his attendance, but also his speech in support of any cause which needed his help. He had also had the gift of not pressing himself forward when he was not wanted. (*Cheers.*) Mr. Fawcett had to overcome difficulties of a moral kind, greater than any physical one,—the difficulty of the moral atmosphere of the House of Commons. (*Applause.*) Many a young man enters that House with all good intention, but, when there, comes under the influence of that atmosphere which, stifling to the moral feeling as an atmosphere is stifling to the physical senses, takes all the fealty out of a man. He comes among a number of persons of Lord Palmerston's school of Liberalism, who have no particular intentions. What little intention they do have is good, but the only thing that affrights them is whether people should do it. Whenever anything is proposed they are always afraid that it will make mischief; or disturb the party; or prevent things from going on smoothly; or make somebody or other vote against them; or, perhaps, make the Liberals go out, or, perhaps, prevent them from coming in. (*Laughter.*) Mr. Fawcett had been as much exposed to their influence as anybody else. He (*Mr. Mill*) knew there had been people going round Mr. Fawcett and saying "For God's sake don't do this;" or, "For heaven's sake don't do that. You will offend this man and that, and you won't do any good." There never is any good to be done in the opinion of those men. (*Laughter and cheers.*) Mr. Fawcett had been assailed in that way, but he just told them in all boldness that he thought it right and therefore must do it. That would not be a safe course to take if a man was wrong-headed or obstinate; but he (*Mr. Mill*) had watched Mr. Fawcett from his first entrance into Parliament (which exactly coincided with his own); he had watched Mr. Fawcett with the deep interest inspired by a knowledge of him and with the great hope he entertained of him, he had watched Mr. Fawcett with the anxiety he felt for a young man in his position, and he had deliberately formed the opinion that Mr. Fawcett's parliamentary conduct had been as much distinguished by judgment as

[1]William Coningham (1815–84), a Liberal who had represented Brighton 1857–64 (and had unsuccessfully stood for Westminster in 1852).

[2]He had been blinded in a shooting accident.

by courage. (*Loud cheers.*) When Mr. Fawcett speaks it is always on something he has studied and which he understands; and when he does, what he has done oftener than any man of his standing in Parliament,—when he has come forward and taken up a question for himself, he has not only done so as well but better than most other people. (*Loud cheers.*) He touched upon three instances,—the reform of the Universities;[3] the cost of elections;[4] thirdly, the subject on which Mr. Fawcett has distinguished himself as much as any member of Parliament, and that he had made his own during the greater part of his parliamentary life, the condition, the lamentable, deplorable condition—a condition which cries out to the whole people of England for remedy,—the condition of the agricultural labourer.[5] (*Cheers.*) These were some of the reasons which make all lovers of improvement who have attended to what Mr. Fawcett has done, anxious that he should be re-elected. And it was very natural that those friends of improvement, when they found such a man going to be opposed, should wonder very much and should be desirous of knowing the reason for such opposition. He (*Mr. Mill*) tried to find out by reading all the accounts he could get of what was said; but he had entirely failed to find any other reason than that a gentleman who lives in this place, and who is very much respected by his fellow-townsmen, and who once represented Brighton (*Voices: Never any more*), would like to represent it again.[6] Well, that is a legitimate object of ambition when a man can show he deserves it; but unfortunately it was only to be gratified in this instance by turning out one of the honourable members who now sit for the Borough. He (*Mr. Mill*) had not yet mentioned his worthy and honourable friend the senior member for the Borough, for the opposition had not been expressly directed against him, and he was almost tempted, after what we read in Scripture,[7] to condole with his friend Mr. White, for nobody speaks any harm of that honourable gentleman. (*Cheers and laughter.*) He supposed the fact was Mr. White was thought to be so deeply rooted in the affections of the people of Brighton that it is no use attempting to dislodge him. (*Cheers.*) But Mr. Fawcett, being a more recent acquaintance, not residing amongst us,—they say that is very invidious,—they think they have a chance of

[3]See, e.g., *PD*, 3rd ser., Vol. 186, cols. 1431–2 (10 Apr., 1867); Vol. 187, cols. 1630–2 (5 June, 1867); Vol. 188, cols. 55–8 (18 June, 1867); and Vol. 193, cols. 1054–8 (10 July, 1868).

[4]See No. 120.

[5]See, e.g., *PD*, 3rd ser., Vol. 186, cols. 1011–14 (2 Apr., 1867); Vol. 187, cols. 559–61 (14 May, 1867); and Fawcett, "What Can Be Done for the Agricultural Labourers?" *Macmillan's Magazine*, XVIII (Oct. 1868), 515–25.

[6]I.e., Coningham.

[7]Though the phrasing of the final clause echoes Acts, 28:21, Mill appears to allude to the Beatitudes: "Blessed are ye, when men shall revile you, and persecute you, and shall say all manner of evil against you falsely, for my sake. Rejoice, and be exceedingly glad: for great is your reward in heaven: for so persecuted they the prophets which were before you." (Matthew, 5:11–12; cf. Luke, 6:22–3.)

decreasing the good opinion formed of Mr. Fawcett; but that good opinion having been formed would be found much harder to shake than some people imagine. (*Cheers.*) With respect to the gentleman who is endeavouring, at the expense of Mr. Fawcett, to regain the seat he once held for Brighton, he (*Mr. Mill*) was tempted to ask, "If he wishes you to elect him in preference to Mr. Fawcett, what does he offer you as his inducement to do so?" (*Cheers.*) During the time that gentleman served Brighton in parliament he conducted himself as a good and faithful Radical; but what did he do during that time for the advancement of the Radical cause, or any other great cause, that could be compared with what Mr. Fawcett, although a young man, had already done during the three years,—for it was no longer,—he had represented this borough in Parliament? (*Loud cheers.*) If it was said that Lord Palmerston's parliament was not a good place for such exertions, or that the time was not favourable,—granting this candidate such allowance,—what did he say for the future? (*Cheers.*) What good things did the gentleman opposing Mr. Fawcett say he would do that would not be equally well done by Mr. Fawcett if re-elected? (*Cheers.*) Indeed, he could not yet find out that Mr. Fawcett had been attacked for anything which was not amongst his merits, and he could prove that if he went through the list of them. He would not say anything of the Tories who would split with that gentleman; though he thought they would not give him a vote because they thought him a surer, a better, a more determined Radical than Mr. Fawcett (*cheers*); but he might give one piece of advice to Liberal electors. If there is any Liberal candidate that the Tories split their votes with, don't let the Liberals split their votes with him, and if there is any Liberal candidate that the Tories are particularly anxious to get out of the way, that is the man for the Liberals and let them vote for him. *Mr. Mill then most elaborately and at great length defended Mr. Fawcett from the charges made against him by his opponents.* Mr. Coningham was reported to have blamed Mr. Fawcett because he desired that persons who took a bribe for their votes should be severely punished. Was the condemnation of that sentiment Radicalism, Liberalism, public morality, or even common honesty? (*Cheers.*) He thought the William Coningham he once knew could never have said so. It must be a misreport. One of Mr. Coningham's supporters said Mr. Fawcett never came here to confer a favour; only to ask one. As to asking for favours that was simple nonsense. What Mr. Fawcett asked was to do the work of this constituency—to devote days of study and nights of expression for the interest of this borough; to expose himself to all sorts of obloquy; and to do so with nothing whatever to gain by it. As to conferring favours—what favours was he to confer? He (*Mr. Mill*) did not think this constituency wanted favours from their representatives. (*Cheers.*) The gentleman could hardly mean bribes. Did he mean that it was a shame Mr. Fawcett did not job for them; or did he mean that he should hold out that very slight inducement of subscribing to the local charities? Mr. Fawcett was opposed, too, because he was the friend of co-operation. He (*Mr. Mill*) did not believe the tradesmen of Brighton would refuse to vote for Mr. Fawcett on that ground, for co-operation was simply a movement that would greatly benefit the working classes without injuring the tradesmen, or, if at all, in a very slight degree. Besides, even if it did injure the tradesmen a little they must be told what the working men had often been told in relation to the introduction of machinery, that they must suffer a little for a time in order to further the general well-being in the end. If a shopkeeper supplies goods as pure, as unadulterated, as honestly measured, and of as good quality as the co-operative stores, his custom would not be injured; and if he could not do that, did he deserve to keep his custom? (*Hear, hear.*) Then there was the lucrative custom of the rich which they were always sure to have. In fact, shopkeepers need not suffer much from the most extended and rapid advance of the co-operative principle. (*Cheers.*) Another thing Mr. Fawcett was opposed for was because he had said that the necessary expenses of elections, which should in fairness be borne by the constituencies, ought to be placed on the constituencies. His clause to carry out that opinion[8] was supported by Mr. Gladstone[9] and all the best Liberals in the house. That would, if carried out, give the constituencies a greater choice of candidates, and would prevent the representation being monopolised by rich men, who often went into Parliament with the hope of getting back their money with great interest. What did they think of those capable of selling their birthright for such a miserable mess of pottage as these expenses would amount to?[10] He hoped the electors of Brighton would fling it back in their faces. (*Cheers.*) Another one of Mr. Fawcett's alleged demerits,—in his (*Mr. Mill's*) eyes they were great merits,—was that he had voted for compulsory education.[11] He would just ask those who condemned him for that if they thought that any man had a right to exclude his own children from the benefit of the education they could get. That was all compulsory education amounted to,—the making parents recognise the duty incumbent upon them to educate their children. If parents could not exclude their children from the advantages of education, then the state had the right to compel all parents to allow their children to be educated. Even parents would not lose anything in the long run. Their children would work better while at work, and in future years they would be able to take advantage of their position and improve themselves and help their parents all the more. (*Cheers.*) He had now gone through all the allegations made against Mr. Fawcett which were worthy of being

[8]Moved on 18 July, 1868; see No. 120.

[9]Gladstone, Speech on Election Petitions and Corrupt Practices at Elections Bill (18 July, 1868), *PD*, 3rd ser., Vol. 193, cols. 1447–8.

[10]Cf. Genesis, 25: 29-34.

[11]On 29 March, 1867, Fawcett had asked the Home Secretary, Walpole, whether it was the Government's intention to introduce compulsory education clauses into "A Bill for Regulating the Hours of Labour for Children, Young Persons, and Women Employed in Workshops"; the provisions appeared in Clauses B, C, and D of the Bill as amended by the Select Committee on which Fawcett served (16 July, 1867; *PP*, 1867, III, 133–47). It was accepted on 14 August without debate, and enacted as 30 & 31 Victoria, c. 146 (1867).

touched upon, and he thought he had shown that the so-called demerits were really conspicuous merits. He supposed that, as Mr. Fawcett was opposed for doing those things, the candidate who opposed him would not do them, but would strive to do exactly the opposite. The candidate would, therefore, be against co-operation; he would be for expensive elections; and he would be against compulsory education. He (*Mr. Mill*) wanted the electors to realise what they were doing, and, as one means of their doing so, he would suppose that these things were put on a placard. How would Coningham like to see these things,—"Coningham and Jobbery!" "Coningham and Expensive Elections!" "Coningham and Ignorance!"—for that would be the result if nobody wanted compulsory education. "Coningham and No Co-operation!" or perhaps as one of the very greatest and surest effects of co-operation would be to do away with the system of credit and substitute a system of paying ready money, he would put it "Coningham and Tick!" (*Great laughter.*) If Mr. Coningham would like a placard so drawn up well and good. In any case, he thought he might now commend Mr. Coningham to the consideration of the Tories and leave him in the hands of the Liberal Electors. *(Mr. Mill sat down amid vehement and continued cheering.)*

[*The usual motion of support of the candidates was made, questions were put and answered, a special motion of thanks to Mill was passed, and the meeting concluded with thanks to the Chair.*]

138. The Westminster Election of 1868 [7]

11 NOVEMBER, 1868

Daily Telegraph, 12 November, 1868, p. 2. Headed: "Election Movements. / Westminster." Also reported in the *Morning Star*, and the *Daily News*. The evening meeting of the electors of St. Martin's-in-the-Fields and St. Mary-le-Strand was held in the Polygraphic Hall, King William Street, James Beal in the Chair (the *Morning Star* says the Rev. D. Bailey chaired). Grosvenor spoke first. Mill was greeted with "immense cheering" (*Morning Star*) by the large audience.

MR. MILL BEGAN, *amid some cheering, by saying* it was very gratifying to see what is going on in the country just now when the Reform Bill has been given to the people. While Mr. Disraeli held out the Reform Bill in his hand to them, they would persist in saying, "Thank you, Mr. Gladstone!" (*Laughter.*) All his talking could not alter their opinion. Had the Tories said that the bill which Mr. Gladstone brought in[1] did not go far enough, and that no invidious distinctions should be made, what a pleasant time the Commons would have had, what a happy family they would have been! (*Laughter.*) They would have carried the Amendment Bill,

[1]In 1866; see No. 15.

would have saved a vast deal of time, a good many broken palings, and perhaps a few broken heads. (*Laughter and cheers.*) Perhaps Mr. Disracli might say he had not then educated his party.[2] He did not think Mr. Disraeli intended to educate his party at that time, but he could not help thinking that Mr. Disraeli and Lord Derby, being religious men, as shown by their wish to preserve the Irish Church, intended to carry out a text of Scripture, but had forgotten what it was. (*A laugh.*) Christ said, if a man wants you to go with him a mile, go with him twain.[3] Lord Derby and Mr. Disraeli evidently thought that in order to get their party to go with them a mile one way, they must take them two miles in another. [a]No man or body of men who desired to stand well with the people of England could succeed by saying one thing and meaning another, the very suspicion of anything of the kind being enough to destroy such persons in popular estimation (*hear, hear*).[a] They had in Mr. Gladstone a statesman whose yea is yea and whose nay is nay [b]. (*Cheers.*) When he made up his mind he followed it out and therefore the people reposed a confidence in him which they could not do in a man whose policy, feelings, and intentions were not as they should be in order to be popular with what was called the multitude, namely, transparent as the day. (*Cheers.*)[b] If they wanted to know the truth about a man they should hear what his enemies said of him. They could not say he was an hypocrite. They said he was precipitate and rash in divulging his opinions. He (*Mr. Mill*) denied that Mr. Gladstone spoke his mind too freely or without due consideration. It was Mr. Gladstone who, in Lord Palmerston's Government, spoke out, and said that Reform had been promised and must be given.[4] [c]When he (*Mr. Mill*) read that in a foreign country he predicted that Mr. Gladstone would be the best abused man in England by a certain class.[c] And had not that been so? (*Yes.*) Did they believe one word of the aspersions cast on him? (*No.*) The move the Liberal party was making related to no grievance to England, but to the injury done to Ireland by the maintenance of the Irish Church.[5] Englishmen knew that to be a source of irritation to a people with whom they wish to be in close friendship, therefore they wished to get rid of it. They could not make the English Church an Irish Church. If the English Church wanted a branch there, let them endow it from their own funds, without taking anything of the lands or

[2]In his speech at Edinburgh on 29 October, 1867; cf. No. 135.

[3]Matthew, 5:41.

[4]E.g., speech of 11 May, 1864, *PD*, 3rd ser., Vol. 175, cols. 312–27.

[5]Gladstone gave notice of his intended resolutions in his Speech on the Irish Church Establishment (23 Mar., 1868), *ibid.*, Vol. 191, cols. 32–3.

[a-a]+MS] DN No man who wished to . . . *as* MS . . . England would . . . *as* MS . . . another. (*Hear, hear.*) The very suspicion of that was enough to destroy a man in the popular estimation. (*Hear, hear.*)

[b-b]DN] DT , and to that he attributed the placing in Mr. Gladstone of a degree of confidence which had been rare indeed in England of late years.] MS , and who, when he had made up his mind upon a subject, was not to be swerved away from carrying out the intentions he had formed.

[c-c]MS Mr. Gladstone could boast of being the best abused man in England, but the time had come when the people of England found how base were those inventions, as the result of the elections would sufficiently show.

tithes of Ireland. (*Hear, hear.*) He related many instances of the severity practised under English rule in Ireland for centuries, remarking that the Irish Church is the one relic left of the system which treated the Irish as a conquered and alien people. [d]He entered at some length on the question of the tenure of land in Ireland[d], recommending the establishment of a tenant right similar to that which has worked so well under the 30 years' lease system in some parts of India. If this security, not to be turned out, were given to the Irishman, he would know that any improvement he might make would be for the benefit of himself and his family, and that he was safe in his possession so long as he paid his rent. That, however, was a question which was much more likely to be properly dealt with by a Liberal than by a Tory Government, inasmuch as the latter would be entirely bound up in the landlords [e]; and he hoped that in the approaching election they would send the Liberal party to power, and that that party would approach these questions in a sincere spirit[e]. If the Irish Church were abolished, and the land question were settled on some such basis as he had sketched, the Irishman would give his hand to the Englishman, and the two nations would be as they had never yet been before—an united people. (*Cheers.*)

[f]*An elector in the body of the room said he had heard it stated that Mr. Mill had been guilty of forging an order for some theatre. (Laughter.) He wanted to give Mr. Mill an opportunity of denying it.*

Mr. Mill: I am much obliged to the gentleman for giving this new instance of what length the Tories will go to, which justifies what I have said in another place, that they stick at nothing. I need hardly say I never heard one word of this charge before, and if it ever happened to anybody there must be some mistake about the name.

Another elector asked if the honourable candidates were in favour of closing the public houses on Sunday. [*Grosvenor would not pledge himself to the view that the public houses should be closed altogether.*]

Mr. Mill: It would not be just, while the rich are able to get access to wine and other intoxicating drinks on Sundays at their clubs, to pass a law that would make it impossible for the poor to obtain refreshment of a similar character on that day.[f]

[g]*Another elector asked whether the candidates were in favour of retaining the law by which the goods of the lodger might be seized for the debts of the landlord.*[6]

[6]4 George II, c. 28 (1731) had extended the landlord's right under common law to seize the personal chattels of a tenant to include the goods of lodgers. (Lodgers were protected later by 34 & 35 Victoria, c. 79 [1871].) In the text the questioner uses "landlord" to signify a tenant who leases from the primary landlord, and himself lets to lodgers.

[d-d]DN As to the land question, he said a government, whig, tory, or liberal, must soon turn its attention to this great sore

[e-e]+MS

[f-f]+MS

[g-g]MS] DT *Both candidates agreed that* a tenant ought not to be liable for the debts of his landlord. *Mr. Mill was of opinion that* in some cases bankrupts should be liable to more severe punishment than can be inflicted under the present laws.

Captain Grosvenor was against the law; as was Mr. Mill, who criticised the present law as an abominable one.

Another elector asked respecting bankruptcy and imprisonment for debt.

Mr. Mill said he did not think there should be any punishment—which imprisonment was—for debtors who were blameless. But there should be punishment for debtors who were not blameless. [g] *Mr. Mill, in answer to another question, said that* no law could be too strong to enforce the education of the community.

In reply to questions, Captain Grosvenor declined to say anything as to the disunion of Church and State.

Mr. Mill believed all connection between Church and State to be an injury to both; but as the State was more liberal than the Church, and might exercise an influence on clergymen, he thought the question might be allowed to sleep for a time.

A middle-aged man in the meeting asked the honourable candidates if they were against the separation of married couples in workhouses. The querist seemed to be so likely to have a direct interest in the matter, that the audience laughed loudly at his question.

Captain Grosvenor: I am very much against married couples going into workhouses at all. (Great laughter arose at the pointed application of this reply to the able-bodied man who had introduced the subject.) I do not see what they should marry for if they go to a workhouse; but if unfortunate circumstances reduce them to poverty, they will have become so sick of one another that in the workhouse they will be very glad to be separated. (Hisses. That will not do, Grosvenor!)

Mr. Mill: Then see if this will do. I think that for old people and for infirm people the workhouse should be made a place of comfort (*hear, hear*), but I think that for young people and for able-bodied people the workhouse should be a place of discomfort. (*Cheers.*) They ought not to be able to enjoy all the advantages of self-support while receiving support from others. I would separate married people if young and able-bodied; but I would not separate them if old. (*Hear, hear.*)

[*The customary vote of confidence in the candidates was moved, seconded, and carried unanimously amid great cheering, and a vote of thanks to the Chair concluded the meeting.*]

139. The Westminster Election of 1868 [8]

13 NOVEMBER, 1868

Daily Telegraph, 14 November, 1868, p. 4. Headed: "The General Election. / Westminster." Also reported fully in the *Daily News*; Mill's speech appeared in less full form on 16 November in *The Times* and the *Morning Star*. The Friday evening meeting of Mill and Grosvenor with the electors was held in St. James's Hall. The huge room was overflowing long before the hour of the meeting. Thomas Hughes, who had intended to take the Chair, was detained by the contest in his own constituency, Frome, and Serjeant Parry was elected to his place. Grosvenor spoke first, quoting a version of Mill's remark in No. 138: "the people, while accepting a household bill from Mr. Disraeli, seemed to say mechanically 'Thank you, Mr. Gladstone.' (*Cheers and laughter.*)" Mill's "reception was enthusiastic, the audience rising *en masse* . . . waving hats and handkerchiefs for several minutes" (*Daily Telegraph*), and "cheering at the top of their voices" (*Daily News*).

SILENCE *having been with some difficulty restored, the honourable gentleman said* every person he was addressing must be aware of the issue which was going to be decided by the constituencies of the country. What they had to decide was whether the Reform Bill should have any consequences. Every one who voted to return a Tory must mean that the Reform Bill should have no consequences. (*Hear, hear.*) If the Tories had intended that the people should have the consequences of Reform, they would not have opposed Reform as long as possible, and then only have granted it on compulsion—the compulsion being that they would not have been allowed to remain in office if they had not. The very best thing that could be said in their excuse—no one believing in the sudden conversion of a whole party—was that they thought, as they saw that the poison would be sure to be administered to the patient whether they did it or not, they might as well administer it in a double dose, and so preserve for a short time longer the advantage of being the patient's physician. (*Cheers.*) As sensible men they would not entrust particular work to people who disliked it, and who would rather it should miscarry than succeed. They were told that the Conservatives were the fittest people to be Reformers, because they would hold the people back when they were going too fast. Though horses did, now and then, need to be held back, it was not usual to choose those to be harnessed which were the best hands at pulling back. (*Hear, hear.*) When people wished to be held back they applied a drag, and that was what the Tories were good for. (*Cheers.*) Their place was not in harness, but to be a drag on the wheel, or to hang on behind and pull back the carriage when it was going down hill. (*Hear, hear.*) If that was their proper function it was now known that it was not a function that they would perform unless they were out of office; for when they were in office they were ready and eager to gallop down hill twice as fast as the others. The Tories were too fond of the old era to be fit to inaugurate the new. A different kind of Parliament and a different kind of Government were wanted from what the country had been used to heretofore. They did not want either a Tory Government or a Palmerstonian Government. It had often been said that Lord Palmerston had demoralised the House of Commons. He did not think Lord Palmerston was responsible for the demoralisation, if it was to be so called, into which the House of Commons had fallen, but he had proved an extremely suitable leader for the House of Commons which had fallen into that state; for, instead of meeting earnestness with earnestness, Lord Palmerston knew how, with serene good humour, to laugh and joke earnestness away. Men often failed to fulfil the hopes of those who returned them; but sufficient allowance was not made for the atmosphere they entered and the company they found themselves in in the House of Commons. They found themselves amongst hundreds of gentlemen who did not belong to the classes who suffered by the evils which at present afflicted society. (*Hear, hear.*) They were comfortable, and did not like to have their comfort interfered with; accordingly they very much disliked those who disturbed them, by meddling with great questions; because such questions were difficult, and required a great deal of thinking, which was very troublesome to men who did not always feel confident that they should think to much purpose, and who did not know whom they could trust to think for them. [a]Comfortable people did not much like those who would not let a sleeping dog lie. (*Laughter and cheers.*) He had observed throughout life that when a man has made up his mind not to do any good, he soon persuaded himself that there was no good to be done.[a] If a young man came into Parliament with high hopes, and really wished to do something, he was [b]told, "For God's sake don't meddle with this or that, the party would not be so safe in office, or would not get into office so soon;" and what was worse, if anyone raised new questions and voted on them, they were sure to offend some of their constituents. In the old Palmerstonian days there had grown up a general feeling in favour of letting things[b] alone. To that system of letting things alone there was one remarkable exception in Mr. Gladstone—(*loud cheers*)—who, in his department, over which he alone had control, constantly busied himself to do something good for the nation, which the nation had not the wit to ask him for. (*Cheers.*) Nobody had forced Mr. Gladstone to give the Post-office Savings' Banks and Life Assurance,[1] to take off taxes year after year by means of retrenchment, or to repeal the paper duties.[2] (*Hear, hear.*) Mr. Gladstone, however, had done something more, for in 1864 he had broken out of harness, and disturbed the sleep of many in the House of Commons by proclaiming that Reform had been promised, and that Reform must be granted.[3] He [c]again had raised the question of the Irish Church in 1864 or '65,[4] and again practically last year,[5][c] so suddenly, as the Tories said,

[1]By 24 Victoria, c. 14 (1861) and 27 & 28 Victoria, c. 43 (1864).

[2]By 24 Victoria, c. 20 (1861).

[3]Speech of 11 May, 1864, cols. 312–27.

[4]Speech on the Church Establishment (Ireland) (28 Mar., 1865), *PD*, 3rd ser., Vol. 178, cols. 420–34.

[5]Speech on the Established Church (Ireland) (7 May, 1867), *ibid.*, Vol. 187, cols. 121–31.

[a-a]+DN

[b-b]DN] DT assailed in every sort of way to desist from action; so that in the old Palmerstonian state of things there had grown up a general feeling not to meddle with anything which could possibly be left

[c-c]DN it was who had conceived the propriety of giving justice to Ireland—

though Ireland had only been waiting for it for three centuries. (*Cheers.*) These were the sort of things which made some people call Mr. Gladstone an unsafe Minister; but he called upon the electors to support Mr. Gladstone for the very reason for which he was called unsafe. They wanted a Minister who would do things merely because they were right, and who would not mind risking a few votes for his party, if by that risk he could do right and effect a great object. (*Cheers.*) He hoped from the elections that were about to commence there would go forth a sound which would proclaim in thunder to the whole world that the Palmerstonian period was at an end. (*Cheers.*) Mr. Gladstone, and those who were sent to his support, would have to apply their minds in the next Parliament to great questions. But first they would have to begin with clean hands, by removing from themselves the reproach of oppression. For seven hundred years, up to a very late period, we had been tyrannising over Ireland. We repented it now, even the Tories repented it; but repentance was not worth much without atonement and reparation—(*cheers*)—and until that atonement and reparation were made the memory of the past would not be extinguished. The Irish required some tangible proof that we felt very differently from our predecessors, and they had a right to expect not only that we should remove that miserable last vestige of our past tyranny which still existed in the shape of a foreign and intrusive Church Establishment, but that for a generation at least Ireland should be the spoilt child of this country. Means also must be found to put an end to the miserable relations now existing in that country between the owners and the cultivators of the land. [d]They must put an end to a system of tenure the like of which had not existed in England since the people were serfs. (*Cheers.*) They would have to consider the same things by and bye with respect to the tenure of land in England. (*Hear, hear.*) He did not wish to conceal the difficulties of the question. [e]It was not very easy to find landlords in the House of Commons without prejudice; but the land question must be put into the hands of people who would not, because there was a seeming resemblance between the systems of the two countries, refuse to apply to Ireland remedies which might appear too strong for England.[e] With respect to education, all admitted that it was necessary, except a few who said that they hated this question of education, because there would soon be no labourers or servants. Better say that they would soon have no more slaves, because a man who was not

[d–d]DN] DT They must be prepared to see very different laws enacted for Ireland than would commend themselves to English landlords. That must be done to enable Englishmen to stand erect before the world, and when matters were set right in Ireland they might think of themselves. *The honourable member then referred to* national education, which he said, emphatically, was not to be trusted to the "Church party," whom he defined to be those laymen and clergymen who took their stand on being peculiarly for the Church and against the Nonconformists. The great sanitary questions of the health of great cities and towns and the state of the dwellings of the mass of the people required bolder men to deal with them than the Tories

[e–e]TT Inasmuch as Irish landlords and Irish tenants differed widely from the same class in England a different method of legislation should be adopted in their regard.

educated must necessarily be a slave. Education was opposed by what was termed the church party as long as they could. When the Bell and Lancaster system was first started,[6] that party cried down the movement for teaching the people to read; but when they found that the people would be taught in schools in which, though the Bible was read, the church catechism was not, they founded what was termed the national schools. He admitted that the Tories did now make great sacrifices to promote education, both by giving and begging money for it; but the church party always confounded the interest of the establishment with that of religion, and were not fit to have the control of education. [f]*He then alluded, with caustic sarcasm, to the conduct of the Duke of Beaufort regarding the support of schools on his Grace's property.*[7][f] Clergymen were deplorably ignorant. Kings, great noblemen, great ladies, and clergymen were generally profoundly ignorant of men and the world; and 200 years ago Lord Clarendon said that clergymen understood the least and took the worst views of human affairs of all men who could read and write.[8] (*Cheers.*) He did not mean that there were not numerous admirable exceptions among the clergy, but he felt bound to say that they were not fit to be trusted with education, especially at the present time, when all the bigotry and prejudice had come to the front. (*Hear, hear.*) They had a vast population and wealth, but with them terrible poverty and enormous taxes. They had a right to expect that government should try to alleviate that poverty. First of all, the health of great cities, towns, and dwellings should be considered. There was no objection on the part of the Tories to make improvements of this kind, but it wanted bolder men to form large plans to benefit the people[d] —men who would have bold, well-considered plans, and carry them partially into operation at every opportunity, and into complete operation as soon as possible. (*Cheers.*) With regard to the two tremendous subjects of crime and pauperism, any Parliament and Government that was fit to exist in this country would place before itself no less grand an object than [g]their extinction. He did not suppose they would succeed; but Christ had said,

[6]Andrew Bell (1753–1832) had used the monitorial system in the infant school in the Madras Male Orphan Asylum; he became Superintendent of the National Society (Church of England) to promote the system. His ideas were closely paralleled by those of Joseph Lancaster (1778–1838), promoted by the dissenting British and Foreign School Society. Proponents of the two systems were at odds in the early years of the nineteenth century over religious issues.

[7]Henry Charles Fitzroy Somerset (1824–99), 8th Duke of Beaufort, had just refused to contribute towards the national school in Winterbourn (where he owned land) because the incumbent had worked against his interest in a by-election for West Gloucester in July 1867. (See *The Times*, 4 Nov., 1868, p. 4.)

[8]Edward Hyde, Lord Clarendon (1609–74), *The Life of Edward, Earl of Clarendon* (Oxford: Clarendon Press, 1759), Vol. I, p. 34.

[f-f]+TT

[g-g]DN] DT the extinction of both; not that such a result could be attained, but because if we placed before ourselves as our aim anything less than perfection, we should fall far short in practice of even the degree of improvement that we were perfectly capable of attaining

"Be ye perfect as your Father is perfect."[9] Christ did not suppose that we could be perfect, but His words implied that we should endeavour to attain that perfection which humanity was capable of. Education would do something, and improvements of all sorts would effect more[g]. [h]These great evils should be grappled with by the great minds of the country—minds accustomed to look on public affairs in a comprehensive light. Mr. Gladstone was eminently distinguished for his broad and enlightened views. That gentleman was inspired by a spirit that would not brook the existence of an evil if he found that he had the power to redress it. Let Mr. Gladstone obtain the support of the country, and a Government animated by his sentiments would inaugurate a policy which would redound to the prosperity of the nation.[h] Mr. Gladstone was the one statesman in his recollection whom he could follow as a leader, and he believed he was the leader for the English people. (*Loud cheers.*)

On the conclusion of the honourable gentleman's speech he was greeted with a second most flattering demonstration of respect and admiration.

After a few questions had been put and replied to by the candidates, [*Fawcett moved a vote of confidence and support, which was carried unanimously; the "proceedings, which were protracted to an unusually late hour"* (The Times), *concluded with a vote of thanks to the Chair.*]

140. W.E. Gladstone [2]

14 NOVEMBER, 1868

Daily Telegraph, 16 November, 1868, p. 3. Headed: "The General Election. / Greenwich." Abbreviated versions of the same report appeared in *The Times* and the *Daily News*. The Saturday evening meeting of the electors of Deptford was held in the hall of the Mechanics' Institute, High Street, the purpose being to hear Mill's speech. A letter was read from Alderman David Salomons (1797–1873), the sitting Liberal M.P. for the borough, now running with Gladstone, in favour of his candidature. The densely crowded meeting greeted Mill with loud cheers.

AFTER A FEW PREFATORY REMARKS, HE OBSERVED, in reference to Mr. Gladstone not taking an active part in the contest in that borough, that he had heard there were

[9]Matthew, 5:48.

[h-h]TT] DT For such work they wanted men accustomed to look at things on a large scale. Where would they find such men amongst statesmen unless they found it in Mr. Gladstone—(*cheers*)—who must have plans, and who, if supported, would go on from one thing to another?] DN But there must be minds to direct the state sufficiently powerful to grasp these great things, and he knew of no other man capable of the work than Mr. Gladstone, who would never allow a great evil to exist without attempting to alleviate it. (*Cheers.*) The more supporters they sent to parliament for Mr. Gladstone the more good he would do; and if they made him sufficiently powerful they would never repent it.

some few among the electors who thought that gentleman should have given his assent to become their representative if elected; but although he was not surprised that they should regret the loss of those splendid specimens of oratory which they would have heard from Mr. Gladstone had he been present among them, yet they knew how impossible it was that Mr. Gladstone should have taken any other than a passive part, seeing the immense importance of the contest then taking place in South-West Lancashire, where, had Mr. Gladstone shown any sign of taking part in the contest for Greenwich, his enemies in Lancashire would at once have put the falsehood forward that he despaired of success in that division of their county; for no falsehood was too false to be taken up and spread by his enemies. (*Hear, hear.*) That was the reason why the electors of Greenwich had not the pleasure of receiving from Mr. Gladstone an expression of his adhesion in their borough contest. (*Hear.*) But Mr. Gladstone was entitled not only to the warmest support from the constituency of Greenwich, but to the warmest support of all Liberal constituencies. (*Loud cheers.*) He was entitled to that support on many grounds. (*Hear, hear.*) It was not necessary that he should dilate on that occasion at length upon all the claims that Mr. Gladstone had to the support of every Liberal constituency—(*cheers*)—and therefore he would pass a few only in review. (*Hear, hear.*) The first claim he had was, that he was the only possible leader of the Liberal party. (*Loud cheers.*) They all knew how difficult it was, and it had often been found most difficult, to induce the Liberal and the Radical party to act together. (*Hear, hear.*) They had had experience at times of how one class would not trust those who were trusted by other classes; but there was no such state of things when they had seriously determined that their cause should be led by Mr. Gladstone, who was more popular with, and had more the confidence of, the middle and working classes of the country, than any other statesman. (*Loud cheers.*) They had in Mr. Gladstone a statesman whom they all trusted. (*Cheers.*) He would be a Minister who knew his business well, and would do it for the good of the country, without being forced to do it. (*Cheers.*) Mr. Gladstone possessed the friendly connection and co-operation of the old Liberal party; and even those who were lukewarm accepted him as the best man—not that there was no rival to him, but because they knew that, however much Mr. Gladstone wished to do, he would not consent to do anything unjust to any class. (*Hear, hear.*) No class wished for injustice. (*Hear, hear.*) He (*Mr. Mill*) did not think the Tories wished for anything unjust, knowingly. (*Hear, hear.*) But they had in Mr. Gladstone a leader in whom they could all confide. (*Cheers.*) These were not all the points upon which Mr. Gladstone ought to receive their support. Mr. Gladstone was the only statesman within their own time who knew properly the duties of leader of a party; and he was distinguished by that characteristic, that he did not stand still and wait to be summoned by the loud voice of people out of doors, by the thundering demands of the people for some measures of public good. (*Hear, hear.*) Mr.

Gladstone [a]sought for[a], arduously and continuously, things which had not been thought of before. (*Hear, hear.*) When Chancellor of the Exchequer, so soon as it was seen anything was wanting, he was not for leaving things alone, but he was a singular exception to all others, and there was scarcely a year during which he did not bring some plan forward, from his own knowledge and ability, and important for the benefit of the poor and labouring classes. (*Cheers.*) It was not from compulsion that Mr. Gladstone introduced the Post Office Savings Bank Bill.[1] (*Hear.*) It was not from compulsion that he introduced, also, the Post Office Life Insurance system[2]—(*hear, hear*)—and it was not from compulsion that he succeeded in making reductions in the expenditure of the country, by means of which to pay off some portion of their National Debt. (*Cheers.*) Neither was it from compulsion that Mr. Gladstone took the duty off paper,[3] thus securing the spread of knowledge among the people. (*Loud cheers.*) Mr. Gladstone was not content with making those improvements in departments only, but he sought improvement in Parliamentary Government. (*Cheers.*) He (*Mr. Mill*) would venture to say that there was no other member in Lord Palmerston's Government but Mr. Gladstone who would have dared to have got up and raised the signal for Parliamentary Reform. (*Cheers.*) No one knew that he was going to do it; and although he would not vote against a measure of Reform as then proposed, he gave warning that Parliamentary Reform had been solemnly promised, and the people expected that promise to be kept.[4] (*Loud cheers.*) That was the beginning of the Reform which they now had. (*Hear, hear.*) It was Mr. Gladstone who had given them the power they now possessed, and not Mr. Disraeli—(*loud cheers*)—for the moment Mr. Gladstone was in power he kept to his word, and tried to do it; but the Tories opposed, and, in succeeding to power, had kept office for two years by granting that, and more than they had before denied to the people. (*Hear, and cheers.*) That which he had named did not make Mr. Gladstone popular with the Palmerston party. (*Hear.*) It was a sort of thing which made them say, "Gladstone is not a safe man"—(*laughter*)—that was, a man who would not give himself the trouble of doing anything—(*hear, hear*)—or a man who would leave questions alone. An unsafe man was a Minister in whom it was high treason to bring forward good measures, or who threw out ideas for good measures. (*Cheers.*) He hoped that in the future, with Mr. Gladstone, they would not be without such a man. (*Hear.*) It was Mr. Gladstone who had brought forward the great Irish Church question, when he reminded the House it was a question which would have to be

[1]"A Bill to Grant Additional Facilities for Depositing Small Savings at Interest," 24 Victoria (11 Feb., 1861), *PP*, 1861, III, 781–8 (enacted as 24 Victoria, c. 14 [1861]).

[2]By 27 & 28 Victoria, c. 43 (1864).

[3]By 24 Victoria, c. 20 (1861).

[4]E.g., in his speech of 11 May, 1864.

[a-a]DN] DT thought of] TT thought for

taken up, for it could not be permitted to wait much longer[5]—(*cheers*)—and as soon as the question of Reform was settled he took the question up of the Irish Church,[6] and in which they were now called upon to support him. (*Loud cheers.*) If they did not support him, what would be the consequences? (*Hear, hear.*) To act wisely would be to give reparation to Ireland for the many wrong laws which had existed for many centuries; for until a recent period they had not treated Ireland like a sister, but more like a slave—(*cheers*)—and even worse than many slaves; for there were such things as petted slaves, but Ireland had been trampled on. (*Hear, hear.*) Having referred to the tenure of land in Ireland, where no man was safe from being turned out of possession at the end of six months without compensation, Mr. Mill said it was a difficult question, what exact system of legislation was required to meet it; but Mr. Gladstone was the man who had the mind to solve it, and he was the man to do it. (*Hear, hear.*) If they did not answer the appeal made to them at the coming elections, and place the right man in the right place, the opportunity for reconciliation with Ireland would be lost. (*Hear, hear.*) If they did not choose this opportunity to be lost, they would return Mr. Gladstone with a triumphant majority. (*Loud cheers.*) But there was still a great deal more depending upon what they might do. There was a vast deal to be done, not only in England, but Ireland also. (*Hear.*) They had to turn over an entire life of half a century, and to undo what former Governments had done. (*Hear.*) In a country where there existed so much wealth with so much poverty, there were difficulties to be got over by the help of brain, energy, and earnestness—(*hear*)—and if they wanted either brain, energy, or earnestness, they would not lay their claim for them on those who had opposed them. (*Hear, hear.*) There were also the questions of national education, and capital, and labour, which required the same brain, energy, and earnestness; and it was for the constituencies to say whom they would have for their leader. (*Cries of Gladstone!*) It was very much to be hoped that Mr. Gladstone would be returned for South-West Lancashire, and that he would not need to take his seat for Greenwich. (*Hear, hear.*) But he might require the seat. If he did not need it, they would have done honour to themselves and [b]given[b] valuable support, showing to other great constituencies that they had given their adhesion in supporting the most illustrious Liberal representative they could select. (*Cheers.*) If Mr. Gladstone should not succeed, and should require their suffrages—and it was said that Lord Derby had consented to spend £20,000 to prevent his election—(*Shame*)—but if only £10,000, or £5,000, he (*Mr. Mill*) believed they would agree with him that the money might be more wisely spent—(*hear, hear*)—if, as he had said, Mr. Gladstone should require their

[5]E.g., in his speeches of 28 Mar., 1865, and 7 May, 1867.
[6]In his speech of 23 Mar., 1868.

[b-b]+TT

suffrages, it would be a joy of triumph to the constituency that they had provided a harbour of refuge for him, to enable him to take his seat at the assembling of the new Parliament, as the head of the Liberal party. (*Cheers.*) *In conclusion, Mr. Mill* called on all the Liberal electors in the borough to be early at the poll on Tuesday morning, and to split their votes by voting for Salomons and Gladstone, *resuming his seat amid considerable applause.*

[*A motion was unanimously accepted pledging support to Salomons and Gladstone, and the meeting concluded.*]

141. The Westminster Election of 1868 [9]

16 NOVEMBER, 1868

Daily Telegraph, 17 November, 1868, p. 2. Headed: "The General Election. / Nominations. / Westminster." Reports (in the third person) appeared in the *Morning Star*, the *Daily News*, and *The Times*. The nomination of candidates took place at noon on the hustings in front of Nelson's Column, Trafalgar Square (the location also being referred to as Charing Cross). The "arrangements were an immense improvement over the old *regime* of dirt and disturbance at Covent Garden Market, where a candidate and his friends seldom escaped without making acquaintance with the flavour of decaying turnips and cabbage-stalks" (*Morning Star*). Smith arrived first, and then Grosvenor and Mill, with a large group of supporters, who had walked in procession from their committee rooms. After the proclamation and the writ had been read, Erskine Perry, seconded by N.N. Seymour, proposed Grosvenor. Mill was nominated by Malleson, who said in part: "Three years ago you did yourself the honour to solicit Mr. Mill to leave his study, where he had already acquired a world-wide reputation—(*cheers*)—and, what he values more, a world-wide usefulness—to represent you in the House of Commons, and there with wonderful rapidity he achieved an astonishing success. (*Cheers.*) As an argumentative debater he is second to none in the House of Commons; and, more than that, the people respect and admire him for his pure courage, his straightforwardness, his simplicity, and his intense devotion to the popular cause. (*Cheers.*) It may be said of him that he has a double title—that he is not only one of the greatest, but one of the best-loved of living Englishmen. (*Cheers, and counter cries of Oh.*) He has been assailed on the occasion of this election with abuse, insult, and calumny of every kind; but the gentlemen who have thus assailed him do not dare to accept the challenge to be present at one of their public meetings, and there defend himself. (*Hear, hear; and a voice, What about Bradlaugh?*)" Beal, who seconded the nomination, summed "up Mill's qualifications by saying that the rancorous hatred of that honourable gentleman's opponents was the best guarantee of the value of his services. (*Cheers.*)" Up to this point the speeches had been quite well heard, but when Smith's supporters began to speak, "there was a surging movement . . . by the rougher element immediately beneath the hustings" which produced "reaction and uproar, and the clamour thus initiated continued without abatement till the end of the proceedings, and little more than a few stray expressions could be caught here and there from the different speakers" (*The Times*). George Cubitt, "in the midst of a deafening uproar," proposed W.H. Smith, interjecting the comment that while the Tories had no complaint to make of Grosvenor, "they did complain that Mr. Mill had indulged in abuse, and had charged the Tories with sticking at nothing. Mr. Mill," he continued, "had been asked to retract, and had declined to do so; and he . . . now asked him to do so that day, or when he went to his retirement at Avignon he would regret it." Tavener Miller (who also could barely be heard) seconded Smith's nomination, and then Grosvenor addressed the crowd. Next Mill rose, to be greeted with "a tumult of applause" and "considerable hooting" (*Daily News*).

GENTLEMEN—This is not the time or the place for many words, and, if it were, you could not possibly hear them; so I will only say this, you and the people of this country generally have got to decide something more important than the particular merit or demerit of candidates that present themselves for your suffrages. You have got to decide whether this country shall have a Tory Government or a Gladstone Government. (*Cheers, cries of Gladstone, and interruption.*) [a]If the new electors who have supported Reform care nothing about the rights that have been acquired, and desire things should go on after the Reform Act exactly as they went on before it, they will do quite right to vote for the Tory candidate; but if the old electors are as much attached to Reform as ever—if the new electors desire that their newly-acquired rights should be exercised to the best advantage—and if both new and old electors wish the Reform Bill to bring forth abundant fruits, then they will, I have no doubt, vote for the two Liberal candidates. (*Cheers.*)[a]

[*The noise constantly increased, and Smith, like Mill, could not be heard easily. On the show of hands, the High Bailiff declared the election to have fallen on Mill and Smith, though the* Morning Star *thought the vote had clearly gone to Mill and Grosvenor; a poll was demanded on behalf of Grosvenor, which was announced to begin at 8 a.m. and continue until 4 p.m. on the 17th, with the result to be declared at 2 p.m. on the 18th. The meeting (which had lasted less than an hour) ended after "some confusion about the customary vote of thanks to the returning officer. A message was sent to Mr. Mill on the part of Mr. Smith, offering to second the vote if he would propose it, but no move to that effect being made, Mr. Smith himself proposed the motion, and in the absence of a Liberal seconder this duty was discharged by the Hon. R. Grimston [Smith's agent]"* (The Times). *"Upon leaving the hustings Mr. Mill with his friends returned to the Liberal committee-room in Cockspur-street, and presenting himself upon the balcony bowed his acknowledgments to his supporters"* (The Times).]

[a-a]MS If the electors regretted the support they had given to the Reform Bill, they might show their feeling properly by returning a Conservative; but if they felt with him, that the destiny of the country depended upon maintaining a policy of progress, and if they did not expect the Legislature to go on after the passing of a new Reform Bill exactly as it had done before, but to pass measures for the moral and social improvement of the community, then he trusted he and his colleague might again represent them. (*Loud cheers.*)

142. The Westminster Election of 1868 [10]

18 NOVEMBER, 1868

Daily Telegraph, 19 November, 1868, p. 8. Headed: "The General Election. / Declarations. / Westminster." Similar reports (also in the first person) appeared in the *Morning Star* and the *Daily News*; *The Times* had a third-person report. Though the declaration of the poll was scheduled for 2 p.m., the number of voters and the consequent difficulty of making up the lists delayed the High Bailiff until 4 p.m. When he appeared on the hustings, the front was occupied by "a number of roughs of the worst type" who, annoyed at the delay, "held high carnival," with the result that "any decently-clad individual wearing a chimney-pot hat had good reason to remember his imprudence." "The principal speaker in the crowd was a little boy whose age could not have been more than ten or twelve years"—*The Times* guesses fourteen—"whose platform was the shoulders of a young man. This youthful political orator expatiated very intelligently upon all the prominent questions of the day, gave the Liberal party full credit for all they had done and intend doing, criticised the Tories rather severely, even going as far as to wish to see the distinguished educator of that party well hung; accused the successful Tory candidate for Westminster of all sorts of bribery and corruption, and prophesied that gentleman's speedy rejection from the seat for Westminster." (*Morning Star.*) Mill and Grosvenor, with their supporters, had arrived before 2 o'clock, to enthusiastic cheers. After waiting an hour, however, Mill, "who was indisposed," rose, whereupon "the little fellow on the man's shoulders called for 'Cheers for Mr. Mill,' a cry which was readily responded to; and, addressing Mr. Mill, said, 'Don't mind, Mr. Mill, we'll pop you in for Greenwich.' (*Great cheering.*)"

GENTLEMEN—So much unexpected delay having occurred, and as I have a bad cold, I will take the opportunity of saying at once the few words I have to say. To be defeated in a contested election is so common an occurrence that there is no reason why any sensible man should be much moved by it—and least of all is that any reason in my case, who, as you know, did not seek the honour which you conferred on me; but, on the contrary, the acceptance was and has been throughout a sacrifice to me. (*Hear, hear.*) Whatever regret I feel, therefore, at the result of yesterday's election is solely on public grounds. (*Cheers.*) I regret the loss of a vote to Mr. Gladstone and the Liberal party. (*Great cheering.*) I regret that Westminster, which was so long at the head of the Liberal interest, should have had the unenviable distinction of being the only metropolitan constituency which has at this election sent a Tory to the House of Commons by the vote of the majority. (*Hisses.*) And I am sorry for one reason more. I think it was an encouragement to young men ambitious of parliamentary distinction—it was a good lesson to them when they found that a great constituency like this was willing to be represented by a man who always told you plainly when he differed in opinion from you—who told you that he differed on a few important points, though he agreed on more, and that he should maintain his opinion by his vote, and who never, for the sake of preserving his seat, ever said or did anything which he would not have thought it his duty to if he had not been your representative. (*Cheers.*) It only remains for me to make my warmest acknowledgments to those who have laboured on my behalf, [a]which I do most heartily,[a] and to the electors who have not only given me their support, but an amount of [b]support, favour, and countenance[b] very far above my deserts. (*Cries of No, and cheers.*)

[*As he left the hustings with his friends, Mill was again warmly cheered, and was joined by a large crowd in walking back to the Liberal committee rooms in Cockspur Street. The display of a Tory placard offended some in the crowd, and a rush on the hustings resulted in the reporters being "walked over"* (Morning Star), *and the police were required to restore order. An hour later, William James Farrer, the High Bailiff, appeared, accompanied by Smith, who was greeted by "a storm of mingled cheers and groans." The poll was announced: Smith, 7,648; Grosvenor, 6,584; Mill, 6,284; and Smith and Grosvenor were declared elected. Smith spoke amidst an uproar, and then Grosvenor, who was heard with much greater ease, expressed his thanks, mixed with regret at the loss of Mill as a colleague. A vote of thanks to the High Bailiff terminated the proceedings more peacefully than had been earlier feared.*]

[a-a]+MS
[b-b]DN] DT kindness and favour

"Nomination of Candidates for Westminster at the Hustings, Charing Cross"
Illustrated London News, 21 November, 1868, p. 485
Metropolitan Toronto Library